1998
26/05/2011 (79)
2 in 2011
1 in 2016

The BIG Book of
GARDEN
DESIGN

TIME
LIFE
BOOKS

Alexandria, Virginia

4

FURNISHING
YOUR LANDSCAPE

124

5

DESIGNING
WITH PLANTS

150

REFERENCE

CHAPTER ONE

Garden Styles

No matter what type of garden you desire—a cool woodland retreat, a backyard kitchen garden, or a fragrant showstopper of roses—your personal imprint is an important part of the design. While the gardens you see in books or magazines may evoke a particular style or theme and follow accepted design principles, invariably something of the designer's personality comes through that makes the garden uniquely his or her own.

Your house and surroundings might indicate a certain style, but in the end the choice is yours. You may opt for an entryway garden that reflects the architecture of your home, while saving backyard or side gardens for a more personalized touch. This can be as easy as selecting plants, such as sweet peas and lilacs, that evoke fond memories of a childhood garden or colorful, drought-resistant perennials that remind you of the American Southwest. Or you might take elements of one style and mix them with compatible elements of another, as some of the gardeners have done in the examples presented here, for a garden style all your own. For a planting guide to each garden, see pages 22-27.

The owner of this stone cottage near Philadelphia opted for a formal design yet filled the beds with plants that evoke a colorful cottage garden—lilies, delphiniums, summer phlox, and astilbe.

A love of the Provence region of France was the inspiration behind this northern California garden. Cool grays and greens were purposely selected to suggest a sunny Mediterranean landscape; mounds of French and English lavender and sprays of deep pink *Erysimum* (wallflower) provide harmonious waves of color. Reflecting the undulating rhythm of the border planting, a stepped pathway of rounded Colorado River-washed stones leads to the back entrance of the house, which is flanked by olive trees. The massive *Plectostachys* at the entrance to the path (lower left) began as a small 1-gallon container plant; it owes its healthy growth both to careful pruning and to the addition of turkey manure to this garden's sandy loam.

Reminiscent of an Early American dooryard planting, this delightful Maine garden of herbs, vegetables, and flowers combines such traditional elements as a straight path—leading here to a bench instead of a door—a profusion of plants, and a fence enclosure with an unusual location: The garden is installed on the site of an abandoned clay tennis court. The plants were carefully chosen and arranged to maximize color, texture, and fragrance and to provide a bounty for the kitchen as well. Tall Phlox paniculata in striking pink welcomes a visitor entering the path, which is lined with 'Lemon Gem' marigolds. Feathery yellow-headed dill off to the left of the walkway fronts raspberry brambles, while purplish blue bellflowers and lilies in pale pink and yellow create a pleasing combination on the right.

8

Perfect for quiet reflection and restoration of the spirit, this Japanese-inspired garden near Boston borrows the elements of a traditional rock-and-water planting. A stream, defined by well-placed fieldstone, encircles an island bed dominated by a simple, evocative ornament. But rather than rely on a few strategically placed and perfectly manicured plants, the gardeners have indulged their desire for lush flowers and foliage, including in the mix Spiraea japonica 'Little Princess' (foreground), Geranium endressii, and a variety of ferns, along with colorful splashes of azalea and iris, a magnolia, and a Japanese maple.

Swimmers in this pool in Phoenix, Arizona, might think themselves afloat in the midst of a prairie meadow— except that this planting is composed of wildflowers native to the desert. Scarlet flax, purple arroyo lupine, and California poppies combine with Indian fig, prickly pear, and saguaro to rim the edge of a man-made oasis, providing privacy for sunbathers as well as sanctuary for the quails, doves, hummingbirds, owls, hawks, and butterflies that flock to this inviting, low-maintenance garden.

The glossy dark green leaves and large blush pink flowers of the vigorous climber 'New Dawn' adorn a pergola in this elegant Alabama garden. Leading the eye upward, the climber helps frame the view of the bench beyond, beckoning visitors to that part of the garden. A low hedge of Camellia hiemalis sets off the walkway beneath the pergola, while the bright green foliage of 'Nastarana' adds a lively note to the foreground. A tall Ternstroemia hedge describes the garden's boundary and provides a handsome background for the white bench.

High walls and a bright blue gate enclose this Santa Barbara, California, garden, making a private haven and an enchanting transition from the outside world to the house. The long-stemmed fragrant flowers of English lavender (left foreground) lean over a Mexican evening primrose, whose pale pink petals surround bright yellow stamens. Spilling onto the tile walk is a drift of Mexican fleabane sprinkled with dainty pink-and-white daisylike flowers. Enormous upward-branching rosemaries flank the gate in the wall, which is adorned with a brilliant red trumpet creeper.

Masses of blue catmint highlight the vivid red of Jupiter's-beard, used sparingly as a color accent in this low-maintenance New Mexico perennial garden. In the background, the contrasting golden columbine also appears more intense against the cool tone of the catmint. By allowing the bright yellow to leap forward in the mind's eye, this combination and placement of colors makes the garden seem more lushly planted.

White baby's-breath and yellow beggar-ticks spill onto the stone walk in front of an antique fence and gate, softening this formal entryway garden in Seattle. Along with pink petunias and the white trumpets of variegated nicotiana, the plants were chosen both for their pleasing color contrasts and their dainty forms, which accent the Victorian setting. Low, deep green mounds of common thrift and other foliage plants unite the composition.

Set against the lush green backdrop of a tall thuja hedge, a medley of foliage plants supply a breathtaking exhibition of colors, sizes, forms, and textures as they sweep alongside a pebble walk in Washington State. Irregular repetitions of yellow-leaved hakonechloa and arching spires of Chinese silver grass, combined with plantings such as the mounded 'Jackman Blue' rue, add color and textural excitement when the flowering plants are not blooming. When they are, the garden is punctuated by splashes of flowering orange alstroemeria, pink geraniums, and yellow daylilies, a composition tied together by interweaving vines of clematis bearing indigo blossoms.

A Guide to the Gardens

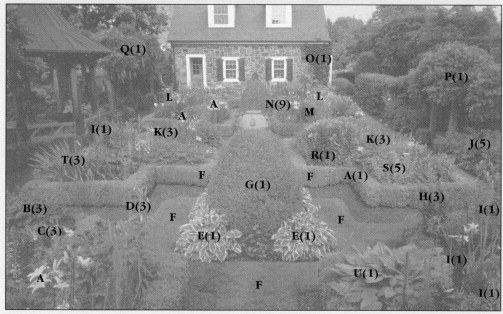

pages 4-5

A. *Lilium 'Luxor'* (lily) (many)
B. *Paeonia officinalis* (peony) (3)
C. *Filipendula ulmaria* (queen-of-the-meadow) (3)
D. *Lilium speciosum 'Rubrum'* (showy Japanese lily) (3)
E. *Hosta fortunei 'Francee'* (plantain lily) (2)
F. *Buxus sempervirens 'Suffruticosa'* (edging boxwood) (many)

G. *Buxus sempervirens 'Arborescens'* (boxwood) (1)
H. *Monarda didyma* (bee balm) (3)
I. *Delphinium elatum 'Pacific Giants'* (candle larkspur) (4)
J. *Astilbe thunbergii 'Straussenfeder'* (astilbe) (5)
K. *Astilbe chinensis* var. *taquetii 'Superba'* (astilbe) (3)
L. *Achillea filipendulina 'Gold Plate'* (fern-leaf yarrow) (many)
M. *Liatris spicata 'Kobold Rose'*

(button snakewort) (many)
N. *Lilium tigrinum* (tiger lily) (9)
O. *Hedera helix* (English ivy) (1)
P. *Wisteria sinensis* (Chinese wisteria) (1)
Q. *Castanea dentata* (American chestnut) (1)
R. *Phlox paniculata* (summer phlox) (1)
S. *Lilium 'Apollo'* (lily) (5)
T. *Iris ensata* (sword-leaved iris) (3)
U. *Hosta fortunei 'Aoki'* (plantain lily) (1)

NOTE: The key lists each plant type and the total quantity needed to replicate the garden shown. The diagram's letters and numbers refer to the type of plant and the number sited in an area.

pages 8-9

A. *Phlox paniculata*
(summer phlox) (4)
B. *Anethum graveolens*
(dill) (many)
C. *Antirrhinum majus*
'Rocket Mix' (snapdragon) (24)
D. *Delphinium* (larkspur) (1)
E. *Digitalis purpurea 'Foxy*
Hybrids' (common foxglove) (12)

F. *Tagetes 'Lemon Gem'*
(marigold) (60)
G. *Rubus* sp. (raspberry) (21)
H. *Lathyrus odoratus*
(sweet pea) (20)
I. *Campanula lactiflora*
(milky bellflower) (3)
J. *Lilium Asiatic hybrids*
(lily) (15)

K. *Papaver* sp. (poppy) (12)
L. *Lilium* x *aurelianense*
'Golden Splendor'
(aurelian lily) (15)
M. *Pinus strobus*
(white pine) (1)
N. *Prunus pensylvanica*
(wild red cherry) (1)

pages 10-11

A. *Spiraea japonica*
'Little Princess' (spirea) (2)
B. *Geranium endressii*
(Pyrenean cranesbill) (2)
C. *Magnolia stellata*
(star magnolia) (1)

D. *Acer palmatum 'Bloodgood'*
(Japanese maple) (1)
E. *Cedrus atlantica* (Atlas cedar) (1)
F. *Pieris japonica*
(lily-of-the-valley bush) (2)
G. *Rhododendron 'Hinodegiri'*
(azalea) (7)
H. *Rhododendron 'Polar Bear'* (4)

I. *Rhododendron 'Hinocrimson'* (3)
J. *Athyrium filix-femina*
(lady fern) (2)
K. *Iris ensata* (sword-leaved iris) (4)
L. *Athyrium goeringianum*
(Japanese fern) (2)
M. *Iris cristata* (crested iris) (3)

pages 12-13

A. *Lupinus succulentus* (arroyo lupine) (many)
B. *Linum grandiflorum 'Rubrum'* (scarlet flax) (many)
C. *Eschscholzia californica* (California poppy) (many)
D. *Larrea tridentata* (creosote bush) (2)
E. *Olneya tesota* (desert ironwood) (3)
F. *Acacia farnesiana* (sweet acacia) (1)
G. *Carnegiea gigantea* (saguaro) (1)
H. *Lycium fremontii* (wolfberry) (1)
I. *Opuntia violacea* var. *santa-rita* (purple prickly pear) (1)
J. *Opuntia ficus-indica* (Indian fig) (5)

pages 14-15

A. *'Nastarana', noisette* (2)
B. *Camellia hiemalis* (4)
C. *Ophiopogon japonicus* (mondo grass) (12)
D. *Vinca rosea* (periwinkle) (9)
E. *'White Pet', polyantha* (rose) (1)
F. *'New Dawn', large-flowered climber* (rose) (8)
G. *Salvia 'Victoria Blue'* (sage) (6)
H. *Cycas revoluta* (sago palm) (2)
I. *Ternstroemia* sp. (6)
J. *'American Beauty', hybrid perpetual* (rose) (1); *'Reine des Violettes', hybrid perpetual* (rose) (1); *'Rosa Mundi', gallica* (rose) (1); *'Gruss an Teplitz', bourbon* (rose) (1)

NOTE: The key lists each plant type and the total quantity needed to replicate the garden shown. The diagram's letters and numbers refer to the type of plant and the number sited in an area.

pages 16-17

A. *Lavandula angustifolia*
'Hidcote Giant'
(English lavender) (7)
B. *Oenothera berlandieri*
(evening primrose) (9)
C. *Erigeron karvinskianus*
(fleabane) (5)
D. *Alyssum* spp. (many)
E. *Salvia leucantha* (sage) (2)
F. *Rosmarinus officinalis*
(rosemary) (6)

page 18

A. *Nepeta* x *faassenii*
(catmint) (8)
B. *Centranthus ruber*
(red valerian) (5)
C. *Aquilegia chrysantha*
(columbine) (9)
D. *Pinus edulis* (pinyon) (1)
E. *Hemerocallis*
'September Gold' (daylily) (4)
F. *Aronia melanocarpa*
(chokeberry) (4)
G. *Populus tremuloides*
(quaking aspen) (4)

pages 18-19

A. *Nicotiana langsdorffii 'Variegata'* (2)
B. *Tagetes x 'Striped Marvel'* (2)
C. *Tagetes 'Lemon Gem'* (2)
D. *Petunia integrifolia* (3)
E. *Gypsophila paniculata* (1)

F. *Chamaecyparis pisifera 'Plumosa Compacta'* (2)
G. *Armeria maritima 'Sea Thrift'* (2)
H. *Fuchsia x 'Checkerboard'* (1)
I. *Bidens ferulifolia*

'Variegata' (1)
J. *Fragaria x 'Pink Panda'* (1)
K. *Liatris spicata* (1)
L. *Hibiscus moscheutos 'Lady Baltimore'* (1)

pages 20-21

A. *Cotinus 'Velvet Cloak'* (1)
B. *Clematis x durandii* (2)
C. *Agapanthus 'Bressingham White'* (3)
D. *Sedum spectabile 'Meteor'* (1)
E. *Helleborus x sternii 'Blackthorn Hybrids'* (1)
F. *Onosma alboroseum* (1)
G. *Hakonechloa 'Aureola'* (3)

H. *Ruta 'Jackman's Blue'* (2)
I. *Artemisia x 'Huntington Botanic'* (1)
J. *Alstroemeria Ligtu Hybrids* (3)
K. *Hemerocallis 'Happy Returns'* (6)
L. *Achillea 'W. B. Child'* (1)
M. *Geranium x 'Mavis*

Simpson' (1)
N. *Stachys byzantina 'Silver Carpet'* (1)
O. *Miscanthus sinensis 'Variegatus'* (2)
P. *Salvia guaranitica* (1)
Q. *Thuja 'Pyramidalis'*
R. *Hydrangea anomala* ssp. *petiolaris* (1)

NOTE: *The key lists each plant type and the total quantity needed to replicate the garden shown. The diagram's letters and numbers refer to the type of plant and the number sited in an area.*

27

CHAPTER TWO

Designing Your Garden

There is much more to designing a flower garden than selecting your favorite plants and putting them in the ground. Before you touch your trowel, you must ask yourself how you intend to use the garden, how you would like it to look, and—most important—you must get to know the property itself.

The Berkeley, California, garden at left strikes a fine balance between style and practicality, demonstrating how plants and landscape elements can work together to create a cohesive design. The lush plantings of pink-flowered fleabane, spiky lavender, and the common garden polebean lead the eye upward to take in the wood trellis and the garden gate. The trellis serves as both a boundary and a backdrop for the plants, while the gate's window breaks the horizontal line and offers a glimpse of what lies beyond. In the foreground, a sundial reinforces the geometric design of the garden's structural elements.

On the following pages you'll learn how to create your own design—one that makes the most of your property and fulfills your fondest dreams for a garden of beautiful blooms.

Planning for Outdoor Living

Your garden should make as important a contribution to your home life as your house, and its design deserves the same careful attention given your interior decor. Like your house, the garden can be a source of pleasure and relaxation. It can express your interests and tastes. And by projecting beauty and interest to the passing public, it can be an asset to your community.

To design such a space successfully, follow the steps that landscape architects do. First, ask yourself some questions to determine your wants and expectations for a garden. Next, take a discerning look at your property. Then, assess the potential for improvement—what can be upgraded, what should be replaced, what is fine just as it is. Finally, decide on a style *(pages 42-46)*. At that point you are ready to plan—first the hardscape (terraces, walkways, and the like), then the plant choices and the planting arrangement.

Executing a good garden design takes time. A garden will evolve as it matures, changing character as plants grow taller and broader. While this is going on, your needs and interests may change as well. At some point you may have to hire a professional for difficult jobs such as earth grading or tree removal. You might also need to implement your design in stages so you don't break your budget. Fortunately, the design process does not have to be rushed. You can give yourself plenty of time to make the right choices. Begin by asking a basic question:

What Is a Garden?

A garden is fundamentally a humanized outdoor space, an idealized form of the natural landscape. The term *garden* can mean a discrete planting, such as a perennial border or a vegetable patch. At other times it can refer to an entire property as the object of a comprehensive garden design.

A garden can occupy various locations in relation to the house. It can be located on a remote part of the property, as might be typical of a vegetable or cutting garden. Or it can be adjacent to the house—a kind of outdoor room. And, of course, it can encompass all the grounds, including the house itself.

In summer (far left), a climbing rose scrambles up an arched trellis gateway in this Connecticut garden, drawing the eye also to the tall stand of globe thistles and deep orange Asiatic lilies surrounded by a sweep of English lavender. The fine foliage of Artemisia and Dianthus adds texture and cooling shades of green to the scene. In winter (left), the underlying plant framework of the garden emerges, including the hedge of evergreen eastern hemlocks that marks the border.

In practice, most properties are made up of more than one garden, each in its own space, according to its use. The individual gardens are then linked into a whole by a unifying network of pathways and sightlines.

Rewards of a Good Design

By linking all parts of your property with the house, a well-designed garden will increase your living space. Various areas will become cherished parts of daily life as places to entertain, play, or relax in comfort and safety. The sense of security afforded you by your house will extend to the surrounding property.

The character of your neighborhood can be a starting point for design decisions. You may want to block a sightline to a neighbor's property or frame a distant view. The style of your house and the history of your area are other possible cues. To complement a 19th-century southern farmhouse, for example, a dooryard flower garden surrounded by a white picket fence, with a stone path leading from fence to door, might be just right. Or you may be influenced by the local ecology, choosing plants to either attract or repel wildlife.

But your garden could also be designed to satisfy less tangible impulses—to create a mood, conjure up memories, or express certain ideals. You might be inspired by the soft feel of pine needles underfoot or the fluttering of swarms of

butterflies on a butterfly bush. Such ideas can be the beginning of a highly satisfying garden plan.

Deciding What You Want

Your first step is to assemble a wish list of attributes for your garden. For most people, the top priority is year-round interest. It is a good idea to study your site first in winter to get the clearest idea of its structural framework—the hardscape, made up of imposed features such as walks and fences; and the softscape, composed of trees, shrubs, and ornamental grasses. Another important criterion for most gardeners is conservation—of energy, money, and natural resources. This means devising a plan that minimizes mowing, watering, fertilizing, weeding, and pruning, and choosing plants that have proved themselves.

Although the design of your house will directly affect the design of your garden, you should also consider the garden's effect on the house. Shade trees, for example, can reduce the cost of cooling your house. On the other hand, some plants can be destructive and should be grown away from the house. A wisteria vine, for example, can pull down your gutters. And tree limbs overhanging your roof can come crashing down in a storm.

Consult the other members of the family who will be using the garden. What kind of play area will the children want? Do you want a cook's garden with fruits, vegetables, and herbs? Also consider the kinds of pets you have and what their impact may be on a garden.

If you have particular horticultural interests, look for suitable places to realize them—a stony slope for a rock garden, a soggy area for a bog garden, a south- or east-facing wall for an attached greenhouse. The site itself will suggest intriguing possibilities to add to your wish list.

Assessing Your Property

The next step is to make an informal survey of your property. Eventually, you will need to make detailed sketches and keep a record of your observations *(page 35)*, but at this stage you should only be taking an overall look at the site.

Start beyond its boundaries. From here you will see the public face of your property. Walk or drive past and try to look at the site with the eyes of someone encountering it for the first time. Is the house open to view or shrouded by trees? Is the entryway welcoming or obscured by shrubs? What kind of impression does the garden make, and is it harmonious with the architecture of the house?

Ask your neighbors for permission to walk your boundary line from their side, and look at your house from their point of view. From here you'll see what privacy screening you may want or need. Then go inside your house and look out each window and door. From this vantage you'll see opportunities to feature certain sightlines. Inspecting the grounds from upstairs windows is particularly revealing of patterns that are not otherwise apparent. Areas visible from important viewpoints such as a picture window in the living room or the window over the kitchen sink are obvious spots for a garden.

The view from a door might reveal a destination—an inviting, sun-dappled bench, for example—and the passage toward it should begin with a comfortable transition space to the outdoors, such as a wide landing with a pathway leading to a patio or to another part of the garden. You might decide that it is worth enlarging a window or replacing a small door with wider French doors to give the house better views to the garden.

Developing Focal Points

As you explore the views on your property, you will discover eye-catching spots you may wish to feature. These will be the focal points on which to base your garden design.

Focal points occur wherever sightlines intersect. They usually lie within the property but sometimes occur beyond it. In the front of the house, for instance, the focal point is the entranceway, where the strong vertical lines of the front door meet the horizontal of the threshold. In a landscape, a focal point will exist where the curve of a path disappears around a row of shrubs or the corner of a house. It could also be an imposing feature beyond your boundaries—a graceful tree or a pond, perhaps.

The sightline leading to a focal point is known as an axis, and your garden may have more than one. An axis creates movement in the garden, inviting the eye to follow it to the focal point. Together, axes unify the design by linking the viewer to all its parts. These links can be strengthened in several ways. First, a focal point itself will become more prominent if an object or a plant is placed there, or if it is framed or enclosed. Also, an axis will be accentuated if a pathway is built along it and the line enhanced with plantings. For instance, the focal point of a view from a patio might be a small flower bed. Adding a flagstone walk from the patio to the bed and framing the view

The metal wall sculpture at the rear of this elegant circular terrace garden in New Orleans provides a dramatic focal point that beckons a visitor. Twin pillars topped with geraniums, as well as the potted palms at the entrance, frame the view and strengthen the axis.

with a pair of vertical shrubs or an arched trellis will create a unified arrangement.

Moving through the Garden

Just as you surveyed your property from the vantage points of the street and the house, you should also stroll through the garden itself to find existing or potential focal points. These will become stopping places and the sightlines leading to them will become pathways.

You can best create this delightful effect by establishing a series of spaces, or rooms, that are either open or closed, beginning with the enclosed space of the house, moving away from the house, and then back again. For example, a network of axes might start from the living room, conveying the visitor through sliding glass doors to the deck, then across a lawn to an intimate shade garden with a hammock under a tree, then over to a sunny, open vegetable garden, and finally back to an herb garden beside the kitchen door.

A garden subdivided into such separate rooms, each with its own character, is both inherently interesting and functional. As in a house, each space has its own purpose: A sunny corner near a hedge might be a retreat; the open lawn, a playing field; the patio, a place for dining alfresco.

How you or your visitors move through the garden—the route you take and what you see along the way—will affect your experience of it. You can determine whether someone strides along quickly or lingers to admire the view. For instance, a walk along a narrow, winding path bordered with interesting flowers is likely to be slower than one along a straight, wide path crossing a lawn. Gates at transition points and steps built into a sloping path also affect the pace of your walk, forcing you to slow down and take in the scene.

Finally, it is the stopping places—a deck, patio, walled courtyard, clearing, or shady bench overlooking a view—that lend a garden a feeling of shelter and restfulness. Be sure to have several such stops on your garden journey, and keep them separate and discreet so that they are a pleasure to rediscover each time you arrive.

Although the meandering gravel path in this Los Angeles garden is its "official" walkway, steppingstones interplanted with sweet alyssum allow for the human tendency to create shortcuts. The low, drystone wall provides an appealing spot for garden strollers to sit and rest, while a decorative birdbath and garden urn create interesting focal points along the way.

Highlighting a Property's Strengths and Weaknesses

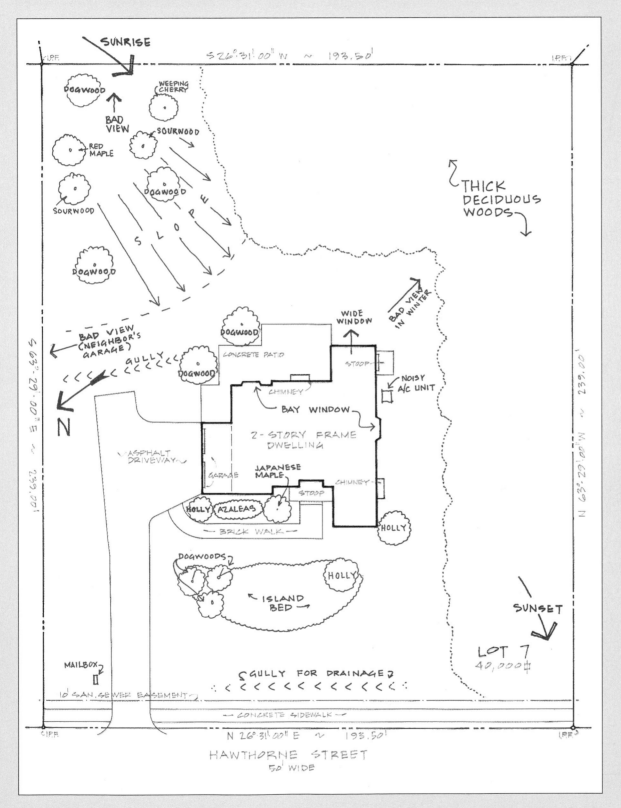

On a property-survey plat serving as a base map, the homeowner has used red ink to indicate existing plantings and record notes on topography, views to emphasize or screen, and possible drainage problems. The assessment reveals minimum landscaping but plenty of potential for an outstanding garden on this nearly one-acre property. Two obvious problems demand attention: The overgrown woods to the south and west take up considerable space and loom over the house to such an extent that it is not even necessary to mark on the map the oppressive shade they cast. Another target for major redesign is the steep slope in the eastern corner, planted with randomly scattered trees.

The Principles of Design

The cottage-like feel of this house in southern California, painted Colonial blue with white shutters, is matched by the plain picket fence and backyard border of 'Heritage' climbing roses, pinks, pansies, and Mexican bush sage. A path of irregular paving stones and a venerable shade tree complete the picture.

Historically, gardeners have relied on certain widely accepted conventions of design to organize the landscape around them. These visual guidelines evoke a feeling of order and harmony in what might otherwise seem an ungovernable wilderness. Properly applied, design principles unify the landscape while maintaining interest by juxtaposing contrasting elements. Thus your garden plan might include a cool oasis at the wooded edge of your property balanced by a sunny kitchen garden closer to your house. Or within a single perennial bed you may choose a unifying color contrasted with a variety of plant textures and forms.

Unity

The first governing principle of garden design is unity—the perception that all the elements of the garden have coalesced into a coherent composition. These elements include the materials and plants used to build a garden and their positions relative to each other.

You can achieve unity in several ways. First, the house and the garden should complement each other in style. For example, a Federal house typically would be surrounded by a formal garden *(pages 42-43)*. Further, the materials of the house and the garden should be similar. If a house is built of brick, unity is furthered when the garden walls are also brick. By the same token, a rustic wooden house is enhanced by a wooden fence.

The materials you use should also be compatible with the land itself. In a seaside garden on a granite shore, for example, you might use a similar rough stone for the retaining walls. You might even incorporate some large stones into the design of a flower border.

Another approach to establishing unity is to repeat an existing line, form, texture, or color in

your design. You could mirror the curve of a dramatically arched doorway in the contour of a flower bed or the rounded edge of a patio. Repeating a foliage or flower color is a familiar device to tie together the design of a border. Such visual rhythms, as with musical rhythms, carry you from one point to another in a composition.

And, of course, you strengthen the unity of your design by providing strong focal points to orient the parts of your garden to one another.

Simplicity

As a rule of thumb, you should strive to keep your design as simple and straightforward as possible. Too much ornamentation, too many focal points, too great a variety of plants and other materials can create an impression of disorder and confusion. Even if you're designing a garden that is meant to perform many different functions, try to keep it simple. A successful design will provide a unifying structure for all the elements in your landscape, from open areas for entertaining and

play to shady glades and backyard herb gardens. You can separate each garden area with screening plants and provide clear pathways or transitional areas that allow you to move easily from one part of the landscape to another.

Proportion and Scale

Proportion is the size relationship among parts of a whole—the dimensions of a single tree, for example, seen against an entire grove. Scale is the measurement of one object or space in relation to another. In a garden, we relate the size of objects and spaces primarily to the size of our bodies. By that measure, alpine plants in a rock garden are tiny and a redwood tree is huge.

Designers understand that the principles of proportion contribute to the mood of a garden. For example, a garden will feel cramped and constrained if enclosed within disproportionately high vertical elements such as buildings, walls or fences. A planting of small trees and shrubs in a city garden surrounded by apartment buildings

The contrast between the bright openness of the lawn and the darkness of the shady patch under the river birch adds weight and dimension to the streamside plantings in this Charlottesville, Virginia, garden. Cheerful splashes of yellow 'Hyperion' daylilies glow next to the dark Hosta sieboldiana 'Elegans'. The stream itself cuts through the greensward like a shiny black ribbon.

would help counteract the looming effect of the tall buildings. On the other hand, if your garden reaches out in a vast expanse from your house, a space enclosed within vertical human-scale elements—a trellis, wall, or hedge—would provide a welcome sense of intimacy and security.

Human scale is not the only measuring stick in matters of proportion. For example, the flowers in a border are usually arranged by height, with the tallest in the back and the shortest in the front. Likewise, your house is an important determinant of scale; nearby trees and structural elements should be in proportion to the size of your house.

When designing your garden, keep in mind that the size of an object is also relative over distance. This can be a useful tool for manipulating space. The farther an object is from the viewer, the larger it must be to stand out clearly. For a perennial border at the back of your property to make an impact from your deck, for example, it should be at least half as wide as the distance between the deck and your garden.

Study the relative size of every object and plant in your garden to find a balance that pleases you. You will notice that the combinations you like will tend to be harmonious—composed of related forms, textures, and colors.

Harmony and Contrast

A good garden design is based on a balance between harmony and contrast. Closely related colors, comparable textures and forms, and similar qualities of line blend together like the musical tones that make a harmonious chord. If objects or plants are too much alike, however, they may tend to blend together and lose their distinction. It is best to set up contrasting groupings of plants so that they complement each other. Textural contrasts are particularly effective in a predominantly single-color garden. In a shady foliage garden, for example, lacy fern fronds and astilbe offset smooth-leaved hosta and the upright spears of iris.

When planning your garden, keep in mind that too much contrast may seem chaotic and jumbled,

A meandering gully of river stones in this Greenwich, Connecticut, garden mimics a stream as it flows through a lawn and around an embankment of dwarf mountain pine and lily-of-the-valley bush. The illusion is furthered by the granite rocks and the spikes of Siberian iris, recalling water-loving yellow flag. This streambed has a practical function as well; it is also used as a drainage channel.

The Delights of Water

A water feature such as a pool, fountain, or stream adds a cooling touch to the landscape and can be a decorative focal point as well. The soothing trickle of water masks unwanted background noises and evokes a touch of the countryside even in the heart of the city.

If you don't have a natural water feature on your property, it is relatively easy to build one *(pages 145-147)*. You can simulate a stream or waterfall by using a simple recirculating pump to draw water from a pool to a higher point where it will run down in a rivulet. The pool below, in Missouri, is built to look like a stream flowing through rocky outcrops at a meadow's edge. Dotting the rocks are colorful native plants such as yellow Ozark sundrops and rosy poppy mallow. Pink prairie phlox and lance coreopsis, behind the phlox, also do well in the fast-draining, rocky soil.

This pool's irregular shape, rough materials, and native plants harmonize with the naturalistic design of this garden. In a more formal garden, a rectilinear, round, or oblong pool accented by a simple arrangement of water lilies or a central fountain can act like a glistening mirror. If you lack the space for such a pool, try a wall fountain that trickles a stream of water into a basin.

while too little contrast can seem monotonous. Begin by juxtaposing open and enclosed areas. Think of your garden as space, and the structures and blocks of plantings as solid elements within that space. Balance the proportion of empty and solid spaces and carefully plan how they will flow together and connect.

Similarly, the alternations of light and shade in the garden create an interesting contrast. They can be used to subdivide the space into discrete areas, each with its own purpose, such as a shady deck for reading and relaxing, a sunny area for a swimming pool, a dappled woodland for strolling. At night, skillfully arranged artificial lighting can carve out still other spaces in the garden.

Harmony and contrast also figure in the selection and arrangement of plants. Most important for the purposes of design is a plant's form, or habit. Most plants are round, prostrate (or carpeting), vase shaped, arching, conical, or columnar. Plants of different forms can be combined to create a coherent and interesting design. In a dry garden, for example, a mound of mountain marigold and a silvery, horizontal mat of snow-in-summer may be used to offset the upright forms of agave and cactus.

But don't omit the other senses from your planning. The contrast between the feel of grass and that of moss along a woodland path, the sudden fragrance of a rosebush in bloom, and the gentle sound of a burbling fountain help enrich the garden experience.

Natural Patterns

With gardens that are ornamental versions of the natural landscape, it is logical to look to nature for basic shapes when designing them. One of these shapes is the meandering stream. This is a sweeping curve that repeats itself and often includes clusters of vegetation on the outward side of each arc or on an island within the stream. In a garden, such a shape could be used for pathways, beds, and even a deck or patio, mimicking the place in nature where a blockage in a stream has widened it into a pool.

There are rarely any hard edges or boundaries in the natural world. Areas of contrasting texture are more likely to merge into each other. You might think of this principle when you blend the edge of a patio into a lawn, perhaps by using sections of flagstone matching those of the patio to begin a pathway

In this San Francisco terrace garden attached to a one-story house, a eucalyptus tree provides midsummer shade. The white 'Alister Stella Gray' rose will reach only to the roof, and the musk rose 'Ballerina', between the chairs, grows just high enough to waft its fragrance to anyone seated there.

Several visual tricks in this Massachusetts garden— bright colors and large foliage up front, a mirroring symmetry to strengthen the archway focal point, and a tapering lawn—suggest a large plot leading into the woods. In fact, it ends just behind the row of hemlocks.

onto the lawn. Or, at a transition to a woodland, you could plant a small grove of trees just at the edge of the woodland to welcome you in.

In nature, plants and rocks tend to cluster. Do the same with your arrangements, whether you have a group of trees at a focal point, perennials in a bed, rocks in a rock garden, or bulbs naturalized in a lawn. The clusters will eventually merge into drifts and come into contact with one another.

Finally, plants in nature grow at different levels. This establishes a layered pattern that you can mimic in your garden. Tall trees will create a top layer or canopy. Under this canopy, you can plant smaller shade-tolerant trees and shrubs typical of a shady understory. At the lowest level will be flowers and ground covers. Such a design is inherently unified and harmonious.

TIPS FROM THE PROS

Creating an Illusion of Space

To create the illusion that a small garden is larger than it really is, designers use a variety of optical tricks. If you have a small or awkwardly shaped lot, one or more of these design tips might work for you.

• Place large objects in the foreground and small ones at a distance. For example, front your patio with large planters and place smaller pots at a focal point at the back. Decrease the size of paving blocks as they recede to the rear.

• Group plants by size and texture. Position those with large leaves in the foreground and those with finer foliage toward the back.

• Simulate the perception that parallel lines converge toward a focal point by slightly tapering a pathway, lawn, or pool so that it narrows at the far end.

• Use a hedge, trellis, or bed to partially block the view to a focal point.

• Subdivide your garden and make strong transitions from one space to another.

• For an illusion of greater depth, plant bold, hot-colored flowers in the foreground and cooler pastels toward the rear of the garden.

Garden Styles

A garden may have a certain character or style, just as houses do. Styles have historical associations, but they are also influenced by regional cultures and growing conditions. Your first consideration should be to keep the style of your garden in harmony with that of your house. Next, take into account climate, soil, and the lay of the land. In fact, many popular garden styles have developed over the years specifically to address regional environmental conditions.

But the style you choose should not be the result of practical considerations alone. It should reflect your taste, your sense of beauty, and your desires. Thus you might decide to have one style of garden in the front yard—a formal one, perhaps—and a totally different look for the side or back yard, where you entertain or where your children play. The garden types described here are only an indication of the range of possibilities.

Formal and Informal Gardens

A house with a strong classical design calls for the strong axes and crisply defined focal points of a formal garden. Building materials such as brick or stone block look appropriate in a formal setting. Formal gardens are boldly geometric in structure. Straight lines, simple curves, precise angles, and sharp edges all contribute to a formal feeling. Symmetrical pairings mirroring each other and framing a central feature—such as two roses pruned into standards flanking a garden sculpture; carpet planting of a single type of plant; and ornate pruning are all elements of a formal design.

Despite this rigidity, formal gardens come in great variety and include rose and herb gardens, flower beds arranged like mosaics, water gardens that reflect the sky in yet another kind of symmetry, and walled vegetable gardens called potagers. Their strong ground plans are easy to read, and they retain a presence even in winter's landscape.

If you like the formal look but only up to a point, you can soften the formal geometry with a cascade of wisteria or a climbing rose on a wall or with a naturalistic planting of herbaceous perennials that billows over a border's straight edge. This softening of the formal style became the basis for the traditional English cottage garden, typically a charming, informal mix of annual and perennial blossoms set within a well-defined garden space.

During Colonial times, American houses had cottage or dooryard gardens that were similar to their English cottage counterparts, with a profusion of flowering plants blooming in beguiling disarray on either side of the front door and along the front of the house. Today, a more structured version of the dooryard garden has become the most popular American landscape style—an informal garden with a somewhat loose, natural appearance featuring irregular or compound curves. But this is not laissez-faire gardening. The style calls for crisply defined beds forming a strong ground pattern. Planting arrangements, though not usually symmetrical, are carefully balanced. Brick, stone, and concrete effects borrowed from the house are built into paths and walls.

The axes and focal points in an informal garden are subtler and the patterns less regular than in a formal arrangement. They may exist naturally on your land, needing only a little emphasis from you to bring them out. Or a focal point might be implied by making a clearing in a line of trees, and the axis leading to it may be no more than an irregularly spaced line of shrubs.

In addition, the mechanism for framing a focal point by bracketing it will be more naturalistic than in a formal garden. For example, rather than balancing two identical clipped shrubs on either side of a focal point, you might achieve an informal balance with a small conifer and a clump of soft foliage to one side and a large rock on the other. The two masses may be equivalent in visual weight, but their textures and forms are quite different.

Japanese-Inspired Gardens

The Japanese-style garden blends some of the principles of formal design—strong, clean lines, for example—with the asymmetry of the informal garden. Each element is carefully chosen to achieve an exquisite effect—a rock is placed just so, a tree is sited to weep over a pool and be reflected in the water, the sinuous motion of a stream is captured in the flowing bends of a path.

The plants and building materials in a Japanese garden reflect a fine attention to detail and are generally kept to a small scale. The emphasis is on the texture and form of plant foliage, rock, and wood, with occasional splashes of flower color.

Enclosed by a low hedge of Japanese holly, this Atlanta, Georgia, parterre—four rectangular beds laid out in a carpetlike pattern—lends a formal accent to the stone steps leading up to the back garden. Wall germander outlines the central beds, which are filled with red wax begonias surrounding a pot of trained ivy.

Regional Gardens

Regional garden designs reflect local climate and growing conditions. They incorporate native plants best suited to that environment and include structural elements, such as walls and water features, that temper the effects of the weather.

Desert gardens thrive in extremes of drought and heat. A desert is not hot all year round, but it is dry, with annual rainfall of less than 10 inches. Plants grow low to the ground, and trees are spaced widely to conserve water. A desert garden follows that model, using plants like prickly pear, ocotillo, and spiky yucca. Trees such as carob, acacia, and common olive have deep taproots to reach underground water, and cast cooling shade. High courtyard walls and sun-screening trellises help moderate the heat and glare.

Mediterranean gardens are a variation on the desert garden. Originating in the arid climate of Spain, North Africa, and the eastern Mediterranean, they have transplanted easily to California and the American Southwest. Suited to contemporary, stucco, or Spanish-style houses, these gardens nestle in the shelter of a courtyard or an atrium. The plantings can be lush, featuring exotically colored and scented tropical trees such as citrus, banana, and palm, all surrounding a central fountain. Vines such as jasmine and bougainvillea climb the garden's walls, and ferns, hibiscus, oleander, and bird-of-paradise grow in pots and raised beds.

Landscape Plants for Specific Styles

Formal

TREES
Acer
(maple)
Cedrus
(cedar)
Cupressus sempervirens
(Italian cypress)
Fagus sylvatica
(European beech)
Magnolia
(magnolia)
Picea
(spruce)
Quercus
(oak)

SHRUBS
Berberis thunbergii
(Japanese barberry)
Ilex crenata
(Japanese holly)
Ilex vomitoria
(yaupon)
Prunus laurocerasus
(cherry laurel)
Rosa hybrids
(hybrid roses)
Taxus baccata
(English yew)

VINES
Rosa
(climbing hybrid rose)
Wisteria
(wisteria)

GROUND COVERS
Calluna vulgaris
(heather)
Hosta
(plantain lily)

Informal

TREES
Acer rubrum
(red maple)
Acer saccharum
(sugar maple)

SHRUBS
Euonymus alata
(winged spindle tree)
Lagerstroemia indica
(crape myrtle)
Rhododendron
(rhododendron)
Rosa rugosa
(rugosa rose)
Syringa
(lilac)

Japanese

TREES
Acer palmatum
(Japanese maple)
Malus floribunda
(Japanese flowering
crab apple)
Pinus densiflora
(Japanese red pine)

SHRUBS
Chaenomeles
(flowering quince)
Juniperus
(juniper)
Pieris japonica
(lily-of-the-valley bush)
Pinus mugo
(dwarf mountain pine)

VINES
Wisteria floribunda
(Japanese wisteria)

GROUND COVERS
Liriope muscari
(big blue lilyturf)

Acer rubrum
(red maple)

Woodland Gardens

Wherever it might appear, a woodland garden consists of the same two elements: a number of large trees to create an overhead canopy, and a succession of underlayers—smaller trees, shrubs, and ground-level plants like wildflowers, ferns, and mosses. To create a successful design, reduce the natural abundance of a woodland to a few simple elements. Build in a clearing to let in light for the less shade-tolerant plants and to bring about a contrast of light and dark. But make sure a few saplings are interspersed among the older trees to ensure successive generations of shade trees. Then make

a path through the garden to take you from place to place and to keep visitors from trampling delicate plants. If you choose plants that produce berries and flowers to create a habitat for wildlife, after a time you will develop a self-sustaining environment that requires little further effort.

Meadow and Prairie Gardens

While woodland gardens provide a shady oasis, wildflower meadow and prairie gardens are open, sunny, and alive with color and texture. They also are more precarious, requiring periodic mowing to prevent unwanted saplings from taking over and to allow desirable seedlings to become established. These gardens work especially well as transition areas between the more structured part of the garden and the openness of the surrounding countryside. Plant mixtures for meadows and prairies will vary according to soil and rainfall, but all will require full sun. You can purchase seed mixes suited to your area from seed companies. These mixes will include annual and perennial wildflowers, such as daisies, sundrops, butterfly weed, and Texas bluebonnet. The annuals should reseed themselves after the first year. Also included will be native bunch grasses like switch grass, big bluestem, and little bluestem. Bulbs planted in broad swaths also naturalize well in a wild meadow.

A North Carolina garden sets the simplicity of the Japanese style within a Western border and lawn. Plants indigenous to Japan, such as red laceleaf Japanese maple, multicolored Houttuynia cordata, and two varieties of Japanese cedar, harmonize beautifully. The shape of the pyramidal rock, for example, is echoed in the smaller cedar 'Bandai-Sugi'.

Composing with Color

You can ensure maximum year-round interest in your garden by weaving threads of seasonal color throughout its beds and borders. The first step is to sketch out color ideas on paper, so that when you are ready to plant you will be able to create a sense of unity throughout the garden. Your personal preferences will guide you in your initial choice of colors. You may lean toward hues from the warm end of the spectrum, such as red, orange, and yellow, rather than the cool end, which includes the greens, blues, and violets. Perhaps you prefer delicate tints over strong shades, and harmonious blendings over bright contrasts. Before you make any final decisions, however, there are a number of other things you must consider.

Color, Light, and Mood

How colors appear in your garden will depend on two factors—whether a planting is located in sun or shade and the way light changes from morning to night and through the seasons. Pastels stand out in the soft light of early morning or evening, for example, and fairly glimmer in the shade, but their pale presence is lost in bright midday sun, where strong, bright colors like reds and oranges do best. Colors that glow warmly in autumn light, such as bronze or purple, may look drab on hazy summer days or in the cold glare of winter.

One way to plan for successful seasonal colors is to observe the hues nature reveals over time. Spring is a symphony of pastel-blooming trees, shrubs, and bulbs, followed by deeper tints of blue, yellow, and pink as summer gets under way. Late summer is dominated by highly saturated colors—vibrant yellow, Day-Glo orange, hot red, deep pink, fuchsia, and violet. By contrast, fall is cloaked in muted shades of gold, bronze, rust, plum, and purple.

Certain color groupings will create different moods in the garden. Try planting pink, purple,

or blue pastels interspersed with neutral whites and grays for a cooling and soothing effect. A garden theme mixing the neutral colors with various shades of green will create a cool retreat in the heat of summer. To add a little warmth, introduce soft creams and buttery yellows to the mix.

If you want a more vibrant atmosphere, choose strong yellows, golds, oranges, and reds. But use red with care; it is the most dominant color in the spectrum and can be overpowering. A backdrop of dark green foliage can tone down even the brightest reds, but a bright green background will make the reds pop out even more.

Color and Space

Through creative placement of colors, you can define spaces and change perspectives in a garden design. Cool colors lengthen distances, warm colors make them appear closer. Your choice of color groupings, therefore, should be based on the perspective you want to achieve.

Setting the landscape afire with its glowing orange-red fall foliage, a katsura tree (Cercidiphyllum japonicum) stands out from the subtler lime yellow coloring of Hydrangea anomala ssp. petiolaris (climbing hydrangea) and Idesia polycarpa (iigiri tree).

Anchored by a Colorado blue spruce, drifts of Zinnia elegans 'Sun Red', orange Helichrysum bracteatum 'Bright Bikini' (strawflower), pink Phlox maculata 'Alpha' (wild sweet William), and yellow Lilium 'Citronella' put on a dazzling summer show. In the foreground, a broad green drift of Sedum spectabile 'Brilliant' (showy stonecrop) completes the planting.

When planning beds and borders close to the house, consider how you can accentuate or complement the color of the roof, sides, or trim with foliage and flowers. Also, select herbaceous plants with colors that will tie in with those of adjacent small shrubs, ground covers, and larger plantings. This way, you will maintain a unified color theme.

You can also choose flower colors to attract butterflies and hummingbirds, which favor strong pinks, reds, yellows, and oranges. (Hummingbirds prefer tubular flowers; butterflies, flat and cup-shaped flowers.) To reduce the potentially overwhelming visual impact of these bright colors, use white flowers or dark green, gray, and variegated foliage to separate vivid pinks and reds from equally intense yellows and oranges.

Color from Bulbs and Annuals

To color your landscape from late winter into fall, be sure to include masses of small- and large-flowering bulbs in your design. Select different varieties that bloom simultaneously or those whose bloom times coincide with those of other flowering plants. For example, create a pleasing contrast by teaming up spring-blooming yellow tulips with blue forget-me-nots or with deep blue grape hyacinths. Or, for a harmonious combination, plant purple pansies next to pale lavender crocuses.

Many summer- and fall-flowering bulbs, such as lilies, dahlias, and begonias, bloom for several weeks and will brighten your beds and borders with a rich tapestry of hues ranging from deep pink to brick red, from apricot to bronze. For a blooming sequence that lasts from late winter through fall, plant a sunny border with a mixture of bulbs and perennials—daffodils, Siberian irises, flowering onion, peonies, daylilies, dahlias, rudbeckias, perennial phlox, asters, and chrysanthemums.

Because of their long bloom periods, which can span three seasons, annual bedding plants are good additions to planting schemes that focus on color. Choose their colors carefully, though, so that they will continue to complement the perennials and bulbs in the bed. You can also plant annuals to cover bare spots in the early years of a garden and to fill gaps between shrubs and trees.

Color in the Shade

Areas dominated by trees and shrubs are typically shady, and many varieties of annuals, perennials, and bulbs can brighten these shadowy spots.

Begin with late-winter and early-spring bulbs that bloom before deciduous trees leaf out to block the sun. Snowdrops, crocuses, squill, Grecian windflowers, and daffodils are early bloomers that will naturalize into colorful masses.

For the rest of the growing season, fill spaces that receive partial or dappled shade with brightly colored, long-lasting, shade-tolerant perennials such as astilbe, foxglove, spurge, cardinal flower, alumroot, Virginia bluebells, monarda, St.-John's-wort, and red valerian *(Centranthus ruber)*. The most reliable annual for a shady nook is *Impatiens wallerana* (busy Lizzie). If you'd like to draw attention to a planting of dark green shrubs, illuminate them with a grouping of white or pastel flowers, such as impatiens, columbine, lily of the valley, primrose, and bleeding heart.

Foliage Plants

Flowering plants bring a rainbow of colors to a border or bed, but herbaceous foliage plants also have their place. By no means confined to green, the foliage colors of these plants range all over the rest of the spectrum. Used in contrast with the blooms surrounding them, they can turn a merely pleasing border into a visual feast.

The texture of the foliage, which can vary from fine to coarse, also plays a major role. When foliage plants of different texture and shape are planted next to each other, for example, they add a dramatic dimension to the design. Ferns are a good example of plants with fine and feathery foliage. The leaves range in color from dark green to bright green, but one, *Athyrium nipponicum* 'Pictum', is dramatically edged in silver. Other fine, feathery-leaved plants include astilbe, *Artemisia* x 'Powis Castle', goatsbeard, *Perovskia* (Russian sage), yarrow, and *Dicentra eximia* 'Luxuriant'.

A good combination for a shade garden is to plant ferns beside smooth-leaved hostas. Depending on the variety, hosta leaves may be small and narrow or large and flat; tinted with blue, cream, yellow, chartreuse, or dark green; variegated with spots and stripes, or one intense solid color.

Other winning texture combinations include furry silver-gray lamb's ears planted with spiky gray-green lavender or green *Santolina;* the large, glossy, purple leaves of *Heuchera micrantha* 'Palace Purple' with the fragile, feathery leaves of achillea; the thick, vertical, sword-shaped leaves of *Yucca filamentosa* with the small, rounded leaves of *Sempervivum* (houseleek); and the narrow, stiff leaves of ornamental grasses with the low-growing lacy foliage of *Astilbe chinensis* 'Pumila'.

A medley of shade-loving plants, their low-growing, rounded habits broken by spiky leaves and filigrees of flowers, receives morning sun and then dappled shade in this east-facing Oregon garden.

Finalizing Your Plan

When you are ready to commit your final planting plan to paper, you'll need to keep in mind how large each plant you choose will grow and how far and how fast it will spread. It takes about 3 years for most herbaceous perennials to spread into drifts, and 5 years for many shrubs to reach maturity. Depending on the growth rate of trees (slow, moderate, or fast) it can take anywhere from 8 to 20 years for them to reach significant size. You'll need to consider whether the trees you have in mind will eventually branch out so broadly that they'll turn your sunny garden into a shady one.

If you're planting slow-growing trees and shrubs, it's important to select a combination of evergreen and deciduous species that will continue to complement each other at maturity. Careful planning in the beginning will save you from the unpleasant and possibly expensive task of removing major plantings after several years of growth because they are crowding each other or simply no longer look good together.

Spacing shrubs to allow for future growth need not leave your garden looking bare and uninteresting during its first few years. To create fullness, you can interplant with perennials, annuals, and filler bulbs, such as tulips, hyacinths, or lilies. And once the shrubs start spreading, it's a simple matter to relocate the herbaceous plants as needed.

Planning for Seasonal Interest

To create a garden that provides four seasons of interest, you will need a mixture of plants that includes some that are visually appealing throughout the year and others that bloom in different months. Before you break ground, your paper plan should indicate which plants produce long-lasting foliage or flowers and which overlap their blooming cycles.

Perhaps the surest way to formulate a successful year-round planting plan is to superimpose on your base map a different tissue overlay for each season. Indicate on each overlay which features— bloom color, leaf texture, distinctive bark, berries, and the like—will be prominent at which locations during that season.

Noting life cycles of flowers, trees, and shrubs will allow you to group plants to advantage. For

In this Connecticut garden, tulips and daffodils share a bed with perennials that will help disguise the bulbs' fading foliage. At the far end, a scarlet Japanese maple contrasts pleasantly with the pastel purple blossoms of a Higan cherry, while a backdrop of rhododendrons provides year-round greenery and the promise of summer flowers.

Tracking the Growth of a New Garden

A new bed, if properly planted, *will show a lot of bare ground. In the bed at right, widely spaced astilbes thrust up white spires beneath a young Korean mountain ash tree. Three red Japanese barberry shrubs and a dwarf hinoki false cypress have space for modest growth, while the pink-flowered sedums, variegated hostas, and tiny ajuga plants require more room.*

By the third year, the astilbes have filled in, *the sedums have spread widely, the hostas have doubled in size, and the ajugas have put out runners in all directions, thickening into a ground cover. The canopy of the Korean mountain ash has expanded 3 to 5 feet, while the barberries and false cypress have yet to reach mature size.*

The bed has attained a pleasing fullness by the fifth year. *While the shrubs show steady but compact growth, the mountain ash continues to expand at 2 feet or so a year, toward its maximum size of 40 feet tall with a canopy 25 feet wide. The astilbes, sedums, and hostas require little maintenance or division, meaning that this bed need not be disturbed for many years to come.*

example, when daffodils have finished blooming, you will want their withering leaves out of view. The best way to accomplish this is to grow them in the midst of colorful foliage or tall swaths of annual or perennial flowers, which will come into full growth just as the bulb foliage begins to fade.

And although annuals have a life cycle of just a few months, they create a continuous flow of color from late spring to summer's end. Some, such as impatiens, scarlet sage, pot marigold, zinnia, cleome, cosmos, and zonal geranium, keep on producing blooms until they are killed by a hard frost. Overlapping with these warm-weather favorites are late-summer perennials, which also carry their colorful flowers until nipped by cold temperatures.

You can plan for even more fall color by choosing deciduous shrubs and trees with leaves that take on intensely brilliant hues and by planting perennials such as asters, *Sedum* x 'Autumn Joy' (stonecrop), goldenrod, *Chrysanthemum* x *morifolium* (florist's chrysanthemum), Japanese anemone, *Caryopteris* (bluebeard), *Colchicum autumnale* (autumn crocus), *Colchicum speciosum* 'Album' (showy autumn crocus), *Rosa* Meidiland varieties, and ornamental grasses.

Brightening Winter Months

In the winter, when trees and shrubs have dropped their fiery leaves, you can still enjoy ample color in the various shades of evergreen foliage, tree and shrub bark, berries, dried grasses, and the seed heads of some perennials and shrubs. The bark of certain deciduous trees, such as birch, eastern sycamore, and *Stewartia pseudocamellia* (Japanese stewartia), and the shiny leaves of holly, bull bay, and ivy will delight your eye after most herbaceous plants have gone dormant for the winter.

By late winter, small-bulb shoots are already pushing their way out of the soil. The delicate snowdrops are among the first to bloom, quickly followed by crocuses and other small bulbs and by the blossoming of shrubs such as witch hazel, forsythia, and *Prunus mume* (Japanese flowering apricot). From then on there is no stopping the show of spring-flowering squill, hyacinths, daffodils, and tulips. And if you have planned carefully, you can enjoy the sequential blooms of rhododendron species, flowering cherries, magnolias, dogwoods, lilacs, viburnums, and a host of other blooms that creep over the ground, wind their tendrils up fences, and blossom overhead.

Putting in the Plants

Begin with the largest trees, which involve the greatest amount of digging and the most extensive trampling on surrounding soil. Because cultivated soil is easily compacted, don't till any soil for planting smaller shrubs and herbaceous plants until you are sure you no longer have any need to walk on it. After the large trees are in, add medium-size shrubs and trees. Follow this stage by planting small decorative specimens, dwarf shrubs, perennials, vines, and ground covers and other filler plants, such as bulbs, annuals, and herbs.

When planting small shrubs, place them in groups of two, three, or even five if space allows. If they are slow growing, shrubs can be sited fairly close together to form a mass that makes a strong impression; you can also plant them farther apart at regular intervals to impart rhythm and continuity to a bed or border. Perennials look better when they are planted close to one another in groups of three or five; but if the plants are young, leave ample room between them. Annuals are more effective when planted in drifts or massed along the edges of a border. It doesn't matter if they crowd one another. Avoid planting flowers singly at random intervals, where their impact would be lost.

In this East Hampton, New York, garden, low-growing bird's-nest spruce, bloodleaf Japanese maple, and variegated hinoki false cypress (far right) furnish year-round interest. The ground-hugging lady's-mantle combined with the large ribbed leaves of hosta, the tall spires of foxtail lily, and the lacy heads of hydrangea contribute more seasonal texture. 'Just Joey' roses, 'Johnson's Blue' geraniums, and other perennials provide weeks of color.

Bringing It All Together

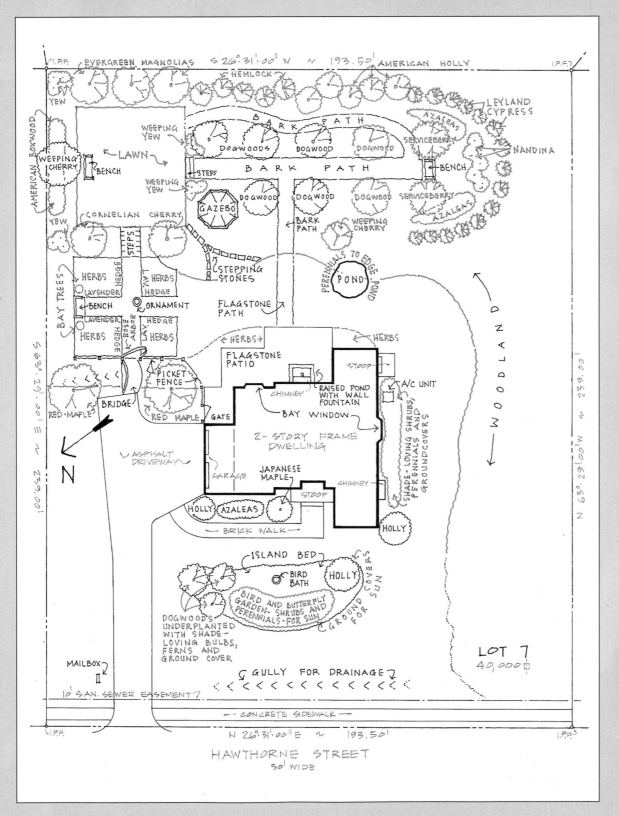

The final phase of this sample garden design is to impose a planting plan on the property map. The map now shows in black ink the regrading and transplanting to be done, and the installation of hardscape elements—such as a brick path and a flagstone patio—the gardener has chosen. Using green ink, she has laid out an ambitious project that will probably take several years to complete. Included are a screen of ornamental trees along the rear property line, a foliage cul-de-sac in the south corner, a lawn framed by shrubs and ornamental trees on the new terrace in the east corner, a formal herb garden, a mixed shade border on the southwest side of the house, and a bird-and-butterfly garden in the existing bed at the front of the house.

Successful Garden Plans

Your garden, as well as your home, reflects your personal idea of beauty. If you prefer modern styles, you may design a garden that has strongly defined lines and bold-colored plants. On the other hand, if you're a romantic at heart, you may choose to create an evocative, fragrant garden, such as the small lavender garden at left. But whatever its style, every garden requires a plan to make it work.

This chapter will show you how to select, place, and maintain plants for a wide range of garden designs. From waterwise gardens to backdoor cutting gardens, you'll learn, step by step, how to create a workable, easily maintained design. Each basic plan is accompanied by two alternate plans for the same garden site. The alternates may reflect regional variations, different environments, or simply alternative approaches to plant selection. Armed with these flexible plans you can easily create a garden that reflects your personal sense of style.

Create Your Own Cottage Garden

One of the most popular gardening styles is the charming, informal cottage garden. The cottage garden's origins lie in 15th-century English villages, where the occupants of small, rustic cottages filled their gardens with a colorful mix of flowers, herbs, and vegetables. The garden provided much of the cottager's daily necessities: medicinal teas, herbal balms and insect repellents, and fresh vegetables for the soup pot.

Today's American-style cottage garden relies on a mix of low-maintenance annuals, perennials, and self-sowing biennials. The casual, densely planted style is perfectly suited to today's busy gardener. Close plantings shade the ground, reducing weeding and watering chores. The occasional removal of spent flowers and unwanted seedlings will keep your garden looking its best.

While the cheerful tumble of flowers in a cottage garden looks casual, the effect takes planning. The mix of annuals, biennials, perennials, and woody plants shown here produces a colorful tapestry that peaks in early summer. Alternate designs on the next two pages focus on a garden of easy-going plants that self-sow from year to year, creating changing color combinations, and an all-summer garden that offers something new to anticipate throughout the growing season. Any of these three gardens is suited to the picket-fenced front yard of a true cottage, but they are all adaptable to any sunny spot in your landscape. Whether it is nestled outside the kitchen door, fronts a patio, or is tucked between the house and garage, the cottage garden should be located for both ease of use and beauty.

Luxurious Floral Abundance

The cottage garden at left relies on old-fashioned biennial sweet Williams, foxgloves, and wallflowers for its nostalgic appeal and early summer bloom. Annual blue bachelor's-buttons and brilliant nasturtiums begin in midsummer and flower into fall. The foliage of perennial lamb's ears and Siberian irises add structure all summer. The bougainvillea provides a flowery backdrop and enclosure that is the essence of the cottage style. It is hardy only in Zone 10, and gardeners in other zones can achieve similar results with clematis or a climbing rose.

In keeping with the spirit of true cottage gardening, this one has a variety of useful plants. Lamb's ears, bachelor's-buttons, and spireas dry well for flower arrangements, and nasturtium blossoms add peppery flavor to salads.

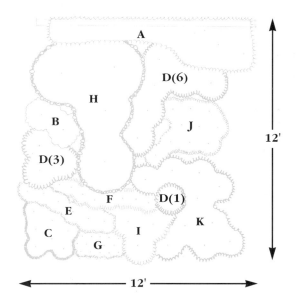

Plant List

A. *Bougainvillea* x *buttiana* (bougainvillea) (1)
B. *Centaurea cyanus* (bachelor's-button) (2)
C. *Dianthus barbatus* (sweet William) (7)
D. *Digitalis purpurea* (foxglove) (10)
E. *Erysimum* 'Bowles Mauve' (wallflower) (6)
F. *Iris sibirica* (Siberian iris) (8)
G. *Papaver nudicaule* (Iceland poppy) (15)
H. *Spiraea* x *bumalda* 'Lime Mound' (spirea) (4)
I. *Stachys byzantina* (lamb's ears) (3)
J. *Tropaeolum majus* (nasturtium) (10)
K. *Salvia* x *superba* 'May Night' (violet sage) (10)

◆ How to Plant This Garden ◆

1. Sow Iceland poppies in spring.

2. Plant bougainvillea in early spring, close to a support.

3. Sow bachelor's-buttons and nasturtiums directly in the ground in spring; plant violet

sage after the last frost.

4. Plant lamb's ears, Siberian irises, and spirea in midspring.

5. Start sweet Williams, foxgloves, and wallflowers outdoors from seed in midsummer. Transplant into the

garden in early fall.

Aftercare and Maintenance
• *Deadhead spent flowers to keep the plants blooming.*
• *Water Siberian irises regularly during dry spells.*

A Cottage Garden of Self-Sowing Flowers

The annuals, biennials, and perennials that contribute the bulk of summer color in this cottage garden range from 3-inch English daisies to 6-foot hollyhocks. Once planted, they perpetuate from self-sown seed, needing only a rigorous thinning in spring to give each plant room to develop.

Certain permanent plant fixtures provide continuity and structure for the effervescent display of summer flowers, such as beautybush, a large shrub with soft pink late-spring flowers; 'Dropmore Scarlet' honeysuckle, a woody vine with fragrant summer blooms; 'Lavender Lassie' shrub rose; and rhubarb, a long-lived perennial that produces edible red stalks in spring and decorative foliage all summer. These four cold-hardy plants need a period of winter dormancy and will not grow well in subtropical climates. All require full sun and well-drained soil to perform well.

In addition to flowers for generous bouquets, this cottage garden produces rhubarb stalks for pies and conserves, pot marigold petals to add golden color to stocks and soups, and feverfew leaves to brew into an astringent tea that is a traditional headache remedy. This garden also will yield rose petals for cake decoration or to dry for potpourri, small sunflower seeds for songbirds, honeysuckle blossoms to attract hummingbirds, and hollyhocks for children to fashion into dolls.

Plant List

A. Alcea 'Country Romance Mix' (hollyhock) (2)
B. Bellis perennis (English daisy) (9)
C. Calendula officinalis (pot marigold) (4)
D. Chrysanthemum parthenium (feverfew) (5)

E. Cleome hasslerana 'Colour Fountain' (spider flower) (7)
F. Helianthus x multiflorus 'Flore Pleno' (perennial sunflower) (5)
G. Kolkwitzia amabilis (beautybush) (1)
H. Lonicera x brownii 'Dropmore Scarlet'

(honeysuckle) (1)
I. Lychnis coronaria (rose campion) (4)
J. Papaver rhoeas (Shirley poppies) (7)
K. Rheum rhabarbarum 'Valentine' (rhubarb) (1)
L. Rosa 'Lavender Lassie' (shrub rose) (2)

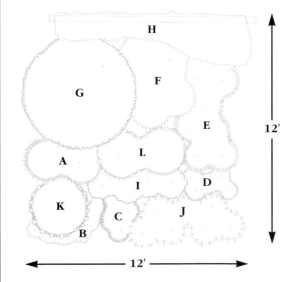

❖ How to Plant This Garden ❖

1. Double dig the garden site.

2. Plant beautybush, shrub rose, and honeysuckle in early spring or fall. Plant honeysuckle 1 foot from trellis. Add plenty of compost to generous holes for root systems.

3. In early spring, plant rhubarb with the crowns 1 to 2 inches below the surface. Add soil gradually to fill in the hole as plants grow.

4. Sow Shirley poppies and pot marigold seeds in early spring. Thin plants to 8 to 10 inches apart.

5. Sow spider flower seeds in midspring. Thin to 10 to 12 inches.

6. Set out the remaining plants in midspring. Water after planting.

Aftercare and Maintenance
• Remove old wood from beautybush, shrub rose, and honeysuckle in late winter or early spring.

A Cottage Garden for All-Summer Bloom

The plants in this cottage garden provide a succession of bloom, beginning with the early-summer flowers of lavender chives and multi-colored columbines shown here, and finishing the season with the last huge, rosy blossoms of Clematis 'Dr. Ruppel' in early fall. This is a pink-and-blue garden, with white highlights provided by the fragrant early blooms of a mock orange shrub and the graceful late-summer spires of gooseneck loosestrife. Most of the plants are long-lived perennials that flower each summer with minimal care. The annual cosmos and globe amaranth are exceptions, but both self-sow reliably and require only the removal of unwanted seed-lings each spring. All these plants will do well in mild to very cold climates; this is not a garden for subtropical or tropical locales. Plant this garden in full sun in loamy, well-drained garden soil, amended with several inches of compost. Position it where it will be convenient to snip a few chives for cooking or to assemble an impromptu bouquet. Its long-blooming season and beautiful combinations of colors and forms qualify this cottage garden for a highly visible location, such as near a patio or front entrance.

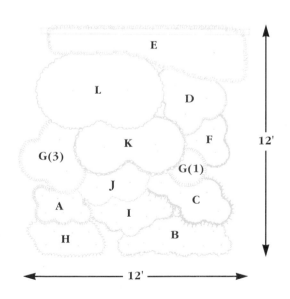

Plant List

A. Allium schoenopra-sum (chives) (6)
B. Aquilegia 'Music Series' (columbine) (10)
C. Artemisia absinthium (wormwood) (5)
D. Campanula lactiflora 'Pritchard's Variety' (bellflower) (3)

E. Clematis 'Dr. Ruppel' (clematis) (1)
F. Cosmos bipinnatus 'Versailles Series' (cosmos) (3)
G. Delphinium 'Blue Bird' and 'Galahad' (delphinium) (4)
H. Dianthus barbatus (sweet William) (8)

I. Gomphrena globosa (globe amaranth) (8)
J. Lysimachia clethroides (gooseneck loosestrife) (2)
K. Paeonia 'Sarah Bernhardt' (peony) (2)
L. Philadelphus 'Belle Etoile' (mock orange) (2)

◆ How to Plant This Garden ◆

1. Plant mock orange in early spring, leaving room for it to reach its full 6-foot spread.

2. Plant clematis in early spring, providing a support to climb.

3. Plant chives, columbines, wormwood, bellflowers, delphini-ums, and loosestrife 2 feet apart.

4. Plant sweet William seedlings in midspring, 1 foot apart.

5. Sow cosmos and globe ama-ranth in midspring, raking lightly

over seeds. Thin to 10 to 12 inches apart.

6. Plant peonies in late summer with their eyes (buds) no more than 1 to 2 inches below the soil's sur-face. Add straw mulch the first win-ter to prevent frost heaving.

Aftercare and Maintenance
•Restrain invasive loosestrife by pulling up unwanted stems. Dig and divide every 2 to 3 years.

Create Your Own Formal Garden

Formal gardens are best known for their strong lines, balanced geometric designs, and classical sense of beauty and repose. The formal garden is often built along a central axis oriented to the house. Minor axes may intersect the central axis, and decorative focal points such as an urn or a pool can punctuate these axes. There may be an oval or rectangular garden "room" at the end of an axis, with walls composed of stone, clipped hedges, or a line of narrow trees.

The choice of plants in a formal garden and the way they are cultivated reflect a planned consistency of line and effect. Ornate pruning, carpet planting of a single type of plant, and flower beds laid out in carefully proportioned designs are typ-ical of formal design. Unlike the casual profusion of the cottage garden, the variety of plants is kept to a minimum. Geometric-shaped beds are neatly outlined by carefully clipped hedges. These can be filled with densely spaced annuals to create solid blocks of color, or a few carefully chosen perennials for a long-lasting formal design. All the formal parterre gardens shown here and on the following pages begin with a strong framework of neat, angular, hedge-bordered beds and brick walkways following a straight axis. The parterre on this page consists primarily of foliage plants, giving it a year-round permanence. The alternate designs *(pages 62 and 63)* incorporate fragrant herbs or flowers for color and plant variety.

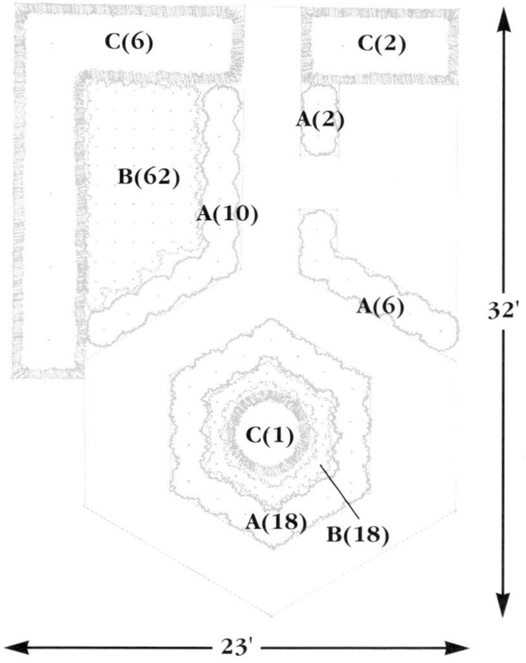

C(6) C(2) A(2) B(62) A(10) A(6) C(1) A(18) B(18)

32'

23'

Plant List

A. Buxus micro-phylla 'Compacta' (boxwood) (36)
B. Pelargonium x

hortorum (zonal geranium) (80)
C. Taxus baccata (English yew) (9)

The Elegance of Simplicity

Straight lines and a clear central axis make this formal garden easy to lay out. The lines and symmetrical beds draw attention to the central hexagon, the main focal point. An urn at the end of the central axis provides another focal point, drawing your gaze to the distant view.

Simple plant choices of dwarf boxwood and yew border the self-contained beds. In the traditional manner, both plants are sheared into round or rectangular forms, but their contrasting leaf shapes, textures, and shades of green sharply accent one another. The variegated foliage of the geranium provides further subtle color, while its pink blossoms echo the warm hues of the patterned brick walkway that unifies the design.

Simplicity, restraint in the use and number of colors, and carefully orchestrated geometry—characteristics of all formal gardens—are the keys to this successful plan.

◆ How to Plant This Garden ◆

1. In the early fall, plant yews in the central and rear beds. Plant boxwoods along the edges, spacing them 9 to 12 inches apart for a dense border.

2. In the spring, plant geraniums in even rows, spaced at 1-foot intervals. Keep them 2 feet away from the base of the shrubs. Cover soil surface with a finely ground mulch of compost, bark, or leaf mold to preserve soil moisture.

3. Water all plants at planting time. Water yews and boxwoods regularly until well established.

Aftercare and Maintenance
• Keep plants evenly moist until they are established, then water when the surface dries.
• As soon as growth begins, clip boxwoods and yews to promote rapid branching and fullness. Do not allow them to grow beyond their planned height.
• Deadhead geraniums regularly. Trim stems periodically to keep plants compact.

A Formal Garden with Fragrant Herbs

A thick, 4-foot-tall sheared privet hedge serves as a dramatic backdrop for this fragrant herb-and-flower garden. The privet, a deciduous shrub, frames the garden with its rich green, lance-shaped leaves in summer. In winter, it takes on a striking architectural appearance while maintaining the garden's formal lines.

A low border of clipped lavender cotton makes a compact, fresh-scented edging for the beds. Echoing its silvery foliage, a tall, unclipped English lavender stands at the center of the bed. The dark purple spires of lavender contrast boldly with the tiny, yellow button-flowers of lavender cotton. Sweet William, a reliable, self-seeding biennial, and mass plantings of cool white ageratum complete the garden's elegant color scheme.

Plant List

A. Ageratum houstonianum 'Neptune White' (ageratum) (62)
B. Dianthus barbatus (sweet William) (12)
C. Lavandula angustifolia 'Hidcote' (English lavender) (3)

D. Ligustrum vulgare 'Lodense' (privet) (9)
E. Santolina chamaecyparissus (lavender cotton) or **Lavandula angustifolia** 'Dwarf Blue' (English lavender) (74)

◆ How to Plant This Garden ◆

1. In the fall, plant privets 1½ feet apart, mixing several inches of compost into clay or sandy soils.

2. In the spring, after the last frost, improve the soil in each herb bed by mixing in 2 inches of compost—more if soil is clay.

3. Plant each bed, crowding ageratums and sweet Williams (every 6 to 8 inches) for a fast, finished look.

4. Position English lavender and lavender cotton 1 foot apart. At planting, pinch tips of herbs to encourage a bushier habit.

5. Regularly water all plants. Keep soil moist until growth begins.

Aftercare and Maintenance
• To maintain a full, dense hedge, prune the privets after their sweet-smelling blooms fade.
• Water sweet Williams and ageratums when soil surface begins to dry out, directing the water with a hose or can.
• Water privets and lavenders when soil is dry to 1 inch beneath the surface.
• Deadhead ageratums and sweet Williams regularly for a longer season of bloom and a tidy, compact appearance.
• In cold climates, overwinter English lavender in pots indoors, or plant new seedlings each spring.
• In spring, in all but the warmest climates, prune winter-damaged growth of both English lavender and lavender cotton and reshape them into low, compact mounds.

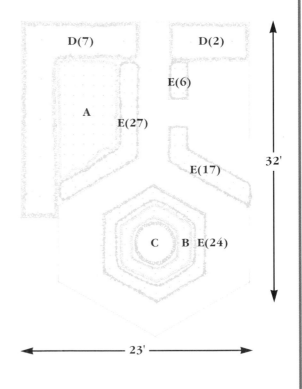

A Formal Flower Garden

The hedge-lined parterre in this plan is restricted to a limited palette of flowers and hues, although a larger variety could be used with an equally striking effect. The pastel rose and New Guinea impatiens add an elegant touch of color to the composition. For a brighter color scheme consider substituting lemon-yellow marigolds and a yellow shrub rose for the pastels used in this plan.

The low 'Kobold' barberry hedge brings further color to this garden through several seasons. New foliage is intensely green, deepening by summer, and in autumn the leaves take on a handsome yellow cast tinged with red. The barberry edging may be pruned for precise formality, as shown here, but left alone it naturally forms neat mounds approximately 2 feet tall.

The dense background hedge 'Sarcoxie' euonymus requires periodic shearing to maintain its shape and size. Its glossy, dark green leaves with whitish veins are a perfect foil for the delicate tints of the 'Lilac Rose' impatiens. Their placement draws the viewer's eye naturally to the garden's center, where the fragrance of the 'Tiffany' rose mingles with that of the surrounding 'Monarch White' pinks to create a sweet-and-spicy centerpiece.

◆ How to Plant This Garden ◆

1. In fall, plant wintercreeper euonymus *and barberries 1½ feet apart in soil amended with compost.*

2. Plant the rose *in a hole at least 18 inches deep and wide. Mix in several shovelfuls of compost and a handful of bone meal. Set the bud union at ground level in warm climates, and 1 to 2 inches below ground in cold regions.*

3. Plant pinks and New Guinea impatiens *in spring after danger of frost has passed. Amend soil with*

2 inches of compost or leaf mold.

4. Water all plants well after planting. *Mulch with shredded bark.*

Aftercare and Maintenance
• *Deadhead roses to promote continuous bloom. Remove dead, diseased, or damaged canes in early spring.*
• *Keep floral beds moist throughout the growing season. Fertilize on a regular basis with a balanced, all-purpose fertilizer.*

Plant List

A. *Berberis thunbergii* 'Kobold' (barberry) (36)
B. *Dianthus* 'Monarch White' (pinks) (18)
C. *Euonymus fortunei* 'Sarcoxie'
(winter creeper euonymus) (9)
D. *Impatiens* x 'Lilac Rose' (New Guinea impatiens) (62)
E. *Rosa* 'Tiffany' (hybrid tea rose) (1)

C(7)   C(2)
A(2)
D   A(10)
A(6)
E   B   A(18)
32'
23'

Create Your Own Fragrant Garden

While colorful gardens please the eye, fragrant gardens evoke many fond memories—from the sweet peas of childhood gardens to the clean smell of linens freshened with lavender sachets.

Some of the most fragrant plants are the old, subtly colored species. While these richly scented antiques have shorter blooming periods than modern hybrids, they are relatively hardy and easy to maintain. Unfortunately, many newer cultivars often sacrifice fragrance for bigger, bolder blossoms and a longer blooming period.

Enjoying fragrant plants depends as much on their location in the garden as on careful selection. To prevent even the most intense fragrance from wafting away in the breeze, try enclosing your garden with fences, walls, or tall plants that provide a windbreak. Try planting some of your favorite fra-

grant species in containers or raised beds near entrances, below bedroom windows, or beside decks and patios, where you will notice them easily. Highly scented, old-fashioned flowers like heliotrope, spicy cottage pinks, and some roses are well suited to containers.

The following gardens are carefully laid out for fragrance as well as beauty. In the purple-and-white garden shown opposite, fragrant herbs and shrubs combine to create an enchanting scene and bouquet. If you prefer sweeter, headier scents, or have a passion for old roses, consider the alternate gardens on the following pages. The first is composed of a variety of roses for a garden filled with traditional fragrance and form. The second is less traditional in its plant selection but equally rich in fragrance.

An Aromatic Blend of Herbs and Shrubs

Gardeners in temperate climates can enjoy the perfumes that pervade the garden shown here. The design includes a weathered gray perimeter fence that helps hold in the honeyed scents of the tall butterfly bush and 'Iceberg' floribunda rose. The feverfew, catmint, and lavender will release their perfume as visitors stroll along the brick paths and brush against their foliage.

Easy to grow in average soil, these low-maintenance plants develop casual arching branches and sprawling mounds, softening the garden's somewhat formal design. With their subtle colors, billowing forms, and evocative scents, these plants create a restful retreat you'll savor all summer long.

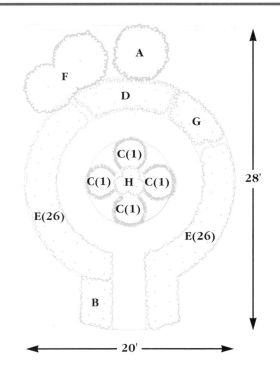

Plant List

A. *Buddleia davidii* 'Lochinch' (butterfly bush) (1)
B. *Chrysanthemum parthenium* (feverfew) (6)
C. *Lavandula angustifolia* 'Hidcote' (lavender) (4)
D. *Lychnis coronaria* 'Alba' (rose campion) (12)
E. *Nepeta* x *faassenii* (catmint) (52)
F. *Rosa* 'Iceberg' (floribunda rose) (2)
G. *Salvia* x *superba* (violet sage) (7)
H. *Santolina chamaecyparissus* (lavender cotton) (3)

◆ How to Plant This Garden ◆

1. In a porous potting mix, plant lavender cotton with the rootball at the same level as in its container.

2. Plant catmints 1 foot back from the walkway. Space lavenders evenly around the central bed, and set sages 12 inches apart.

3. Plant butterfly bush 2 feet from the fence and mulch well.

4. Plant rosebushes so bud union is at ground level in warm regions and 2 inches deep in cold ones.

5. In spring, plant feverfews and rose campions in full sun.

Aftercare and Maintenance
• Pinch growing tips of butterfly bush to encourage bushiness.

A Fragrant Garden Based on Roses

Perhaps no garden is more intensely fragrant than one filled with antique roses. The companion herbs shown here, with their sprawling mounds of scented foliage, complement the roses' casual look. All of the plants featured in this garden are relatively easy to maintain and will thrive in average, well-drained soil.

The circular design of this garden gives easy access to all of the plants, allowing close-up appreciation of the spicy gallica rose 'Camaieux' and even the climbing 'Dr. J. H. Nicolas'. Most antique roses flower only once in early summer, but the raspberry-scented 'Madame Isaac Pereire' blooms again in the fall. Complementing the white and pink roses, catmint, sage, and purple-hued English lavender spill along the path and out of their containers, inviting you to brush up against their aromatic leaves.

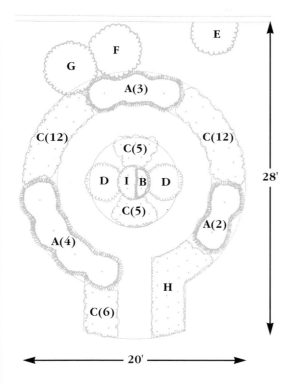

Plant List

A. *Lavandula angustifolia* 'Grosso' (English lavender) (9)
B. *Lavandula stoechas* ssp. *pedunculata* (Spanish lavender) (2)
C. *Nepeta* x *faassenii*

(catmint) (40)
D. *Rosa* 'Camaieux' (gallica rose) (2)
E. *Rosa* 'Dr. J. H. Nicolas' (climbing rose) (1)
F. *Rosa* 'Madame Hardy' (old garden rose) (1)

G. *Rosa* 'Madame Isaac Pereire' (bourbon rose) (1)
H. *Rosa* 'Popcorn' (miniature rose) (27)
I. *Salvia officinalis* (garden sage) (2)

◆ How to Plant This Garden ◆

1. Fill a container with a porous potting mix. *Plant garden sage and Spanish lavender plants close together for a full look.*

2. Dig holes for roses *18 inches wide and just deep enough to accommodate the roots. Spread roots out and cover with fine, compost-rich soil. Water roses well.*

3. Plant English lavender *at even intervals in the areas shown.*

4. Plant catmints *1 foot back from the walkway and 1 foot apart.*

Aftercare and Maintenance
• *Water roses monthly with a fish emulsion solution.*
• *Feed roses a balanced fertilizer in early spring and again in summer.*
• *In spring, add a deep layer of compost mulch around roses.*
• *Control vigorous 'Madame Isaac Pereire' by removing the largest canes every few years in winter.*
• *Divide sages every few years.*

A Sweet-and-Spicy Garden

Spring fragrance gets off to an early start in this garden planted with spicy-scented viburnum. Old-fashioned purple dame's rocket follows with its soft evening aroma. By early summer the potent fragrance of tall, arching mock orange penetrates every corner. Madonna lilies and pinks add their own sweet-and-spicy scents from early to midsummer.

This garden is at the peak of bloom from late spring to early summer. The Peruvian daffodils and 'David' phlox provide mid-summer fragrance and color, and the low carpets of pink-and-white flowering thyme continue blooming until frost. They release a delightfully spicy fragrance if you brush by their foliage.

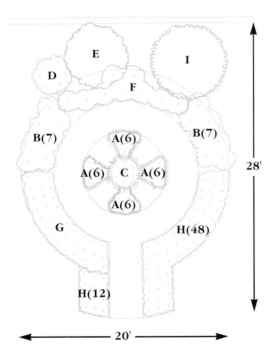

◆ How to Plant This Garden ◆

1. In early summer set three to five bulbs of Peruvian daffodils in loose potting soil in the urn with their tips 1 inch below the surface.

2. Dig a hole slightly wider and as deep as mock orange and Burkwood viburnum rootballs. Loosen the soil on the sides of the holes and spread out any circled roots before covering them with soil.

3. Plant Madonna lilies while the bulbs are dormant in late summer, covering them with no more than 2 inches of soil. Water well.

4. Sow seed for dame's rockets when the soil has warmed in the spring. The plants will bloom the following year. For faster bloom, set out bedding plants, allowing 1 to 2 feet of space between plants for expansion and air circulation.

5. Plant thyme 1 foot apart and 8 inches back from the walkway.

6. Plant garden phlox 2 feet apart.

Aftercare and Maintenance
• North of Zone 8, lift Peruvian daffodil bulbs after foliage yellows. Dry the bulbs and store upside down with roots still attached.
• Prune mock orange annually after bloom, removing the oldest, weakest stems at the base of the plant.
• Divide garden phlox every 2 to 3 years.

Plant List

A. Dianthus 'Bath's Pink' (pinks) (24)
B. Hesperis matronalis (dame's rocket) (14)
C. Hymenocallis narcissiflora (Peruvian daffodil) (7)
D. Lilium candidum 'Cascade Strain' (Madonna lily) (7)
E. Philadelphus coronarius (mock orange) (1)
F. Phlox paniculata 'David' (garden phlox) (9)
G. Thymus serpyllum 'Albus' (mother of thyme) (34)
H. Thymus serpyllum 'Coccineus' (mother of thyme) (60)
I. Viburnum x burkwoodii (Burkwood viburnum) (1)

Create Your Own Secret Garden

Whether set deep within a wooded glade or enclosed by the green walls of an outdoor room, a garden can be a peaceful hideaway. Your leafy retreat may be an oasis of cool shade and bubbling water where you can rest on a hot summer day, or perhaps a small dining area in a walled enclosure covered with rambling roses and clematis vines.

Whether made of brick, stone, lattice, or hedging, walls help define a secret garden. Sheared hedges such as hawthorn, holly, box, yew, privet,

or hornbeam create a more formal enclosure than vine-covered walls, but either style provides a sense of privacy. You can complete the structure of your outdoor room with a living carpet of grass or creeping thyme.

To create a secluded room, follow the plan here. If you prefer an abundance of old-fashioned flowers, or would like your garden to reach its peak later in the summer, then consider the two alternate plantings that follow.

Structuring a Garden Room

In the garden pictured opposite, you will find an inexpensive and quick way to create a secluded garden room. Instead of building a costly fence or wall, install sturdy stands of latticework planted with 'New Dawn' climbing roses. You won't have to wait 10 years for the new hedge to mature; you should feel comfortably enclosed in this private retreat in about 3 years. The rose-covered lattice walls will block out most views beyond the garden's confines, providing a pleasant seclusion and insulating your private bower.

This garden is not large, but it is rich enough in detail to seem a world of its own. A garden seat furnishes a place to rest and to appreciate the many plants springing up among the paving stones. The rustic path draws attention to the fragrant edging plants. Sharp scents of thyme and oregano blend with spicy pinks and the sweet perfume roses.

Color plays a role in the garden's look. Golden flowers of tree lupine and feverfew contrast with purple-flowered thyme, while pink roses and foxgloves complement the garden's abundant green foliage. Gardeners north of Zone 8 can substitute 'Father Hugo' roses for the tree lupines.

As your garden grows and its plants mature, you can change the room's decor by trying out new varieties of your favorite bedding plants or tucking a variety of different herbs in between the paving stones.

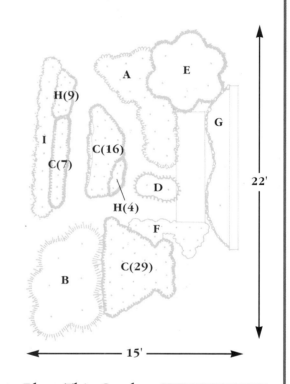

Plant List

A. Anemone hupehensis (Japanese anemone) (14)
B. Chrysanthemum parthenium 'Aureum' (feverfew) (6)
C. Dianthus deltoides 'Flashing Light' (maiden pinks) (52)
D. Digitalis purpurea (common foxglove) (2)
E. Lupinus arboreus (tree lupine) (7)
F. Origanum onites 'Aureum' (pot marjoram) (10)
G. Rosa 'New Dawn' (climbing rose) (2)
H. Sisyrinchium bellum (California blue-eyed grass) (13)
I. Thymus praecox (thyme) (9)

◆ How to Plant This Garden ◆

1. Amend soil with compost.

2. Work an all-purpose granular fertilizer into the site, following package directions. Water well.

3. In the early fall or spring, plant roses 1 foot from the base of a trellis. Loosely tie canes to the trellis with soft twine.

4. Allow 1 foot of space around each lupine and foxglove, but cluster other plants closer together.

5. Slip the marjorams and pinks in between paving stones, blending colors so that they are evenly dispersed over the area.

Aftercare and Maintenance
• Continue to tie rose canes to the lattice as they grow, arching canes to promote flowering stems.
• Trim herbs annually to 2 to 3 inches to keep them compact; replace them every other year.

A Hideaway Among Old-Time Flowers

Whether it is the lure of nostalgia or romance, planting a secret garden filled with old-fashioned flowers recalls a simpler time. Lovely clematis shelters this garden from the bustling world beyond. The abundant, vigorously growing vine quickly covers the trellis in a dense screen of foliage and flowers.

Red valerians give long-lasting color to the garden, and their pinkish red panicles above gray-green foliage make beautiful cut flowers. Drifts of catmints add a bright blue accent to the composition, while a small clump of carmine-hued pinks sweetly scent the air.

The hortensia hydrangea blossoms abundantly—enough to cut a few stems to dry for colorful, long-lasting arrangements.

The daylilies and evening primroses provide masses of yellow blooms in late spring and early summer that yield to the bright white flowers of 'Miss Lingard' phlox later in the season.

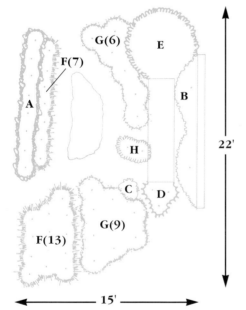

◆ How to Plant This Garden ◆

1. Dig several inches of compost into the soil and work in a balanced granular fertilizer. Water well.

2. After the last frost in spring, plant evening primroses, red valerians, Allwood pinks, lemon daylilies, catmint, and thick-leaf phlox.

3. Plant clematis about 1 foot in front of the base of the trellis. Cover the soil with several inches of mulch to shade its roots.

4. Allow 5 feet of space at the side of the bench for the hydrangea.

Aftercare and Maintenance
• *In spring, cut back the hortensia hydrangea stems to the ground, or as high as 18 inches if you prefer a taller shrub.*
• *Tie clematis to the lattice with soft twine as stems grow. Cut out all dead clematis wood in early spring. Cut stems back to the topmost pair of large buds.*
• *Deadhead red valerians and thick-leaf phlox frequently to induce more flowers and prevent rampant self-sowing.*
• *Remove faded flowers and foliage from the plants to add to your compost pile.*

Plant List

A. Centranthus ruber (red valerian) (8)
B. Clematis 'Bees Jubilee' (clematis) (2)
C. Dianthus x allwoodii (Allwood pinks) (1)
D. Hemerocallis lilioasphodelus (lemon daylily) (3)
E. Hydrangea macrophylla 'Nikko Blue' (hortensia hydrangea) (1)
F. Nepeta x faassenii (catmint) (20)
G. Oenothera tetragona 'Fireworks' (evening primrose) (15)
H. Phlox carolina 'Miss Lingard' (thick-leaf phlox) (2)

A Secret Garden for Late-Summer Repose

In the heat and glare of deepest summer, a hidden retreat filled with flowers and fragrance is a most welcome resting place. Butterflies flutter around a fragrant, white-flowered buddleia, while jasmine scrambles over the trellis, filling the garden with a sweet scent. For cooler climates, try substituting a hardy, fast-growing vine such as sweet autumn clematis or coral honeysuckle in place of the jasmine.

The blue-gray foliage and white flowers that light up this garden room for evening enjoyment also seem to cool it down on hot August days. Quiet lavenders and catmints produce mounds of pale, scented foliage and bluish purple flowers, while the strap-shaped leaves and lilac-blue sprays of lily-of-the-Nile arch gracefully above. Spiky Adam's-needle and its towering blooms supply a touch of drama matched only by the silvery sheen of the wormwood foliage.

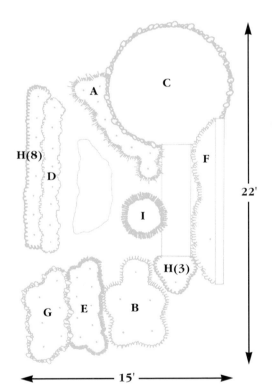

Plant List

A. Agapanthus Headbourne Hybrids (lily-of-the-Nile) (8)
B. Artemisia absinthium 'Lambrook Silver' (wormwood) (5)
C. Buddleia davidii 'White Bouquet' (butterfly bush) (1)
D. Campanula carpatica 'Blue Chips' (Carpathian bellflower) (8)
E. Calamintha nepeta (calamint) (9)
F. Jasminum officinale (jasmine) (2)
G. Lavandula angustifolia (English lavender) (6)
H. Nepeta x faassenii 'Six Hills Giant' (catmint) (11)
I. Yucca filamentosa (Adam's-needle) (1)

◆ How to Plant This Garden ◆

1. Amend the entire site with a thick layer of compost.

2. In cold climates, plant lilies-of-the-Nile in pots.

3. Plant the yucca in the background, where its sharp leaves will be out of the way.

4. Water all plants well to keep the soil continuously moist.

5. Cover all the planting beds with 2 inches of fine bark or chopped-leaf mulch.

Aftercare and Maintenance
• If soil is poor, apply an all-purpose fertilizer in midspring and again in early summer. Water well after fertilizing.
• Deadhead butterfly bush to encourage bloom into autumn. Cut stems to the ground in spring.
• Cut lily-of-the-Nile flower stems to the base after blooms fade.
• In spring, trim catmints to a small mound.
• Overwinter the potted plants indoors.

Create Your Own Evening Garden

The silvery foliage and cool white flowers of the evening garden will continue to be enjoyed long after sunset. With few color contrasts, the garden is fresh and serene by day, while at night it brightens even the darkest corner. For gardeners who spend their days away from home, a garden composed of white-flowering or night-scented plants offers a pleasurable setting for dining or relaxing after a busy day.

Some evening gardens rely on a foundation of blue-gray or variegated foliage plants for their brightening effect, while others consist largely of white-flowering plants. Pale foliage reflects evening light, often from countless tiny hairs that cover the leaves of some species. White blossoms glow resplendently in moonlight, especially those with large or doubled petals.

Garden rooms on patios or in sheltered corners of the landscape are especially pleasant in the evening. They provide a sense of privacy and seclusion. A garden room may also provide a setting for tender, container-grown plants that need protection in cool climates.

If you are drawn to delicate, flowering exotics, you may want to try the white-flowering plant combinations illustrated here. Alternate gardens on the following pages include an evening garden consisting only of plants with silvery foliage, and one composed of fragrant flowers that give off their scent after dark.

A White Garden Room

The evening garden featured here is a dazzling display of both tender and hardy white-flowering plants. The tiers of raised beds and rows of tall pots lift the floral bouquets, creating levels of reflected evening light. Elevated beds bring interesting features, such as the clustered flowers of the primroses and the fluted petals on cyclamen, into close view.

The neatly sheared row of boxwood provides an effective backdrop for dozens of sparkling pansies and clearly accents the gardenia and the exotic-looking calla lily.

The tender plants in this collection—primrose, cyclamen, gardenia, and calla lily—can be grown in cool-weather climates only in planters and containers, as they are here. Potting mixes provide excellent drainage, and containers allow the plants to be moved inside for protection during winter. The hardier ivy and boxwoods remain in place year round to provide welcome color.

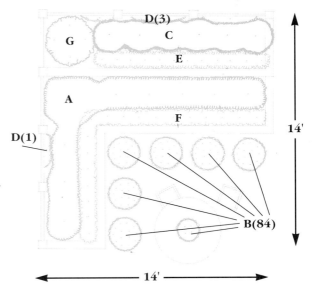

Plant List

A. *Buxus semper-virens* 'Suffruticosa' (dwarf boxwood) (9)
B. *Cyclamen per-sicum* (florist's cyclamen) (84)
C. *Gardenia jasmi-noides* (gardenia) (6)
D. *Hedera helix*
(English ivy) (4)
E. *Primula malacoides*
(fairy primrose) (12)
F. *Viola* x *wittrock-iana* (pansy) (18),
G. *Zantedeschia aethiopica*
(calla lily) (5)

◆ How to Plant This Garden ◆

1. Plant the ivy close to the trellis.

2. Amend soil with compost before planting the gardenias.

3. Set the boxwood plants 8 inches apart in the raised bed.

4. Plant florist's cyclamens in tubs approximately 8 inches apart.

5. Loosen soil and set the calla lily rhizomes 2 inches deep.

Aftercare and Maintenance
• Mulch gardenias with compost.
• Clip the boxwoods to 6 inches at planting, then trim regularly once they are established.
• Lightly fertilize pansies, florist's cyclamens, and primroses every 2 weeks during blooming season.
• Water the calla lilies lightly until leaves appear, then increase watering, and feed weekly. Store the rhizomes in sawdust in a cool location over the winter.

A Silver-Gray Garden

This evening garden, suitable for a temperate climate, relies on unusual silver-gray and variegated foliage for its striking effect. The 'Silver Carp' lamb's ears and nearly white dusty-millers, the brightest foliage in the garden, provide a frosted effect in evening light. Male *Actinidia kolomikta* vines produce showy heart-shaped leaves touched with white and pink. This is a relative of the edible kiwi, and with a female actinidia nearby, will produce edible grape-size fruits. Also dramatic are the gray-green, thistlelike leaves of the cardoon, which can grow up to 8 feet long.

Although foliage predominates, white flowers are also a feature in this evening garden. Small blossoms float on the sturdy rose campion stems, while tall, narrow clusters of the Adam's-needle tower above its dramatic swordlike leaves.

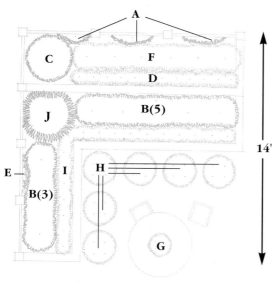

Plant List

A. *Actinidia kolomikta* (actinidia) (3)
B. *Artemisia absinthium* 'Lambrook Silver' (wormwood) (8)
C. *Cynara cardunculus* (cardoon) (1)
D. *Eryngium bourgatii* (sea holly) (12)
E. *Hedera helix* 'Eva' (English ivy) (1)
F. *Lychnis coronaria* 'Alba' (rose campion) (6)
G. *Nephthytis afzelii* (nephthytis) (1)
H. *Senecio cineraria* 'Cirrus' (dusty-miller) (24)
I. *Stachys byzantina* 'Silver Carpet' (lamb's ears) (18)
J. *Yucca filamentosa* 'Golden Sword' (Adam's-needle) (1)

◆ How to Plant This Garden ◆

1. Position Adam's-needle and cardoon *where their sharp leaves will be out of the way.*

2. Plant actinidias *in front of a support, at least 5 feet apart.*

3. Crowd dusty-millers together, *leaving only a few inches between plants.*

4. Plant wormwoods *at the same depth as they were in their containers, and 18 inches apart.*

5. Plant nephthytis *in a pot when night temperatures stay above 40°.*

6. Set sea hollies *6 to 12 inches apart, being careful not to disturb the long taproots during planting.*

Aftercare and Maintenance
• *Mulch plants with shredded bark to keep soil moist. Keep mulch 1 to 2 inches away from plant stems to prevent rot.*
• *Tie actinidia stems to trellis during the growing season. Prune hard in the winter to restrict their vigorous growth.*
• *Trim dusty-millers regularly to prevent them from becoming leggy.*
• *In spring, prune wormwoods to within 6 inches of the ground.*

A Garden of Evening Scent

At dusk, when most gardens appear to rest, a garden of fragrant flowers like the one shown here imparts a sensory parade. The light vanilla scent of pinkish white clematis hangs in the evening air. Winter daphne's heady aroma perfumes the air in spring. Climbing sweet peas and tall summer-sweet along the patio walls supply a privacy screen in summer that also holds in their light fragrances. As shown here, by early fall, white, waxy tuberoses release their potent perfume, and evening light is reflected from their tall, spikelike wands.

Blooming from spring through fall, heliotrope, sweet alyssum, and pincushion flower offer a constant invitation to this garden. 'Defiance' verbena closes the season with its scarlet flowers in autumn.

All of the plants here thrive in containers filled with a loose, rich potting mix. These combinations produce spreading masses of foliage and flowers that reliably fill the evening garden with several seasons of beauty and light fragrance.

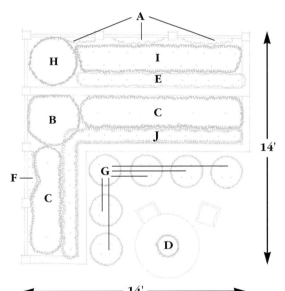

Plant List

A. Clematis montana 'Elizabeth' (clematis) (3)
B. Clethra alnifolia 'Hummingbird' (summer-sweet) (1)
C. Daphne odora 'Aureo-marginata' (winter daphne) (8)
D. Dianthus x allwoodii (Allwood pinks) (4)
E. Heliotropium arborescens 'Marine' (heliotrope) (12)
F. Lathyrus odoratus 'White Supreme' (sweet pea) (6)
G. Lobularia maritima 'Snowcloth Improved' (sweet alyssum) (24)
H. Polianthes tuberosa 'The Pearl' (tuberose) (37)
I. Scabiosa atropurpurea 'Mixed Doubles' (pincushion flower) (21)
J. Verbena x hybrida 'Defiance' (verbena) (18)

◆ How to Plant This Garden ◆

1. Set the clematis, winter daphnes, and summer-sweet in soil to the tops of their rootballs.

2. Plant the pincushion flowers and heliotropes 8 to 10 inches apart in rows in front of the clematis.

3. Sow seed of fast-growing sweet peas in front of the trellis, 4 inches apart and covered with ½ inch of soil.

4. Sow seed of alyssum on top of soil, as they require light for germination.

5. Set the tuberoses 4 to 6 inches apart in rows, or plant six in a 12-inch pot. Cover them with 2 inches of soil.

6. Plant Allwood pinks in an 8-inch pot; plant verbenas in front of the winter daphnes 8 inches apart.

Aftercare and Maintenance
• Prune summer-sweet in early spring. Keep it evenly moist.

Create Your Own Patio Garden

A patio expands the living area of your house and becomes an outdoor space that connects the indoors with the garden. It also provides a place where people can sit, with room for an arrangement of potted plants or edging beds that bring a part of the garden close to the house.

Gardening in containers allows you to move plants into sun or shade as necessary or to group plants with diverse cultural needs for visual effect. Tall containers and raised beds also protect garden plants from pets and children.

Groups of pots and planters can display favorite plant collections close to your house or patio, with easy access for garden maintenance. Terra cotta, which ages from orange to brick red, is an attrac-

tive, practical material for patio containers. It allows air to penetrate to plant roots and provides excellent drainage, critical for potted plants. Wooden tubs and half barrels are rustic alternatives, while stoneware and metal urns contribute a more artistic touch. But bear in mind that container plants tend to dry out faster than garden plants, so you must be vigilant about watering them.

You may want to begin container gardening with the easy-care ornamentals shown in the garden opposite. The alternate plan on the next page adds a few edibles such as basil and strawberries. The tender plants in the second alternate garden *(page 79)* are most suitable for a partially shaded site in a warm or coastal climate.

A Country Look for an Urban Patio

The patio garden at left is informal and full of variety, and its scale is appropriate for a small backyard. The garden features a mix of annuals and perennials in a charming array of pots. The interplay of flowers and foliage will continue to decorate this garden over several seasons, provided plants get off to a good start in a rich soil mix that is kept evenly moist.

Wooden and terra-cotta planters spill over with a profusion of grasses, herbs, bulbs, and flowers. Crimson-leaved fountain grass plays counterpoint to the garden's emerald leaves and golden blooms, while sweet alyssum and elegant foxgloves offset the Johnny-jump-ups, sweet violets, and lemon balms.

Lilies, which need some winter cold to promote blooms, are planted in a ground-level bed along the low brick retaining wall. The plant-crowded containers in the foreground and on top of the wall sustain the illusion that the garden and its patio are one.

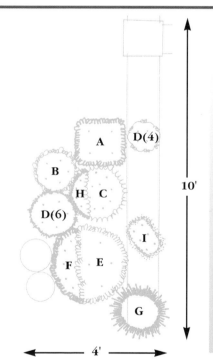

Plant List

A. *Digitalis purpurea* (common foxglove) (4)
B. *Galium odoratum* (sweet woodruff) (6)
C. *Lilium* (Asiatic hybrid lily) (10)
D. *Lobularia maritima* 'Snowdrift'(sweet alyssum) (10)
E. *Melissa officinalis* (lemon balm) (4)
F. *Ocimum basilicum* (common basil) (5)
G. *Pennisetum setaceum* 'Rubrum' (crimson fountain grass) (1)
H. *Viola odorata* (sweet violet) (6)
I. *Viola tricolor* (Johnny-jump-up) (6)

◆ How to Plant This Garden ◆

1. In the fall or early spring, plant lily bulbs 8 inches deep in the garden, or grouped in a 10-inch pot.

2. Plant crimson fountain grass in a container wider and deeper than its rootball. Use a knife to cut any wrapped roots.

3. Plant alyssum, lemon balm, and basil in the ground in Zones 9 or 10, or

in 10- or 12-inch pots suitable for either indoors or out.

4. Plant Johnny-jump-ups in spring. They are a self-seeding annual; once planted, they'll show up in other places in following years.

5. Plant sweet violets in the ground or in 8-inch pots for easy rearranging.

6. Tuck foxgloves in next to the lilies.

Aftercare and Maintenance
• *Fertilize and mulch lilies when they begin to grow.*
• *Pinch the growing tips of basil to promote fullness. Use the leaves to flavor salads.*

A Container Garden of Annuals and Edibles

This small garden nook is a delightful mix of flowering ornamentals and edibles in a variety of attractive and unusual containers. The rich blend of purple basil with the vibrant yellows, pinks, and oranges of the annuals is at its peak when the garden is in full summer bloom.

Variegated houttuynias and nasturtiums are good choices in this colorful patio garden. The pale splotches in their foliage highlight the bright red-and-orange nasturtium blooms as well as the Transvaal daisies. They also combine well with the yellow Dahlberg daisies and black-eyed Susans.

In this garden, purple basil and Swiss chard are charming as ornamentals but, like the strawberries, are also welcome in the kitchen.

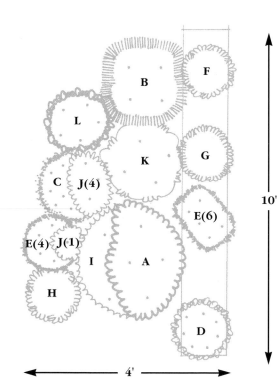

Plant List

A. *Beta vulgaris* 'Rhubarb' (Swiss chard) (4)
B. *Canna* x *generalis* (dwarf canna) (4)
C. *Dyssodia tenuiloba* (Dahlberg daisy) (7)
D. *Fragaria* 'Ozark Beauty' (garden strawberry) (8)
E. *Gazania rigens* 'Sunshine' (treasure flower) (10)
F. *Gerbera jamesonii* 'Dwarf Frisbee Pink' (Transvaal daisy) (1)
G. *Gerbera jamesonii* 'Dwarf Frisbee Scarlet' (Transvaal daisy) (1)
H. *Gerbera jamesonii* 'Dwarf Frisbee Yellow' (Transvaal daisy) (1)
I. *Houttuynia cordata* 'Chameleon' (houttuynia) (3)
J. *Ocimum basilicum* 'Purple Ruffles' (common basil) (5)
K. *Rudbeckia hirta* 'Rustic Dwarfs' (black-eyed Susan) (4)
L. *Tropaeolum majus* 'Alaska' (garden nasturtium) (6)

◆ How to Plant This Garden ◆

*1. **Start seed indoors** in early spring for Dahlberg daisies, black-eyed Susans, Swiss chard, and basil. Set out transplants after all danger of frost has passed.*

*2. **Sow nasturtium seed** outdoors in a container about 1 to 2 weeks after the last frost.*

*3. **Set strawberries** with their crowns above the soil surface and their roots spread out below.*

*4. **Since Transvaal daisies** are difficult to grow from seed, plant nursery seedlings. Keep their crowns above the soil level.*

Aftercare and Maintenance
• For continued flowering and fruit pro-duction, pick strawberries frequently and remove runners.
• Keep container plants well watered but not soggy; hot, windy weather can cause them to dry out quickly.
• Remove the leaves of daisies and Swiss chard that become ragged with age.
• To stimulate continued flowering, regularly deadhead flowers and cut them for indoor use.

A Shady Patio for Tender Plants

This patio sits in partial shade, creating a cool, lush setting for tender, moisture-loving plants. Plants whose colors may seem muted in direct sunlight appear richer in the soft, dappled light of this garden.

The shadiest areas of the garden are best for the colorful foliage of caladium and Japanese fern. The hydrangea, tuberous begonias, Johnny-jump-ups, lobelias, and sweet cicely all flower more profusely in brighter light. Catching partial sunlight in the front, lobelia adds brilliant blue highlights, and 'Little Bunny' pennisetum waves bright bottle-brush clusters above wispy leaves.

All of these luxuriant and shade-loving plants grow best in soil amended with leaf mold or compost. Keep them well fed and slightly moist, and they'll reward you with richly colorful foliage and a summer-long display of flowers.

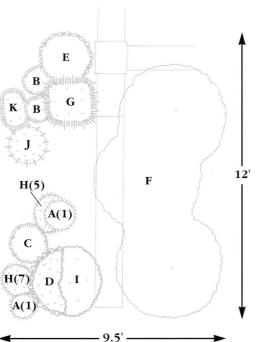

Plant List

A. *Athyrium nipponicum* 'Pictum' (Japanese painted fern) (2)
B. *Begonia* x *tuberhybrida* 'Nonstop' (tuberous begonia) (2)
C. *Begonia* x *tuberhybrida* 'Skaugum' (tuberous begonia) (1)
D. *Caladium* x *hortulanum*
(caladium) (15)
E. *Fuchsia* x *hybrida* 'Estelle Marie' (fuchsia) (1)
F. *Hydrangea arborescens* 'Annabelle' (hydrangea) (3)
G. *Iris pallida* 'Variegata' (sweet iris) (9)
H. *Lobelia erinus* 'Riviera Blue Splash'
(edging lobelia) (12)
I. *Myrrhis odorata* (sweet cicely) (4)
J. *Pennisetum alopecuroides* 'Little Bunny' (Chinese pennisetum) (8)
K. *Viola tricolor* (Johnny-jump-up) (6)

◆ How to Plant This Garden ◆

1. Start begonia and caladium tubers *indoors in early spring. Transplant outside after all danger of frost has passed.*

2. Plant lobelias and Johnny-jump-ups *close together for a massed effect.*

3. Loosen soil *to 8 inches for sweet irises. Set the rhizomes close to the surface of the soil.*

4. Set fuchsia, Japanese painted ferns, *and pennisetums in pots with the tops of the rootballs at the soil surface.*

5. Plant hydrangeas *1 to 1½ feet from the base of the wall.*

Aftercare and Maintenance
• *Feed caladiums, tuberous begonias, and fuchsias every 2 weeks with a fish emulsion or other liquid fertilizer.*
• *To encourage foliage on caladiums, remove any flowers that appear.*
• *Keep tuberous begonias and fuchsias evenly moist but not wet.*
• *Withhold water from begonias and caladiums when foliage fades in the fall. Dry tubers outdoors before storing in a frost-free place over the winter.*

Create Your Own Garden for a Small Yard

Although limited in space, small yards have the potential for becoming showplaces for favorite plants. If you have a small yard or a confined yet promising space to personalize with plants, you can do so with creative and surprising results.

When designing your small garden, consider the potential for vertical expansion. Without taking up precious bed space, many versatile and exciting plants can grow up hedges, walls, fences, trellises, and even trees. You can also train shrubs or small trees to grow flat against a vertical element using the technique called espalier, by which their trunks and branches are encouraged to conform to a supporting framework.

Manipulating space can make your yard look larger than it actually is. Adjust the scale and boundaries of your site by installing raised beds or by varying the height of your fence. For example, a low fence, as in the garden design shown opposite, allows you to see over it to the larger landscape beyond and appropriate its expanse. Even a small slice of a borrowed view adds a sense of spaciousness. A meandering path or a small center oval of lawn can also create the illusion of space.

If you are a novice gardener, you may want to begin with the simple plan shown on this page. If you like the challenge of managing a broader plant palette, try one of the two alternate plans on the following pages, which include more perennials and shrubs.

A Private Garden

In this seaside garden plan, the fence provides a sense of privacy and shields the plants from the wind and the ocean's salt spray. An angular layout with a patterned brick path opens onto a small patch of lawn that extends to a herbaceous border at the far end. The boxwood hedge lined with sweet alyssum repeats the shape of the walk and thus helps define the garden's somewhat formal character.

The boxwoods and other evergreens provide year-round interest, while annual and perennial flowers offer seasonal color and texture. Trees and a tall hedge rise above the fence, expanding the horizon. The low-flowering plants emphasize the contrasting levels, their colors carefully selected to harmonize with the deep, earthy rose of the bricks. All of these plants do well in average soil conditions inland or along a seashore.

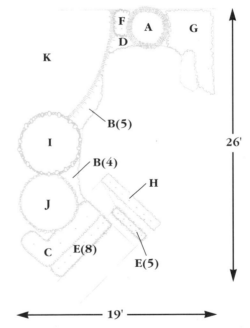

Plant List

A. Artemisia ludoviciana (western mugwort) (1)
B. Browallia speciosa 'Marine Bells' (bush violet) (9)
C. Buxus sempervirens 'Suffruticosa' (dwarf boxwood) (5)
D. Dianthus deltoides 'Ruber' (maiden pinks) (2)
E. Lobularia maritima (sweet alyssum) (13)
F. Malva alcea var. **fastigiata** (mallow) (2)
G. Oenothera erythrosepala (evening primrose) (11)
H. Oenothera speciosa (evening primrose) (7)
I. Rosa rugosa 'Blanc Double de Coubert' (rugosa rose) (1)
J. Rosa 'Sexy Rexy' (rose) (1)
K. Taxus baccata (English yew) (1)

◆ How to Plant This Garden ◆

1. In spring, after danger of frost, dig compost into the soil.

2. Set boxwoods 1 foot apart at approximately the same depth as in their containers.

3. Plant western mugwort in a 1-gallon pot; keep soil evenly moist.

4. Plant roses, keeping bud unions just above ground in warm climates and 1 to 2 inches below ground in colder areas.

5. Sow sweet alyssum seed, or set out bedding plants from cell packs.

6. Plant annuals: bush violet, maiden pinks, and evening primrose.

Aftercare and Maintenance
• Trim boxwood hedge to 1½ feet regularly during growing season.
• Shear sweet alyssums before seeds set to keep compact and prevent self-sowing.

Midsummer Bloom in a Small Yard

Although small, this yard includes a diverse collection of plants that display a variety of colors and forms. The shortest plants, dwarf zinnias and low-growing, evergreen maiden pinks, provide bright accents of color. Taller, but still only 10 inches high, 'Little Miss Muffet' Shasta daisies produce 2- to 3-inch-wide creamy white flowers with sunny yellow centers. In late spring, 'Abbotswood Rose' campion brings a new form to the garden with a compact, showy mound of bright pink blooms. After the flowers fade, gray-green clumps of foliage harmonize all summer with spiky silver stems of Russian sage.

Evergreen germander makes the most of limited space in this yard. Small, even at maturity, it easily can be kept as a 1-foot-high hedge. Although this garden is at its peak in midsummer, compact dwarf blue spruce provides form and color that maintains interest throughout the seasons.

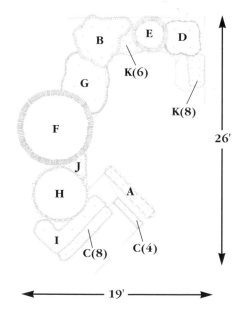

Plant List

A. *Chrysanthemum* **x** *superbum* 'Little Miss Muffet' (Shasta daisy) (7)
B. *Delphinium* 'Chelsea Star' (delphinium) (8)
C. *Dianthus deltoides* (maiden pinks) (12)
D. *Lychnis* x *walkeri* 'Abbotswood Rose'

(campion) (4)
E. *Perovskia atriplicifolia* (Russian sage) (1)
F. *Picea pungens* 'Fat Albert' (Colorado blue spruce) (1)
G. *Potentilla fruticosa* 'Abbotswood' (cinquefoil) (4)

H. *Rosa rugosa* 'Rosea' (rugosa rose) (1)
I. *Teucrium chamaedrys* (germander) (5)
J. *Veronica spicata* 'Blue Charm' (speedwell) (6)
K. *Zinnia* Thumbelina Series (zinnia) (14)

◆ How to Plant This Garden ◆

1. Set the dwarf blue spruce and the rose *in the ground at the same depth as they were in their containers, preferably in full sun.*

2. Dig in a 3-inch layer of compost *before planting daisies, delphiniums, pinks, campions, Russian sage, speedwells, and zinnias.*

3. Locate campions, delphiniums, *Russian sage, and speedwells behind the lower-growing daisies, pinks, and zinnias.*

4. Add a 1-inch layer of compost *to beds for germanders and cinquefoils.*

Aftercare and Maintenance
• *Keep the spruce moist but not wet, since it cannot tolerate dry soil.*
• *Pinch the main buds on delphiniums when the plants are 5 inches tall.*
• *Leave hips on the rose for brilliant fall color.*
• *Deadhead Shasta daisies throughout the growing season to encourage more blooms and keep plants compact.*

A Small Yard in Pink and Yellow

Rich pinks and yellows create a cheerful, bright design for this small yard. The strong, sculptural lines of a pyramidal yew are complemented by sprays of variegated 'Morning Light' grass and the compact, free-flowering polyantha rose, 'The Fairy'. The edges of the brick pathway are softened with low-growing lemon thyme, a fragrant herb that gives off a fresh scent when touched. 'Golden Showers' azalea bears peach-yellow, vanilla-scented blooms. 'Wargrave Pink' cranesbill is planted nearby, with complementary salmon-pink flowers that bloom from early summer through fall. Festive red, pink, orange, yellow, and white blooms of 'Bright Bikini' strawflowers light up this summer garden and make long-lasting dried flowers to enjoy throughout the year.

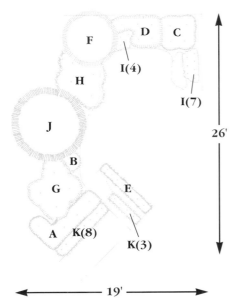

Plant List

A. Berberis thunbergii var. atropurpurea (Japanese barberry) (5)
B. Coreopsis rosea (pink tickseed) (1)
C. Coreopsis verticillata 'Moonbeam' (tickseed) (4)
D. Geranium endressii 'Wargrave Pink'

(cranesbill) (5)
E. Helichrysum bracteatum 'Bright Bikini' (strawflower) (7)
F. Miscanthus sinensis 'Morning Light' (Japanese silver grass) (1)
G. Rhododendron 'Golden Showers' (azalea) (4)

H. Rosa 'The Fairy' (polyantha rose) (4)
I. Tagetes 'Antigua Gold' (marigold) (11)
J. Taxus x media 'Hatfieldii' (Hatfield's yew) (1)
K. Thymus x citriodorus (lemon thyme) (11)

◆ How to Plant This Garden ◆

1. Prepare a planting bed *for each azalea by incorporating several shovelfuls of peat moss into an area twice the width of the rootball. Plant at the same depth as in the container.*

2. Add well-rotted manure or compost *to beds before planting the roses and barberry plants. Check their rootballs for tightly wrapped roots. Loosen or*

cut the roots free before planting.

3. Loosen the soil in beds *before planting the yew, Japanese silver grass, tickseeds, strawflowers, thymes, and marigolds. Leave 10 feet for the yew to spread and 8 feet for the grass.*

Aftercare and Maintenance
• *Mulch azaleas with chopped leaves. Re-*

plenish the mulch annually. Avoid cultivating around their shallow roots.
• *Trim polyantha roses in late winter after the second year to shape the plants. Trim deadwood anytime.*
• *Shear tickseed plants toward the end of summer to encourage a second flush of bloom.*
• *Cut clumps of Japanese silver grass to the ground in late winter.*

Create Your Own Entryway Garden

The entryway garden should be planned to enhance the architecture of your house. Formal, traditional houses call for symmetrical plantings while less formally designed homes are complemented by well-laid-out, asymmetrical gardens. While the style of the architecture dictates the main lines of the entryway garden plan, your climate, setting, and personal preferences leave plenty of room for creative design. The most formal entryway garden, for instance, may be softened with summer flowers, while a small clipped hedge can add just the right balance of control to an exuberant mix of blooms.

The plants for your entryway garden should look good in all seasons. In every region, it is important to include some plants that will provide color and shape throughout the year, connecting your home with the landscape and preventing a bare, out-of-season look. Plants with evergreen foliage are especially valuable for this purpose.

A welcoming setting for any entry must have a broad, easily negotiated path to the door. While plants can cover its edges, they shouldn't spill more than several inches into the walkway.

If privacy is important, an entry design may include a hedge or fence that is large and thick enough to shield the house from passersby without creating a forbidding barrier to friends.

The design here, suitable for the Northeast, Midwest, and mid-Atlantic regions, combines casual, colorful bloomers and a tidy but not overly formal hedge. The effect is easygoing but controlled. For a more romantic look in the Southeast, consider the alternate design on the following page. Or, to create an oasis in the Southwest, you might try the planting described on page 87.

Extending a Traditional Welcome

The combination shown here of shrubs, vines, and flowers for a sunny front entrance in a temperate region has a traditional look that suits this colonial-style house. A handsome boxwood hedge flanks the front door, providing year-round symmetry and matching the lines of the low white fence at the beginning of the path.

The formal effect is softened by a seemingly random scattering of annuals lining the pathway. Morning-glories along the fence rails, perennial lilies, and delicate Queen Anne's lace reinforce the unpretentious period charm of the house.

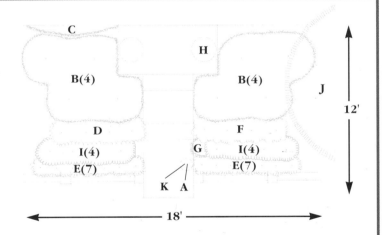

◆ How to Plant This Garden ◆

1. Create a rich, well-drained site by digging 2 inches of compost into the soil.

2. Dig 12-inch-deep holes for lily bulbs. Spread roots and fill, covering the top of the bulbs with 9 inches of soil.

3. Plant the trumpet creeper on a strong trellis 24 inches from the house. Gently tie the main stems onto the trellis. Next, plant the yew and boxwoods.

4. Sow morning-glories, Queen Anne's lace, and zinnias in deeply worked soil. Keep soil moist until germination.

5. Grow geraniums in containers.

6. Plant snapdragons and rose campion in a sunny spot.

Aftercare and Maintenance
• In colder climates, screen boxwood with burlap to protect it from winter damage.
• Divide the coneflowers every 4 years.
• Top-dress established lilies with compost or well-rotted manure each fall.

Plant List

A. Antirrhinum majus (snapdragon)
B. Buxus spp. (boxwood) (8)
C. Campsis radicans (trumpet creeper) (1)
D. Daucus carota var. carota (Queen Anne's lace) (4)
E. Ipomoea tricolor (morning-glory) (14)
F. Lilium spp. (lily) (4)

G. Lychnis coronaria (rose campion) (1)
H. Pelargonium x hortorum (zonal geranium) (1)
I. Rudbeckia laciniata 'Goldquelle' (coneflower) (8)
J. Taxus cuspidata (Japanese yew) (1)
K. Zinnia elegans (zinnia)

An Entryway Garden for the Sultry South

This lush, romantic garden suits the gardening style of the Southeast. This region favors durable plants that must be tolerant of the heat and humidity common in the South, and must do well in either full or partial sun. Such plants also provide year-round interest in a region where the gardening season never really ends.

Golden-rain tree is a colorful focal point, with bronze or shrimp pink spring foliage and languid, graceful clusters of yellow blooms all summer. The shiny green gardenia hedge scents the entry from summer into early winter and requires little upkeep. Heat and humidity intensify its rich, sweet scent. Occasional pruning keeps it blooming freely at a 4- to 6-foot height. The clematis vine softens the hard lines of the building with purple summer blooms that give way in fall to picturesque, feathery, silver seed heads.

Deceptively modest-looking lilyturf may be the most hardworking plant in this garden. Its evergreen foliage provides year-round structure to the garden and sets off the other flowers, including long-blooming Peruvian lilies and tender black-eyed Susan vines, which must be replaced annually.

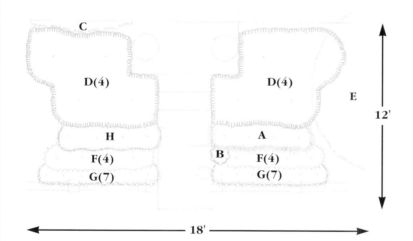

Plant List

A. *Acanthus dioscoridis* (lesser bear's-breech) (4)
B. *Alstroemeria aurantiaca* 'Lutea' (Peruvian lily) (1)
C. *Clematis* x *jackmanii* (Jackman clematis) (1)
D. *Gardenia jasminoides* 'August Beauty' (common gardenia) (8)

E. *Koelreuteria paniculata* (golden-rain tree) (1)
F. *Liriope muscari* 'Variegata' (variegated blue lilyturf) (8)
G. *Thunbergia alata* 'Susie' (black-eyed Susan vine) (14)
H. *Trachelium caeruleum* 'Violet Blue' (blue lace flower) (4)

◆ How to Plant This Garden ◆

*1. **Prepare the site** by digging in 1 to 2 inches of compost to a depth of 2 feet to increase the root depth, making the plants more drought-resistant.*

*2. **Plant the golden-rain tree** in spring in a bowl-shaped hole as deep at its center as the rootball. Before planting, loosen soil out to the branch spread of the tree.*

*3. **Grow Peruvian lilies**, lesser bear's-breech, black-eyed Susan vine, gardenias, and lilyturfs under the golden-rain tree.*

*4. **To plant the Peruvian lilies**, spread the tubers and cover with 2 inches of soil.*

*5. **After planting clematis** and garde-*

nias, cover soil with 3 inches of mulch.

Aftercare and Maintenance
• Mulch the gardenias with compost to protect the roots, and add organic matter to the soil. If leaves turn yellow, the soil may be too alkaline. Test and adjust pH.

An Entryway Garden for the Sundrenched Southwest

If you garden in the Southwest, you need plants that thrive in this region's hot, dry conditions. You may also have to contend with alkaline soil that is unfriendly to many plants. The region's brilliant sunshine and low rainfall call for plants whose colors and forms can hold their own in such a challenging environment.

This entryway, planted with shades of blue and green, makes a cool oasis from the hot sun. Evergreen Texas mountain laurel, with its showy violet blooms, and the white flowers of star jasmine both offer appealing fragrance while soothing the eye with lush, green foliage.

The soft, hazy effect of the sea lavender's tiny blossoms is balanced by purple coneflowers and nasturtiums, whose bright colors are powerful enough to withstand the glare of the sun.

In autumn, the evergreen cotoneaster is bright with orange berries that will, along with the seed heads of the coneflower, feed the birds of winter. The fernlike leaves of yarrow and the plumes of crimson fountain grass add soft texture and bright color. All these plants grow well in these demanding conditions and reward minimal care with an abundance of colorful blooms.

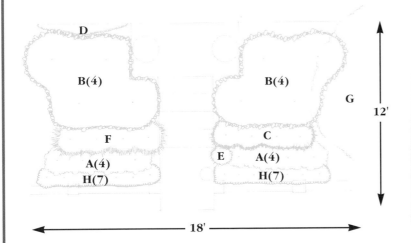

Plant List

A. *Achillea millefolium* 'Sulphur Beauty' (common yarrow) (8)
B. *Cotoneaster congestus* (Pyrenees cotoneaster) (8)
C. *Echinacea purpurea* (purple coneflower) (4)
D. *Jasminum multiflorum* (star jasmine) (1)
E. *Limonium latifolium* (sea lavender) (1)
F. *Pennisetum setaceum* 'Rubrum' (crimson fountain grass) (4)
G. *Sophora secundiflora* (Texas mountain laurel) (1)
H. *Tropaeolum majus* 'Climbing Mix' (garden nasturtium) (14)

◆ How to Plant This Garden ◆

1. Test the soil and, if it is alkaline, adjust with powdered sulfur to bring it closer to neutral.

2. Spread amendments and compost, working them into the soil.

3. Plant Texas mountain laurel and cotoneaster first. Container specimens of cotoneaster will transplant easily.

4. Train the star jasmine vines, planted 18 inches from the house, on wires.

5. Next, plant the crimson fountain grass, followed by the sea lavender and drifts of yarrow and purple coneflower.

6. Plant nasturtium seed 1 inch deep in full or part sun.

Aftercare and Maintenance
• *Divide the yarrow every 3 years.*
• *Unlike most fountain grasses, crimson fountain grass does not self-seed. Propagate by dividing large clumps.*

Create Your Own Backdoor Garden

The joy of a backdoor garden is in its easy access. Herbs and flowers grow only a few steps from the kitchen, where food is cooked, or from the utility room, where cut blooms are prepared and arranged. From windows in rooms at the rear of your house or from a nearby patio, you can see your backdoor garden every day, watch it grow, and delight in its changes.

Raised beds are ideal for a backdoor garden, because of their added convenience and accessibility. Planting areas are clearly defined, and the plants are elevated out of harm's way and within easy reach. Best of all, raised beds are a practical solution to the problem of soil compaction near

the house, the result of years of foot traffic.

Assemble the walls of the beds using sturdy pressure-treated wood, railroad ties, or even large boulders, and fill with good quality soil mixed with plenty of compost and other organic matter. You will find that you can work this soil weeks earlier in the spring than the rest of the garden, and that it drains more quickly. In winter, however, it will freeze to a greater depth.

The three plans shown here give you guidelines for easy-to-grow, colorful backdoor gardens. You can create the mixed bed shown opposite, design a garden of cutting flowers, or plant a colorful, early-blooming garden to welcome spring.

Mixed Beds of Perennials and Herbs

The backdoor garden here is useful as well as beautiful. It invites you to snip rosemary to season a dish or flavor a bottle of vinegar, or to cut a few yarrows, pinks, irises, or roses for the table. The plants are easily accessible by virtue of the handsome brick paths between the raised beds. This attractive design provides a practical approach to intensive gardening, presenting a variety of perennials and herbs in a well-ordered style. The garden works well in average soil located in mixed sun-and-shade spots.

The raised beds display a tightly woven tapestry of contrasting colors and textures. Fine lavender foliage sets off broadly lobed lady's-mantle leaves, while the thick woolly gray foliage of lamb's-ears stands out against the upright sweeps of iris. Sage and rosemary tumble over the side walls and soften the geometric layout, an effect enhanced by yarrow's soft foliage and gracefully bending flowers.

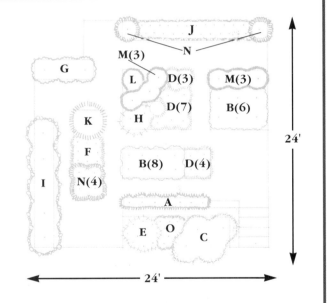

Plant List

A. Achillea millefolium (yarrow) (7)
B. Alchemilla mollis (lady's-mantle) (14)
C. Cotoneaster microphyllus (small-leaved cotoneaster) (4)
D. Dianthus sp. (pinks) (14)
E. Impatiens walierana 'Double Pink' (garden impatiens) (12)
F. Iris sp. (bearded hybrid iris) (9)
G. Lamium maculatum (spotted dead nettle) (3)
H. Lavandula angus-

tifolia (English lavender) (3)
I. Pyracantha coccinea 'Lalandei' (scarlet firethorn) (5)
J. Rosa 'Dreamglo' (miniature rose) (24)
K. Rosmarinus officinalis (rosemary) (1)
L. Salvia officinalis (sage) (1)
M. Salvia officinalis 'Purpurea' (sage) (6)
N. Stachys byzantina (lamb's-ears) (6)
O. Viola x wittrockiana 'Atlas Purple' (pansy) (10)

◆ How to Plant This Garden ◆

1. Plant dead nettles 15 to 18 inches apart, as they will spread.

2. Mix a 2-inch layer of compost in bed and plant lady's-mantle, pinks, sage, pansies, garden impatiens, and miniature roses. Cluster pinks evenly, about 8 inches apart.

3. Before planting irises in fall, work bone meal and low-nitrogen fertilizer into topsoil. Loosen soil to a depth of 10 inches. Bury the rhizomes so tops are just above the soil surface.

4. Plant lamb's-ears, yarrow, and rosemary along edges, and lavender at center.

5. Plant small-leaved cotoneaster and scarlet firethorn in a spot protected from winter winds.

Aftercare and Maintenance
• Check raised beds for moisture, as they dry more quickly than surrounding ground in hot weather.

A Backdoor Cutting Garden

This annual cutting garden provides brilliantly colored blooms right outside your back door all summer long. Fast-growing annuals only a few steps away will keep you supplied with bouquets during the entire growing season. The garden also produces blooms for drying, some that draw butterflies, and others that self-sow and continue the garden next year.

The old-fashioned 'Rose Queen' cleome blooms continually until frost, adding height to the garden. Cosmos is marked by fernlike foliage and 3-inch daisylike blooms ranging in color from white to pink to deep red.

'Blue Horizon' ageratum and mealy-cup sage add cool notes to the composition, while tickseed, pot marigold, and zinnia turn up the heat with red, yellow, and orange hues. Mixed colors of globe amaranth and flowering tobacco make a festive parade from summer through early fall. All of these annuals are tremendously productive, reblooming each time stems are cut, and providing you with an incentive to visit the cutting garden often.

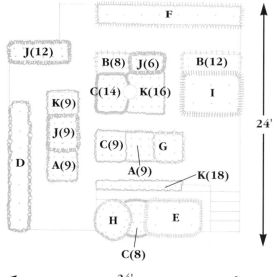

Plant List

A. *Ageratum houstonianum* 'Blue Horizon' (flossflower) (18)
B. *Antirrhinum majus* 'Tahiti' (snapdragon) (20)
C. *Calendula officinalis* 'Geisha Girl' (pot marigold) (31)
D. *Cleome hasslerana* 'Rose Queen' (spider flower) (7)
E. *Coreopsis grandiflora* 'Early Sunrise' (large-flowered tickseed) (6)
F. *Cosmos bipinnatus* 'Sensation Mix' (cosmos) (8)
G. *Gomphrena globosa* (globe amaranth) (4)
H. *Nicotiana* x *sanderae* 'Nikki Mix' (flowering tobacco) (17)
I. *Salvia farinacea* (mealy-cup sage) (6)
J. *Tagetes tenuifolia* 'Lemon Gem' (signet marigold) (27)
K. *Zinnia elegans* (zinnia) (43)

◆ How to Plant This Garden ◆

1. Layer 3 inches of compost over beds and dig in thoroughly.

2. Start flossflowers, snapdragons, globe amaranths, mealy-cup sage, flowering tobacco, and signet marigolds indoors in late winter. Transplant to garden after last frost.

3. Sow seeds of pot marigold, spider flower, cosmos, and zinnia directly in garden, where they will grow after last frost.

4. Arrange plants so that taller ones do not shade lower-growing plants. Set in evenly spaced rows, 10 inches apart for smaller plants, 15 inches for taller ones.

Aftercare and Maintenance
• *Fertilize annuals every 2 weeks with a balanced fertilizer.*

A Backdoor Garden That Heralds Spring

This garden is the perfect design for lovers of spring flowers. Tulips, bleeding hearts, Spanish bluebells, and forget-me-nots form a mosaic of pink, white, and blue. Mountain bluet adds silvery foliage and deep blue flowers. A big tub of multi-colored pansies next to angel's-tears narcissus brings early color to the garden.

As spring progresses, emerging leaves of white 'Triumphator' lily-flowered tulips, pink-and-white 'Angelique' peony tulips, and yellow-and-white 'Sweet Harmony' tulips fill the beds with color. All of these varieties make excellent cut flowers, allowing you to bring the freshness of spring into your home. Variegated 'Francee' hosta hides fading narcissus foliage.

Dramatic bleeding heart anchors the corner of two beds, while pale yellow primrose holds its own next to Spanish bluebells. Late spring and early summer host the Dutch iris 'Blue Ribbon' and blooming hostas. In early spring, 'Toyo-Nishiki' quince erupts in clouds of white flowers.

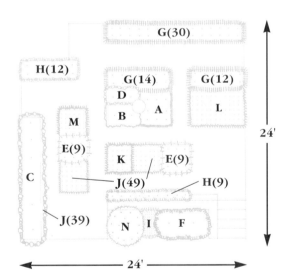

Plant List

A. Allium aflatunense 'Purple Sensation' (Persian onion) (9)
B. Centaurea montana (mountain bluet) (2)
C. Chaenomeles speciosa 'Toyo-Nishiki' (flowering quince) (6)
D. Dicentra spectabilis (bleeding heart) (2)
E. Endymion hispanicus (Spanish bluebells) (18)

F. Hosta fortunei 'Francee' (variegated hosta) (2)
G. Iris 'Blue Ribbon' (Dutch iris) (56)
H. Myosotis scorpioides var. semperflorens (forget-me-not) (21)
I. Narcissus triandrus (angel's-tears narcissus) (28)
J. Primula vulgaris

(primrose) (137)
K. Tulipa 'Angelique' (peony tulip) (64)
L. Tulipa 'Sweet Harmony' (lily-flowered tulip) (120)
M. Tulipa 'Triumphator' (tulip) (64)
N. Viola x wittrockiana 'Maxim Mix' (pansy) (15)

◆ How to Plant This Garden ◆

1. Plant Persian onion, tulip, narcissus, Dutch iris, and Spanish bluebell bulbs in the fall. Set the base of the bulbs at a depth equal to three times their average diameter and mix a handful of bone meal into the soil at the bottom of each planting hole.

2. In early spring, plant pansies in a tub filled with a light potting mix. Plant forget-me-nots closely for a mass effect.

3. Choose a location for quinces, giving space to expand to 5 feet tall and wide.

4. Plant hostas, primroses, and *bleeding hearts* where they will receive partial shade and protection from direct afternoon sun.

5. If soil is acidic, add lime before planting mountain bluets.

Aftercare and Maintenance
• To encourage flowering, divide mountain bluets every 2 to 3 years.
• Remove bulb foliage 12 weeks after blooms have faded, or when it turns completely yellow.
• Cut back forget-me-nots to control rampant self-seeding.

Create Your Own Driveway Edging

Of all areas in a home landscape, the driveway is the most frequently used and is also the place where visitors may form their first impression of the home. But making a driveway attractive and welcoming poses a special set of problems. Surrounding plants must survive exhaust fumes, salt runoff from roads and walks, extra heat reflected by paving in summer, occasional trampling, and perhaps abuse from snow-removal equipment.

Driveway landscaping also presents a unique visual problem. Most driveways consist of a large, flat area. Surrounded by equally flat lawn or ground covers, the scene can seem open and barren. The solution is to introduce vertical elements—trees, shrubs, ornamental grasses, and flowers—with a variety of forms, textures, and colors to soften and contrast with that commanding slash of driveway.

The realities of gardening around a driveway rule out delicate or demanding plants and those that look less than presentable at anytime during the growing season. Fortunately, there are still plenty of excellent choices that meet these challenging criteria.

The plan shown here combines sturdy perennials that perform well in full sun or partial shade and could be worked into a planting of existing shrubs and trees. The alternate shrub garden that follows is especially low in maintenance requirements and offers attractions for all seasons. The other alternate planting, an annual driveway garden for full sun, provides the most colorful effect.

Tough Plants That Soften Hard Lines

The durable flowering perennials in this design all have a long period of bloom and foliage that remains attractive throughout the growing season. They will do fine in full sun, but will also bloom well with as little as 4 hours of sun a day. In fact, the astilbe is happiest in partial shade; with more sunlight it requires extra water. In summer, the garden is sheltered from drying winds by a high hedge at the back. A low rock wall between the plants helps shield them from the occasional wayward tire for an enduring roadside existence—except for the lilies. Tuck the lilies into a safe spot, as shown here. In winter, the plants retreat to ground level or below, thus escaping the rough treatment of errant snowplows and the weight of high-piled snow.

◆ How to Plant This Garden ◆

1. Till the soil 12 to 15 inches deep and work in 2 to 3 inches of compost to improve drainage and moisture retention.

2. Plant lily bulbs with 9 inches of soil over the bulb tip.

3. Plant astilbes and coral bells in a lightly shaded, moist spot.

4. Locate remaining plants in a spot with at least 8 hours of sun.

5. Mulch all plantings with a light layer of shredded bark.

Aftercare and Maintenance
• Spray Shasta daisies with a strong jet of water from a hose to rid plants of aphids or spider mites in summer.
• Spot-water astilbes weekly to keep soil evenly moist during dry weather.
• Deadhead chamomile throughout the growing season to keep it blooming all summer.

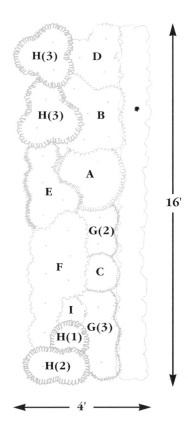

Plant List

A. Artemisia ludoviciana var. albula 'Silver King' (wormwood) (1)
B. Astilbe x arendsii (astilbe) (5)
C. Chamaemelum nobile (chamomile) (1)
D. Chrysanthemum x superbum (Shasta daisy) (3)
E. Coreopsis lanceolata (lance-leaved coreopsis) (4)
F. Hemerocallis citrina (citron daylily) (7)
G. Heuchera sanguinea (coral bells) (5)
H. Lilium cv. (Asiatic hybrid lily) (9)
I. Stachys byzantina (lamb's ears) (1)

A Driveway Planting with Shrubs

This driveway edged with shrubs looks good year round with minimal attention. The shrubs give permanent structure to the landscape, unlike perennials and annuals that disappear by late fall in most cold climates. Once established, these slow-growing plants need little more than an annual pruning and mulching to look their best. Shrubs such as these are big enough to complement a large driveway, whereas small plants may look lost unless planted in great masses.

This shrub garden works best in mild-winter areas in Zones 5 through 8. Several species, including cinquefoil, cotoneaster, and juniper, are hardy in much colder zones. This plan includes two shrubs, a hydrangea species and cinquefoil, that will grow to reasonable size and bloom well even if cut to the ground each winter.

The garden emphasizes seasonal interest, from the spring flowers of weigela to the evergreen junipers that brighten the winter landscape.

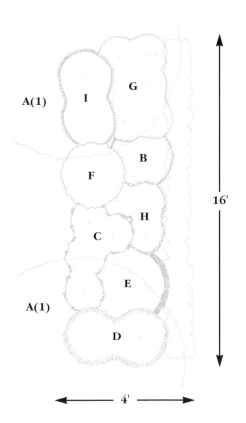

Plant List

A. *Chionanthus virginicus* (white fringe tree) (2)
B. *Cotoneaster dammeri* 'Royal Beauty' (bearberry cotoneaster) (1)
C. *Hibiscus syriacus* 'Woodbridge' (rose-of-Sharon) (4)

D. *Hydrangea macrophylla* 'Domotoi' (bigleaf hydrangea) (2)
E. *Juniperus horizontalis* 'Hughes' (creeping juniper) (1)
F. *Kerria japonica* 'Pleniflora' (kerria) (1)
G. *Potentilla fruticosa*

'Katherine Dykes' (cinquefoil) (6)
H. *Spiraea japonica* 'Little Princess' (Japanese spirea) (3)
I. *Weigela florida* 'Variegata Nana' (dwarf variegated weigela) (2)

◆ How to Plant This Garden ◆

1. Assess the amount of sun and shade in your garden site.

2. In spring, plant white fringe trees in a sunny spot. Prepare a hole as deep as the rootball at the center. Loosen soil beyond the edges of the hole and work in compost.

3. Plant spirea, cotoneaster, juniper, and cinquefoil in sunny sites, and hydrangea, rose-of-Sharon, weigela, and kerria in part shade.

Aftercare and Maintenance
• Prune hydrangea immediately after flowering, since it blooms on the previous season's wood.
• Prune cotoneaster and juniper if they need shaping.

A Driveway Planting with Annuals

Spring brings a clean slate and the opportunity to try new color combinations in this garden. The annuals here produce maximum color and bloom throughout summer and early fall. While this planting is an excellent choice for cold-climate areas where the space around the driveway may be piled high with snow, a driveway garden of annuals is also sensible for situations such as a summer cottage or rental.

The plants have been chosen to grow to a variety of heights, avoiding the frequent pitfall of monotonous flatness in annual plantings. All withstand pollution, salty breezes, and residual road salt in the soil, and none require especially fertile soil, so preparing the bed and planting is fast and easy.

All of these plants grow well in the heat of summer and full sun, except the pot marigolds, which may falter. If they do, cut them back to rebloom as the weather cools, providing color through the first light frosts of fall.

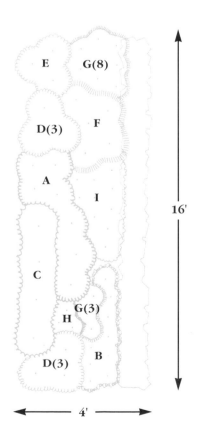

Plant List

A. *Calendula officinalis* 'Prince' (pot marigold) (7)
B. *Catharanthus roseus* 'Bright Eye' (periwinkle) (9)
C. *Celosia argentea* var. *cristata* 'Amazon' (celosia) (4)
D. *Cosmos bipinnatus* 'Sensations Pink' (cosmos) (6)
E. *Cosmos bipinnatus* 'Sensations White' (cosmos) (3)
F. *Gomphrena globosa* 'Strawberry Fields' (globe amaranth) (5)
G. *Salvia farinacea* 'Strata' (mealy-cup sage) (11)
H. *Senecio cineraria* 'Cirrus' (dusty-miller) (3)
I. *Verbena* x *hybrida* 'Imagination' (verbena) (10)

◆ How to Plant This Garden ◆

1. Assess your site to be sure it has at least 6 hours of sun per day to encourage flowering.

2. To prepare the site, till 2 to 3 inches of compost into the soil. Rake soil smooth.

3. Sow seeds of calendula and cosmos after the last frost. Cover with a ¼-inch layer of soil and keep moist. Thin so seedlings are 12 inches apart.

4. Plant periwinkle, celosia, globe amaranth, sage, dusty-miller, and verbena seedlings after last frost.

5. Keep soil moist until plants are growing. Mulch when seedlings are 3 to 4 inches tall, keeping mulch 1 inch from plant stems.

Aftercare and Maintenance
• Pinch tips of sage, globe amaranth, and cosmos when plants are about 12 inches high to make them bushy and full.
• Lightly fertilize all plants in early summer.

Create Your Own Garden of Varied Light

It is best, if possible, to plant tall deciduous trees, such as maples and oaks, on the south side of your property. In the summer, they will provide welcome shade and channel fresh breezes toward the house, while in winter, warming sunlight will shine through their bare branches.

Observing the time of day when parts of your garden are in sun and shade will help you understand your site and ensure the success of your garden plan. On a site plan, mark sun and shade patterns in your garden for each season over a year. Date your drawings and note both morning and afternoon light. You may discover that the amount of sun your garden receives is affected by the shadows of houses and trees on neighboring properties. Using this information, you can create successful designs or make plans to cut down or prune some trees to create new sunny spaces.

If you have a wet and wooded or otherwise partly shaded spot, you might choose the garden featured here. Its perennials do well in moist, rich soil, and their colors add brightness to the dappled sunlight. Or use the first alternate planting on the following page; it features flowers, such as phlox and goatsbeard, that also fare well in sunny sites. If your location is partly shaded but the soil is dry, the second alternate planting *(page 99)* will produce the best results.

A Garden for a Moist, Shaded Site

The garden opposite combines an interesting mix of moisture- and shade-loving perennials in a wide range of textures and forms. A wide, grassy path rambles through patches of dappled light, leading to a pond partially hidden by landscaped banks, while perennials spill onto the path.

Japanese irises thrive in this garden, standing in wet soil at the pond's edge. Their flat flowers and clumps of broad, swordlike leaves make a dramatic contrast with the fluffy, pointed panicles of the astilbes nearby.

If you have enough room, you may want to add a dramatic clump of variegated hosta. A birdhouse or two on poles will provide nesting sites for songbirds, adding a lively note to your garden.

Plant List

A. Allium giganteum (giant onion) (5)
B. Astilbe x arendsii (astilbe) (4)
C. Astilbe thunbergii 'Straussenfeder' (astilbe) (1)
D. Clethra alnifolia 'Hummingbird' (summersweet) (3)
E. Hakonechloa macra 'Aureola' (golden variegated hakonechloa) (9)
F. Iris ensata (sword-leaved iris) (16)
G. Primula florinadae (Tibetan primrose) (16)
H. Rodgersia pinnata 'Superba' (rodgersia) (1)

◆ How to Plant This Garden ◆

1. Test your soil before planting irises, which require acid-to-neutral conditions. If soil is alkaline, apply powdered sulfur or iron sulfate (1 ounce to 2 gallons of water). Plant irises in the spring at the same depth they were growing in their containers.

2. Locate astilbes in sheltered sites with morning sun and giant onions in sunny spots. Dig several shovelfuls of compost into the bed at planting time.

3. Plant rodgersia, Tibetan primrose, summersweet, and golden variegated hakonechloa in moist soil for best growth.

Aftercare and Maintenance
• *Check soil acidity regularly during the growing season. Amend as needed.*
• *Divide irises when they become overcrowded and do not flower as abundantly.*
• *Water astilbes regularly to keep soil moist.*

A Native Wildflower Garden in Dappled Shade

This garden combines some of the most beautiful native and naturalized wildflowers with conventional perennials. Their blossoms of pink, red, blue, and white brighten the area, and their contrasting plant forms add structure to the path after the garden has bloomed. Together, these plants create a cool, restful mood in the garden as they adapt to sun and dappled shade. With this flexibility, you can plant them in an area already lightly shaded by the high canopy of deciduous trees and lower shrubs, or you can site them near newly planted trees that do not yet cast much shade. The plants were chosen for their ability to thrive in the moist conditions found by the pond.

Plant List

A. Aquilegia caerulea (Rocky Mountain columbine) (6)
B. Aruncus dioicus (goatsbeard) (2)
C. Asclepias incarnata (swamp milkweed) (6)
D. Aster novae-angliae (New England aster) (4)
E. Cimicifuga racemosa (black cohosh) (1)
F. Dicentra eximia 'Snowdrift' (wild bleeding heart) (11)
G. Filipendula rubra (queen-of-the-prairie) (2)
H. Iris versicolor (blue flag) (3)
I. Lobelia cardinalis (cardinal flower) (7)
J. Phlox paniculata 'Cotton Candy' (perennial phlox) (4)
K. Phlox paniculata 'Mt. Fuji' (perennial phlox) (3)

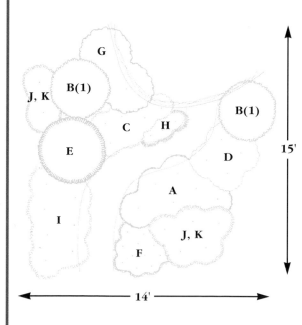

◆ How to Plant This Garden ◆

1. Plant queen-of-the-prairie, goatsbeard, and swamp milkweed close to the water's edge in a bright spot.

2. Site blue flag in a sunny area in damp soil or water to a maximum of 6 inches deep.

3. Plant Rocky Mountain columbines and New England asters in a raised or sloping spot where soil drains.

4. Before planting phlox, amend soil with compost or aged manure. Space approximately 2 feet apart for good air circulation.

5. Place cardinal flower and black cohosh where their tall, showy spikes become focal points. Both plants do best in acid soil amended with leaf mold.

6. Scatter wild bleeding heart in the shadiest spots, but away from standing water. Add leaf mold to the soil to keep it moist and rich.

Aftercare and Maintenance
• Dig and divide blue flags and queen-of-the-prairie in the fall every 2 to 3 years.
• Pinch back asters twice before midsummer for denser, more compact plants. Divide clumps every 2 to 3 years.
• Divide phlox every 2 to 3 years in early fall, keeping the strong outer divisions. In spring, thin the clumps to five or six stems to improve air circulation.
• Covering cardinal flowers with a light straw mulch after the ground freezes in winter protects them in cold climates.
• Leave the seedpods on the Rocky Mountain columbines intact to encourage reseeding and to attract birds.
• Fertilize all plants lightly each spring after growth begins.

A Dry Garden in Partial Shade

Here is a colorful garden that uses plants suited to a dry, partly shaded site. The plants may not grow as tall or as lush as those found in more moist and fertile conditions, but they are equally attractive, with agapanthus and speedwell adding vertical contrast. This planting borders a crushed stone walk leading to a red brick patio. The dark reddish brown colors of this hardscape allow the rich floral blues and yellows to assume prominence, with white and pink tones emerging as sharp accent colors.

Dry soil in shade can be a difficult place to garden successfully. Therefore, before you plant your garden, double dig the soil and enrich it with large amounts of moisture-retentive materials such as compost, leaf mold, and manure. This work will pay off in moister soil and stronger plants.

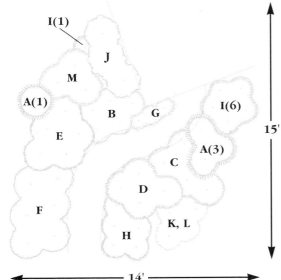

Plant List

A. Agapanthus africanus (agapanthus) (4)

B. Alchemilla mollis (lady's-mantle) (5)

C. Campanula medium 'Alba' (Canterbury bells) (4)

D. Campanula medium 'Caerulea' (Canterbury bells) (4)

E. Centaurea macro- cephala (knapweed) (5)

F. Dennstaedtia punctilobula (hay-scented fern) (6)

G. Hyacinthoides hispanica (Spanish bluebell) (3)

H. Geranium sanguineum 'Album' (cranesbill) (5)

I. Iris foetidissima (scarlet-seeded iris) (7)

J. Rudbeckia hirta 'Goldilocks' (black-eyed Susan) (3)

K. Tradescantia x andersoniana 'Osprey' (spiderwort) (2)

L. Tradescantia x andersoniana 'Zwanberg Blue' (spiderwort) (2)

M. Veronica longifolia (speedwell) (3)

◆ How to Plant This Garden ◆

1. Plant clumps of Canterbury bells every spring to bloom the following year.

2. Plant black-eyed Susans, ferns, knapweeds, speedwells, and spiderworts in drifts.

3. Add compost to soil before planting lady's-mantle, cranesbill, and iris.

4. In Zones 7 to 10, plant agapanthus in the ground. In colder climates, sink potted plants in the ground.

5. In fall, plant Spanish bluebell bulbs 3 inches deep in mild climates and 6 inches deep in colder regions. Spread them in drifts running through neighboring plants.

6. Apply a pine bark mulch to preserve soil moisture.

Aftercare and Maintenance
• To promote strong, compact growth in knapweeds, spiderworts, and speedwells,

apply a balanced fertilizer sparingly once a month to midsummer.
• Cut back spiderwort and geranium foliage in midsummer if it becomes untidy.
• Sow biennial Canterbury bells the following spring to promote earlier and more abundant blooms.
• Lift and overwinter the potted agapanthus indoors.

Create Your Own Hillside Shade Garden

Beautifying a partly shaded bank presents several challenges for gardeners. Variations in steepness, degrees of shade, drainage, and soil quality play critical roles in developing a solid cover that will flourish on the hillside throughout the year. Fortunately, a wide array of low ground covers and shrubs, as well as perennials and vines, is available to survive difficult conditions and even help control erosion.

The effect of such a garden can be dramatic. Even though flower color is sometimes limited in shady gardens, combinations featuring variegated foliage add brightness. Interesting leaf shapes that cast shadows in dappled sun provide striking patterns of light and color as well.

When selecting plants for shade, look for contrasting foliage textures. Combine plants with large, leathery leaves, grasslike spikes, and finely fringed leaf margins. These will become the focal points around which you can add less striking plants that work hard to cover and stabilize the slope. Ivy or other hardy vines and ground covers, such as periwinkle or spurge, are good examples.

Your garden site may be like the one featured here, which has slow drainage and stays moist after heavy rainfall. If your site features well-drained soil, consider the first alternate planting on the following page; but if you have a site with drier, poorer soil, the shade garden plan *(page 103)* will be more suited to your needs.

A Far-East Feel

The Oriental pavilion at the top of the shaded slope shown opposite gives this garden a contemplative aura and underscores the quiet harmony of the plant combinations. Like a Chinese landscape painting, this garden design draws your gaze up the winding path to the hilltop and invites you to scale the path for a view from the crest. Springtime visitors who make the effort will be rewarded with a tapestry-like view of the flowering shrubs.

Moisture-loving rhododendrons and azaleas offer splashes of welcome color in the spring against vivid green foliage that persists for most of the year. Masking the bare lower stems of the larger shrub behind are masses of large, puckered hosta leaves. They add contrasts in color and texture, anchoring the sloping landscape and providing a sense of balance to the base of this design.

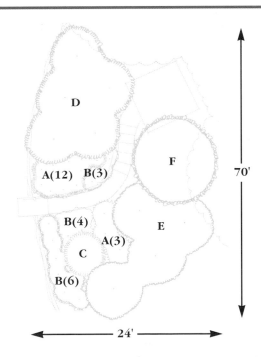

Plant List

A. *Aquilegia flabellata* var. *pumila* (dwarf blue columbine) (15)
B. *Hosta* 'Big Boy' (hosta) (13)
C. *Hosta sieboldiana* (hosta) (1)
D. *Rhododendron* Gable Hybrids 'Karen' (azalea) (5)
E. *Rhododendron* Leach Hybrids 'Bali' (rhododendron) (4)
F. *Rhododendron smirnowii* (Smirnow rhododendron) (1)

◆ How to Plant This Garden ◆

1. Plant azaleas and rhododendrons in light to medium shade at the top of the slope in holes 2 feet deep and wide. Fill holes, mixing two to three shovelfuls of organic matter with soil. Protect soil around the shrubs with a layer of pine bark mulch.

2. Locate hostas in partial shade at the bottom of the slope, where moisture is constant. Enrich soil in their planting area with compost or leaf mold.

3. Tuck columbines into shaded areas around the bases of shrubs. Crowd them together for a mass effect. Add mulch between plants.

Aftercare and Maintenance
• *Monitor soil moisture on the slope; irrigate fast-draining areas.*
• *Apply acid fertilizer to azaleas and rhododendrons in the spring.*
• *Divide hostas after 6 to 8 years.*

A Rich Hillside of Blooms and Foliage

Many plants prosper in the shady, rich, well-drained soil of this hillside woodland setting. The design features plants notable for their striking foliage as well as for their blooms. Both the barrenwort and the viburnum have reddish-tinted leaves early in the growing season and more dramatic color in the fall. The glossy mountain laurel foliage reflects the filtering sunlight and adds color with early summer blooms. Most dramatic of all, the ligularia spreads its broad leaves near the base of the slope. It will become the central landscape feature when its towering spires of yellow flowers emerge in late summer. Nearby ostrich ferns, Japanese anemones, and yellow globeflowers complete the woodland scene.

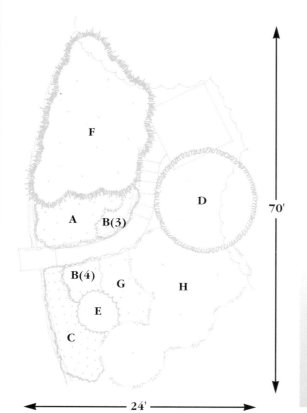

Plant List

A. Anemone x hybrida 'Whirlwind' (Japanese anemone) (12)
B. Aquilegia canadensis (wild columbine) (7)
C. Epimedium x versicolor (barrenwort) (46)

D. Kalmia latifolia 'Fuscata' (mountain laurel) (1)
E. Ligularia x przewalskii 'The Rocket' (ligularia) (1)
F. Matteuccia pennsylvanica (ostrich fern) (12)

G. Trollius europaeus 'Lemon Queen' (globeflower) (6)
H. Viburnum trilobum 'Bailey Compact' (American cranberry bush viburnum) (4)

◆ How to Plant This Garden ◆

1. In spring or early fall, plant mountain laurel and viburnums in loosened, unamended soil to encourage their roots to spread. Mulch with chopped leaves.

2. In spring or very early fall, install the remaining plants in soil amended with compost. Plant ligularia in a spot with naturally damp soil. If plants are potbound and have circled roots, loosen them with your fingers or slice the root-balls with a knife, then spread roots out in the planting holes.

3. Water well after planting. Apply a 1- to 2-inch layer of bark mulch between the plants.

Aftercare and Maintenance
• Replenish the mulch layer around the shrubs and perennials annually.
• Water ligularia regularly, keeping soil moist to wet. Keep ostrich ferns moist.

• For an added bonus of summer-long color, underplant the viburnums with shade-loving annuals such as impatiens, begonias, or coleus.
• Collect and crush dried seedpods of columbines. Sprinkle seed where more plants are needed.
• If leaf miner attacks foliage of columbine, remove affected leaves immediately and discard.

A Garden for a Dry, Shady Slope

Dry, shady conditions that appear only seasonally in parts of a property may exist year round under evergreen trees and shrubs. Despite such difficult garden conditions, it is still possible to create an attractive landscape. The garden illustrated here features trees, shrubs, and perennials that will thrive in partial shade to create an interesting four-season landscape.

Spring- and early summer-flowering wild columbine and fairy-lantern in the lower reaches of the garden give way to summer mallow blossoms and the fall color of decorative Indian currants midway up the slope. Glossy evergreen holly grape foliage and bright red-osier dogwood stems add winter interest, while the red cedar provides a year-round presence with its density and texture.

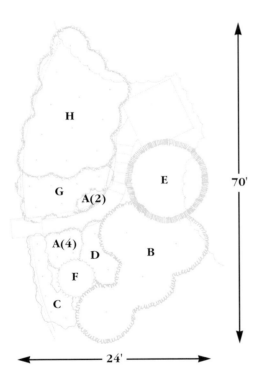

Plant List

A. *Aquilegia canadensis* (wild columbine) (6)
B. *Cornus sericea* (red-osier dogwood) (4)
C. *Disporum smithii* (fairy-lantern) (7)
D. *Filipendula vulgaris* 'Flore Pleno' (dropwort) (3)
E. *Juniperus virginiana* 'Hillii' (red cedar) (1)
F. *Mahonia aquifolium* 'Compacta' (holly grape) (1)
G. *Malva alcea* (hollyhock mallow) (6)
H. *Symphoricarpos orbiculatus* 'Foliis Variegatus' (variegated Indian currant) (12)

◆ How to Plant This Garden ◆

1. Plant dropworts, red-osier dogwoods, red cedar, holly grape, and Indian currants in spring or early fall. Once established, they tolerate dry conditions, but must receive water frequently after planting and during their first year.

2. Dig a 2- to 3-inch layer of compost or leaf mold into the soil before planting the columbines and fairy-lanterns.

3. Water entire planting site thoroughly, then cover with a 2- to 4-inch layer of organic mulch. Be sure to keep the mulch 2 to 3 inches away from the trunks of the trees, the bases of the shrubs, and perennial stems.

Aftercare and Maintenance
• *Replace the mulch annually in the spring to control weeds, regulate soil temperature, and retain soil moisture.*
• *Water the garden every 2 to 3 weeks to prevent soil from drying out completely.*
• *Deadhead fading mallow blooms to encourage a redisplay of color.*
• *Thin out suckers that arise around Indian currants to keep the plants in bounds.*

Create Your Own Waterwise Garden

Perhaps your community restricts the amount of water you can use in summer, or you are concerned about conserving natural resources. Maybe you live in a hot, dry climate like the Southwest, or you travel in summer and have little time for watering lawn and flowers. Whatever the reason, xeriscaping—the practice of combining drought-adaptive plants with thrifty water use—makes good sense.

Principal elements of waterwise gardening include little or no turf grass, use of native species when possible, and minimal paving to reduce runoff. Digging deep into the soil and amending it with organic matter such as rotted manure, compost, and leaf mold will increase the soil's water-retention capacity. If you can't redig your whole garden, then top-dress the existing beds, add organic matter when you plant, or mulch heavily. Where organic mulches are not available or would be too expensive, crushed stone makes

an effective mulch for a xeriscape garden. The sun's heat warms the stones by day, and water condenses on them in the cool of night, increasing the amount of moisture that enters the soil.

The choice of plants is one of the most important factors in xeriscaping. Plants native to or compatible with your environment will be tougher and less prone to disease and insect damage. Regular maintenance will help control weeds and insects that compete with your garden plants for moisture and nutrients.

The design on this page features a southwestern garden abounding in cacti, which require minimal water or care once established. The first alternate planting focuses on drought-resistant perennials that can be planted in most zones; the second shows a garden laid out according to the varying water needs of different groups of plants, a principle that can be applied in any location. All are gardens for full sun.

Southwestern Cactus Garden

The plants in this garden evolved in the dry climate of the Southwest and can cope with the harshness of a hot desert. This plan combines the cacti in an arrangement of columns, spheres, and clusters to arrive at a pleasing contrast of forms, textures, and colors. All the plants have been given enough space to achieve their mature size, but the amended soil allows for closer spacing than in their natural desert environment, dramatizing the juxtaposition of forms and creating a strikingly artistic whole.

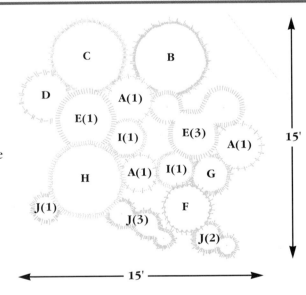

Plant List

A. *Agave victoriae-reginae* (century plant) (3)
B. *Cephalocereus senilis* (old-man cactus) (1)
C. *Cereus hildmannianus* (curiosity plant) (1)
D. *Cleistocactus strausii* (silver-torch) (1)
E. *Echinocactus grusonii* (golden barrel cactus) (4)
F. *Echinocerus* sp. (hedgehog cactus) (1)
G. *Ferocactus pilosus* (fishhook cactus) (1)
H. *Parodia magnifica* (parodia) (1)
I. *Rebutia albopectinata* (crown cactus) (2)
J. *Uebelmannia flavispina* (Uebelmannia) (6)

◆ How to Plant This Garden ◆

1. Dig a planting area *deep enough to accommodate a 3- to 4-inch layer of coarse gravel topped by 1 foot of soil mix made of half loam and half sand or grit. Wet soil gently with spray from a hose.*

2. To protect yourself from sharp spines, *wrap folded burlap around plants that need moving.*

3. Pack soil mix around plants. *Stake tall plants until established.*

4. Leave room for clump-forming cacti (silver-torch, parodia, and fishhook) *to spread.*

5. Mulch soil with granite chips *up to the crowns of the plants. Moisten the soil, and shade the plants with burlap until established.*

Aftercare and Maintenance
• Water cacti only when dry; remove dust with hose spray.

A Drought-Resistant Perennial Garden

Suitable for a wide range of climates, this garden is perfect if you travel often or have little time to spend watering. Many of these tough, low-maintenance perennials are actually native wildflowers or cultivars of wildflowers that combine ornamental leaves or flowers with the sturdiness of native plants. The garden is really a small, refined version of the American prairie, and includes ornamental grasses to underscore the theme. Be sure to buy nursery-grown specimens rather than plants taken from the wild.

Yarrow, black-eyed Susan, and tickseed provide informal bouquets, and the sturdy rugosa rose produces attractive red hips after its white flowers fade. All these plants thrive in full sun and average, well-drained soil.

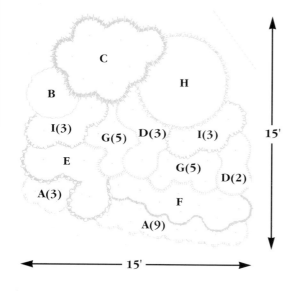

Plant List

A. Achillea millefolium (yarrow) (12)
B. Baptisia australis (blue false indigo) (1)
C. Calamagrostis acutiflora 'Karl Foerster' (feather reed grass) (8)

D. Coreopsis verticillata 'Moonbeam' (tickseed) (5)
E. Euphorbia griffithii 'Fireglow' (spurge) (3)
F. Gaillardia x grandiflora 'Golden Goblin'

(blanket-flower) (9)
G. Linum perenne (perennial flax) (10)
H. Rosa rugosa 'Alba' (rugosa rose) (1)
I. Rudbeckia hirta (black-eyed Susan) (6)

◆ How to Plant This Garden ◆

1. Spread 2 inches of compost *over the soil, work in to a depth of 12 inches, and rake smooth.*

2. Plant false indigo *4 feet from other plants.*

3. Arrange remaining perennials *in loose, natural-looking drifts. Space tickseed, spurge, blanket-flower, and flax*

1 to 1½ feet apart. Space others 2 feet apart.

Aftercare and Maintenance
• Deadhead self-seeding tickseed to encourage more blooms. Near the end of the growing season, shear back to keep it neat.
• Divide yarrows, blanket-flowers, and

black-eyed Susans every 2 to 3 years.
• Apply a 2- to 3-inch-deep layer of mulch to keep weeds down. Reapply as necessary.
• Prune roses to shape in the spring. Once plants are established, remove the oldest canes and any winter damage each spring.

A Garden Zoned by Water Needs

This drought-tolerant garden is designed according to the water needs of the plants. Grouping plants with similar needs for moisture makes gardening easier and reduces maintenance time, even where water availability is not an issue. Here, the cosmos, coneflowers, Russian sage, and asters at the back and sides of the garden are quite drought resistant. Those requiring more moisture, such as lamb's ears, baby's-breath, mullein, and cinquefoil, are placed at the front of the garden where they are easily accessible for watering. This garden of annuals and perennials could work well if part of the site is close to a water source and other parts are difficult to reach.

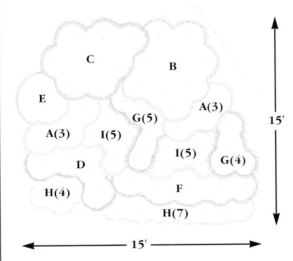

15'

15'

Plant List

A. *Aster novae-angliae* 'Harrington's Pink' (New England aster) (6)
B. *Cosmos bipinnatus* 'Versailles White' (cosmos) (9)
C. *Echinacea purpurea* (purple coneflower) (8)
D. *Gypsophila paniculata* 'Perfecta' (baby's-breath) (4)
E. *Perovskia*

atriplicifolia (Russian sage) (1)
F. *Potentilla nepalensis* 'Miss Willmott' (cinquefoil) (5)
G. *Salvia x superba* 'East Friesland' (violet sage) (9)
H. *Stachys byzantina* (lamb's ears) (11)
I. *Verbascum phoeniceum* 'Pink Domino' (purple mullein) (10)

◆ How to Plant This Garden ◆

1. Prepare the garden site by double-digging soil to a depth of 2 feet. Dig 2 to 3 inches of compost into the top layer of soil when returning it to the bed. The extra digging promotes longer plant roots and more efficient water use.

2. Sow cosmos seeds after the last frost, covering them with a thin layer of soil, and gently pat down. Sprinkle with water daily until seeds germinate.

3. Plant perennial asters, purple coneflowers, baby's-breath, cinquefoil, lamb's ears, Russian sage, and

violet sage in groups for clumps of color. Space baby's-breath and Russian sage 3 feet apart, all others 2 feet apart.

Aftercare and Maintenance
• Pinch 2 to 3 inches of tip growth from asters during early summer in cool climates and midsummer in hot climates to encourage branching.
• Cut Russian sage to 6 inches in early spring to encourage new growth and abundant flowers.

Create Your Own Bird and Butterfly Haven

A garden is a natural stopping point for hummingbirds, songbirds, and butterflies attracted to the food, water, and shelter that home landscapes provide. With careful planning, you can attract a variety of birds and butterflies to your backyard. Be sure to include an array of nectar-rich blooms in summer, brightly colored berries and fruits in the fall and winter, nesting sites safe from prowling predators, and both high and low sheltering foliage. Your hard work will be rewarded with a built-in garden pest control system, and pollinators aplenty for your seeding and fruiting plants. You will also have a setting that gives you and your family hours of pleasurable garden viewing and interest.

Bright colors are the signal that attracts birds and butterflies into your garden in search of energy-giving nectar. Explosive bursts of vivid reds, oranges, yellows, pinks, and some blues lure them best. The predominantly red-and-orange garden opposite caters to hummingbirds; the one on the following page offers a home to a variety of songbirds; the subsequent garden gives food and shelter to butterflies. You can put in a garden to attract one type of winged creature, or plants from each plan to create a habitat for all three.

Attracting Hummingbirds

Pendant flowers with tubular blooms are hummingbird favorites. Mass plantings of fiery orange Peruvian lily in this warm-climate garden will draw in the hummers, as will red rose campion and bold yellow tickseed. The protective canopy of the western redbud offers them a sheltered observation point, if and when they should come to rest. In addition, the birdbath in the middle of the garden provides drinking water and a bathing spot. Because these tiny fliers are drawn to water, consider installing an ornamental pool or a cascading waterfall.

For gardeners in the Northeast, a reliable substitute for the western redbud is its hardier eastern relative, *Cercis canadensis*. Other cold-hardy hummingbird favorites include bee balm, honeysuckle, and *Campsis*. You can also draw hummingbirds right to your house with trailing petunias and fuchsias in hanging pots.

Plant List

A. *Alstroemeria aurantiaca* (Peruvian lily) (29)
B. *Brugmansia x candida* (angel's-trumpet) (2)
C. *Cercis occidentalis* (western redbud) (1)
D. *Coreopsis lanceolata* (lanced-leaved tickseed) (30)
E. *Gazania rigens* (treasure flower) (23)
F. *Lychnis coronaria* (rose campion) (20)

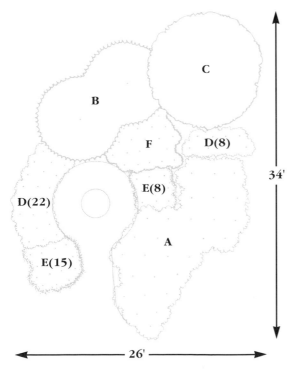

◆ How to Plant This Garden ◆

1. Plant western redbud in a hole as deep as the rootball and twice as wide. Stake during the first growing season.

2. Plant Peruvian lily tubers 1 foot apart on mounded soil in planting holes. Cover with 2 inches of soil. Water well.

3. Set tickseeds 12 to 15 inches apart in a section of unamended soil. Water well.

4. Cluster rose campions 8 to 10 inches apart.

5. Set low-growing treasure flowers close together to provide a quick, attractive ground cover.

6. In warm climates, plant angel's-trumpets in full sun or partial shade; in cold climates, plant them in a 5-gallon container for overwintering indoors.

Aftercare and Maintenance
• Avoid overwatering western redbud, since it is native to regions with dry summers.
• Mulch Peruvian lilies in winter in Zones 6 and 7 to protect them from heavy frost. Dig up and store indoors in colder regions.

A Songbird Garden

Songbirds bring beautiful sound and color to the garden year round. Fortunately for the bird-loving gardener, they are easy to attract.

In the garden illustrated here, shrubs make up most of the songbird's nesting and feeding habitat, providing protective cover, food, and shelter for insects, and ample supplies of fall berries. Serviceberry bears white flowers followed by sweet, juicy, blackish purple fruit. This shrub grows to 20 feet tall and spreads vigorously from the base by erect sucker growth. Its attractive yellow-and-gold fall color gives it an extra season of interest in your garden.

Arrowwood viburnum, another colorful shrub, spreads 6 to 15 feet wide and grows nearly as tall. Birds flock to its blue-black fruit, which appears in late September through October. This tough, useful plant adapts to many soil conditions and brings reddish purple fall color into the garden.

Low-growing 'Coral Beauty' cotoneaster produces many attractive coral-red berries. It makes a wonderful evergreen ground cover with its glossy foliage and abundant fruit.

Brilliant scarlet cardinal flowers and bee balm both provide a middle level of color at 3 feet high from summer to fall. The cardinal flower's lance-shaped leaves are often tinted a reddish bronze. The birdbath provides songbirds with essential water for drinking and bathing. Be sure to clean it regularly.

Plant List

A. *Amelanchier canadensis* (serviceberry) (1)
B. *Aronia arbutifolia* (red chokeberry) (1)
C. *Cotoneaster dammeri* 'Coral Beauty' (bearberry cotoneaster) (1)
D. *Lobelia cardinalis* (cardinal flower) (7)
E. *Mimulus* Malibu Series (monkey flower) (25)
F. *Monarda didyma* 'Gardenview Scarlet' (bee balm) (34)
G. *Solidago sphacelata* 'Golden Fleece' (goldenrod) (11)
H. *Tagetes* 'Crackerjack' (African marigold) (9)
I. *Tagetes patula* 'Naughty Marietta' (French marigold) (39)
J. *Viburnum dentatum* (arrowwood viburnum) (1)
K. *Viburnum trilobum* 'Compactum' (American cranberry bush) (1)

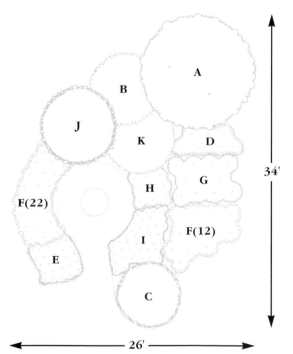

34'

26'

◆ How to Plant This Garden ◆

1. Plant arrowwood viburnum *3 feet from path. Plant red chokeberry, bearberry cotoneaster, and American cranberry bush in sun for maximum fruit production.*

2. Locate serviceberry, *monkey flowers, and cardinal flowers in the dampest area of the garden.*

3. Cluster bee balms *1 foot apart.*

4. Plant goldenrods and marigolds *8 inches apart in the driest areas.*

Aftercare and Maintenance
• *Leave faded flowers on the plants to form berries and seeds that will help attract birds.*

A Butterfly Garden

The happy lilt of songbirds is a welcome sound in any garden. Fortunately for the bird-loving gardener, songbirds are easy to attract and will provide year-round color and melody.

Microclimate is important when planning a butterfly garden. The garden illustrated here is situated in a sunny spot, a necessity for butterflies that need the sun to warm their wings for flight. Butterfly bush, summer-sweet, and glossy abelia, all flowering shrubs, not only feed butterflies, but also act as windbreaks to protect them from harmful gusts. Butterfly favorites such as 'Fantasy Mix' petunias, rosy perennial Jupiter's-beard, 'Brilliant' showy stonecrop, butterfly weed, and pincushion flower bloom from midsummer to early fall.

Planting a variety of native meadow plants, such as asters, butterfly bush, and Joe-Pye weed, also assures colorful butterfly blooms and foliage through fall.

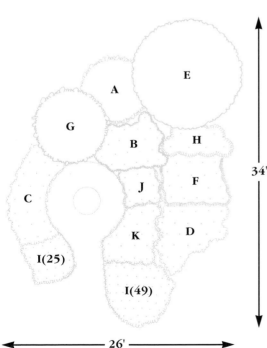

Plant List

A. *Abelia x grandiflora* (glossy abelia) (1)
B. *Asclepias tuberosa* (butterfly weed) (20)
C. *Aster x frikartii* 'Mönch' (Frikart's aster) (22)
D. *Aster novae-angliae* 'Purple Dome' (New England aster) (22)

E. *Buddleia davidii* 'Pink Delight' (butterfly bush) (1)
F. *Centranthus ruber* (Jupiter's-beard) (19)
G. *Clethra alnifolia* 'Rosea' (summer-sweet) (1)
H. *Eupatorium maculatum*

(Joe-Pye weed) (7)
I. *Petunia x hybrida* 'Fantasy Mix' (garden petunia) (74)
J. *Scabiosa caucasica* 'Pink Mist' (pincushion flower) (9)
K. *Sedum spectabile* 'Brilliant' (showy stonecrop) (18)

◆ How to Plant This Garden ◆

1. Plant summer-sweet, *glossy abelia, and butterfly bush in ordinary well-cultivated soil.*

2. Amend soil with organic matter *before planting asters, Jupiter's-beard, Joe-Pye weed, petunias, pincushion flowers, and stonecrop.*

3. Plant butterfly weed *in unamended soil.*

Aftercare and Maintenance
• *Place large, flat stones in birdbath to allow safe access to water for butterflies.*
• *Water regularly, keeping soil moist until plants are established.*
• *Deadhead butterfly bush to prolong bloom into fall; cut stems halfway back in spring.*

Waves of Color from Spring to Fall

Gardeners dream of a sequence of blooms and colorful foliage that will transform their landscape into a continuously evolving display. With the right combination of plants, you can step into your garden almost anytime and be surrounded by waves of color. To create such color succession, go beyond the use of annuals and perennials and include bulbs, vines, shrubs, and trees.

Bulbs bring primary hues, soft pastels, and even variegated colors in spring and summer. You can select annuals to fill in when perennials are just beginning to sprout in spring and to obscure yellowing leaves as the perennials die back in autumn. Deciduous trees, shrubs, and vines provide year-round interest, with their sculptural woody structures becoming most noticeable during winter. Some of the shrubs and trees add berries, varied leaf color, and seasonal blooms to ensure an always-changing picture.

Often you can find creativity in simplicity. For example, you can extend the flowering season by taking advantage of the full range of a single genus. Daffodils, tulips, peonies, lilies, and daylilies are all available in varieties that flower early and late, throughout the growing season.

For a splash of spring color, follow the garden plan on this page. This design offers gently rolling waves of blue and white blooms that thrive in partial shade. For a display of spring and late-summer color in a sunny site, consider the first alternate plan of several early- to late-blooming plants. Or fill your garden with contrasting color from spring to frost with the second alternate planting of pink, purple, and yellow blooms.

A Sequence of Blooms for Shade

Shade can work to your advantage. A mix of newly planted and established trees and undulating drifts of cool colors create the shady garden shown here. The flowering plants, which flourish in the dappled light of the trees, are framed by the rich green lawn and conifer foliage. All of the plants thrive in well-drained average to rich soil.

The pendant flower clusters of the Carolina silverbell illuminate the darkest corner of the garden in midspring. Waves of cool blue forget-me-nots carpet the garden floor with tall, bright tulips popping through. Peonies take center stage in late spring with their spectacular blooms. Wall rock cress and columbine will continue to flower into summer.

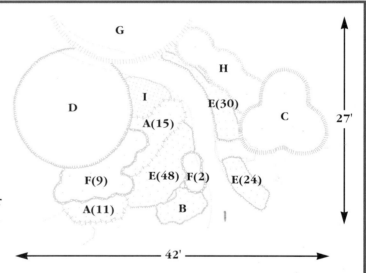

Plant List

A. *Aquilegia vulgaris* (columbine) (26)
B. *Arabis caucasica* (wall rock cress) (23)
C. *Chamaecyparis pisifera* 'Filifera aurea' (goldthread false cypress) (3)
D. *Halesia carolina* (Carolina silverbell) (1)

E. *Myosotis sylvatica* (forget-me-not) (102)
F. *Paeonia lactiflora* (garden peony) (11)
G. *Pinus strobus* (eastern white pine) (1)
H. *Syringa* x *persica* (Persian lilac) (3)
I. *Tulipa* Darwin Hybrids (tulip) (92)

◆ How to Plant This Garden ◆

1. Mix a spoonful of bone meal into each 8-inch-deep planting hole before planting hybrid tulip bulbs about 8 inches apart.

2. Set out peonies with their eyes 2 inches below the soil surface. Peonies planted too deeply may not bloom.

3. Set wall rock cress rosettes in a checkerboard pattern and plant 6 inches apart.

4. Plant Carolina silverbell, eastern white pine, Persian lilac, and goldthread false cypress in holes as deep as the rootball and twice as wide.

5. Plant forget-me-nots with columbine in a moist, shady spot.

Aftercare and Maintenance
• Cut tulip stems as the petals begin to drop. Leave fading foliage to replenish the bulb's food supply.
• Deadhead garden peonies to encourage more robust growth.

A Garden of Spring and Fall Color

If you travel in the summer or have little time for garden care, this planting may be for you. It maximizes color with an artful combination of early- to late-blooming plants, including different cultivars of daffodils and lilies, whose sequential blooms prolong the flowering season. A temperate climate and well-drained soil in full sun are ideal for these plants. Various lilies bloom from early to late summer, while 'Wide Brim' hosta adds handsome variegated leaves. The chrysanthemums, dwarf euonymus, and hydrangea imbue the garden with autumn color.

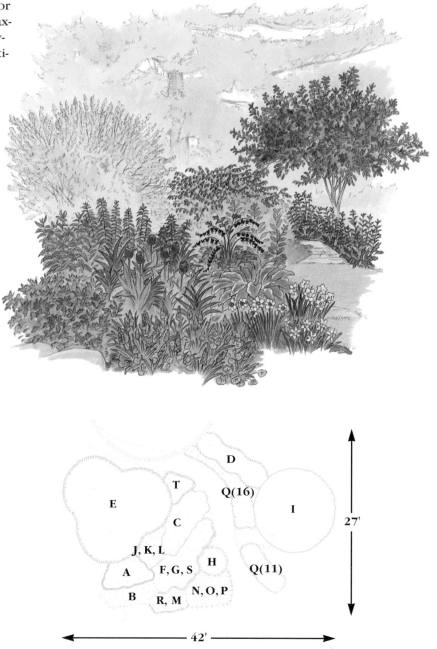

Plant List

A. *Campanula persicifolia* 'Telham Beauty' (peachleaf bellflower) (12)

B. *Chrysanthemum x morifolium* 'Shades of Autumn' (chrysanthemum) (22)

C. *Dicentra spectabilis* (bleeding heart) (17)

D. *Euonymus alata* 'Compacta' (winged euonymus) (3)

E. *Forsythia x intermedia* (forsythia) (3)

F. *Hemerocallis* 'Hyperion' (daylily) (11)

G. *Hemerocallis* 'Lacy Queen' (daylily) (10)

H. *Hosta* 'Wide Brim' (hosta) (1)

I. *Hydrangea paniculata* 'Grandiflora' (peegee hydrangea) (1)

J. *Lilium* 'Amber Gold' (lily) (3)

K. *Lilium lancifolium* var. *splendens* (tiger lily) (5)

L. *Lilium mackliniae* (lily) (6)

M. *Muscari armeniacum* (grape hyacinth) (90)

N. *Narcissus* 'Ice Follies' (daffodil) (35)

O. *Narcissus* 'Jack Snipe' (daffodil) (35)

P. *Narcissus* 'Kilworth' (daffodil) (35)

Q. *Scabiosa caucasica* 'David Wilkie' (pincushion flower) (27)

R. *Tropaeolum* 'Double Dwarf Jewel Series' (nasturtium) (16)

S. *Tulipa* 'Pine Diamond' (tulip) (100)

T. *Veronica spicata* (speedwell) (6)

◆ How to Plant This Garden ◆

1. In the fall, plant daffodils and tulips at a depth three to four times the diameter of the bulb. Plant grape hyacinths 3 inches deep. Set lily bulbs in holes at a depth two times the diameter of the bulb.

2. Set daylily crowns no more than 1 inch below soil.

3. Sow nasturtium seed or set out seedlings after the last frost.

4. Plant forsythia, winged euonymus, and hydrangeas in holes as deep as the rootballs and twice as wide.

5. Plant bellflowers, speedwell, pincushion flowers, and chrysanthemums in groups. Plant bleeding hearts and hostas in the shadiest garden spot.

Aftercare and Maintenance
• Tuck fading tulip and daffodil leaves under nearby foliage.
• Deadhead lilies regularly throughout summer.

A Garden of Continuous Color

This garden plan creates a three-season color symphony from spring through fall. In spring, the large double pink flowers of *Prunus serrulata* harmonize with crocus, tulip, iris, primrose, and horned violet. In a summer show of yellow and orange, golden Marguerite, 'Golden Showers' azalea, and long-blooming Stella de Oro daylily are set off by spurge's grayish evergreen foliage. Summer-blooming perennials, including 'Rose Queen' sage, Russian sage, and astilbe, add touches of lilac and pink. The composition closes in autumn, as the flowering cherry's red leaves are set off by the Colorado blue spruce, more daylily blossoms, and spurge.

This plan places late-blooming perennials and annuals that flower all summer long next to early-blooming bulbs, so summer foliage discreetly covers the wilting leaves of the spring bloomers. Thus, daylilies will hide crocus leaves, petunias will overtake primroses, spurge will replace browning iris leaves, and violet sage will mask the dormant tulips.

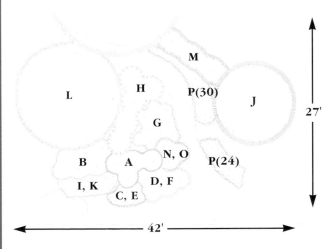

Plant List

A. *Anthemis tinctoria* 'Moonlight' (golden Marguerite) (4)
B. *Astilbe x arendsii* 'Finale' (astilbe) (6)
C. *Crocus* spp. (crocus) (24)
D. *Euphorbia characias* spp. *wulfenii* (spurge) (5)
E. *Hemerocallis* 'Stella de Oro (daylily) (14)
F. *Iris reticulata* 'Harmony' (iris) (70)

G. *Kniphofia* 'Shining Sceptre' (torch lily) (3)
H. *Perovskia atriplicifolia* (Russian sage) (5)
I. *Petunia* x *hybrida* 'Total Madness Mix' (common garden petunia) (24)
J. *Picea pungens* 'Fat Albert' (Colorado blue spruce) (1)
K. *Primula denticulata* (drumstick primrose) (24)

L. *Prunus serrulata* 'Kwanzan' (Japanese flowering cherry) (1)
M. *Rhododendron* Weston Hybrids 'Golden Showers' (azalea) (3)
N. *Salvia* x *superba* 'Rose Queen' (violet sage) (3)
O. *Tulipa* 'Beauty Queen' (tulip) (6)
P. *Viola cornuta* (horned violet) (54)

◆ How to Plant This Garden ◆

1. Plant cherry, azaleas, and Colorado blue spruce in spring.

2. In the fall, plant crocuses 2 to 3 inches deep, tulips 6 to 8 inches deep, and irises 3 to 4 inches deep.

3. Wear gloves when planting spurge, because its white sap can irritate skin.

Allow at least 3 feet of space around its planting site.

4. Plant horned violets when frosts are light. After the last frost in spring, plant torch lilies, astilbes, Russian sage, golden Marguerites, petunias, drumstick primroses, violet sage, and daylilies.

Aftercare and Maintenance
• After the first frost, cut Russian sage to about 6 inches high, removing all old stems. Protect with winter mulch and remove it in spring.
• Keep soil moist around astilbes and azaleas.
• Deadhead astilbes, daylilies, torch lilies, petunias, and sage as needed.

Create Your Own Winter Garden

For some gardeners, winter is a dull, colorless season, a time to retreat indoors and dream of spring. But with a little planning, you can create a garden to provide visual pleasures through the frigid months. Choose plants that provide color and texture with evergreen foliage, beautiful bark, or colorful berries.

Evergreen trees and shrubs are the backbone of any frost-to-thaw garden. From spring to fall, they provide a soothing green background for more colorful annuals and perennials. But after the frost kills the last of the fall flowers, the evergreens are still there to remind you of spring and summer. By choosing a variety of evergreens with different foliage colors, you can also add shades of blue and gold to your winter plantings.

Some deciduous trees and shrubs, too, can offer winter beauty, in their colorful stems, fruits, and berries. Many ornamental grasses are also wonderful in winter, with their graceful, arching foliage and fluffy seed heads. You can even experience fragrance in your winter garden; a few shrubs blossom during the colder months, and their sweetly scented flowers bring a touch of spring to the crisp winter air.

The garden featured opposite relies on evergreen foliage and brightly colored berries to liven up the winter landscape. The first alternate garden highlights plants that are best suited for winter in southern gardens. The second showcases tough, cold-hardy plants to entice northern gardeners outdoors during the dull winter months.

Welcome Winter Color

This winter garden would fit perfectly in an outlying corner of your property. A sunny, well-drained site with slightly acid soil is ideal for all these plants. The broad central path will encourage you to stroll through the plantings often to admire the bright red berries of the American holly, cotoneaster, and flowering dogwood. An extra dividend of this garden is in watching the winter birds that will come to eat the berries. Even when the berries are gone, you'll still enjoy the beautiful horizontal branching structure of the dogwood and the cotoneaster. The purple foliage of the wintercreeper euonymus complements the bright green leaves of the holly and the 'Pfitzerana' juniper, as well as the gold-marked, blue-green branches of the compact 'Gold Star' juniper.

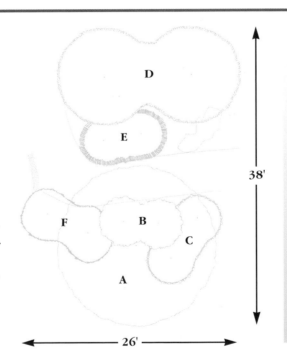

38'

26'

Plant List

A. *Cornus florida* (flowering dogwood) (1)
B. *Cotoneaster horizontalis* 'Compacta' (cotoneaster) (2)
C. *Euonymus fortunei* 'Colorata' (winter creeper euonymus) (2)
D. *Ilex opaca* 'Brilliantissima' (American holly) (2)
E. *Juniperus chinensis* 'Gold Star' (Chinese juniper) (2)
F. *Juniperus chinensis* 'Pfitzerana' (Chinese juniper) (2)

◆ How to Plant This Garden ◆

1. Spread a 2- to 3-inch layer of compost or leaf mold over the whole planting area, and work it into the top 8 to 12 inches of soil.

2. Plant one male and one female holly tree, spaced 8 to 10 feet apart. Only the female tree will produce berries, but it needs a male tree nearby for pollination to occur.

3. In a sunny spot, plant flowering dogwood.

4. Allow about 4 feet between the junipers and the cotoneasters, and 4 to 6 feet between the wintercreepers.

Aftercare and Maintenance
• Mulch to a depth of 2 to 3 inches. Keep mulch clear of the plants' trunks

or stems to prevent rot.
• Prune young hollies in winter as needed; use the trimmings for decorations.
• Prune dogwood lightly to develop shape.
• If junipers start to get leggy, cut the longest shoots back to a branch union. Prune in late spring or early summer.

A Garden for Mild Winters

Southern gardeners may experience milder winters than their northern counterparts, but they still welcome plants that add interest to the off-season. Gardeners in mild climates can enjoy such winter-blooming shrubs as wintersweet and winter daphne. Besides producing pretty flowers at this somewhat barren time of year, these shrubs also perfume the air.

Once the flowers lure you out into the garden, you'll stay to admire the steely blue foliage of the dwarf Colorado blue spruce, the red buds and berries of the skimmia, and the arching evergreen leaves and fluffy seed heads of the pampas grass. Worth admiring, too, is the smooth, dark red bark of the Sargent cherry. It grows quickly and, with proper pruning, will provide a canopy high enough to walk under.

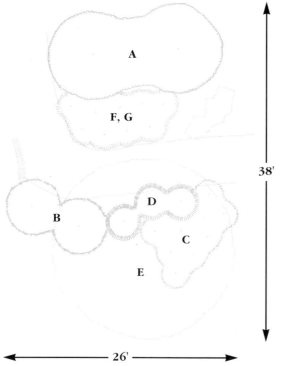

38'

26'

◆ How to Plant This Garden ◆

1. Plant in early to midspring *so plants will have a chance to get established before winter. Loosen soil over the entire site and work in a 2- to 3-inch layer of compost.*

2. Dig a hole *for the Sargent cherry that is as deep as the rootball and twice as wide.*

3. Plant both male and female skimmias. *The females will produce berries only if males are there for pollination.*

4. Space skimmias and winter daphnes *2 feet apart within their clumps. Allow 5 feet between spruces, 8 feet between pampas grasses, and 6 to 8 feet between*

wintersweets to accommodate their spread. Cut roots that circle the rootball or spread them out when planting.

Aftercare and Maintenance
• *Spread a 2- to 3-inch layer of mulch, such as shredded bark or bark chips, to control weeds and keep the soil moist. Keep mulch 2 to 3 inches from plant trunks and stems.*
• *Each spring, pull back the mulch around winter daphnes and add a 1-inch layer of compost or leaf mold, then replace the mulch.*
• *To keep wintersweets bushy, prune one or two of the oldest stems to the ground after they have finished flowering.*
• *Cut pampas grasses to the ground in late winter.*
• *Water regularly to keep the soil evenly moist.*

Plant List

A. Chimonanthus praecox (wintersweet) (2)
B. Cortaderia selloana 'Pumila' (pampas grass) (2)
C. Daphne odora

D. Picea pungens 'Glauca Globosa' (dwarf Colorado blue spruce) (3)
E. Prunus sargentii

(Sargent cherry) (1)
F. Skimmia japonica 'Nymans' (skimmia) (4)
G. Skimmia japonica 'Rubella' (skimmia) (5)

A Winter Garden for the North

Northern gardeners need all the help nature offers to make it through the raw winter days. With its mix of evergreen foliage, attractive bark, and fabulous fruits, this colorful garden is the perfect remedy for cold weather.

All of the plants in this garden are hardy to at least Zone 5, and many thrive well into Zone 3. Whether you view your garden from the comfort of your house or slog through the snow to get closer, you'll be warmed by the winter colors of the rose, with its large, orange-scarlet hips, which are echoed on the other side of the path by the small, glossy, bright red fruits of the crab apple. The young shoots of the red-osier dogwood add another touch of welcome color. Color and form alike come from the silvery blue, scalelike foliage of 'Blue Vase' juniper, which stands out beautifully against the broader, dark green to purplish leaves of 'Olga Mezitt' rhododendrons. Add the attractive dried flower heads of peegee hydrangea, and you'll have a planting that's packed with cold-season interest.

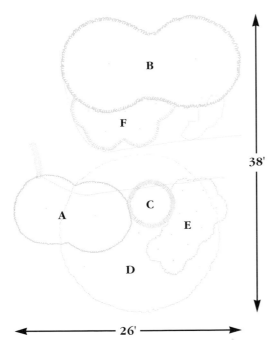

38'

26'

◆ How to Plant This Garden ◆

1. Prepare the site and set plants out in early to midspring so they'll have a chance to get established before the first winter.

2. Add compost or leaf mold to the dogwood planting holes to enrich the soil.

3. If any of the container-grown shrubs shows a mass of circling roots when you remove the pot, use a knife to make a few vertical slits around the rootball. This will encourage cut roots to grow out into the surrounding soil.

4. Set rhododendrons about 2 feet apart and roses about 2 to 3 feet apart. Allow 4 to 6 feet between dogwoods and 8 to 10 feet between peegee hydrangeas.

Aftercare and Maintenance
• *Apply a 2- to 3-inch layer of bark mulch over the bare soil.*
• *Cut all stems of peegee hydrangeas to just above the ground in late winter for best flower display, or trim off the lowest branches to encourage a treelike form that shows off the ridged bark.*
• *Prune roses in late winter to remove one-third of the oldest canes. Also shorten the remaining canes by about one-third. Wear gloves to protect your hands from the prickly stems.*
• *Starting 2 to 3 years after planting, prune dogwoods in early spring to promote new growth. Cut one-third to one-half of the stems to the ground each year, or cut all stems to the ground every other year.*

Plant List

A. *Cornus sericea*
(red-osier dogwood) (2)
B. *Hydrangea paniculata*
'Grandiflora' (peegee hydrangea) (2)

C. *Juniperus chinensis*
'Blue Vase' (Chinese juniper) (1)
D. *Malus* 'Donald Wyman'
(crab apple) (1)

E. *Rhododendron* 'Olga
Mezitt' (rhododendron) (10)
F. *Rosa rugosa* 'Albo-plena' (rugosa rose) (5)

Create Your Own Four-Season Garden

Think of your four-season garden as a roomlike enclosure of small trees and tall shrubs framing the walls and supplying the "furniture," larger trees providing a canopied roof, and a floor carpeted with lawn and beds of herbaceous plants. The plants in this "room," must have year-round presence to hold the design together. You'll need a balance of deciduous and evergreen plants that complement one another in shape, substance, and mood. Then fill in with plants that display their best in all the different seasons.

Begin your planning in winter. The evergreens, and the deciduous shrubs and trees stripped of their foliage, will reveal the inherent structure of your garden. You may find that many of your plants already have seasonal strengths of their own—brightly colored berries, fascinating bark patterns, or dormant foliage that whispers and shivers in the breeze. You may only need to move plants around to play their winter colors, textures, and forms against each other.

Then embellish the winter framework with plants from the garden opposite, shown in early summer, or from the two alternate gardens that follow. The first alternate planting makes use of the quiet contrasts of shrubs and ornamental grasses. The second features heaths and heathers for coastal climates or areas with acid soil.

Interest Through the Seasons

The garden illustrated here artfully mixes conifers, small deciduous trees, shrubs, and flowering perennials for a rich, ever-changing effect. Colorado blue spruce, rich green savin juniper, and the plume-like foliage of Japanese cedar supply the strongest structural elements that carry the garden year round.

Silhouetted against the evergreen backdrop in winter are the lower-growing deciduous trees that make their impact in summer. The decorative leaves of Japanese maple glisten from spring until they drop in the fall, and accent the bright red blossoms of red buckeye in midspring and the perky yellow flowers of broom in summer.

Filling in along the central path, peonies are the star performers in spring, but they also carry bright green color into summer and burnished hues into fall. Variegated hosta leaves introduce summer-long color and textural interest and underscore the tall, sturdy spikes of iris.

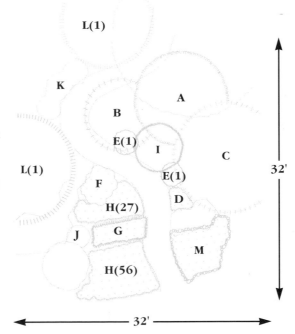

Plant List

A. Acer palmatum 'Atropurpureum' (Japanese maple) (1)
B. Aesculus pavia (red buckeye) (1)
C. Cryptomeria japonica (Japanese cedar) (1)
D. Cytisus decumbens (broom) (8)
E. Hosta fortunei 'Aureo-marginata' (variegated hosta) (2)
F. Hosta fortunei 'Francee' (variegated hosta) (10)
G. Iris germanica (bearded iris) (21)
H. Iris sibirica (Siberian iris) (83)
I. Juniperus sabina (savin juniper) (1)
J. Paeonia lactiflora 'Beersheba' (garden peony) (1)
K. Paeonia lactiflora cv. (garden peony) (3)
L. Picea pungens 'Glauca Hoopsii' (Colorado blue spruce) (2)
M. Sedum sieboldii (stonecrop) (43)

◆ How to Plant This Garden ◆

1. In mild climates, *plant trees, shrubs, and perennials in the fall. In cold regions, plant in the spring as soon as the soil has warmed.*

2. In fall, set peony roots *on mounds in planting holes. Spread roots, keeping the eyes no more than 1 to 2 inches below the soil surface.*

3. Plant bearded irises in sun, *keeping rhizomes partially uncovered.*

Aftercare and Maintenance
• Replenish organic mulch annually as it biodegrades.

A Garden of Shrubs, Grasses, and Perennials

Tall, rustling flame grass stands as a sentinel in this garden, ever-present, but in changing colors. In summer, its silvery flowering plumes rise above wispy green leaves. By autumn, however, the grass develops the burnished orange and purplish tones shown here. Flame grass continues to stand as the garden's focal point during winter, when its tones mellow.

Sturdy evergreens—a pendant hemlock and a bulky juniper—provide structural weight and contribute to the changing seasonal colors. The deep, dark greens of the juniper and mugo pine make the silvery blue fescue look even bluer, and late in the season their green color softens the harsh winter landscape.

Flowering heartleaf bergenia, bright pink catchfly, and rich blue plumbago scatter pockets of floral color throughout the year. Masses of daffodils and daylilies create a constantly varying stream of color from spring through autumn.

In fall, orange fothergilla foliage stands out, while the flame grass provides brillant color. The reddish foliage of brilliantly blue-flowered heartleaf plumbago takes on a rusty brown cast, and the waxy leaves of bergenia turn glossy red.

Plant List

A. Bergenia cordifolia 'Silberlicht' (heartleaf bergenia) (8)
B. Ceratostigma plumbaginoides (plumbago) (1)
C. Cornus mas (cornelian cherry) (1)
D. Festuca ovina var. glauca 'Elijah Blue' (blue fescue) (26)
E. Fothergilla major (fothergilla) (1)
F. Hemerocallis multiflora (Mayflower daylily) (21)
G. Juniperus virginiana 'Hillii' (red cedar) (1)
H. Miscanthus sinensis 'Purpurascens' (flame grass) (3)
I. Narcissus cv. (daffodil) (50)
J. Pinus mugo var. mugo (mugo pine) (1)
K. Silene x 'Longwood' (catchfly) (46)
L. Tricyrtis formosana var. stolonifera 'Amethystina' (toad lily) (10)
M. Tsuga canadensis 'Pendula' (weeping Canada hemlock) (1)

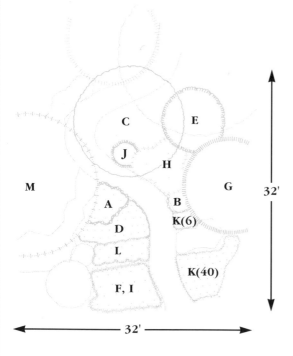

◆ How to Plant This Garden ◆

1. In cold climates, plant red cedar, pine, and cornelian cherry in spring. Plant in the fall in warm climates.

2. Plant fothergilla in acid soil.

3. Set rootballs of flame grass and blue fescue at the same depth as in their containers.

4. Plant daylilies in spring or fall, setting them in holes 2 feet apart.

5. Set catchflies and heartleaf bergenias in clumps with individual plants 8 to 10 inches apart.

6. Plant plumbagos in the spring, after the last frost.

7. In the fall, plant daffodils in 8-inch-deep holes.

Aftercare and Maintenance
• Tuck fading daffodil foliage under the arching daylily leaves.
• Mark the location of plumbagos to avoid damaging them in spring.

A Garden of Heaths and Heathers

This garden provides a dramatic year-round spectacle of colors and variety. Heaths and heathers make perfect all-season companions to broadleaf evergreens and conifers. In spring, the dark green foliage of spring heath is draped with bright red flowers, while in late summer, pale lilac blossoms adorn the golden mounds of heather.

The vertical shapes of 'Crippsii' false cypress and arborvitae are set off by the rich, spreading blue-green mantle of juniper and bright green spray of winter-creeper euonymus. 'Blue Emerald' phlox adds to the spring show with a colorful blue carpet of flowers across the garden. Variegated sedge, hellebore, and yucca supply a sharp textural contrast to the plump, red fruits of holly and cornelian cherry that punctuate the muted winter landscape.

This garden plan is best suited to cool, humid coastal climates, but it can be enjoyed in most mild climates if you supply moist, acid soil.

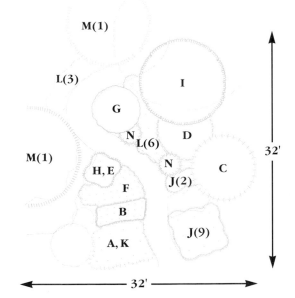

Plant List

A. *Calluna vulgaris* 'Blazeaway' (heather) (13)
B. *Carex morrowii* 'Variegata' (sedge) (21)
C. *Chamaecyparis* 'Crippsii' (false cypress) (1)
D. *Cornus mas* (cornelian cherry) (1)
E. *Dryopteris erythrosora* (wood fern) (4)
F. *Erica carnea*

'Myretown Ruby' (spring heath) (25)
G. *Euonymus fortunei* 'Greenlane' (winter creeper euonymus) (1)
H. *Helleborus* x *hybridus* (hellebore) (16)
I. *Ilex* 'Sparkleberry' (holly) (1)
J. *Juniperus horizontalis* 'Mother Lode' (juniper) (11)

K. *Muscari armeniacum* (grape hyacinth) (300)
L. *Phlox subulata* 'Blue Emerald' (phlox) (9)
M. *Thuja occidentalis* 'Elegantissima' (arborvitae) (2)
N. *Yucca filamentosa* 'Color Guard' (yucca) (2)

◆ How to Plant This Garden ◆

1. Plant false cypress, junipers, winter-creeper euonymus, yuccas, and arborvitae so that the tops of the rootballs are just below the soil.

2. To ensure berry production by Ilex 'Sparkleberry', which is a female, plant I. 'Apollo', a male, within 100 feet.

3. Add large quantities of moist compost or peat moss to the soil before planting heaths and heathers. Mulch

with additional compost or peat moss after planting.

4. Plant sedges, ferns, hellebores, grape hyacinths, phlox, and cornelian cherry in a well-drained site.

CHAPTER FOUR

Furnishing Your Landscape

Once you've settled on your garden style, but before you choose any plants, it's time to select landscape elements. Whether it's pathways, lighting, terraces, or pools, the decorative elements of a garden should not only be stylish and beautiful but functional as well.

The Montchain, Delaware, garden at left strikes a fine balance between style and practicality, demonstrating how decorative elements can work with the landscape to create a cohesive design. In this informal, wooded landscape, two pools cut into a gently sloping hill simulate a natural, stone-edged pond and waterfall. Brightly colored, sun-loving Hemerocallis (daylilies) are planted in masses at the pool's far edge, while in the foreground, pink clematis, Allium, daylilies, and lantana border a small terrace overlooking the landscape. A sculpture placed atop a large boulder provides a unique finishing touch to this garden's natural setting.

Pathways and Pavings

Paths and walkways create physical links between one place and another. In working them into your garden plans, keep in mind that no matter where they go or what they are made of, walkways should be compatible with the style of your house and with your landscape.

Start by deciding where you want the walkways to begin and end. Stroll around your property, examining its dimensions and contours. Do your design ideas lend themselves to pathways that follow a straight line, as in a formal garden? Or are meandering routes more appropriate, paths that induce the visitor to stop here and there along the way?

Take plenty of time in your exploratory walk through the garden, following natural routes from place to place. Once you've chosen the likeliest lines for your paths to follow, wait for a good heavy rain to come along, and then go out and check drainage patterns along and adjacent to these lines. Improperly positioned walkways can act like dams, exacerbating drainage problems.

In general, heavily traveled walkways, such as those leading to the house from the front sidewalk or the driveway, should be formal in design and constructed from hard, durable materials like concrete, brick, unglazed tile, or stone. They should follow straight lines and right angles or simple curves, and their edges should be well defined. For safety's sake, all walkways should present smooth but nonslick surfaces, and, ideally, they should be wide enough—4 to 5 feet across—for two people to walk abreast comfortably.

Informal Paths

Informal styles are usually chosen for less traveled paths, such as those leading into and through the garden, and can be constructed with softer paving materials. Such paths often have a meandering quality, but they can take any form you want them to. Merely setting out stone slabs in an irregular pattern through your garden will create a simple walkway and add visual interest. A winding gravel path with wood rounds set into the gravel at intervals would not only be aesthetically pleasing

The path in this New Hampshire garden is paved with long rectangular stones set in a zigzag pattern; within the frame they create are multicolored cobblestones and round and diamond-shaped concrete slabs. Simple plantings, including a compact Rhododendron 'Ramapo' and an arborvitae hedge, line one side of the path; yellow shrubby cinquefoil spills in from the other.

but would also encourage a leisurely stroll. Informal paths are usually narrower than main walkways—from 2½ to 3 feet wide—but should still be wide enough for you to traverse comfortably with garden equipment. For an even more informal look, you can soften the effect of paving materials by letting plantings spill over onto them. Place small mound-forming plants like moss, thyme, or alyssum around paving stones to add texture, beauty, and softness to the surface.

Selecting Pavement Styles

The mood a hardscape material contributes to your overall design is a major consideration in choosing it. But equally important are such practical matters as cost and ease of installation and maintenance. If you don't have a lot of time to devote to plant care, you may want to invest in an intricate paving pattern or a mosaic tile that will act as a focal point, and then put in plants and ground covers that virtually look after themselves. If, on the other hand, you have considerable time for gardening, select a simple garden paving material and offset it with glorious flower borders.

Weather is another practical matter to consider. Some paving materials are more susceptible than others to damage by frost or hot, baking sun. And some, such as smooth concrete, tile, wood, brick, and stone, can be slippery when wet.

When you've worked out the practical questions, it's time to consider aesthetics. First look at the style and colors of your house and at the colors and textures of your present plantings. Decide how you want your pathways to fit in with them.

The gray stones of this Berkeley, California, pathway take a backseat to the Dianthus 'Rose Bowl', thrift, and Dalmatian bellflowers that grow between them. Geraniums and Santa Barbara daisies offer a profusion of blooms, while spotted dead nettle, lamb's ears, and Siberian iris add texture and lushness.

Making a Natural Fieldstone Pathway

Using only a shovel, you can build an informal pathway of natural fieldstone. This material, an unquarried stone, fits in well with rustic, naturalistic landscape designs. The one drawback is that the stones are heavy, so it's best to have your local stone yard or quarry deliver them and deposit them beside the site of the pathway.

Choose randomly sized stones that are flat on top and large enough to tread upon comfortably. Then experiment with different arrangements, mapping out a route that is underlain by firm soil. Working along the route, but before you have begun digging, set the larger stones in place to get the general shape of the path. Then fill in the gaps with smaller stones. Leave a natural stepping distance between large stones laid in a line—about 18 inches. If your path is curved, set a large stone at the points where the path bends, to serve as stopping areas. Vary the size of the stones, and try to match shapes of adjoining stones so that their sides align fairly well.

To set a steppingstone path of large, widely spaced stones, dig a hole for each stone, add a little builder's sand or stone dust (available where you buy the fieldstone), and position the stone in the hole. Adjust the material underneath the stone and replace the soil around it until the stone is firm and stable. For a path of closely set stones, follow the directions below for laying the stones in a trench.

1. Before you dig your trench, do a practice run by laying the stones down in a pattern that's both comfortable to walk on and aesthetically pleasing. Once you have settled on a workable path, dig a trench 5 to 6 inches deep and spread a 3-inch-deep bed of builder's sand or stone dust over it. Then lay the stones in place, aligning their irregular sides as much as possible.

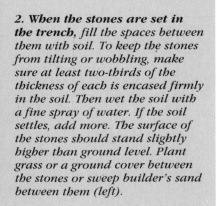

2. When the stones are set in the trench, fill the spaces between them with soil. To keep the stones from tilting or wobbling, make sure at least two-thirds of the thickness of each is encased firmly in the soil. Then wet the soil with a fine spray of water. If the soil settles, add more. The surface of the stones should stand slightly higher than ground level. Plant grass or a ground cover between the stones or sweep builder's sand between them (left).

Paving Materials

The possibilities for paving are almost limitless. Your choices range from such hard materials as brick, concrete, flagstone, fieldstone, granite, tile, and wood to softer materials, including loose aggregates such as gravel, cobbles, crushed rock, woodchips, or bark chips. And, of course, you can combine hard and soft materials very successfully.

Stone works especially well in naturalistic settings; you can find it in many sizes and in both regular and random shapes. In making a choice, remember that different types of stone vary in durability, slipperiness, and resistance to frost damage. Tiles—both terra cotta and the more durable high-fired types—though relatively expensive are highly decorative, conveying a feeling of elegance. Tile is a poor choice, however, in climates where cycles of freezing and thawing occur, because wide cold-weather temperature fluctuations can cause it to crack. Remember, too, that in the rain, glazed tiles are more slippery than unglazed types.

Wood is a versatile paving material and conveys a warmth difficult to achieve with a harder material such as concrete. Woods that can be left to weather naturally, such as red cedar, cypress, and redwood, can be especially attractive. Although easy to install and fairly inexpensive, wood pavings will eventually decompose. You can extend their life somewhat by installing them in a way that allows for ventilation on the underside.

Loose Aggregates

Gravel is a popular choice among loose-aggregate paving materials. Inexpensive and easy to install, it is especially useful in spots where a less porous paving might create or worsen a drainage problem. Some maintenance is required, however. You'll need to rake gravel periodically, because it gets squeezed out of place when walked on. Your pathway will also require an edging to keep the migrating gravel from spilling over onto plantings.

Gravel tends to refract and absorb light, which can help soften the appearance of the entire garden. Remember, though, that gravel may look a bit boring when used exclusively, so plan to interrupt the line of a simple gravel path by introducing other paving materials at random, such as stone pavers or wood rounds.

The same holds true for other visually neutral materials, such as woodchips. It is best to combine them with other, more intricate-looking pavers. And no matter what type of loose-aggregate material you use, be sure to place layers of newspaper under it to help control weeds.

Patterns and Textures

As you plan your walkways, consider the roles that color, pattern, and texture play in the appearance of your garden. Simple, neutral paving works best with complex planting schemes. If your garden is filled with flowers, for example, brick might clash with red, pink, or orange blooms. Consider using gravel or flagstone and save brick for areas where the focus is on evergreens or foliage.

You can use pattern and texture in paving to convey various moods. Woodchips used together with steps created from landscape timbers, for example, lend a quiet, woodland feel. Wood planks set in a base of gravel give a more dynamic feeling—the mixture of textures, patterns, and materials keeps the eye moving.

Straight lines that run away from a particular viewpoint intensify a sense of direction and depth, whereas lines that cross the field of vision create a sense of breadth. Patterns that have a static quality—regular, symmetrical shapes such as squares, circles, and hexagons, for example—can help create a restful effect. Use them in places where you might want guests to linger. If you do choose a static arrangement, pay attention to the size of your paving units. A broad expanse of small units can create a fussy or dull appearance.

Edgings

There are several good reasons for bordering your pathways with some sort of hard edging. First, if you pave a path with a soft material such as gravel, bark, or woodchips, you will need some sort of edging to contain the material and prevent it from spreading out onto the surrounding ground and thinning out on the path until bare earth shows through. Second, if the path cuts across the lawn, edging will serve the dual purpose of keeping the turf grass within bounds and providing a hard surface for the wheels of your lawn mower as you mow the edge of the lawn.

You will find a variety of edgings at home stores. Brick can be set on edge or on end, for example. You can also buy stone or concrete pavers or concrete sections designed to be set end to end. For rustic or woodsy landscapes, pressure-treated 4-by-4 or 6-by-6 timbers and uncut stone work well.

Paving with Brick

Brick comes in many colors, shapes, and textures, and adds warmth and interest to virtually any landscape. It can be arranged in a variety of different patterns and looks equally appropriate in formal and informal settings. It is also durable and easy to work with.

In selecting a specific brick, first consider your climate. Where frost occurs, look for brick designated SX, which means it will resist the effects of freezing and thawing. Then select a brick texture: Some have smooth, sleek surfaces and sharp edges, whereas others are more porous, with rounded edges.

The way in which you lay the brick can create moods. A running pattern—used alone, as shown below, or in combination with a stacked bond pattern—conveys fluidity and movement. By contrast, a basket-weave pattern gives a feeling of containment.

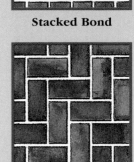

Stacked Bond

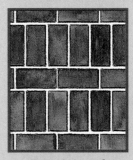

Herringbone

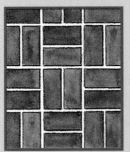

Basket Weave

Diagonal Herringbone

Running and Stacked Bond

Entrances and Exits

The journey through your garden should be punctuated by entrances and exits that not only provide access to its spaces but also organize them. As points of arrival and departure between house and garden and within the garden itself, they will unite the separate parts of your property and set the stage as you move from one area to the next.

Extending an entranceway welcome almost to curbside, a Los Angeles garden fills the strip of earth between the sidewalk and the road with Tulbaghia violacea (society garlic), Geranium incanum, and a red-flowered Leptospermum scoparium (New Zealand tea tree). In many gardens, such island beds are the only locations in full sun. Before planning a sidewalk garden, find out if your municipality has height restrictions on sidewalk plantings.

The Front Entry

Because your front door is the first destination for visitors, the passage to it should allow clear access from the front sidewalk without sacrificing privacy. Paradoxically, this passageway can seem more inviting if it is fronted by a hedge or a fence. An enclosure around the front of your property conveys a sense of shelter from the outside world. A gate or a trellised archway will frame the view to the house and help direct visitors to the front door.

For the shape and dimensions of your front pathway, look to the style of your house and the contours of your land. Keep the design simple, and use appropriate materials and scale. But don't forget the practicalities. The front door should be visible and the path direct. Look closely to find natural traffic patterns: People and pets will instinctively take the shortest route to a destination, crossing over lawns and even through hedges to get there (for more on pathways, see pages 126-127).

From House to Garden

When guests walk out of your house on their way to the garden, whether through a front, side, or rear door, the area outside the door should give them the impression of linking the interior with the exterior. This space can be as small as a doorstep or as large as a patio or deck. It can incorporate elements that are extensions of the house—lighting, furniture, even an awning or a roof. At the same time, it can introduce elements of the garden, such as a small pool, a climbing rose, or clusters of plants in decorative containers.

The transition from one space to another

within the garden can be marked or signaled in several ways. The subtlest is a change in the materials underfoot. For example, the transition from lawn to a woodchip path can mark the entrance to a woodland. A gravel walkway that becomes a concrete sidewalk may indicate an exit from the garden to the driveway. More obvious are the portals created by open or gated passages, standing free or as part of a hedge or fence. The simplest is a passage between two shrubs at either side of a pathway. More elaborate would be an archway or pergola. A picket or wrought-iron gate will give the visitor a glimpse of the space beyond, whereas one of solid wood, if tall enough, will block the view and make the entrance a surprise.

A picket gate mounted on rough-hewn posts has been embellished by a rustic archway of interwoven boughs. The style fits in with the informal pebbled path leading to the utility area of this southern California garden. Wild lilac, snakebeard, and 'Bonica' shrub roses edge the pathway.

Choosing Openness or Privacy

The impression made by the entrance to your house can be altered with a few simple landscaping changes, depending on the design of the house. A dramatic front door or a handsome roofline may call for an arrangement that boldly displays them. On the other hand, you may want more screening if, for example, you have large windows that look out on the street.

The house below is fronted by an open expanse of lawn, its foundation softened by a line of shrubbery. Vertical accent shrubs flank the entranceway and strengthen it as a focal point. To a visitor, such an exposed design may seem imposing, if not slightly forbidding. Curtains or shutters in the windows are needed to maintain a sense of privacy.

Planting a screen of trees and a hedge creates a sheltering enclosure in front of this house. The trees block upper-window sightlines from the street. Indoors, the house is bright because curtains can be left open. Outdoors, the hedge-enclosed space feels more intimate and inviting to a visitor than an open space would.

131

Places for Stopping and Viewing

Nestled against the side of a small gatehouse in this Atlanta, Georgia, garden, a bed of boxwood, peonies, ferns, and ivy makes a tranquil resting place at the edge of a walled flagstone terrace. The formal gateway, crowned with an evergreen arch, announces the beginning of an excursion into the garden.

Whether you seek a cozy spot to rest after an afternoon of planting and pruning or a vantage point from which to admire the perennials in bloom, your garden should include places to stop, rest, and reflect. Benches have long been used along the garden path as popular stopping places, but you can create a number of other arrangements as well. A hammock swinging from a venerable old tree, an outdoor table and chairs, or a seat built into an arbor will all add individuality and style to your garden.

Patios and decks are something of a middle ground between the house and the garden. They allow a comfortable transition between indoors and outdoors, and can be treated as an extra "room" in which to relax and entertain. Because of its proximity to the house, a patio should be built of materials that complement the house. A brick house might have a brick or colored concrete patio, for example, and a clapboard house a patio surface of flagstone or terra-cotta tile.

Decks extend out over the property and can be used to deal with difficult gradients, such as a site too steep for walking or even for steps. With their elevated vantage point, they also offer a unique view of the garden. And the materials typically used to construct decks—pressure-treated pine, redwood, and cedar—work well aesthetically with the design and building materials of most houses.

Planting Arrangements

Your garden design can include beds of spectacular plantings arranged to be stopping places at the ends of pathways or along their length—

especially when the spot is equipped with a bench for restful viewing. With plantings calculated to provide interest through a long season of growth, these stopping places will maintain their appeal for much of the year.

An Elevated Perspective

If an overlook, such as a balcony or an accessible rooftop, is part of your property, it can become the visitor's ultimate destination. From there, an appealing view of your garden or of a distant vista can be a delightful surprise.

Roof gardens and balcony plantings can be part of your overall garden design. If the view from your overlook is less than captivating, you can minimize it by creating a focal point within the roof garden or screen offending views with a simple garden structure such as a latticework trellis.

Designing a roof garden is always a challenge. Your plants will generally grow in large containers or planters, which must be designed to allow for adequate drainage. The drain water must, in turn, be effectively channeled off the roof. Also keep in mind that the soil mix must be light enough to be supported by the roof once the plants are in place. One technique to ensure safety is to position heavy plantings directly over the supporting pillars of the structure.

Balconies are interesting places to experiment with container gardening. Make sure you take note of the growing conditions before you make plans—sun angles and the direction and strength of the wind will affect your plant choices.

Depending on the size of your balcony, you may be able to grow climbing vines against the building walls for green cover as well as have annual and perennial plantings for seasonal interest. Before you move any containers onto the balcony, however, find out how much weight it can safely support.

An arbor made of ginkgo trees supports the weight of a fragrant climbing white Rosa soulieana. Such a sheltered stopping place provides shade and seclusion and even some protection from a light summer rain in this East Hampton, New York, garden. The white-edged leaves of the variegated hostas thriving in its corners pick up the white of the blossoms.

Trees for Shade

Abies
(fir)
Aesculus hippocastanum
(common horse chestnut)
Betula
(birch)
Cedrus atlantica
(Atlas cedar)
Cladrastis lutea
(American yellowwood)
Cornus florida
(flowering dogwood)
x *Cupressocyparis leylandii*
(Leyland cypress)
Fagus
(beech)
Koelreuteria paniculata
(golden-rain tree)
Liquidambar
(sweet gum)
Magnolia grandiflora 'Bracken's Brown Beauty'
(southern magnolia)
Magnolia stellata
(star magnolia)
Malus floribunda
(Japanese flowering crab apple)
Picea
(spruce)
Pinus strobus
(eastern white pine)
Prunus subhirtella 'Pendula'
(Higan cherry)
Quercus phellos
(willow oak)
Stewartia pseudocamellia
(Japanese stewartia)
Tilia
(linden)
Tsuga
(hemlock)
Ulmus
(elm)
Zelkova
(zelkova)

Enclosing the Garden

The fences, walls, and gates you place around the outskirts of your property and at the boundaries of its internal "rooms" should act like picture frames, defining and showcasing the space within. But these elements must be useful as well as beautiful. On the practical side, walls and fences enclose your property, provide protection and privacy, act as windbreaks, and muffle street sounds. Walls generally make more formidable barriers than fences because they are usually made of such weighty, permanent materials as poured concrete, stone, or brick. Fences can be solid structures, too, but they are typically constructed of wood in decorative, open patterns. They offer less privacy but let in more light and air.

Walls and fences play a major role in garden design because of the strong vertical dimension they impose. They also provide wonderful planting

opportunities. A wall might double as a support for a raised bed; a fence might serve as a trellis for climbing flowers or vines.

You can also use walls and fences to espalier shrubs and ornamental trees: The patterns created by flowers, fruit, and seasonal foliage color will ornament the structure as well as enliven the garden. Even the simplest of planting strategies—for example, just setting a few containers of flowers at its base—will add interest to an expanse of wall or fence.

An important focal point in either a wall or a fence is its gateway. An attractive or unusual garden gate serves not only as a passageway but also as an accent in its own right, framing a view within or beyond the garden. Gates can add ornamental interest, focus the eye, and break up the solid line of a garden boundary.

By their bulk, weight, and strength, walls contribute a sense of stability and permanence to your landscape. The commonest building materials for walls are concrete block, poured concrete, brick, and stone. If you decide on a stone wall,

Bright red bougainvillea (left) crests a concrete wall in this garden in Rancho Santa Fe, California. Echoing the tawny hues of the surrounding desert, the wall also serves as a backdrop for a profusion of native plantings, including Agave, Sedum, Aconitum, and Euphorbia.

Living Garden Boundaries

Hedges are a lovely natural alternative to walls and fences. But remember that some trees and shrubs can take 10 years to grow to a useful height for a hedge. One tree that is ideal for this purpose is x *Cupressocyparis leylandii*, a handsome, fast-growing tree with a columnar habit. In cool, temperate climates, choose from such evergreens as *Viburnum tinus* 'Spring Bouquet', *Prunus caroliniana* 'Bright 'n' Tight', *Rhododendron* 'Fragrantissimum', *Euonymus japonica*, *Pieris, Taxus, Buxus, Pyracantha, Thuja, Spiraea, Ilex crenata,* and *Prunus lusitanica.* For tropical gardens, *Griselinia* and *Olearia* perform well, as does a ficus hedge like the one at right.

If you prefer a flowering hedge, forsythia is inexpensive and easy to grow. And if you want roses, both *Rosa rugosa* and *R. eglanteria* make beautiful informal hedges that produce not only blooms but also bright rose hips in the fall.

A Gallery of Wooden Fences

Wooden fences can range from the simple to the ornate. Slats can be diagonal, horizontal, or vertical; picket fences can have various intervals between pickets and tops that are pointed or rounded, spearheaded, or double- or triple-saw-toothed. The look of the fence will also be affected by the finish. Unfinished wood creates a rustic appearance as it ages. Or, if you prefer, you can stain the wood or paint it.

Pressure-treated pine is the least expensive fence wood that offers resistance to insects and decay. But typical pressure-treated pine fencing will often be poorly cured and subject to warping, and it will have knots, holes, and splits. Furthermore, it will be considerably darker than untreated pine and may have a greenish cast from its chemical treatment. Thus, it will not weather handsomely if it is left unfinished. If the design of your fence will be intricate, opt for redwood, cypress, or cedar, which are more expensive but are better choices when fine workmanship is required and appearance is a priority.

Concave-topped Double Picket

Interwoven Slat

select a stone that will help merge the style of your house with the landscape. Keep in mind that stone can be either dry-laid or mortared in place. If you choose brick or concrete block, you have the further option of building with pierced brick or block, which will make your wall a bit more like a screen, allowing for a limited pass-through of air and light.

To decide on a building material, you must first consider the purpose of the wall, which will, in turn, help you select its location, height, and length. If, say, you want a barrier to prevent children and small dogs from wandering into the street, you may need a wall only 3 feet high. If you want to keep out intruders or large animals, you'll need a wall at least 6 feet high.

Remember that a wall will become a prominent feature in your garden. The strong line it introduces might not necessarily fit best along the property line, so experiment with various possible positions.

Doing It Yourself or Contracting Out

Some walls have heavier work to do than merely enclosing the perimeter of your property. For these, you will have further choices to make.

If you want to build a retaining wall, for example, you may need to consult a professional about materials, siting, and design before tackling the job. Something so relatively uncomplicated as a

dry-laid retaining wall made of stone—or even broken chunks of sidewalk—can be an efficient way to control erosion on a slope or to change grade. But you must be sure your wall will withstand the downhill pressure of soil and water.

In a few locales a retaining wall as low as 18 inches is subject to building regulations concerning construction methods and form—although in most jurisdictions the code doesn't apply unless the wall is at least 3 feet tall. It's best to hire a contractor if the wall you want will be tall enough to come under the local code. And if you are planning a wall with a height of 6 or more feet, or one that will run near the property line, make sure you're clear on local height and setback restrictions.

Adorning a Wall with Plants

The right plantings, of course, can provide the perfect finishing touch for a stone wall. Consider installing succulents or rock plants such as alyssum or campanula in the crevices to help soften the look of the wall. Espaliered apple or pear trees can lend year-round interest and interrupt the unbroken expanse of a high wall. Vines with long, supple branches can do the same for a long, low wall. Good choices include *Euonymus fortunei* (winter creeper) and *Campanula poscharskyana* (Serbian bellflower).

To support vines or espaliered limbs, drill holes in the wall at mortar intersections, hammer in expandable steel plugs, and screw in steel eyes.

Prominent wooden posts interrupt the expanse of latticework fencing that encloses this Long Island, New York, garden. The open design of the fence allows air to circulate and affords a sense of privacy that is enhanced by the plants— sage, strawberries, phlox, and hibiscus— growing in borders and containers alongside it. Red 'Queen Elizabeth' roses and the pale pink blooms of the climbing rose 'Compassion' spill over the top of the fence at intervals, breaking its horizontal line.

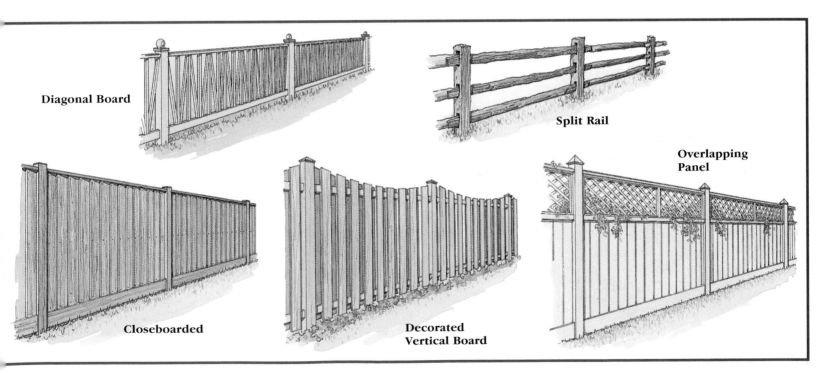

Diagonal Board

Split Rail

Closeboarded

Decorated Vertical Board

Overlapping Panel

Then string braided metal wires through the eyes in any pattern you like, and attach the growing stems to the wires with plastic ties.

Fences

Fences, like walls, should serve as far more than boundary markers. They offer almost limitless opportunities for introducing pattern and texture as well as vertical and horizontal interest.

Fences are generally less imposing, easier to install, and less expensive than walls. And they can, like walls, lend unity to your landscape if you use construction materials that harmonize with the overall style of your house and complement your garden. The more formal the look of the garden, the more architectural the fence should be.

Choosing a Fence Design

Decide in the planning stages how much privacy you want. Depending on style and design, fences may offer substantial privacy or virtually none at all. Fences of interwoven slats or louvered wood, for example, let in limited light and air, leaving you quite enclosed within your garden. A louvered fence is a good choice for encircling a patio, as it offers a degree of ventilation, filters sunlight, and softens wind. You can paint a louvered fence, stain it, or allow it to age naturally.

Open fence styles like lattice and wrought iron are more for decoration than privacy, although they can serve as effective psychological barriers against casual intrusions. They also make wonderful mounting surfaces for a variety of plantings and allow good ventilation. Lattices made of vinyl look good, last longer than wooden ones, and are available in several colors. Wrought iron has a quiet, distinguished look that is particularly suited to urban areas. And a split-rail fence, often made from untreated wood, is so open that it merges your property with the surrounding landscape.

Picket fences blend easily with a variety of house styles, and can look just right in the city or in rural and suburban settings. When painted white, they are bright and cheerful additions to the landscape. But white fences look their best when freshly painted, so keep time and maintenance requirements in mind when you choose a finish. If you don't want the obligation of repeated upkeep, consider a dark stain for your picket fence—it will give a more formal appearance with far less maintenance.

Before you install a fence, find out about local regulations regarding allowable fence heights. In many places the height limit is 42 inches for front-yard fences and 6 feet for backyard fences. If you are not sure of the exact location of the property line, contact a surveyor when building a fence on a boundary. You may want to position the fence a few inches inside the line to be sure of avoiding legal entanglements with touchy neighbors.

Anchoring Wooden Fence Posts

To delay rot, set fence posts in concrete. First dig a posthole deep enough to set one-third the total length of the post below-ground. Then place a flat stone in the hole to act as a base. Insert the post, then pour in and tamp down 4 to 6 inches of gravel. Fill the hole with concrete 2 to 3 inches at a time, tamping it in as you go. Use a level to make sure the post is vertical. To allow for expansion, cut two pieces of plywood into wedges that are several inches long, as wide as the post, and an inch thick; coat them with motor oil, then position them on either side of the post as you pour the concrete. Remove them after the concrete dries and fill the spaces with sand or tar.

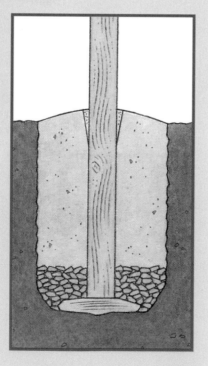

Gates

Gates can be plain and sturdy or highly detailed and ornamental. They can be either traditional or contemporary in style but work best, of course, when the design and materials of the gate are coordinated with the dominant architecture of the property. Because a gate is the focal point of a wall or fence—or even of a dense hedge—it can communicate a certain style or feeling. A solid wooden gate with a lattice design on top, for example, suggests openness without sacrificing privacy. A white wooden gate placed midway along a brick wall and decorated with climbing roses lends color and charm. And a wrought-iron gate looks elegantly formal at the entrance to a Victorian-style home. Whatever type of gate you choose, you can add ornamental interest with catches, hinges, and locks that enhance the overall effect.

Accessories for the Garden

Culinary plantings of thyme, oregano, fennel, sage, tarragon, and mint share space with ornamental daisies, pinks, heliotrope, and alyssum in a trio of terra-cotta containers at the edge of a brick patio.

Decorative elements such as containers, statuary, benches, and sundials can help you create a garden that's more than just a pretty collection of plants. Thoughtfully selected and placed, outdoor decorative pieces can create a focal point, complement foliage and flowers, define boundaries, provide smooth transitions between plantings, and increase the area available for cultivation. Before you select your garden decorations, make sure you know your garden well, and let its size, style, and purpose guide you. Classical statues look appropriately imposing in a formal garden with well-defined beds; a stone frog hiding under parsley sprigs might better suit a kitchen garden.

Container Gardening

Containers, a favorite of the city gardener with limited space for cultivation, come in many shapes, sizes, and materials. Filled with annuals or perennials, they can go almost anywhere to brighten an existing plant bed or to extend your growing area on patios, decks, balconies, sidewalks, and even walls. People confined to wheelchairs or those for whom bending and kneeling are difficult may find containers a pleasing gardening alternative to

Making a Log Planter

A fallen tree trunk can be recycled into a distinctive wooden planter that will hold a mixture of perennials and annuals. First, dig out the center of the log to a depth of about a foot, then cut a V-shaped groove from the center opening out to one end of the log; this will provide drainage. Fill the hole with an appropriate soil mix, then plant easy-care varieties such as begonias, hostas, impatiens, or bulbs.

Place one or more logs around a patio or along a garden path; or place your log planter in a less structured setting. Set several small boulders around the log to stabilize it and help it blend with its setting.

working in the ground. Containers can also become garden focal points or accents if they have a striking shape or texture.

Be sure to choose containers that will suit their contents. If you want to highlight your plantings, simple containers are best. If, on the other hand, you wish to feature a lovely pot, choose a simpler plant. And if an outdoor container is to hold perennials, be sure it is large enough to keep freezing temperatures from reaching the roots.

Choosing Containers

Pick a container that is the correct size and weight for your plant and your purposes. If you are hanging plants from a ceiling or wall, lightweight plastic planters or a wire-and-moss arrangement may be best. Heavier trees and shrubs need to be based in sturdy tubs or barrels so that they are not blown over by a strong wind. And always locate your containers where they're not too difficult to reach for watering.

Anything from a wheelbarrow to an old sink can be turned into a container for plants. Most of the containers available commercially are made of terra cotta, wood, plastic, cast stone, or concrete or fiberglass molded to look like stone.

Terra cotta works well in both formal and informal settings, and its neutral color harmonizes with almost any color of flower or foliage. But it may not stand up to repeated freezing and thawing, and glazed terra cotta is even less resistant to fluctuating hot and cold temperatures.

Wood containers, such as barrels or tubs, are unaffected by frost and can be treated to resist rot. They look better in casual settings and, because they are available in large sizes, are often used for permanent plantings such as ornamental fruit trees, juniper trees, and some varieties of cypress, azalea, and rhododendron. Small wooden boxes are attractive underneath windows, on porch or deck railings, or along the perimeter of a patio. You can paint them for added visual interest.

Because plastic and composite containers start to look shabby relatively quickly, it's best to limit their use to annuals. Petunias, impatiens, geraniums, and snapdragons will flourish in a plastic container hung from the porch ceiling. Plastic is

Vinca 'Little Bright Eyes', Cleome 'Royal Queen', Zinnia elegans 'Bouquet White', and Artemisia schmidtiana 'Silver Dust' surround this New Jersey garden's sundial in summer. In winter, the absence of flowers will bring out its elegant form even more strongly.

available in a variety of colors. Green and other neutral colors are a safe bet with any planting; white containers quickly show scratches and dirt.

Cast-stone and concrete containers are appropriate for both formal and informal gardens. They resist damage from rain, snow, and freezing temperatures. Plan the placement of a large stone container carefully—once it is filled it will be difficult to move. Some fiberglass containers look like stone but are much lighter.

Decorative Details

Garden ornaments can make a garden uniquely your own. Adornments help set a garden's tone, be it whimsical, understated, formal, practical, or sentimental. An ornament might be a focal point, or you might tuck one in an out-of-the-way corner to be come upon unexpectedly.

Heavy stone objects like urns look best in a formal garden with well-defined paths. In this sort of setting you might use an obelisk or a sundial on a pedestal as a centerpiece. A fragrant herb garden would be a prime location for a conical beehive shape; small stone sculptures of dogs, cats, frogs, rabbits, turtles, or gnomes are popular additions to a woodland garden.

Ornaments of all sorts are available in gardening stores and through catalogs, but if you're creative, you can turn almost anything into a garden decoration. Birdbaths and old birdcages are an inviting touch. Or if an old weather vane or lantern appeals to you, try it out. After all, it's your garden.

Seating

Before you choose seating for your garden, consider these questions: Will a seat at a given location serve as a brief rest spot, an afternoon lounging retreat, or a vantage point from which to view a certain portion of the landscape? Will the seating be permanent, or will you want to shift it as the sunlight fades and the seasons change?

A bench or chair for the garden is more than just a place to sit; it can be used as a decoration as well. Various kinds of seats are available in a range of sizes, materials, and colors. The challenge is to make sure that your seat, bench, or swing harmonizes with its surroundings. A formal scrolled-iron bench, for example, may look out of place among plant containers created from rusted milk pails and weathered wine cases.

In formal gardens, stone benches might be used to define boundaries between cultivated

beds; they can also work in tandem with such stone ornaments as statues, vases, and urns to contribute to the stately tone of such gardens.

You might also place a bench at the end of a path, grass alley, or arbor to provide a visual focal point and a convenient resting place after a stroll in the garden. Cast-iron furniture looks at home in a formal setting, while rustic twig furniture adds a homey touch to a more informal garden. Wicker and rattan contribute an exotic flavor to many settings; they will survive longer if they are somewhat protected from the elements.

Traditionally, garden furniture has been green, white, or black. White contrasts most sharply with the surrounding foliage; green blends more smoothly with the varied tints of leaves, bushes, and grasses; and black is the most stately. But many colorful alternatives are now available.

The owner of this Los Angeles garden, not Mother Nature, provided the large flat-topped stone on which to sit and enjoy the scenery. Set atop flagstones among plumes of rose fountain grass, feather grass, and drifts of sweet alyssum, the stone seat also provides a visual transition between the two plant groupings.

Vertical Garden Structures

Vertical elements—trellises, arbors, pergolas, lath houses, and gazebos—can be the most interesting and decorative structures in your garden. They create design interest in the landscape by leading the eye upward. And, like the walls or fences that enclose your garden, they strengthen its sense of composition by framing what lies beyond them.

Whether simple or elaborate, vertical landscape elements perform practical as well as aesthetic functions. They can provide shade for plants and people, sheltered spots for seating, and alcoves or other places for repose. They can serve as focal points. They can provide niches for container plants or act as supports on which to train climbing flowers and vines.

Vertical elements should be aesthetically pleasing, blending with your overall garden design and the architectural style of your house. When planning for these elements, keep in mind that unless the vertical structure supports an evergreen climber, over the long winter the framework of your arbor or pergola will be clearly visible.

Construction materials used for vertical elements include wood, stone, brick, metal, and wrought iron. You can also fashion appealing rustic structures from willow or grapevines gathered

in your own garden or a nearby field *(below, right)*.

While vertical structures can add greatly to the visual impact of your garden, they are also capable of overpowering it if installed without forethought. One such architectural element goes a long way, so exercise restraint. As with any garden structure, a vertical one should be proportioned to match the scale of the garden and home so that it complements and does not overwhelm the landscape.

An arched trellis laden with pink clematis beckons visitors to pass beneath it and into the Salem, Oregon, garden beyond. Along with the fence, the trellis acts as both a focal point and a garden divider. A border hedge of boxwood lines the walkway, and white hawthorn blooms in front of the fence.

Freestanding Structures

Pergolas, arbors, trellises, and gazebos are usually ornamental—even fanciful—elements within the garden. An arch or a pergola can resemble a piece of sculpture, beautiful in its own right and enhanced even further by the adornment you choose for it. Beyond their aesthetic appeal, freestanding garden structures provide shade along with privacy and protection—all without sacrificing light or air. They make wonderful supports for all manner of plantings. A trellised archway draped with wisteria or fragrant roses makes a lovely frame for a garden pathway. Keep in mind that your plantings must be in proportion to the size of your structures. Small, wispy climbers may look skimpy, or even sickly, when grown on a large, bold frame such as a pergola. On the other hand, heavy vines such as Japanese wisteria will overwhelm a more delicate trellis. In either case, prune your plantings regularly to control their growth.

Pergolas and Arbors

Pergolas, elongated structures of columns supporting a sturdy, overhead gridwork of wood rafters, are bold, linear affairs. Traditionally, they function as covered walkways and should therefore lead somewhere, connecting one area to another or perhaps just ending a garden stroll at a seat or ornament. Plan the location of a pergola with care—it will take up considerable room. You might build one over a patio as an extension of your house, or locate it as a freestanding unit at a distance from the house, creating a garden retreat.

Pergolas originated as frameworks for such climbing plants as grapevines. *Vitis vinifera* 'Purpurea' and the hybrid 'Brant' provide wonderful color on a pergola in the fall. Other climbing vines also do well on pergolas.

Arbors, with their graceful arches and enclosed seats, are generally less imposing than pergolas. An arbor can be used to create a private nook off the beaten path, a quiet spot for resting or reading,

Making a Rustic Trellis

Fashioning your own trellis from flexible grapevines or willow twigs is not difficult and can lend a pleasant rustic touch to an informal garden design. To make a trellis like the one shown below, first construct a rectangular frame of sturdy branches—cedar, maple, walnut, or sycamore—by nailing the pieces of wood together to form posts and crosspieces. Then bend flexible grapevines or willow shoots so that they arch over the frame, and attach them to the supporting pieces with twine or plastic ties.

Wind additional grapevines around the crosspieces for a decorative touch. Then prop your finished trellis against a garden wall or fence and train climbing roses, vines, or even vegetables to scurry up it.

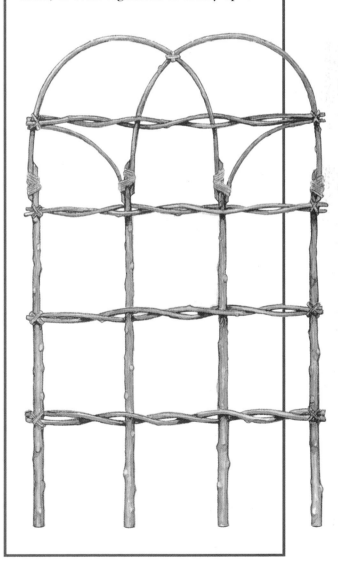

or for just enjoying your garden in solitude. If you design it so that it faces a lovely view in the garden or occupies a particularly warm and sunny spot, you'll be sure to enjoy it to the fullest. Arbors are usually associated with climbing plants—classically, grapes and roses. Train them to climb up the sides of the structure and cascade over the top.

Trellises

A trellis acts like a screen, creating a partial barrier that provides a measure of shade, shelter, and privacy but never completely blocks out air and light. A traditional trellis has panels of wood latticework that can either abut a wall, a fence, or the side of the house, or stand freely. If you incorporate a seating area into your trellis, it can provide a wonderful spot for enjoying tranquillity and repose.

Traditionally, trellis panels are made from a grid of perpendicular wood slats attached to a frame. The design of the trellis can be simple or intricate, incorporating a variety of arches and posts. You can build a trellis from decay-resistant woods such as redwood, cypress, or cedar that weather naturally into a handsome hue over the years. If you

use pine, however, it should be pressure-treated; otherwise, you will have to treat it with a preservative and either stain or paint it to prevent rotting.

Although a trellis primarily serves as a plant support, don't mask the underlying wood pattern with too much vegetation. Take into account the style and intricacy of your trellis design and balance that with the habit and vigor of your climbing and twining plants. If your trellis is of a tightly woven crisscross pattern, for example, it's better to use a light, airy climber like clematis than a larger-leaved climber, which would look too heavy.

Gazebos and Lath Houses

A gazebo is a roofed and often elevated pavilion that serves as a kind of ornate freestanding deck and gives a whimsical focus to the garden. It is usually circular, square, or octagonal, with low latticework sides that often support pretty flowering vines. A lath house is similar to a pergola in form but much more lightly constructed. Its main purpose is to create dappled shade rather than to support climbing plants, though it may well bear light herbaceous vines.

This pergola constructed over a patio in Santa Barbara, California, creates a garden room for outdoor relaxation. The chairs and the table, with its tree-trunk pedestal, echo the natural look of the pergola. Juniper shrubs flank the structure, and Laurentia fluviatilis 'Blue Star Creeper' fills the spaces between the flagstones.

Rock Gardens and Water Features

Adding rock gardens or water features to your property is not a simple undertaking; it requires thoughtful planning to make the finished elements look as if they belonged in a particular spot. Yet nothing compares with the topographical texture, color, variety, and focus these features bring to a garden, to say nothing of the elegance they impart.

If a rock garden is high on your list of wants, you should first candidly assess whether it will look natural in its setting. Don't try to impose one on a region lacking natural rock formations. And remember that once it is set in place, a rock garden is not easily rearranged, so before you undertake any heavy lifting, prepare carefully. Concentrate first on the overall design for placement of the rocks, as this task will be more demanding than that of drawing up a planting plan.

Begin by sketching a design on paper. If your garden will be larger than a few square yards, work out a schedule for building it—perhaps in stages over several seasons. Good drainage is important,

so avoid low, wet places. A possible exception to a location with good drainage is a spot on a slope with a drainage problem that might be solved or at least ameliorated by installing a rock garden.

As you create your design, take advantage of existing features—rock formations, a mound or rise, or shrubs that will provide background. If your garden already contains a single large rock or an attractive collection of them, use these as your starting point.

Adding Elevation

If your rock garden will be large, include minor grade changes in your plan—stones and rocks generally look best in layers, just as they occur in nature. Choose stones that are flat and wide and are native to your area.

If you'd like a sloping rather than a vertical rise in elevation, place each succeeding tier of stones

Fluffy white double arabis tumbles downward through the grade changes in this upstate New York rock garden, finding a foothold in gravelly patches along the way. Composed of native granite stones in various shapes and sizes, the man-made outcrop provides a home for pink phlox, golden Aurinia, and shade-tolerant Ajuga.

several inches back from the one beneath it. Position each stone to slant downward toward the rear so rainwater will seep back among the stones.

Installing a Water Feature

Planning for a water feature begins with assessing its purpose. Will it be a dominating feature in your landscape or brighten a hidden corner? From what spot on your property would you like to view it? How will it fit into the rest of your garden plan? What wildlife do you expect to attract? Do you want to have fish? If your landscaping style is informal, you might want to simulate a natural pond. Such a free-form basin requires considerable space. If you prefer straight lines and geometric patterns, a formal pool with a fountain or a piece of sculpture might suit you best. Given its shape, a formal pool will most likely require a concrete bottom and sides—and, in most cases, installing these is a job for a contractor.

For the health of your pool, choose a site that receives direct sunlight for at least 3, and preferably 6, hours each day. Containers that hold less than 100 gallons, however, do need shade in the middle of the day to prevent overheating of the water, which could be fatal to fish and plants. Avoid low places where runoff might collect under your

The lush textures of a full-blown summer morning are reflected in the dark, velvety waters of this garden pond in Birmingham, Alabama, where bog plants, water lilies, and other aquatics thrive in submerged containers. Potted caladiums and ferns complete the cheerful setting and tie the water garden to the soft lawn beside it.

pond and damage concrete or masonry during freezes and thaws. If possible, avoid overhanging trees, whose falling leaves could pollute the water.

As you plan your pond, consider the visual effect you want to create. The color of the pond liner—the sheet of waterproof material laid along the bottom and sides to serve as the actual container for the water—is important. A dark liner intensifies reflections and creates a mirrorlike effect; a light liner cuts down reflections and invites the observer to look deeply into the pond.

Building the Pond

If your pond is not of Olympic proportions and does not require concrete, you can probably do the work yourself—or at least oversee it. Lay out the shape of the pond in any design you choose, using a garden hose or a rope. To line an irregularly shaped pond, you will need a strong synthetic-rubber liner at least 45 millimeters thick. Its length and width should be the same as that of your excavation plus twice the maximum depth.

You might wish to plan for both a shallow area in your pond where birds can drink and a deeper one that will provide fish with cool temperatures and security. Depending on the climate, the depth of your pond should vary from a minimum of 4 inches to a maximum of 3½ feet. Dig two or three tiers in your pond, finishing with a shelf around the perimeter to lodge the coping stones that will form the edging of the pond and anchor the lining in place. Line the excavation with sand, carpet padding, or even newspapers to protect your pond liner from being punctured by sharp stones or roots. Lay the liner in the excavation and weight the edges with brick or stone coping.

Fill the pond with water and let it stand at least 1 week to reduce the chlorine levels before you introduce any fish or plants. In a well-balanced pond—one stocked with oxygenating grasses—algae growth will be restrained and the pond will remain reasonably clean. Bog plants and flowering aquatics will thrive along with water lilies submerged in widemouthed pots.

Avoid stocking the pond with more fish than the miniature ecosystem can support. To prevent a buildup of toxic ammonia and solid waste, you will probably need a filtration system. A pond of a capacity of less than 1,000 gallons needs only a small pump to circulate at least half the water every hour through a filter box and up to a fountain that aerates the water. You can purchase effective systems that use either biological, mechanical, or chemical means of filtering.

TIPS FROM THE PROS

Making a Pond Self-Sustaining

A new pond is likely to become cloudy with algae at first, because its natural chemical balance, its microorganisms, and the plant populations you put in need time to establish themselves. To keep unicellular algae—the floating cloudy stuff—under control while that process takes place, you can use a commercial algicide. However, don't try to get rid of all the mosslike algae that clings to the sides of the pond. It may be unsightly, but it is also useful to the health of your water garden. And natural scavengers, especially snails and tadpoles, will graze on it and help keep it in check.

To maintain a good ecological balance in the pond, include the following elements:
- One bunch of submerged plants for each 1 to 2 square feet of pond surface. Small ponds (fewer than 100 square feet in surface area) and those that receive a great deal of sun will need a higher ratio of plant material than larger and shadier ones.
- Floating leaf plants to cover roughly 50 percent of the pond's surface.
- One scavenger fish for each 1 to 2 square feet of pond surface.
- Up to 20 gallons of water for each 4-inch fish.

Lighting Your Garden for Utility and Beauty

Bathing the evening landscape with the glow of soft light will add hours of enjoyment, as well as increase the security of your garden. Whether your plans call for decorative lanterns along a garden path, entranceway lampposts, recessed lights in walls or steps, or dramatic accent lights, the key is to use soft, low-wattage lighting for a more natural effect.

Safety First

You'll need to plan your lighting scheme so that it not only shows off your plantings to best advantage but also helps your guests avoid bumping into objects or tripping on steps or walkways. At a minimum, you should focus the lighting on paved surfaces. Ankle-level lights along the edges of pathways, for example, will deflect light downward, both illuminating the walkway and lending a flattering glow to plants and flowers bordering the path. You should also install lighting in or alongside steps, on walls, or underneath railings to help people see where they are walking, and illuminate pools, decks, and patios for safety as well as for aesthetic reasons.

Advanced Lighting Technology

If you thought you needed an electrician or a landscape architect to install lighting in your garden, think again. The advent of low-voltage outdoor lighting systems has changed all that. Operating at 12 to 24 volts of electricity instead of the 120 volts that household fixtures require, these lighting systems are inexpensive to install, maintain, and use. No permits are required, the cables don't need to be heavily protected and buried, and the only special equipment you need is a step-down transformer to reduce your household current to the correct voltage. Do-it-yourself lighting kits, complete with the transformer, are available at most garden centers. Many of these kits also come with timing devices to turn the lights on and off automatically.

Another advancement in garden lighting has been the introduction of new, smaller bulbs. These bulbs are more energy efficient than older models and can cast light with laserlike accuracy or great subtlety, giving you a choice of design effects not previously available.

Types of Installations to Choose From

Garden lights range in type from freestanding lamps and lanterns to ground-level path lights, recessed step lighting, floodlighting, and accent lighting. In regions that receive plentiful sunlight, small, pagoda-shaped, solar-powered walk lights require no wiring and can be placed at any sunny spot in the garden.

Lighting fixtures are made of all types of materials—plastic, cast brass, bronze, copper, steel, aluminum, granite, and stone. As a rule of thumb, outdoor lights should be inconspicuous—it is their effect, not their design, that should have the greatest impact on your garden. Of course, some fixtures are meant to be decorative, such as lampposts at the entrance to a path or lanterns to frame a gate. But ideally, your lighting plan will be designed so that, once installed, the fixtures will be virtually unnoticeable during the day. Placing fixtures high in trees is one way of hiding them while at the same time creating intriguing shadows and diffusing the light (page 149).

Bulbs of clear, white light can be used anywhere in the landscape. Color filters are usually reserved for illuminating water features; overuse of colored lights can create a garish effect. Yellow lights, however, are good for discouraging mosquitoes and other flying insects.

All fittings must be grounded for safety; and cables, above- or belowground, must be weather- and childproof. Of course, installations in wet spots and pools must use submersible fixtures.

Using Lighting to Create an Effect

To achieve the effect you want, think about what parts of the garden you wish to illuminate—not only what must be lit for safety reasons, but which structural accents, trees, or shrubs you want to highlight for aesthetic reasons. Take a powerful flashlight outdoors and shine it in various directions, playing up light and shadow to see where lighting will have the best impact. You will most likely have to use trial and error to find the right lighting scheme for your property. A simple change in the location, intensity, angle of beam, or the number of lights you use can dramatically affect the outcome.

For the most natural look, it is better to err on the side of caution; overlighting will give an artificial look to your plants. Instead of installing one or two powerful lights, use five or six low-wattage ones for a softer, warmer glow.

Plants to Light Up the Night

White blooms are particularly lovely at night. Under soft illumination, flowers like *Phlox paniculata* 'Mount Fuji', *Nicotiana alata*, and *Ipomoea alba* appear to float above their dark greenery. Plants with silver or variegated leaves also produce a beautiful effect under night lighting. Since white flowers tend to be more heavily scented than brightly colored ones, planting jasmine or lily of the valley along the edge of a pathway or along steps will send up a wonderful perfume to add to the pleasure of your nighttime garden strolls.

Artful Highlighting

Lights can be positioned to illuminate objects in your garden in dramatic or subtle ways, allowing you to showcase trees, shrubs, and ornaments. Whether you wish to highlight a particular plant feature or perhaps imitate moonlight, you can find a fixture and a mounting position to create the desired effect. Some of the methods shown here require a wall as a backdrop; others rely solely on clever positioning of the lights. Modern lighting fixtures are easily moved, making it simple to change the lighting scheme when desired.

Silhouetting: *If a small tree or shrub with attractive symmetry or unusual form is growing in front of a wall, you can feature it by placing a light behind the plant to show it in full relief.*

Shadow lighting: *Another treatment for a tree or shrub in front of a wall is to aim a light source at the plant from the front. The light will do double duty, both illuminating the plant and casting its form in shadow against the wall.*

Uplighting: *Placing light sources in front of your trees and angling them upward highlights bark and foliage, accentuating textures and shapes.*

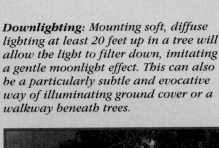

Downlighting: *Mounting soft, diffuse lighting at least 20 feet up in a tree will allow the light to filter down, imitating a gentle moonlight effect. This can also be a particularly subtle and evocative way of illuminating ground cover or a walkway beneath trees.*

Crosslighting: *Placing fixtures high in trees so that beams of light cross each other will accentuate depth and texture, highlighting the three-dimensional forms of your plantings and softening shadows falling within the combined beams.*

CHAPTER FIVE

Designing with Plants

By the time you sit down to choose the plants for your garden, you will already have a picture in your mind—and a plan on paper—based on the style of the garden you want, the purpose behind the design, the size of your property, and any plants already in the ground.

Once your basic garden plan has been determined, you will need to select plants whose forms, textures and colors complement your design and blend in with the surrounding landscape. In the Ashton, Maryland, garden, at left, an archway adorned with a blush-pink tea rose leads the eye upward and beyond, into the surrounding woodland. Plantings of bright, yellow-green Japanese barberry highlight the dark cerise blooms of a single antique rose, 'Belle de Crecy'.

On the following pages you'll learn how to make selections based on the entire panoply of plants—beginning with the garden's most stalwart members, the trees and shrubs. With an understanding of basic design principles and a palette of carefully chosen plants, you can create a garden that both unifies and enhances your entire landscape.

Laying Down the Framework

The structure of a garden is formed by its trees and shrubs. They serve as visual linchpins that hold the entire planting scheme together. Some may already be growing on your property and are sited just where you want them; others may need transplanting to fit into your design. In addition, you will unquestionably want to put in a number of new shrubs and trees—both deciduous and evergreen. If you select these plants carefully for shape, winter silhouette, and visual density, they will create shade, accent focal points, define spaces, provide backdrops, and screen out unwanted views.

But there is much more to garden design than just these architectural plants. Evergreen ground covers and small areas of lawn, for example, will help balance the design of your garden. Like trees and shrubs, they are permanent elements in the landscape. Vines also have a part to play: They can climb walls and fences or stand in for a shrub in a

This house and garden in Washington, D.C., are shielded from the scorching summer sun by mid-size deciduous trees. Twelve river birches and two each of dogwood, redbud, and serviceberry create dappled light and ideal growing conditions for the ivy, sweet woodruff, wild ginger, and other shade-loving plants growing in this formal space.

narrow space. Ornamental grasses, too, can partially fill the role of shrubs. While not as permanent as woody plants, they will provide interest for 10 or 11 months of the year. Tall varieties can be used as focal points, and smaller, weeping specimens are ideal for planting around a patio or a pond.

The most prominent of all these garden inhabitants are the trees that tower over the landscape and give your garden its fundamental character. Large trees that flourish in full sun not only bestow generous amounts of shade but also lend an air of maturity to even a newly installed garden. Because such trees link your property with the surrounding land, it's a good idea to choose species similar to those growing nearby, which are likely to be native or adapted types.

Deciduous trees are the best choice for providing shade next to the house. In summer their leafy canopies block out the sun and naturally cool your

home's interior; in winter the bare branches allow the sun to brighten and warm the rooms. To create shade for a bed or border, choose deciduous species with fine-textured foliage or an open habit that will cast dappled shade. Avoid trees with shallow roots, such as silver and Norway maples and American sweet gum, because they will outpace the roots of smaller plants in the competition for growing room, moisture, and nutrients. If space is limited, use small varieties of ornamental trees that won't overwhelm the house or the landscape or require constant pruning to restrain their size. Install cultivars of dogwood, Japanese maple, sassafras, birch, and hawthorn in groupings of three or more to screen an area from late afternoon sun.

Keep your intended location in mind when choosing trees. For example, don't plant fruiting types near a deck, patio, or walkway, where the dropping fruits will make a mess underfoot and may stain stonework, decks, or outdoor furniture.

Accent Plants

An easy way to create anchors or focal points is to plant individual accent trees and shrubs—also known as specimens. Some specimen trees and shrubs add color to a planting design with spring or summer flowers or brilliantly hued fall foliage, while others capture interest with such features as textured bark, twisted limbs, or distinctive leaves.

A tree with contorted or sculptural lines will take on a more dramatic appearance if it rises from a ground cover or a sward of green grass. The simplicity of the setting will allow you to focus on the strong lines of a trunk or spreading branches. To maintain this feeling of openness when planting a specimen tree in an island bed, surround it with plants that grow only a few feet tall.

You can also place two specimen plantings in such a way that they call attention to each other. Plant low-growing *Acer palmatum* 'Dissectum Atropurpureum', for example, in the same bed with *Cedrus atlantica* 'Glauca' (Atlas cedar). In winter, the weeping leafless branches of the maple will set off the cedar's pale bluish green needles.

An accent tree can also be used as a focal point in front of an evergreen hedge or a fence or to soften a corner of the house. But take care not to overwhelm the scene with an outsize or excessively showy selection. Your accent tree should match the scale of its surroundings.

Flowering Sargent cherries and blue pansies are among the plants that provide springtime color in this Charlottesville, Virginia, garden. Rounded boxwood, the long horizontal line of the wall, and garden steps linking the upper and lower gardens make a striking, year-round composition.

Recommended Trees and Shrubs

FAST-GROWING SHADE TREES
Acer rubrum
(red maple)
Aesculus glabra
(Ohio buckeye)
Fraxinus americana
(white ash)
Fraxinus pennsylvanica
(red ash)
Gleditsia triacanthos
(honey locust)
Liquidambar styraciflua
(American sweet gum)
Liriodendron tulipifera
(tulip poplar)
Pistacia chinensis
(Chinese pistachio)

SPECIMEN AND ACCENT TREES
Acer palmatum 'Bloodgood'
(Japanese maple)
Acer palmatum 'Dissectum Atropurpureum'
(threadleaf Japanese maple)
Chilopsis linearis
(desert willow)
Cornus kousa
(kousa dogwood)
Cotinus coggygria
(smoke tree)
Euonymus alata 'Compacta'
(winged spindle tree)
Magnolia stellata
(star magnolia)
Prunus subhirtella var. *pendula*
(weeping Higan cherry)
Punica granatum 'Legrellei'
(pomegranate)
Stewartia pseudocamellia
(Japanese stewartia)
Syringa reticulata
(Japanese tree lilac)

EVERGREEN TREES
Cedrus atlantica 'Glauca'
(blue Atlas cedar)
Cedrus deodara
(deodar cedar)
Chamaecyparis obtusa 'Crippsii'
(hinoki false cypress)
Ilex opaca
(American holly)
Ligustrum ovalifolium 'Aureum'
(California golden privet)
Magnolia grandiflora
(bull bay)

TREE AND SHRUB SHAPES

Columnar Plants	Type/Growth Pattern	Height	Zones
Acer platanoides 'Columnare' (Norway maple)	fast-growing deciduous tree	40-50 ft.	4-9
Acer rubrum 'Columnare' (red maple)	fast-growing deciduous tree	40-50 ft.	3-7
Ginkgo biloba 'Princeton Sentry' (maidenhair-tree)	slow-growing deciduous tree	50 ft.	4-8
Malus 'Sentinel' (crab apple)	fast-growing deciduous flowering/fruiting tree	15-20 ft.	4-8
Pinus sylvestris 'Fastigiata' (Scotch pine)	fast-growing needled evergreen tree	25-40 ft.	2-8
Rhamnus frangula 'Columnaris' (alder buckthorn)	fast-growing deciduous flowering/fruiting shrub	12 ft.	2-8

Pyramidal Plants	Type/Growth Pattern	Height	Zones
Oxydendrum arboreum (sourwood)	slow-growing deciduous flowering tree	25-30 ft.	5-9
Pseudolarix kaempferi (golden larch)	slow-growing needled deciduous conifer	30-50 ft.	6-8
Quercus palustris (pin oak)	fast-growing deciduous tree	50-80 ft.	2-9
Sciadopitys verticillata (Japanese umbrella pine)	slow-growing needled evergreen tree	40-80 ft.	4-8
Thuja occidentalis 'Pyramidalis' (American arborvitae)	moderate-growing evergreen shrub	10-20 ft.	3-8

Fan/Vase Plants	Type/Growth Pattern	Height	Zones
Amelanchier canadensis (shadblow serviceberry)	fast-growing deciduous flowering/fruiting tree	6-20 ft.	4-9
Cercis (redbud)	moderate-growing deciduous flowering tree	20-30 ft.	4-9
Magnolia x soulangiana (saucer magnolia)	moderate-growing deciduous flowering/fruiting tree	20-30 ft.	4-9
Prunus x blireiana (blireiana plum)	moderate-growing deciduous flowering tree	25 ft.	5-8
Salix matsudana 'Tortuosa' (dragon-claw willow)	moderate-growing deciduous tree	35 ft.	4-9

Weeping/Arching Plants	Type/Growth Pattern	Height	Zones
Buddleia alternifolia/ B. davidii (butterfly bush)	fast-growing deciduous flowering shrub	6-10 ft.	5-9
Fagus sylvatica 'Pendula' (weeping beech)	moderate-growing deciduous tree	40 ft.	4-7
Forsythia x intermedia 'Spring Glory' (golden-bells)	fast-growing deciduous flowering shrub	6 ft.	5-9
Pyrus salicifolia 'Pendula' (willow-leaved pear)	moderate-growing deciduous flowering tree	25 ft.	5-7
Tsuga canadensis 'Pendula' (Canada hemlock)	slow-growing needled evergreen tree	20 ft.	2-8

Broad-Spreading Plants	Type/Growth Pattern	Height	Zones
Aesculus parviflora (bottlebrush buckeye)	fast-growing deciduous flowering shrub	15 ft.	4-8
Castanea mollissima (Chinese chestnut)	moderate-growing deciduous tree	30-60 ft.	4-9
Cephalotaxus harringtonia (Japanese plum yew)	slow-growing needled evergreen shrub	20 ft.	6-9
Crataegus x mordenensis 'Toba' (hawthorn)	fast-growing deciduous flowering/fruiting tree	25 ft.	4-9
Photinia x fraseri (Fraser photinia)	fast-growing evergreen flowering/fruiting shrub	10-15 ft.	8-9

Rounded Plants	Type/Growth Pattern	Height	Zones
Aesculus x carnea 'Briotii' (red horse chestnut)	slow-growing deciduous tree	40 ft.	3-7
Amelanchier arborea (downy serviceberry)	moderate-growing deciduous flowering/fruiting tree	20 ft.	4-9
Buxus sempervirens (common boxwood)	slow-growing evergreen shrub	15 ft.	5-8
Chaenomeles speciosa (flowering quince)	medium-growing deciduous flowering/fruiting shrub	2-10 ft.	4-8
Malus 'Coralburst'; M. 'Snowdrift' (crab apple)	moderate-growing flowering/fruiting tree	8-20 ft.	3-8
Raphiolepis indica (Indian hawthorn)	fast-growing evergreen flowering/fruiting shrub	5 ft.	9-10

Plant Features as Accents

When trees with fine and feathery foliage are sited alongside trees bearing large, bold leaves, they create a pleasing contrast, adding variety and texture to beds of massed plantings. Tree foliage comes in many shapes, sizes, and textures, including the heart-shaped leaves of *Cercis canadensis* 'Forest Pansy' (eastern redbud), the fan-shaped leaves of maidenhair-tree, and the large compound leaves of *Aesculus parviflora* (bottlebrush buckeye). For gracefully long leaves look to sourwood. If you want foliage of a finer texture, consider the feathery foliage of *Sambucus racemosa* 'Plumosa Aurea' (European red elder), threadleaf Japanese maple, and evergreens such as *Chamaecyparis* (false cypress) and Atlas cedar.

Flowering and fruiting ornamentals provide double pleasure. In the spring or summer they produce lovely blooms, and in the fall, colorful foliage and fruits. Among the best examples are two trees, Washington thorn and *Prunus maackii* (Amur chokecherry), and several shrubs, including shadblow and *Viburnum dilatatum* (linden viburnum). You can get the same effect with a number of plants that may be shaped as either shrubs or small trees: kousa dogwood, *Sorbus alnifolia* (Korean mountain ash), golden-rain tree, *Stranvaesia davidiana* (Chinese stranvaesia), pomegranate, and *Prunus* x *blireiana* (blireiana plum).

Shrubs that produce both showy flowers and strikingly colored leaves include *Pieris japonica* 'Red Mill', *Nandina domestica* 'Nana Purpurea', Oregon grape, and witch alder. These plants can be chosen to harmonize or contrast with the house trim or a facade of brick or stained wood siding. If nestled against a backdrop of evergreen plantings, they will stand out even more dramatically.

Some deciduous trees and shrubs continue to provide interest in the winter with shaggy, mottled, corky, or richly colored bark or with gnarled, twisted, knotted, or multiple trunks or branches. Those with the most striking bark are 'Heritage' river birch, *Acer palmatum* 'Senkaki' (coral bark maple), Amur chokecherry, *Salix alba* 'Britzensis' (coral bark willow), *Pinus bungeana* (lace-bark

Perfuming the air with their delicate flowers, Lonicera heckrottii (goldflame honeysuckle) and Trachelospermum jasminoides (star jasmine) climb an arbor in Columbia, South Carolina. The jasmines were planted against the adjoining fence—a good 10 feet away on either side of the arbor—and have worked their way onto the support over the years.

Beginning with a box-wood in the left fore-ground, this garden room in Doylestown, Pennsylvania, is en-closed by a display of (clockwise) cherry lau-rel, Japanese barberry, a yew hedge, a star magnolia, and a low-growing azalea. In early summer the dark hedging is punctuated with the bright flowers of the azalea and the star magnolia, as well as with astilbes and rose mallows.

pine), *Platanus occidentalis* (eastern sycamore), and Amur cork tree. The eastern sycamore has an intriguingly shaped trunk, as does *Crataegus* x *mordenensis* 'Toba' (hawthorn). And *Corylus avellana* 'Contorta' (Harry Lauder's walking stick) grows strikingly twisted branches.

Focusing on Evergreens

A planting design that features the shapes, tex-tures, and colors of evergreen trees and shrubs will ensure year-round structural interest. But be careful not to overuse evergreens, which can evoke a dark, heavy feel to your garden. It's best to strike a balance between the weight of evergreens and the airiness of deciduous ornamentals.

Evergreens range in shape from miniature cones to tall pyramids, from neat mounds to weep-ing giants. Their foliage also varies dramatically: It may be needled or broad-leaved, with needle tex-tures ranging from soft and feathery to coarse and stiff, from glossy and prickly to smooth and silky. Broad-leaved varieties might be long and droop-ing, small and round, or narrow and pointed. Col-ors run the gamut from palest to darkest green, as well as blue-green, blue-gray, silvery blue, or varie-gated yellow and green or cream and green.

Some evergreen shapes and foliage textures are suited to particular landscape styles. For example, the loose, irregular forms of broad-leaved rhodo-dendrons, *Pieris japonica*, and mountain laurel go well in a woodland garden or a shaded formal gar-den. The stiff, pyramidal shape of Colorado blue spruce, the cone-shaped *Sciadopitys verticillata* (Japanese umbrella pine), and the almost perfectly rounded littleleaf boxwood add formality to a de-sign. The rangy shapes of x *Cupressocyparis ley-landii* (Leyland cypress) and deodar cedar are at home in an informal garden, while the irregular but compact hinoki false cypress and Atlas cedar are equally suited to a formal or an informal design.

Dwarf evergreens are good choices for a rock garden, and can give shape and weight to any loose arrangement of foliage and flowers. Good choices include *Ilex cornuta* 'Carissa', *Ilex crenata*, *Picea abies* 'Nidiformis', *Picea glauca* 'Conica', *Rhododendron* 'Moonstone' and *R.* 'Ramapo', and *Taxus baccata* 'Repandens'. For vertical accents, plant taller evergreen varieties such as cedar, English holly, bull bay, Norway spruce, and Douglas fir. They will stand out dramatically when surrounded by low or round shapes.

Plants for Screening

Hedges are the workhorses of the garden. They not only perform as stately backdrops for herbaceous borders, they can also provide privacy, block undesirable views, and muffle street noises. They can direct the flow of traffic in a garden and lead the eye toward a focal point. They can be planted to form intimate, enclosed garden rooms, and they can give structure to a flat, featureless expanse of lawn. A row of shrubs or trees can also act as a windbreak, keeping the house and garden warmer. When planted near a vegetable garden, a windbreak can create a warmer microclimate, shielding tender young plants and extending the growing season.

When you buy trees and shrubs for hedges or windbreaks, keep in mind both aesthetics and utility. If you wish to complement a formal garden design, choose stiff varieties or those that lend themselves to close clipping for a hedge; floppy or arched varieties are best for an informal garden. And be sure the mature size of the varieties you choose is appropriate for the location.

You can manipulate the sense of space on your property through the height of your hedges: Masses of tall, dense evergreens will make an area look smaller; a hedge of low shrubs or open and airy deciduous trees will create an expansive effect.

A hedge of fast-growing evergreens will screen an unsightly view or object. A more natural-looking alternative, however, would be to install a mixed selection of evergreens in clumps. To block unwelcome sightlines projecting from your neighbors' upper windows, consider a combination of tall columnar or pyramidal evergreens and twiggy deciduous trees such as hornbeam or *Pyrus calleryana* (Callery pear), whose high canopies will put the screening where you most need it.

If your property is large and deep, you can form a multilayered screen by planting tall trees behind lower-growing shrubs, or slow-growing evergreens on the boundary and fast-growing deciduous trees

inside. When the purpose of a hedge is to delineate property lines without producing a closed-in look, deciduous shrubs can be very effective. Make sure, however, that such an installation fits in with the garden's overall design. To create a barrier that keeps your pets in and those of your neighbors out, plant fruiting shrubs that bear thorns or prickly leaves, such as barberry, hawthorn, rose, firethorn, or holly. These plants have the added benefit of providing food for wildlife.

Vines

The fastest way to block an ugly view or create a sense of privacy is to install a fence or trellis and grow a perennial vine on it. This almost instant barrier makes a good alternative to the dense shade and screening offered by a mid-size hedge. It can also enclose a space that is too small or narrow for trees or shrubs. Few vines, however, are evergreen, and many deciduous ones die back or need cutting back annually. And some varieties, such as trumpet vine, yellow jessamine, *Akebia quinata* (five-leaf akebia), *Actinidia chinensis* (kiwi fruit), and Japanese wisteria, are such sturdy, heavy growers they need pruning regularly to keep them from getting out of hand or even pulling down the structure they are growing on.

Most of these vines must be trained to climb a support, or be secured to it with wire or twine. Other fast growers, such as clematis, climbing hydrangea, cross-vine, *Polygonum aubertii* (China fleece vine), and star jasmine, twine and grip with tendrils. Vines that climb with extreme ease and cling to any vertical surface with suction roots include *Hedera colchica* 'Dentata' (Persian ivy), Boston ivy, Virginia creeper, *Euonymus fortunei* (winter creeper), and *Ficus pumila* (climbing fig).

Ornamental Grasses

With their graceful foliage and fluffy plumes, perennial ornamental grasses add form and texture to the landscape for most of the year. And their nodding seed heads and rustling leaves provide appealing sound and movement during the winter, when most of the garden is in the doldrums. Varieties range in height from 6 inches to 14 feet. The shorter varieties, such as *Carex morrowii* 'Aurea Variegata' (variegated Japanese sedge), *Arrhenatherum elatius* var. *bulbosum* (bulbous oat grass), *Festuca amethystina* (large blue fescue), and *Hakonechloa macra* 'Aureola' (golden variegated hakonechloa), make striking

Capitalizing on Ornamental Grasses

Most ornamental grasses need not be divided for propagation; they are fast spreading or self-seeding. But like many other herbaceous perennials, they may start to look straggly and die off in the center after years of growth. When they do, it's time to divide them. Do this in early fall so the plants can reestablish themselves before the onslaught of winter; otherwise, wait until midspring.

There are many creative uses for divided clumps. Install low- to mid-height grasses to control erosion on a slope, to replace a lawn, or to screen the base of a deck. They also add diversity in sunny herbaceous borders.

Use medium and tall varieties in place of shrubs to create a hedge. Where it may cost a small fortune to edge a sizable property with shrubs or trees, tall perennial grasses are an inexpensive and fast-growing alternative.

If space is limited, you can plant a compact, slow-growing variety, such as *Miscanthus sinensis* 'Gracillimus' (maiden grass), *Carex morrowii* 'Aurea Variegata' (variegated Japanese sedge), or *Hakonechloa macra* 'Aureola' (golden variegated hakonechloa).

Consider planting some of the smaller grass varieties in containers so they can decorate your front entrance, deck, or patio. To keep the roots from freezing in extremely cold weather, you may have to overwinter the pots in a garage or cool basement.

The weeping green foliage of Pennisetum alopecuroides (fountain grass) softens the lines of the stonework and creates an intimate seating area in this garden near Baltimore. In the background, the golden foliage of Calamagrostis acutiflora 'Stricta' (feather reed grass) adds warmth and privacy to the scene.

combinations when planted as edging companions to low-growing creeping ground covers.

Among those grasses that grow to a middle height are *Pennisetum alopecuroides* (fountain grass), *Calamagrostis acutiflora* 'Stricta' (feather reed grass), *Cortaderia selloana* 'Pumila' (dwarf pampas grass), and *Miscanthus sinensis* 'Purpurascens'. The taller grasses, which can be planted as a privacy screen, include *Cortaderia selloana* (pampas grass), *Miscanthus sinensis* (eulalia), and *Erianthus ravennae* (Ravenna grass).

The leaf colors of most ornamental grasses range from creamy yellow to bright green. Some types have variegated hues, and others—including such low-growing species and cultivars as *Festuca ovina* var. *glauca* (blue fescue), *Imperata cylindrica* 'Red Baron' (Japanese blood grass), *Ophiopogon planiscapus* 'Nigrescens' (black mondo grass), and *Carex elata* 'Bowles' Golden' (Bowles' golden sedge)—are distinctively colored.

Ornamental grasses are not only visually appealing but also desirable as fast-growing plants with minimal cultural requirements. In most regions they require no watering or fertilizing and will grow in poor soils. However, perennial varieties will need cutting back once a year in very early spring, before they start to send up new shoots.

Although ornamental grasses spread by root systems and seeds, they are easy to control. Simply remove the young volunteers, taking care to remove all roots, as soon as they germinate in late summer or the following spring.

Lawns and Meadows

A lawn—even a small one—can be an asset to a garden. It will set off the house and separate the beds from the borders and the driveway. It will serve as a tranquil foil for the diversity of surrounding plants and garden elements. And it can provide a place for relaxation and play. Turf grass, however, needs constant attention. So you might want to consider replacing part of your lawn with an evergreen ground cover or converting some of it to a sizable island bed planted with a combination of small trees, shrubbery, and ground covers.

One of the most colorful and carefree kind of open expanses is one that has been converted from a lawn into a wildflower meadow. Planted with native annuals and perennials, it requires no feeding or watering and need be mowed only once a year. It also provides food and shelter for butterflies, bees, and beneficial insects. In putting in a meadow, you will want to plant a variety of native flowers. Perennial wildflowers that are good in a wide variety of meadow environments include goldenrod, milkweed, aster, rudbeckia, *Echinacea purpurea* (purple coneflower), tansy, sunflower, yarrow, *Oenothera caespitosa* (twisted evening primrose), *Ranunculus* (buttercup), oxeye daisy, wild bergamot, *Phlox paniculata* (garden phlox), and *Liatris* (gay-feather). Although annual or biennial wildflowers such as *Centaurea cyanus* (cornflower) and Queen Anne's lace die at the end of

their flowering season, they also work well in a carefree meadow environment. Because they self-seed prolifically, they will return year after year with almost the same certainty as perennials.

A Ground-Cover Carpet

Offering dense growth, year-round color, and interesting texture, ground covers make a fine alternative to turf grass. They can also define, separate, or unify portions of the landscape. When choosing a ground cover to replace an area of lawn, look for a type that meets your needs for speed of growth, ability to withstand light foot traffic, tolerance for sun or shade, and seasonal flower or foliage colors.

Ground covers that will accept moderate foot traffic include *Thymus praecox* (creeping thyme), wintergreen, ivy, winter creeper, bearberry, *Ajuga reptans,* and periwinkle. For shady areas, choose pachysandra, *Chrysogonum virginianum* (goldenstar), *Lamium maculatum* (spotted dead nettle), *Potentilla verna* (spring cinquefoil), or *Ophiopogon* (lilyturf). Ground covers that spread quickly in full sun and are effective in controlling erosion on a slope include *Verbena peruviana* (Peruvian verbena)*, Hypericum calycinum* (creeping St.-John's-wort), *Cerastium tomentosum* (snow-in-summer), *and Chamaemelum nobile* (Roman chamomile). One of the best ground covers to grow in moist or wet ground, whether sunny or shady, is *Lysimachia nummularia* (loosestrife). If the soil is moist and well drained, plant Corsican mint.

Annuals for Accent

Among the many reasons to grow annuals—length of bloom period, ease of care, minimal expense—perhaps the most compelling is that you can choose from an enormous variety of colors. During their short life spans, annuals produce seed so rapidly that hybridizers have been able to tinker with them endlessly, introducing new colors far more quickly than is possible with other types of plants.

The temporary nature of annuals also allows you to experiment with compositions and color schemes that are more daring than any you might be willing to undertake with your more permanent plantings. You can let your imagination run wild with the lavish selection of annuals that are available for your garden.

The Mixed Border

Annuals bring a vitality to the mixed border. If your garden is newly planted, their colors and shapes can supply eye-catching contrasts and harmonies during the time it takes for perennials and shrubs to fill out and mature. For example, soft pink *Diascia barberae* and a pale blue cultivar of *Lobelia erinus* contrast soothingly with the large, lustrous dark green leaves of Oregon grape or the simple blue-green to gray-green foliage of *Daphne mezereum*. Tall pink *Cleome hasslerana* can supply height at the back of the border and pull the composition together by repeating tints of pink.

If it's bold color you like, try yellow and crimson 'Double Madame Butterfly' snapdragons with a smattering of 'Giant Double Mixed' zinnias in red, scarlet, orange, and golden yellow. Low-growing clusters of white *Iberis umbellata* nestled among the fiery hues will help temper them.

Other annuals combine marvelous color with a flower shape so distinctive that they are worthy of a spot in the most prominent border. Perfectly at home among showy perennials are the jewel-like red-orange blooms of *Emilia javanica*, which look like miniature paintbrushes atop wiry 2-foot

Blazing red Salvia splendens 'Hot Shot' sizzles around 'Ultra White Madness' petunias, deep purple Salvia farinacea 'Rhea', and the coarse foliage of rose daphne (right), igniting this Pacific Northwest garden with hot color.

'Raspberry Rose' and 'Jolly Joker' pansies and pink and peach 'Oregon Rainbow' Iceland poppies (below) brighten the front of this mixed border in Oregon. Pink and creamy white spires of Digitalis purpurea 'Excelsior' and ruby blooms of 'Red Charm' peony are shaded by a backdrop of white, yellow, and salmon azaleas.

stems; the quill-petaled, urn-shaped, rose red flowers of *Cirsium japonicum,* which hover 2 feet above dark green spiny leaves; and the enormous sunburst-shaped pink, lavender, or white flower clusters of cleome, which float on 3- to 4-foot stems. When designing with such striking flowers, plant each species together in large groups, weaving in drifts of gray-leaved plants such as *Stachys byzantina* (lamb's ears), *Artemisia, Senecio,* and *Santolina* to soften the color scheme.

Some annuals with distinctive blooms have forms that are equally elegant. Consider *Lavatera trimestris* (rose mallow), which grows 3 feet tall and wide. Its densely branching stems, large, cup-shaped pink or white flowers, and lower leaves that resemble those of a maple blend in effortlessly with border regulars such as iris, fluffy lady's-mantle, cabbagy bergenia, and old-fashioned shrub roses. In a border with big, downy, early-summer-blooming peonies, rose mallow can carry the flower show from midsummer to early fall.

Annuals that have sparse foliage are at their best when mated with plants that have abundant leaves. Stiff stands of easy-to-grow *Verbena bonariensis,* with its pale lilac-colored flat-topped blooms, pair well with lemon yellow daylilies, whose slender,

arching leaves mask the strong but spindly stems of the verbena. The verbena offers summer color long after the perennial's petals have dropped. Simply pull up the stalks of the daylilies once they turn dry and brown, and leave the foliage intact to provide a green backdrop for the verbena.

The Annual Border

Simple borders composed of only a few judiciously chosen flowering plants often have the greatest impact. *Cuphea ignea,* an eye-catcher whose abundant scarlet cigar-shaped flowers have black-and-white tips resembling cigar ash, forms a compact foot-high mat of color; place it before soaring red-blooming cannas with their curled, wide-bladed leaves to create a pleasing contrast in form and a harmony of color. An ideal backdrop for this marriage would be a yellow-green hedge of *Philadelphus coronarius* 'Aureus' (mock orange) or tall, woody layers of fast-growing green-leaved *Spiraea prunifolia* (bridal wreath).

For a tall border with a tropical effect, try combining gold, yellow, and apricot cannas with the 5-foot stems of *Abelmoschus manihot* (sunset hibiscus), a Brazilian native whose large, fragile-looking flowers come in shades of pale to buttery yellow with maroon centers. To create a striking border in limited space, pair the red-plumed form of *Celosia cristata* (feather amaranth) with deep yellow marigolds and golden-hued calendulas. In back of the combination plant a fountain of *Miscanthus sinensis* 'Zebrinus', a perennial ornamental grass whose 5- to 6-foot-tall arching, straplike leaves display horizontal bands of creamy yellow and green.

Color Massing

Probably the easiest way to make the most of annual color is to plant a solid mass of a single variety that has especially striking blossoms. Choose an area of your yard that you want to highlight, and plant enough of the annual variety to make a bold statement. Because dramatic shocks of color dominate the area in which they're placed, resist the temptation to repeat the bold planting all around your property—or else the sheer numbers of the one color will overwhelm the viewer and lose its impact.

No matter how stunning the hue of an individual bloom, however, a stretch of unbroken color tends to tire the eye. Masses of color look best in out-of-the-way settings seen briefly and from a distance. The far corner of your backyard or the side

Four beds filled with pansies—yellow 'Crown Cream', peach, red, and pink 'Imperial Antique Shades', and purple 'Blue Perfection' —square off at the intersection of paths in a Virginia garden. Perennial orange 'Harvest Moon' Oriental poppies rise above the symmetrical arrangement.

wall of your garage is ideal; a mass of color in such removed, even remote, locations comes as a pleasant surprise when the viewer's eye discovers it. And you can extend the pleasure for months by changing the planting as the growing season progresses—replacing an expanse of fading summer-blooming purple petunias, for instance, with the fall flowers of lemon yellow chrysanthemums.

Design Bedding

Compact, profusely blooming annuals are ideal for decorative plantings called design beds, where the creative range is limited only by the gardener's imagination. These plantings can be simple, composed of, say, deep yellow *Rudbeckia hirta* 'Double Gold' blooming behind neat, squat mounds of pink, white, and red 'Prince', 'Princess', and 'Gaiety' *Dianthus chinensis,* all planted in a free-form island in your lawn. Or the beds can be formal, tracing strict geometric lines or neatly defined shapes.

If you prefer the ornate, try fashioning a circle

Low-growing orange and russet nasturtiums and white candytuft edge an Oregon bed layered with red and pink zinnias and deep gold marigolds and capped by radiant yellow sunflowers. The hedge runs along the edge of the yard, hiding a busy road from view.

How to Keep Annuals Blooming All Season Long

Once an annual has formed seeds, its life cycle is over and the plant stops producing flowers. For this reason, you'll need to prune off spent flowers before they go to seed if you want your annuals to bloom continuously through the season. In addition, cutting back plants that have become tall and scraggly encourages new, leafy growth. Pruned stems usually form new flower buds within 2 to 3 weeks.

Cut main stems just above a leaf or pair of leaves *(left).* The joint where the leaf or leaves emerge from the stem is the place from which side shoots will grow. Make a clean cut with pruning shears, removing about one-third or more of the stem. This will

stimulate branching and the production of new flowers throughout the summer *(right).*

Salvia, zinnias, and most annuals with daisylike blooms take readily to this degree of pruning. Trailing and soft-stemmed annuals such as nasturtiums, petunias, portulaca, and sweet alyssum that have grown shabby-looking benefit from a more drastic treatment that removes all but a few inches of leafy stem. For annuals with decorative seedpods such as love-in-a-mist and those whose seed you plan to collect, stop cutting back at least 2 months before the first fall frost to give them time to mature.

163

bed divided into four equal pie-like slices of color by flagstone paving. Within the structured bed, plant scarlet geraniums in opposite quadrants and bright blue petunias in the other two; soften them by ringing the perimeter of the bed with the bronzy-leaved 'Early Splendor' cultivar of *Amaranthus tricolor* and by planting an outermost rim of silver *Senecio cineraria* (dusty-miller).

The fancier the bed's design, the more formal its appearance. Beds in the shapes of rectangles, circles, and half-moons can be any size that suits your property, but for a large-scale bed, avoid the overused combination of a solid block of one color edged with another color. A mass of blue ageratum skirted with pink wax begonias or yellow marigolds is rescued from the realm of the ordinary when clusters of other varieties that grow or can be trimmed to the same uniform height are interspersed among the rim plantings. Hybrid petunias in violet, blue, and yellow are easy-care annuals that respond well to trimming in such a design.

When planting an edging or a row in a formal design, situate your annuals so that you achieve a lush, unbroken line. Planted single file or on a straight grid, the row will be pocked with unsightly holes. Instead, arrange the plants in a zigzag, or for wider perimeters, position them in slanted, overlapping rows three, four, or five plants deep.

Less formal bedding designs reflect the planting patterns of a border: bands of color interwoven throughout the groupings of plants. A delightful annual bed for a somewhat dry spot in your yard might combine two popular annuals—yellow and white snapdragons and cream and peach-colored common nasturtiums—with the lesser known *Linaria maroccana* (Moroccan toadflax), whose blooms resemble small snapdragons, and lacy-leaved *Foeniculum vulgare* 'Purpureum' (bronze fennel). Choose white and yellow toadflax and group it near a mass of the snapdragons for a contrast in scale; repeat the pairing as space allows, placing the taller fennel in the middle of the bed and letting the nasturtiums wander throughout.

Multicolored Annuals

Among the most interesting annuals are those that display contrasting colors on a single bloom in zoned, striped, and spotted patterns. Pansies, for example, have been bred to produce symmetrical blotches, with as many as three colors on one flower. Some petunias have bicolored designs in red, purple, blue-violet, or pink with white stripes that look like the spokes of a wheel. The beautiful funnel-shaped flowers of *Salpiglossis sinuata*

(painted tongue) carry velvety swatches of purple, red, and brown with overtones of white, yellow, and pink, with prominent veining in dark, contrasting shades. The dianthus tribe, including sweet William and *D. chinensis* (China pink), comprises virtually all types of variegation. In one prevalent type, called picotee, petals sport a thin outer margin in a color that contrasts with the rest of the blossom. Impatiens, wax begonia, and *Nicotiana alata* hybrids are just a few of the many annuals that can have picotee markings.

An ideal plant to blend with multicolored flowers is *Cynoglossum amabile* (Chinese forget-me-not), renowned for its exquisite clear blue color. For early-spring display in Zones 7 through 10, sow Chinese forget-me-nots in late summer and early fall with creamy yellow, dusty pink, and purplish many-toned blooms of 'Imperial Antique Shades' pansies. Add the delicate pastels of the multicolored *Papaver rhoeas* 'Mother of Pearl' (corn poppy); each bloom boasts shades of gray, lilac, peach, and palest pink that blend together like a parfait. For summer bloom in cooler areas, sow Chinese forget-me-nots in early spring with hybrid verbena 'Peaches and Cream' and apricot, peach, lavender, and salmon *Clarkia amoena* (farewell-to-spring), which features speckled and picotee markings.

In this northern California garden, the pink blossoms of the shrub rose 'Bonica' reconcile the potentially clashing colors of two annual vines—hyacinth bean, with its flat, red-violet seedpods, and common morning-glory, with blue-violet trumpet-shaped flowers.

In this Missouri border, yellow 'Castle Series' celosia spotlights the fuchsia and red blooms of 'Cut and Come Again' zinnias and round 'Globosa Mix' gomphrena. Pale blue 'Belladonna' delphiniums contrast with orange butterfly weed in a composition that spans the spectrum.

Alcea rosea (hollyhock)

Annuals with Multicolored Blooms

***Abelmoschus* spp.**
(abelmoschus)
Agrostemma githago
(corn cockle)
Alcea rosea
(hollyhock)
Antirrhinum majus
(snapdragon)
Arctotis stoechadifolia
(African daisy)
Callistephus chinensis
(China aster)
Chrysanthemum carinatum
(chrysanthemum)
Clarkia amoena
(farewell-to-spring)
Cosmos bipinnatus
(cosmos)
Dahlia hybrids
(dahlia)
Dianthus barbatus
(sweet William)
Dianthus chinensis
(China pink)
***Digitalis* spp.**
(foxglove)
Gazania rigens
(treasure flower)
***Impatiens* spp.**
(impatiens)
Layia platyglossa
(tidytips)
Linaria maroccana
(Moroccan toadflax)
Lobelia erinus
(lobelia)
Mimulus* x *hybridus
(monkey flower)
Mirabilis jalapa
(four-o'clock)
Nemesia strumosa
(nemesia)
***Nemophila menziesii* 'Pennie Black'**
(baby-blue-eyes)
Papaver rhoeas
(corn poppy)
***Pelargonium* spp.**
(geranium)
Petunia* x *hybrida
(petunia)
***Rudbeckia hirta* 'Gloriosa Daisy'**
(gloriosa daisy)
Salpiglossis sinuata
(painted tongue)
***Tropaeolum* spp.**
(nasturtium)
***Viola* spp.**
(pansy)

Note: The abbreviation "spp." stands for the plural of "species"; where used in lists it means that many, but not all, of the species in a genus meet the criterion of the list.

Heat-Tolerant Annuals

Annuals are unequaled when it comes to landscaping around paved driveways, brick paths, stone terraces, concrete walls, and a variety of other hard or rocky surfaces, known collectively as hardscapes. Hardscapes pose special challenges to plants growing close to them. For one thing, they absorb and radiate heat: On a sunny summer day a blacktopped driveway or stuccoed wall can significantly raise the temperature in the immediate area, so anything planted nearby must be reliably heat tolerant. Also, soil that is close to buildings or pavement may contain high levels of minerals deposited by water that has first washed over these surfaces. And driveways are sources of chemical pollution in the form of oily runoff and vehicle exhaust fumes.

Fortunately, there are many heat-loving, poor-soil-tolerant annuals that flourish unfazed in these locales. In addition, the microclimates created by hardscapes can even make it possible for you to grow more kinds of plants than would otherwise be possible under the normal conditions on your property. The warm environment created by a stone patio with a southern exposure, for example, might allow tender annuals to do well in a region where summers are short and cool.

Assessing Your Hardscapes

When planning any garden, you'll get the best results if you consider the conditions of the site and choose plants that are best suited to them. This is especially so of hardscape locations, which may be dramatically affected by patterns of light and shade, heat, and traffic. Start by noting how many hours of sunlight the site receives. Be aware that the amount may vary widely from one spot to the next because vertical hardscapes such as walls and buildings can block light, forming pools of shade in the midst of sun. Bear in mind, too, that the heat given off by pavement or other hardscape surfaces will cause the surrounding soil to dry out

Sweet alyssum, purple pansies, silver dusty-miller, and white geraniums fill the beds of this California garden in the spring. The alyssum guards the pansies from contact with heat-retaining gravel and also softens the straight lines and sharp corners created by the bricks. Pink geraniums make a grand focal point in the stone planter.

Flowering undaunted through a sultry Virginia summer, purple blooms of verbena overflow their raised planter. The dry heat produced by the bricks enclosing the bed is increased by a brick sidewalk beneath. But with regular watering the verbena—descended from plants native to the Americas—is thriving.

faster than normal, and that walls can keep rainfall from reaching ground adjacent to them. Plan on watering plants in these areas more often, and for added ensurance, use annuals that are especially drought resistant. A thick layer of mulch will also help keep the soil cool and moist. For plants that will prefer the conditions around your hardscapes, check the Plant Selection Guide on pages 228-231 and the encyclopedia section on pages 238-355.

Last, look at the size and use patterns of walkways and driveways. Broad paths and lightly used hardscapes have the room to accommodate annuals that sprawl over their borders. On the other hand, narrow, heavily trafficked hardscapes—the paths to back or side doors, for instance—are best edged with upright plants that won't spill onto the walkway and get trampled. Varieties of *Tagetes* (marigold), *Begonia* (wax begonia), and *Senecio* (dusty-miller) are just a few candidates for tight situations. The list at right features plants with both neat, vertical habits and more relaxed attitudes.

Choosing the Right Plants

Bare hardscapes seem to cry out for the beauty annuals can bring. Grow the plants in beds and borders along patios, terraces, and wooden decks. If space is narrow, try planting a mixed-color variety of a bushy annual such as *Salvia splendens* (sage) or *Zinnia elegans* (common zinnia) that will grow 8 to 12 inches tall. If you have room for a wide swath of color, place low-growing, compact plants such as *Gazania* species and *Ageratum houstonianum* (flossflower) along the edges of the hardscape and larger accent plants—*Zinnia angustifolia* (narrowleaf zinnia) or *Kochia scoparia* (burning bush), for example—behind them.

You need not restrict the beauty to the perimeter of your hardscape. For a weed-inhibiting carpet of blossoms in the midst of a sunny patio where foot traffic is light, plant *Portulaca grandiflora* (moss rose) and *Lobularia maritima* (sweet alyssum) between the pavers. Just remove any grass or weeds, and then fill the spaces with a fast-draining soil that contains 1 part gardener's sand for every 2 parts topsoil. Sow seeds in the soil or set out seedlings, and water lightly. And in your search for hardscape plants, don't overlook herbs. Many, such as basil and sweet marjoram, will like the hot, dry microclimate furnished by sunny hardscapes.

On sloping terrain alongside a flight of stone or

Plants for Hardscapes

UPRIGHT
***Abelmoschus* spp.**
(abelmoschus)
Ageratum houstonianum
(flossflower)
Antirrhinum majus
(snapdragon)
Arctotis stoechadifolia
(African daisy)
Begonia* x *semperflorens-cultorum
(wax begonia)
Calendula officinalis
(pot marigold)
Canna* x *generalis
(canna lily)
Catharanthus roseus
(Madagascar periwinkle)
***Cosmos* spp.**
(cosmos)
***Dimorphotheca* spp.**
(Cape marigold)
Foeniculum vulgare
(fennel)
***Gazania* spp.**
(gazania)
Kochia scoparia
(burning bush)
Ocimum basilicum
(basil)
***Salvia* spp.**
(sage)
Senecio cineraria
(dusty-miller)
***Tagetes* spp.**
(marigold)
***Zinnia* spp.**
(zinnia)

SPRAWLING
Brachycome iberidifolia
(Swan River daisy)
Browallia speciosa
(browallia)
Celosia cristata
(celosia)
Dyssodia tenuiloba
(Dahlberg daisy)
Gaillardia pulchella
(Indian blanket)
Gypsophila elegans
(baby's-breath)
***Impatiens* spp.**
(impatiens)
Lobelia erinus
(lobelia)
Lobularia maritima
(sweet alyssum)
Pelargonium peltatum
(ivy-leaved geranium)
Petunia* x *hybrida
(petunia)
Portulaca grandiflora
(moss rose)
***Tropaeolum* spp.**
(nasturtium)
***Verbena* spp.**
(verbena)

Note: The abbreviation "spp." stands for the plural of "species"; where used in lists it means that many, but not all, of the species in a genus meet the criterion of the list.

concrete steps, plant annuals that are naturally sprawling. They will drape gracefully on the incline, whereas more-upright species will tend to lean uphill or downhill in their efforts to resist gravity. Raised flower beds with sides of brick or other stonework are also pretty when dressed with these trailing plants to soften their edges.

If a wall runs beside your driveway, patio, or walk, with a narrow strip of land separating the two hard surfaces, try planting *Cobaea scandens* (cup-and-saucer vine) or *Ipomoea* species (morning glory) along the wall's base. These robust climbers should form a lavish upper growth in a short period of time.

Like other hardscapes, a rock garden creates a special microclimate since its stones absorb heat and block precipitation and wind. Rocks also help maintain moisture in the soil below them by shading it from the sun—and by returning water to the soil at night as humidity condenses on their cool surfaces and seeps into the ground. For these

reasons, well-chosen plants in rock gardens often require little maintenance.

In general, the most appealing rock gardens include a combination of small, mounded plants and sprawlers that can be trained over the edges of the rocks, brightening the surfaces with their flowers and foliage. Petite flowering annuals are well suited to the task because their small roots adapt to the confined spaces between stones and to the shallow soil on rocky outcrops. Also, they are ideal for providing color and interest in the hot season, when many perennials rest.

Spreading *Phlox drummondii* (annual phlox), brightly colored *Brachycome iberidifolia* (Swan River daisy), and dwarf varieties of *Cheiranthus cheiri* (English wallflower) are just a few annuals that thrive in sunny rock gardens. If your site is partially shaded, try snapdragon-like *Collinsia heterophylla* (Chinese houses) or delicate *Exacum affine* (German violet). The lee side of a partially shaded rock may be moist and chilly enough

Nestled between pavers on a southern Pennsylvania patio, Portulaca grandiflora (moss rose) self-sows from year to year. Blooms stay open through the day, providing maximum beauty in a cheerful mix of bright colors that hug the ground at heights of about 6 inches. The flowers do tend to attract bees, so barefooted visitors should beware.

to let cool-loving *Iberis* species (candytuft) and *Nemophila menziesii* (baby-blue-eyes) bloom all summer long.

If you have a natural rocky area on your property, try planting it with annual wildflowers that are native to your locale or from regions with comparable climates. Natives often self-sow, and they also blend well with the other aspects of the landscape where they evolved. Talk to your local Cooperative Extension Service or check catalogs that sell seeds and young plants specifically for your region to find the right annual wildflowers for your rock garden.

To plant rock-garden annuals, create pockets of well-draining soil, using 2 parts topsoil to 1 part gardener's sand. If the site is partially shaded and you're installing plants that prefer fertile soil, add 1 part compost or leaf mold and 1 part peat moss to the mix as well. Either sow seeds or transplant seedlings into the spaces. Once the seedlings are a few inches high, spread a mulch of shredded bark around them to keep the soil cool and moist.

Heat-loving annuals in this Connecticut garden add a touch of softness to the stone surfaces in this walled niche. Red-violet Petunia integrifolia surrounds the base of the center sculpture, while tall white Nicotiana alata, which self-sows from year to year, lightens and brightens the entire space.

Petite yellow Dahlberg daisies, open-faced Gaillardia aristata 'Burgundy', spiky Salvia coccinea 'Lady in Red', and orange California poppies flourish through the summer in the rocky Missouri garden at left. The limestone chunks bordering the raised bed prevent rainwater from draining through the soil too quickly.

The Many Styles of Perennial Gardens

This Pennsylvania garden uses the symmetry of an arbor to impose formality on its plantings of dark violet Salvia x superba, pale violet Nepeta, pink Dianthus deltoides, and blue oat grass. The bench provides an eye-level focal point against the backdrop of the towering hedge.

As you search for an appropriate style for your perennial garden, the possibilities will be almost endless. You might wish to recreate all or part of a garden fondly remembered from childhood, or one seen on a memorable vacation. Your inspiration might come from a fictional garden in a favorite novel, or from a particular time in history: perhaps the plantation gardens of the South, the wildflower meadows of Texas, the mission gardens of California, or the prairie landscapes of the Midwest. Or your model garden could have a horticultural theme—a rock garden, a cutting garden, and a shade garden are examples.

Be careful not to design a garden that will be too difficult for you to construct, plant, and take care of. A 200-foot double border—one that flanks both sides of a walkway or driveway—on an English country estate is magnificent to see, but it takes hundreds of hours, great professional expertise, and a lot of money to install the border and maintain it in peak condition. Similarly, a serene Japanese garden you may once have admired most likely required major earth working, backbreaking placement of stones, and meticulous pruning of trees and shrubs to achieve its stylistic simplicity and grace.

Garden Ideas to Borrow

Countless gardeners before you have wrestled with making gardens, and their successes—the

results of their hard work and imaginations—are evident in the pages of gardening books and magazines. These are great resources when it comes time to plan your own garden. You can also look for ideas in the gardens of friends and neighbors, and in public gardens, which are useful to study because they give a true measure of how well specific plants will grow in your area.

Use these gardens for inspiration—to borrow an idea or two or mix and match a few plant combinations—but resist the urge to copy them plant for plant. Tempting as it might be to simply duplicate a planting that appeals to you, even if you were to succeed at recreating one of these elaborate productions, you would rob your garden of its own character and deprive yourself of the satisfaction of creating something unique.

Nor is it necessary to recreate a whole landscape to capture its essence. Some pairings of columbine and Solomon's-seal in your own shady corner might be just enough to remind you of the plantings along a woodland path. Likewise, a single mature lavender plant in a terra-cotta container placed just so on the patio might be all that is necessary to conjure up the appealing look of an entrance to a French country inn.

Choosing Your Design Framework

One thing you will want to decide on from looking at other gardens is your design framework—whether you prefer your garden to be formal or informal, or a mixture of both. These are loose concepts; what is formal to you might seem quite relaxed or even chaotic to a neighbor. Clearly, however, some gardens are laid out in an orderly manner, with straight, architectural lines, while other gardens use plants in a more casual style.

Within both formal and informal design frameworks, you can choose from a number of different garden styles. Perennials will have a major role regardless of the style you select. They form such a rich and diverse family of plants that they can fit comfortably into virtually any planting scheme.

The mossy path curving through this informal shade garden evokes a woodland scene. Framed by a blanket of mondo grass, the path meanders through a thicket of white foamflower, and, in the foreground, purple phlox and a variegated variety of Solomon's-seal.

The daisies, delphiniums, poppies, and snapdragons of this garden are grouped tightly in a color plan of blues, pinks, and whites, with yellow added as an accent. Such a jumble of plants in rich, vibrant colors is the essence of the cottage garden style.

Perennials for a Cutting Garden

Achillea
(yarrow)
Allium
(flowering onion)
Aster
(aster)
Campanula
(bellflower)
Chrysanthemum
(chrysanthemum)
Coreopsis
(tickseed)
Delphinium
(delphinium)
Digitalis
(foxglove)
Echinacea
(purple coneflower)
Echinops
(globe thistle)
Eryngium
(sea holly)
Gaillardia

(blanket-flower)
Gypsophila
(baby's-breath)
Heliopsis
(false sunflower)
Iris
(iris)
Lavandula
(lavender)
Liatris
(gay-feather)
Paeonia
(peony)
Phlox
(phlox)
Rudbeckia
(coneflower)
Solidago
(goldenrod)
Thalictrum
(meadow rue)
Veronica
(speedwell)

Formal Gardens

Generally, the mark of a formal garden is the straight line—in its paths, pools, borders, hedges, and even in the way a view is directed along an axis, or sightline. In the most formal gardens, spaces are crafted into open-air rooms by the use of walls or hedgerows. Often, columns of marble, stone, wood, or even living trees are used to suggest walls. In classical gardens, the formality is reinforced through symmetry, with one side of the garden mirroring the other.

Most such elements would overpower the typical suburban garden, of course, but it is possible to have formality on a more intimate scale. You might put in a small knot garden—so called for its knotlike shape—where you arrange the beds in a balanced geometric pattern with, perhaps, brick walkways in between the plantings. The beds in a knot garden can be curved or have squared corners, and are usually edged in miniature boxwood.

However, some gardeners in warmer climates outline the edges of the beds with perennials and herbs, including lavender, germander, and rosemary, instead of using the evergreen shrubs.

You might choose to adopt an even more subdued level of formality, using a patio's straight edge as the boundary of your garden, for example, or choosing to plant perennials in borders instead of in beds with a freer form. A simple curve with a fixed radius can lend a formal air to a border in a way that a winding curve will not.

Without changing the outlines of a rectangular garden plot, you can either enhance or soften its air of formality by your choice of plantings. If you prefer the less formal, plant the garden's straight borders with perennials of different colors and with a relaxed form that will creep over the edges of the border. On the other hand, if order and regularity are to your liking, you could lay out a neat pathway through the plot with a mass planting on both sides of a graceful perennial like *Nepeta* (catmint) or a showy one like peony.

Informal Gardens

Curving lines and asymmetry are the key characteristics of the informal garden. The landscape is no less crafted than in a formal garden, but the borders, if there are any, might take a rambling course alongside a lawn. Often, the plantings are in beds rather than borders, the walkways are curved rather than straight, and trees and shrubs are located randomly and pruned only for their health, not to conform to a particular shape.

Cottage Gardens

One of the most popular and enduring styles is the cottage garden, whose air of rustic domesticity may be a better match for a suburban property than would a grand, classically formal garden. The cottage garden's origins lie in the old-fashioned villages of England, where the occupants of small thatched- or tile-roofed cottages filled their gardens with annuals and perennials. These were species plants—not today's highly developed cultivars and hybrids, which usually cannot reproduce themselves faithfully from seed. The old plants set seed freely, however, perpetuating themselves and producing a riot of color amid a rambling growth of foliage—and, best of all, requiring little care from the owner.

In the late 19th and early 20th centuries, some of England's leading gardeners developed a style

The same general color scheme and some of the same plants used in the cottage garden at left appear in this perennial border in Atlanta, Georgia. However, this garden's neat edging of brick and the layers of plants rising against a vertical backdrop—the clipped hedge—give it a more elegant and formal aspect.

173

based on the cottage garden but refined to a high level of sophistication. They took pains to design herbaceous borders that would bloom in rolling waves of color throughout the summer months.

The American cottage garden so in favor now lies somewhere between its two predecessors. Crafting color schemes and choosing plants for their foliage, form, and ease of care—as well as their flowers—are more important to today's gardeners than to those who tended the appealing but unruly tangle of plants dominating the early dooryard gardens. Even so, today's standards are not as rigid or demanding as those that produced the refined English border. The variety of plants to choose from is different, too, with a greater reliance on hardy perennials that are distinctly American, such as daylilies and rudbeckias.

Cutting Gardens

Nothing announces serious gardeners—or a serious love of flowers—more than choosing to grow

The rocket larkspurs, irises, and daisies in this wide perennial flower bed remain accessible to the gardener, whose design included a maintenance path paved in woodchips.

A handsome fence adds strength and completeness to this border, which includes pale yellow Achillea 'Moonshine' (foreground), reddish Alstroemeria, and tall, lilac-colored Verbena bonariensis. Without such backdrops, which define the plants' shapes and highlight their colors, some borders might lose their visual impact and become harder to see.

a cutting garden. There, plants are raised for the sole purpose of producing beautiful blooms for indoor arrangements. Although the cutting garden is less common in the American landscape than other garden styles, it deserves a second look.

Again, perennials are an ideal ingredient, especially long-stemmed plants like delphinium, solidago, and iris. Most will not rebloom, as cut annuals do, but they will present an array of flowers across the growing season if enough different kinds are planted.

Traditionally, the cutting garden occupies its own bed or beds away from the main garden; plants grow in well-spaced rows, allowing the gardener to reach them easily. Even a small area, about 10 by 10 feet, will yield hundreds of blooms in a season. But if space is at a premium, you can grow flowers for cutting in between plants in the vegetable plot or within display beds and borders.

Perennial Borders and Beds

The two most common ways to display perennials are in a border or a bed. The border typically forms the edge of a garden space and lies next to a vertical element—a wall of the house, a fence, or a hedge, for example.

The width of the border can vary, but it is an important factor in choosing plants. In a conventional border, the rule of thumb is that no plant should be taller than one-half the width of the space. If your border is a thin strip of ground between a wall and a sidewalk, for example, the scale of the perennials you place there must be modest—perhaps a row of petite plants such as candytuft, threadleaf coreopsis, or ajuga.

One advantage of the border garden is that its vertical element offers a handsome backdrop for the flowers. A white fence or wall, for instance, spotlights the color and form of the plants growing in front of it. Be careful, though, of color clashes, particularly against red brick walls, where bold red or orange blooms might be jarring.

A flower bed doesn't have the visual anchor that is inherent in a border; it often takes the form of a free-floating island. But the bed does valuable service: It can direct views across a lawn, and spotlight such landscape features as decks, patios, and swimming pools. Also, a bed might be the only place on your property where you can grow perennials in the full sun that most require.

There are pitfalls to watch out for, however, in deciding to create island beds. Islands must be made large enough to hold their own in an overall design. Even at that they might need the added

visual weight of some shrubs or small trees in order not to be overshadowed by imposing elements—such as the house—that are nearby.

Both borders and beds, if they are broad enough, will need maintenance paths—narrow, hidden trails that give you access to plants without the risk of your stepping on them or compacting their soil. In a bed, you might create a path from woodchips or river stones that, from a distance, is hidden by plant foliage. In a border, your path might run between the back of the plantings and the wall or hedge backdrop. Apart from the access it affords you, the path will also improve air circulation among the plants and prevent lingering dampness that might cause fungal infections.

Borders and beds also benefit from edging, especially if the adjacent ground is a lawn. Brick, stone, or concrete pavers laid just 6 to 12 inches wide will keep the lawn mower away from the plants and keep the plants from smothering the grass as they flop forward. Edging also acts as a unifying element for the whole plant display.

The deep pink hardy geranium and the catmint at the front of this perennial border (above) spill forward but, thanks to an edging of paving stones, remain well clear of the lawn. The line of stones also sharpens the formality of the border.

An Explosion
of Perennial Choices

Selecting plants to fit your garden style is the most challenging and rewarding aspect of perennial gardening. The complexities of selecting perennials for their bloom colors, their shapes, and their foliage and textures can appear overwhelming, but by taking a systematic approach and learning all you can about the plants and how they might look in your garden, you can become a master.

The whole idea of composing with herbaceous plants can be a new one for many home gardeners. In the past, gardeners were able to find beauty in only a limited range of old-fashioned species of such perennials as daylilies, hostas, peonies, bearded iris, and phlox. Shrub borders were old favorites, as were foundation plantings of broad-leaved evergreens and a well-trimmed lawn. Color was achieved by planting a few perennials, some spring-blooming bulbs, flowering trees, shrubs, and, especially, beds of bright, cheery annuals.

In recent years, gardeners have found in mail-order catalogs and local nurseries alike a sumptuous and sometimes bewildering array of perennials. At the same time, a distinct type of perennial garden plant, the ornamental grass, has gone from being a relative unknown in the garden to a sought-after addition to any planting, particularly given the development of many fine cultivars.

The enduring popularity of perennials has changed the face of the American garden. In an age when people want beauty and color in their garden but have little time to nurture it, well-chosen perennials provide ready solutions. Diverse and versatile, perennials can be used in any

A drift of Echinacea purpurea, the purple coneflower, shows up nicely against a backdrop of unfinished fenceboards (right). Lending a different character to the species is a cultivar called E. purpurea 'Alba', or white purple coneflower (above), which can be used in a color scheme where purple would clash. Echinacea purpurea is one of many enduring species that have been bred to produce new colors.

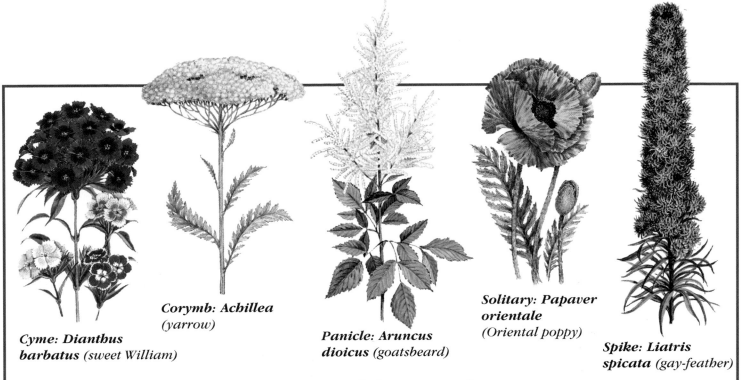

Cyme: Dianthus barbatus (sweet William)

Corymb: Achillea (yarrow)

Panicle: Aruncus dioicus (goatsbeard)

Solitary: Papaver orientale (Oriental poppy)

Spike: Liatris spicata (gay-feather)

A Variety of Flower Heads

The flower heads of perennials (inflorescences) can be grouped into several types, each lending its particular character to a plant and even influencing the length of its blooming season. Spikes, for example, generally have a long season, as the tiny individual flowers open in sequence from bottom to top. Other factors also influence the duration of flowering, such as the speed of pollination, the number of blooms produced, and the durability of the petals. Besides the inflorescences shown above, perennial flowers also take the form of racemes, such as *Polygonum bistorta* 'Superbum' *(page 294);* umbels, *Asclepias tuberosa (page 272);* and heads, *Echinacea purpurea (page 280).*

setting but are particularly well suited to looser, more natural landscape styles. They are also tougher in their ability to withstand climatic extremes and troublesome pests and diseases.

If you do not have a ready source of free perennials from gardening friends or relatives eager to divide mature plants, or if you can't take advantage of low-cost perennials from garden-club plant sales, your initial investment in perennials can be high. But with your expenditure comes the chance to create landscapes full of color and vitality using plants that require relatively little care. You'll also save the money you would spend on replacing annuals year after year, and in a fairly short period of time you'll have mature plants from which to propagate new ones.

Choosing Perennials for Color

The most important task perennials perform in the garden is enlivening the landscape with color. It is this decorative factor that places the well-designed perennial bed or border at the heart of any garden plan.

If you consciously choose a color scheme for a part or all of your perennial garden, it is best to start not with a specific plant in mind but with a particular color or colors. Once you decide on an all-white garden, say, or a grouping of soft yellows, white, and blue, you can select plants that will fall into those color bands and bloom throughout the growing season *(for information on perennials organized by color, see the Plant Selection Guide that begins on page 228).* Interplanting foliage perennials that echo the selected hues—silvery foliage plants in an all-white garden, for instance—or provide a buffer of green between potentially clashing colors, will help tie the entire arrangement together.

One color is virtually unavoidable in the garden—green. But green comes in many different shades and tints. (Shades are colors darkened by black, such as deep purple from violet; tints are colors that have been lightened by white, such as pink from red.) The careful selection of the right quality of green will enhance your color scheme.

Mixing and Matching Colors

Red, yellow, and blue are the primary colors on the color wheel. When equal amounts of two primary colors are mixed, secondary colors—orange, green, and violet— result. A primary color mixed with an adjacent secondary hue creates a third level of colors. Colors said to be harmonious share a portion of color; contrasting colors do not.

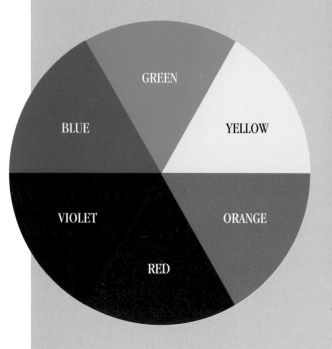

In the planting above, *the gardener has used the neutral gray foliage of Stachys byzantina to link the harmonious colors of Veronica 'True Blue' and the pink-flowered cranesbill Geranium x oxonianum 'Claridge Druce'.*

For example, the mauve-pink *Dianthus plumarius* 'Agatha' blends well with its own blue-green foliage but would jar disagreeably when paired with the yellow-green fringes of *Hosta fortunei* 'Aureo-marginata'. Successful pairing of colors is made much simpler if you understand the basics of the color wheel.

Using the Color Wheel

Different versions of the color wheel have been devised over the years, some reflecting the great scientific lengths to which color theory has been taken. However, most gardeners rely on the simple, standard version that starts with the three primary colors— red, yellow, and blue.

An equal mix of two primary colors produces one of the three secondary colors; hence orange is a mix of yellow and red and lies between them on the wheel, violet appears between red and blue, and green between blue and yellow. Mixing primary colors with their adjacent secondary colors yields the further gradations yellow-orange, red-orange, red-violet, blue-violet, blue-green, and yellow-green.

Conventional wisdom holds that the most pleasing color combinations are either contrasting, meaning that they stand directly opposite each other on the color wheel, or harmonious, found next to each other on the wheel and sharing a common pigment. A contrasting color combination might be blue and orange, violet and yellow, or red and green. Harmonious pairings include green and yellow-green, red-orange and orange, or blue-violet and blue.

Tints and shades, as well as blends of different colors—mauve, for example, which combines red and violet—add more variables. So do such elements as the amount and strength of the light the plants receive (pastels show up better in low light, bright colors look better in full sun), how well the the flower's petals reflect light, and the tendency for light colors to seem to come forward toward

The robust blooms of the popular daylily Hemerocallis 'Bejeweled' team with the dainty pink flowers of Achillea 'Rose Beauty' to produce a striking monochromatic effect (above).

Coming from opposite sides of the color wheel, the rich blue of Nepeta mussinii and the pale yellow, umbrella-shaped blossoms of Achillea 'Moonshine' demonstrate the striking combinations that are possible with the use of contrasting colors (below).

the viewer's eye and for dark colors to recede.

Clearly, with all these considerations to be taken into account, it is easy to become bogged down in the complexities of color. The best course is to use the color wheel to follow the basic rules of composing contrasting and harmonious color groupings but to let your garden plants, your eye, and your taste have the final say. If you occasionally create combinations that simply don't work well together, you won't be the first gardener to make a mistake. Keep in mind that you can move perennials from one spot in the garden to another if you have to.

Marrying Cool and Hot Colors

Besides combining plants for harmony or contrast, it is generally considered preferable to group cool colors such as violets, blues, and off-whites together. Such combinations work particularly well in those areas that receive filtered light or partial shade, where there will be no glaring sun to wash out the lighter hues. Within this family of cool colors you can use yellows or reds to create accents, but for a better blending consider a red leaning toward violet rather than toward orange, and yellows that are lemon and pastel, not the pure and brilliant yellow of some achilleas or euphorbias, for example.

A garden of hot colors—reds, oranges, and pure yellows—works best in beds or borders that receive full sun. Here, you can have fun with fiery-colored varieties of such plants as geums,

The robust, coarse-veined leaves of Hosta sieboldiana create a bold contrast in size and texture when placed next to the delicate foliage of Saxifraga stolonifera (strawberry saxifrage). Texture can provide visual interest for a garden well after the flowers have faded.

poppies, daylilies, and gaillardias. Be careful with rich colors such as magenta, blue-violet, or purple, however; they sometimes create a strident note in a bed or border unless they are somehow tempered. One way to handle such dominant colors is to isolate them in a separate bed where their brilliance will not overshadow more subdued colors. If you lack the space for this, try planting them in partial shade (if they are suited for these conditions), which will reduce their impact. When viewed in shadows, colors that were once overpowering or garish will softly glow.

Foliage is an another important component of color in the perennial garden. It might not present itself as vividly as flowers, but it lasts much longer. A color scheme of reds, purples, and grays, for instance, might be constructed of the gray foliage of artemisia and one of the purple-leaved varieties of heuchera with coral red flowers. For a color combination of violet, yellow-green, and gray, you might plant *Stachys byzantina* (lamb's ears) between *Alchemilla mollis* (lady's-mantle), lavender, and euphorbia. Note that gray is of immense value in the perennial garden: It calms the colors around it and, as a neutral, ties them together.

Planning for Texture and Mass

Plant foliage not only contributes color, it also gives the garden texture and mass. Many perenni-als are grown principally for their foliage, among them hostas, artemisia, lamb's ears, epimedium, santolina, and lamium. A number of others—ajuga, lady's-mantle, and Solomon's-seal, for example—produce foliage at least as valuable as their flowers. Even such prominent flowering plants as Japanese and Siberian iris, ligularia, acanthus, and blackberry lily accompany their blooms with a display of handsome leaves.

The fineness or coarseness of the leaves gives a plant its texture. Just as light colors advance to the eye and dark hues recede, a coarse-textured plant leaps forward into view and a fine-textured one retreats. With careful attention to the placement of fine-textured plants, for example, you can create an illusion of depth in a small garden.

More to the point, you can add interest to your garden through the thoughtful positioning of plants of varying textures. A coarse-leaved plant like ligularia would have greater visual impact set against the fine foliage of veronica than if it were next to an equally big-leaved plant like hosta.

If a plant's character comes from its leaf and flower texture, then its overall shape, or mass, dictates its stature. Mature miscanthus grass, for example, though it is fine in texture, may grow 6 feet high and 4 feet across—the size of a large shrub. Wild ginger, on the other hand, though it has coarse foliage, grows only a few inches high.

Just as you should think about associations of different colors and textures in planning your garden, you should also consider mass. For example,

a flowering mound of phlox will look more imposing when given space to show off than when it is surrounded by other perennials of similar bulk.

Putting It All Together

With all these components in mind, it is time to put your planting ideas down on paper. Assemble those ideas first according to the colors, textures, and shapes you have decided on and then select the plants to produce them. For a long border or bed, it is best to work in short sections, mindful that the most pleasing designs have some unifying element, such as a repeated pattern of color, a progression of color, or a recurring plant.

The perennial garden should present itself in layers—tall plants at the back, medium ones in the middle, and smaller ones up front. There are exceptions, of course: You might plant a tall perennial like macleaya at the front of a border to serve as an accent at a strategic spot. In island beds, which are viewed from all sides, the layering generally moves from the center outward in all directions. And in a garden to be seen from within the house as well as outside, you would not want tall plants blocking the view of the rest of the flowers.

It is best to plant in odd numbers—threes, fives, sevens—so that identical plants are not rigidly grouped and can flow easily into and among the others. You can give structure to a bed through the regular and rhythmic placement of bulkier perennials or drifts of plants, and then fill in gaps with buffers like gray-leaved neutrals or other foliage plants. By limiting the types of plants and planting individuals en masse, you will achieve a garden with less variety in color but with a simple, strong, and effective design.

Finally, as you combine plants consider scale. A bear's-breech, with its tall flower spikes and coarse leaves, would be a minor accent in a long border; next to a patio, however, it would dominate the scene. Within the confines of a small garden in the city or in the suburbs, or in the small subgardens of larger properties, it is usually best to limit the use of large-scale plants.

The gentle undulation of this California perennial border is achieved by combining plants of similar mass. A fan of Iris 'Victoria Falls' and the compact mounds of deep purple Spanish lavender, spiky English lavender, and fleabane, a member of the daisy genus Erigeron, echo the shapes of the background shrubs and provide a transition to the creeping thyme in the foreground.

Designing with Bulbs

Gardeners today use bulbs with abandon, incorporating them into traditional beds and borders *(page 186)* and using them as colorful accents in combination with other plants. Bulbs shine in these settings. Yet there is something undeniably satisfying about all-bulb groupings, with their rich, simultaneous burst of color—especially in spring, when the rest of the garden is just beginning to stir. With such unlimited design choices, it's often a good idea to create a plan on paper first, to help you see how you might include bulbs in your garden; the first chapter of this book *(pages 4-27)* explains how to map out such plantings.

The Elements of Design

Just as certain homes lend themselves to particular styles of gardens—a Federal-style brick house, for instance, with its elements of balance and symmetry, seems an apt setting for a formal garden—certain plants lend themselves to particular styles of planting. The garden surrounding such a house would likely have tidy beds of uniform plantings, outlined in straight edges and simple curves. The bulbs chosen would have simple, strong forms and compact blooms, and they would be closely grouped to create the effect of a stunning carpet of color. Tulips, hyacinths, and daffodils, placed in upright, soldierly formations and edged with annuals, make good formal plantings.

Since different types of bulbs bloom at different times you can highlight certain parts of the formal garden as the seasons progress. For example, in the early spring you can brighten the entrance to the front door and the path leading to it with a mass planting of early-blooming crocuses. As the weather warms up, shift attention to a pool or a slope edged with a bank of blooming lilies and allium or perhaps to a shady bench flanked by groupings of caladium and calla lilies. On a shady terrace, arrange large pots of colorful begonias.

The grounds around a simple frame house might be planted in mixed drifts of bulbs that would multiply over the years. Such an informal approach is characterized by irregular curves and asymmetrical shapes. A cluster of lilies, for example, might be balanced by a dwarf conifer on one side and a stand of low-growing blue fescue grass on the other.

The star-burst shape of spiky Eryngium (sea holly) beautifully echoes the open trumpet form of 'Golden Pixie' lilies. Strengthening the combination is the contrast between the lily's golden yellow color and the sea holly's lavender-blue.

An informal garden plan could also include naturalized plantings—drifts of robust species able to spread on their own from year to year. Such plantings might be started at the edge of a lawn, along a woodland floor, or around trees or shrubs. A rock garden made of randomly spaced stones set into a hillside also expresses a natural, informal look when planted with bulbs. Depending on the space, you could plant delicate-looking bulbs, such as scillas or allium, or larger bulbs such as daffodils or tulips *(pages 190-191)*. Just be sure to keep the planting in scale; you don't want the tall bulbs to dwarf the small ones.

Of course, your garden style may also combine some formal and informal elements. Deliberate contrast can be effective—a jewel-like formal bed, say, next to a naturalized woodland shade garden. But keep proportions in mind; plant large plants in large places, small plants where they can be isolated and featured.

Choosing Bulbs for Color

Deciding on a color scheme will help organize your choice of bulbs. Bulbs come in nearly every color you could want, from whites and the palest tints to the richest, most saturated hues. For vivid, energetic arrangements select plants in contrasting colors, such as yellow and violet, orange and blue-violet, or red and yellow. To create a more relaxed and peaceful mood, appropriate for an informal garden, consider harmonious color combinations such as blue-violet and mauve or shades of plum and rose. Remember, however, that these are guidelines, not hard and fast rules. If your heart is set on a particular color scheme, give it a try; your garden should reflect your tastes and your imagination. And part of the beauty of bulbs is that they can be lifted and moved easily.

Bulbs can contribute color to your garden as accent plants or in broad swaths. For example, a small group of *Allium giganteum,* with large purple globes on 4-foot stems, would highlight the foliage of a nearby planting of *Heuchera* 'Palace Purple' (alumroot) and the flowers of blooming *Lavandula* (lavender). But if you plant the allium in large bands among ornamental grasses and the rich yellow flowers of a few *Achillea* 'Coronation Gold' (yarrow), the contrast in colors and the scale of the planting will make the allium stand out from the other plants.

It is generally best to cluster like colors together and to group the clusters next to each other to make patterns. An exception might be when you combine different colors of the same type of bulb—a spring bed of *Anemone blanda* (Greek anemone) in blue, white, and pink, for example, can be quite cheery.

White-flowered bulbs such as tulips can be quite striking when planted as part of an all-white garden, especially when paired with the creamy-edged leaves of *Hosta* 'Northern Halo' and other silvery foliage plants. They are also useful to break up overly dominant color patterns or subdue strident colors. Plan for about a fourth of your bulbs at any given time to be white: crocus, narcissus, or tulip in spring; lily or dahlia in summer. In a shady location, the natural light-reflecting qualities of white flowers attract the eye and brighten shadowy curves and corners. In fact, whites and pale hues show up best in shady locations and at twilight.

Yellow is another color that makes a beautiful accent. A proportion of one yellow bloom to about three violet or blue ones creates a vivid combination. Green, a steady presence in the garden, forms a bridge between the two colors. Yellow also harmonizes with orange, a tricky hue to weave into a color scheme.

Texture and Form

Although color is a bulb's dominant attribute, the texture and overall shape of the plant can also add to the garden design. To begin with, there can be enormous variations in flower heads. Parrot tulips, for example, have developed ragged-edged petals that are wildly mottled in color. Lilies exhibit a wide range of trumpet shapes. Other lilylike flowers, such as the *Gloriosa superba,* have a lacy, airy quality.

Polianthes tuberosa 'Dangerous Pleasures' (tuberose)

Bulbs yield some of the largest and tallest of all flowers, such as the 9-inch-wide "dinner-plate" dahlia and the equally extraordinary *Eremurus himalaicus* (Himalayan desert-candle), with a flowering stalk reaching as high as 9 feet. These giants never fail to make an impression. On the other hand, the miniature detailing of a *Cyclamen coum* or the dangling bells of a *Fritillaria meleagris* require a close inspection for the viewer to fully appreciate their delicate form.

Decorative Foliage

A few bulbs are grown solely for their interesting foliage. Notable is the caladium, whose heart-shaped leaves are speckled and striped in pink, red, lavender, and white. A common houseplant, caladium is frost-tender but will do well in a shady, moist spot in the garden. The gigantic elephant's ear, or *Colocasia esculenta,* also thrives in shady and damp conditions.

Many flowering bulbs also have attractive foliage, which gives the plants interest after their blooms fade. Some cannas, for example, have purplish leaves, and the foliage of *Canna* x *generalis* 'Pretoria' has startling green-and-gold variegation. Several small tulip cultivars—'Red Riding Hood', 'Cape Cod', and 'Oriental Splendor', to name a few—have red-striped leaves. And *Tulipa aucheriana* has wavy-edged leaves that radiate from its short stem.

The foliage of flowering bulbs such as arum, oxalis, and cyclamen, when planted in masses, makes a beautiful ground cover. And in Zones 8 to 10, agapanthus, clivia, and canna foliage is evergreen, preserving their position in the garden throughout the year.

For most bulbs, however, foliage is viewed as the price a gardener must pay to enjoy the beauty of the flower. It takes some ingenuity to deal with the sprawl of daffodil foliage or the withering of allium or hyacinth leaves. With careful planning, though, you can take advantage of the emerging foliage of perennials to disguise the bulbs' progressively unsightly leaves. Ferns, for example, come into leaf just as snowdrops, crocuses, and winter aconites are fading. *Astilbe* (false spirea), *Epimedium* (bishop's hat), *Paeonia* (peony), and Siberian iris are also good camouflage.

A Bulb for Every Season

Once you have settled on the bulbs and colors you like, select for bloom season. The flowering glory of most bulbs is brief—2 to 3 weeks. The Plant Selection Guide on pages 228-231 will help you pick bulbs that bloom when you want them to and in the colors and shapes you prefer. Happily, many bulbs of the same genus bloom at different times. So if you love tulips, you can extend their presence in the garden for months by planting early-spring-blooming species tulips, followed by Triumph and Darwin tulips, which flower in midspring, and finishing with single and double late varieties, which will carry you into summer.

The Bewitchment of Scent

The scents exuded by bulb flowers range from lemony to sweet. Scent evolved to attract pollinators, and the fragrance emitted by some lilies and narcissus may seem overpowering at times. By contrast, the delicate perfume of small spring bulbs such as crocuses, scilla, and snowdrops may be hardly noticeable. Most fragrant bulb flowers come in white, pale pink, mauve, or yellow, and their petals are waxy, like those of hyacinth, tuberose, and lily. To get the most enjoyment from scented bulbs, plant them in a border close to where you walk, near the front entrance to your house, or near a patio or window.

Practical Considerations

Any garden design has to take into account the growing requirements of plants. With a few exceptions, bulbs prefer soil with a more or less neutral pH of about 7.0, and good drainage. Generally, spring bloomers such as daffodils require a dry period in the summer, when they are dormant. Cyclamen, trout lily, and other woodland bulbs need protection from hot summer sun. Plants that evolved in mountain meadows—crocuses and tulips are examples—can tolerate a good baking.

Meeting these requirements is made easier by the use of companion plants. Shrubs and perennials not only conceal the long spindly stems of tall bulb plants such as lilies—and, of course, help hide withering bulb foliage after flowering—but their roots also take up excess moisture in the soil. And later, when the bulbs are dormant, perennials shade the ground and moderate soil temperature.

You'll want to bring all these variables together when you create the detailed map of your garden design *(page 53)*. For example, a hard-to-mow slope might be just the place for a rock garden or a drift of naturalized bulbs. A diagram also helps you keep track of where your bulbs are planted.

Showy deep blue Agapanthus 'Bressingham Blue' (African Lily) stands out in bold contrast to golden mounds of orange coneflower, slender trumpets of Cape fuchsia, and yellow daylilies in this Washington State garden. Vigorous summer-flowering tubers, the African lilies bloom throughout the season.

Bulbs in the Bed and Border

Beds and borders are the building blocks of most garden designs. These self-contained plantings give the garden its shape and character, and afford the gardener an opportunity to combine plants in myriad ways, using color, form, and texture for maximum effect. The strong hues of flowering bulbs have an immediate and vivid impact in such a setting. Indeed, many of the more formal bulbs that produce uniform shapes and colors, such as tulip, iris, narcissus, and hyacinth, look most at home in a bedding display.

Use a bed or border to position plants where they can best be appreciated—along a walkway or near an entrance, around a pool or patio or a garden bench. Beds and borders are a versatile way of organizing your plants for viewing, presenting lovely vistas from afar or up close.

Cultivating a Bed or Border

Beds and borders also allow you to group your plants according to their growing requirements. They are the part of the garden where you can most easily focus your cultivation efforts to im-

prove soil texture and fertility specifically for the plants you have chosen.

Bulb experts agree that the most important factor for success in growing bulbs is your soil's drainage. The soil must allow water to percolate away from the bulbs, but it also must contain enough compost or other organic matter to hold nutrients and to retain sufficient moisture to keep the bulbs from drying out completely. In a bed or border you can prepare the soil to meet those needs and thus protect your sometimes considerable investment in growing stock.

Serving a Purpose

Although they share a common purpose in the garden, beds and borders accomplish it slightly differently. A border forms the edge of a garden space and usually lies along a vertical element—a fence, a hedge, or a wall. The vertical element serves as a backdrop to set off the plants, which are typically laid out with the tallest at the back and the shortest in front and are generally viewed from the front only. A bed, on the other hand, is often a free-standing area visible from all sides. It can be geometric or irregular in shape and surrounded by lawn, ground cover, or even gravel.

A bed must be in proportion to the space around it—neither so small that it fades from view at a modest distance nor so large that it overpowers its surroundings. On a small lot, you can give a bed of limited size more visual weight by adding shrubs or small trees, or by mounding earth to form a raised bed *(left)*. The height of the plants should be proportional to the width of the plot. As a general guideline, no plant should be taller than one-half the width of the space. And when designing either a bed or a border, be sure to give yourself enough room to move around the plantings to perform routine maintenance chores.

Formal Beds and Borders

Bulbs in massed plantings make spectacular formal designs. Expect to plant the bulbs rather densely in a formal bed—inches apart—and to think of the planting as a one-season affair, good for drawing attention to an area for a short period of time. Try, for example, a spring bed of clusters of pink, red, and yellow tulips, surrounded by an edging of vivid blue grape hyacinths. Other good edging plants include pansies, impatiens, rock cress, candytuft, primroses, coleus, or ornamental kale. Forget-me-nots are a traditional foundation

---

TIPS FROM THE PROS

Making a Mounded Bed

One way to make your bulb bed more visible from a distance is to create a gentle hillock or mound. The extra elevation adds dimensional interest and increases the color impact you will get from plants of similar height—for example, a grouping of tulips and daffodils. In addition, the eye will naturally be carried to the top of the mound, where you can place a special feature—a dwarf shrub with an interesting shape, perhaps, or a large ornamental rock.

Besides its decorative appeal, a mounded or raised bed is an ideal location for bulbs because you can easily mix up your own soil recipe on the site to ensure that it will have good drainage.

To make a raised bed, pile topsoil at least a foot high, so there will be enough to envelop completely the roots of your plants. A few artfully arranged rocks will help keep the soil in place until the plants can establish a root system. Depending on your preference for a formal or an informal arrangement, the raised bed can be centered within an available space on your property or given an off-center position. Orient the slope of the bed to the point from which you will view it.

A line of nodding 'Ice Follies' daffodils leads to a cascading white wisteria in this formal San Francisco garden. Extending the white theme, creamy tulips and a snowy azalea glow against dark masonry walls.

The flowing curves of this informal early-spring border burst with colorful naturalized bulbs, including crown imperial, emerging scilla, and a variety of daffodils. Interspersed are ivory and purple pansies and primulas to fill in the bare spots.

plant for bulb displays, creating a misty blue haze through which the bulbs grow.

You might want to experiment with a single-color scheme. For an all-white spring garden, plant *Crocus vernus* 'Snowstorm', *Narcissus* 'Thalia' and 'Mount Hood', *Hyacinthus orientalis* 'L'innocence', *Anemone blanda* 'White Splendor', *Leucojum aestivum,* and *Tulipa* 'Ivory Floridale' and 'White Dream'.

A summer bed could have clusters of red or yellow canna with a central group of red and yellow gladiolus, surrounded by mixed dahlias. For accents, try marigold, petunia, lobelia, and alyssum.

Informal Plantings

In contrast to the uniformity of a formal bed, an informal planting should offer some surprises. Give it an irregular, asymmetrical shape, and choose a wider variety of plants.

Consider, for example, creating dramatic pairings of bulbs with trees and shrubs. Blue-flowered bulbs such as scilla, muscari, and chionodoxa can create a beautiful effect when clustered in a ring around the base of a white-barked birch or small flowering cherry. Bulbs also combine well with spring-blooming shrubs—witch hazel and forsythia are two excellent examples.

Certain shrubs benefit from a screen of plants around their bare stems. For example, a hedge of lilacs, such as *Syringa* x *chinensis*, looks better with a skirt of bulbs and ferns at the beginning of the year. A succession of early-spring bulbs such as snowflakes and snowdrops, followed by crocuses and winter aconites, will finish blooming just as the dark red and pale green fronds of the maidenhair fern and the royal fern begin unfurling at the base of the lilacs. The ferns will then fill out to mask the bulbs' dying foliage.

Pastel tulips in an informal bed or border can pick up the pale blue of a *Wisteria* or lilac or the pink of spirea. Position them in front of glossy green *Ilex* (holly) or the deep maroon foliage of *Berberis thunbergii* 'Rose Glow' (barberry), and the tulips will shine. Dark purple tulips pair well with the burgundy in a cut-leaf *Acer palmatum* (Japanese maple). Their waxy blooms create a stimulating contrast with the lacy maple foliage.

Similarly, bold, waxy hyacinth flowers contrast with the fine, delicate blossoms of arabis, goldentuft, and myosotis. While hyacinths are at their best massed in a formal bed, they can serve as a good accent dotted among other plants, and their perfume is a bonus.

A specimen tree or shrub anchoring a bed can be accented with a group of bulbs. The number of bulbs should vary with the mature size of the variety chosen—a dozen daffodils, tulips, or hyacinths, for example; half a dozen large fritillaries, lilies, or galtonias; or minor bulbs in groups of three to four dozen.

Going for a Large Effect

Whether your bedding plot is formal or informal, you can strengthen its impact by choosing bulbs for height. The white-veined green leaves of an elephant's ear, for example, would contrast dramatically with the spiky foliage of a yucca or with an upright temple juniper. Or place an immense *Dahlia imperialis* next to a mass of burgundy-leaved cannas and a vining gloriosa lily.

Lilies are generally tall plants with long, relatively bare stems. They combine well with plants that rise to conceal those stems. Low grasses work well, as do dwarf conifers. For example, plant copper-colored *Lilium* x *dalhansonii* with blue-gray *Pinus flexilis* 'Glauca Pendula' (limber pine). The purple bells of a 'Betty Corning' clematis climbing over such a pair would make a stunning display.

Other tall bulb plants include *Fritillaria imperialis, Camassia, Cardiocrinum giganteum,* the tender *Watsonia,* and the giant *Canna iridiflora*—all of which grow to more than 4 feet tall in the right conditions.

Managing Bulb Foliage

Since bulb leaves should not be cut back until they are withered and brown, you'll need various planting strategies to hide them as they decline. Daffodils, for example, develop a floppy habit, especially as their foliage yellows in the sun. Plant them with hostas, daylilies, peonies, leopard's-bane, astilbe, ferns, and grasses—perennials that emerge in time to hide the homely daffodil leaves. Or put them at the base of flowering shrubs or among ground covers such as ivy, vinca, or low-growing cotoneaster, allowing you to tuck the daffodil leaves out of sight.

Crocus foliage is shorter and thus not so troublesome, getting conveniently lost among low ground covers such as vinca, sedum, bugleweed, euonymus, ivy, and carpet junipers. Do not plant

Towering Lilium 'Golden Splendor' and the smaller white 'Gypsy' shine among the pastel pink of filipendula and the blue of campanula in this Oregon garden. Clipped box bushes anchor the corner of the bed.

crocuses with pachysandra, however; it will smother the bulbs and cause them not to return.

Another way to hide withering bulb foliage is to plant annuals such as pansy, iberis, and *Lobularia maritima* (alyssum) among the bulbs just before the latter start to grow. Since the roots of annuals are shallow, the growing bulbs will find a way through them. The annuals will remain in flower through the summer, attracting attention away from the withering bulb leaves.

The foliage of certain autumn-flowering bulbs appears in the spring, long before the flowers arrive, and can be a nuisance if you have not planned for it in your garden design. Fall-blooming crocus and cyclamen have tidy, decorative leaves that add interest to the scene, but the foliage of the belladonna lily and colchicum is broad and floppy and should be tucked unobtrusively among other plants, such as hostas, in the spring.

Orange-trumpeted Asiatic hybrid lilies and purple-petaled columbine burst from a rock-edged bed in Idaho. Low-growing, plum-colored oxalis climbs between the stones.

Bulbs for Specific Conditions

MOIST SOIL
Caladium
(angel-wings)
Camassia quamash
(camassia)
Canna
(canna)
Convallaria majalis
(lily of the valley)
Eranthis byemalis
(winter aconite)
Erythronium americanum
(dogtooth violet)
Fritillaria meleagris
(checkered lily)
Lilium superbum
(Turk's-cap lily)
Narcissus cyclamineus
(daffodil)

SHADE
Achimenes
(magic flower)
Anemone blanda
(Greek anemone)
Arum italicum
(painted arum)
Begonia
(begonia)
Clivia miniata
(Natal lily)
Convallaria majalis
(lily of the valley)
Crocus tomasinianus
(crocus)
Cyclamen
(Persian violet)
Erythronium americanum
(dogtooth violet)
Eucharis grandiflora
(Amazon lily)
Fritillaria
(fritillary)
Galanthus
(snowdrop)
Hyacinthoides hispanica
(Spanish bluebell)
Iris xiphioides
(English iris)
Leucojum aestivum
(summer snowflake)
Lilium candidum
(Madonna lily)
Lycoris squamigera
(magic lily)
Muscari
(grape hyacinth)
Oxalis spp.
(shamrock)
Zantedeschia
(calla lily)
Zephyranthes
(zephyr lily)

Note: The abbreviation "spp." stands for the plural of "species"; where used in lists it means that many, but not all, of the species in a genus meet the criterion of the list.

The nodding bells of Hyacinthoides hispanica seem to splash their way gaily past the mossy rocks in an Oregon garden in April. Bright pink arabis flows through a crevice alongside.

Bulbs for the Rock Garden

A rock garden reproduces on a small scale the growing conditions of the mountain plants known as alpines. These tough little plants can thrive in pockets of gritty soil sandwiched among rocks in wind-scoured heights.

Located on a terraced slope or in a natural outcrop, a rock garden is a sheltered environment that provides plants with a variety of microclimates. Those areas shaded by the rocks are shadowy and cool, while those in full sun are warm and sheltered. The rocks protect the plants from wind, keep their roots cool, and channel water to them. In winter the rocks absorb the sun's heat by day and release it at night, moderating root-damaging temperature fluctuations in the soil. And adding a coarse gravel mulch helps keep the plants' crowns and leaves from rotting.

Tailoring the Soil for Bulbs

Alpines are usually planted in a mixture of garden soil, sand or grit, and leaf mold. Additional coarse grit will create the pockets of quick-draining soil favored year round by iris, crocus, narcissus, oxalis, and tulip. To mature well, iris, calochortus, and brodiaea plants need rapid drainage in summer. By adding more humus to the mixture, you can give erythronium, cyclamen, and anemone the rich, moisture-retentive soil they need. You can also apply water and food as needed. For example, anemone and colchicum like extra water in summer; erythronium and fritillaria need extra fertilizer.

Nestling such early-spring bloomers as *Iris reticulata,* species tulips, and crocus against rocks will give them shelter and warmth. The periods of shade the rocks provide will give cyclamen, fritillary, galanthus, oxalis, and scilla a needed respite from the summer sun.

Showcasing Smaller Bulbs

A rock garden has just the right scale for those smaller bulbs that might get lost at ground level

Species Tulips: Tiny but Tough

Species tulips like these *Tulipa bakeri* 'Lilac Wonder' naturalize easily in a sunny spot. Natives of the Mediterranean, they bloom very early in spring in Zones 5 to 7; *T. clusiana* even grows in Zone 9. With multiple flowers on each stem, species tulips look best in an uncrowded position in a rock garden. They combine well with other bulbs that bloom at the same time—*Pulsatilla vulgaris, Adonis vernalis,* or bulbous iris. Evergreen dwarf shrubs, such as *Ilex crenata* (Japanese holly), *Chamaecyparis obtusa* (Hinoki false cypress), and *Arctostaphylos uva-ursi* (bearberry), also make good companions.

among larger plants. The rocks help set off the plants. For instance, elevated in a terraced rock garden and silhouetted against dark stones, the pale blue, purple-veined petals of *Crocus speciosus* stand out. And because the plants are elevated, the scents of species tulip, crocus, narcissus, iris, and grape hyacinth more easily reach your nose. Rock gardens for hardy spring and summer bulbs like *Allium cyaneum* and *Lilium cernuum* can be as small as 3 square feet. A larger garden would be appropriate for ixia, freesia, romulea, brodiaea, babiana, or bletilla. They generally grow from 12 inches to 18 inches high.

Bulbs for the Mixed Rock Garden

Bulbs combine handily in rock gardens with dwarf shrubs and perennials, which discreetly cover the spots left bare when the bulbs go dormant. Low-growing, mat-forming herbs such as thyme, mint, and oregano protect the bulbs from splashing mud. They also provide ground-covering greenery for colchicum or *Cyclamen hederifolium,* which bloom without foliage in the fall.

Look for drought-tolerant plants that prefer fast-draining soil. Dwarf evergreens and other small shrubs such as heather, daphne, dwarf cotoneaster, ground-cover azalea, and blue spruce offer excellent possibilities for combinations with bulbs. The bulbs' upright form rising through these sprawling plants makes an interesting and colorful contrast.

Finally, choose companion perennials for color: pinks and white from saxifrage, arabis, phlox, primula, and pink; blues and lavender from bellflower, gentian, and mint; yellow and orange from dwarf aster and chrysanthemum in the fall. The silver-blue foliage of blue fescue is a good foil for brightly colored bulbs. In a shady, damp spot, plant small astilbe, fern, and hosta.

Designing with Roses

An arbor blanketed with 'Cl. First Prize' and 'Abraham Darby' serves as a threshold between rose beds with such beauties as deep red 'Chrysler Imperial' and a cutting garden beyond. The formality of this Long Island garden is emphasized by the straight lines of a trim yew hedge, low edgings of boxwood, and a wide brick walk.

With their multitude of colors, shapes, and sizes, roses exist for almost any garden situation. In choosing the plants that bring the most beauty into your garden, you'll be considering the hues of both flower and foliage, the texture of the leaves, and even the winter charm of hips. But it is the form of the plant that will help you decide how best to use it. Plump shrubs make sumptuous hedges, stiffly elegant bushes are for formal beds, tall climbers enliven a trellis or fence, and low growers blanket the ground—and these are only some of the ways to introduce roses into your landscape.

For many gardeners, the thought of a rose garden conjures up an image of upright bushes neatly arranged inside a formal, geometric frame of dense, clipped greenery. This stately, even spare, look can be magnificent, showcasing the beautiful long-stemmed blooms of hybrid teas such as the deep red 'Mister Lincoln' or the pale yellow 'Elina' and grandifloras such as the elegant pink 'Queen Elizabeth'. If growing roses for cutting and exhibiting in competitions is your goal, devote space solely to these showy types, and—because hybrid teas and grandifloras are typically scant on leaves—enclose the bed with a low hedge of yew, holly, or boxwood to contribute foliage to the overall picture. A protective barrier of greenery also creates a pleasant microclimate for roses, shielding them from strong winds and shading the soil to slow the rate of evaporation. Partial afternoon shade will help keep the blossoms looking their best longer and preserve their fragrance.

If you're planning a large traditional garden, plant a network of several rose beds, divided by paths of brick, stone, or turf grass. The straighter the paths and the more symmetrical their arrangement, the more formal your rose garden will look. And any number of special touches can be added. For variety in height, try planting climbers and ramblers, trained along arches and tripods. Ornaments such as urns, a sundial, or statuary will give the garden a sense of whimsy, dignity—or whatever personality you wish to convey.

Hedges: Double-Duty Roses

Roses can also play a substantial role outside of the formal setting. Define the perimeter of your property with species roses; separate one area from another with teas and shrubs; edge a walkway with miniatures or clustering floribundas. The floribunda 'Betty Prior', for example, makes a lush yet tidy hedge to guide visitors to your front door. Plant a single row of 'Betty Prior' 3 feet apart and keep the bushes trimmed to shorter than 5 feet. Unlike 'Betty Prior', modern shrub roses such as pink 'Bonica' and the snow white hybrid rugosa 'Blanc Double de Coubert' spread out and form a loosely cascading hedge. Use these shrubbier roses as a transition between the patio and the lawn or as a low screen to block the view of your neighbor's yard. Planted in staggered rows about 2½ feet apart, the shrubs create an impenetrable barrier of thorny canes and foliage. Roses suitable for both formal and informal hedges are listed on page 195.

Woody Shrubs and Roses

If you have room for only one hedge, try combining evergreen shrubs with roses. In moist, well-drained soil in the hot southeastern United States,

Upright and vase shaped in habit, the floribunda 'Iceberg' rises to 5 or 6 feet and spreads only slightly, making it an ideal rose for use as an open hedge. Its plush, pure white 3-inch flowers offer a textural contrast to this driveway of concrete pavers in southern California.

Roses and Herbs: Sharing a Gardening Heritage

Roses and herbs have made ideal garden companions for centuries. The oldest known gallica and the first rose known to be cultivated for medicine and perfume, *Rosa gallica officinalis*—'Apothecary's Rose'—shared a bed with fragrant herbs and, in time, with other roses in the enclosed walls of medieval monastery gardens. For hundreds of years, essences were distilled from the plants and combined into conserves, syrups, balms, and ointments that were used for treating ailments ranging from lung and liver disorders to headaches and hangovers. These mixtures contained the petals of gallicas and their citrus- and clove-scented damask descendants such as 'York and Lancaster' and 'Celsiana', vitamin-rich hips of rugosas, and such pungent herbs as lavender and chamomile.

Today, a garden of herbs and roses is still an enticing blend of function and beauty. Herbs may be grown for their culinary and possible medicinal value, and their powerful aromas help keep insects and pests away from prized roses. In addition, the striking foliage of such plants as gray-green santolina, silvery artemisia, and lacy-textured tansy offers an ideal foil for roses' showy blooms. Bushy herbs like germander also have a place, forming short, dense hedges of tiny, glossy green leaves, which add a sober note to the heady tumble of color and fragrance. In planting roses and herbs together in your own garden, you can create anything from a casual cottage version, with roses spotted here and there, to a dramatic setting that echoes the walled gardens of the past, like the Atlanta, Georgia, garden shown above.

Traditionally, roses were awarded the prime sites within a walled garden, surrounded by low hedges outlining island beds in ornamental shapes. In the garden above, the narrow, walled space is divided into three main diamond-shaped beds, each defined by a clipped hedge of true dwarf box and ground-hugging marjoram. At the rear of the garden, a rustic pergola draws the eye upward to a stand of trees beyond the garden wall. A weeping rose standard, 'The Fairy', adds a vertical dimension to each bed, and underplantings of herbs and vegetables fill the areas inside the hedges. At left center, a potted standard lemon verbena and a rosemary topiary echo the upright form of the roses and relieve the strict symmetry of the patterns, creating a garden that is lush yet orderly, and a feast for the senses.

plant *Photinia* x *fraseri* (Fraser photinia), whose new foliage is tipped with red, and *Raphiolepis indica* 'Springtime' (Indian hawthorn), which forms stiff mounds of dark green foliage, behind 'Buff Beauty' and 'Mrs. Dudley Cross' to get a gorgeous living fence. 'Buff Beauty' is a fragrant hybrid musk with 2-inch pale apricot blooms that grows to 6 feet, and 'Mrs. Dudley Cross'—a 4-foot tea rose that does especially well in warm climates—has smaller, pink-tinged yellow flowers. The photinia grows quite straggly if left untamed and should be pruned to 6 feet, while the Indian hawthorn tops out at 6 feet and needs only occasional shaping.

Farther north, alternate cool-climate needled and broad-leaved evergreens with the hardy silvery pink rugosa 'Frau Dagmar Hartopp', pruned to 4

Beside a trickling fountain in this garden in Vancouver, British Columbia, apricot 'Leander' blooms mingle gently with the off-white peony 'Coral Sunset'. The blue foliage of common rue, the pure green leaves of a pink shrub rose, and the glossy evergreen foliage of a cherry-laurel hedge bring the soft tints into sharper focus.

feet in height and width. *Picea pungens* 'Montgomery', a spruce with a bluish cast that forms a dwarf pyramid, and *Ilex glabra* 'Compacta' (dwarf inkberry), with dark green foliage and black berries in fall, will complement the rugosa's flashy passage to winter as its foliage turns deep maroon, then golden yellow, and its large hips ripen to red.

Color Schemes for Beds and Borders

Get the most out of your roses' vibrant color display by placing them in beds and borders with other flowering plants. The opportunities to compose a stunning picture of color and form are infinite; just make certain that the companions you choose share the same cultural conditions required by most roses—fairly acid, well-drained, loamy soil, and plenty of sunlight and water.

Tall or spiky plants such as lilies, hollyhocks, and foxgloves complement the arching or rounded shapes of rosebushes. Low-growing plants, including annual 'Carpet of Snow' sweet alyssum and candytuft, conceal the bare, twiggy ankles of hybrid teas—and they produce white flowers that go with roses of any color. When combining roses with other colorful plants, keep in mind that pleasing arrangements are usually harmonious—composed of colors that are within the same color family—or contrasting—meaning that the colors are from the opposite side of the color spectrum. The

Recommended Roses for a Hedge

Formal Hedges

UNDER 3 FEET
'Cécile Brunner'
'La Marne'
'Marie Pavié'
'Nearly Wild'
'White Pet'

3 TO 5 FEET
'Archduke Charles'
'Autumn Damask'
'Betty Prior'
'Carefree Beauty'
'Elina'
'French Lace'
'Iceberg'
'Old Blush'
'Olympiad'

TALLER THAN 5 FEET
'John Cabot'
'Penelope'
'Queen Elizabeth'

Informal Hedges

3 TO 5 FEET
'Ballerina'
'Belle Poitevine'
'Blanc Double de Coubert'
'Bonica'
'Erfurt'
'Hansa'
'Sea Foam'

TALLER THAN 5 FEET
'Belinda'
'Cl. Pinkie'
R. glauca
R. palustris
R. rugosa alba
'Simplicity'
'Will Scarlet'

195

vivid magenta flowers of *Geranium psilostemon*, for example, harmonize well with the perfumed deep pink bourbon 'Madame Isaac Pereire'. As an added bonus, the rose acts as a brace for the tall geranium.

Since roses come in virtually every color except blue, try pairing them with perennials and annuals in tints or shades of blue or violet. The yellow-pink blooms of the hybrid tea 'Peace' or the bright pink trusses of the bourbon 'Louise Odier' rising above the pale blue, cloudlike flowers of *Nigella damascena* (love-in-a-mist)—a self-sowing annual—paints a portrait of soothing pastels. For more drama, plant the clear yellow shrub 'Graham Thomas' with deep violet 'Black Knight' delphiniums. If you want truly eye-popping color, pair 'Playboy'—whose blooms are splashed with orange, yellow, and scarlet—with blue-violet flower stalks of *Nepeta* x *faassenii* (catmint) and *Salvia* x *superba* 'May Night' (sage). If the combination seems too garish, add bright yellow 'Moonshine' achillea to temper the mix.

The Many Tones of White

White roses come in creamy tones tinged with yellow—the climbing tea 'Sombreuil' is one example—and blush tones flushed with the lightest tints of pink, such as 'Celestial', an alba. When placed amid delicate pastel flowers of pink and apricot, these near-white roses seem to deepen the tints of their neighbors. And in a garden of hot colors—orange, scarlet, fiery red—a mass of pure white roses is a refreshing respite.

For a cool midsummer display, plant white 'Frau Karl Druschki', using a technique called pegging to create a low habit and encourage prolific blooms. Back the rose with the sculpted foliage of sea kale and its lacy mounds of dainty white flowers, then let tall, steel blue spherical flower heads of *Eryngium* x *tripartitum* (three-lobed eryngium) lean on the sea kale for support.

The large floribunda 'Iceberg' helps make a gleaming white statement when it is combined with the almost translucent white cups of *Campanula persicifolia alba* (white bellflower) and a pure white cultivar of fireweed, *Epilobium angustifolium* 'Album'. In back of this trio—which will bloom from early summer through fall—plant a tall stand of the big-leaved foliage

Saucer-shaped semi-double pink blooms of the floribunda 'Simplicity' contrast merrily with sunny yellow bearded iris. At upper right, the deep blue spikes of rocket larkspur and white and lilac dame's rocket add a sedate note to the cheery scene.

The Whitest Roses

'Alba Semi-plena'
'Blanc Double
   de Coubert'
'Boule de Neige'
'Fair Bianca'
'Frau Karl Druschki'
'Iceberg'
'Irresistible'
'Lamarque'
'Linville'
'Madame Alfred
   Carrière'
'Madame Hardy'
'Madame Legras
   de St. Germain'
'Madame Plantier'
'Marie Pavié'
'Nastarana'
R. banksiae banksiae

R. rugosa alba
'Sally Holmes'
'Sea Foam'
'Silver Moon'
'Snow Bride'
'Sombreuil'
'White Meidiland'
'White Pet'

'Frau Karl
Druschki'

of *Macleaya cordata* (plume poppy), which should reach at least 7 feet by July, lending an otherworldly quality to the luminous landscape.

Bicolored/Multicolored Roses

Not all rose blooms are one solid color. Apricot-and-salmon 'Party Girl' and yellow-and-red 'Rainbow's End', for instance, are blends, which means that varying degrees of each color merge in the blooms. A bloom can also be striped, blotched, or mottled with separate colors, or there may be an "eye" of a second color at its center. The oldest striped rose of record, 'Rosa Mundi', a sport of the gallica 'Apothecary's Rose', has pale pink blooms blotched with the vivid pink of its parent. Alternate plants of 'Rosa Mundi' and 'Apothecary's Rose' for an enchanting hedge or border.

'Camaieux', with crimson, purple, and lilac stripes on a creamy background, is at home with solid colored flowers such as the wine red and pink hybrids *Penstemon campanulatus* 'Garnet' and 'Evelyn'. The colors of the two penstemons match the rose's stripes, but the shape of their blooms is tubular, making for a pleasing contrast in form against the roundness of the rose. Add white foxglove to complement the red and pink.

Companions Worth Cultivating

Pair roses and ornamental grasses for a sensational-looking garden, says Mike Shoup, founder of the Antique Rose Emporium in Brenham, Texas. Ornamental grasses come in many colors, to be combined with roses of all hues, and their graceful, linear growth habit—tufted, mounded, arching, and upright—offers a refreshing counterpoint to the more rounded shapes of rosebushes and their blooms. To delight the eye with a planting composed of varying forms, textures, and colors, try the following combinations:

- Tufted, fine-textured, icy blue *Festuca ovina* var. *glauca* 'Blaufuchs' with soft pastels such as light pink 'Old Blush' and 'Cécile Brunner', rose pink 'Duchesse de Brabant', and pink-apricot 'Perle d'Or'.
- Arching, burgundy-leaved *Pennisetum setaceum* 'Rubrum' (purple fountain grass) with yellow-pink 'Lafter', 'Dr. Eckener', and yellow 'Graham Thomas' for dramatic contrast.
- Metallic blue *Panicum virgatum* 'Heavy Metal' (switch grass) and *Elymus arenarius* 'Glaucus' (blue Lyme grass) with mauve 'Reine des Violettes' and 'Cardinal de Richelieu', bright pink 'Betty Prior', and rose pink 'Nearly Wild'.
- Tall *Miscanthus sinensis* 'Morning Light' (Japanese silver grass), whose slender green leaves have a narrow margin of clear white, with red shrub rose 'John Franklin' and in front of climbers such as bright pink 'Zéphirine Drouhin' and dark red, tiny-leaved 'Red Cascade'.

'Gruss an Aachen' and Helictotrichon sempervirens (blue oat grass)

Designing Your Herb Garden

Snow cloaks the simple yet beautiful forms in this Connecticut herb display. A plain knot garden made of squares of germander and rue sits at the point where an alley of bare 'Seckel' pears and evergreen 'Wichita Blue' junipers intersects with two short rows of 100-year-old boxwood hedges. A trellised fence with an arched gateway separates the orderly refuge from the woods beyond.

For all their traditional appeal, herbs lend themselves well to gardening in modern landscapes. Most garden settings today are similar to those of the past in that each area of a home landscape tends to have its own purpose. Some gardens within the overall scheme may be purely decorative, while others may be used for recreation, escape, or the cultivation of special plants. Some open to a distant vista, while others offer shelter and repose. Whatever the nature of the garden, herbs have a place.

Understanding some simple design principles will help simplify the work of planning a visually appealing herb garden. At the same time, you'll need to factor in such practicalities as finding the right site, situating pathways, and selecting plants for year-round interest. Once you've considered all of these variables, you'll be ready to put your plan into action.

Even if you're only designing a small herb-filled niche, it should be unified with the rest of the setting. You can accomplish this by using materials for edging that are similar to those used for other features in the landscape. For example, if you have a brick terrace, outline a nearby garden with a row of the same bricks set on end. Also, make the outline of the garden follow or repeat the lines of the house, the garden walls, the patio, or some primary feature within the garden itself, such as a pond.

The size of your garden in relation to the landscape around it is another critical consideration. While a narrow city garden lends itself to a few herbs tucked here and there, a larger site may be best suited to the formal, patterned expanse of a knot garden. Whatever the scope of your garden, it should neither overpower nor be diminished by its surroundings.

In a garden, the most important measuring rod used to establish scale is the human body. Raised beds should be comfortable to reach across and

At the same time, keep in mind that a bit of color contrast will prevent the monotony that can result from reliance on a narrow palette. Pink or lavender nicely accents a white garden, for instance, and yellow pops out among blue or purple flowers. Especially pure yellows are found in the buttons of 'E. C. Buxton' dyer's chamomile, yellow foxglove (Digitalis lutea), French marigolds, the yarrow cultivar 'Moonshine', and the wide, daisylike disks of elecampane. For delicate yellow flowers tinged with green, plant lady's-mantle, angelica, mustard, and rue. Calendulas in shades of orange-yellow, or red-flowered pineapple sage and bee balm can also warm up a blue garden.

Foliage size, shape, and texture create another source of contrast. The feathery leaves of dill, fennel, and French marigold create a misty filigree, while fine-toothed santolina, caraway, artemisia, fringed lavender (Lavandula dentata), parsley, tansy, and yarrow contrast with the bold foliage of comfrey or castor bean, the spires of foxglove, or the flat-faced leaves of lady's-mantle.

Finally, a plant's overall form makes an important statement. Spiky iris or towering cardoon add vertical movement and dramatic contrast when placed next to mounding plants like dwarf basil, rue, lavender, or artemisia. Mat-forming or clumping ground huggers such as thyme, chamomile, creeping savory, dwarf santolina, pinks, and lady's-mantle link taller plants to each other visually and to the landscape, as well as softening craggy slopes and rounding off the sharp edges of retaining walls, stone steps, and rock edging.

Choosing a Style and Making a Plan

If your taste leans toward the formal, consider planting a knot garden, composed of intertwined bands laid out like a bas-relief carpet in a mirroring symmetry. Achieved with careful planning (page 200), it is beautiful even in winter, embossed with a blanket of snow. Herbs for each band of the knot garden should be of markedly different foliage colors to create a strong contrast between the intertwining areas of the design.

Choose plants that are roughly the same height at maturity—less than 24 inches tall and wide—and dense enough to create a seamless and solid design when pruned. Some naturally compact herbs are dwarf basil, curly chives, 'Blue Mound' rue, 'Twikel' English lavender, and burnet (Poterium sanguisorba), as well as the more traditional knot-garden members like germander, santolina, hyssop, low-growing artemisias, lemon thyme, and

An informal garden suits this rustic Texas home and provides the kitchen with herbs. Fennel and bay laurel grace the front of the bed, while silver artemisia and a border of lavender-flowered onion chives lead the eye toward the house. Mexican oregano, growing behind the fennel, is a native herb used in Southwest cuisine.

paths should offer easy access to the garden for both maintenance and harvesting. The traditional knot garden should be planted in an open, level area of your landscape, ideally where you can view its elaborate pattern from above.

You can also unify your herb garden by repeating the same plant at regular intervals. Or you can establish a color theme. For example, a blue-and-lavender garden would group catmint, bachelor's-buttons, lavender, spiderwort, and blue flag irises. A white garden would include angelica, artemisia, sweet woodruff, and the white-flowering cultivars of hyssop, bee balm, and creeping thyme (Thymus praecox ssp. arcticus 'Albus'). For pink, look for pink-flowering allium (Allium neapolitanum), marsh mallow, dittany-of-Crete, summer and winter savory, clary sage, and pink creeping thymes.

How to Construct and Plant a Knot Garden

The 10-by-10-foot closed knot garden described below consists of three bands of contrasting plants that make interlocking rectangles with a circle weaving through them. Site your knot garden in full sun on level ground; shade may cause the plants to grow unevenly.

To obtain true 90° square corners, lay out your bed as shown below. Materials you will need include wooden stakes and pegs; string; and sand, bone meal, or powdered lime to mark lines on the soil. After marking the bed's perimeter, prepare the soil, and install a brick or wooden edging to keep the look neat and trim.

Space the plants closely, and buy several extra plants in case you need replacements during the season. You will also need to mulch the ground between the bands with woodchips or gravel, or, alternatively, plant a low-growing ground-cover herb such as caraway thyme, creeping thyme, or woolly thyme. Install a dwarf boxwood near each corner to finish the design.

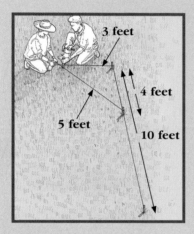

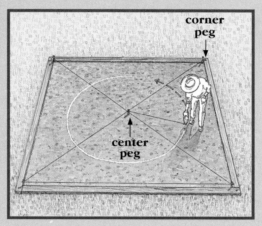

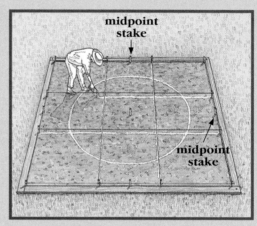

1. To create square corners, mark off one 10-foot side of the bed with stakes and string. Then, with a helper, set a peg 4 feet from the first stake and tie a string to it; mark the string at a point 5 feet from the peg. Tie a string to the first stake and mark it 3 feet from the stake. Cross the strings at the marks and set a new peg at that point. To stake off the next side, run a string from the first stake out to a length of 10 feet; repeat the squaring process. Repeat for remaining corners. Install edging along the string line and prepare the soil for planting.

2. Run string to link opposite corners; set a peg where the strings intersect at the center of the square. Next, to mark a circle at the garden's center, tie a string to a nail in the top of the center peg. Mark your string at a point that is half the distance from the center peg to a corner stake. Tie a sand- or lime-filled bottle to the string at the mark and, keeping the string pulled taut, walk around the peg with the bottle inverted so the sand pours out and marks a circle.

3. To outline the two interlocking rectangles, set stakes at the midpoint of each side of the bed. Then set two pegs on either side of each midpoint stake, 1½ feet away, so that the pegs are 3 feet apart. Run string between each of the opposite pegs to make two sets of parallel lines. Then mark the lines on the ground by dribbling sand or lime along the string lines. Remove the string, but keep the stakes and pegs in place.

4. Working outward from the center, space the plants 3 to 6 inches apart along the sand lines, adding a dose of slow-release fertilizer for each plant, following package directions. Plant a same-size dwarf box at each corner, as shown in the diagram. In the spaces between the bands of plants, spread gravel or woodchips, or plant a ground cover. As the garden matures, trim the herbs every few weeks so that the bands appear to go under or over each other, like a lattice piecrust (inset).

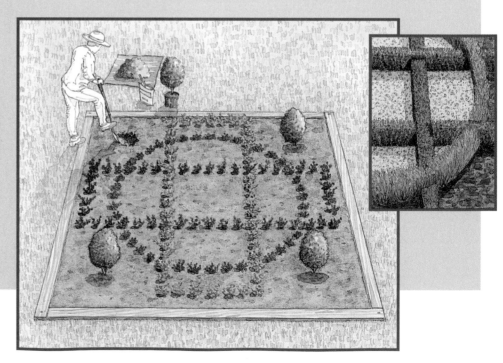

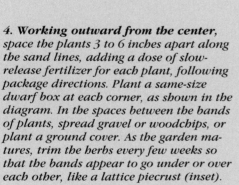

200

dwarf sage. Fill in the ground between the bands with low-growing flowers or herbal ground covers such as creeping thyme, pennyroyal, or curly parsley, which makes an interesting ground cover when mass-planted. Or spread woodchip mulch, crushed brick, tile, slate, seashells, or colored sand.

If you prefer an informal garden, remember that it will still need careful planning. Although such gardens don't contain any strict geometric lines, they take on a satisfying sense of balance with sinuous lines of beds and paths that lead you to a focal point. Without this focal point, the garden will appear jumbled and formless. Consider a garden bench or an ornament to draw the eye and create atmosphere. Traditionally, a sundial, a stone or iron urn, or a small statue appears at a central focal point in a formal garden—whereas a birdhouse, a birdbath, or a bee skep can transform an informal setting into a homey and inviting sanctuary.

Once you have decided on the ideal place for your herb garden, you're ready to lay it out. Either plot your design on paper, or plan your garden at the site itself. Mark the outer corners of the garden with stakes, and tie string from one stake to the other to approximate the garden's perimeter.

This will allow you to "see" the finished garden from all angles and to determine the best location for your plants. At the same time, mark features such as benches, ornaments, and pathways, keeping in mind that for two people to walk side by side—or to accommodate a wheelbarrow—your paths will need to be at least 4 feet wide.

Plan for a sheltering enclosure to keep out the wind and hold in the herbs' scents. Even one wall or hedge can make a difference. A trimmed boxwood hedge nicely complements formal architecture, while lattice or low walls of wattle—vines woven between stout branches driven into the earth—are especially well suited to informal or naturalistic settings.

Once you have planned the layout and the hard structures of your garden, draw up your list of herbs, noting their heights so that you can assign their positions in the garden. Also take into account their bloom times; with a little planning you can have flowers all season long. Last, plan for a generous proportion of the herbs to be evergreen. Many herbs, such as English lavender, thyme and wintergreen, will maintain a presence all through the winter.

The billowing herbs in this Mobile, Alabama, garden are contained within the straight lines of brick-edged garden beds. Laid out in a traditional quartered design, the garden features a sundial at its center, surrounded by low-growing hollies and culinary herbs, including yellow-flowering dill and fennel, in the four outer sections. White blooms of flowering tobacco at the edge of the lawn perfume the evening air.

Designing Container Gardens with Herbs

Planting herbs in pots allows you to grow a lavish garden where—and when—you choose. If your in-ground growing space is small, containers can expand it by incorporating surrounding areas—such as a walkway or a set of stairs—into your overall scheme. And if you have a roomy garden, you can use container-grown herbs to embellish a design or to emphasize special plantings.

Whether you allow them to develop their natural form or train them as espaliers or topiaries, herbs in containers are excellent accents in a garden. A pair of large containers filled with tall herbs can become a dramatic way to flank the entrance to a garden path. And matching topiaries can be set up to march in a rhythmic geometric pattern across a bare wall or along a stockade fence.

A Portable Visual Feast

The simplest way to create a lovely display of container-grown herbs is to cluster together small pots holding different plants. The herbs for this type of arrangement may be chosen for appearance' sake alone or may be related by a theme of color, scent, or use—a grouping of culinary herbs, for example, can be situated right outside your kitchen door. A more ambitious design technique is to plant a large container with a variety of complementary herbs to form what will amount to a movable garden. You can take the container to any part of the property or—if it suits you—take it into your home or greenhouse. Using a dolly to transport your pots makes even heavy concrete containers portable.

Inside, the kitchen is a logical setting for a grouping of culinary herbs. Scented and decorative herbs would be worthwhile additions to any part of your living quarters, and bathrooms are humid quarters for plants that thrive on moisture. In cold climates you can grow long-lived tender herbs such as sweet bay laurel, camphor tree, and lemon grass outdoors in pots during the summer months and move them indoors when temperatures drop and nights grow cold.

Containers also allow you to bring herbs that are at the peak of their season and are looking their best into prominent spots in the garden for viewing. If you want to dress up a shady spot for a party, for instance, you can move in containers planted with sun-loving herbs, display them there

A Victorian-style urn, bursting with Aloe vera, becomes the focal point of this Pennsylvania garden. Standing the urn on a concrete pedestal—painted to match—adds extra height while balancing the proportions of the bowl to the base. The blades of iris foliage at the foot of the pedestal mimic the spiky aloe, while the velvety silver lamb's ears lining the walk pick up the pale color of the urn.

Cinnamomum camphora (camphor tree)

Long-Lived Container Herbs

Aloe vera
(aloe)
Aloysia triphylla
(lemon verbena)
Cinnamomum camphora
(camphor tree)
Cinnamomum zeylanicum
(cinnamon tree)
Citrus aurantium
(bitter orange)
Citrus limon
(lemon)
Cymbopogon citratus
(lemon grass)
Elettaria cardamomum
(cardamom)
Eucalyptus citriodora
(lemon-scented gum)
Laurus nobilis
(bay laurel)
Myrtus communis
(myrtle)
Pelargonium spp.
(scented geranium)
Punica granatum var. nana
(pomegranate)
Rosmarinus officinalis
(rosemary)
Tulbaghia violacea
(society garlic)

Note: The abbreviation "spp." stands for the plural of "species"; where used in lists it means that many, but not all, of the species in a genus meet the criterion of the list.

Herbs for Kitchen Gardens

Agastache foeniculum
(anise hyssop)
Allium schoenoprasum
(chives)
Allium tuberosum
(Chinese or garlic chives)
Aloysia triphylla
(lemon verbena)
Artemisia dracunculus
var. *sativa*
(French tarragon)
Cymbopogon citratus
(lemon grass)
Foeniculum vulgare
(fennel)
Foeniculum vulgare
'Purpurascens'
(copper fennel)
Levisticum officinale
(lovage)
Melissa officinalis
(lemon balm)
Mentha x piperita
(peppermint)
Mentha spicata
(spearmint)
Ocimum basilicum
(sweet basil)
Origanum majorana
(sweet marjoram)
Origanum onites
(Greek oregano)
Petroselinum crispum
(parsley)
Rosmarinus officinalis
(rosemary)
Rumex acetosa
(sorrel)
Salvia officinalis
(sage)
Satureja hortensis
(summer savory)
Thymus x citriodorus
(lemon thyme)
Thymus vulgaris
(thyme)
Tropaeolum majus
(nasturtium)

Culinary herbs are kept close at hand on a New Jersey deck (above) and outside a Washington State kitchen door (below). The rustic planter filled with thyme and a cluster of clay pots containing mint, oregano, parsley, basil, and sage create an interesting display as well as provide fresh herbs for cooking.

for the few hours they are needed, and then whisk them back to their more hospitable location.

Selecting Plants for Containers

Choosing different herbs to mix in a container can be as much of a creative challenge as designing a garden bed or border. Keep in mind the growth habits of the plants as well as which ones look good together. As a starting point, perennials are logical companions for other perennials, annuals for other annuals. For best success, combine plants with similar needs. Mediterranean herbs such as sage, lavender, and rosemary require well-drained soil and can tolerate a degree of drought. Don't mix them with plants like parsley, pennyroyal, valerian, or lady's-mantle, which prefer rich, moist conditions.

Also consider the mature shape and size of each herb so the finished effect will show off all of the plants to best advantage. Be careful not to set a slow-growing or naturally small plant next to one that will quickly envelop its smaller companion in foliage. Lemon verbena and lovage, for example, reach heights of 6 feet or more if left to grow unchecked. Marjoram, nasturtium, French tarragon, and parsley tend to get choked out by that sort of vigorous plant.

Most herbs need a minimum of 6 hours of sunlight to flourish. When you plan your containers, make sure sun-loving plants aren't shaded by taller neighbors. One likely trio for a sunny site would feature sweet basil, lemon basil, and sweet marjoram. Herbs that tolerate some shade include angelica, costmary, lovage, mint, and tarragon. Chervil, coriander, and parsley all enjoy a cool, moist environment.

Designing Plant Combinations

As you work out what plants will mix well because of similar growing requirements, use your imagination to create displays that are beautiful as well as functional.

Plant herbs with trailing habits on the edges of pots, where they can cascade down over the sides. Among your choices might be silver or golden lemon thyme, marjoram, and prostrate rosemary. To cover bare soil in a container planted with a tall-growing plant or a standard, use low-growing herbs such as creeping thymes or Roman chamomile (Chamaemelum nobile).

Pairings for Color and Texture

Consider planting a container with a color theme, combining—for example—the variegated pink, green, and cream foliage of tricolor sage with pink-flowering chives. Tricolor sage would also look stunning against the deep purple foliage of purple basil. For a golden motif, you might choose gold-leaved forms of sage (Salvia officinalis 'Icterina'), feverfew (Tanacetum parthenium 'Aureum'), marjoram (Origanum vulgare 'Aureum'), and thyme (Thymus x citriodorus 'Aureus'). Herbs with gray or silver foliage include lamb's ears, southernwood, silver thyme, santolina (Santolina chamaecyparissus), and French lavender (Lavandula dentata var. candicans). For a large container, consider sweet bay (Laurus nobilis), vetiver, horsetail (Equisetum hyemale) or silver horehound (Marrubium incanum), which can grow 2 feet or more in height.

To create a look that is subtle but no less striking, combine herbs that have contrasting leaf textures. Intermingle the lacy foliage of southernwood with the wrinkled, bumpy leaves of tricolor sage (Salvia officinalis 'Tricolor'), or contrast the large leaves of purple sage (S. officinalis 'Purpurea') with delicate thyme foliage.

Perfuming the Air with Geraniums

Scented geraniums, tender perennials native to Africa's Cape of Good Hope, were introduced in England around 1795. Growers soon found that the plants would thrive indoors in winter if given ample light. The geraniums were an instant success because of their diverse, fascinating leaf forms—the herb mutates readily, and bee-crossed hybrids are common—and distinctive scents: Victorian women would brush their skirts against large pots of geranium to release its fragrance into a room. Ardent collectors amassed hundreds of varieties.

Today, although nursery catalogs may claim scents as diverse as clove, apricot, and coconut, most experts agree that the possibilities for perfume are limited to variations of lemon, mixed citrus (combining lemon, lime, and orange), mint, rose, rose-lemon, apple, pepper, and a pungent odor—more or less pleasant depending on the cultivar—that can only be described as spicy.

Fragrant geraniums boast leaf forms to satisfy just about any gardener. Size varies from the crinkly ½-inch-diameter leaf of lemon-scented Pelargonium crispum 'Minor' to the pungent P. hispidum, with leaves that measure 4 to 5 inches across. Leaf shapes range from the ruffled round of apple geranium (P. odoratissimum) to the deeply indented of rose geranium (P. graveolens). Leaves come in many shades of green, some with a light brush of velvet, as well as in variegated mixtures of green with cream, white, brown, and even maroon.

With so many cultivars available, choosing scented geraniums for your garden can seem overwhelming. If your growing space is limited, opt for a citrus-, rose-, or mint-scented plant since these are the most useful for cooking and for making sachets and potpourri.

Pelargonium quercifolium 'Fair Ellen' (oak-leaved geranium)

Wildflowers for Every Garden

It is very likely that you are already growing wild-flowers in your garden. Many of the old standbys of the traditional herbaceous borders that have long been the hallmark of English gardens trace their ancestry to North America. Such plantings would be far poorer without New World asters, wild indigos, columbines, lupines, coneflowers, coral bells, phloxes, and their progeny.

In many instances, the plants have been changed through selection and breeding. When horticulturists find a truly outstanding individual and want to reproduce it, they do so vegetatively, from cuttings or tissue culture. That way, the results will be clones, identical to the mother plant. (On the other hand, when plants are grown from seed, the results are often unpredictable.) These cloned plants are called *cultivars*—short for "cultivated variety." Cultivars usually possess some distinctive quality—a long flowering period, an unusual color, small stature, or handsome foliage. They are not necessarily better than seed-grown plants, but they *are* predictable, identical, and, therefore, uniform in appearance. This is a great advantage in formal gardens.

A Formal Setting for Wildflowers

There are many types of formal gardens, from small island beds to intricate parterres. All, however, are guided by the geometric principles of scale

The brilliant pink flowers and willowlike leaves of Epilobium angustifolium—called fireweed because it is one of the first plants to germinate after a fire—make a delicate tracery against a house in Crested Butte, Colorado. Fireweed can be invasive, but a less vigorous white variety is well behaved in a perennial bed.

and proportion. Shorn hedges, well-defined planting beds, and the use of symmetry are all typical of formal gardens.

Formal gardens are most often designed to reflect the architecture of a formal house. When the owner of a Georgian-style house chooses straight-edged, geometric beds and neatly clipped hedges, it is because these features enhance the simple, elegant lines of the house. Next to a brick path, mass plantings of a discreetly hued cultivar such as the pale, creamy-yellow *Coreopsis verticillata* 'Moonbeam' (threadleaf coreopsis) enclosed by a clipped hedge of dwarf edging boxwood yields a neat, tailored look that harmonizes with more formal architectural styles.

Wildflowers for Beds and Borders

The predictability of cultivars also makes them good choices for traditional perennial beds and borders because a particular color, height, or width is a given. Gardeners design such ornamental plantings around specific color schemes, so being able to count on a particular shade is all-important. For example, in a pink to purple border that is meant to be soothing, the vivid scarlet of *Lobelia cardinalis* (cardinal flower) would be jarring. The darker wine of its cultivar 'Ruby Slippers', however, adds just the right touch of color.

Of course, cultivars are not the only natives suitable for perennial borders. Dozens of others, often not as well known, serve beautifully. *Baptisia alba* (white wild indigo), a midborder star, has clusters of pea-like flowers for nearly a month in spring and remains a neat 30-inch shrub until frost. Also for the midborder is golden threadleaf coreopsis, which adds tiny flowers and airy volume. Like its better-known, shorter cultivars 'Zagreb' and 'Moonbeam', it blooms for weeks on end, carrying the border through the summer.

Designing for a Natural Look

When gardens take inspiration from nature rather than from architectural or traditional styles, they almost seem to have evolved on their own. Rather than being geometric in form, the beds in such gardens flow and curve, following the natural contours of the land. Slopes, stands of trees, and the banks of streams or creeks are good places to site free-form beds, where they will also save on maintenance by eliminating the need to mow.

The gardener augments this less constrained look by placing plants in irregular groups of mixed textures and varying sizes and heights. If shrubs are combined with the herbaceous plants, they should reflect the diversity found in nature; fewer than half should be evergreen. And save the task of regular shaping for some other part of the garden. Instead, allow deciduous shrubs like the native *Callicarpa americana* (beautyberry), with its long, arching stems and purple berries, to grow into their natural shapes.

The Versatility of Ornamental Grasses

Most herbaceous plants change with the seasons, tying the garden to the natural world, but the ornamental grasses do it with exceptional flair. In summer their graceful forms serve as cool green and blue fillers when planted in natural drifts, providing a subtly textured background for the shifting colors of perennials and annuals. Throughout fall and winter, the grasses remain standing, turning shades of almond, russet, tan, and gold. Grasses also bring year-round movement and sound to the garden as they sway and rustle in the wind.

Lively in form but restrained in color, the boltonia in the foreground above enhances the monochromatic color scheme of a formal garden in Potomac, Maryland. Blooming from late summer into fall, its airy flowers contrast with the thick, plush texture of the lamb's ears that edge the border.

tus. If form is paramount in a planting scheme, consider dividing this grass every 2 years, since it may lose its neat outline with age.

Two other evergreen or semievergreen grasses are *Muhlenbergia capillaris* (pink muhly) and *Deschampsia caespitosa* (tufted hair grass). Found growing in moist, rich soil in the Southeast, pink muhly makes a 1½-foot clump of extremely fine-textured leaves surmounted in fall by airy panicles of pink flowers that are lovely when backlit by the afternoon sun. *Muhlenbergia rigens* (deer grass) is another delicate-looking species suitable for dry-climate gardens in the West.

In silhouette, tufted hair grass is similar to muhly grass, but its foliage is a darker green. Its delicate flowers open green, then change to buff, gold, or a purplish bronze, depending on the cultivar. One of the few ornamental grasses that tolerate shade, it is lovely juxtaposed against ferns and hostas or massed as a ground cover in a woodland garden.

Tall Grasses

Prairie grasses attaining heights of 4 feet and more are ideal for the back of a sunny border, but they needn't be relegated solely to supporting roles. If you have a pool in your garden, the slim, graceful leaves of *Panicum virgatum* (switch grass), *Sorghastrum nutans* (Indian grass), or *Andropogon gerardii* (big bluestem) would make elegant reflections on its surface. Placed in front of a dark broad-leaved evergreen such as the native *Ilex glabra* (inkberry), any of these grasses presents a striking contrast of color and texture. If you juxtapose them with the red berries of *Aronia arbutifolia* (chokeberry) or the scarlet autumn leaves of *Itea virginica* (Virginia sweetspire), for instance—the composition fairly sparkles.

The height and mass of these grasses equip them to serve as architectural elements within the garden. To turn an area of lawn open to public view into a private seating area, partially surround it with clumps of grass planted in a sinuous curve or, for a more formal look, in an L shape. Because a tall grass reaches its mature size about 3 years af-

Prairie wildflowers cover a sunny slope in the Wisconsin garden at left. In midsummer the white spires of Culver's root are surrounded by black-eyed Susans and pink bee balm. Later in the season, the feathery plumes of goldenrod will dominate. After frost the slope is peppered with the dark round seed heads of the black-eyed Susans.

The Low-Growing Grasses

The arching leaves of grasses spilling onto a paved terrace, driveway, or walk make a pretty edging. Among the low-growing grasses suitable for this purpose are *Sporobolus heterolepis* (prairie dropseed), whose ⅟₁₆-inch-wide emerald green leaves form a fountainlike hummock. Prairie dropseed grows well in dry soil, as does the dwarf evergreen *Festuca ovina* var. *glauca* (blue fescue). Sometimes no more than 6 inches in height, blue fescue has dome-shaped tufts of needlelike leaves that color best in full sun and dry soil. Its dense, mounded form makes this grass a striking accent among trailing plants in a rock or trough garden. For textural contrast, mass blue fescue in front of the flattened, leathery pads of a prickly pear cac-

ter planting, the new garden room it defines will assume its character sooner than it would if shrubs were used.

Along a property line, a tall grass makes a low-key three-season herbaceous hedge that is cut to the ground by late winter to make way for new growth. A less restrained, more colorful alternative is to embellish the leafy screen with stately wildflowers. Choose a mix of annuals, biennials, and perennials ranging in height from 3 to 6 feet or more: *Helianthus maximiliani* (Maximilian sunflower) and *H. annuus* (common sunflower); *Ipomopsis rubra* (standing cypress), with brilliant red flowers that are magnets for hummingbirds; goldenrods; a dusky purple *Vernonia* (ironweed); yellow-flowered *Agastache nepetoides* (giant hys-

sop); or splashes of blue from *Baptisia australis* (blue wild indigo). Your choices will depend not only on growing conditions but also on the space available. A useful guideline is to limit the height of the tallest plant to no more than half of the width of the planting.

Meadows and Prairies

Whether growing in hedges, beds, or borders, ornamental grasses interplanted with colorful wildflowers evoke prairies or meadows. *Prairie*, the French word for meadow, denotes the complex, grass-dominated, treeless ecosystem that once covered much of the central United States and

Canada. The special, untamed beauty of an expanse of flowering plants and grasses in a treeless clearing has caught the eye and won the heart of many a gardener.

Even though most people notice the flowers first, grasses are the major component of a prairie, making up more than 50 percent of its biomass. Such proportions account for the subtle, color-flecked green of the prairie, compared with the intense color of a conventional bed or border. If the grasses tone down the brilliance of the flowers, they also help to hide their demise. And in winter when other herbaceous plants have withered, grasses add volume and a tawny presence.

A pleasing possibility for the gardener who yearns for a bit of the prairie but has a small yard is a "pocket meadow," which is simply a prairielike mixture of flowering plants and grasses scaled down in height and mass to suit the space. By choosing plants that stay under 3 feet tall, a gardener can create a meadow in as few as 60 to 100 square feet.

A pocket meadow looks best when it is framed with a fence or shrub border as a background. In front, a path or a row of a grass with a mounding habit, such as prairie dropseed, gives it a finished edge. Another option is to mow a curving path through the meadow. Even in a small space where the plants are only hip high, a path gives the illusion of greater depth. It also allows whoever walks on it the wonderful sensation of being surrounded by a miniature ecosystem alive with the sound and sight of insects drawn to the flowers.

Establishing a pocket meadow is not substantially different from planting a border. Within the allotted space, intersperse grasses and flowering plants at intervals of a foot or so. Position flowering plants in irregular drifts. Even though the end product will appear to have evolved naturally, the young plants require care. Mulch the meadow well, and keep it watered and weed free while the plants establish themselves.

A cooling sight on a hot July day in Milwaukee, a man-made garden pond (below) features the cupped blossoms of a nonnative water lily. Natives include the dark green fringe of sedge in the foreground and two clumps of dark green arrowhead that offer a vertical accent to the water lily's flat, round leaves.

Shade Gardening with Style

The lacy blue foliage of Dicentra eximia (fringed bleeding heart) daintily accents the broad, powdery-surfaced leaves of Hosta 'August Moon' and yellow-edged H. 'Golden Tiara'. The bright new growth on the tips of the spiky yew echoes the golden tones of the hostas, completing the shady vignette.

Just as a flowering garden changes from month to month and from season to season as plants bloom and fade, a shady foliage garden also presents a series of new faces over time. Spring-blooming bulbs, growing in the sunlight that filters through the bare branches of deciduous trees, can give way to winter-dormant perennials known for their appealing foliage, such as hostas, astilbes, ferns, and daylilies. The fresh leaves of these plants will conceal those of the spent bulbs and will remain attractive throughout the summer.

Keeping company with the perennials can be a mixture of evergreen and deciduous shrubs. To form a tapestry that will engage the eye through the growing season and beyond, combine shrubs that have contrasting leaf colors and textures. Vivid fall color is assured if you choose shrubs such as *Amelanchier canadensis* (shadblow serv-iceberry), a large plant that turns brilliant orange-red; *Aronia* (chokeberry), showing red in fall; or *Hamamelis mollis* (Chinese witch hazel), *H. vernalis* (American witch hazel), or *H. virginiana* (common witch hazel), with yellow autumn color.

In cold climates, evergreens enhance the shade garden's winter appeal. Yew, boxwood, rhododendron, *Pieris,* and holly are among the many shrubs that remain green year round. In addition, a number of perennial foliage plants manage to survive above ground during the winter. Some, such as *Polystichum setiferum* (soft shield fern) and *P. lonchitis* (northern holly fern), become large enough to assume the design role of a small shrub.

To alleviate bare ground during the winter months, plant evergreen ground covers such as *Ajuga* (bugleweed), pachysandra, *Mazus reptans,* and *Heuchera* (alumroot).

Combining Foliage Plants

Once you've decided which foliage plants to include in your shade garden, your next step is to fit them into a harmonious design. As you plan your garden's layout, take time to consider each plant's form, texture, mature height, and color. If you will be including flowering plants in the design, plan for them as well.

The form, or shape, of a plant is often its most noticeable feature. When small plants have distinctive forms, mixing them together willy-nilly can create a discordant design. To unify a composition, group three or more of one type of plant together and arrange clusters of perennials in naturalistic drifts that flow through the garden. If you are planting a shady border, occasionally repeat the pattern of plants to create a visual rhythm. The exception to planting in groups occurs when you want to use one dramatic plant as a specimen.

Sometimes a plant whose greatest virtue seems to be its ability to complement others in a harmonious grouping can also make a powerful statement when mass-planted on its own. *Polygonatum biflorum* (small Solomon's-seal), for example, is delightful combined in a woodland garden with *Trillium* (wake-robin), *Smilacina* (false Solomon's-seal), ferns, and *Mertensia virginica* (Virginia bluebells). Yet when it is mass-planted, its arching stems form an impressive display. Likewise, a mass planting of a hosta cultivar with a low-growing habit can prove a dramatic variation on a ground cover.

Marrying Foliage Textures and Colors

Juxtaposing plants of different textures can create fascinating effects in your garden. For an intriguing composition, try mixing fine-leaved plants with those that have larger, coarser leaves. A broad-leaved hosta paired with a feathery fern, for example, or the straplike foliage of daylilies or *Liriope* (lilyturf) with the heart-shaped foliage of *Epimedium* (barrenwort) creates an appealing contrast.

Color adds yet another dimension to plant pairings. Use accents of gold, lime green, or bluish green to enrich a combination, or use gold or variegated leaves where you need a flash of light. For example, the yellow-green and bronze-purple varieties of the Japanese barberry shrub *(Berberis thunbergii)* create a vivid pairing in light shade, with the darker foliage seeming to recede behind the brighter leaves. In fact, you can visually enlarge a shady spot by placing dark or cool-colored foliage toward the back of the garden, where it will subtly blend into the shadows. If a cozier space is what you want, put brighter-colored foliage in the back; it will appear to leap forward, foreshortening the distance.

Demonstrating how a shady border can depart from the traditional floral emphasis of a sunny one, this planting in Vancouver, British Columbia, features a pleasing mix of leafy perennials. The Solomon's-seal in back arches over the hostas and maidenhair ferns in front, adding height and movement to the design.

Designing with Shade-Tolerant Herbaceous Plants

Although most shade-tolerant herbaceous plants are grown primarily for their bloom, many of them also have lovely foliage. And because such plants are generally shallow rooted, they are ideal for shade gardens, where competition with the roots of trees and shrubs is often intense.

Cimicifuga (bugbane) sends up beautiful plumelike flower spikes in summer, but its ferny foliage is equally attractive during the rest of the season. A tall plant that will tolerate partial shade, bugbane should be placed in the back of flower borders or on the fringes of woodlands. For the edge of a path or in a rock garden, consider *Corydalis lutea* (yellow corydalis), a low-growing, clumping plant with gray-green fernlike leaves. Its delicate yellow flowers will persist through most of the growing season if it is kept well watered.

Other flowering perennials with fine, feathery foliage include bleeding heart, astilbe, *Aruncus* (goatsbeard), and *Aquilegia* (columbine). For interesting contrast, try mixing them with the strappy leaves of shade-tolerant daylilies, the large heart-shaped leaves of *Begonia grandis* (hardy begonia), or the geranium-like foliage of *Alchemilla* (lady's-mantle).

If you're looking for a plant to light up a dark spot or act as an accent, combine variegated *Pulmonaria saccharata* (Bethlehem sage) with the deep purple leaves of *Heuchera micrantha* 'Palace Purple'. Another heuchera with striking foliage is *H. americana* 'Garnet' (rock geranium), which has a geranium-shaped leaf with apple green margins and deep purple veins.

The Wide World of Hostas

Hostas, also known as plantain lilies, are an astonishingly varied group of plants, the majority of which prefer shade. They grow in most of North America, although they are less successful in regions that don't get winter chill or are extremely arid. Because of the diversity of size, texture, and color in this genus, there is a hosta to meet almost any landscape requirement. Some grow only a few inches tall with petite leaves; others have large paddlelike leaves and grow to a substantial 36 inches tall and wide. *Hosta fortunei* 'Gold Standard', a chartreuse-leaved cultivar edged with dark green, makes clumps that grow to a width of 5 feet or more. Foliage color among hostas

ranges from bright yellow, gold, and creamy white, usually in the form of variegation, to the entire spectrum of greens and blues. Leaves can be long and thin, broad and round, oval, heart shaped, or pointed. Foliage textures vary as well, from smooth to deeply ribbed.

Hostas adapt to a variety of growing conditions; they thrive in both dry and wet locations. The yellow varieties tend to do best when their shade is no more than partial; those with blue foliage usually prefer more time in the shade. While hostas are easy to propagate by division, a single clump can grow in the same place for several years.

Petasites japonicus var. giganteus 'Fuki' (giant butterbur) blankets a New Jersey border with leaves that can grow up to 4 feet in diameter. In early spring this spreading perennial produces cones of daisylike, pale yellow flowers before the large leaves appear.

Mining Hostas' Assets

Put hostas to work in your shade garden. Edge a path or walkway with midsize cultivars such as *H.* 'So Sweet', which has green leaves with white margins and very fragrant flowers; 'Golden Tiara', with long heart-shaped green leaves edged in gold; or the cream-edged *H. undulata* 'Albo-marginata'.

Create a striking ground cover by mass-planting small hostas such as *H.* 'Kabitan', a narrow, gold-leaved variety, or *H.* 'Ginko Craig', a green-and-white beauty. Although hostas don't spread by means of runners like traditional ground covers, you can space the clumps so that the leaves overlap to completely cover the ground. For spring color, plant early-blooming daffodils between the hostas; the hosta foliage will appear just as the daffodils are fading.

Large hostas perform well as foundation plantings, in mixed-flower borders, or as specimen plants. Giants—as tall as 3 feet and 5 feet or more across—include the blue *H. fortunei* var. *hyacinthina*; *H. sieboldiana* 'Elegans', a blue-green cultivar; *H.* 'Sum and Substance', prized for its 2-foot-wide heart-shaped chartreuse leaves; and *H.* 'Blue Angel', which has striking, heart-shaped, deeply ridged blue leaves.

Experiment with hostas and other plants to create exciting color and texture combinations. Plant a broad-leaved hosta such as *H. sieboldiana* 'Frances Williams' next to a feathery *Athyrium filix-femina* (lady fern). Or combine *H.* 'Gold Edger', a chartreuse-leaved cultivar, with a variegated ivy that picks up the same yellow-green color. Equally eye-catching is a collection of different hostas that echo and accent one another's colors and forms. Don't be afraid of trial and error. Hostas are sturdy, and you can move them around without much damage if they don't marry happily.

Ferns: Prehistoric Wonders

Ferns are another group of adaptable and intriguing shade performers. There are ferns suited to just about any garden condition, from full sun to deep shade, from wet conditions to dry, and from alkaline to acid soil. The less fussy ones will put up with whatever situation they are given. *Thelypteris noveboracensis* (New York fern), for example, prefers damp, acid soil and light shade but will tolerate fairly dry conditions, neutral soil, and medium shade.

The diversity of ferns provides the shade gardener with a wealth of choices. There are creepers that make excellent—although sometimes invasive—ground covers. *Dennstaedtia punctilobula*

Mass plantings of colorful hostas brighten shady areas of the garden where grass will not survive. Cultivars encircling a tree are (counterclockwise from top) H. 'Kabitan', H. x tardiana 'Blue Wedgewood', H. 'Antioch', H. fortunei 'Francee', and H. sieboldiana 'Elegans'.

(hay-scented fern), for example, will quickly fill a space with its 30-inch-tall fronds. It tolerates wet or dry conditions and deep shade. Other good ground covers include *Gymnocarpium dryopteris* (oak fern), *Polypodium aureum* (rabbit's-foot fern), and *Polypodium glycyrrhiza* (licorice fern).

Designing with Ferns

To create a soft, lacy effect in your garden, choose a genus with dainty foliage, such as one of the many maidenhair ferns. Depending on the species, these ferns form dense clumps ranging in height from 8 to 20 inches. One of the best is the hardy *Adiantum pedatum* (northern maidenhair). For a splash of color, add the purple-and-silver *Athyrium nipponicum* 'Pictum' (painted lady fern).

Ferns are particularly attractive when planted around woodland ponds and along streams. Delicate, aerial ferns grow happily at the water's edge and will quickly naturalize, softening the shoreline. *Osmunda cinnamomea* (cinnamon fern), *O. regalis* (royal fern), and *Dryopteris marginalis* (marginal shield fern) are ideal for such settings.

Ferns as Woodland Companion Plants

In woodland gardens, combine ferns with rhododendrons, azaleas, and delicate woodland flowers. Members of the genus *Dryopteris*, also known as fancy ferns, have finely cut rich green foliage that rises from a central crown; they mix admirably with trillium, bleeding heart, phlox, and primrose.

A diminutive woodlander, growing just 4 inches tall, is the oak fern. It looks especially charming mixed with *Linnaea borealis* (twinflower), *Claytonia virginica* (spring beauty), and *Dicentra cucullaria* (Dutchman's-breeches). When the Dutchman's-breeches foliage dies back in early summer, the fern can fill in the gap.

Because of their striking foliage and forms, ferns make excellent accents in a shady flower bed or border. Good candidates for this role include many *Dryopteris* species. And *Asplenium nidus* (bird's-nest fern) also does the trick with thin, leathery, tonguelike fronds that will grow an impressive 4 feet high in warm, humid conditions.

In cooler zones, *Matteuccia* (ostrich fern) is a good choice. With its erect feathery fronds that stand 3 feet tall and resemble a shuttlecock, this fern makes a dramatic display. Combine it with spring-flowering bulbs or woodland flowers, or let a clump of the ferns make a showing on their

A dependable shade performer, Athyrium filix-femina (lady fern) grows to a height of 3 feet and thrives in moist soil. The wild species, shown above in its springtime glory, often looks tired and tattered by summer's end; try one of its hybrids, such as A. filix-femina 'Victoriae', instead.

In this Seattle shade garden, northern maidenhair ferns (Adiantum pedatum)—also known as five-finger ferns—display their "fingers" against leathery spears of Asplenium scolopendrium (hart's-tongue fern). Overarching fronds of Polystichum munitum (western sword fern) add weight to the design.

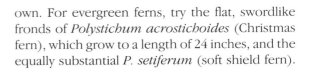

The dark olive shade of the broad, crinkled Heuchera (alumroot) leaves accentuates the dark ribs of Athyrium nipponicum 'Pictum' (painted lady fern) in the St. Louis, Missouri, shade garden at left. The fern's silvery fronds add streaks of light to the composition.

Hairy leaf buds known as fiddleheads mark the early appearance of Osmunda cinnamomea (cinnamon fern). As the season progresses, the fiddleheads unfurl into fertile cinnamon-colored fronds, later to be joined by sterile green fronds.

own. For evergreen ferns, try the flat, swordlike fronds of *Polystichum acrostichoides* (Christmas fern), which grow to a length of 24 inches, and the equally substantial *P. setiferum* (soft shield fern).

A Perfect Match: Ferns and Rocks

Tiny, shallow-rooted ferns are ideal for growing in rock gardens, on the earthen risers of garden steps, and even in the crevices of walls. In fact, the warmth radiated by a wall may create a microclimate that enables you to grow a fern that is only borderline hardy in your zone. For such spots, try *Cystopteris fragilis* (fragile fern), which is much tougher than its name suggests; *Polypodium virginianum* (rock polypody), which will grow happily in just 2 inches of soil; the 6-inch-tall *Asplenium trichomanes* (maidenhair spleenwort), or *A. scolopendrium* (hart's-tongue fern), with its crinkled, tongue-shaped fronds.

In a shady, moist rock garden, plant *A. rhizophyllum* [also classified as *Camptosorus rhizophyllus*] (walking fern). It especially appreciates limestone rocks. An intriguing miniature for Zone 10 is the spreading *Selaginella kraussiana* (mat spike moss), which grows only half an inch tall.

Caladiums

The brightly colored heart- or arrowhead-shaped leaves of caladiums come in a beautiful silvery white that is veined with dark green, or in striking mixtures of pink, green, and cream. Well suited to shrub and flower borders as well as containers, caladiums grow in clumps about 12 inches tall and will thrive in either full or partial shade. They prefer evenly moist but well-drained soil, and their favorite weather condition is hot and humid; they are hardy perennials only to Zone 10. Caladiums do produce flowers, but they are so undistinguished that connoisseurs generally remove them, along with spent foliage, to encourage more leaf production. The broad, colorful leaves make caladiums a delightful foil next to any lacy green plant, including ferns, columbine, and astilbe. Use the silvery varieties in front of deep green plants such as yew; they will shimmer in contrast.

Coleus

Like caladiums, coleus will grow as a perennial in very warm regions but in colder climes must be

217

Nestled comfortably around rocks and beneath a blooming mountain laurel, dainty sweet woodruff and spotted lungwort (lower left), glossy wild ginger (lower right), and the blue-green arrowhead-shaped leaves of astilbe (right), create an arresting combination of perennials in this Connecticut garden.

treated as an annual. Coleus flaunts a wide range of foliage colors, including solids or mixtures of salmon, pink, red, maroon, chartreuse, yellow, and bronze. Dwarf varieties grow to about 6 inches tall, with leaves as small as an inch long; others may reach 36 inches, with leaves from 3 to 6 inches long. Leaf texture may be velvety to crinkled, with smooth, scalloped, or serrated edges.

Put the dwarf varieties to work in the front of a shady border. The larger varieties look handsome combined with tall ferns, which help isolate the multiple bold colors. Because of the diversity of color and textures, coleus is an excellent plant to combine with other shade plants to create your own unique plant marriages. Try a pink-leaved coleus next to the deep purple foliage of *Heuchera micrantha* 'Palace Purple', or combine a red or maroon specimen with a blue hosta.

Coleus does best in indirect light or light shade. Pinch back the stems in early summer to encourage bushy growth, and remove the inconspicuous flower spikes that emerge throughout the summer. This will help the plant focus its energy on foliage production.

You can create an unusual specimen by training a potted coleus as a standard. Remove side growth to encourage the plant to grow a tall stem and to leaf out on top. The plants are easy to propagate from cuttings in either water or a rooting medium, so you can reproduce your present inventory—and even increase your supply—by taking cuttings in autumn and overwintering them indoors.

Woodland Foliage Plants

A woodland setting is a shade gardener's paradise, for this is the natural habitat for many of the shade-loving species. It presents a classic opportunity to create a foliage garden that is not only in tune with nature but also complements it by adding a measure of order and design. Many woodland plants have an exquisite but ephemeral bloom season; their foliage is the dominant feature for the rest of the growing season. Think in terms of massing and combining plants to produce a pleasing flow of foliage color and texture in the woods.

Ornamental Grasses for Shade

Although the list of ornamental grasses for full shade is not long, you should be able to find something to meet your needs. One of the best is *Hakonechloa macra* 'Aureola' (golden variegated hakonechloa), shown above tucked in next to a hosta and beneath a blue spruce. Hardy in Zones 5 to 9, it grows in clumps 16 inches tall and 18 to 24 inches wide. Other grasses that do well in full shade include *Carex* (sedge) and *Deschampsia caespitosa* (tufted hair grass). For partial shade, try *Miscanthus sinensis* 'Variegatus' (eulalia) or *Chasmanthium latifolium* (northern sea oats). *Liriope* (lilyturf) works well along shady borders.

Some of the woodland plants, such as Virginia bluebells, *Dicentra*, and Dutchman's-breeches, have pretty foliage and flowers in spring, but then die back in early summer. Combine them with plants such as columbine, ferns, hostas, and Solomon's-seal, which will fill in the bare spots created by the summer-dormant woodland plants.

For a fascinating foliage mix, combine *Trillium erectum* (purple trillium), with its whorl of three leaves on a 6- to 18-inch tall stem; *Tiarella cordifolia* (foamflower), which spreads over the ground by runners; *Sanguinaria* (bloodroot), another colonizing plant with rounded, shallow-lobed pale green leaves; *Viola* (violet); Solomon's-seal; and *Clintonia borealis* (corn lily), which grows clusters of oval leaves about 6 inches long.

Another attractive woodland composition is achieved by joining purple trillium with *Asarum canadense* (wild ginger), a ground cover with velvety heart-shaped medium green leaves, and *Aquilegia canadensis* (wild columbine). Equally admirable—and unusual—is *Podophyllum* (May apple). On each stem is one broad, deeply lobed leaf that opens each spring like an umbrella. The foliage carpets the ground until midsummer, when it withers and dies back. As an encore to the May apple, interplant *Galium odoratum* (sweet woodruff). It doesn't mind the deep shade under the May apples, and it will provide a pretty green cover when they are gone. For information on which woodland species will do best in your area, contact local botanical gardens, arboretums, nursery and garden centers, and local plant societies.

The mottled magenta-and-lime-green foliage of a St. Louis, Missouri, planting of Coleus 'Bellingrath Pink' assumes the role of a floral accent next to the lacy bluish green leaves of Pelargonium denticulatum (fern-leaf geranium).

Answers to Common Questions

I have many garden ideas for different parts of my property, but I have a hard time visualizing how they might all fit together. How can I work them out?

Go out into the landscape and try them. Place tall stakes where you think you would like trees; use hose, string, or powdered lime to define lawn shapes, paths, and beds; string up lines to represent fencing; spread out sheets or blankets where you might like a small paved area. Set outdoor furniture in places where you might want seating. Then look at these elements from different angles and keep making adjustments until you feel satisfied.

I don't intend to develop my whole property. Do I really need a plan for the entire area before I start a small front garden?

Making a cohesive plan for the whole property is essential, even if you don't expect to carry it all out or may change the plan later on. Individual projects like the front garden might end up well, but the cumulative effect of such efforts may not be fully satisfactory unless you have an overall plan.

Why do designers recommend looking at a garden in winter to determine what needs improvement?

Professionals see the garden first as a visual and spatial composition, and only secondarily as a collection of plants and garden elements. During warmer months the allure of foliage and flowers can distract a gardener from possible weaknesses in the composition. In winter it's easier to see plants as shapes or silhouettes and judge them in relation to other shapes (buildings, paving, walls) in the garden.

I've recently bought an older home with a rather boring landscape. I can't afford to redo the entire property at once. How can I phase the garden development over a period of, say, 5 years? In what order should I proceed?

Spend the first year getting to know your garden. Keep a notebook to record such data as when the plants bloom and how the sun strikes different areas throughout the day and in different seasons. Test the soil, and begin correcting any deficiencies. Bring in an arborist to evaluate the trees. The autumn and winter of the first year is a good time for removing diseased or poorly placed trees and planting new ones. The second year, put your money into "hardscape" items—an irrigation system, if needed, and patios, walkways, retaining walls, and fences. Protect trees during the construction process by surrounding the root zone with temporary fencing. Concentrate on shrubbery during the third year, thinning, transplanting, and adding color and texture. Use the fourth year to establish herbaceous beds. By the fifth year you should be ready to add the finishing touches—a sundial, perhaps, or garden art to serve as focal points.

I have planted different gardens in our large suburban lot over the years, but now I don't have the time to keep up all the areas as well as I would like to. How can I revamp the gardens so they will look good with less maintenance?

Categorize the different garden areas according to the levels of maintenance needed to keep each looking good: intensive, moderate, or casual. Are the intensive areas too many, too scattered, and too far away to be noticed or enjoyed? If so, concentrate your efforts where they matter. Let the farther reaches revert to woodland. Turn a mixed border into a low-maintenance shrub border. Replace a struggling woodland garden with a hardy ground cover. Put your main effort into pruning for shape a few key specimen trees and shrubs and intensively maintaining a close-in flower border.

I loved a planting scheme I saw in a garden book, but when I tried to copy it in my garden it didn't look right. How can I tell what will work in my garden?

Apart from incompatible cultural requirements among plants, the most common cause for an unsuccessful duplication of a garden scheme in another location is the difference in scale, proportion, and conformation of the surrounding space. When you see a design that you like, check to determine whether the setting of the locale where you want to duplicate it is similar to that of the original. You're almost certain to be disappointed, for example, if you pick out an arrangement set against a fenced-in corner for reproduction at the edge of a lawn opening onto woods.

DESIGN

I like formal garden styles, but I've heard that informal gardens require less maintenance. Is that true?

Formality or informality does not determine maintenance requirements. Whatever the style, complex garden patterns and intricate plant combinations take considerable effort to keep all the parts in balance. On the other hand, a simple ground shape like an oval lawn or a square terrace imparts a sense of formal order that can carry a casually maintained planting. A strong horizontal line like a wall, fence, or clipped hedge does the same thing on the vertical plane. And bold sweeps or groups will always look neater than a hodgepodge of unrelated materials scattered all over.

I was surprised to find on my trip to England that many houses there do not have foundation plantings. What is the purpose of foundation plantings, and are they really needed?

Foundation plantings gained widespread popularity in America during the Victorian era. Heavy evergreen shrubs helped stabilize the bulk of the then-new style of large Victorian houses. Foundation plantings have since acquired a life of their own and are used indiscriminately even when not needed. They are useful for hiding an ugly foundation, or when a house lacks a stable base of level ground, or when a softer transition is needed between house and ground. Otherwise, they are neither necessary nor desirable.

Many design books emphasize the importance of shape and mass in planting design, but I can't seem to get past the flower colors when I am making plant arrangements. How can I begin to see plants the way designers see them?

To see shape only, first try to look at your plant groupings as if they were all one color. Use a black-and-white photocopy of a garden view and trace an outline of trees, shrubs, and groups of smaller plants in the picture. Don't try to follow the outline shape in detail; generalize as much as possible, so that you end up with a diagram of circles, ovals, cones, horizontal lines, and so on. If the diagram turns out to be a series of boring circles, try adding vertical spikes or a taller cone shape to vary the composition. Once you have hit upon a pleasing combination of shapes, use this as the basis for working out a detailed planting plan, into which you can introduce texture and color.

I need immediate screening from my neighbors. Should I put in a fence along my property line?

This only makes sense when you want to mark your property or keep out intruders and animals. A more effective way of screening unwanted views is to place a fence or screen where it gives you the greatest protection. On a sloping lot, for example, a screen placed at the edge of an elevated terrace will be more effective than one at the property line, where you may be able to see over the fence from where you sit. Also, fences and screens are expensive garden elements, and you should take full advantage of their architectural features by locating them where you gain the most from the definition they provide, as near a terrace.

The only cool side of our house on summer evenings is the front yard. Is there any way we can make this into a quiet and private sitting area?

There's no rule that says a patio must open only off a back or side door. A front courtyard can be a wonderful place for dining outdoors or for reading the paper, and it can create a pleasant vista from a sitting room or dining room. If local building codes permit, you could build a walled front courtyard in a style that is compatible with the architecture of the house. In your planning, consider wind patterns, the effects of rain, cooling breezes, and drainage. If solid walls are not feasible, put in accent trees and shrubs of varying sizes and perhaps a section of decorative fencing. Complete the area with attractive furniture, add a small fountain to drown out traffic noises, and decorate with lots of colorful plants in containers.

Should a garden have a color scheme?

Yes. Nature can get away with combining every imaginable color in a wildflower meadow, but gardeners may ruin a landscape with clashing hues. One possible scheme is to repeat the colors of your living and dining rooms in the landscape. The colors of the exterior of your house are also important to consider in selecting a color theme for your garden. For example, if you have an orange brick house, avoid hot pinks or reds in favor of predominantly white-flowering trees, shrubs, and perennials, perhaps combined with blues, yellows, purples, and peachy tones. Against a neutral-colored house it's hard to go wrong with a pastel garden in tones of pink, with blue, yellow, and white accents. A bright red or an orange theme goes beautifully with a white house. If the house is dark or the site is heavily wooded, brighten it with lots of white and yellow.

CONSTRUCTION

The back of my lot slopes down so steeply from my house that the soil is washing away. I want to terrace the land for planters, but I'm concerned because the area is large and I might be creating a monster in terms of maintenance. What do you suggest?

Why not terrace the upper portion closest to your house and clothe the lower part in shrubs and ground covers? Plants with dense root systems, such as cotoneaster, *Hypericum calycinum* (St.-John's-wort), or juniper, will help prevent erosion. You would be well advised to call a landscape architect to prepare a plan for the terraced portion. A professional can help you select the most cost-effective material for a retaining wall and can engineer the wall to stand up to the force of soil and water pushing against it.

We plan to lay a new driveway and walkway, doing the work ourselves. We're trying to decide between natural brick and concrete pavers. What are the advantages and disadvantages of each? What should we know to do a professional job?

For residential use, the look of natural, or fired-clay, brick is generally preferable to that of concrete pavers. And both materials cost about the same, so for walkways and patios alone there's no real advantage in using pavers. A driveway is a different story. If you want to pave it in clay bricks you will need a reinforced concrete base, which may require hiring skilled labor, whereas interlocking concrete pavers need only a sand base that you can lay down yourselves. Thus, if you want the driveway and walkways to have the same surface, concrete pavers become the more cost-effective choice. Walkways should be laid with a slight crown along the center to shed water. Where they adjoin planting beds, lay them slightly higher than the soil level so that soil and mulches won't wash out onto the paving every time it rains. Slope all walks away from the house. Put down a layer of polyethylene or roofing felt before laying in the sand to reduce the chance of vegetation growing up between any cracks that may develop over the years.

We will be moving into a new house that is under construction. We want to plan for a garden, but cannot do it all right now. What should we do first?

Apart from having a plan, the most important first step is to grade the land to the contours you want while the equipment is still on site. This is the time to create flat spots for lawns or terraces, to shape the ground so that the house sits gracefully on it instead of perching awkwardly. Once the grading is done, you can add plantings and hardscape elements gradually over time.

PLANTS

We have a plan for our backyard that includes a flowering shrub border backed by an evergreen hedge. But we can't afford to execute the design with all large plants. How can we stay within our budget and still get some immediate effect?

It would be a mistake to try to spread out your budget evenly and compromise on the size of all the plants in your design. Instead, start off with a few large plants to carry the design until the rest grow in. Buy the hedge plants in larger sizes so that you get an effective backdrop right away. Buy moderate-size plants of a few key shrubs that form a corner. The rest can be started out very small.

What are some good trees to plant in front of a new two-story townhouse on a very small lot?

Choose deep-rooted species; avoid such trees as sweet gum and Norway maple, which have greedy, shallow roots that compete with nearby shrubbery and make it impossible to grow grass. In the past few years nurseries have introduced several narrow-crowned, upright selections of familiar shade trees suitable for use in small gardens and as street plantings. Trees with less than a 15-foot spread include *Pyrus calleryana* 'Chanticleer' (Callery pear), pyramidal *Carpinus betulus* 'Fastigiata' (European hornbeam), *Quercus robur* 'Fastigiata' (English oak), or one of the several red maples selected for upright form, such as *Acer rubrum* 'Armstrong'.

How can I design for the most bloom in my perennial border?

First, make sure your border is large enough—at least 5 feet deep—to contain three tiers of plants for the front, middle, and back. Choose plants for a sequence of bloom over a long period, making sure that there will always be something in flower. Choose perennials with long bloom periods, and plant them in overlapping horizontal drifts rather than in blocks so the nonflowering gaps will look less obvious. Use annuals to fill in spaces left by plants whose foliage dies back after bloom. If you don't have room for a large bed, choose plants for a limited flowering season rather than diffusing the effect by trying to spread bloom over a longer period.

I have a tiny city garden that is walled in on all sides with almost no planting space around the patio. How can I make it a year-round garden that is full of plants that bloom in succession?

If you can't go outward go up: Plant the space thickly with climbers. Combine vines, so that when one is finished, another will bloom—for example, a planting of *Clematis montana,* 'New Dawn' climbing roses, and *Clematis paniculata (C. maximowicziana)* to cover spring, summer, and fall. Use bold foliage plants like *Yucca filamentosa* and *Mahonia bealei* for accents. Make a dense evergreen background by planting ivies or *Clematis armandii*. On the patio, set pots of annuals and bulbs in groups or arrange them on a baker's rack so you gain even more planting space.

Troubleshooting Guide

Even the most carefully tended beds and borders can fall prey to pests and diseases. To keep them in check, regularly inspect your plants for warning signs. Lack of nutrients, improper pH levels, and other environmental conditions may cause symptoms that could be confused with disease. If wilting or yellowing appears on neighboring plants, the source is probably environmental; pest and disease damage is usually more random.

This guide is intended to help identify and solve most of your pest and disease problems. In general, proper drainage, fertile soil, and good air circulation help prevent diseases. To aid in controlling pests, consider using any of the common beneficial insects, such as ladybugs and lacewings, that prey on pests. Natural solutions to garden problems are best. For persistent infestations, use horticultural oils, insecticidal soaps, and neem tree-based insecticides; these products are the least disruptive to beneficial insects and will not destroy the soil balance that is the foundation of a healthy garden. If you must use chemicals, treat only the affected plant.

PESTS

PROBLEM: Leaves curl, are distorted, and may be sticky and have a black, sooty appearance. Buds and flowers are deformed, new growth is stunted, and leaves and flowers may drop.

CAUSE: Aphids are pear-shaped, semitransparent, sucking insects about ⅛ inch long, and range in color from green to red, pink, black, or gray. Aphids suck plant sap, and in so doing may spread viral disease. Infestations are most severe in spring and early summer, when the pests cluster on new shoots, undersides of leaves, and around flower buds. Winged forms appear when colonies become overcrowded. Aphids secrete a sticky substance known as honeydew onto leaves. This substance fosters the growth of a black fungus called sooty mold.

SOLUTION: Spray plants frequently with a steady stream of water from a garden hose to knock aphids off plants and discourage them from returning. In severe cases, prune infested areas, and use a diluted insecticidal soap solution or a recommended insecticide. Ladybugs and lacewings, which eat aphids, may be introduced into the garden. *SUSCEPTIBLE PLANTS: MANY, AND IN ALL CATEGORIES, BUT INFESTATIONS ARE USUALLY LIMITED TO THE SOFT STEMS AND LEAVES OF NEW GROWTH.*

PROBLEM: Holes appear in leaves, buds, and flowers; entire leaves and stems also may be eaten.

CAUSE: Caterpillars, including the larvae of violet sawfly, verbena bud moth, sunflower moth, and painted lady butterfly, come in a variety of shapes and colors, and can be smooth, hairy, or spiny. These voracious pests are found in gardens in spring and summer.

SOLUTION: Handpick to control small populations. The bacterial pesticide Bacillus thuringiensis (Bt) kills many types without harming beneficial insects. If caterpillars return to your garden every spring, spray Bt as a preventive measure. Identify the caterpillar species to determine the control options and timing of spray applications. Introduce beneficial insects that prey on caterpillars, including spined soldier bugs, assassin bugs, minute pirate bugs, and lacewings. *SUSCEPTIBLE PLANTS: ANNUALS AND PERENNIALS, ESPECIALLY TENDER NEW SHOOTS.*

PROBLEM: Ragged or neat, round holes are eaten into leaves, leaf edges, and flowers. Leaves may be reduced to skeletons with only veins remaining.

CAUSE: Japanese beetles, iridescent blue-green with bronze wing covers, are the most destructive of a large family of hard-shelled chewing insects ranging in size from ¼ to ¾ inch long. Other genera include Asiatic garden beetles (brown), northern masked chafers (brown with dark band on head), and Fuller rose beetles (gray), as well as blister beetles (metallic black, blue, purple, or brown), and flea beetles (shiny dark blue, brown, black, or bronze). Adult beetles are voracious in summer. Larvae (white grubs) feed on plant roots from midsummer through the next spring, when they emerge as adults.

SOLUTION: Handpick small colonies, placing them in a can filled with soapy water. (Caution: Use gloves when picking blister beetles.) Japanese beetles can be caught in baited traps. Place traps in an area away from susceptible plants so as not to attract more beetles into the garden. The larval stage can be controlled with milky spore disease, which can be applied to the whole yard. For heavy infestations, contact your local Cooperative Extension Service. *SUSCEPTIBLE PLANTS: ASTILBE, AZALEA, CLEMATIS, FOXGLOVE, HOLLYHOCK, NEW YORK ASTER, PURPLE CONEFLOWER, ROSE, AND ROSE MALLOW.*

PROBLEM: White or light green tunnels are bored through leaves; older tunnels turn black. Leaves may lose color, dry up, and die. Seedlings may be stunted or die.

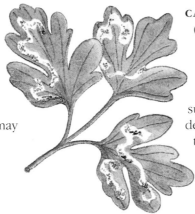

CAUSE: Leaf miners—minute (¹⁄₁₆ to ⅛ inch long), translucent, pale green larvae of certain flies, moths, or beetles—are hatched from eggs laid on plant leaves. During spring and summer, the larvae eat the tender interior below the surface of the leaf, leaving behind serpentine trails of blistered tissue known as mines.

SOLUTION: Damage may be unsightly but is usually not lethal. Pick off and destroy infested leaves as they appear. In the fall, cut the plant to the ground and discard stalks. Do not compost. Remove and destroy leaves with egg clusters. Keep the garden well weeded. Inspect plants before purchase and do not buy any with trails in leaves. *SUSCEPTIBLE PLANTS: MANY ANNUALS AND PERENNIALS, ESPECIALLY COLUMBINE; MANY SHRUBS, INCLUDING AMERICAN HOLLY.*

PROBLEM: Leaves become stippled or flecked, then discolor, turning yellow or nearly white with brown edges; the leaves of some shrubs become speckled with gray. Entire leaves may turn yellow or bronze and curl. Flowers and buds discolor or dry up. Webbing may be seen on undersides of leaves and on the branches of shrubs. Growth is stunted; leaves may drop.

CAUSE: Mites are pinhead-size, spider-like sucking pests that can be reddish, pale green, or yellow. These insects can become a major problem in hot, dry weather when several generations of mites may occur in a single season. Adults of some species hibernate over the winter in sod, in bark, and on weeds and plants that retain foliage.

SOLUTION: Damage is worst to plants in full sunlight and hot areas. Detect by gently shaking branch or leaf over paper; if dust moves, it's mites. Keep plants watered and mulched. Regularly spray the undersides of leaves, where mites feed and lay eggs, using water or a diluted soap solution. Horticultural oils also may be applied to undersides. Insecticidal soaps control nymphs and adults but not eggs. Introduce natural predators such as green lacewing larvae. *SUSCEPTIBLE PLANTS: MANY PERENNIALS, INCLUDING ROSE, DAYLILY, GARDEN PHLOX, AND IRIS; ANNUALS SUCH AS ZINNIA AND SALVIA; SHRUBS SUCH AS AZALEA, BOXWOOD, AND JUNIPER; ELM, HOLLY, FIR, AND PINE TREES.*

PROBLEM: Ragged holes appear in leaves, especially those near the ground. New leaves and entire young seedlings may be eaten. Telltale shiny silver streaks appear on leaves and garden paths.

CAUSE: Slugs and snails are serious pests in the shade garden, favoring such an environment over hot, sunny conditions. They prefer damp, cool locations and are most damaging in summer, especially in wet regions or during rainy years.

SOLUTION: Keep the garden clean to minimize hiding places. Handpick, or trap them by placing saucers of beer near plants. Slugs also will collect under citrus or melon rinds. Salt kills slugs and snails but may damage plants. Strips of coarse sand, cinders, or copper garden edging placed around beds, or small amounts of diatomaceous earth worked in around new transplants will deter both slugs and snails. Spading in spring destroys dormant slugs and eggs. *SUSCEPTIBLE PLANTS: VIRTUALLY ALL, PARTICULARLY THOSE WITH YOUNG OR TENDER FOLIAGE. HOSTAS ARE ESPECIALLY SUSCEPTIBLE. NOTE: CHOOSE LESS SUSCEPTIBLE PLANTS, INCLUDING CORAL BELLS, HELLEBORE, AND LUNGWORT.*

DISEASES

PROBLEM: Foliage develops irregular, yellow to purplish brown spots that darken with age. These spots also may expand and join to cover the leaves. Leaves turn brown and drop. Purplish lesions form along stems, and plant growth is often stunted.

CAUSE: Anthracnose is a fungus disease that is especially severe in wet weather.

SOLUTION: Grow resistant varieties. Thin stems and tops to improve air circulation, and water plants from below to keep the disease from spreading. Remove and destroy infected plants. For trees, prune deadwood and water sprouts. Water during dry spells and keep the root zone mulched to prevent drought stress. To keep a severe infection from spreading, spray plants with a fungicide according to directions while new leaves are growing in spring. *SUSCEPTIBLE PLANTS: PEONY, ROSE, AND SHRUBS, MANY TREES, INCLUDING ASH, BOX ELDER, DOGWOOD, ELM, MAPLE, AND OAK.*

PROBLEM: A brownish gray moldy growth appears on flowers and foliage. Stalks are weak and flowers and foliage droop. Buds may not open. Discolored blotches appear on leaves, stems, and flowers. Stem bases rot. Plant parts eventually turn brown and dry up. Flowering plants are most often affected.

CAUSE: Botrytis blight, known as gray mold, thrives in moist air and cool temperatures, survives winter in the soil or on dead plants, and spreads on wind or water.

SOLUTION: Limit watering to early in the day and avoid overhead watering. Place plants in well-drained soil, and thin to provide more light and air. Cut and destroy all infected plant parts. Spray plants with Bordeaux mixture. *SUSCEPTIBLE PLANTS: FLOWERING PLANTS ARE MOST AT RISK, INCLUDING RHODODENDRON, HELLEBORE, LILY, ROSE, AND TULIP.*

PROBLEM: Leaves develop small yellow, brown, or black spots that are surrounded by a rim of discolored tissue. Spots often join to produce large, irregular blotches. Entire leaf may turn yellow, wilt, and drop. Spotting usually starts on lower leaves and moves upward.

CAUSE: The many leaf-spot diseases are caused by a number of fungi or bacteria. All are particularly severe in wet weather because they are spread by splashing water.

SOLUTION: Clean up all fallen leaves before winter. Water overhead only in the morning, as damp foliage in cool night air encourages spreading of the diseases. Prune and destroy infected leaves of perennials and shrubs. A fungicide can protect healthy foliage but will not destroy fungus on infected leaves. *SUSCEPTIBLE PLANTS: ALL TYPES OF PLANTS.*

PROBLEM: Leaves are covered with spots or a thin layer of grayish white powdery material. Infected parts may distort and curl, then turn yellow or purplish; leaves may finally drop off. Badly infected buds will not open properly.

CAUSE: Powdery mildews are fungus diseases that thrive when nights are cool and days are hot and humid. The diseases are most noticeable in late summer and fall, and at times when plant growth is vigorous.

SOLUTION: Plant mildew-resistant varieties. Susceptible plants should receive full sun with good air circulation. Water overhead only in the early morning. In the fall, cut infected perennials to the ground and discard. Do not compost. Spray a solution of 1 teaspoon baking soda and ¼ teaspoon summer horticultural oil to 1 gallon water every 5 to 7 days until symptoms disappear. *SUSCEPTIBLE PLANTS: MANY PERENNIALS; YOUNG GROWTH OF MANY WOODY PLANTS, ESPECIALLY ROSE, LILAC, AND EUONYMUS.*

PROBLEM: Upper leaf surfaces have pale yellow or white spots, and undersides are covered with orange or yellow pustules. Leaves wilt or shrivel and hang down along the stem, but do not drop off. Pustules may become more numerous, destroying leaves and occasionally the entire plant. Plants may be stunted.

CAUSE: Rust, a fungus disease, is a problem in late summer and early fall and is most prevalent when nights are cool and humid. Rust spores are spread easily by wind and splashing water and overwinter on infected plant parts.

SOLUTION: Buy rust-resistant varieties whenever possible. Water early in the day and avoid wetting leaves. Remove and destroy infected plant parts in the fall and again in the spring. Do not compost. Spray with sulfur, lime sulfur, or Bordeaux mixture—a traditional antifungal treatment first used in vineyards. *SUSCEPTIBLE PLANTS: VIRTUALLY ALL.*

PROBLEM: Plants suddenly lose color, turn yellow, and wilt. Stems and branches may die back, or the whole plant may die. Roots are damaged or deformed and have knotty growths and swellings.

CAUSE: Soil nematodes—colorless microscopic worms that live in the soil and feed on plant roots—inhibit a plant's intake of nitrogen. Damage is at its worst in warm, moist soils. Nematodes overwinter in infected roots or soil and are spread by soil transplants and tools.

SOLUTION: Only a laboratory test will confirm the presence of soil nematodes. Be suspicious if roots are swollen or stunted. There are no chemical controls; dispose of infected plants and the soil that surrounds them, or solarize the soil. Plant resistant species and cultivars. Add nitrogen fertilizer. *SUSCEPTIBLE PLANTS: VIRTUALLY ALL.*

Plant Selection Guide

Organized by plant type, this chart provides information needed to select species and varieties that will thrive in the particular conditions of your garden. For additional information on each plant, refer to the encyclopedia that begins on page 238.

	ZONES	SOIL		LIGHT			BLOOM SEASON				PLANT HEIGHT					Form	NOTED FOR			
		Dry	Moist	Full sun	Partial shade	Shade	Spring	Summer	Fall	Winter	Under 3 ft.	3-6 ft.	6-10 ft.	10-20 ft.	Over 20 ft.	Form	Foliage	Flowers	Fruit/seeds	Bark/twigs
PERENNIALS AND GRASSES																				
Artemisia x *'Powis Castle'*	5-8	✔		✔							✔						✔			
Bergenia cordifolia	3-8		✔	✔	✔		✔				✔						✔	✔		
Calamagrostis acutiflora 'Stricta'	6-9	✔	✔	✔				✔				✔				✔	✔	✔		
Cyrtomium falcatum	8-10		✔		✔	✔					✔					✔	✔			
Fargesia murielae	5-9	✔	✔		✔									✔		✔	✔			
Helleborus niger	4-8		✔		✔					✔	✔						✔	✔		
Hemerocallis 'Stella d'Oro'	4-9	✔	✔	✔	✔			✔	✔		✔							✔		
Heuchera micrantha 'Palace Purple'	4-8		✔	✔	✔			✔			✔						✔			
Hosta 'Krossa Regal'	3-9		✔		✔	✔		✔				✔				✔	✔			
Iris sibirica 'Caesar's Brother'	3-9		✔	✔	✔			✔				✔				✔	✔	✔		
Lavandula angustifolia	5-9	✔		✔				✔			✔						✔	✔		
Lavandula stoechas	8-10	✔		✔				✔			✔						✔	✔		
Miscanthus sinensis 'Zebrinus'	5-9		✔	✔					✔				✔			✔	✔	✔		
Pennisetum setaceum 'Rubrum'	8-10	✔	✔	✔				✔			✔					✔	✔	✔		
Potentilla nepalensis 'Miss Wilmott'	5-7	✔	✔	✔	✔			✔			✔						✔	✔		
Rudbeckia fulgida 'Goldsturm'	3-9		✔	✔	✔	✔		✔	✔		✔							✔		
Sedum x *'Autumn Joy'*	3-10	✔		✔	✔	✔		✔	✔		✔					✔	✔	✔		
GROUND COVERS																				
Calluna vulgaris 'Mrs. Ronald Gray'	4-7		✔	✔	✔			✔			✔					✔	✔	✔		
Ceanothus griseus var. *horizontalis*	8-10	✔		✔				✔			✔							✔		
Cotoneaster dammeri 'Skogholm'	5-8	✔	✔	✔	✔		✔				✔					✔	✔			
Cotoneaster salicifolius 'Autumn Fire'	6-8	✔	✔	✔	✔		✔				✔					✔	✔	✔	✔	
Erica carnea 'Springwood Pink'	6-9		✔	✔	✔					✔	✔							✔		
Euonymus fortunei 'Colorata'	4-9	✔	✔	✔	✔	✔					✔						✔			
Hypericum calycinum	5-9	✔		✔	✔			✔	✔		✔							✔		
Juniperus horizontalis 'Wiltonii'	3-9	✔	✔	✔							✔					✔	✔			
Juniperus procumbens	3-9	✔	✔	✔							✔						✔			
Liriope muscari 'Variegata'	7-10	✔	✔	✔	✔	✔		✔			✔						✔	✔	✔	
Mahonia repens	5-10		✔		✔	✔					✔						✔	✔	✔	

	ZONES	SOIL		LIGHT			BLOOM SEASON				PLANT HEIGHT					NOTED FOR				
		Dry	Moist	Full sun	Partial shade	Shade	Spring	Summer	Fall	Winter	Under 3 ft.	3-6 ft.	6-10 ft.	10-20 ft.	Over 20 ft.	Form	Foliage	Flowers	Fruit/seeds	Bark/twigs
VINES																				
Clematis armandii	7-9		✓	✓	✓		✓							✓			✓	✓		
Clematis paniculata	5-8		✓	✓	✓				✓						✓			✓		
Gelsemium sempervirens	6-9		✓	✓	✓		✓							✓				✓		
Hydrangea anomala ssp. *petiolaris*	4-7		✓	✓	✓	✓	✓								✓			✓		✓
Ipomoea alba	10		✓					✓	✓					✓				✓		
Lonicera heckrottii	4-9	✓	✓	✓	✓			✓						✓				✓		
Rosa 'New Dawn'	3-10		✓	✓				✓						✓				✓		
Wisteria floribunda	4-9	✓	✓	✓			✓								✓			✓		
DECIDUOUS SHRUBS																				
Abelia x *'Edward Goucher'*	6-10		✓	✓	✓			✓	✓			✓					✓	✓		
Acer palmatum 'Dissectum'	5-8		✓	✓	✓		✓						✓			✓	✓			✓
Berberis thunbergii 'Crimson Pygmy'	4-8	✓	✓	✓			✓				✓						✓		✓	
Chaenomeles speciosa 'Cameo'	4-8	✓	✓	✓			✓					✓						✓	✓	
Cotinus coggygria 'Velvet Cloak'	5-8	✓	✓	✓				✓						✓			✓	✓	✓	
Enkianthus campanulatus	4-7		✓	✓	✓		✓						✓				✓	✓		
Euonymus alata 'Compacta'	5-8	✓	✓	✓	✓	✓	✓						✓				✓		✓	✓
Forsythia x *intermedia 'Spectabilis'*	6-9	✓	✓	✓			✓						✓			✓		✓		
Hamamelis x *intermedia 'Arnold Promise'*	5-8		✓	✓	✓					✓				✓			✓	✓		
Hydrangea arborescens 'Annabelle'	3-9		✓	✓	✓	✓		✓				✓						✓		
Jasminum nudiflorum	6-10	✓	✓	✓	✓					✓		✓					✓	✓		✓
Lagerstroemia indica 'Seminole'	7-10		✓	✓				✓					✓				✓	✓		✓
Ligustrum ovalifolium 'Aureum'	5-10	✓	✓	✓	✓			✓						✓			✓	✓	✓	
Myrica pensylvanica	3-7	✓	✓	✓	✓		✓						✓				✓		✓	
Potentilla fruticosa 'Klondike'	3-7	✓	✓	✓	✓			✓	✓		✓						✓	✓		
Punica granatum 'Legrellei'	8-10		✓	✓	✓			✓						✓				✓	✓	
Rhododendron mucronulatum	4-7		✓		✓					✓	✓	✓					✓	✓		
Rhododendron schlippenbachii	4-7		✓		✓		✓						✓				✓	✓		
Rosa rugosa 'Hansa'	3-7		✓	✓				✓				✓					✓	✓	✓	
Spiraea x *bumalda 'Gold Flame'*	3-8		✓	✓	✓			✓			✓						✓	✓		
Stewartia ovata	5-9		✓	✓	✓			✓						✓			✓	✓		✓
Syringa patula 'Miss Kim'	3-8		✓	✓			✓					✓					✓	✓		
Viburnum plicatum var. *tomentosum*	5-8		✓	✓	✓		✓						✓			✓	✓	✓	✓	
Vitex agnus-castus 'Rosea'	7-9		✓	✓				✓	✓				✓	✓				✓		

	ZONES	SOIL		LIGHT			BLOOM SEASON				PLANT HEIGHT					NOTED FOR				
		Dry	Moist	Full sun	Partial shade	Shade	Spring	Summer	Fall	Winter	Under 3 ft.	3-6 ft.	6-10 ft.	10-20 ft.	Over 20 ft.	Form	Foliage	Flowers	Fruit/seeds	Bark/twigs
EVERGREEN SHRUBS																				
Aucuba japonica 'Variegata'	7-10		✓		✓	✓	✓						✓				✓		✓	
Berberis buxifolia var. *nana*	5-8		✓	✓	✓	✓	✓				✓						✓	✓	✓	
Berberis julianae	5-8		✓	✓	✓	✓	✓						✓				✓	✓	✓	
Chamaecyparis obtusa 'Nana Gracilis'	4-8		✓	✓	✓							✓				✓	✓			
Cistus x *hybridus*	8-10	✓		✓			✓					✓					✓	✓		
Cistus x *purpureus*	8-10	✓		✓				✓				✓						✓		
Cotoneaster salicifolius	6-8		✓	✓	✓		✓							✓		✓	✓		✓	
Eriobotrya japonica	8-10		✓	✓	✓				✓					✓	✓		✓		✓	
Escallonia x *langleyensis* 'Apple Blossom'	8-10	✓	✓	✓			✓	✓	✓			✓					✓	✓		
Euonymus fortunei 'Emerald Gaiety'	5-9	✓	✓	✓	✓	✓	✓					✓				✓	✓			
Fatsia japonica	8-10		✓		✓			✓					✓				✓	✓	✓	
Hebe 'Autumn Glory'	8-10	✓		✓				✓	✓		✓						✓	✓		
Ilex cornuta 'Berries Jubilee'	7-9		✓	✓	✓		✓						✓				✓		✓	
Juniperus chinensis 'Mint Julep'	3-9	✓	✓	✓								✓				✓	✓			
Ligustrum japonicum	7-10	✓	✓	✓	✓	✓	✓						✓	✓			✓	✓	✓	
Mahonia bealei	7-10		✓			✓				✓			✓				✓	✓	✓	
Nandina domestica 'Harbour Dwarf'	6-9		✓	✓	✓	✓	✓				✓					✓	✓	✓	✓	
Picea abies 'Nidiformis'	3-7		✓	✓	✓						✓					✓	✓			
Pieris japonica 'Variegata'	5-8		✓	✓	✓	✓	✓					✓	✓			✓	✓	✓		
Pittosporum tobira	8-10	✓	✓	✓	✓	✓	✓						✓				✓			
Prunus laurocerasus 'Otto Luyken'	6-10		✓	✓	✓		✓					✓					✓	✓		
Raphiolepis indica	9-10		✓	✓			✓					✓					✓	✓		
Rhododendron 'Scarlet Wonder'	6-8		✓		✓	✓	✓				✓						✓	✓		
Rosmarinus officinalis 'Lockwood de Forest'	7-10	✓	✓	✓	✓		✓		✓	✓	✓					✓	✓	✓		
Viburnum davidii	8-9		✓	✓	✓		✓				✓						✓	✓	✓	
DECIDUOUS TREES																				
Acer griseum	4-8		✓	✓	✓		✓							✓			✓			✓
Acer rubrum 'October Glory'	3-9		✓	✓	✓		✓								✓		✓			✓
Betula nigra	4-9		✓	✓	✓		✓								✓	✓				✓
Carpinus betulus 'Columnaris'	4-7	✓	✓	✓	✓		✓								✓	✓	✓			✓
Chilopsis linearis	8-10	✓		✓			✓							✓	✓		✓	✓		
Cladrastis kentukea	4-8	✓	✓	✓			✓								✓	✓	✓	✓		✓
Cornus alternifolia	3-7		✓	✓	✓		✓							✓	✓	✓		✓	✓	

DECIDUOUS TREES

	ZONES	SOIL		LIGHT			BLOOM SEASON				PLANT HEIGHT					NOTED FOR				
		Dry	Moist	Full sun	Partial shade	Shade	Spring	Summer	Fall	Winter	Under 3 ft.	3-6 ft.	6-10 ft.	10-20 ft.	Over 20 ft.	Form	Foliage	Flowers	Fruit/seeds	Bark/twigs
Cornus kousa var. *chinensis*	5-8		✓	✓	✓		✓	✓							✓	✓	✓	✓	✓	✓
Fagus sylvatica 'Aurea Pendula'	4-7		✓	✓	✓		✓								✓	✓	✓			✓
Fraxinus americana 'Champaign County'	3-9	✓	✓	✓			✓								✓		✓			
Gleditsia triacanthos var. *inermis* 'Imperial'	4-7	✓	✓	✓			✓								✓		✓			
Koelreuteria paniculata	5-9	✓	✓	✓	✓			✓							✓		✓	✓	✓	
Lagerstroemia indica 'Natchez'	7-10		✓	✓				✓	✓					✓			✓	✓		✓
Magnolia stellata 'Royal Star'	4-8		✓	✓	✓					✓				✓			✓	✓		
Magnolia virginiana	5-9		✓	✓	✓			✓						✓		✓	✓	✓	✓	
Malus 'Red Jade'	4-8		✓	✓			✓							✓		✓		✓	✓	
Phellodendron amurense	3-8	✓	✓	✓			✓								✓					✓
Pistacia chinensis	6-9	✓	✓	✓			✓								✓		✓		✓	
Populus tremuloides	3-7	✓	✓	✓			✓								✓	✓	✓			✓
Prunus mume	6-9		✓	✓	✓					✓				✓				✓	✓	
Pyrus calleryana 'Chanticleer'	5-8	✓	✓	✓			✓								✓	✓	✓	✓		
Quercus shumardii	5-9	✓	✓	✓			✓								✓	✓	✓			
Sapindus drummondii	6-9	✓		✓	✓		✓								✓	✓	✓		✓	✓
Stewartia pseudocamellia	5-7		✓	✓	✓			✓							✓	✓	✓	✓		✓
Styrax japonicus	5-8		✓	✓	✓		✓								✓	✓		✓		✓
Syringa reticulata	3-7		✓	✓				✓							✓			✓		
Taxodium distichum	4-9		✓	✓			✓								✓	✓	✓			✓
Ulmus parvifolia	4-9		✓	✓				✓							✓		✓			✓
Zelkova serrata 'Green Vase'	5-8		✓	✓			✓								✓	✓	✓			✓

EVERGREEN TREES

	ZONES	Dry	Moist	Full sun	Partial shade	Shade	Spring	Summer	Fall	Winter	Under 3 ft.	3-6 ft.	6-10 ft.	10-20 ft.	Over 20 ft.	Form	Foliage	Flowers	Fruit/seeds	Bark/twigs
Abies concolor	3-7	✓	✓	✓											✓	✓	✓			
Cedrus deodara	7-8	✓	✓	✓											✓	✓	✓			
x *Cupressocyparis leylandii* 'Silver Dust'	6-10	✓	✓	✓											✓	✓	✓			
Cupressus sempervirens	7-9	✓		✓											✓	✓	✓			✓
Ilex opaca	5-9		✓	✓	✓		✓								✓		✓		✓	
Ilex vomitoria	7-10	✓	✓	✓	✓		✓							✓		✓			✓	✓
Picea glauca	3-6		✓	✓	✓										✓	✓	✓			
Pinus contorta var. *contorta*	7-10		✓	✓											✓	✓				
Pinus nigra	4-7	✓	✓	✓											✓	✓	✓			
Taxus x *media* 'Hicksii'	4-7	✓	✓	✓	✓									✓		✓	✓	✓	✓	

Color Guide to Herbaceous Plants

Organized primarily by flower color, this chart provides information needed to select species and varieties of perennials, bulbs, annuals, and biennials that will thrive in the particular conditions of your garden. For more information on each plant, refer to the encyclopedia that begins on page 238.

	ZONES	SOIL			LIGHT			BLOOM SEASON				PLANT HEIGHT					NOTED FOR			
		Dry	Well-drained	Moist	Full sun	Partial shade	Shade	Spring	Summer	Fall	Winter	Under 1 ft.	1-3 ft.	3-6 ft.	6-10 ft.	Over 10 ft.	Flowers	Foliage	Fruit/seeds	Fragrance
WHITE																				
Achillea ptarmica 'The Pearl'	4-9		✓		✓				✓				✓				✓	✓		
Ageratum houstonianum 'Summer Snow' [2]			✓	✓	✓				✓	✓		✓					✓	✓		
Anemone x hybrida 'Honorine Jobert'	4-9		✓	✓	✓	✓			✓	✓			✓	✓			✓	✓		
Aruncus dioicus	4-9			✓		✓			✓					✓			✓	✓		
Chrysanthemum parthenium	4-9		✓		✓				✓	✓			✓				✓	✓		✓
Crambe cordifolia	5-9		✓		✓	✓	✓		✓					✓			✓	✓		✓
Datura metel 'Alba' [1]			✓	✓	✓				✓					✓			✓	✓		✓
Dicentra spectabilis f. alba	4-8		✓			✓	✓	✓					✓				✓	✓		
Galanthus nivalis	3-8		✓	✓		✓		✓			✓	✓					✓			
Gaura lindheimeri	6-9		✓		✓				✓					✓			✓			
Helianthus annuus 'Italian White' [1]			✓	✓	✓				✓	✓				✓			✓			
Ipomoea alba [4]	9-10		✓		✓				✓	✓						✓	✓	✓		✓
Leucojum vernum	4-8			✓		✓		✓				✓					✓			
Lysimachia clethroides	4-8			✓	✓	✓			✓				✓				✓	✓		
Mandevilla laxa	8-10		✓	✓		✓			✓							✓	✓	✓		✓
Phlox stolonifera 'Bruce's White'	3-8			✓	✓	✓	✓	✓					✓				✓	✓		
Polygonatum commutatum	3-9			✓		✓	✓	✓							✓		✓	✓	✓	
Tiarella cordifolia	3-8		✓	✓		✓	✓	✓	✓				✓				✓	✓		
Yucca glauca	4-8	✓	✓		✓				✓				✓	✓			✓	✓		
PINK																				
Acanthus spinosus	7-10	✓	✓		✓				✓				✓	✓			✓	✓		
Antirrhinum majus 'Pink Rocket' [4]	8-11		✓		✓				✓				✓	✓			✓			
Bergenia 'Abendglut'	4-8		✓	✓	✓	✓		✓					✓				✓	✓		
Chrysanthemum coccineum 'Helen'	3-7		✓			✓	✓		✓				✓				✓	✓		
Fuchsia x hybrida 'Pink Chiffon' [4]	9-11		✓	✓		✓			✓				✓				✓			
Geranium cinereum	4-9	✓	✓	✓	✓	✓			✓			✓					✓	✓		
Gypsophila paniculata 'Pink Fairy'	4-9		✓	✓	✓				✓				✓				✓			
Origanum vulgare	3-10	✓	✓		✓				✓	✓			✓				✓	✓		✓
Sedum sieboldii	5-9	✓	✓		✓					✓		✓					✓	✓		

[1] Tender annual   [2] Half-hardy annual   [3] Hardy annual   [4] Tender perennial grown as an annual in colder zones

	ZONES	Dry	Well-drained	Moist	Full sun	Partial shade	Shade	Spring	Summer	Fall	Winter	Under 1 ft.	1-3 ft.	3-6 ft.	6-10 ft.	Over 10 ft.	Flowers	Foliage	Fruit/seeds	Fragrance
MIXED/MULTICOLORED																				
Alcea rosea 'Chater's Double'	3-9		✓		✓				✓						✓		✓			
Anemone coronaria 'de Caen'	7-9		✓	✓	✓	✓		✓				✓					✓	✓		
Antirrhinum majus 'Tahiti' [4]	8-11		✓		✓	✓			✓	✓		✓					✓			
Aristolochia macrophylla	4-8		✓	✓	✓	✓			✓							✓	✓	✓		
Cosmos bipinnatus 'Candy Stripe' [1]		✓	✓		✓	✓			✓	✓			✓				✓	✓		
Impatiens wallerana 'Shady Lady' [4]	10		✓	✓		✓	✓		✓	✓			✓				✓	✓		
Lathyrus odoratus 'Royal Family' [3]			✓	✓	✓	✓		✓	✓					✓			✓	✓		✓
Nicotiana alata 'Domino Hybrids' [1]			✓	✓	✓	✓			✓	✓			✓				✓	✓		
Papaver rhoeas 'Fairy Wings' [3]		✓	✓		✓	✓		✓	✓				✓				✓			
Tagetes patula [1]			✓		✓				✓	✓		✓	✓				✓	✓		
YELLOW																				
Achillea 'Moonshine'	3-8	✓	✓		✓				✓	✓			✓				✓	✓		✓
Alchemilla mollis	3-7		✓	✓	✓	✓		✓	✓				✓				✓	✓		
Allium moly 'Jeannine'	3-9		✓	✓	✓	✓		✓				✓					✓	✓		
Arum italicum	5-9		✓	✓		✓	✓	✓					✓				✓	✓	✓	
Caltha palustris	3-8		✓	✓	✓	✓		✓					✓				✓	✓		
Digitalis grandiflora	3-9		✓	✓		✓		✓	✓				✓				✓	✓		
Doronicum 'Harper Crewe'	4-8		✓	✓	✓	✓		✓						✓			✓			
Helianthus angustifolius	6-9			✓	✓				✓	✓					✓	✓	✓	✓		
Lysimachia punctata	4-8			✓	✓	✓			✓				✓				✓	✓		
Rudbeckia fulgida var. *sullivantii 'Goldsturm'*	4-9		✓		✓	✓			✓	✓			✓				✓			
Rudbeckia nitida 'Herbstsonne'	4-9		✓		✓	✓			✓	✓					✓		✓			
Tanacetum vulgare	3-9		✓		✓	✓			✓				✓	✓			✓	✓		✓
Tropaeolum peregrinum [1]		✓	✓		✓				✓						✓		✓	✓		
ORANGE																				
Asclepias tuberosa	4-9		✓		✓				✓				✓				✓			
Calendula officinalis 'Geisha Girl' [3]			✓		✓			✓	✓	✓			✓				✓			
Cosmos sulphureus 'Diablo' [1]		✓	✓		✓	✓			✓	✓			✓				✓			
Euphorbia griffithii 'Fireglow'	4-9		✓		✓				✓				✓				✓			
Helenium 'Moerheim Beauty'	4-8		✓		✓					✓			✓				✓			
Hemerocallis fulva	3-9		✓	✓	✓	✓			✓				✓				✓	✓		
Sphaeralcea ambigua	9-10		✓		✓				✓				✓				✓	✓		
Thunbergia alata 'Aurantiaca' [4]	10-11		✓	✓	✓	✓			✓						✓		✓			
Tithonia rotundifolia 'Torch' [1]			✓		✓				✓	✓			✓				✓			

[1] Tender annual   [2] Half-hardy annual   [3] Hardy annual   [4] Tender perennial grown as an annual in colder zones

		ZONES	SOIL			LIGHT			BLOOM SEASON				PLANT HEIGHT					NOTED FOR			
			Dry	Well-drained	Moist	Full sun	Partial shade	Shade	Spring	Summer	Fall	Winter	Under 1 ft.	1-3 ft.	3-6 ft.	6-10 ft.	Over 10 ft.	Flowers	Foliage	Fruit/seeds	Fragrance
RED	*Achillea millefolium 'Red Beauty'*	3-8	✓	✓		✓				✓	✓			✓				✓	✓		✓
	Astilbe 'Fanal'	5-9			✓		✓			✓				✓				✓	✓		
	Centranthus ruber	5-9		✓		✓			✓	✓	✓			✓				✓	✓		
	Dianthus deltoides 'Flashing Light'	4-7		✓	✓	✓	✓		✓				✓					✓	✓		
	Hemerocallis 'Anzac'	3-9		✓	✓	✓				✓				✓				✓	✓		
	Knautia macedonica	5-9		✓		✓				✓				✓				✓	✓		
	Lobelia 'Queen Victoria'	3-8			✓	✓				✓	✓			✓				✓	✓		
	Lychnis chalcedonica	4-9		✓	✓	✓	✓			✓				✓				✓	✓		
	Monarda didyma 'Cambridge Scarlet'	4-8		✓	✓	✓				✓				✓				✓	✓		
	Pelargonium x hortorum 'Ringo Scarlet' [4]	9-10		✓	✓	✓			✓	✓	✓		✓	✓				✓	✓		
	Penstemon 'Garnet'	4-9		✓		✓				✓	✓			✓				✓	✓		
	Phaseolus coccineus [4]	9-10		✓	✓	✓			✓	✓	✓							✓			
	Primula japonica 'Miller's Crimson'	6-8			✓		✓	✓	✓	✓				✓				✓			
	Rheum palmatum 'Atrosanguineum'	5-9		✓		✓				✓						✓		✓	✓		
	Salvia splendens [4]	10-11		✓		✓	✓			✓	✓		✓	✓				✓	✓		
	Thymus praecox 'Coccineus'	4-9	✓	✓		✓			✓				✓					✓	✓		✓
PURPLE	*Ageratum houstonianum 'North Sea'* [2]			✓	✓	✓				✓	✓		✓					✓	✓		
	Allium giganteum	5-8		✓	✓	✓				✓					✓			✓			
	Campanula glomerata 'Superba'	3-8		✓	✓	✓	✓			✓				✓				✓			
	Centaurea montana	3-8		✓		✓				✓				✓				✓	✓		
	Cleome hasslerana 'Purple Queen' [1]			✓	✓	✓	✓			✓	✓				✓			✓		✓	
	Cynara cardunculus	9-10		✓		✓				✓						✓		✓	✓		
	Lavandula dentata [4]	8-9		✓		✓				✓				✓				✓	✓		✓
	Linaria triornithophora	6-9		✓		✓				✓				✓				✓	✓		
	Liriope muscari	6-10	✓	✓	✓	✓	✓	✓		✓	✓			✓				✓	✓	✓	
	Mentha spicata	4-9			✓	✓	✓			✓				✓				✓	✓		✓
	Pelargonium peltatum 'Amethyst' [4]	9-10		✓	✓	✓			✓	✓	✓		✓					✓	✓		
	Petunia x hybrida 'Heavenly Lavender' [1]			✓		✓				✓	✓		✓					✓			
	Platycodon grandiflorus	4-9		✓		✓				✓				✓				✓	✓		
	Salvia x superba 'East Friesland'	5-8		✓	✓	✓	✓		✓	✓				✓				✓	✓		
	Teucrium chamaedrys	5-10		✓		✓	✓			✓				✓				✓	✓		
	Veronica longifolia 'Romiley Purple'	4-8		✓		✓				✓					✓			✓	✓		

[1] Tender annual   [2] Half-hardy annual   [3] Hardy annual   [4] Tender perennial grown as an annual in colder zones

	ZONES	SOIL			LIGHT			BLOOM SEASON				PLANT HEIGHT					NOTED FOR			
		Dry	Well-drained	Moist	Full sun	Partial shade	Shade	Spring	Summer	Fall	Winter	Under 1 ft.	1-3 ft.	3-6 ft.	6-10 ft.	Over 10 ft.	Flowers	Foliage	Fruit/seeds	Fragrance
BLUE																				
Agapanthus africanus	8-10		✓	✓	✓				✓	✓			✓	✓			✓	✓		
Ajuga reptans 'Bronze Beauty'	3-9	✓	✓	✓	✓	✓		✓	✓			✓					✓	✓		
Allium azureum	4-10		✓		✓				✓				✓				✓			
Aquilegia flabellata	3-9		✓	✓	✓	✓		✓	✓			✓					✓	✓		
Borago officinalis ³			✓		✓				✓	✓			✓				✓			
Campanula latifolia	4-8		✓	✓	✓	✓			✓					✓			✓			
Cyananthus microphyllus	5-7		✓			✓			✓			✓					✓	✓		
Echinops bannaticus	8-10		✓		✓				✓					✓			✓			
Gentiana sino-ornata	5-7			✓		✓				✓		✓					✓			
Geranium x 'Johnson's Blue'	5-8	✓	✓	✓	✓	✓		✓	✓				✓				✓	✓		
Ixiolirion tataricum	7-10		✓		✓			✓	✓			✓					✓			
Lobelia erinus 'Crystal Palace' ³			✓		✓				✓	✓		✓					✓	✓		
Meconopsis betonicifolia	8			✓		✓	✓	✓	✓				✓				✓			
Mertensia virginica	3-8		✓	✓		✓	✓	✓					✓				✓	✓		
Nepeta x faassenii	4-8		✓		✓			✓	✓				✓				✓	✓		✓
Perovskia atriplicifolia	5-9		✓		✓			✓	✓					✓			✓	✓		✓
Polygala calcarea	5-7		✓		✓			✓	✓			✓					✓			
Rosmarinus officinalis	7-10	✓	✓	✓	✓	✓			✓	✓	✓	✓	✓				✓	✓		✓
Scabiosa caucasica 'Fama'	4-9		✓		✓				✓				✓				✓			
Scilla siberica 'Atrocoerulea'	1-8		✓		✓			✓				✓					✓			
Sisyrinchium angustifolium	3-10			✓	✓	✓		✓	✓				✓				✓	✓		
Veronica longifolia	4-8		✓		✓	✓			✓	✓			✓	✓			✓	✓		
Vinca major ⁴	7-9		✓	✓	✓	✓	✓	✓				✓					✓	✓		
GRASSES																				
Andropogon glomertatus	6-9			✓	✓					✓	✓			✓				✓	✓	
Bouteloua curtipendula	3-10	✓	✓		✓				✓	✓			✓					✓	✓	
Calamagrostis acutiflora 'Stricta'	6-9	✓		✓	✓				✓					✓			✓	✓		
Imperata cylindrica rubra	5-9		✓	✓	✓				✓			✓						✓		
Miscanthus sinensis 'Morning Light'	5-9	✓	✓		✓				✓	✓	✓			✓			✓	✓		
Muhlenbergia lindheimeri	6-10		✓		✓	✓			✓					✓				✓	✓	
Panicum virgatum 'Haense Herms'	5-9			✓	✓				✓	✓			✓				✓	✓	✓	
Pennisetum alopecuroides	5-9		✓	✓	✓				✓	✓				✓			✓	✓		
Schizachyrium scoparium	3-10	✓	✓		✓				✓	✓				✓				✓		

¹ Tender annual   ² Half-hardy annual   ³ Hardy annual   ⁴ Tender perennial grown as an annual in colder zones

235

Zone and Frost Maps of the U.S.

To determine if a plant will flourish in your climate, first locate your zone on the map below and check it against the zone information given in the Plant Selection Guide that begins on page 228 or in the Encyclopedia entries that begin on page 239. For annuals and biennials, planting dates depend on when frosts occur: Hardy annuals can be safely sown 6 weeks before the last spring frost, whereas tender annuals should be sown only after all danger of frost is past. Also, while cool-season annuals can withstand some frost, warm-season plants can be grown without protection only in the frost-free period between the last and first frosts. Used together, the zone map and the frost-date maps shown opposite will help you select plants suited to your area and determine when to plant them. Frost dates vary widely within each region, however, so check with your weather service or Cooperative Extension Service for more precise figures, and record the temperatures in your own garden from year to year.

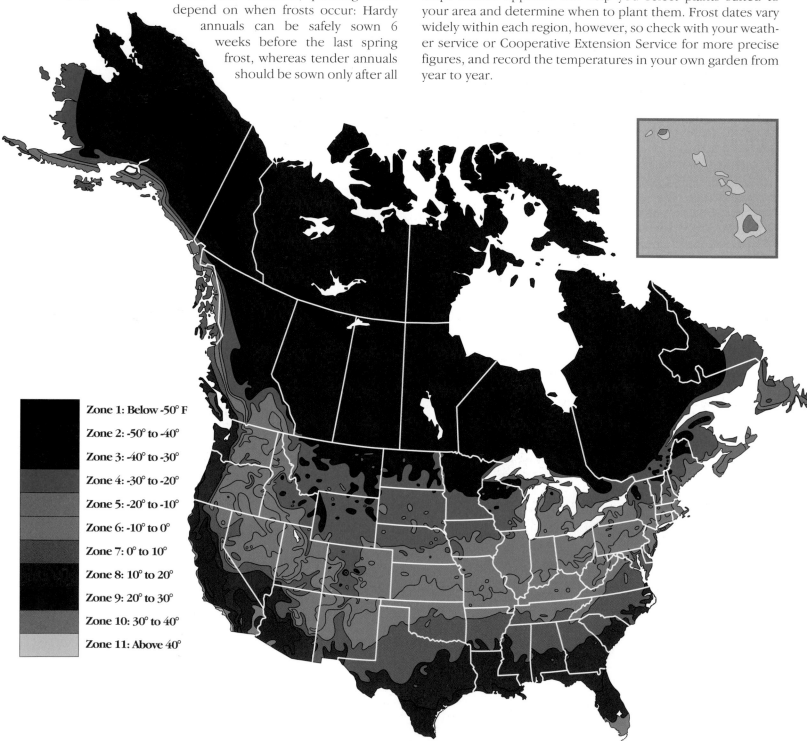

Zone 1: Below -50° F

Zone 2: -50° to -40°

Zone 3: -40° to -30°

Zone 4: -30° to -20°

Zone 5: -20° to -10°

Zone 6: -10° to 0°

Zone 7: 0° to 10°

Zone 8: 10° to 20°

Zone 9: 20° to 30°

Zone 10: 30° to 40°

Zone 11: Above 40°

AVERAGE DATES OF LAST SPRING FROST

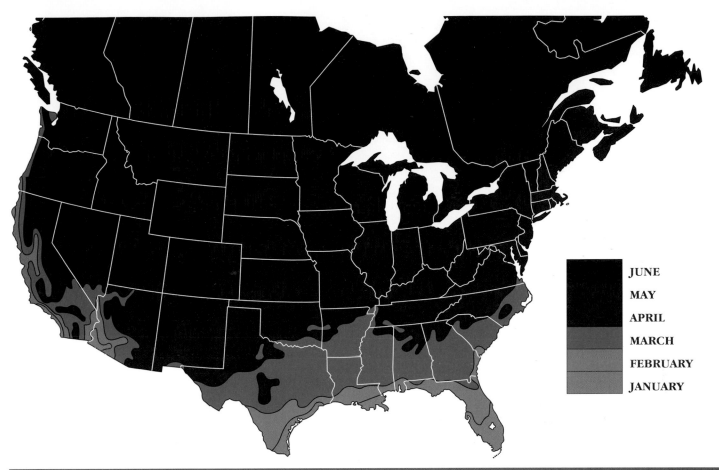

JUNE

MAY

APRIL

MARCH

FEBRUARY

JANUARY

AVERAGE DATES OF FIRST FALL FROST

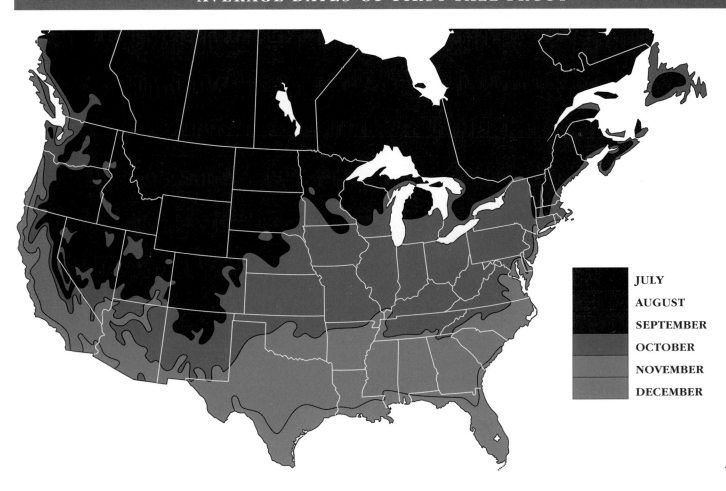

JULY

AUGUST

SEPTEMBER

OCTOBER

NOVEMBER

DECEMBER

237

Encyclopedia of Plants

Presented on the following pages is information on most of the plants mentioned in this volume. Each genus is listed alphabetically by its Latin botanical name, followed by a pronunciation of the Latin and the genus's common name. (If you know a plant only by its common name, see the index.) A botanical name consists of the genus and, usually, a species, both written in italics. Species often have common names of their own, which are given in parentheses in each entry, and many species have one or more cultivars, which are set off by single quotation marks.

Information is given for plant hardiness, flowering season, height, flower color, and soil and light needs. Selected species and varieties are discussed, as well as a plant's optimum growing conditions and maintenance requirements.

ANNUALS & BIENNIALS
pages 239-267

Entries designate these plants as either annuals, biennials, or tender perennials. Since the planting dates for most annuals and biennials depend on the dates of the last spring frost and the first fall frost, refer to the maps on page 237 to determine which plants will grow most successfully in your region.

PERENNIALS
pages 268-300

Perennials are likely to have a home in your garden for a long time to come, so use the information in the entries on the following pages to choose those plants that are the most compatible with your garden's conditions and fulfill your desires for a garden design.

BULBS
pages 301-323

In addition to identifying whether a plant is a true bulb, rhizome, corm, or tuber, the entries that follow designate some bulbs as "tender"; these bulbs are able to survive winter in the ground only in warm zones. Elsewhere, they must be dug up in fall and stored for the winter or grown in containers.

ROSES
pages 324-337

The roses presented in this section have been chosen for their enduring appeal, availability, bloom colors, and landscape uses. Many are notable for disease resistance, winter-hardiness, or low-maintenance requirements—and sometimes all three. The American Rose Society's (ARS) evaluation of overall quality is given for each rose that has received a rating. Winners of the coveted All-American Rose Selections (AARS) award are also identified.

TREES & SHRUBS
pages 338-355

Trees and shrubs are important structural plants for your garden. While expensive at the outset, most are long-lived once established. The entries that follow provide you with information on many popular species, including mature heights and forms, pruning tips, and rates of growth.

Ageratum
(aj-er-AY-tum)
FLOSSFLOWER

Ageratum houstonianum 'Blue Horizon'

Plant type: *annual*

Height: *6 to 30 inches*

Interest: *flowers, foliage*

Soil: *moist, well-drained*

Light: *full sun*

A profusion of fluffy flowers with thread-like petals crown flossflower's clumps of heart-shaped leaves. With soft colors and a compact, mounding habit, dwarf varieties create excellent garden edgings. Taller varieties combine well with other flowers in the middle or back of a border and are good candidates for indoor arrangements.

Selected species and varieties: *A. houstonianum* bears tiny blue or bluish purple flowers in dense, fuzzy clusters from summer through fall; white- and pink-flowered varieties are available; 'Blue Horizon' grows to 30 inches with deep blue flowers that are excellent for cutting; 'Capri' grows to a uniform 12 inches, producing bicolored flowers that are medium blue with white centers, and it is heat tolerant; 'Summer Snow' grows 6 to 8 inches tall with pure white flowers that begin early and continue to frost.

Growing conditions and maintenance: Sow seed indoors 6 to 8 weeks before the last expected frost. Space plants 6 to 12 inches apart. Pinching early growth will promote compactness, and removing spent blooms will encourage continuous production of flowers.

Agrostemma
(ag-roe-STEM-a)
CORN COCKLE

Agrostemma githago

Plant type: *annual or biennial*

Height: *1 to 4 feet*

Interest: *flowers, foliage*

Soil: *poor, well-drained*

Light: *full sun*

Corn cockles are trouble-free plants from Europe that have naturalized throughout the eastern United States. They provide a long season of bright blooms for borders. Abundant 1- to 2-inch flowers in shades of pink, lilac, cherry red, or magenta top their stems throughout the summer. Their old-fashioned appearance is effective massed or in combination with other flowers in a cottage garden. Blooms are excellent for cutting.

Selected species and varieties: *A. githago* is a hardy annual with willowy stems up to 4 feet tall and narrow leaves covered with a silvery down; each flower has five petals that sport delicate stripes or spots seeming to radiate from the center; the black seeds are plentiful—and poisonous.

Growing conditions and maintenance: Corn cockle is easy to grow. Sow seed in place in late fall or early spring. Thin plants to stand 6 to 12 inches apart. They tolerate dry conditions and almost any soil. Deadhead to encourage reblooming and prevent excessive self-seeding.

Amaranthus
(am-a-RAN-thus)
AMARANTH

Amaranthus caudatus

Plant type: *annual*

Height: *18 inches to 6 feet*

Interest: *flowers, foliage*

Soil: *dry to well-drained*

Light: *full sun*

Amaranths are large, brilliantly colored plants that hail from the tropics of the Far East. They add a bold touch to borders with their long-lasting tasseled flowers and colorful leaves. Tall types are effective as accents, while shorter selections are suited to beds or containers. Flowers are suitable for both fresh and dried arrangements.

Selected species and varieties: *A. caudatus* (love-lies-bleeding) grows 3 to 5 feet tall with green or red leaves and huge drooping tassels of red flowers that may reach 2 feet in length; 'Viridis' grows 2 to 3½ feet with greenish yellow flower tassels. *A. cruentus* (purple amaranth, prince's-feather) produces huge 12-inch leaves along erect 6-foot stems, and drooping red or purple flower spikes. *A. tricolor* (Joseph's-coat amaranth, tampala) grows from 1½ to 5 feet tall with variegated leaves up to 6 inches long that sport shades of green, red, and gold.

Growing conditions and maintenance: Seed requires very warm temperatures and can be started indoors 4 to 6 weeks prior to the last frost. In warm areas sow seed directly. Thin to allow 1 to 2 feet between plants. Water sparingly.

Antirrhinum
(an-tir-RYE-num)
SNAPDRAGON

Antirrhinum majus 'White Sonnet'

Plant type: *tender perennial*

Height: *6 inches to 4 feet*

Interest: *flowers*

Soil: *well-drained, fertile*

Light: *full sun to partial shade*

Snapdragons, with their wide range of heights and flower colors and long season of bloom, have been cultivated since ancient times. Short varieties add color to rock gardens and edgings, while taller types are well suited to the middle and rear of mixed borders, where they provide a vertical accent. They are outstanding in fresh arrangements.

Selected species and varieties: *A. majus* bears terminal clusters of flowers that open from the bottom up. Each bloom has five lobes, divided into an upper and a lower lip. Varieties are classified by height: small (6-12 inches), intermediate (12-24 inches), and tall (2-4 feet); 'Black Prince' is 18 inches with deep crimson flowers and bronze foliage; 'Madame Butterfly' grows to 3 feet with flaring blossoms in a range of colors; 'White Sonnet' is 22 inches with white flowers that are superb for cutting.

Growing conditions and maintenance: Start seed indoors in late winter for transplanting in mid- to late spring. Space plants 6 to 18 inches apart. Deadhead to encourage continuous flowering. Taller types may need staking. Perennial in Zones 8 to 11.

Asclepias
(as-KLEE-pee-as)
MILKWEED

Asclepias curassavica

Plant type: *tender perennial*

Height: *2 to 6 feet*

Interest: *flowers, seedpods*

Soil: *moist to dry*

Light: *full sun*

Often referred to as weeds in South America, *Asclepias* species are suited to the rear of a herbaceous border, where their clusters of flowers put on a fine display from summer until frost. Flowers are followed by attractive seedpods that are useful in dried arrangements.

Selected species and varieties: *A. curassavica* (bloodflower) develops sturdy branched stems 2 to 4 feet tall and narrow 5-inch dark green leaves that clasp the stems in pairs. The 6-inch flower clusters arise from branch tips and axils and are made up of many tiny purplish red and orange flowers. Flowers are followed by 4-inch brown seedpods. *A. fruticosa* (gomphocarpus) grows 3 to 6 feet tall and bears creamy white flowers and spiny silvery green pods.

Growing conditions and maintenance: Start seed indoors in midwinter for transplanting to the garden after all danger of frost has past. Space plants 15 to 18 inches apart and pinch when they reach 4 to 6 inches to promote branching. Plants thrive in warm weather and can be grown as perennials from Zone 8 south.

Begonia
(be-GO-nee-a)
WAX BEGONIA

Begonia 'Cocktail Series'

Plant type: *tender perennial*

Height: *5 to 16 inches*

Interest: *flowers, foliage*

Soil: *moist, fertile*

Light: *partial shade to shade*

Wax begonias add color to the shady garden with both their perpetual clusters of delicate flowers and their glossy rounded leaves. Flowers range from white to pink to red, and leaves may be green, bronze, or variegated green and white. They are useful for edging, massing, and growing in containers both indoors and outside.

Selected species and varieties: *B.* x *semperflorens-cultorum* (bedding begonia) has a mounding habit and produces flowers nonstop from spring until frost. In Zones 9 and 10 they bloom almost year round. Selections vary in both flower and leaf color, flower size, and height; 'Cocktail Series' offers white, pink, rose, salmon, and red flowers on dwarf 5- to 6-inch plants with glossy bronze foliage; 'Pizzazz Mixed' grows to 10 inches with large red, pink, or white flowers and glossy green leaves.

Growing conditions and maintenance: Start seed 4 to 6 months prior to the last frost, or purchase bedding plants in spring. Plants can also be propagated by cuttings. Space 8 to 12 inches apart. Although the ideal site is filtered shade, plants will tolerate full sun if given sufficient water, especially in cooler regions.

Borago
(bor-RAY-go)
BORAGE

Borago officinalis

Plant type: *annual*

Height: *2 to 3 feet*

Interest: *flowers, foliage*

Soil: *well-drained*

Light: *full sun to light shade*

This European native makes an attractive addition to flower or herb gardens, fresh flower arrangements, and summer salads. Both leaves and flowers are edible, with a refreshing cucumber-like flavor, and can be used to garnish salads or fruit cups. It has a somewhat sprawling habit that is best suited to an informal garden, where its soft-textured leaves and sky blue flowers add a cool, gentle touch.

Selected species and varieties: *B. officinalis* (talewort, cool-tankard) is a hardy annual with a rounded, sprawling habit, bristly gray-green foliage, and succulent stems. Flowers are arranged in drooping clusters. Each is ¾ inch across and star shaped, with five petals. Though usually clear blue, they are sometimes light purple. Flower buds are covered with fine hairs.

Growing conditions and maintenance: Sow seed directly in the garden at monthly intervals beginning 2 to 3 weeks prior to the last frost for continuous summer bloom. Once established, plant will self-seed. Allow 12 to 18 inches between plants. Where summers are very hot, afternoon shade is recommended. Borage tolerates drought.

Brachycome
(bra-KIK-o-me)
SWAN RIVER DAISY

Brachycome iberidifolia

Plant type: *annual*

Height: *9 to 14 inches*

Interest: *flowers*

Soil: *moist, well-drained, fertile*

Light: *full sun*

The Swan River daisy is a tender annual from Australia with a neat, mounding habit and colorful daisylike flowers. Although small, the brightly colored flowers are produced in masses, making this plant a good choice for rock gardens, edgings, and containers, including hanging baskets.

Selected species and varieties: *B. iberidifolia* grows to 14 inches tall with a compact habit and a 12-inch spread. The delicate pale green leaves are 3 inches long and are borne on slender stems. Flowers are about 1 inch across and appear for 4 to 6 weeks in the summer, tapering off toward the end of the season. Colors include white, pink, lavender, and blue.

Growing conditions and maintenance: Start seed indoors 5 to 6 weeks prior to the last frost, or sow directly in the garden when the soil has warmed. Successive plantings will lengthen the flowering season. Allow 6 to 12 inches between plants. Water during dry spells.

Brassica
(BRASS-i-ka)
ORNAMENTAL CABBAGE

Brassica oleracea

Plant type: *biennial*

Height: *10 to 15 inches*

Interest: *foliage*

Soil: *moist, well-drained*

Light: *full sun*

This ornamental cousin of the familiar vegetable side dish is highly valued for the splash of color it provides in the fall and winter landscape. A biennial, it is grown as an annual for its brightly colored and intricately curled foliage, which grows in a flowerlike rosette.

Selected species and varieties: *B. oleracea,* Acephala group (ornamental kale) does not form heads but produces an open rosette of leaves that typically spreads 12 inches across. Foliage colors include lavender-blue, white, green, red, purple, pink, and assorted variegations. Color improves in cool weather. Leaves of 'Cherry Sundae' are a blend of carmine and cream; 'Color Up' displays a center of red, pink, cream, white, and green surrounded by green margins; 'Peacock' series has feathery, notched and serrated leaves in a variety of colors.

Growing conditions and maintenance: For spring planting, start seed indoors 4 to 6 weeks prior to the last frost. For fall gardens, start seed 6 to 8 weeks prior to the first anticipated frost. Space plants 18 to 24 inches apart. Plants will last all winter in Zones 8 to 10.

Browallia
(bro-WALL-ee-a)
BUSH VIOLET

Browallia speciosa

Plant type: *tender perennial*

Height: *8 to 16 inches*

Interest: *flowers*

Soil: *moist, well-drained*

Light: *partial shade to shade*

A good choice for the shady border, bush violet bears clusters of blue, violet, or white flowers from early to late summer. It has a low-growing rounded habit that is well suited for use as an edging, and it's an outstanding choice for window boxes or hanging baskets, where it cascades gracefully over the edge. In fall, plants can be cut back severely and potted to be grown as flowering houseplants through the winter.

Selected species and varieties: *B. speciosa* has a rounded to sprawling habit with 1½- to 2-inch long-throated, star-shaped flowers; 'Blue Bells' bears blue-violet flowers with prominent white centers; 'Jingle Bells' bears flowers in a mixture of colors including shades of blue, white, and lavender; 'Silver Bells' bears large white blooms.

Growing conditions and maintenance: Start seed indoors about 8 weeks prior to the last frost. Plant in the garden after all danger of frost is past, spacing plants 8 inches apart. Avoid overwatering and overfertilizing.

Calendula
(ka-LEN-dew-la)
POT MARIGOLD

Calendula officinalis

Plant type: *annual*

Height: *12 to 24 inches*

Interest: *flowers*

Soil: *moist, well-drained*

Light: *full sun*

The long-lasting blooms of pot marigolds are daisylike with flattened, wide-spreading rays ranging in color from deep orange to yellow or cream. They are a good choice for mixed beds, containers, or indoor arrangements. Native to the Mediterranean, this hardy annual has long been grown as an ornamental and used as a flavoring for puddings and cakes.

Selected species and varieties: *C. officinalis* has a neat, mounding habit and grows 1 to 2 feet tall with a similar spread. Leaves are 2 to 6 inches long, blue-green, and aromatic. The solitary 2½- to 4½-inch flower heads close at night; 'Bon-Bon' grows 12 inches tall with a compact, early-blooming habit and a mixture of flower colors.

Growing conditions and maintenance: Start seed indoors 6 to 8 weeks prior to the last frost, for transplanting to the garden after the last hard frost. In areas with mild winters it can be sown directly outdoors in fall or early spring. Space plants 12 to 18 inches apart. Deadhead to increase flowering. Calendulas thrive in cool conditions and tolerate poor soils if they have adequate water.

Canna
(CAN-ah)
CANNA

Canna x generalis 'Lerape'

Plant type: *tender perennial*

Height: *18 inches to 6 feet*

Interest: *flowers*

Soil: *moist, well-drained*

Light: *full sun*

Cannas produce 4- to 5-inch flowers with a tousled arrangement of petal-like stamens from summer through frost. Bold leaves provide a dramatic backdrop to the flowers. They are well suited to the back of borders and to massing. Grow dwarf cultivars as edgings or in patio containers.

Selected species and varieties: *C. x generalis* (canna lily) is available in standard varieties that grow 4 to 6 feet tall or dwarfs that are less than 3 feet. The flowers are carried on stiff, erect stems; colors include red, orange, salmon, yellow, pink, white, and bicolors. The broad leaves, up to 24 inches long, are usually a deep glossy green but are sometimes bronzy red or striped or veined in white or pink; 'Lerape' bears yellow flowers with bright orange spots; 'Seven Dwarfs Mixed' grows to 18 inches with a wide range of flower colors.

Growing conditions and maintenance: Soak seed prior to planting indoors in midwinter, or start rhizomes indoors 4 weeks before the last frost and move them to the garden when night temperatures reach 60° F. In Zones 9 and 10, plant directly in the garden in spring, spaced 1 to 2 feet apart.

Capsicum
(KAP-si-kum)
PEPPER

Capsicum annuum 'Treasure Red'

Plant type:	*tender perennial*
Height:	*6 to 20 inches*
Interest:	*fruit*
Soil:	*moist, well-drained, fertile*
Light:	*full sun*

Bushy, rounded pepper plants produce brightly colored fruit that is well displayed against dark green leaves. In their native environment of tropical North and South America, peppers are woody perennials, but in temperate climates they are treated as annuals. Ornamental varieties make tidy and colorful edgings for beds and are superb for containers.

Selected species and varieties: *C. annuum* (ornamental pepper) has a bushy, compact habit with evergreen leaves from 1 to 5 inches long. Flowers are white and small. Fruit ranges from ¾ to 2 inches long and may be red, purple, yellow, green, black, cream, or variegated; 'Holiday Cheer' grows to 8 inches with round 1-inch fruit that turns from cream to red; 'Red Missile' grows to 10 inches with tapered 2-inch fruit; 'Treasure Red' grows 8 inches tall with conical fruit that turns from white to bright red.

Growing conditions and maintenance: Start seed indoors in late winter to transplant to the garden after all danger of frost has past. Space plants to stand 8 to 15 inches apart. Dig and pot plants in the fall to grow as houseplants; perennial in Zones 10 and 11.

Catharanthus
(kath-ah-RAN-thus)
PERIWINKLE

Catharanthus roseus

Plant type:	*tender perennial*
Height:	*3 to 18 inches*
Interest:	*flowers, foliage*
Soil:	*moist, well-drained*
Light:	*sun to partial shade*

Periwinkle provides summer-to-fall color for temperate gardens. Its flowers resemble those of *Vinca,* and it is available in both creeping and upright varieties. Use it as a summer ground cover or in mass plantings, annual borders, or containers.

Selected species and varieties: *C. roseus* [sometimes listed as *Vinca rosea*] (Madagascar periwinkle) produces glossy oblong leaves, 1 to 3 inches long. Creeping varieties grow 3 inches tall, spreading 18 to 24 inches across. Erect strains grow 8 to 18 inches tall. Flowers are 1½ inches wide and cover the plant throughout the summer; colors range from shades of pink or mauve to white; 'Parasol' produces large 1½- to 2-inch white flowers with pink eyes on 12- to 18-inch plants; 'Tropicana' grows to 12 inches and produces flowers in several shades of pink from pale blush to deep rose, with contrasting eyes.

Growing conditions and maintenance: Start seed indoors 10 to 12 weeks prior to the last frost for late-spring transplanting to the garden; space 1 to 2 feet apart. Plants can also be started from cuttings. They thrive in warm, humid conditions and are perennial in Zones 9 to 11.

Celosia
(sel-OH-see-a)
CELOSIA

Celosia cristata 'Pink Tassels'

Plant type:	*annual*
Height:	*6 to 24 inches*
Interest:	*flowers, foliage*
Soil:	*moist to dry, well-drained*
Light:	*full sun*

These vibrant annuals are native to the tropics of Asia. Their crested or plumed flowers are extremely long-lasting, making them ideal for bedding and cutting for both fresh and dried arrangements.

Selected species and varieties: *C. cristata* displays a range of heights and flower types. Leaves may be green, purple, or variegated. Flowers appear from midsummer to fall and are usually deep shades of red, orange, yellow, or gold. The species is divided according to flower type: Childsii group (crested cockscomb) produces crested or convoluted flower heads that resemble lumps of coral. Plumosa group (feather amaranth) bears feathery 6- to 12-inch flower heads. Spicata group bears flowers in slender spikes; 'Pink Tassels' bears long pale pink spikes with bright pink tips.

Growing conditions and maintenance: Start seed indoors 4 to 6 weeks before transplanting to the garden after all danger of frost has passed. In warm areas, sow directly outside. Space plants 6 to 18 inches apart. Celosias thrive in warm weather and tolerate dry soils. For use in winter arrangements, cut flowers at their peak and hang them upside down to dry.

Centaurea
(sen-TOR-ee-a)
KNAPWEED

Centaurea cyanus

Plant type: *annual*

Height: *1 to 6 feet*

Interest: *flowers*

Soil: *well-drained*

Light: *full sun*

The tufted blooms of these popular annuals come in shades of pink, blue, lavender, yellow, and white. Sprinkle them liberally in informal borders, wildflower gardens, and the cutting garden. They can be used for both fresh and dried arrangements.

Selected species and varieties: *C. americana* (basket flower) grows to 6 feet tall with sturdy stems and 4- to 5-inch pink flowers with cream centers. *C. cyanus* (bachelor's-button, cornflower) produces gray-green leaves on erect stems to 3 feet; perky 1-inch flowers appear from early summer until frost and are available in many colors. *C. moschata* (sweet-sultan) grows 2 to 3 feet with 2- to 3-inch musk-scented flowers; the hybrid 'Imperialis' grows to 4 feet with pink, purple, or white flowers.

Growing conditions and maintenance: Sow seed in place in late winter or early spring; in areas with mild winters it can also be sown in fall. Space 6 to 12 inches apart. Once established, plants often self-seed. For continuous bloom, make successive plantings 2 weeks apart throughout the season.

Cheiranthus
(ky-RAN-thus)
WALLFLOWER

Cheiranthus cheiri 'Bowles' Mauve'

Plant type: *tender perennial*

Height: *6 to 24 inches*

Interest: *flowers*

Soil: *well-drained, fertile*

Light: *full sun*

This Eurasian native bridges the flowering season between early bulbs and bedding plants. Fragrant 1-inch flowers are borne in clusters resembling stock; colors include deep shades of yellow, orange, red, purple, and brown. Dwarf varieties are perfect for rock gardens or growing in gaps of stone walls. Plant taller types in borders.

Selected species and varieties: *C. cheiri* (English wallflower) has a low, erect habit; dwarf varieties grow 6 to 9 inches, while tall varieties may reach 2 feet. Early-flowering strains often bloom their first year from seed, but most varieties are treated as biennials; 'Bowles' Mauve' produces large clusters of deep pink flowers.

Growing conditions and maintenance: Sow seed outdoors in spring or fall for bloom the following season. Provide winter protection in areas with severe winters. Early-flowering varieties can be started indoors in midwinter, hardened in a cold frame, and transplanted to the garden as soon as the soil can be worked in spring. Space plants about 12 inches apart. Wallflowers thrive in cool climates and do well in coastal and mountainous areas such as the Pacific Northwest.

Chrysanthemum
(kri-SAN-the-mum)
CHRYSANTHEMUM

Chrysanthemum coronarium 'Primrose Gem'

Plant type: *annual*

Height: *1 to 3 feet*

Interest: *flowers*

Soil: *well-drained*

Light: *full sun to partial shade*

Annual chrysanthemums, which hail from the Mediterranean region, supply the summer and fall border with a nonstop production of colorful daisylike flowers. They are also cheerful and dependable cut flowers.

Selected species and varieties: *C. carinatum* (tricolor chrysanthemum) grows 2 to 3 feet tall with dark green toothed leaves. It derives its common name from its 2½-inch flower heads that are white with a yellow band surrounding a purple or chocolate brown central disk; 'Court Jesters' produces red, pink, orange, yellow, maroon, and white flowers with red or orange bands. *C. coronarium* (crown daisy, garland chrysanthemum) grows 1 to 2½ feet tall with coarsely cut leaves and yellow and white flowers, 1 to 2 inches across, which may be single, semidouble, or double; 'Primrose Gem' bears semidouble soft yellow blooms with darker yellow centers.

Growing conditions and maintenance: These plants are easily grown from seed planted directly in the garden as soon as soil can be worked in the spring. Thin plants to stand 12 to 18 inches apart. Once established they will self-seed.

Clarkia
(KLAR-kee-a)
GODETIA

Clarkia amoena

Plant type: *annual*

Height: *1 to 3 feet*

Interest: *flowers*

Soil: *dry, sandy*

Light: *full sun to partial shade*

Clarkias are free-flowering annuals from the coastal ranges of the western United States. They are named after the explorer William Clark, who collected their seed during the Lewis and Clark expedition. These species are also listed under the genus *Godetia*.

Selected species and varieties: *C. amoena* (farewell-to-spring) grows 1 to 3 feet tall. Throughout summer, 2- to 4-inch cup-shaped flowers appear in the axils of the upper leaves. Petals number four and are pink to lavender with a red or pink splash at the base; the four sepals are red. *C. concinna* (red-ribbons) grows 1 to 2 feet tall and bears rose purple flowers with deeply cut, fan-shaped petals in late spring and early summer. *C. purpurea* grows to 3 feet tall with 1-inch flowers in shades of purple, lavender, red, and pink, often with a dark eye.

Growing conditions and maintenance: Sow seed outdoors in fall where winters are mild, and elsewhere in spring as soon as the soil can be worked. Sow fairly heavily since crowding will encourage flowering. Plants perform best where nights are cool.

Cleome
(klee-O-me)
SPIDER FLOWER

Cleome hasslerana 'Helen Campbell'

Plant type: *annual*

Height: *3 to 4 feet*

Interest: *flowers, seedpods*

Soil: *moist, well-drained*

Light: *full sun to light shade*

Enormous clusters of 1-inch flowers top the stems of cleome continuously from summer until frost. Pink, lavender, or white flower petals surround 2- to 3-inch-long stamens that protrude from the center, creating a spiderlike effect further enhanced by the slender, conspicuous seedpods that follow the flowers. Cleome makes a graceful summer hedge, accent, or border plant.

Selected species and varieties: *C. hasslerana* [also known as *C. spinosa*] has an erect habit with dark green palmately compound leaves and airy, ball-shaped flower heads. While flowers are short-lived, new ones are produced continuously at the top of the stem; 'Cherry Queen' bears rose red flowers; 'Helen Campbell' has white blooms; 'Pink Queen' bears clear pink blossoms; the flowers of 'Violet Queen' are purple, and leaves display a purple tint at their edges.

Growing conditions and maintenance: Start seed indoors 4 to 6 weeks prior to the last frost, or plant directly in the garden in early spring. Plants often self-seed. Space plants about 24 inches apart. Cleome thrives in warm weather and responds well to abundant moisture.

Consolida
(kon-SO-li-da)
LARKSPUR

Consolida ambigua

Plant type: *annual*

Height: *1 to 4 feet*

Interest: *flowers*

Soil: *well-drained, fertile*

Light: *full sun to light shade*

This native of southern Europe produces dense clusters of flowers upon stately, erect spikes. The flowers are available in shades of blue, lilac, pink, red, purple, and white and are quite long-lasting. Plant tall types toward the rear of a border, where they provide a graceful vertical accent and a fine source of fresh-cut flowers. Shorter varieties can be placed in the mid- or foreground of a mixed border.

Selected species and varieties: *C. ambigua* (rocket larkspur) produces lacy, deeply cut leaves. Spurred flowers in many pastel shades are borne in dense, graceful spikes throughout the summer; 'Imperial Blue Bell' grows to 4 feet with double blue flowers; 'Imperial White King' is similar with double white flowers.

Growing conditions and maintenance: Start seed indoors in peat pots 6 to 8 weeks prior to the last frost. Seed can be sown directly outdoors in fall from Zone 7 south and or in early spring elsewhere. Space plants to stand 8 to 15 inches apart. Tall varieties often require staking. Plants thrive in cool conditions, and where summers are warm will benefit from light shade. Keep soil evenly moist throughout the growing season.

Coreopsis
(ko-ree-OP-sis)
TICKSEED

Coreopsis tinctoria

Cosmos
(KOS-mos)
COSMOS

Cosmos bipinnatus 'Sonata White'

Cynara
(SIN-ah-ra)
CYNARA

Cynara cardunculus

Plant type: *annual*

Height: *2 to 3 feet*

Interest: *flowers*

Soil: *well-drained to dry*

Light: *full sun*

Plant type: *annual*

Height: *10 inches to 6 feet*

Interest: *flowers*

Soil: *well-drained to dry*

Light: *full sun to light shade*

Plant type: *tender perennial*

Height: *4 to 6 feet*

Interest: *flowers, foliage*

Soil: *moist, well-drained, fertile*

Light: *full sun*

This easy-to-grow annual is native to the eastern United States and is a common component of wildflower mixtures. Daisylike flower heads are borne on wiry stems and appear throughout the summer to early fall. Colors include yellow, orange, red, mahogany, and bicolors. Plant them in mixed borders and wildflower gardens, and cut them for fresh indoor arrangements.

Selected species and varieties: *C. tinctoria* (calliopsis) produces wiry, multiple branched stems with opposite-lobed or dissected leaves. Flower heads may be solitary or appear in branched clusters. Ray flowers are notched and often banded, surrounding a dark red or purple center. Double-flowered and dwarf varieties are available.

Growing conditions and maintenance: Start seed indoors 6 to 8 weeks before the last frost or sow directly in the garden in early spring. Space plants 6 to 8 inches apart. Make a second sowing in midsummer for fall flowers. Deadhead to prolong flowering. Plants tolerate hot weather and drought.

Daisylike flowers crown the wiry stems of this tropical American native. Its showy, delicate blossoms appear singly or in long-stalked loose clusters from midsummer until frost. Cosmos makes a graceful addition to mixed borders, where it will attract numerous butterflies, and is an excellent source of long-lasting cut flowers.

Selected species and varieties: *C. bipinnatus* grows to 6 feet with delicate, finely cut leaves and flowers in shades of red, pink, and white; 'Candy Stripe' grows 30 inches tall with white flowers with crimson markings; 'Seashells Mixture' grows 3 to 3½ feet with fluted petals of white, pink, or crimson surrounding a yellow center; 'Sonata White' grows 24 inches tall with snowy white blooms; 'Versailles Pink' develops strong, tall stems and pink flowers and is recommended for cutting. *C. sulphureus* grows to 6 feet—and cultivars to 18 to 36 inches—with yellow, orange, or scarlet flowers.

Growing conditions and maintenance: Sow seed directly in the garden after the last frost in spring. Thin to allow 12 to 18 inches between plants. Do not fertilize. Taller types are subject to lodging and may need staking. Plants often self-seed.

Related to the edible artichoke, this species forms clumps of thick stems lined with spiny, lacy silver-gray leaves with woolly undersides that provide a bold accent in a border or form a fast-growing summer hedge. Fuzzy thistle-like flower globes tip each stem from summer through fall. Both leaves and flowers are prized by floral designers for fresh and dried arrangements. It is native to southern Europe.

Selected species and varieties: *C. cardunculus* (cardoon) will grow 6 feet tall in warm climates, though it often reaches only 4 feet in cooler regions. Leaves grow to 3 feet long. Both the leafstalks and the roots are edible. Flower heads are purplish, up to 3 inches across, and are surrounded by spiny bracts.

Growing conditions and maintenance: Start seed indoors in late winter, transplanting to successively larger pots as needed before moving to the garden in midspring. Allow 3 feet between plants. Cardoon can be grown as a perennial from Zone 8 south.

Dahlia
(DAH-lee-a)
DAHLIA

Dahlia 'Audacity'

Plant type: *tender perennial*

Height: *12 inches to 8 feet*

Interest: *flowers*

Soil: *moist, well-drained, fertile*

Light: *full sun*

Dahlias brighten the border over a long season with diverse blooms whose sizes range from a few inches across to the diameter of a dinner plate. Their tightly packed disk flowers are surrounded by one or more rows of petal-like ray flowers that may be doubled, curved, twisted, cupped, or rolled into tiny tubes. Colors range widely; some are bicolored or variegated. The more than 20,000 cultivars available today descend from a few wild species cultivated by Aztec botanists. Dwarf dahlias are cultivated in beds or borders as low-growing bushy edgings; standard dahlias are grown as medium to tall fillers in beds and borders or as specimens. All make long-lasting cut flowers.

Selected species and varieties: *Anemone-flowered dahlias*—a central disk obscured by a fluffy ball of short, tubular petals and rimmed by one or more rows of longer, flat petals. *Ball dahlias*—cupped, doubled petals crowding spirally into round domes or slightly flattened globes. *Cactus dahlias*—straight or twisted petals rolled like quills or straws over half their length to a pointed tip. *Chrysanthemum-type dahlias*—double rows of petals curving inward and hiding the central disk. *Collarette dahlias*—central disks surrounded by a collar of short petals backed by a second collar of broader, flat petals. *Formal decorative dahlias*—double rows of flat, evenly spaced petals covering the central disk; 'Audacity' produces lavender-pink petals that fade to white at the base. *Informal decorative dahlias*—double rows of randomly spaced flat petals hiding the central disk. *Peony-flowered dahlias*—two or three overlapping layers of ray petals surrounding a central disk. *Pompom dahlias*—small, round balls of tightly rolled petals less than 2 inches in diameter. *Semicactus dahlias*—flat petals curling over less than half their length into tubes at their tips. *Single dahlias*—one or two rows of flat petals surrounding a flat central disk. *Star dahlias*—two or three rows of short petals curving inward. *Water lily-flowered dahlias*—short petals tightly clasped over the central disk like a water lily bud, surrounded by several rows of flat petals. Dahlias are further categorized by flower size.

Growing conditions and maintenance: Start seed indoors in very early spring, or plant tubers directly in the garden in spring, spacing them 1 to 4 feet apart, depending on their type. Provide abundant water and mulch. Remove faded blooms to extend bloom period. Taller types require staking. Dahlias are perennial in Zones 9 to 11; elsewhere tubers may be dug up in fall and stored in a dry, cool location until planting time the next spring.

Datura
(da-TOOR-a)
ANGEL'S-TRUMPET

Datura inoxia

Plant type: *annual or tender perennial*

Height: *2 to 5 feet*

Interest: *flowers*

Soil: *moist, well-drained*

Light: *full sun to light shade*

Datura's large flower trumpets bloom above coarse, oval leaves on shrubby plants that are useful as fillers or as backdrops in a border. Each summer-blooming flower opens at sunset and lasts only a day. Though flowers are sometimes fragrant, the leaves are unpleasantly scented, and most plant parts are extremely poisonous. Plant them only in places where they are completely out of the reach of children and pets.

Selected species and varieties: *D. inoxia* (angel's-trumpet, thorn apple) grows to 3 feet with 10-inch leaves and pendant pink, white, or lavender flowers 8 inches long and 5 inches wide. *D. metel* (Hindu datura) grows 3 to 5 feet tall with 8-inch leaves and 7-inch white or yellow- or purple-tinged flowers. *D. stramonium* (jimson weed) grows to 5 feet with 8-inch leaves and white or purple 2- to 5-inch flowers; it is extremely poisonous.

Growing conditions and maintenance: Start seed indoors 6 to 8 weeks prior to moving outdoors to warmed soil. Space plants 1½ to 2 feet apart. Provide shelter from wind. *D. inoxia* may survive as a short-lived perennial in Zones 9 and 10.

Daucus
(DAW-kus)
DAUCUS

Daucus carota var. carota

Dianthus
(dy-AN-thus)
PINK

Dianthus chinensis 'Telestar Picotee'

Digitalis
(di-ji-TAL-us)
FOXGLOVE

Digitalis purpurea 'Excelsior'

Plant type: *biennial*

Height: *3 to 4 feet*

Interest: *flowers*

Soil: *average to poor, well-drained*

Light: *full sun*

Plant type: *annual, biennial, or tender perennial*

Height: *4 to 30 inches*

Interest: *flowers, foliage*

Soil: *moist, well-drained, slightly alkaline*

Light: *full sun to partial shade*

Plant type: *biennial*

Height: *2 to 6 feet*

Interest: *flowers, foliage*

Soil: *moist, well-drained, acid*

Light: *partial shade*

This native of Eurasia has naturalized in the United States along roadsides and in abandoned fields. It is very closely related to the garden carrot but is grown for its dainty 4-inch flower heads, called umbels, which appear in late spring to midsummer. The flat-topped umbels consist of tiny white flowers with, often, a single dark red flower at the center. Its lacy appearance serves as a nice filler in a sunny border, and it naturalizes easily in wildflower meadows, attracting butterflies and bees. Flowers are valued for both fresh and dried arrangements.

Selected species and varieties: *D. carota* var. *carota* (Queen Anne's lace, Queen's lace, wild carrot) produces a prominent rosette of fernlike leaves in early spring, from which grows a 3- to 4-foot branched flowering stem. Each branch is topped by a 3- to 4-inch umbel.

Growing conditions and maintenance: Sow seed outdoors in late spring for flowers the following year. Once established, plant will vigorously self-seed. To prevent unwanted plants, remove flowers before seeds mature. Plants are easy to grow and thrive in nearly any well-drained soil.

Pinks form mats of grassy foliage with white, pink, red, and bicolored flowers with fringed petals. Low-growing types make delightful edgings or rock-garden or container specimens, while taller selections are useful in the foreground or middle of a border, and as cut flowers.

Selected species and varieties: *D. barbatus* (sweet William) is a biennial that self-seeds freely; dwarf varieties grow 4 to 10 inches tall, while tall varieties may reach 2 feet. Flowers are borne in dense, flat-topped clusters from late spring to early summer. *D. chinensis* (China pink, rainbow pink) is an annual, biennial, or short-lived perennial that grows 6 to 30 inches tall with a dense, mounded habit; 1- to 2-inch flowers, often fragrant, are borne singly or in loose clusters from early summer to fall; 'Telestar Picotee' has a compact habit with deep pink flowers fringed with white.

Growing conditions and maintenance: Sow sweet William seed outdoors in late spring for flowers the following year. Start seed of China pinks indoors 6 to 8 weeks prior to the last frost for transplanting to the garden in midspring. Space plants 8 to 18 inches apart.

Foxglove's striking summer-blooming flower trumpets line the tips of stiff stalks above clumps of coarse, hairy leaves. Most are native to Europe and North Africa but have been grown in the Americas since Colonial times. They add an old-fashioned look and a vertical accent to borders. They also fit well into naturalized plantings such as a woodland garden, and bees love their flowers. Though most bloom their second season, some varieties flower the first year from seed. Because foxglove self-seeds easily, new plants appear each year, giving it a perennial quality. Leaves contain digitalis and are poisonous if eaten.

Selected species and varieties: *D. ferruginea* (rusty foxglove) produces a basal clump of narrow, deeply veined dark green leaves, each up to 9 inches long. A leafy 5- to 6-foot flower stalk rises from the clump, bearing dense clusters of small yellowish blooms that open from mid- to late summer. Each flower is ½ to 1¼ inches long, yellow-brown, and netted with a rusty red. Tiny hairs fringe the flower lip. *D. purpurea* (common foxglove) produces a broad clump of large rough-textured woolly leaves from which an erect flower stem with smaller leaves emerges in early summer. The flower stalk ranges in size from 2 to 5 feet. The 2- to 3-inch pendulous flowers are borne in a one-sided cluster up to 2 feet long. Their colors include purple, pink, white, rust, or yellow, and their throats are often spotted; 'Alba' grows to 4 feet with white flowers; 'Apricot' grows to 3½ feet with flowers ranging from pale pink to bold apricot; 'Excelsior' grows to 5 feet with blooms borne all around the stem rather than on one side, in colors of purple, pink, white, cream, and yellow; 'Foxy' grows 2½ to 3 feet with flowers in pastel shades from rose pink to white appearing the first year from seed; 'Giant Shirley' grows 5 feet or more, producing strong stems with large mottled blooms in shades of pink.

Growing conditions and maintenance: Start seed outdoors in spring or summer, thinning to stand 6 inches apart. Transplant seedlings to their flowering location in fall or early spring. Types that bloom their first year from seed should be started indoors about 10 weeks, and transplanted to the garden 2 weeks, before the last frost. Space plants 18 to 24 inches apart. Foxgloves thrive in a rich, loose soil and benefit from the addition of compost. Provide water during dry periods and mulch after the ground freezes in fall.

Dolichos
(DO-li-kos)
HYACINTH BEAN

Dolichos lablab

Plant type: *tender perennial*

Height: *10 to 20 feet*

Interest: *flowers, foliage, fruit*

Soil: *loose, well-drained*

Light: *full sun*

This lush, tropical twining vine produces purplish stems and purple-veined compound leaves. Attractive clusters of pink, purple, or white pea-like flowers appear in summer and are followed by showy red-purple seedpods. The seeds are edible and are an important food source in many parts of the world. As an ornamental, plants provide a colorful screen or covering for a fence, an arbor, or a trellis.

Selected species and varieties: *D. lablab* climbs to 20 feet in one season by twining stems. Leaves are composed of three heart-shaped leaflets, each 3 to 6 inches long. The loosely clustered flowers stand out against the deeply colored leaves. Pods are 1 to 3 inches long.

Growing conditions and maintenance: Start seed indoors in peat pots 4 to 6 weeks prior to the last frost, or sow directly in the garden after the soil has warmed. Space plants 12 to 24 inches apart and provide support for climbing. Hyacinth bean thrives in warm weather and is perennial in Zones 10 and 11.

Dyssodia
(dis-OH-dee-ah)
DAHLBERG DAISY

Dyssodia tenuiloba

Plant type: *annual or tender perennial*

Height: *4 to 8 inches*

Interest: *flowers, foliage*

Soil: *well-drained to dry*

Light: *full sun*

Their dainty blooms sprinkled on a dense carpet of finely divided foliage, Dahlberg daisies (also called goldenfleece) constantly flower throughout the summer. They are perfect for bedding and edging, in rock gardens, and in hanging baskets. They can be planted between steppingstones to add color to a sunny garden path.

Selected species and varieties: *D. tenuiloba* grows to 8 inches tall but spreads up to 18 inches wide. Its slender stems produce threadlike, bristle-tipped leaves that are aromatic. Flower heads are ½ to 1 inch across with orange-yellow ray flowers surrounding a yellow center.

Growing conditions and maintenance: Start seed indoors 6 to 8 weeks prior to the last frost to transplant to the garden after all danger of frost has passed. In warm areas they can be planted directly in the garden and will self-seed. Allow 6 to 12 inches between plants. Water sparingly and do not fertilize. Plants thrive in sunny, dry locations and tolerate heat, drought, and coastal conditions.

Echium
(EK-ee-um)
VIPER'S BUGLOSS

Echium candicans

Plant type: *biennial*

Height: *1 to 10 feet*

Interest: *flowers, foliage*

Soil: *dry, poor*

Light: *full sun*

These tropical natives provide a striking accent to borders and rock gardens with their brightly colored and closely packed tubular flowers, which appear from early to late summer. Plants often flower their first year from seed. They are especially useful in sunny, dry locations where the soil is poor.

Selected species and varieties: *E. candicans* (pride-of-Madeira) grows 3 to 6 feet tall with narrow gray-green leaves covered with silvery hairs and an erect 20-inch cluster of white or purple ½-inch flowers held well above the leaves. *E. lycopsis* (viper's bugloss) grows 1 to 3 feet tall with a bushy habit; flowers are blue, lavender, purple, pink, or white and appear on dense 10-inch spikes. *E. wildpretii* (tower-of-jewels) grows to a show-stopping 10 feet, with pale red blooms.

Growing conditions and maintenance: Start seed indoors 6 to 8 weeks before the last frost or outdoors as soon as soil can be worked in spring. In Zone 9 and south, seed can be sown in fall for earlier bloom. Space plants 12 to 18 inches apart. They thrive in poor soils and will produce few flowers on a fertile site. Water sparingly.

Eschscholzia
(es-SHOL-zee-a)
CALIFORNIA POPPY

Eschscholzia californica

Plant type: *annual or tender perennial*

Height: *4 to 24 inches*

Interest: *flowers*

Soil: *dry*

Light: *full sun*

This genus includes both annuals and tender perennials native to the grasslands of California and the Southwest. Flowers open during the day and close at night and in cloudy weather. They are effective for massing in beds and borders and compete well in wildflower meadows.

Selected species and varieties: *E. caespitosa* (tufted California poppy, pastel poppy) is an annual with pale yellow flowers on 4- to 12-inch stalks above finely cut basal foliage. *E. californica* is a 1- to 2-foot tender perennial from Zone 8 south but is grown as an annual elsewhere, with 1- to 3-inch yellow or orange flowers from spring to fall and feathery blue-green foliage; 'Aurantiaca' is an old variety with rich orange single blooms; 'Monarch Mixed' bears single and semidouble flowers in yellow, orange, red, and pink; 'Orange King' bears translucent orange flowers.

Growing conditions and maintenance: Plant seed outdoors in early spring; seedlings do not transplant well. Once established, plants self-seed freely. Space them 6 inches apart. Though they tolerate most soils, they prefer a poor, sandy one.

Euphorbia
(yew-FOR-bee-a)
EUPHORBIA

Euphorbia marginata

Plant type: *annual*

Height: *18 inches to 2 feet*

Interest: *flowers, foliage*

Soil: *dry to wet*

Light: *full sun*

This hardy annual is native to many parts of the United States and is grown as much for its neatly variegated leaves as for its tiny green flowers surrounded by white bracts. It is an effective accent for annual beds, especially planted in groups of three or five among plants with dark leaves or brightly colored flowers. The sap may cause skin irritation.

Selected species and varieties: *E. marginata* (snow-on-the-mountain, ghostweed) produces erect, stout, branched stems bearing gray-green oval leaves attractively striped and margined with white. Though the late-summer flowers are small, they are surrounded by showy white leaflike bracts.

Growing conditions and maintenance: Sow seed directly in the garden in late fall or early spring. Allow 10 to 12 inches between plants. Moisture is needed for seed to germinate and for the plants to become established, but they become very drought tolerant as they mature. They self-seed easily and may become invasive. Use gloves when handling stems to avoid contact with the sap.

Gazania
(ga-ZAY-nee-a)
GAZANIA

Gazania rigens 'Fiesta Red'

Plant type: *tender perennial*

Height: *6 to 16 inches*

Interest: *flowers*

Soil: *well-drained to dry*

Light: *full sun*

This tender perennial from South Africa produces daisylike flowers from midsummer to frost. Blossoms open when the sun is out, and close at night and on overcast days. They provide a colorful show in beds or containers.

Selected species and varieties: *G. linearis* grows to 16 inches with narrow leaves and 2¾-inch flower heads with golden rays and orange-brown disks. *G. rigens* (treasure flower) grows 6 to 12 inches tall with 3-inch flower heads, borne on long stalks, that may be yellow, orange, pink, or red; 'Chansonette' grows to 10 inches with a compact habit and flowers in a wide range of colors; 'Fiesta Red' bears deep burnt orange flowers with a dark ring surrounding a yellow disk; 'Harlequin Hybrids' bear flowers in many shades with a brown zone around the central disk; 'Sunshine' grows to 8 inches with 4-inch multicolored flowers.

Growing conditions and maintenance: Sow seed indoors in early spring to transplant to the garden after all danger of frost has passed. Space plants 12 inches apart. Do not overwater. They thrive in sunny, dry locations, and tolerate wind and coastal conditions.

Gomphrena
(gom-FREE-na)
GLOBE AMARANTH

Gomphrena globosa

Plant type: *annual*

Height: *8 to 24 inches*

Interest: *flowers*

Soil: *well-drained*

Light: *full sun*

Colorful cloverlike flower heads of gomphrena top upright stems from summer to frost. A native of India, this half-hardy annual is easy to grow and imparts a cheerful, informal appearance to beds and borders. Plants perform well in patio planters and window boxes. Flowers, which have a papery texture even when fresh, are excellent for both fresh and dried arrangements.

Selected species and varieties: *G. globosa* produces erect, branched stems and somewhat coarse, hairy leaves. The globular flower heads are 1 inch long and may be pink, white, magenta, orange, or red.

Growing conditions and maintenance: Start seed indoors 8 to 10 weeks before the last frost and transplant outdoors after all danger of frost has passed. Seed can be sown directly outside in late spring. Allow 8 to 15 inches between plants. Though slow to start, plants are easy to grow once established, and they thrive in warm weather. To use in dried arrangements, cut before the flowers are fully open and hang them upside down in an airy room until dry.

Gypsophila
(jip-SOFF-il-a)
BABY'S-BREATH

Gypsophila elegans

Plant type: *annual*

Height: *8 to 24 inches*

Interest: *flowers*

Soil: *well-drained, alkaline*

Light: *full sun*

This hardy annual from Europe and northern Asia produces a cloud of delicate, tiny flowers on sprawling, branched stems from midspring to early fall. It is beautiful as a filler between more brightly colored and boldly textured plants in flower borders or rock gardens and in indoor arrangements both fresh and dried.

Selected species and varieties: *G. elegans* has a mounded habit with thin, multibranched stems bearing pairs of narrow gray-green leaves and airy clusters of white, pink, red, or purple flowers. Each flower is ¼ to ¾ inch across.

Growing conditions and maintenance: Sow seed directly in the garden in midspring. Supplement acid soils with limestone. Plants are short-lived, so make successive sowings every 2 to 3 weeks for continuous bloom. Thin plants to stand 9 to 12 inches apart. Taller varieties may need staking. In Zone 9 and south, provide afternoon shade.

Helianthus
(bee-lee-AN-thus)
SUNFLOWER

Helianthus annuus 'Inca Jewels'

Plant type: *annual*

Height: *2 to 10 feet*

Interest: *flowers*

Soil: *moist, well-drained*

Light: *full sun*

The sunflower's daisylike blooms in yellow, cream, mahogany, crimson, and assorted blends appear from midsummer to frost on erect stalks. The flowers make a bold statement in mixed borders, and a row of them makes a delightful temporary screen. Flowers are great for cutting. The seeds are a favorite food of many wild birds.

Selected species and varieties: *H. annuus* (common sunflower) has an erect habit and a coarse texture, producing sturdy stems with broad, bristly leaves and flowers composed of petal-like, often yellow rays surrounding brown or purple disk flowers; 'Inca Jewels' has a multi-branched habit with yellow-tipped orange rays; 'Italian White' grows to 4 feet with multibranched stems and 4-inch cream-colored flowers with a brown center; 'Sunbeam' grows 5 feet tall with 5-inch pollenless flowers ideal for cutting; 'Teddy Bear' produces single and double yellow flowers on 2-foot plants.

Growing conditions and maintenance: Sow seed directly outdoors after the last frost. Thin seedlings to allow 1 to 2 feet between plants. Plants thrive in hot, dry weather conditions.

Helichrysum
(hel-i-KRY-sum)
EVERLASTING

Helichrysum bracteatum

Plant type: *tender perennial*

Height: *1 to 3 feet*

Interest: *flowers*

Soil: *light, well-drained*

Light: *full sun*

This Australian native, also known as immortelle, produces papery-textured flowers in shades of white, yellow, orange, salmon, red, and pink. What appear to be the flower's petals are actually colorful bracts; the true flowers are at the center of the flower head. Use dwarf types for adding color to a rock garden or the edge of a border. Taller varieties are highly valued for cutting, especially for winter arrangements. Flowers retain their colors very well when dried.

Selected species and varieties: *H. bracteatum* (strawflower) produces narrow, coarsely toothed leaves on wiry, branching stems. Flower heads appear from midsummer to early fall and are 1 to 2½ inches across.

Growing conditions and maintenance: Start seed indoors 6 to 8 weeks prior to the last frost. In warm climates, seed can be sown directly in the garden. Allow 12 inches between plants. Once established, plants thrive in dry soil and often self-seed. They do not perform well in areas with very high humidity. For winter arrangements, cut flowers when they are about half open and hang them upside down in an airy room to dry.

Heliotropium
(hee-lee-oh-TRO-pee-um)
HELIOTROPE

Heliotropium arborescens 'Marine'

Plant type: *tender perennial*

Height: *1 to 3 feet*

Interest: *flowers*

Soil: *well-drained, fertile*

Light: *full sun to partial shade*

Heliotrope is a tender perennial from Peru grown as an annual in temperate zones. Large clusters of summer flowers range from deep purple to white and bear a lovely vanilla fragrance. Site plants in the foreground of a mixed border; they are especially effective in groups located where their fragrance will be appreciated. They are ideal container plants, and flowers can be cut for fresh arrangements.

Selected species and varieties: *H. arborescens* (cherry pie) grows 1 to 3 feet in the garden, though plants grown in a greenhouse or in their native range may reach 6 feet. Foliage is dark green and wrinkled. Five-petaled flowers are ¼ inch across, occurring in clusters as large as a foot across; 'Marine', a compact variety reaching 2 feet, has large deep purple flowers and is excellent for bedding, although it lacks intense fragrance.

Growing conditions and maintenance: Start seed indoors 10 to 12 weeks prior to the last frost, or buy young plants in spring. Plants can also be started from cuttings. Do not transplant to the garden until soil has warmed, as plants are very frost sensitive. Allow 12 inches between plants and keep them well watered.

Hibiscus
(hy-BIS-kus)
MALLOW, ROSE MALLOW

Hibiscus acetosella

Plant type: *tender perennial*

Height: *18 inches to 8 feet*

Interest: *flowers, foliage*

Soil: *moist, well-drained*

Light: *full sun to light shade*

These shrubby tender perennials are attractively grown as annuals in many temperate gardens. Some are grown for their ornamental foliage, while others produce large, funnel-shaped, five-petaled flowers with prominent stamens that add a tropical flavor to a border. You will find many uses for these bold-textured plants. Plant them individually as specimens or in groups as a fast-growing summer hedge. Tall types are effective as a background for mixed borders or as the centerpiece of an island bed. Shorter ones are useful for fronting shrub borders or planting in the foreground of annual beds. Both large and small types are excellent choices for patio containers.

Selected species and varieties: *H. acetosella* hails from Africa and is grown primarily for its attractive foliage. Purple flowers form so late in the season in most areas that they fail to open before frost. The plant grows to 5 feet tall, with glossy red leaves and stems. Leaves may be smooth in outline or deeply lobed. This plant makes a bold accent mixed with other annuals, or a stunning summer hedge; the variety 'Red Shield' produces burgundy leaves with a metallic sheen that resemble maple leaves in shape. *H. moscheutos* (common rose mallow, swamp rose mallow, wild cotton) grows 3 to 8 feet tall with a shrubby habit. It is native to marshlands of the eastern United States and can be grown as a perennial in Zone 7 and south, but is often grown as a half-hardy annual. The large gray-green leaves provide a soft foil for the huge white, pink, rose, or red summer flowers that are often 8 inches across; 'Southern Belle' grows 4 to 6 feet tall with red, pink, or white flowers with a distinct red eye, up to 10 inches across. *H. trionum* (flower-of-an-hour) grows 18 to 36 inches with a bushy habit and dark green three- or five-lobed leaves. Flowers are 2 inches across and are creamy yellow with a deep maroon throat. Though flowers are short-lived, they appear in abundance from mid-summer to late fall.

Growing conditions and maintenance: Start seed of *H. acetosella* and *H. moscheutos* indoors about 8 weeks prior to the last frost and transplant outdoors after all danger of frost has passed. Space *H. acetosella* 12 to 14 inches apart, *H. moscheutos* 3 feet apart. Because *H. trionum* is difficult to transplant, seed should be sown directly in the garden after all danger of frost has passed, allowing 12 inches between plants. Plants tolerate heat as long as abundant moisture is supplied.

Iberis
(eye-BEER-is)
CANDYTUFT

Iberis umbellata

Plant type: *annual*

Height: *6 to 18 inches*

Interest: *flowers*

Soil: *well-drained*

Light: *full sun*

These European wildflowers are easy to grow and free flowering. Like the perennial species *[I. sempervirens]*, annual candytufts produce clusters of tiny four-petaled flowers above dark green leaves. They flower throughout the summer and are effective in rock gardens and borders, or as an edging or in a planter, where their sweet fragrance will be noticed.

Selected species and varieties: *I. amara* (rocket candytuft) grows 12 to 18 inches tall with fragrant white flowers in cone-shaped spikes that can be cut for fresh arrangements. *I. odorata* (fragrant candytuft) grows 6 to 12 inches with flat clusters of white flowers. *I. umbellata* (globe candytuft) grows 8 to 16 inches with clusters of pink, red, lilac, or violet flowers that are not fragrant.

Growing conditions and maintenance: Sow seed in the garden in fall or as soon as soil can be worked in the spring, thinning to allow 6 to 9 inches between seedlings. Make successive sowings to extend the flowering season. Cut back lightly after bloom to stimulate growth. Plants thrive in city conditions.

Impatiens
(im-PAY-shens)
BALSAM, JEWELWEED

Impatiens wallerana 'Super Elfin Twilight'

Plant type: *annual*

Height: *6 inches to 8 feet*

Interest: *flowers, foliage*

Soil: *moist, well-drained*

Light: *full sun to full shade*

Massed as edgings or ground covers, impatiens brighten a shady garden with flowers in jeweled hues from summer through frost. Low-growing types are ideal for planters and hanging baskets.

Selected species and varieties: *I. balsamina* (garden balsam, rose balsam) grows to 3 feet, producing 1- to 2-inch flowers in mixed colors. *I. glandulifera* (Himalayan jewelweed) grows to 8 feet with 2-inch purple, pink, or white flowers in mid- to late summer. *I.* x *New Guinea* (New Guinea impatiens) grows to 2 feet with showy, often variegated leaves with flowers up to 3 inches across. *I. wallerana* (busy Lizzie) grows 6 to 18 inches tall with a compact, mounded habit and 1- to 2-inch flat-faced flowers available in many colors; 'Super Elfin Twilight' bears deep pink flowers on spreading plants.

Growing conditions and maintenance: Plant *I. glandulifera* seed outdoors in fall. Start impatiens indoors 3 to 4 months prior to the last frost, or purchase bedding plants to transplant to the garden after all danger of frost has passed. Space *I. glandulifera* 2 feet apart, others 12 to 18 inches apart. Most species prefer some shade and abundant water.

Kochia
(KOE-kee-a)
BURNING BUSH

Kochia scoparia f. trichophylla

Plant type: *annual*

Height: *2 to 4 feet*

Interest: *foliage*

Soil: *moist, well-drained*

Light: *full sun*

This Eurasian annual has naturalized in some parts of the United States. Its fine-textured foliage and neat, symmetrical form make it an attractive summer hedge, screen, or background for a flower border.

Selected species and varieties: *K. scoparia f. trichophylla* (summer cypress, firebush) has an erect, uniform habit with dense, feathery foliage that is light green in summer, turning bright red in fall, while flowers are insignificant; 'Acapulco Silver' produces variegated silver-tipped leaves.

Growing conditions and maintenance: Start seed indoors in individual peat pots 6 to 8 weeks prior to the last frost or plant directly in the garden after all danger of frost has passed. Do not cover the seed; it needs light for germination. Plants often self-seed and may become invasive. Allow 1½ to 2 feet between plants. Plants can be sheared to maintain their shape or size, and they tolerate heat. Avoid overwatering. In windy locations, plants may require staking.

Lathyrus
(LATH-er-us)
LATHYRUS

Lathyrus odoratus

Plant type: *annual*

Height: *6 inches to 6 feet*

Interest: *flowers*

Soil: *moist, well-drained*

Light: *full sun to partial shade*

The sweet pea is a hardy annual from southern Europe that bears puffy flowers on branching flowering stalks. It can be used as a trailing ground cover, a climbing vine for a screen or backdrop, or a bushy accent among bulbs.

Selected species and varieties: *L. odoratus* (sweet pea) produces fragrant spring or summer flowers up to 2 inches wide on compact 6-inch- to 2½-foot-tall annual bushes, or on a twining vine 5 to 6 feet long. Flower colors include deep rose, blue, purple, scarlet, white, cream, salmon, pink, and bicolors; 'Bijou Mixed' is a bush type that grows to 12 inches with a full range of colors; 'Royal Family' is a vining type that comes in a wide range of colors, grows to 6 feet, and is heat resistant.

Growing conditions and maintenance: Sow seed 2 inches deep in well-prepared soil in late fall or early spring. Provide climbing types with support. Mulch to keep soil cool, and provide abundant water. Remove faded blooms to prolong flowering.

Lavatera
(lav-a-TEER-a)
TREE MALLOW

Lavatera trimestris

Plant type: *annual*

Height: *2 to 6 feet*

Interest: *flowers*

Soil: *well-drained*

Light: *full sun*

Native to the Mediterranean region, lavatera is a hardy annual with a bushy habit and cup-shaped summer flowers that resemble hollyhocks. Their long blooming season makes these plants a good choice for the mixed border. They are also useful as a summer hedge, and flowers can be cut for fresh arrangements.

Selected species and varieties: *L. trimestris* produces pale green rounded leaves on branched stems that may reach 6 feet, although most varieties are between 2 and 3 feet; both leaves and stems are hairy. Solitary 2½- to 4-inch flowers, each with five wide petals, are borne in great numbers throughout the summer. Colors include shades of pink, red, and white; 'Mont Blanc' grows only 2 feet tall and bears pure white flowers; 'Silver Cup' also grows to 2 feet, bearing salmon pink flowers with darker veins.

Growing conditions and maintenance: Sow seed outdoors in midspring, thinning to allow plants to stand 1½ to 2 feet apart. Young plants require abundant water and should be mulched. Once established, plants are drought resistant. Deadhead to prolong flowering.

Layia
(LAY-ee-ah)
TIDYTIPS

Layia platyglossa

Plant type: *annual*

Height: *1 to 2 feet*

Interest: *flowers*

Soil: *well-drained*

Light: *full sun*

Layia is a member of the sunflower family and is native to California, where it grows as a wildflower. Its common name refers to the showy white-tipped ray petals that surround a golden disk. It is a good choice for beds, borders, rock gardens, and sunny banks. Flowers are excellent for fresh arrangements.

Selected species and varieties: *L. platyglossa* has a neat habit and coarsely toothed gray-green leaves covered with dense hairs. Flowers appear from spring to early summer; they are bright yellow, single, 2 inches across, and daisylike. This species is often included in wildflower mixes.

Growing conditions and maintenance: Start seed indoors 6 to 8 weeks prior to the last frost, or sow outdoors in early spring. In Zone 9 and warmer, seed can be sown in fall. Space plants 9 to 12 inches apart, and provide abundant moisture to seedlings. Once plants are established, they are quite drought tolerant. Remove flowers as they fade to prolong blooming period.

Limonium
(ly-MO-nee-um)
STATICE

Limonium sinuatum

Plant type: *annual or biennial*

Height: *10 to 24 inches*

Interest: *flowers*

Soil: *well-drained, sandy, slightly alkaline*

Light: *full sun*

Statice, also called sea lavender, is native to the Mediterranean region and bears clusters of brightly colored flowers surrounded by a papery calyx that remains after the rest of the flower drops. This long-lasting display is useful both in beds and for cutting. Flowers dry easily and retain their color well so are often used in dried arrangements.

Selected species and varieties: *L. sinuatum* (notchleaf statice) grows 18 to 24 inches with a clump of 4- to 8-inch basal leaves and branched, winged flower stems. The papery-textured flowers are borne in short one-sided clusters; colors include pink, blue, lavender, yellow, and white. *L. suworowii* [also known as *Psylliostachys suworowii*] (Russian statice) grows 10 to 20 inches tall with large basal leaves and spikes of lavender and green flowers from summer to frost.

Growing conditions and maintenance: Start seed indoors in individual peat pots 8 weeks prior to the last frost, or sow directly outdoors in midspring in warm climates. Allow 9 to 18 inches between plants. They tolerate drought and seaside conditions but will rot in soil that remains wet.

Lobularia
(lob-yew-LAIR-ee-a)
SWEET ALYSSUM

Lobularia maritima

Plant type: *tender perennial*

Height: *4 to 12 inches*

Interest: *flowers*

Soil: *well-drained*

Light: *full sun to partial shade*

This Mediterranean native spreads to nearly twice its height, producing tiny fragrant flowers from late spring to frost. It makes a good choice for an edging, for a rock garden, along dry walls, or for window boxes. In the front of a mixed border, it neatly covers the dying foliage of spring-flowering bulbs.

Selected species and varieties: *L. maritima* is a fine-textured plant with alternate narrow leaves 1 to 2 inches long. It has a low-branching and spreading habit. Four-petaled flowers are borne in clusters and bear a honeylike scent; colors include white, lilac, pink, and purple.

Growing conditions and maintenance: Start seed indoors 6 to 8 weeks prior to the last frost, or sow directly in the garden in early spring. Avoid overwatering seedlings. Space plants 6 inches apart; they tolerate crowding. In warm areas, they will self-seed. They thrive in cool weather; flowering may stop in hot temperatures. Cutting back plants will encourage further flowering.

Lunaria
(loo-NAY-ree-a)
HONESTY, MONEY PLANT

Lunaria annua

Plant type: *biennial*

Height: *2 to 3 feet*

Interest: *fruit*

Soil: *well-drained*

Light: *full sun to partial shade*

This old-fashioned biennial is native to southern Europe. It is grown primarily for its fruit, a flat, oval, translucent seedpod. Plants are best suited to the cutting garden, an informal border, or a wildflower meadow. Their papery seedpods are highly valued for dried arrangements.

Selected species and varieties: *L. annua* (silver-dollar, bolbonac) has an erect habit with broad, coarsely toothed leaves and fragrant pink or purple flowers, each with four petals, borne in terminal clusters in late spring. Flowers are followed by the seedpods, which fall apart, revealing a thin, silvery white disk, 1 to 2 inches across, to which the seeds cling; 'Alba' produces white flowers well displayed when grown against a dark background.

Growing conditions and maintenance: Lunaria can be grown as an annual or a biennial. For flowers and seedpods the first year, sow seed outdoors in very early spring, or plant in midsummer to early fall for flowers and seedpods the following year. Once established they will reseed through Zone 4. Space plants 8 to 12 inches apart. They tolerate wet and dry conditions and are not fussy about soil quality, as long as it is well drained.

Matthiola
(ma-THY-o-la)
STOCK

Matthiola incana

Plant type: *annual or biennial*

Height: *12 to 30 inches*

Interest: *flowers*

Soil: *well-drained, fertile*

Light: *full sun to light shade*

The blossoms of stock perfume a garden throughout summer. Plant them in beds, window boxes, or patio containers where their fragrance can be appreciated. Flowers add a dainty appearance and sweet scent to fresh indoor arrangements.

Selected species and varieties: *M. bicornis* [also known as *M. longipetala* ssp. *bicornis*] (night-scented stock, evening stock, perfume plant) has a bushy habit and grows 12 to 18 inches tall. It bears single ¾-inch flowers in shades of lilac and pink that open at night from mid- to late summer and are extremely fragrant. *M. incana* (common stock, gillyflower) grows 12 to 30 inches with gray-green oblong leaves and terminal clusters of 1-inch-long flowers that may be single or double and bear a spicy fragrance; colors include pink, purple, white, and blue.

Growing conditions and maintenance: Start seed indoors 6 to 8 weeks prior to the last frost, or sow directly in the garden in early spring. Space plants to stand 6 to 12 inches apart; they tolerate crowding. Plants thrive in cool weather and may stop flowering when temperatures rise. *M. bicornis* will tolerate poorer soil and drier conditions than will *M. incana*.

Mimulus
(MIM-yew-lus)
MONKEY FLOWER

Mimulus x hybridus

Plant type: *tender perennial*

Height: *10 to 14 inches*

Interest: *flowers*

Soil: *moist, well-drained, fertile*

Light: *partial to full shade*

Blooming from midsummer to fall, this native of both North and South America provides bright color to shady beds and borders. It fits well alongside a garden pond or stream and also makes an attractive container plant. Funnel-shaped, two-lipped flowers are thought to resemble monkeys' faces.

Selected species and varieties: *M.* x *hybridus* has a mounded habit with glossy 2- to 2½-inch leaves and 2-inch tubular flowers in shades of red, yellow, orange, rose, and brown, usually with brown or maroon spotting or mottling.

Growing conditions and maintenance: Start seed indoors 10 to 12 weeks prior to the last frost for transplanting to the garden after all danger of frost has passed. Space plants 6 inches apart. Plants benefit from the addition of organic matter to the soil. They require some shade and ample moisture. In fall, plants can be dug and potted to continue flowering indoors over the winter.

Myosotis
(my-oh-SO-tis)
FORGET-ME-NOT

Myosotis sylvatica 'Ultramarine'

Plant type: *annual or biennial*

Height: *6 to 10 inches*

Interest: *flowers, foliage*

Soil: *moist, well-drained*

Light: *full sun to partial shade*

Airy clusters of dainty flowers with prominent eyes open above the forget-me-not's low mounds of delicate foliage. Forget-me-nots provide a soft filler or a delicate border edging. They are particularly attractive in combination with spring-flowering bulbs such as tulips.

Selected species and varieties: *M. sylvatica* (woodland forget-me-not, garden forget-me-not) produces 8- to 10-inch stems in clumps almost as wide, lined with soft, elongated leaves and tipped with loose clusters of ¼-inch yellow-centered blue flowers from spring through early summer; 'Ultramarine' is very dwarf, growing to 6 inches, with dark blue flowers; 'Victoria Blue' grows 6 to 8 inches, forming neat mounds and producing early flowers of gentian blue.

Growing conditions and maintenance: Start seed outdoors in late summer to early fall for flowers the following spring. Once established, forget-me-nots self-seed readily, performing like a perennial. Enrich the soil with organic matter. Allow 6 to 12 inches between plants, and water during dry periods.

Nemophila
(nem-OFF-i-la)
BABY-BLUE-EYES

Nemophila menziesii

Plant type: *annual*

Height: *6 to 10 inches*

Interest: *flowers*

Soil: *moist, well-drained*

Light: *full sun to partial shade*

Baby-blue-eyes hails from California and Oregon, where it grows as a wildflower. In the garden its low, mounded habit and dainty flowers make good edgings, rock-garden specimens, and companions for spring-flowering bulbs. They are also attractive when planted so that their trailing stems spill over the edge of a wall.

Selected species and varieties: *N. menziesii* produces trailing stems to form a mounding plant, usually about 6 inches tall and 12 inches across, with deeply cut light green leaves. Flowers are tubular, 1 to 1½ inches across, and sky blue in color with white centers; 'Pennie Black' has deep purple ¾-inch blooms edged with silvery white.

Growing conditions and maintenance: Sow seed directly in the garden in early spring, thinning the seedlings to stand 6 inches apart. Enrich the soil with organic matter and provide abundant moisture. Plants thrive in areas with cool summers and will self-seed under favorable conditions.

Nicotiana
(ni-ko-she-AN-a)
TOBACCO

Nicotiana sylvestris

Plant type: *annual*

Height: *1 to 6 feet*

Interest: *flowers, foliage*

Soil: *moist, well-drained*

Light: *full sun to partial shade*

Flowering tobacco produces clusters of fragrant, flat-faced flowers with elongated tubular throats growing at the tips of soft stems, and clumps of large leaves. Plants are useful as border fillers or specimens. Flowers of some varieties close in sunlight but open on cloudy days or in the evening. Leaf juices are poisonous.

Selected species and varieties: *N. alata* (jasmine tobacco) produces 1- to 2-foot-tall clumps with flowers that bloom from spring to fall; 'Domino Hybrids' have compact cushions of foliage to 15 inches and early-spring flowers in mixed colors; 'Nikki' grows to 18 inches tall with pink, red, white, yellow, or lime green flowers; 'Sensation Mixed' grows 2 to 2½ feet tall with red, pink, purple, white, and yellow blooms. *N. langsdorffii* produces nodding green flowers with turquoise anthers at the tips of 5-foot stems. *N. sylvestris* (woodland tobacco) produces drooping white flowers tinged pink or purple on branching plants 3 to 6 feet tall.

Growing conditions and maintenance: Start seed indoors 6 to 8 weeks prior to the last frost, or sow directly outdoors in late spring. Space plants about 12 inches apart. Deadhead spent blooms.

Nigella
(nye-JEL-a)
LOVE-IN-A-MIST

Nigella damascena

Plant type: *annual*

Height: *18 to 24 inches*

Interest: *flowers, seed heads*

Soil: *well-drained*

Light: *full sun*

Love-in-a-mist adds a delicate, fine texture to any border or flower arrangement in which it is used. Its fernlike leaves are light green, and solitary flowers are nestled in a mist of foliage at the ends of stems throughout the summer. Interesting seed capsules replace the flowers and are attractive in dried flower arrangements. This annual is native to southern Europe and North Africa.

Selected species and varieties: *N. damascena* has an erect multibranched habit with delicate leaves divided into thread-like segments. Flowers are 1 to 1½ inches across with blue, white, or pink notched petals. The papery 1-inch seed capsules are pale green with reddish brown markings.

Growing conditions and maintenance: Start seed directly outdoors in early spring, and make additional sowings every 2 or 3 weeks until early summer to extend the flowering season. Plants are not easily transplanted. Thin to allow 6 to 10 inches between plants. Water during dry periods. If pods are allowed to remain on plants, they will self-seed.

Oenothera
(ee-no-THEE-ra)
EVENING PRIMROSE

Oenothera biennis

Plant type: *biennial*

Height: *2 to 8 feet*

Interest: *flowers*

Soil: *well-drained to dry*

Light: *full sun to partial shade*

Among this genus of mostly perennial plants are a few hardy biennials that can be treated as annuals. Their pale yellow funnel-shaped blooms appear from early summer to midfall, opening in the evening atop tall, erect stems. They are suitable for massing at the rear of a border or for use in a wildflower garden.

Selected species and varieties: *O. biennis* produces a clump of coarse basal leaves from which a stout, erect flower stem rises. Stems may reach 6 feet and bear 1- to 2-inch flowers that open pale yellow and turn gold. *O. erythrosepala* [also called *O. glaziovinia*] grows 2 to 8 feet tall with yellow flowers that turn orange or red; 'Tina James' grows 3 to 4 feet with showy yellow flowers that burst open in 1 to 2 minutes and are pleasantly fragrant.

Growing conditions and maintenance: Start seed indoors 8 to 12 weeks prior to the last frost, or outdoors in early spring. Where winters are mild, seed can be sown outdoors in fall. Once established, plants will often self-seed, and may become invasive. Space plants 12 inches apart. They thrive in warm weather and tolerate poor soil.

Papaver
(pa-PAY-ver)
POPPY

Papaver nudicaule

Plant type: *annual or tender perennial*

Height: *1 to 4 feet*

Interest: *flowers*

Soil: *well-drained loam*

Light: *full sun to partial shade*

Poppy's showy spring flowers surround prominent centers above clumps of coarse, hairy, deeply lobed leaves. The brightly colored flower petals are extremely delicate in appearance, with a tissuelike texture. Flowers may be single, with four overlapping petals, or double, with many petals forming a rounded bloom. They are borne on solitary stems, and are suitable for mixed borders and good for cutting.

Selected species and varieties: *P. nudicaule* (Iceland poppy, Arctic poppy) produces a fernlike clump of 6-inch lobed gray-green leaves from which 12- to 18-inch leafless flower stems rise from spring to early summer. Flowers are fragrant, 2 to 4 inches across, and saucer shaped; colors include white, yellow, orange, salmon, pink, and scarlet. *P. rhoeas* (corn poppy, Flanders poppy, Shirley poppy, field poppy) grows to 3 feet with wiry, branching stems and pale green deeply lobed leaves. Flowers may be single or double, and are borne from late spring to early summer in colors of red, purple, pink, and white; 'Fairy Wings' produces flowers in soft shades of blue, lilac, dusty pink, and white with

faint blue margins; 'Mother of Pearl' bears flowers in shades of blue, lavender, pink, gray, white, and peach, and the flowers may be solid or speckled. *P. somniferum* (opium poppy) grows 3 to 4 feet tall with large white, red, pink, or mauve flowers that appear throughout summer and are often double or fringed; 'Alba' bears white blooms; 'Pink Chiffon' produces double bright pink flowers; 'White Cloud' bears large double white blooms on sturdy stems.

Papaver rhoeas

Growing conditions and maintenance: *P. nudicaule* can be started indoors 10 weeks prior to the last frost for transplanting in late spring. Handle seedlings carefully because they are difficult to transplant. You can also sow directly in the garden in late fall or early spring. Other species are so difficult to transplant that they are best sown in place. Papaver seed is very small and can be mixed with sand for easier handling. Thin *P. nudicaule* to stand 8 to 10 inches apart, *P. rhoeas* about 12 inches apart, and *P. somniferum* 4 to 8 inches apart. Double-flowered varieties of *P. somniferum* often require staking. Poppies will often self-seed. Deadhead plants to prolong flowering season. For use in indoor arrangements, cut the flowers as the buds straighten on their nodding stems but before the flowers actually open.

Perilla
(per-RILL-a)
BEEFSTEAK PLANT

Perilla frutescens 'Crispa'

Plant type: *annual*

Height: *2 to 3 feet*

Interest: *foliage*

Soil: *well-drained to dry*

Light: *full sun to partial shade*

This Asian native is grown for its attractive foliage, which resembles that of coleus or purple basil. Plants are useful as accents in borders, especially toward the back, where the dark leaves contrast well with brightly colored flowers. Leaves are used as a seasoning in oriental cooking.

Selected species and varieties: *P. frutescens* has an upright habit with the square stems and opposite leaves typical of the mint family. Leaves are up to 5 inches long, have a quilted texture, and are purple-bronze, green, or variegated in color; 'Crispa' develops bronze leaves with wrinkled margins; 'Atropurpurea' has very dark purple leaves.

Growing conditions and maintenance: Start seed indoors 6 weeks prior to the last frost, or sow directly in the garden after the soil has warmed. Space plants 15 to 18 inches apart. Once established, perilla will self-seed and may become invasive; to avoid this problem, remove flowers as they develop. Plants will tolerate poor soil.

Phaseolus
(faz-ee-OH-lus)
BEAN

Phaseolus coccineus

Plant type:	*tender perennial*
Height:	*6 to 10 feet*
Interest:	*flowers, foliage, fruit*
Soil:	*moist, well-drained, fertile*
Light:	*full sun*

This tender perennial twining vine from tropical America produces abundant dark green leaves that are a perfect foil for its brilliant scarlet flowers. The vine will grow quickly to cover a trellis or fence, or climb up a porch railing. It also forms a dense and dramatic backdrop for a flower border. The flowers attract hummingbirds.

Selected species and varieties: *P. coccineus* (scarlet runner bean) produces twining stems with 5-inch dark green leaves composed of three leaflets. Flowers are bright red and pea-like and appear in large clusters from early to midsummer, followed by flat 4- to 12-inch pods filled with black-and-red mottled seeds. Both flowers and beans are edible.

Growing conditions and maintenance: Plant seed outdoors in spring after danger of frost has passed. Thin to allow 2 to 4 inches between plants. Provide support for climbing, and water when dry.

Phlox
(flox)
PHLOX

Phlox drummondii 'Palona Rose with Eye'

Plant type:	*annual*
Height:	*6 to 20 inches*
Interest:	*flowers*
Soil:	*dry, sandy*
Light:	*full sun to partial shade*

This Texas native provides a long season of colorful blooms on low, spreading plants that are useful as edgings, in rock gardens, massed in beds, and in containers. Flowers are also good for cutting. Their colors include white, pink, red, purple, yellow, and bicolors.

Selected species and varieties: *P. drummondii* (annual phlox, Drummond phlox) grows to 20 inches with a spreading, mounded habit, hairy leaves and stems, and five-lobed flowers that are 1 inch across; 'Palona Rose with Eye' is compact, 6 to 8 inches tall, with rose flowers with contrasting white eyes; 'Petticoat' series are compact 6-inch plants that come in a mix of colors with good drought and heat tolerance; 'Twinkle' series are 8 inches with small, early, star-shaped flowers in mixed colors.

Growing conditions and maintenance: Start seed indoors 8 weeks prior to the last frost. In Zone 8 and warmer, seed can also be sown in fall. Remove spent flowers to extend bloom, and provide water when dry. Flowering often declines in midsummer but will resume in fall.

Rhodochiton
(ro-DOH-ki-ton)
RHODOCHITON

Rhodochiton atrosanguineum

Plant type:	*tender perennial*
Height:	*5 to 15 feet*
Interest:	*flowers, foliage*
Soil:	*well-drained, fertile*
Light:	*full sun*

Native to Mexico, where it is a perennial, the purple bell vine is grown as an annual north of Zone 9. It climbs by twisting its long petioles around any nearby support. From summer to frost, tubular deep purple flowers hang from thin stalks and are surrounded by a four-pointed fuchsia calyx. Plants make an attractive cover for a fence or trellis, or can be allowed to cascade from a hanging basket.

Selected species and varieties: *R. atrosanguineum* [also called *R. volubile*] (purple bell vine) grows to 15 feet in its native habitat but usually reaches 5 to 8 feet in temperate zones. Its thick-textured, heart-shaped leaves are tipped with purple. Elongated bell-shaped flowers are about an inch in length.

Growing conditions and maintenance: Start seed indoors in individual peat pots 3 to 4 months prior to the last frost. Place several seeds in each pot because germination may be spotty. Cut out all but the strongest seedling. Transplant to the garden after soil has warmed, allowing 1 foot between plants. They thrive in warm weather. Fertilize and water regularly.

Rudbeckia
(rood-BEK-ee-a)
CONEFLOWER

Rudbeckia hirta 'Double Gold'

Plant type: *annual, biennial, or tender perennial*

Height: *1 to 3 feet*

Interest: *flowers*

Soil: *moist to dry, well-drained*

Light: *full sun to partial shade*

Rudbeckias have prominent dark centers fringed with petal-like ray flowers. The yellow summer flowers bloom on stems lined with large, hairy leaves. They are useful as a filler or backdrop in a border or sunny meadow garden.

Selected species and varieties: *R. hirta* (black-eyed Susan) may be an annual, a biennial, or a short-lived perennial with single or double 2- to 3-inch flower heads whose drooping yellow rays surround dark centers; 'Double Gold' produces spectacular double yellow blooms; 'Gloriosa Daisy' bears flowers in shades of yellow with mahogany centers, and other bicolors; 'Goldilocks' grows to 15 inches with 3- to 4-inch double flowers; 'Green Eyes' (also called 'Irish Eyes') grows to 30 inches and bears 5-inch flowers with golden rays around a green eye.

Growing conditions and maintenance: Start seed indoors 8 to 10 weeks prior to the last frost, or sow directly outdoors in fall or early spring. Allow 9 to 24 inches between plants. Once established they may self-seed. They tolerate a wide range of soils and drought.

Salpiglossis
(sal-pi-GLOSS-is)
PAINTED TONGUE

Salpiglossis sinuata 'Bolero'

Plant type: *annual*

Height: *2 to 3 feet*

Interest: *flowers*

Soil: *well-drained, fertile*

Light: *full sun*

The flowers of salpiglossis come in an incredible range of colors, including red, pink, purple, blue, white, yellow, and brown. Blooms are typically veined or spotted with a contrasting color. Plants add a cheerful accent to beds and borders, and are excellent for cutting.

Selected species and varieties: *S. sinuata* has an erect, bushy habit with narrow 4-inch leaves. Both leaves and stems are slightly hairy and sticky. Flowers resemble petunias, are 2 to 2½ inches wide, have a velvety texture, and appear in terminal clusters; 'Bolero' is 18 to 24 inches tall with flower colors that include gold, rose, red, and blue.

Growing conditions and maintenance: Start seed indoors 6 to 8 weeks prior to the last frost for transplanting to the garden after all danger of frost has passed, or plant directly outdoors in late spring. Space plants 10 to 12 inches apart. Prepare soil deeply to provide excellent drainage. Taller varieties may need staking. Plants thrive in cool weather and die in high heat and humidity.

Salvia
(SAL-vee-a)
SAGE

Salvia coccinea 'Lady in Red'

Plant type: *annual or tender perennial*

Height: *8 inches to 4 feet*

Interest: *flowers, foliage*

Soil: *sandy, dry to well-drained*

Light: *full sun to partial shade*

Whorled spikes of tiny hooded summer-to fall-blooming flowers line the tips of salvia's erect stems above soft, sometimes downy leaves. Salvias are particularly effective in masses that multiply the impact of their flowers. Tender perennial salvias that cannot withstand frost are grown as annuals in Zone 8 and colder.

Selected species and varieties: *S. argentea* (silver sage) produces branching clusters of white flowers tinged yellow or pink on 3-foot stems above rosettes of woolly gray-green 6- to 8-inch leaves. *S. coccinea* (Texas sage) produces heart-shaped leaves on 1- to 2-foot branching stems; 'Lady in Red' has slender clusters of bright red flowers. *S. farinacea* (mealy-cup sage) grows 2 to 3 feet tall with gray-green leaves and spikes of small blue flowers; 'Silver White' grows 18 to 20 inches tall with silvery white flowers; 'Strata' reaches 16 to 24 inches with 6- to 10-inch spikes of bicolored flowers in blue and white that are useful in both fresh and dried arrangements; 'Victoria' grows to 18 inches with a uniform habit and a 14-inch spread with violet-blue flowers. *S. greggii* (autumn sage) grows 2 to 4 feet tall with an erect, shrubby habit, medium green leaves, and red, pink, yellow, or white flowers that bloom from midsummer through fall and attract hummingbirds. *S. leucantha* (Mexican bush sage) grows 2 to 4 feet with gracefully arching stems, gray-green leaves, and arching spikes of purple and white flowers in summer and fall. *S. officinalis* (common sage, garden sage, culinary sage) bears whorls of tiny white, blue, or purple flowers above hairy, aro-

Salvia farinacea 'Victoria'

matic gray-green leaves used for cooking; 'Icterina' grows 18 inches tall with variegated leaves of golden yellow and green; 'Tricolor' grows to 18 inches and produces leaves that are white and purple with pink margins. *S. splendens* (scarlet sage) grows 8 to 30 inches with bright green 2- to 4-inch leaves and terminal clusters of red, pink, purple, lavender, or white flowers up to 1½ inches long; 'Blaze of Fire' grows 12 to 14 inches with bright red blooms; 'Laser Purple' bears deep purple flowers that resist fading; 'Rodeo' grows to 10 inches with early red flowers. *S. viridis* (clary sage, painted sage) grows to 18 inches with white and blue flowers with showy pink to purple bracts throughout summer and fall, and is superb for fresh and dried arrangements.

Growing conditions and maintenance: Start seed indoors 6 to 8 weeks prior to the last frost. Space smaller types 12 to 18 inches apart, larger types 2 to 3 feet apart. Salvias are generally drought tolerant. Remove faded flowers to extend bloom.

Sanvitalia
(san-vi-TAY-lee-a)
CREEPING ZINNIA

Sanvitalia procumbens

Plant type:	*annual*
Height:	*5 to 6 inches*
Interest:	*flowers*
Soil:	*well-drained to dry*
Light:	*full sun*

This low-growing annual from Mexico produces a nonstop display of flowers from early summer to frost. Flowers resemble zinnias, but each head is only ¾ inch across. Sanvitalia makes a superb edging or ground cover, and it is well suited to a sunny rock garden.

Selected species and varieties: *S. procumbens* (trailing sanvitalia) grows to a height of 6 inches, although its trailing stems spread to 18 inches, with pointed, oval leaves that are ½ to 1 inch long. Flowers are composed of yellow or orange rays surrounding a dark purple center and may be single, semidouble, or double; 'Gold Braid' produces double yellow blooms; 'Mandarin Orange' bears semidouble orange flowers.

Growing conditions and maintenance: Start seed indoors 4 to 6 weeks prior to the last frost, or sow directly outdoors in late spring. Allow 6 to 12 inches between plants. Sanvitalia thrives in hot, humid weather and is drought tolerant.

Scabiosa
(skab-ee-O-sa)
SCABIOUS

Scabiosa atropurpurea

Plant type:	*annual*
Height:	*18 inches to 3 feet*
Interest:	*flowers*
Soil:	*well-drained, fertile*
Light:	*full sun*

Scabiosa is easy to grow and produces long-lasting flowers that are well suited to borders, massing, and both fresh and dried arrangements. Flower heads are 1 to 2 inches across with prominent stamens that resemble pins stuck in a pincushion; colors include lavender, pink, purple, maroon, red, and white.

Selected species and varieties: *S. atropurpurea* grows 2 to 3 feet tall with an erect habit and showy, domed flower heads on long stems. *S. stellata* (paper moon) grows 1½ to 2½ feet tall with pale blue flowers that become papery when dry and are highly valued for dry arrangements; 'Drumstick' bears faded blue flowers that quickly mature to bronze; 'Ping-Pong' bears white flowers on heads the size of a Ping-Pong ball.

Growing conditions and maintenance: Start seed indoors 4 to 6 weeks prior to the last frost and transplant to the garden after danger of frost has passed, or sow directly outdoors in late spring. Space plants 8 to 12 inches apart. Water during dry periods.

Schizanthus
(ski-ZAN-thus)
BUTTERFLY FLOWER

Schizanthus pinnatus

Plant type:	*annual*
Height:	*1 to 4 feet*
Interest:	*flowers*
Soil:	*moist, well-drained, fertile*
Light:	*full sun to partial shade*

Schizanthus is a native of Chile that produces exotic flowers resembling orchids. Borne in loose clusters, the two-tone flowers, which come in many colors, are pleasantly displayed against fernlike foliage. They are useful in beds or containers and are excellent for cutting.

Selected species and varieties: *S. pinnatus* grows to 4 feet with light green finely cut leaves and 1½-inch flowers produced in open clusters from early summer to early fall. Flowers have a tropical appearance, and colors include pink, rose, salmon, vivid red, lavender, violet, and cream. Each displays contrasting markings on the throat.

Growing conditions and maintenance: Start seed indoors 8 weeks before the last frost, or plant directly outdoors in midspring. Make successive plantings to extend the blooming season. Space plants 12 inches apart. Provide abundant moisture in a soil with excellent drainage. Grow in light shade where summers are hot. Tall varieties require staking; shorter types are better for borders.

Silybum
(sil-LY-bum)
BLESSED THISTLE

Silybum marianum

Plant type:	*annual or biennial*
Height:	*to 4 feet*
Interest:	*flowers, foliage*
Soil:	*well-drained*
Light:	*full sun*

Silybum is grown primarily for its spiny, glossy foliage, which is dark green with silvery white spots. The 12- to 14-inch deeply lobed basal leaves form an attractive wide-spreading rosette from which 2-inch thistlelike flowers rise in late summer. It is useful as a ground cover in dry, sunny sites. The roots, leaves, and flower heads can be eaten as a vegetable.

Selected species and varieties: *S. marianum* grows to 4 feet with coarse, prominently veined and spotted leaves and solitary nodding flower heads ranging in color from rose to purple. Flowers are surrounded by curved, spiny bracts.

Growing conditions and maintenance: Sow seed directly outdoors in early spring. Once established, plants often self-seed and may become weedy. Space plants 2 feet apart. They tolerate poor soil and dry conditions.

Tagetes
(ta-JEE-tez)
MARIGOLD

Tagetes erecta 'Primrose Lady'

Plant type:	*annual or tender perennial*
Height:	*6 inches to 3 feet*
Interest:	*flowers, foliage*
Soil:	*well-drained*
Light:	*full sun*

Marigolds are among the most popular bedding plants in the United States. They are easy to grow, provide a reliable display, and are available in a wide range of heights. Their flowers typically range from pale yellow to bright orange and burgundy and are produced nonstop from early summer to frost in many varieties. Some species are grown for their fernlike foliage, which is often quite aromatic. Marigolds are suited to many uses, depending on their size: They can be placed in the background of a border, used as an edging, or massed in a bed. They are suitable for cutting for fresh arrangements and can be effectively grown in patio planters and window boxes. Despite some of their common names, marigolds are native to Mexico and Central and South America.

Selected species and varieties: *T. erecta* (American marigold, African marigold, Aztec marigold) has an erect to rounded habit and a wide range of heights, categorized as dwarf—10 to 14 inches, medium—15 to 20 inches, or tall—to 36 inches; flower heads are solitary, single to double, and 2 to 5 inches across; 'Primrose Lady' is 15 to 18 inches with a compact habit and double yellow carnationlike flowers. *T. filifolia* (Irish lace) is grown primarily for its finely divided fernlike foliage; it grows 6 to 12 inches tall and wide and produces small white blooms in late summer. *T. lucida* (Mexican tarragon, sweet-scented marigold) grows 2 to 2½ feet tall with dark green tarragon-scented leaves and small, single yellow flowers in clusters; it may be

Tagetes tenuifolia

perennial in warm climates. *T. patula* (French marigold, sweet mace) grows 6 to 18 inches tall with a neat, rounded habit and deeply serrated bright green leaves; flower heads are solitary, up to 2½ inches across, and may be single or double; double flowers often display a crest of raised petals at their center; colors include yellow, orange, maroon, and bicolors. *T. tenuifolia* (dwarf marigold, signet marigold) grows 6 to 12 inches tall with compact mounds of fernlike foliage and single yellow or orange 1-inch flowers that are so profuse they almost completely cover the leaves; excellent for edgings and window boxes.

Growing conditions and maintenance: Start seed indoors 6 to 8 weeks prior to the last frost, or sow directly outdoors 2 weeks before that date. Space plants 6 to 18 inches apart, depending on the variety, and pinch the seedlings to promote bushiness. Marigolds thrive in a moist, well-drained soil but tolerate dry conditions. Remove dead blossoms to encourage continuous flowering. Avoid overwatering.

Thunbergia
(thun-BER-jee-a)
CLOCK VINE

Thunbergia alata

Plant type:	*tender perennial*
Height:	*3 to 6 feet*
Interest:	*flowers*
Soil:	*moist, well-drained, fertile*
Light:	*full sun to partial shade*

Thunbergia, native to South Africa, is a small climbing or trailing vine that produces a mass of neat, triangular leaves and trumpet-shaped flowers in shades of yellow, orange, and cream, usually with a very dark center, throughout the summer. Plants are attractive in window boxes and hanging baskets, and are excellent as a fast-growing screen on a trellis or fence.

Selected species and varieties: *T. alata* (black-eyed Susan vine) develops stems with 3-inch leaves with toothed margins and winged petioles. The solitary flowers are 1 to 2 inches across with five distinct, rounded petal segments, usually surrounding a black or dark purple center.

Growing conditions and maintenance: Start seed indoors 6 to 8 weeks prior to the last frost, or sow directly outdoors after danger of frost is past. Space plants 12 inches apart and provide support if you wish them to climb. Plants thrive where summer temperatures remain somewhat cool. Water during dry periods.

Tithonia
(ti-THO-nee-a)
MEXICAN SUNFLOWER

Tithonia rotundifolia

Plant type:	*annual*
Height:	*2 to 6 feet*
Interest:	*flowers*
Soil:	*well-drained*
Light:	*full sun*

This native of Mexico and Central America is exceptional in its ability to withstand heat and dry conditions. Its daisylike flowers range in color from yellow to red and are borne atop erect stems with coarse-textured leaves. Plants are suitable for the background of borders and for cutting; they can also be used as a fast-growing summer screen.

Selected species and varieties: *T. rotundifolia* has a vigorous, erect habit with broadly oval, velvety, serrated leaves that may reach 10 inches in length. Flower heads consist of orange, yellow, or scarlet raylike petals surrounding an orange-yellow disk; 'Goldfinger' grows 2 to 3 feet with 3-inch orange-scarlet blooms.

Growing conditions and maintenance: Start seed indoors 6 to 8 weeks prior to the last frost, or sow directly outdoors after all danger of frost has passed. Do not cover seed. Space plants 24 to 30 inches apart. Plants tolerate poor soil, heat, and drought. When cutting flowers for indoor arrangements, cut in the bud stage and sear the stem.

Torenia
(to-REE-nee-a)
WISHBONE FLOWER

Torenia fournieri

Plant type: *annual*

Height: *6 to 12 inches*

Interest: *flowers*

Soil: *moist, well-drained*

Light: *partial to full shade*

The blossoms of wishbone flower, also called blued torenia, have upper- and lower-lobed lips and are borne above a mound of foliage from midsummer to early fall. Because they thrive in shady locations, they are the perfect choice for a woodland bed or shady border. They are also well suited to hanging baskets and patio planters.

Selected species and varieties: *T. fournieri* (bluewings) has a rounded, compact habit with neat, oval leaves 1½ to 2 inches long. The 1-inch flowers appear in stalked clusters; each bloom displays a pale violet tube with a yellow blotch and flaring lower petal edges marked with deep purple-blue. A pair of fused yellow stamens resembles a poultry wishbone, hence the common name.

Growing conditions and maintenance: Start seed indoors 10 to 12 weeks prior to the last frost; in Zone 9 and warmer, seed can be sown directly outdoors in early spring. Space seedlings 6 to 8 inches apart. Plants thrive in humid areas, and they tolerate full sun only in cool climates.

Tropaeolum
(tro-PEE-o-lum)
NASTURTIUM

Tropaeolum majus

Plant type: *annual*

Height: *6 inches to 8 feet*

Interest: *flowers, foliage*

Soil: *poor, well-drained to dry*

Light: *full sun*

Nasturtiums' bright flowers and attractive shieldlike leaves make them excellent fast-growing screens or bedding plants. Blooms appear from summer through frost. Young leaves and flowers are edible, and flowers are ideal for cutting.

Selected species and varieties: *T. majus* (common nasturtium) may be bushy, about 1 foot tall and twice as wide, or climbing, reaching 6 to 8 feet; leaves are round, 2 to 7 inches across, with long stems, and the showy 2- to 3-inch flowers are red, yellow, white, or orange and may be spotted or streaked. *T. minus* (dwarf nasturtium) reaches 6 to 12 inches in height, with a bushy habit suitable for edgings or massing; 'Alaska Mixed' grows 8 to 15 inches with variegated leaves and a wide range of flower colors. *T. peregrinum* (canary creeper, canarybird vine) is a climbing vine up to 8 feet long with pale yellow fringed flowers and deeply lobed leaves that resemble those of a fig.

Growing conditions and maintenance: Sow seed directly outdoors after danger of frost has passed. Nasturtiums do not transplant well. Space dwarf types 12 inches apart, vines 2 to 3 feet apart. Do not fertilize.

Verbascum
(ver-BAS-cum)
MULLEIN

Verbascum bombyciferum

Plant type: *biennial*

Height: *2 to 8 feet*

Interest: *flowers, foliage*

Soil: *well-drained*

Light: *full sun*

Mulleins develop a rosette of coarse leaves and tall, sturdy spikes of long-lasting summer flowers followed by attractive dried seedpods. Plant them in the rear of a border or in a wildflower garden.

Selected species and varieties: *V. blattaria* (moth mullein) grows 2 to 6 feet with dark green glossy leaves and slender spikes of pale yellow flowers with a lavender throat. *V. bombyciferum* (silver mullein) produces rosettes of oval leaves covered with silvery, silky hairs and 4- to 6-foot spikes of sulfur yellow flowers; 'Arctic Summer' is a heavy-flowering form with powdery white stems and leaves; 'Silver Candelabra' grows to 8 feet, with silver leaves and pale yellow blooms; 'Silver Lining' produces cool yellow flowers and metallic silver leaves and stems. *V. thapsus* (flannel mullein) bears felt-textured leaves and 3-foot spikes of yellow flowers, and may be found growing wild along the roadside.

Growing conditions and maintenance: Sow seed directly outdoors in spring to bloom the following year. Established plants will self-seed. Space 1 to 2 feet apart. Plants tolerate dry conditions.

Verbena
(ver-BEE-na)
VERVAIN

Verbena bonariensis

Plant type: *annual or tender perennial*

Height: *6 inches to 4 feet*

Interest: *flowers*

Soil: *moist, well-drained*

Light: *full sun*

From summer through frost, small, vividly colored flowers bloom in clusters on wiry stems with soft green foliage. Verbenas are useful as ground covers or as fillers in a border; smaller types are a good choice for containers, while taller types are excellent for cutting.

Selected species and varieties: *V. bonariensis* (Brazilian verbena) grows to 4 feet tall with slender, multibranched stems; wrinkled, toothed leaves grow primarily on the lowest 12 inches of the stem so that the fragrant rosy violet flower clusters seem nearly to float in the air. *V. x hybrida* (garden verbena) grows 6 to 12 inches tall and spreads to 2 feet, with wrinkled leaves and small flowers in loose, rounded heads to 2 inches across in shades of pink, red, blue, purple, and white; 'Peaches and Cream' bears flowers in shades of apricot, orange, yellow, and cream; flowers of 'Silver Ann' open bright pink and fade to blended pink and white.

Growing conditions and maintenance: Start seed indoors 12 weeks prior to the last frost and transplant outdoors after all danger of frost has passed. Allow 12 inches between plants of common verbena and 2 feet between Brazilian verbenas.

Viola
(vy-O-la)
PANSY

Viola tricolor

Plant type: *annual*

Height: *3 to 12 inches*

Interest: *flowers*

Soil: *moist, well-drained, fertile*

Light: *full sun to partial shade*

Although many pansies are technically short-lived perennials, they are considered annuals because they bloom their first year from seed and their flowers decline in quality afterward, regardless of region. They may also be treated as biennials, sown in late summer for bloom early the following spring. Their vividly colored and interestingly marked flowers are borne over a long season, often beginning with the first signs of spring and lasting until the summer heat causes them to fade, although a bit of shade and water may encourage the blossoms to continue throughout most of the summer. The rounded flower petals overlap, and their patterns often resemble a face. Pansies are a good choice for planting with bulbs, combining well with the flower forms and providing cover for fading foliage. They are attractive when massed in beds and useful as edgings or combined with other annuals in patio planters or window boxes.

Selected species and varieties: *V. rafinesquii* (field pansy) is a true annual that is native to much of the United States and grows 3 to 12 inches tall. Its ½-inch flowers are pale blue to cream, often

with purple veins and a yellow throat. *V. tricolor* (Johnny-jump-up, miniature pansy) is a European native that has naturalized in much of the United States. It typically grows to 8 inches with a low, mounded habit and small, colorful flowers that have been favorites in the garden since Elizabethan times. The 1-inch flowers are fragrant, and colors include deep violet, blue, lavender, mauve, yellow, cream, white, and bicolors; flowers are edible and are often used as a garnish; 'Bowles' Black' bears blue-black flowers. *V. x wittrockiana* (common pansy)

Viola 'Melody Purple and White'

grows 4 to 8 inches tall and spreads to 12 inches. The 1- to 2-inch flowers are usually three-tone in shades of purple, blue, dark red, rose, pink, brown, yellow, and white. Many varieties are available; 'Melody Purple and White' bears flowers with white and purple petals marked with deep violet-blue.

Growing conditions and maintenance: Sow seed outdoors in late summer for earliest spring blooms or purchase transplants. Pansies started in late summer should be protected over the winter in a cold frame or by covering plants after the first hard frost with a light mulch or branches. They can also be started indoors in midwinter to transplant to the garden in midspring. Germination can be enhanced by moistening and chilling the seed (between 40° and 45° F) for 1 week prior to planting. Space plants about 4 inches apart. Pansies prefer a cool soil. Remove faded blooms and keep plants well watered to extend flowering.

Xeranthemum
(zer-RAN-the-mum)
EVERLASTING

Xeranthemum annuum

Plant type: *annual*

Height: *18 inches to 3 feet*

Interest: *flowers*

Soil: *moist, well-drained to average*

Light: *full sun*

Xeranthemum's fluffy flower heads in purple, pink, and white are displayed on long stems from summer to early fall. This Mediterranean native is a good choice for the midground of a mixed border and is exceptional for cutting, for both fresh and dried arrangements.

Selected species and varieties: *X. annuum* has an erect habit and gray-green leaves that are concentrated toward the bottom of the wiry stems. The 1½-inch flowers may be single or double, and they are surrounded by papery bracts that are the same color as the true flowers at the center of the head.

Growing conditions and maintenance: In colder zones, start seed indoors in individual peat pots 6 to 8 weeks prior to the last frost, but handle carefully because they are difficult to transplant. In warmer climates, sow seed directly in the garden in spring after all danger of frost has passed. Allow 6 to 9 inches between plants. They adapt to most soils. For use in winter arrangements, cut flowers when they are fully open and hang them upside down in a well-ventilated room until dry.

Zinnia
(ZIN-ee-a)
ZINNIA

Zinnia elegans

Plant type: *annual*

Height: *8 to 36 inches*

Interest: *flowers*

Soil: *well-drained*

Light: *full sun*

Zinnias brighten the border with pompom or daisylike blooms whose petal-like rays may be flat and rounded, rolled into fringes, or crowded around yellow or green centers that are actually the true flowers. Hues range from riotous yellows, oranges, and reds to subdued pinks, roses, salmons, and creams, and maroon and purple. Flowers bloom from summer through frost and are best massed for effect as edgings or in the border. Low, spreading types are at home in window boxes and patio planters, while taller forms are excellent for fresh summer arrangements.

Selected species and varieties: *Z. angustifolia* (narrowleaf zinnia) has a compact, spreading habit, grows 8 to 16 inches in height with narrow, pointed leaves and 1-inch-wide single orange flowers, and is excellent as an edging or ground cover; 'White Star' bears abundant 2-inch flowers consisting of white rays surrounding orange-yellow centers. *Z. elegans* (common zinnia) grows 1 to 3 feet with an erect habit, rough-textured, clasping leaves up to 4 inches long, and showy flowers in many colors up to 6 inches across; 'Big Red' bears blood red 5- to 6-inch blooms on vigorous plants that reach 3 feet in height; 'Cut and Come Again' is a mildew-resistant variety that grows 2 feet tall and bears abundant 2½-inch flowers in a wide range of colors on long, sturdy stems that are suitable for cutting; 'Peter Pan' is an early bloomer with a uniform habit reaching 10 to 12 inches tall and 3- to 4-inch flowers in a wide range of colors. *Z. haageana* (Mexican zinnia) grows 1 to 2 feet tall with narrow leaves and 1½- to 2½-inch single or double flowers in colors that include red, mahogany, yellow, orange, and

Zinnia angustifolia 'White Star'

bicolors; 'Persian Carpet' has a bushy habit and 2-inch, mostly bicolored flowers with pointed petals and crested centers in shades from maroon through chocolate to gold and cream.

Growing conditions and maintenance: Zinnias are among the easiest annuals to grow. Start seed indoors 6 weeks prior to the last frost, or sow directly outdoors after all danger of frost has passed. Space seedlings 6 to 12 inches apart and pinch young plants to encourage bushiness. Remove spent blooms to keep plants attractive and to encourage flowering. Zinnias thrive in hot weather but benefit from regular watering. *Z. angustifolia* tolerates dry conditions.

Achillea
(ak-il-EE-a)
YARROW

Achillea 'Coronation Gold'

Hardiness: *Zones 4-8*

Flowering season: *summer*

Height: *6 inches to 4½ feet*

Flower color: *white, yellow, pink*

Soil: *well-drained, poor*

Light: *full sun*

Flat-topped flower clusters grown above green or gray-green fernlike foliage. Long-lasting when cut, the flowers also dry well.

Selected species and varieties: *A. filipendulina* (fernleaf yarrow)—yellow flower clusters up to 5 inches across; 'Gold Plate', 6-inch yellow flower heads on 4½-foot stems. *A.* 'Coronation Gold', a hybrid with 3-inch-deep yellow flower clusters on 3-foot stems. *A.* x *lewisii* 'King Edward'—small yellow flowers on 4-inch stalks. *A. millefolium* (common yarrow)—2-inch white flowers with cultivars in shades from pink to red; 'Red Beauty' has broad crimson flower clusters.

Growing conditions and maintenance: Plant taller species 2 feet apart and dwarfs 1 foot apart. Propagate by division every 2 to 4 years in spring or fall or from midsummer stem cuttings.

Aeonium
(ee-OH-nee-um)
AEONIUM

Aeonium arboreum 'Schwartzkopf'

Hardiness: *Zones 9-10*

Flowering season: *succulent perennial*

Height: *1 to 3 feet*

Flower color: *yellow*

Soil: *light, well-drained*

Light: *full sun*

Aeoniums bear fleshy leaves in attractive rosettes on succulent stems. Flowers in shades of yellow develop in terminal pyramidal clusters. Aeoniums are prized for their long season of interest in West Coast gardens, where they are often used as accents in rock gardens, dry borders, and containers.

Selected species and varieties: *A. arboreum* 'Schwartzkopf'—2 to 3 feet tall, upright and shrubby, with golden yellow flowers and dark, shiny, purple-black leaves appearing in 6- to 8-inch rosettes on branched stems. *A. tabuliforme*—12 inches, with leaves forming saucer-shaped, stemless rosettes 3 to 10 inches across, and pale yellow flowers.

Growing conditions and maintenance: Aeoniums thrive in California coastal conditions, where their soil and light needs are best met and they enjoy high humidity and mild temperatures. They can be grown farther inland, but may require some shade for protection from midday heat. They do not tolerate frost.

Agapanthus
(ag-a-PAN-thus)
LILY-OF-THE-NILE

Agapanthus africanus

Hardiness: *Zones 8-10*

Flowering season: *summer*

Height: *18 inches to 5 feet*

Flower color: *blue, white*

Soil: *moist, well-drained*

Light: *full sun*

Slender stems support loose clusters of 30 to 100 small, tubular flowers, which bloom for 2 months among narrow, glossy, green leaves. Lilies-of-the-Nile make good potted plants north of Zone 8; they are evergreen in warm winters.

Selected species and varieties: *A. africanus*—up to 30 eye-catching deep blue blossoms on 3-foot stems; leaves are 4 to 10 inches long. *A. orientalis*—5 feet tall with up to 100 blue flowers in each cluster; the leaves of the variety 'Variegatus' are striped white. 'Albidus' has white flowers.

Growing conditions and maintenance: Plant agapanthus 2 feet apart and water well during the growing season. Plants tolerate dryness while dormant. South-facing locations are preferable, as agapanthus leans toward light if not in full sun. In northern zones, grow in large containers for porch or patio.

Ajuga
(a-JOO-ga)
BUGLEWEED

Ajuga reptans

Hardiness: *Zones 3-9*

Flowering season: *late spring to summer*

Height: *to 12 inches*

Flower color: *white, pink, violet, blue*

Soil: *well-drained, acid loam*

Light: *full sun to light shade*

An excellent ground cover, ajuga spreads by stolons in or on top of the soil, creating dense mats of attractive foliage that suppress weeds; very vigorous and sometimes invasive. The foliage, growing in shades of green, deep purple, bronze, or creamy white mottled dark pink, is topped by whorled flowers.

Selected species and varieties: *A. genevensis* (Geneva bugleweed)—blue, pink, or white summer flowers on erect stems 6 to 12 inches tall; Zones 4-9. *A. pyramidalis* (upright bugleweed)—blue late-spring flowers on 4- to 6-inch spikes; less invasive than other species; Zones 3-9. *A. reptans* (common bugleweed)—violet flowers ¼ inch long in late spring on 3- to 6-inch prostrate stems. 'Alba' offers white flowers; 'Atropurpurea' bronze leaves; 'Rubra' dark purple leaves; and 'Metallica Crispa' curled metallic leaves and blue flowers. Zones 3-9.

Growing conditions and maintenance: Grows equally well in sun or shade. Sow seed in late summer or fall. Divide in spring or fall.

Allium
(AL-lee-um)
FLOWERING ONION

Allium sphaerocephalum

Hardiness: *Zones 3-9*

Flowering season: *late spring to early summer*

Height: *6 inches to 5 feet*

Flower color: *blue, purple, red, pink, white*

Soil: *moist, well-drained*

Light: *full sun to partial shade*

Flowering onion bears unique globes of tiny blossoms on stiff stalks above leaf clumps that fade after bloom. They make excellent cut flowers.

Selected species and varieties: *A. aflatunense* (Persian onion)—4-inch lilac-purple flowers on 2- to 4-foot stems; Zones 3-8. *A. christophii* (stars-of-Persia)—10-inch violet spheres on 24-inch stems; Zones 4-8. *A. giganteum* (giant onion)—6-inch reddish purple flower clusters on 5-foot stalks; Zones 5-8. *A. sphaerocephalum* (drumstick chives)—green to purple flower clusters atop 2- to 3-foot stalks; Zones 4-8.

Growing conditions and maintenance: Some species form bulbils; others form small bulbs at base of main bulb. Plant bulbs in the fall. Propagate by seed and division. Some species, including *A. aflatunense,* may take 2 years to germinate. Resistant to pests.

Amsonia
(am-SO-nee-a)
BLUESTAR

Amsonia tabernaemontana

Hardiness: *Zones 3-9*

Flowering season: *late spring to early summer*

Height: *2 to 3 feet*

Flower color: *blue*

Soil: *moderately fertile, well-drained*

Light: *full sun to partial shade*

Amsonia produces pale blue star-shaped blossoms. Blooming in late spring and early summer, they are particularly effective combined with more brightly colored flowers. The densely mounded willowlike leaves remain attractive throughout the growing season, providing a lovely foil for later-blooming perennials.

Selected species and varieties: *A. tabernaemontana*—produces blue flowers in terminal clusters on 2- to 3-foot-tall stiff, erect stems with densely occurring leaves 3 to 6 inches long that turn yellow in fall; *A. tabernaemontana* var. *salicifolia* has longer and thinner leaves and blooms later than the species.

Growing conditions and maintenance: Amsonias grown in shade will have a more open habit than those grown in sun. In poor to moderately fertile soil, amsonia stems rarely need staking; avoid highly fertile soil, which produces rank, floppy growth. Other than for propagating, division is usually not necessary.

Anemone
(a-NEM-o-ne)
WINDFLOWER

Anemone pulsatilla

Hardiness: *Zones 2-9*

Flowering season: *spring through fall*

Height: *3 inches to 2 feet*

Flower color: *white, cream, red, purple, blue*

Soil: *well-drained, fertile loam*

Light: *partial shade to full sun*

This diverse genus carries sprightly 1- to 3-inch-wide flowers with single or double rows of petals shaped like shallow cups surrounding prominent stamens and pistils. The flowers are held on branched stems above mounds of handsome deeply cut foliage. Many species brighten the garden during periods when few other plants with similar flowers are in bloom. Native to North America, anemone species can be found in moist woodlands, meadows, and dry prairies.

Selected species and varieties: *A. canadensis* (meadow anemone)—1 to 2 feet tall with deeply lobed basal leaves and 1½-inch white flowers with golden centers on leafy flower stems in late spring; Zones 2-6. *A. caroliniana* (Carolina anemone)—6 to 12 inches tall with numerous 1½-inch white flowers with yellow centers in spring; Zones 6-8. *A.* x *hybrida* (Japanese anemone)—white or pink flowers with a silky sheen on their undersides above dark green foliage from late summer to midfall; Zones 6-8; 'Alba' cultivar grows 2 to 3 feet tall with large clear white flowers; 'Honorine Jobert' has white flowers with yellow centers on

3-foot stems; 'Prince Henry', deep rose flowers on 3-foot stems; 'Queen Charlotte', full, semidouble pink flowers; 'September Charm', single-petaled silvery pink flowers; 'September Sprite', single pink flowers on 15-inch stems. *A. magellanica*—cream-colored flowers bloom from late spring through summer atop 18-inch stems; Zones 2-8. *A. multifida* (early thimbleweed)—loose clump of silky-haired stems up to 20 inches tall with deeply divided leaves on long stalks; sepals of the ⅜-inch flowers that appear from late spring to summer are usually yellowish white but occasionally bright red; Zones 3-9. *A. pulsatilla* [also classified as *Pulsatilla vulgaris*] (pasqueflower)—2-inch-wide blue or purple bell-shaped spring flowers on 1-foot stems above hairy leaves; Zones 5-8. *A. sylvestris* 'Snowdrops' (snowdrops windflower)—1 to 1½ feet tall, with light green foliage topped by dainty, fragrant 2-inch spring flowers. *A. vitifolia* 'Robustissima' (grapeleaf anemone)—branching clusters of pink flowers from late summer to fall on 1- to 3-foot stalks; an invasive variety good for naturalizing; Zones 3-8.

Growing conditions and maintenance: Plant small anemones 1 foot apart, taller varieties 2 feet apart. The latter may require staking. Meadow anemone prefers a moist, sandy soil and needs frequent division to prevent overcrowding. Pasqueflowers need full sun and a neutral to alkaline soil in a cool location. Snowdrops windflowers prefer moist soil; grapeleaf anemones tolerate dry conditions. Protect all anemones from afternoon sun and do not allow to dry out completely. Propagate cultivars of Japanese anemone by root cuttings or division, others from seed. Divide Japanese and grapeleaf anemones in spring every 3 years to maintain robustness. Other species grow slowly and division is rarely needed.

Anthemis
(AN-them-is)
CHAMOMILE

Anthemis tinctoria

Hardiness: *Zones 3-8*

Flowering season: *midsummer through early fall*

Height: *2 to 3 feet*

Flower color: *yellow, orange*

Soil: *well-drained to dry, poor*

Light: *full sun*

Anthemis has daisylike blossoms 2 to 3 inches across. The blossoms grow amid shrubby, aromatic, gray-green foliage and are excellent as cut flowers.

Selected species and varieties: *A. sancti-johannis* (St. John's chamomile)—2-inch bright orange flowers on evergreen shrubs; Zones 5-8. *A. tinctoria* (golden marguerite)—2-inch, upturned gold-yellow flowers above finely cut, aromatic foliage; 'Kelwayi' has bright yellow flowers; 'Moonlight', pale yellow; 'E.C. Buxton', creamy white; Zones 3-8.

Growing conditions and maintenance: Plant anthemis 1½ feet apart. Remove spent flowers for continuous bloom over several months. Propagate by division every 2 years, from seed, or from stem cuttings in spring.

Aquilegia
(ak-wil-EE-jee-a)
COLUMBINE

Aquilegia canadensis

Hardiness: *Zones 3-9*

Flowering season: *spring to early summer*

Height: *8 inches to 3 feet*

Flower colors: *white, yellow, pink, red, blue*

Soil: *moist, well-drained, acid loam*

Light: *full sun to shade*

The flowers of this beautiful and delicate wildflower come in many colors and bicolors, appearing in spring on erect stems; they are nodding or upright and consist of a short tube surrounded by five petals and backward-projecting spurs of varying lengths. The blue-green compound leaves fade early. Many species have a life span of only 3 to 4 years.

Selected species and varieties: *A. caerulea* (Rocky Mountain columbine)—2- to 3-inch blue-and-white flowers. *A. canadensis* (Canadian columbine)—1 to 3 feet tall, with nodding flowers consisting of yellow sepals, short red spurs, and yellow stamens that project below the sepals. *A. flabellata* 'Nana Alba' (fan columbine)—8 to 12 inches tall, with pure white nodding flowers 2 inches wide with spurs to 1 inch long. *A.* x *hybrida* 'Crimson Star'—30 to 36 inches tall, bearing bright red and white upright flowers with long spurs.

Growing conditions and maintenance: Columbines require good drainage; for heavy soils, work pebbles in before planting. Plant 1½ feet apart. Propagate from seed or by careful division in the fall.

Arenaria
(a-ren-AIR-ee-a)
SANDWORT

Arenaria montana

Hardiness: *Zones 5-9*

Flowering season: *spring*

Height: *2 to 8 inches*

Flower color: *white*

Soil: *moist but well-drained, sandy*

Light: *full sun to partial shade*

Sandwort forms mats of small, dainty evergreen foliage crowned with tiny white flowers. This low, spreading perennial is ideal tucked into wall crevices and between pavers.

Selected species and varieties: *A. montana*—trailing stems up to 12 inches long with grasslike leaves and topped by 1-inch star-shaped white flowers with yellow centers. *A. verna caespitosa* [now formally listed as *Minuartia verna* ssp. *caespitosa*] (Irish moss)—narrow mosslike leaves and ⅜-inch star-shaped white flowers in dainty 2-inch clumps that grow rapidly and withstand heavy foot traffic.

Growing conditions and maintenance: Plant sandwort 6 to 12 inches apart. Water well during dry spells in the growing season. Propagate by division in late summer or early fall.

Armeria
(ar-MEER-ee-a)
THRIFT, SEA PINK

Armeria maritima 'Laucheana'

Hardiness: *Zones 3-8*

Flowering season: *spring or summer*

Height: *6 inches to 2 feet*

Flower color: *white, pink, rose*

Soil: *well-drained, sandy loam*

Light: *full sun*

Thrifts produce spherical clusters of flowers on stiff stems above tufts of grassy evergreen leaves.

Selected species and varieties: *A. alliacea* [also called *A. plantaginea*] (plantain thrift)—1¾-inch rosy pink or white flower clusters on 2-foot stems; 'Bee's Ruby' cultivar has intense ruby red flower clusters. *A. maritima* (common thrift)—white to deep pink flowers on 1-foot stems; 'Alba' is a dwarf cultivar with white flowers on 5-inch stems; 'Bloodstone' has brilliant bright red flowers on 9-inch stems; 'Laucheana', rose pink flowers on 6-inch stems.

Growing conditions and maintenance: Plant thrifts 9 to 12 inches apart. Older clumps die out in the middle. Rejuvenate and propagate plants by division every 3 or 4 years.

Asclepias
(as-KLEE-pee-as)
MILKWEED

Asclepias tuberosa

Hardiness: *Zones 3-9*

Flowering season: *summer to fall*

Height: *2 to 4 feet*

Flower color: *rose, orange, yellow*

Soil: *well-drained sandy, or moist and deep*

Light: *full sun*

Milkweed's flower stalks bear brilliantly colored flower clusters followed by canoe-shaped pods, which burst to release silky seeds. The flowers are excellent for cutting, and the decorative pods dry well. Some species may be weedy.

Selected species and varieties: *A. incarnata* (swamp milkweed)—clusters of fragrant, pink to rose ¼-inch flowers on 2- to 4-foot stems. *A. tuberosa* (butterfly weed)—showy, vibrant orange flower clusters on 2- to 3-foot stems; the leaves and stems are poisonous.

Growing conditions and maintenance: Plant asclepias 12 inches apart. Swamp milkweed prefers moist conditions; butterfly weed does best in dry soils, where its long taproot makes plants drought tolerant. Propagate from seed sown in spring to blossom in 2 years.

Aster
(AS-ter)
ASTER

Aster novae-angliae 'Harrington's Pink'

Hardiness: *Zones 3-9*

Flowering season: *early summer to fall*

Height: *6 inches to 8 feet*

Flower color: *white, blue, purple, pink*

Soil: *moist, well-drained, fertile*

Light: *full sun*

Asters are prized for their large, showy, daisylike flowers that appear over weeks and even months. Most varieties are subject to mildew.

Selected species and varieties: *A. alpinus*—a low-growing species forming 6- to 12-inch-high clumps topped by violet-blue 1- to 3-inch flowers with yellow centers; 'Dark Beauty' produces deep blue flowers; 'Goliath' grows a few inches taller than the species, with pale blue flowers; 'Happy End' has semidouble lavender flowers. *A. x frikartii* (Frikart's aster)—2- to 3-foot-tall plants topped by fragrant 2½-inch lavender-blue flowers with yellow centers blooming in summer and lasting 2 months or longer; 'Mönch' has profuse blue-mauve flowers and is resistant to mildew. *A. novae-angliae* (New England aster)—3 to 5 feet tall with 4- to 5-inch leaves and 2-inch violet-purple flowers; less important than its many cultivars, most of which are quite tall and require staking; 'Alma Potschke' has vivid rose-colored blossoms from late summer to fall; 'Harrington's Pink' grows to 4 feet tall with large salmon pink flowers in fall; 'Purple Dome' is a dwarf

variety, growing 18 inches tall and spreading 3 feet wide, with profuse deep purple fall flowers. *A. novi-belgii* (New York aster, Michaelmas daisy)—cultivars from 10 inches to 4 feet tall, blooming in white, pink, red, blue, and purple-violet from late summer through fall; 'Eventide' has violet-blue semidouble flowers on 3-foot stems; 'Professor Kippenburg' is compact and bushy, 12 to 15 inches tall with lavender-blue flowers; 'Royal Ruby' is a compact cultivar with large crimson fall flowers; 'Winston S. Churchill' grows violet-red flowers on 2-foot stems.

Growing conditions and maintenance: Choose sites for asters carefully to avoid mildew problems. Good air circulation is essential; well-drained soils deter rot. Space dwarf asters 1 foot apart, taller ones 2 to 3 feet apart, and thin out young plants to improve air circulation. Taller varieties may require staking. Prompt deadheading encourages a second flowering in early summer bloomers. *A. x frikartii* in Zone 5 or colder must be mulched over the winter and should not be cut back or divided in fall; otherwise, divide asters in early spring or fall every 2 years or so when a plant's center

Aster x frikartii 'Mönch'

begins to die out. Asters can also be propagated by stem cuttings in spring and early summer. Cultivars seldom grow true from seed.

Astilbe
(a-STIL-bee)
PERENNIAL SPIREA

Astilbe chinensis var. taquetii 'Purple Lance'

Hardiness: *Zones 3-9*

Flowering season: *summer to early fall*

Height: *8 inches to 4 feet*

Flower colors: *white, pink, red, lavender*

Soil: *moist, well-drained, fertile*

Light: *bright full shade to full sun*

Feathery plumes in many colors make astilbe one of the treasures of a shade garden. Depending on variety, blooms appear through summer and into early fall atop 1- to 4-foot stalks. The 6- to 18-inch-high foliage, consisting of finely divided fernlike leaves, adds a medium-fine texture to the landscape. Some varieties are nearly as ornamental in seed as they are in flower. Astilbe can be used as a background accent to shorter perennials, or to grace water features. The dwarf forms work well tucked into rock gardens and border fronts.

Selected species and varieties: *A.* x *arendsii* (false spirea)—a hybrid group, 2 to 4 feet tall, with pink, salmon, red, white, and lavender varieties; 'Bridal Veil' blooms early, with elegant creamy white flower spikes to 30 inches; 'Fanal' has carmine red flowers on 2-foot stems with bronzy leaves in early to midsummer; 'Cattleya' has 36-inch rose flower spikes at midseason; 'Feuer' ('Fire') bears coral red flowers on 30-inch stems in late summer; 'Red Sentinel', 3-foot-tall brilliant red flowers and reddish green leaves in midsummer; 'White Gloria' ('Weisse

Gloria'), with white plumes to 2 feet in late summer. *A. chinensis* (Chinese astilbe)—to 2 feet tall, with white, rose-tinged, or purplish blooms; 'Finale' grows 18 inches tall with light pink blooms; 'Pumila' (dwarf Chinese astilbe), a drought-tolerant variety that produces mauve-pink flowers in narrow plumes on 8- to 12-inch stems in late summer and spreads by stolons for a good ground cover; var. *taquetii* 'Purple Lance' ('Purpulanze') (fall astilbe) grows 4 feet tall

Astilbe chinensis 'Pumila'

with purple-red flowers; 'Superba', 3 to 4 feet tall with lavender-pink or reddish purple spikes that bloom from late summer to fall over bronze-green, somewhat coarse foliage. *A. simplicifolia* (star astilbe)—a compact species with simple leaves having several cultivars from 12 to 20 inches tall in white and several shades of pink; Zones 4-8. *A. thunbergii* 'Ostrich Plume' ('Straussenfeder')—salmon-pink plumes to 3 feet in midsummer.

Growing conditions and maintenance: Plant astilbes 1½ to 2 feet apart. In hot climates, they require shade, where the soil does not dry out; in cooler climates, partial or full sun is acceptable if the soil is moisture retentive. Select an area that has good drainage, and enrich the soil with compost, peat moss, or leaf mold. Astilbe is a heavy feeder, so take care not to plant under shallow-rooted trees. Allow soil to dry out in the winter. Apply a high-phosphorus fertilizer such as 5-10-5 each spring. Plants will multiply quickly and lose vigor as they become crowded. Divide clumps every 2 or 3 years to rejuvenate. Leave dried flower spikes on plants through the winter for ornamental effect.

Aurinia
(o-RIN-ee-a)
BASKET-OF-GOLD

Aurinia saxatilis

Hardiness: *Zones 4-10*

Flowering season: *late spring to early summer*

Height: *6 to 12 inches*

Flower color: *yellow, gold*

Soil: *well-drained, sandy*

Light: *full sun*

One of the most widely used rock garden plants, basket-of-gold's tiny flowers mass in frothy clusters on low-growing mats of silver-gray foliage.

Selected species and varieties: *A. saxatilis* [formerly listed as *Alyssum saxatile*]—golden yellow flowers in open clusters; 'Citrina' has pale yellow flowers and gray-green, hairy foliage; 'Compacta' is dense and slow spreading, with vivid yellow blossoms; 'Dudley Neville' grows light apricot blooms.

Growing conditions and maintenance: Space aurinia plants 9 to 12 inches apart. Plants become leggy if overfertilized. Cut plants back by one-third after flowering. Remove and replace plants when they become woody after a few years. Propagate from seed sown in spring or fall or from cuttings. Aurinia plants grow and bloom best in full sun.

Baptisia
(bap-TIZ-ee-a)
WILD INDIGO

Baptisia australis

Hardiness: *Zones 3-9*

Flowering season: *midspring to early summer*

Height: *3 to 4 feet*

Flower color: *blue*

Soil: *well-drained to dry, sandy*

Light: *full sun*

Wild (false) indigo produces dainty blue pealike flowers from midspring to early summer. Its blue-green leaves are an attractive foil for both its own blooms and those of surrounding plants. The leaves remain handsome throughout the growing season. The plant is useful for the background of a border or as a specimen; its pods are often used in dried flower arrangements.

Selected species and varieties: *B. australis*—erect stems to 4 feet in height, producing compound leaves with three leaflets, each 1½ to 3 inches long, and indigo blue flowers in long, terminal racemes, good for cutting. *B. alba*—to 3 feet tall with white flowers; Zones 5-8.

Growing conditions and maintenance: Wild indigo adapts to almost any well-drained soil. It is slow growing and noninvasive. Tall selections may require staking. Remove faded flowers to extend the blooming season.

Begonia
(be-GO-nee-a)
HARDY BEGONIA

Begonia grandis

Hardiness: *Zones 6-9*

Flowering season: *early summer to frost*

Height: *2 feet*

Flower color: *pink, white*

Soil: *moist, rich loam*

Light: *full sun to partial shade*

The popular hardy begonia bears 1-inch flowers at the tips of reddish branched stems. Leaves are hairy, with red-tinted undersides and veins.

Selected species and varieties: *B. grandis*—the hardiest of the begonia genus, with sprays of pink flowers surrounded by heart-shaped leaves; the variety 'Alba' has white flowers.

Growing conditions and maintenance: Plant hardy begonias 1½ feet apart. They tolerate full sun in cooler climates but require partial shade where summers are hot and dry. Propagate by digging and transplanting the sprouts that emerge from the small bulbils that form in leaf junctions, then fall to the ground to root.

Bergenia
(ber-JEN-ee-a)
BERGENIA

Bergenia cordifolia 'Purpurea'

Hardiness: *Zones 3-8*

Flowering season: *spring*

Height: *12 to 18 inches*

Flower color: *white, pink, red, magenta*

Soil: *moist, well-drained, poor*

Light: *full sun to light shade*

Bergenia bears flowers resembling tiny open trumpets in clusters 3 to 6 inches across. Blooms are held above handsome fleshy leaves that are evergreen in milder climates.

Selected species and varieties: *B. cordifolia* (heartleaf bergenia)—pink flower clusters; 'Purpurea' has magenta flowers above leaves that turn purplish in winter. *B. crassifolia* (leather bergenia)—reddish pink blossoms above leaves turning bronze in winter. *B.* hybrids—'Abendglut' ('Evening Glow') has magenta flowers on 1½-foot stems; 'Bressingham White', early-spring white flowers maturing to pale pink; 'Sunningdale', crimson flowers.

Growing conditions and maintenance: Plant bergenias 1 foot apart. Propagate by division after flowering.

Brunnera
(BRUN-er-a)
BRUNNERA

Brunnera macrophylla

Hardiness: *Zones 4-9*

Flowering season: *spring*

Height: *1 to 2 feet*

Flower color: *blue*

Soil: *moist, well-drained loam*

Light: *full sun to light shade*

Brunnera produces airy sprays of dainty azure blue flowers resembling forget-me-nots above large dark green, heart-shaped foliage that grows in loose, spreading mounds. The plant's stems are slightly hairy.

Selected species and varieties: *B. macrophylla* (Siberian bugloss)—boldly textured leaves up to 8 inches across and dainty bright blue flowers; 'Hadspen Cream' has light green leaves edged in cream; 'Langtrees', spots of silvery gray in the center of the leaves; 'Variegata', striking creamy white leaf variegations.

Growing conditions and maintenance: Plant brunneras 1 foot apart. Propagate from seed, by transplanting the self-sown seedlings, or by division in spring.

Campanula
(cam-PAN-ew-la)
BELLFLOWER

Campanula glomerata

Hardiness: *Zones 3-9*

Flowering season: *early summer to late fall*

Height: *6 inches to 5 feet*

Flower color: *blue, violet, purple, white*

Soil: *well-drained loam*

Light: *full sun to light shade*

With spikes or clusters of showy, bell- or star-shaped flowers on stems rising from deep green foliage, bellflowers offer a long season of bloom. Dwarf and trailing varieties enhance a rock garden, wall, or border edge. Taller species form neat tufts or clumps in a perennial border or cutting garden.

Selected species and varieties: *C. carpatica* (Carpathian harebell)—2-inch-wide, bell-shaped, upturned blue flowers bloom on plants up to 1 foot tall; 'Blaue Clips' ('Blue Clips') has 3-inch-wide blue flowers on 6- to 8-inch stems; 'China Doll', lavender flowers on 8-inch stems; 'Wedgewood White' is compact, with white flowers; Zones 3-8. *C. glomerata* (clustered bellflower)—1- to 2-foot stems, with clusters of 1-inch white, blue, or purple flowers; 'Joan Elliott' grows deep violet blooms atop stems 18 inches tall; 'Schneekrone' ('Crown of Snow'), white flowers; 'Superba' grows to 2½ feet, with violet flowers; Zones 3-8. *C. latifolia* (great bellflower)—purplish blue flowers 1½ inches long on spikes, tipping 4- to 5-foot stems; 'Alba' is similar to the species but with white flowers; 'Brantwood' has

large violet-blue trumpet-shaped flowers; Zones 4-8. *C. persicifolia* (peachleaf bellflower)—spikes of 1½-inch blue or white cup-shaped blossoms on stems to 3 feet; 'Alba' has white flowers; 'Telham Beauty', 2- to 3-inch lavender-blue blooms lining the upper half of 4-foot flower stalks; Zones 3-7. *C. portenschlagiana* (Dalmatian bellflower)—a 6- to 8-inch dwarf species with blue flower clusters; Zones 5-7. *C. poscharskyana* (Serbian bellflower)—a mat-forming, creeping dwarf with abundant 1-inch lilac blossoms; Zones 3-8. *C. rotundifolia* (Scottish bluebell)—profuse, nodding, 1-inch-wide blue-violet blooms; 'Olympica' cultivar has bright blue flowers; Zones 3-7.

Growing conditions and maintenance: Plant small bellflowers 12 to 18 inches

Campanula portenschlagiana

apart, larger ones 2 feet apart. Clip faded flowers to encourage further bloom. 'Superba' and Serbian bellflower are heat tolerant. Great bellflower thrives in moist shade. Dalmatian and Serbian bellflowers do well in sandy or gritty soil. Dig up and divide every 3 or 4 years to maintain plant vigor. Propagate from seed or by division every 3 or 4 years.

Centaurea
(sen-TOR-ee-a)
KNAPWEED

Centaurea montana

Hardiness: *Zones 3-8*

Flowering season: *spring to summer*

Height: *1 to 3 feet*

Flower color: *lavender, pink, blue, yellow*

Soil: *well-drained loam*

Light: *full sun*

Excellent plants for a flower garden, centaurea's fringed, thistlelike flowers bloom at the tips of erect stems that are lined with distinctive gray-green foliage.

Selected species and varieties: *C. dealbata* (Persian centaurea)—feathery, lavender to pink 2-inch flowers on stems to 3 feet with coarsely cut, pinnately lobed leaves. *C. hypoleuca* 'John Coutts' (John Coutts' knapweed)—2- to 3-inch pink-and-white flowers on stems to 3 feet tall. *C. macrocephala* (globe centaurea)—yellow flowers up to 3 inches across on erect stems up to 4 feet tall. Globe centaurea is generally planted as a specimen, not in groups. *C. montana* (mountain bluet, cornflower)—2-inch-deep cornflower-blue blooms on 1- to 2-foot stems; *C. ruthenica* (ruthenian centaurea)—2-inch pale yellow flowers on stems 3 feet tall with pinnately divided leaves.

Growing conditions and maintenance: Space centaureas 1 to 2 feet apart. Taller species will need staking. Propagate by transplanting self-sown seedlings, by division, or from seed.

Chrysanthemum
(kri-SAN-the-mum)
CHRYSANTHEMUM

Chrysanthemum morifolium 'Pink Daisy'

Hardiness: *Zones 4-10*

Flowering season: *spring to fall*

Height: *1 to 3 feet*

Flower color: *all colors but blue*

Soil: *well-drained, fertile loam*

Light: *full sun to partial shade*

Chrysanthemum flower forms vary widely but generally consist of tiny central disk flowers surrounded by petal-like ray flowers. Reliable performers in the garden, often blooming throughout summer, they are also valued as cut flowers.

Selected species and varieties: *C. coccineum* (painted daisy)—white, pink, lilac, crimson, and dark red single radiating flowers 2 to 4 inches wide, blooming from late spring to early summer on stems 2 to 3 feet tall; 'Eileen May Robinson' produces salmon pink flowers atop 30-inch stems; 'James Kelway', scarlet flowers with bright yellow centers on 18-inch stems; 'Robinson's Pink', 2-foot-tall plants with medium pink flowers; Zones 3-7. *C. frutescens* (marguerite)—single or double daisylike flowers in pink, white, or pale yellow colors throughout the summer on shrubby plants that grow up to 3 feet tall; perennial in Zones 9 and 10, annual elsewhere. *C. leucanthemum* (oxeye daisy)—solitary flowers 1½ inches across with white rays surrounding yellow disks on stems to 2 feet tall in spring and summer. *C.* x *morifolium* (hardy chrysanthemum, florist's chrysan-

themum)—rounded plants up to 3 feet tall with aromatic gray-green lobed leaves and 1- to 6-inch flowers in all colors but blue and in a wide range of forms; button chrysanthemums are usually under 18 inches tall with small double flowers less than an inch across; cushion mums usually grow less than 20 inches tall in rounded, compact mounds with numerous double blossoms; daisy chrysanthemums have pronounced yellow centers surrounded by a single row of ray flowers on 2-foot stems, the 'Pink Daisy' cultivar having 2-inch rose pink flowers; decorative chrysanthemums have semidouble or double 2- to 4-inch flowers on loose, open plants to 3 feet tall; pompom chrysanthemums, ball-shaped flowers on 18-inch plants; spider chrysanthemums, rolled petals of irregular lengths; spoon chrysanthemums, petals rolled so that open tips resemble spoons. *C. nipponicum* (Nippon daisy)—solitary 1½- to 3½-inch blossoms with single white ray flowers and greenish yellow disk flowers in the fall on erect, branching stems to 2 feet tall over shrubby mounds. *C. parthenium* (feverfew)—pungently scented

Chrysanthemum nipponicum

¼-inch white flower buttons with yellow centers, growing from early summer through fall on plants 1 to 3 feet tall; 'Golden Ball' is a dwarf cultivar with yellow flowers; 'White Star', a dwarf with white flowers. *C.* x *superbum* (Shasta daisy)—white flowers with yellow centers up to 3 inches across from early summer to frost on 3-foot stems with narrow, toothed leaves up to a foot long; 'Alaska' cultivar has large single pure white flowers on 2- to 3-foot stems; 'Little Miss Muffet' is a 12-inch dwarf with semidouble white flowers. Double varieties include 'Horace Read', with 4-inch, ball-like blooms if grown in a cool climate, and 'Marconi', with 6-inch blooms.

Growing conditions and maintenance: Space chrysanthemums 1 to 2 feet apart. Their shallow root systems demand frequent watering and fertilizing. In cooler climates, apply winter mulch to prevent frost heaving. Divide *C.* x *morifolium* and *C.* x *superbum* every 2 years to prevent

Chrysanthemum x superbum

overcrowding, which can lead to disease and fewer flowers. Cut back *C. morifolium* and Nippon daisies two or three times in spring and early summer to develop compact, bushy plants and abundant flowers. Feverfew and oxeye daisies self-sow. Shasta, feverfew, and oxeye daisies are easily propagated from seed. Propagate all chrysanthemums by division or from spring cuttings.

Chrysogonum
(kris-AHG-o-num)
GOLDENSTAR

Chrysogonum virginianum var. virginianum

Hardiness: *Zones 5-9*

Flowering season: *late spring to summer*

Height: *4 to 9 inches*

Flower color: *yellow*

Soil: *well-drained*

Light: *full sun to full shade*

The deep green foliage of goldenstar provides a lush background for its bright yellow, star-shaped flowers, which appear from late spring into summer. Its low-growing, spreading habit makes it useful as a ground cover, for edging at the front of a border, or in a rock garden.

Selected species and varieties: *C. virginianum* var. *virginianum*—6 to 9 inches, with dark green leaves that are bluntly serrated along upright spreading stems and flowers 1½ inches across that bloom throughout the spring in warm areas, well into summer in cooler zones; var. *australe* is similar to var. *virginianum* but more prostrate.

Growing conditions and maintenance: Goldenstar grows well in most soils with average fertility. For use as a ground cover, space plants 12 inches apart. Divide every other year in spring.

Cimicifuga
(si-mi-SIFF-yew-ga)
BUGBANE

Cimicifuga ramosa 'Brunette'

Hardiness: *Zones 3-8*

Flowering season: *late summer to fall*

Height: *3 to 7 feet*

Flower color: *white*

Soil: *moist, well-drained, fertile*

Light: *full sun to partial shade*

Bugbane's lacy leaflets create airy columns of foliage topped by long wands of tiny, frilled flowers. Use it as an accent specimen, naturalized in a woodland garden, or massed at the edge of a stream or pond.

Selected species and varieties: *C. americana* (American bugbane) dense spikes of creamy blossoms on branched 2- to 6-foot-tall flower stalks in late summer to fall. *C. ramosa* (branched bugbane)—3-foot wands of fragrant white flowers on reddish stalks in fall; 'Atropurpurea' grows to 7 feet with bronzy purple leaves; 'Brunette' has purplish black foliage and pink-tinged flowers on 3- to 4-foot stalks. *C. simplex* 'White Pearl'—2-foot wands of white flowers on branching, arched 3- to 4-foot flower stalks followed by round, lime green fruits.

Growing conditions and maintenance: Plant bugbane in cooler areas of the garden in soil enriched with organic matter. Propagate by division in spring.

Coreopsis
(ko-ree-OP-sis)
COREOPSIS, TICKSEED

Coreopsis grandiflora

Hardiness: *Zones 4-9*

Flowering season: *spring to summer*

Height: *6 inches to 3 feet*

Flower color: *yellow, orange, pink*

Soil: *well-drained loam*

Light: *full sun*

Coreopsis bears single- or double-petaled daisylike, predominantly yellow flowers on wiry, sometimes branching stems over a long season of bloom. The blossoms are excellent for indoor arrangements.

Selected species and varieties: *C. auriculata* (mouse-ear coreopsis)—bears 1- to 2-inch flowers in late spring and early summer above fuzzy leaves with lobed bases lining 1- to 2-foot stems; 'Nana' is a creeping variety 4 to 6 inches tall. *C. grandiflora*—yellow or orange single, semidouble, and double flowers 1 to 1½ inches across, blooming from early to late summer on 1- to 2-foot stems; 'Sunburst' grows to 2 feet tall, with large semidouble golden flowers; 'Sunray', 2 feet tall, with 2-inch double yellow flowers. *C. lanceolata* (lance coreopsis)—yellow flowers 1½ to 2½ inches across, with yellow or brown centers, blooming from late spring through summer on stems up to 3 feet tall; 'Brown Eyes' has maroon rings near the center of yellow flowers; 'Goldfink' is a 10- to 12-inch-tall dwarf that blooms prolifically from summer to fall. *C. maritima* (sea dahlia)—

1- to 3-foot stems with long yellow-green leaves and yellow flowers 2½ to 4 inches wide from early spring to summer; suited to the hot, dry summers of southern California. *C. rosea* (pink coreopsis)—delicate pink flowers with yellow centers on stems 15 to 24 inches tall lined with needlelike leaves; can be invasive. *C. verticillata* (threadleaf coreopsis)—yellow flowers 1 to 2 inches across from late spring to late summer grow atop stems that are 2 to 3 feet tall lined with finely cut, delicate leaves 2 to 3 inches long to form dense clumps about 2 feet wide; 'Zagreb' is a 12- to 18-inch-tall dwarf with bright yellow flowers; 'Moonbeam' is a warm-climate variety that grows 18 to 24 inches tall with a prolific output of

Coreopsis verticillata

creamy yellow flowers; 'Golden Showers', 2 to 3 feet tall with 2½-inch-wide star-shaped flowers.

Growing conditions and maintenance: Space coreopsis 12 to 18 inches apart. Remove spent flowers to extend bloom time. Transplant the self-sown seedlings of threadleaf coreopsis. Propagate *C. maritima* from seed, all other coreopsis from seed or by division in the spring.

Cynara
(SIN-ah-ra)
CYNARA

Cynara cardunculus

Hardiness: *Zones 8-9*

Flowering season: *summer to fall*

Height: *6 to 8 feet*

Flower color: *blue-violet*

Soil: *well-drained*

Light: *full sun*

Related to the edible globe artichoke, cynara forms clumps of thick stems lined with spiny, lacy, silver-gray leaves with woolly undersides that provide a bold accent in a border. Fuzzy, thistlelike flower globes tip each stem from summer through fall. Both leaves and flowers are prized by floral designers for fresh and dried arrangements.

Selected species and varieties: *C. cardunculus* (cardoon)—deep blue-violet flower heads at the tips of 6-foot stems lined with spiny leaves up to 3 feet long.

Growing conditions and maintenance: Plant cardoon in moist soil enriched with organic matter. Propagate from seed or by transplanting suckers that grow from the base of established clumps.

Dianthus
(dy-AN-thus)
PINKS, CARNATIONS

Dianthus gratianopolitanus 'Karlik'

Hardiness: *Zones 4-8*

Flowering season: *spring to summer*

Height: *3 inches to 2 feet*

Flower color: *pink, red, white*

Soil: *moist, well-drained, slightly alkaline loam*

Light: *full sun to partial shade*

Pinks are perennials whose fragrant flowers with fringed petals are borne singly or in clusters above attractive grassy foliage that is evergreen in mild climates.

Selected species and varieties: *D.* x *allwoodii* (Allwood pinks)—single or double flowers in a wide range of colors grow for 2 months above gray-green leaves in compact mounds 12 to 24 inches tall; 'Aqua' grows white double blooms atop 12-inch stems. *D.* x *a. alpinus* (Alpine pinks)—dwarf varieties of Allwood pinks; 'Doris' grows very fragrant, double salmon-colored flowers with darker pink centers on 12-inch stems; 'Robin', coral red flowers. *D. barbatus* (sweet William)—a biennial species that self-seeds so reliably that it performs like a perennial; unlike other pinks, it produces flowers in flat clusters and without fragrance; 'Harlequin' grows ball-shaped pink-and-white flowers; 'Indian Carpet', single flowers in a mix of colors on 10-inch stems. *D. deltoides* (maiden pinks)—¾-inch red or pink flowers on 12-inch stems above 6- to 12-inch-high mats of small bright green leaves; 'Brilliant' has scarlet flowers; 'Flashing Light' ('Leuchtfunk'), ruby red flowers. *D. gratianopolitanus* (cheddar pinks)—1-inch-wide flowers in shades of pink and rose on compact mounds of blue-green foliage 9 to 12 inches high; 'Karlik' has deep pink, fringed, fragrant flowers; 'Tiny Rubies', dark pink double blooms on plants just 4 inches tall. *D. plumarius* (cottage pinks)—fragrant single or semidouble flowers 1½ inches across in shades of

Dianthus plumarius 'Essex Witch'

pink and white or bicolors above 12- to 18-inch-high mats of evergreen leaves; 'Essex Witch' produces fragrant salmon, pink, or white flowers.

Growing conditions and maintenance: Space pinks 12 to 18 inches apart. Cut stems back after bloom and shear mat-forming types in the fall to promote dense growth. Maintain vigor by division every 2 to 3 years. Propagate from seed, from cuttings taken in early summer, or by division in the spring.

Dicentra
(dy-SEN-tra)
BLEEDING HEART

Dicentra spectabilis

Hardiness: *Zones 3-8*

Flowering season: *spring to summer*

Height: *1 to 3 feet*

Flower color: *pink, white, purple*

Soil: *moist, well-drained loam*

Light: *partial shade*

Bleeding heart's unusual puffy, heart-shaped flowers dangle beneath arched stems above mounds of lacy leaves.

Selected species and varieties: *D. eximia* (fringed bleeding heart)—pink to purple flowers above 12-inch mounds of blue-green leaves; 'Alba' has white flowers. *D. formosa* (Pacific bleeding heart)—deep pink flowers on 12- to 18-inch stems; 'Luxuriant', cherry pink flowers; 'Sweetheart', white flowers on 12-inch stems. *D. spectabilis* (common bleeding heart) —pink, purple, or white flowers on arching 3-foot stems.

Growing conditions and maintenance: Space fringed and Pacific bleeding hearts 1 to 2 feet apart, common bleeding heart 2 to 3 feet. Propagate from seed or by division in the early spring.

Doronicum
(do-RON-i-kum)
LEOPARD'S-BANE

Doronicum cordatum

Echinacea
(ek-i-NAY-see-a)
PURPLE CONEFLOWER

Echinacea purpurea

Echinops
(EK-in-ops)
GLOBE THISTLE

Echinops ritro 'Taplow Blue'

Hardiness: *Zones 4-8*

Flowering season: *spring*

Height: *1½ to 2 feet*

Flower color: *yellow*

Soil: *moist loam*

Light: *full sun to partial shade*

The daisylike flowers of leopard's-bane stand brightly above mounds of heart-shaped dark green leaves.

Selected species and varieties: *D. cordatum* (Caucasian leopard's-bane)—yellow flowers 2 to 3 inches across on 12- to 18-inch stems above mounds of leaves up to 24 inches across. *D.* 'Miss Mason'—compact 18-inch-tall plants with long-lasting, attractive foliage. *D.* 'Spring Beauty'—double-petaled yellow flowers.

Growing conditions and maintenance: Space leopard's-bane 1 to 2 feet apart in full sun but in cool locations where its shallow roots will receive constant moisture. Foliage dies out after flowers bloom. Propagate from seed or by division every 2 to 3 years.

Hardiness: *Zones 3-9*

Flowering season: *summer*

Height: *2 to 4 feet*

Flower color: *pink, purple, white*

Soil: *well-drained loam*

Light: *full sun to light shade*

Drooping petals surrounding dark brown, cone-shaped centers bloom on purple coneflower's stiff stems over many weeks.

Selected species and varieties: *E. pallida* (pale coneflower)—rosy purple or white flowers up to 3½ inches long on 3- to 4-foot stems. *E. purpurea*—pink, purple, or white flowers up to 3 inches in diameter on stems 2 to 4 feet tall; 'Bright Star' has rosy pink petals surrounding maroon centers; 'Robert Bloom', reddish purple blooms with orange centers on 2- to 3-foot stems; 'White Lustre', abundant white flowers with bronze centers.

Growing conditions and maintenance: Space plants 2 feet apart. Transplant self-sown seedlings or propagate from seeds or by division.

Hardiness: *Zones 3-9*

Flowering season: *summer*

Height: *3 to 4 feet*

Flower color: *blue*

Soil: *well-drained, acid loam*

Light: *full sun*

The round, spiny, steel blue flowers of globe thistle are held well above coarse, bristly foliage on stiff, erect stems. Several stout stems emerge from a thick, branching taproot. Flowers are excellent for both cutting and drying.

Selected species and varieties: *E. exaltatus* (Russian globe thistle)—spiny flowers grow on stems up to 5 feet tall above deep green foliage. *E. ritro* (small globe thistle)—bright blue flower globes up to 2 inches across on stems 3 to 4 feet tall; 'Taplow Blue' has medium blue flowers 3 inches in diameter.

Growing conditions and maintenance: Space globe thistles 2 feet apart. Once established, the plant is drought tolerant. Propagate from seed or by division in the spring.

Erigeron
(e-RIJ-er-on)
FLEABANE

Erigeron speciosus 'Pink Jewel'

Hardiness: *Zones 3-8*

Flowering season: *summer*

Height: *1½ to 2 feet*

Flower color: *blue, lavender, pink*

Soil: *well-drained loam*

Light: *full sun*

Fleabane's asterlike blossoms grow singly or in branched clusters with a fringe of petal-like ray flowers surrounding a yellow center. Flowers sit atop leafy stems above basal rosettes of fuzzy swordlike or oval leaves.

Selected species and varieties: *E. pulchellus* (Poor Robin's plantain)—pink, lavender, or white flowers 1½ inches across on plants up to 2 feet tall. *E. speciosus* (Oregon fleabane)—the most popular species in the genus, *E. speciosus* bears purple flowers 1 to 2 inches across on stems to 30 inches; 'Azure Fairy' has semidouble lavender flowers; 'Double Beauty', double blue-violet flowers; 'Foerster's Liebling', deep pink semidouble flowers; 'Pink Jewel', single lavender-pink flowers; 'Sincerity', single lavender flowers.

Growing conditions and maintenance: Plant fleabane 18 inches apart. Propagate by transplanting self-sown seedlings or by division in spring.

Eupatorium
(yew-pa-TOR-ee-um)
BONESET

Eupatorium coelestinum

Hardiness: *Zones 5-10*

Flowering season: *summer to frost*

Height: *1 to 6 feet*

Flower color: *blue, mauve, purple*

Soil: *moist, well-drained loam*

Light: *full sun to partial shade*

Boneset produces flat, dense clusters of fluffy, frizzy ½-inch flowers on erect stems lined with hairy, triangular leaves. The sturdy clumps will naturalize in marshy areas at the edges of meadows or in wild gardens. The flowers provide a fall foil for yellow or white flowers such as chrysanthemums and are excellent for cutting.

Selected species and varieties: *E. coelestinum* (mist flower, hardy ageratum, blue boneset)—bluish purple to violet ½-inch flowers crowded in clusters at the tips of 1- to 2-foot-tall stalks in late summer to fall. *E. fistulosum* (hollow Joe-Pye weed)—large flat clusters of mauve flowers on hollow purple stems to 6 feet in late summer through fall. *E. maculatum* (Joe-Pye weed, smokeweed)—large flattened clusters of reddish purple or white flowers on 6- to 10-foot stems.

Growing conditions and maintenance: Plant boneset 18 to 24 inches apart (allow 3 feet between taller species) in soil enriched with organic matter. Cut foliage back several times through the summer for bushier plants. Propagate from seed or by division in spring.

Euphorbia
(yew-FOR-bee-a)
SPURGE

Euphorbia griffithii 'Fireglow'

Hardiness: *Zones 3-10*

Flowering season: *spring to late summer*

Height: *6 inches to 3 feet*

Flower color: *yellow-green*

Soil: *light, well-drained*

Light: *full sun to partial shade*

A large, diverse genus, *Euphorbia* includes many easy-care perennials. It produces small flowers that are surrounded by showy bracts. Many species produce attractive foliage with intense fall color.

Selected species and varieties: *E. corollata* (flowering spurge)—1 to 3 feet tall, with slender green leaves that turn red in the fall. In mid- to late summer, bears clusters of flowers surrounded by small white bracts; Zones 3-10. *E. epithymoides* (cushion spurge)—forms a neat, symmetrical mound 12 to 18 inches high, with green leaves that turn dark red in fall. In spring it produces small green flowers surrounded by showy, chartreuse-yellow bracts; Zones 4-8. *E. griffithii* 'Fireglow'—2 to 3 feet tall, with brick red flower bracts in late spring and early summer; Zones 4-8.

Growing conditions and maintenance: Plant in a sunny, dry location and soil that is not too rich. In moist, fertile locations, growth may become rank, unattractive, and invasive. These plants do not like to be transplanted. Use gloves when handling them, as they exude a milky sap that can cause skin irritations.

Geranium
(jer-AY-nee-um)
CRANESBILL

Geranium endressii

Hardiness: *Zones 4-8*

Flowering season: *spring to summer*

Height: *4 inches to 4 feet*

Flower color: *pink, purple, blue, white*

Soil: *moist, well-drained loam*

Light: *full sun to partial shade*

Cranesbill is valued for both its dainty flat, five-petaled flowers and its neat mounds of lobed or toothed leaves that turn red or yellow in the fall. The plants are sometimes called hardy geraniums to distinguish them from annual geraniums, which belong to the genus *Pelargonium*.

Selected species and varieties: *G. cinereum* (grayleaf cranesbill)—summerlong pink flowers with reddish veins above 6- to 12-inch-high mounds of deeply lobed, dark green leaves with a whitish cast. *G. dalmaticum* (Dalmatian cranesbill)—clusters of rosy pink inchwide spring flowers on 4- to 6-inch trailing stems. *G. endressii* (Pyrenean cranesbill)—pink flowers ½ inch across in spring and summer above spreading 12- to 18-inch-high mounds of sometimes evergreen leaves; 'A.T. Johnson' has silverpink flowers; 'Wargrave Pink', deep pink flowers. *G.* 'Johnson's Blue'—1½- to 2-inch blue flowers from spring to summer on plants up to 18 inches tall. *G. macrorrhizum* (bigroot cranesbill)—clusters of magenta or pink flowers with prominent stamens in spring and summer on spreading mounds of aromatic leaves

turning red and yellow in fall; 'Ingersen's Variety' has lilac-pink flowers; 'Spessart', pink flowers. *G. maculatum* (wild geranium)—loose clusters of rose-purple or lavender-pink flowers in spring on 1- to 2-foot stems. *G. psilostemon* (Armenian cranesbill)—vivid purplish red flowers up to 2 inches across with darker centers on plants 2 to 4 feet tall and equally wide. *G. sanguineum* (bloody cranesbill)—solitary magenta flowers 1 to 1½ inches across in spring and summer on 9- to 12-inch-high spreading mounds of leaves turning deep red in fall; 'Album'

Geranium psilostemon

has white flowers; *G. sanguineum* var. *striatum* [also listed as var. *lancastriense*], with dark red veins tracing light pink flowers.

Growing conditions and maintenance: Space Dalmatian cranesbill 12 inches apart, Armenian cranesbill 3 to 4 feet apart, and other species about 1½ to 2 feet apart. Cranesbill grows in full sun to partial shade in cool areas but needs partial shade in warmer zones. Taller species may need staking. Propagate from seed, summer cuttings, or by division. Divide in spring when clumps show signs of crowding—approximately every 4 years.

Geum
(JEE-um)
GEUM, AVENS

Geum x borisii

Hardiness: *Zones 5-8*

Flowering season: *spring to summer*

Height: *8 to 30 inches*

Flower color: *red, orange, yellow*

Soil: *well-drained, fertile loam*

Light: *full sun to light shade*

Geums produce flat-faced flowers in single or double blooms. The flowers, which resemble wild roses with ruffled petals surrounding frilly centers and growing singly on slender stems, make excellent cut flowers. The bright green, hairy leaves, which are lobed and frilled at their edges, form attractive mounds of foliage ideal for the front of a border or for the rock garden.

Selected species and varieties: *G. coccineum* [also called *G. borisii,* which is different from *G.* x *borisii*] (scarlet avens)—early-summer-blooming ½-inch bright orange flowers ride above bright green toothed leaves on 12-inch-tall stems; 'Red Wings' has semidouble scarlet flowers atop 2-foot stems. *G. quellyon* (Chi-lean avens)—scarlet flowers 1 to 1½ inches wide on plants 18 to 24 inches tall; needs winter protection in the North. 'Fire Opal' grows reddish bronze flowers that are up to 3 inches across; 'Mrs. Bradshaw' bears semidouble redorange blossoms; 'Lady Stratheden' produces semidouble deep yellow flowers; 'Princess Juliana', semidouble orange-bronze blooms; 'Starker's Magnificent', double-petaled deep orange flowers. *G. reptans* (creeping avens)—yellow or orange flowers on plants 6 to 9 inches tall that spread by runners; Zones 4-7. *G. rivale* (water avens)—tiny, nodding, bell-shaped pink flowers on 12-inch stems above low clumps of dark green, hairy leaves; 'Leonard's Variety' produces copper-rose flowers on slightly taller stems than the species; Zones 3-8. *G. triflorum* 'Prairie Smoke'—nodding purple to straw-colored flowers on 6- to 18-inch-tall plants; Zones 5-10. *G.* x *borisii*—orange-scarlet flowers on 12-inch plants. *G.* 'Georgenberg'—orange flowers on 10- to 12-inch stems.

Growing conditions and maintenance: Space geums 12 to 18 inches apart in soil enriched with organic matter. They grow best in moist but well-drained sites in cooler climates and will not survive wet winter soil. Most species dislike high temperatures; protect the plants from hot afternoon sun in warmer zones. *G. reptans* requires full sun and alkaline soil. Keep geums robust by dividing annually. Propagate by division in late summer for plants that will be ready to flower the following year, or from seed sown outdoors in fall; *G. rivale* may be sown in early spring.

Gillenia
(gil-LEE-nee-a)
BOWMAN'S ROOT

Gillenia trifoliata

Hardiness: *Zones 4-8*

Flowering season: *spring to summer*

Height: *2 to 4 feet*

Flower color: *white*

Soil: *moist, well-drained loam*

Light: *light to moderate shade*

Gillenia is a tall, delicate, woodland perennial with white, star-shaped flowers, often blushed with pink. The flowers emerge from wine-colored sepals, which remain as ornaments after the petals drop. It is native to the eastern U.S.

Selected species and varieties: *G. trifoliata* [formerly *Porteranthus trifoliata*] (bowman's root)—five-petaled flowers 1 inch wide, growing in loose, airy clusters on wiry, branching stems 2 to 4 feet tall above lacy leaves with toothed edges.

Growing conditions and maintenance: Space gillenia 2 to 3 feet apart in sites with abundant moisture and light to moderate shade. Incorporate organic matter into soil to help retain water. Plants often require staking. Propagate from seed or by division in spring or fall.

Helleborus
(hell-e-BOR-us)
HELLEBORE

Helleborus orientalis

Hardiness: *Zones 3-9*

Flowering season: *winter to spring*

Height: *1 to 3 feet*

Flower color: *white, green, purple, pink*

Soil: *moist, well-drained, fertile*

Light: *partial shade to bright full shade*

The cuplike flowers of hellebores offer such subtle variation in rich coloration that every plant carries a distinctive look. Most species are long-lived, consistent bloomers for borders and perennial beds. Depending on the species, they are stemmed or stemless plants with deeply lobed leaves that may remain evergreen if given winter protection. *Caution:* All parts of the plant are poisonous.

Selected species and varieties: *H. argutifolius* [also listed as *H. corsicus* and *H. lividus* ssp. *corsicus*] (Corsican hellebore)—shrubby growth 1 to 2 feet tall without rhizomes, with glossy, heavily toothed leaves having ivory veins and, sometimes, red margins and producing clusters of yellowish green cups in spring; Zones 6-8. *H. atrorubens*—produces dark red, brownish, or plum-colored flowers on 1½-foot stems in winter or early spring followed by deciduous leaves; hardy to Zone 6. *H. foetidus* (stinking hellebore)—2 feet tall and bearing small green bells edged with maroon over lobed, glossy black-green leaves that form rosettes around the flowers; some hybrids are well scented; hardy to Zone 6.

H. lividus—12 to 18 inches tall, similar to Corsican hellebore, but the 2-inch-wide greenish yellow cups are brushed with pink and gray and borne in clusters of 15 to 20 in spring over deeply toothed, purple-toned leaves; hardy to Zone 8. *H. niger* (Christmas rose)—highly variable in size and bloom time and color, but generally 12 to 15 inches tall, each stalk bearing a seminodding, white or pinkish green flower almost 3 inches

Helleborus niger

across in late fall to early spring; Zones 5-8; ssp. *macranthus* has unusually large flowers in winter and pale blue-green foliage; hardy to Zone 5. *H. orientalis* (Lenten rose)—bears cream, pale to deep pink, plum, brownish purple, chocolate brown, or nearly black flowers 2 inches wide in early to midspring on 18-inch plants; Zones 4-9.

Growing conditions and maintenance: Hellebores are adaptable to most garden soils, but they do best when leaf mold or peat moss has been added to the soil. Although near neutral or alkaline soils are considered ideal, many hellebores seem to do just as well under acid conditions. Space smaller species 1 foot apart, larger ones up to 2 feet apart. Hellebores form clumps and self-seed under suitable conditions. Most species develop rhizomes; the exception is Corsican hellebore, which cannot be cut back because of its unusual habit. Christmas rose appears to thrive and flower best when it receives ample water from spring to midsummer, followed by a dry period in late summer. Stinking hellebores are especially tolerant of dry shade. Hellebore roots are brittle; take special care when dividing, which is best done in early summer.

Hemerocallis
(hem-er-o-KAL-lis)
DAYLILY

Hemerocallis 'Stella de Oro'

Hardiness:	*Zones 3-10*
Flowering season:	*summer to fall*
Height:	*1 to 4 feet*
Flower color:	*all shades but blue*
Soil:	*moist, well-drained loam*
Light:	*full sun to partial shade*

Daylilies produce dainty to bold flower trumpets with petals resembling those of true lilies. Their colors span the rainbow, with the exception of blue and pure white, and blooms are often bi- or tricolored. Sometimes with ruffled edges or double or even triple rows of petals, and occasionally fragrant, the flowers rise above mounds of grasslike, arching leaves on branched stems called scapes. Each flower lasts only one day, but each scape supports many buds that continue to open in succession for weeks, even months. Daylilies have been extensively hybridized, offering a wide choice of plant sizes, flower colors and styles, and periods of bloom. In some hybrids, the normal number of chromosomes has been doubled, giving rise to tetraploid daylilies with larger, more substantial flowers on more robust plants. Miniature varieties with smaller flowers on shortened scapes have also been bred.

Selected species and varieties: *H. fulva* (tawny daylily)—the common orange daylily found along roadsides; 6 to 12 orange flower trumpets per scape on vigorous, robust plants in large clumps;

'Kwanso Variegata' is a larger plant than the species and produces double blooms; 'Rosea' has rose-colored flowers. *H. lilioasphodelus* (lemon daylily) [also known as *H. flava*]—lemon yellow 4-inch flowers on 2- to 3-foot scapes over clumps of slender dark green leaves up to 2 feet long; spreads rapidly by rhizomatous roots; 'Major' grows taller than the species and produces larger, deep yellow flowers. *H.* hybrids—yellow-gold hybrids include 'Golden Chimes', a miniature variety with gold-yellow flowers; 'Stella de Oro', another gold-yellow miniature that blooms from late spring until frost; 'Happy Returns', a hybrid offspring of 'Stella de Oro' with abundant, ruffled lemon yellow blooms and a similarly long flowering season; 'Little Cherub', 3½-inch light yellow flowers on 22-inch scapes over evergreen foliage; 'Alice in Wonderland', with 5½-inch ruffled lemon yellow flowers on 3-foot scapes and beautiful deep green foliage; 'Bountiful Valley', with 6-inch yellow blooms sporting lime green throats; 'Hyperion', an older variety still very popular

Hemerocallis 'Grapeade'

for its fragrant, late-blooming yellow flowers on 4-foot scapes; 'Fall Glow', a shorter alternative with late, golden orange blooms.

Among red hybrids are 'Artist's Dream', a midseason tetraploid bearing red blooms with yellow midribs above a yellow-green throat; 'Anzac', true red blooms with yellow-green throats, 6 inches wide on 28-inch scapes; 'Cherry Cheeks', with cherry red petals lined by white midribs; 'Pardon Me', prolific producer of cerise flowers 2¾ inches across with green throats on 18-inch scapes;

'Autumn Red', sporting late-season red flowers with yellow-green throats.

Pink to purple hybrids include 'Country Club' and 'Peach Fairy', with pink-peach flowers; 'Joyful Occasion', 6-inch medium pink flowers with green throats and ruffled petals over evergreen foliage; 'Flower Basket', with coral pink double flowers; 'Catherine Woodbury', with pale lilac-pink flowers; and 'Grapeade', with green-throated purple blossoms.

Growing conditions and maintenance: Daylilies are among the least demanding of perennials, providing spectacular results with minimal care. Planted in

Hemerocallis 'Artist's Dream'

groups, they spread to create a rugged ground cover that will suppress most weeds. Plant daylilies in spring or fall, spacing miniature varieties 18 to 24 inches apart, taller varieties 2 to 3 feet apart. Daylilies prefer sunny locations but adapt well to light shade. Light-colored flowers that fade in bright sun often show up better with some shade. Fertilize with an organic blend, if necessary, but do not overfeed, as this will cause rank growth and reduce flowering. Propagate by dividing clumps every 3 to 6 years.

Heuchera
(HEW-ker-a)
ALUMROOT

Heuchera sanguinea

Hardiness: *Zones 4-8*

Flowering season: *spring to summer*

Height: *12 to 24 inches*

Flower color: *white, pink, red*

Soil: *moist, well-drained, rich loam*

Light: *partial shade to full sun*

The delicate, bell-shaped flowers of alumroot line slender upright stalks held above neat mounds of attractive evergreen leaves that can be rounded, triangular, or heart shaped.

Selected species and varieties: *H. micrantha* (small-flowered alumroot)—white flowers above gray-green heart-shaped leaves; 'Palace Purple' has dramatic, deep bronze leaves. *H. sanguinea* (coral bells)—the showiest of the genus, with red flowers persisting 4 to 8 weeks; 'Red Spangles' grows scarlet flowers on short stems; 'Chatterbox', rose pink flowers; 'Snowflakes', white flowers.

Growing conditions and maintenance: Space heuchera 1 to 1½ feet apart. Water well during dry spells. Plants tolerate full sun in cooler climates but prefer partial shade in warmer zones. Propagate from seed or by division every 3 years.

Hosta
(HOS-ta)
PLANTAIN LILY

Hosta 'Krossa Regal'

Hardiness: *Zones 3-9*

Flowering season: *summer*

Height: *5 inches to 3 feet*

Flower color: *white, lavender, violet*

Soil: *moist, rich, acid loam*

Light: *partial to bright full shade*

Hostas are valued chiefly for their foliage—mounds of oval or heart-shaped green, blue, or gold leaves in a variety of sizes—but also produce tall, graceful spires of pale lilylike flowers during the summer. They are useful as edging or border plants, as ground covers, and in mass plantings. The variegated and light green forms make beautiful accent plants and brighten shady corners.

Selected species and varieties: *H. decorata* (blunt plantain lily)—1 to 2 feet tall, with white-edged leaves 3 to 8 inches long and dark blue flowers. *H. fortunei* (Fortune's hosta, giant plantain lily)—to 2 feet tall, with 5-inch-long oval leaves and pale lilac to violet flowers; 'Albomarginata' forms a 15- to 24-inch-high clump with white margins on 5-inch leaves. *H. lancifolia* (narrow-leaved plantain lily)—a 2-foot-high cascading mound of 4- to 6-inch-long leaf blades and 1- to 1½-inch blue-purple flowers in late summer; hardy to Zone 3. *H. plantaginea* (fragrant plantain lily)—fragrant pure white flowers 2½ inches wide open in late summer on 2½-foot stems above bright green heart-shaped foliage; Zones 3-8.

H. sieboldiana (Siebold plantain lily)—2½ to 3 feet tall with 10- to 15-inch-long glaucous, gray to blue-green puckered leaves and lavender flowers that bloom amid the leaves in midsummer; hardy to Zone 3; 'Big Mama' has blue leaves and pale lavender flowers; 'Blue Umbrellas' grows 3 feet tall and 5 feet wide, with blue to blue-green leaves; 'Frances Williams', 32 inches tall and 40 inches wide with round, puckered, blue-green leaves having wide, irregular gold margins; var. *elegans* [also classified as *H. sieboldiana*. 'Elegans'], 36 inches tall with lavender-white flowers and large, dark blue puckered leaves. *H. tardiflora* (autumn plantain lily)—glossy dark green medium-

Hosta 'Golden Tiara'

size leaves and large purple flowers on 1-foot scapes in fall. *H. tokudama*—18 inches tall and 40 inches wide, with puckered bluish leaves and white flowers in midsummer; 'Flavo-circinalis' grows to 18 inches tall and 50 inches wide with round, heavily puckered blue-green leaves that have irregular cream-and-yellow margins and white flowers in early summer. *H. undulata* var. *univittata* [also classified as *H. undulata* 'Univittata'] (wavy-leaf shade lily, snow feather funkia)—2 to 3 feet tall and 3 feet wide, with broad white centers in medium green leaves and lavender flowers. *H. venusta* (dwarf plantain lily, pretty plantain lily)—5 inches tall and 8 inches wide with medium green leaves and light purple flowers. *H.* hybrids—'August Moon', to 12 inches tall, with small yellow puckered leaves and midsummer white flowers; 'Fringe Benefit', 36 inches tall and 42 inches wide, with broad cream-colored margins on green heart-shaped leaves

and pale lavender flowers in early summer; 'Ginko Craig', an excellent ground cover, 10 inches tall with narrow, white-edged, dark green lance-shaped leaves and lavender flowers in midsummer;

Hosta sieboldiana 'Frances Williams'

hardy to Zone 4; 'Golden Tiara', a low, compact mound 6 inches high and 16 to 20 inches wide bearing yellow-edged medium green heart-shaped leaves and purple flowers on 15-inch scapes in midsummer; 'Gold Standard', 15 inches tall with dark green margins on greenish gold leaves and lavender flowers on 3-foot scapes in mid- to late summer; 'Halcyon', 12 inches tall and 16 inches wide, with grayish blue heart-shaped leaves having wavy margins and distinct parallel veins and lilac-blue flowers blooming in late summer; 'Honeybells', fragrant lavender flowers and light green leaves to 2 feet tall; 'Krossa Regal', to 3 feet tall, with silvery blue leaves and 2- to 3-inch-long lavender flowers in late summer on 5-foot scapes; hardy to Zone 4; 'Royal Standard', full-sun-tolerant plant with fragrant white flowers on 30-inch stems in late summer to early fall; 'Shade Fanfare', lavender blooms on 2-foot scapes in midsummer above leaves with broad cream-colored margins.

Growing conditions and maintenance: Plant smaller hostas 1 foot apart, larger species 2 to 3 feet apart, in a moist but well-drained soil; wet soil in winter often damages plants. Water during dry spells. The blue forms need bright shade in order to hold color. *H. plantaginea* is tender until established; in the northern part of its range, mulch or cover during the first winter. Once established, hostas are long-lasting and need little attention.

Iberis
(eye-BEER-is)
CANDYTUFT

Iberis sempervirens 'Snowmantle'

Hardiness:	*Zones 4-8*
Flowering season:	*spring*
Height:	*6 to 12 inches*
Flower color:	*white*
Soil:	*moist, well-drained loam*
Light:	*full sun*

The dark green leaves of candytuft are effective year round covering the ground before a perennial border, edging a walkway, or cascading over a stone wall. The delicate white flowers that cover the plant in spring are a delightful bonus.

Selected species and varieties: *I. sempervirens*—to 12 inches high and 24 inches wide, with a low, mounded habit, linear evergreen leaves 1 inch long, semiwoody stems, and very showy white flowers in dense clusters 1 inch across; 'Snowflake' grows 10 inches high, with 2- to 3-inch flower clusters; 'Snowmantle', 8 inches high, with a dense, compact habit.

Growing conditions and maintenance: Incorporate organic matter into the soil before planting candytuft. Space plants 12 to 15 inches apart. Protect the plant from severe winter weather with a loose mulch in colder zones. Cut it back at least 2 inches after it flowers to maintain vigorous growth.

Inula
(IN-yew-la)
INULA

Inula ensifolia

Hardiness: *Zones 4-9*

Flowering season: *summer*

Height: *6 to 12 inches*

Flower color: *yellow*

Soil: *well-drained, average fertility*

Light: *full sun to partial shade*

Inula produces cheerful, bright yellow, daisylike flowers at the tips of wiry stems that form mounds.

Selected species and varieties: *I. acaulis* (stemless inula)—single yellow flowers borne on 6-inch stems in midsummer, over tufts of spatulate leaves 2 inches tall. *I. ensifolia* (swordleaf inula)—dense clumps, 12 inches tall and wide, of wiry, erect stems lined with narrow, pointed 4-inch leaves and tipped with 1- to 2-inch flowers. The blooms last 2 to 3 weeks in warmer zones, up to 6 weeks in cooler areas.

Growing conditions and maintenance: Space inulas 1 foot apart in massed plantings. Propagate from seed or by division in spring or fall.

Kirengeshoma
(ky-reng-esh-O-ma)
YELLOW WAXBELLS

Kirengeshoma palmata

Hardiness: *Zones 5-8*

Flowering season: *summer to fall*

Height: *3 to 4 feet*

Flower color: *yellow*

Soil: *moist, well-drained, acid, fertile*

Light: *bright full shade*

Kirengeshoma is an unusual, semiexotic shade plant that is not often seen in the landscape. Shrubby but a bit spindly in habit, it produces handsome maplelike leaves on dark purple, semiarching stems and upright clusters of nodding yellow flowers in summer and fall. It makes an interesting specimen plant for edgings or borders.

Selected species and varieties: *K. palmata*—nearly round, toothed leaves, each with up to 10 lobes, arise from opposite sides of the stems and give an almost platelike appearance beneath clusters of 1½-inch-long butter yellow bell-shaped flowers whose buds last for months before opening.

Growing conditions and maintenance: Kirengeshoma needs soil that has been liberally supplemented with compost, leaf mold, or peat moss and is lime-free. Water during dry spells, and mulch to retain moisture. Propagate by dividing.

Kniphofia
(ny-FO-fee-a)
TORCH LILY, TRITOMA

Kniphofia uvaria 'Robin Hood'

Hardiness: *Zones 5-9*

Flowering season: *summer to fall*

Height: *2 to 4 feet*

Flower color: *red, orange, yellow, cream*

Soil: *well-drained, sandy loam*

Light: *full sun*

Torch lily's stiff clusters of tubular flowers on bare stems held above tufts of stiff, gray-green leaves are a bold accent in a mixed border and a favorite visiting place of hummingbirds.

Selected species and varieties: *K. uvaria* (red-hot poker)—individual 1- to 2-inch flowers clustered along the top several inches of stem like a bristly bottle brush open a bright red then turn yellow as they mature.

Growing conditions and maintenance: Plant torch lilies 1½ to 2 feet apart in locations protected from strong winds. Propagate from seed, by division in spring, or by removing and transplanting the small offsets that develop at the base of plants. Plants grown from seed require 2 to 3 years to flower.

Lavandula
(lav-AN-dew-la)
LAVENDER

Lavandula stoechas

Hardiness: *Zones 5-9*

Flowering season: *summer*

Height: *1 to 3 feet*

Flower color: *lavender, purple, pink*

Soil: *well-drained loam*

Light: *full sun*

Lavender forms neat cushions of erect stems lined with fragrant, willowy, gray or gray-green leaves tipped with spikes of tiny flowers. Lavender's attractive evergreen foliage blends into rock gardens or at the edges of borders and can be clipped into a low hedge.

Selected species and varieties: *L. angustifolia* (true lavender, English lavender)—whorls of lavender-to-purple ¼-inch flowers in summer on compact, round plants 1 to 2 feet tall; 'Hidcote' produces deep violet-blue flowers and silvery gray foliage. *L. latifolia* (spike lavender)—branched stalks of lavender-to-purple summer flowers above broader leaves than true lavender on plants to 2 feet tall. *L. stoechas* (French lavender)—dense whorls of tufted purple flowers in summer on plants to 3 feet tall.

Growing conditions and maintenance: Plant lavender 12 to 18 inches apart in soil that is not overly rich. Cut stems back to 8 inches in early spring to encourage compact growth and to remove old woody stems that produce few flowers. Propagate from seed or by division.

Liatris
(ly-AY-tris)
SPIKE GAY-FEATHER

Liatris spicata 'Kobold'

Hardiness: *Zones 3-9*

Flowering season: *summer to fall*

Height: *18 inches to 5 feet*

Flower color: *purple, pink, lavender, white*

Soil: *sandy, well-drained*

Light: *full sun to light shade*

The flowers of spike gay-feather are borne on erect stems, and unlike most spike flowers the top buds open first and proceed downward. The effect is that of a feathery bottle brush. It provides a striking vertical accent in both the garden and indoor arrangements.

Selected species and varieties: *L. pycnostachya* (Kansas gay-feather)—bright purple flower spikes on 4- to 6-foot stems. *L. spicata*—usually 2 to 3 feet tall and 2 feet wide but may reach 5 feet tall. Leaves are narrow and tapered, up to 5 inches long, on erect, stout stems; flowers are purple or rose, borne closely along top of stem in mid to late summer; 'Kobold'—18- to 24-inch dwarf form, bright purple flowers, good for the front or middle of the herbaceous border.

Growing conditions and maintenance: Space gay-feathers 1 foot apart. Spike gay-feather prefers a light, well-drained soil and full sun but adapts to light shade and tolerates wet conditions better than other species of liatris. Tall types often need support; however, 'Kobold', with its stout habit, rarely requires staking.

Linum
(LY-num)
FLAX

Linum perenne

Hardiness: *Zones 5-9*

Flowering season: *spring to summer*

Height: *12 to 24 inches*

Flower color: *blue, white, yellow*

Soil: *well-drained, sandy loam*

Light: *full sun to light shade*

Delicate flax blooms prolifically with inch-wide, cup-shaped flowers held aloft on soft stems. Though blossoms last only one day, new buds open continuously for 6 weeks or more.

Selected species and varieties: *L. flavum* (golden flax)—bright yellow flowers on stems 1 to 1½ feet tall. *L. perenne* (perennial flax)—sky blue, saucer-shaped flowers on stems up to 2 feet tall; 'Diamant White' has abundant white blossoms on 12- to 18-inch stems.

Growing conditions and maintenance: Space flax plants 18 inches apart in groups of 6 or more for an effective display. Flax is a short-lived perennial but often reseeds itself. Propagate from seed or from stem cuttings taken in late spring or summer, after new growth hardens.

Lobelia
(lo-BEE-lee-a)
CARDINAL FLOWER

Lobelia cardinalis

Hardiness: *Zones 3-9*

Flowering season: *summer*

Height: *2 to 4 feet*

Flower color: *red, pink, white, blue*

Soil: *moist, fertile loam*

Light: *light shade*

Cardinal flower bears spires of intensely colored tubular blossoms with drooping lips on stiff stems rising from rosettes of dark green leaves. Opening in mid- to late summer, the flowers last 2 to 3 weeks; they are followed by button-shaped seed capsules

Selected species and varieties: *L. cardinalis* (red lobelia)—1½-inch scarlet blossoms on 3-foot-tall flower stalks; pink and white varieties available. *L. siphilitica* (great blue lobelia)—1-inch-long blue flowers persist a month or more. 'Alba' has white flowers.

Growing conditions and maintenance: Plant lobelia 12 inches apart in locations with adequate moisture and in soil with ample organic matter. Lobelia will grow in full sun with sufficient moisture. Though short-lived, it self-sows freely. It can also be propagated by division in early fall. Lobelias are suited to moist-soil gardens, and do well alongside ponds and streams.

Lupinus
(loo-PY-nus)
LUPINE

Lupinus densiflorus var. aureus

Hardiness: *Zones 3-10*

Flowering season: *spring, summer*

Height: *4 inches to 3 feet*

Flower color: *blue, purple, yellow, white, pink*

Soil: *moist to dry*

Light: *full sun to partial shade*

Lupines inhabit prairies, open woodlands, and dry mountain slopes and bear dense, showy terminal clusters of flowers in spring or summer. They have attractive palmately compound leaves.

Selected species and varieties: *L. densiflorus* var. *aureus* (golden lupine)—annual 8 to 16 inches tall with short spikes of yellow flowers in late spring; California Coast Range. *L. palmeri* (Palmer's lupine)—1 to 2 feet in height with blue flowers in late spring; southwestern mountains; Zones 6-9. *L. perennis* (wild lupine)—up to 2 feet tall with elongated clusters of late-spring to early-summer flowers that are usually purplish blue; Maine to Florida; Zones 4-8.

Growing conditions and maintenance: Space lupines 2 feet apart. Most need full sun and dry soils with excellent drainage. Lupines benefit from soil or seed inoculants containing nitrogen-fixing bacteria. Propagate from seed sown in fall or spring. Scarify the seed with sandpaper or by nicking the seed coat.

Miscanthus
(mis-KAN-thus)
EULALIA

Miscanthus sinensis

Hardiness: *Zones 5-9*

Flowering season: *summer*

Height: *3 to 10 feet*

Flower color: *pink, red, silver*

Soil: *well-drained loam*

Light: *full sun*

Eulalia produces feathery flower fans on tall stems above graceful clumps of arching leaves an inch wide. Both the flowers and the foliage remain attractive throughout the winter and are useful as specimens and screens.

Selected species and varieties: *M. sinensis*—5 to 10 feet tall, narrow leaves 3 to 4 feet long with prominent white midrib; flowers are feathery and fan shaped. Varieties offer a selection of colors and blooming periods; 'Condensatus' has purple flowers; 'Gracillimus' (maiden grass), fall flowers above compact clumps of fine-textured leaves; 'Purpurascens', silvery pink summer flowers above red-tinted foliage; 'Strictus' (porcupine grass), upright leaves striped with horizontal yellow bands; 'Yaku Jima', a 3- to 4-foot dwarf; 'Zebrinus' (zebra grass) striped with yellow band.

Growing conditions and maintenance: Space clumps of miscanthus 3 feet apart. Cut plants back to 2 to 6 inches in late winter before new growth begins. Propagate by division in spring.

Monarda
(mo-NAR-da)
BEE BALM

Monarda didyma

Nepeta
(NEP-e-ta)
CATMINT

Nepeta mussinii 'Blue Wonder'

Oenothera
(ee-no-THEE-ra)
SUNDROP

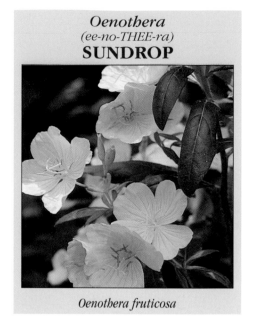

Oenothera fruticosa

Hardiness: *Zones 4-9*

Flowering season: *summer*

Height: *2 to 4 feet*

Flower color: *red, purple, pink, white*

Soil: *moist or dry loam*

Light: *full sun to light shade*

Bee balm has fragrant leaves and shaggy clusters of tiny tubular flowers growing on square stems. Attractive to bees, butterflies, and hummingbirds, these plants are easily cultivated.

Selected species and varieties: *M. didyma*—scarlet flowers on 3- to 4-foot stems; 'Cambridge Scarlet', wine red flowers; 'Croftway Pink', rose pink; 'Mahogany', dark red; 'Marshall's Delight', mildew resistant, with pink flowers on 2-foot stems; 'Blue Stocking', violet-blue; 'Snow Queen', white. *M. fistulosa* (wild bergamot)—lilac to pink flower clusters on plants up to 4 feet tall. *M. punctata* (spotted bee balm)—yellow blossoms with purple spots.

Growing conditions and maintenance: Plant monarda 1½ to 2 feet apart. It thrives in moist areas, although wild bergamot and spotted bee balm tolerate dry conditions. Propagate from seed or from cuttings; divide every two to three years in the spring to maintain vigor. Thin plant occasionally for air circulation and to avoid mildew.

Hardiness: *Zones 3-9*

Flowering season: *summer*

Height: *1 to 3 feet*

Flower color: *lavender-blue, white*

Soil: *average, well-drained loam*

Light: *full sun*

Catmint forms loose cushions of fragrant stems lined with soft, oval, pointed leaves and tipped with spikes of tiny white, mauve, or blue flower whorls that form a haze of color above the foliage. The plant is effective massed as a dense ground cover.

Selected species and varieties: *N.* x *faassenii* (blue catmint)—18- to 36-inch-high mounds of silvery gray foliage with lavender-blue spring-to-summer-blooming flowers; 'Six Hills Giant' grows taller and is more robust than the species. *N. mussinii* (Persian catmint)—sprawling 1-foot-high mounds with lavender summer flowers; 'Blue Wonder' has deep blue blossoms on compact plants to 15 inches.

Growing conditions and maintenance: Plant catmint 1 to 1½ feet apart in any well-drained soil. It can be invasive. Shearing plants after flowering may produce a second season of bloom. Propagate blue catmint from cuttings, Persian catmint from seed, and either species by division.

Hardiness: *Zones 4-8*

Flowering season: *summer*

Height: *6 to 24 inches*

Flower color: *yellow, pink, white*

Soil: *well-drained loam*

Light: *full sun*

Showy, saucer-shaped flowers bloom on sundrops during the day and on evening primroses (night-blooming oenothera) at night.

Selected species and varieties: *O. fruticosa* (common sundrop)—prolific clusters of 1- to 2-inch bright yellow flowers at the tips of 18- to 24-inch stems. *O. missouriensis* (Ozark sundrop)—large 5-inch yellow flowers on 6- to 12-inch plants. *O. speciosa* (showy evening primrose)—white or pink blossoms on spreading stems that grow 6 to 18 inches tall. *O. tetragona*—yellow flowers similar to those of *O. fruticosa* but with young buds and stems tinted red.

Growing conditions and maintenance: Plant Ozark sundrops 2 feet apart, other species 12 to 18 inches apart. Propagate Ozark sundrops from seed, other species either from seed or by division.

Paeonia
(pee-O-nee-a)
PEONY

Paeonia lactiflora

Hardiness: *Zones 3-8*

Flowering season: *spring to summer*

Height: *18 to 36 inches*

Flower color: *white, pink, red*

Soil: *well-drained, fertile loam*

Light: *full sun to light shade*

Peonies are long-lived perennials beloved for their large, showy flowers and attractive foliage. Dramatic in the garden, they are stunning in bouquets. Peony flowers are classified by their form. Single-flower peonies have a single row of five or more petals surrounding a center of bright yellow stamens. Japanese and anemone peonies have a single row of petals surrounding modified stamens that resemble finely cut petals. Semidouble peonies have several rows of petals surrounding conspicuous stamens. Double-flowered peonies have multiple rows of petals crowded into ruffly hemispheres.

Selected species and varieties: *P. lactiflora* (garden or Chinese peony)—white, pink, or red flowers on 3-foot stems. *P. mlokosewitschii* (Caucasian peony)—very early blooming, 2-inch single lemon yellow flowers on 2-foot-tall stems with soft gray-green foliage. *P. officinalis* (common peony)—hundreds of varieties with 3- to 6-inch blooms in various forms and colors from red to light pink to white on 2-foot stems. *P. tenuifolia* (fern-leaf peony)—single

deep red flowers and finely divided, fern-like leaves on 18- to 24-inch stems; 'Flore Pleno' has double flowers.

Hundreds of peony hybrids are available. 'Lobata' (red-pink), 'Lotus Bloom' (pink), and 'Krinkled White' are outstanding singles. 'Isani-Gidui' (white) and 'Nippon Beauty' (dark red) are lovely Japanese types. 'Gay Paree' (pink with white-blush center) grows anemone-type blossoms. Semidouble varieties include 'Ludovica' (salmon pink) and 'Lowell Thomas' (deep red). Among the double-flowered varieties, 'Festiva Maxima' (white with red marking), 'Red Charm' (deep true red, early blooming), 'Mons. Jules Elie' (early, pink), 'Karl Rosenfeld' (deep red), and 'Nick Shaylor' (blush pink) are all exceptional.

Growing conditions and maintenance: Plant peonies 3 feet apart in soil containing some organic matter. Set the buds (eyes) 2 inches below the soil surface;

Paeonia mlokosewitschii

setting them deeper delays flowering. Propagate by dividing clumps in late summer-early fall into sections containing three to five eyes each.

Papaver
(pap-AY-ver)
POPPY

Papaver orientale

Hardiness: *Zones 3-9*

Flowering season: *spring to summer*

Height: *1 to 4 feet*

Flower color: *red, pink, orange, yellow, white*

Soil: *well-drained loam*

Light: *full sun to partial shade*

Poppies bear large, brilliantly colored, silky-textured blossoms on wiry stems above finely cut leaves. The blooms, which last for several weeks, open from nodding buds.

Selected species and varieties: *P. nudicaule* (Iceland poppy)—fragrant flowers up to 3 inches across on 12- to 24-inch stems. *P. orientale* (Oriental poppy)—blossoms up to 8 inches across composed of tissue-thin petals on wiry stems rising from mounds of coarse, hairy leaves; 'Glowing Embers' has orange-red ruffled petals; 'Mrs. Perry', clear pink flowers; 'Beauty of Livermore', deep red petals spotted black at the base; 'Princess Victoria Louise', bright salmon-pink flowers.

Growing conditions and maintenance: Space poppies 1½ feet apart. Propagate Oriental poppies, which are tough, long-lived plants, from seed or from root cuttings. Grow Iceland poppies from seed to flower in their first year; sow in late summer in the North and in fall in southern climates.

Pennisetum
(pen-i-SEE-tum)
FOUNTAIN GRASS

Pennisetum alopecuroides

Hardiness: *Zones 5-9*

Flowering season: *summer*

Height: *2 to 5 feet*

Flower color: *silvery mauve, white*

Soil: *well-drained loam*

Light: *full sun*

Fountain grass forms a spray of arching leaves with bottle-brush flower heads borne on thin, arching stems in summer and fall. Stunning in masses, fountain grass graces borders, rock gardens, water features, and fall-blooming perennial beds. It is also useful as an accent plant.

Selected species and varieties: *P. alopecuroides* (Chinese pennisetum, perennial fountain grass)—silvery mauve 5- to 7-inch blooms on erect stems up to 5 feet tall above a mound of arching 2- to 3-foot leaves that turn a bright almond color in winter; 'Hameln' (dwarf fountain grass) grows only 1 to 2 feet tall; 'National Arboretum', to 2 feet with a dark brown inflorescence; Zones 7-9. *P. caudatum* (white flowering fountain grass)—silvery white bloom spikes 4 to 5 feet tall.

Growing conditions and maintenance: Space plants 2 to 3 feet apart. Cut back to 6 inches before growth begins in the spring. Propagate the species from seed or by division, varieties by division. Divide every 5 to 10 years to prevent the center from falling open. Fountain grass tolerates wind and coastal conditions.

Perovskia
(per-OV-skee-a)
RUSSIAN SAGE

Perovskia atriplicifolia

Hardiness: *Zones 5-9*

Flowering season: *summer*

Height: *3 to 4 feet*

Flower color: *lavender-blue*

Soil: *well-drained loam*

Light: *full sun*

Russian sage's shrubby mounds of fine-textured, deeply toothed aromatic gray foliage are an effective filler in the border and remain attractive through winter. In summer, spires of tiny lavender flowers tip each stem. They combine particularly well with ornamental grasses. Planted in a mass, Russian sage develops into a summer hedge, and the stems remain attractive through the winter.

Selected species and varieties: *P. atriplicifolia* (azure sage)—tubular, two-lipped lavender flowers growing in whorls, spaced along 12-inch flower spikes above downy gray, finely divided leaves. Clumps of woody stems grow to 4 feet tall and as wide. 'Blue Spire' is upright with violet-blue flowers.

Growing conditions and maintenance: Plant Russian sage 2 to 3 feet apart in full sun; shade causes floppy, sprawling growth. Soil should not be overly rich. Cut woody stems to the ground in spring before new growth begins. Propagate by seed or from summer cuttings.

Phlox
(flox)
PHLOX

Phlox divaricata 'Fuller's White'

Hardiness: *Zones 3-9*

Flowering season: *spring, summer, or fall*

Height: *3 inches to 4 feet*

Flower color: *pink, purple, red, blue, white*

Soil: *sandy and dry to moist, fertile loam*

Light: *full sun to full shade*

Versatile phlox produces flat, five-petaled flowers, either singly or in clusters, many with a conspicuous eye at the center. There is a species suitable for nearly every combination of soil and light, as well as for nearly any landscape use, from 3-inch creepers to upright border plants growing 4 feet tall.

Selected species and varieties: *P. divaricata* (wild blue phlox)—blue blossoms on 12-inch-tall creepers; 'Fuller's White' has creamy white flowers. *P. maculata* (wild sweet William)—elegant, cylindrical flower heads in shades of pink to white on 3-foot plants; 'Miss Lingard' [sometimes listed as a variety of *P. carolina*] has 6-inch trusses of pure white blossoms; 'Omega', white petals surrounding a lilac-colored eye; 'Alpha', rose pink petals around a darker pink eye. *P. paniculata* (summer phlox, garden phlox)—magnificent pyramidal clusters of white, pink, red, lavender, or purple flowers on 2- to 4-foot stems; 'Fujiyama' has white flower heads 12 to 15 inches long; 'Bright Eyes', pale pink petals surrounding a crimson eye; 'Orange Perfection', salmon orange blossoms; 'Starfire', cherry red. *P. stolonifera* (creeping phlox)—blue, white, or pink flowers on creeping 6- to 12-inch stems with evergreen leaves that form a dense ground cover; 'Blue Ridge' produces clear blue flowers; 'Bruce's White', white flowers with yellow eyes. *P. subulata* (moss phlox, moss pink)—white, pink, blue, lavender, or red flowers above dense clumps of evergreen foliage 3 to 6 inches tall and 2 feet wide.

Phlox subulata

Growing conditions and maintenance: Space lower-growing phlox 1 to 1½ feet apart, taller species up to 2 feet apart. Wild blue phlox grows well in shady, moist sites; moss phlox thrives in sunny, dry spots. Creeping phlox grows in sun or shade. Both moss phlox and creeping phlox form lush mats of evergreen foliage and make wonderful ground covers. Wild sweet William and summer phlox thrive in full sun, provided they receive ample moisture during the growing season. Space summer phlox for good air circulation to avoid powdery mildew. Propagate phlox by division. Promote dense growth and reblooming by cutting plants back after flowering.

Physostegia
(fy-so-STEE-gee-a)
FALSE DRAGONHEAD

Physostegia virginiana

Hardiness: *Zones 4-8*

Flowering season: *late summer to fall*

Height: *2 to 4 feet*

Flower color: *pink, purple, white*

Soil: *moist or dry acid loam*

Light: *full sun to partial shade*

False dragonhead produces unusual 8- to 10-inch flower spikes with four evenly spaced vertical rows of blossoms resembling snapdragons.

Selected species and varieties: *P. virginiana*—pink flowers tipping each stem in clumps of 4-foot stalks; 'Variegata' has pink flowers above green-and-white variegated leaves; 'Vivid', rosy pink blossoms on compact plants only 20 inches tall; 'Summer Snow', early-blooming white flowers.

Growing conditions and maintenance: Plant false dragonhead 1½ to 2 feet apart. It is so tolerant of varying growing conditions that it can become invasive. Propagate the plants from seed or by division every 2 years.

Platycodon
(plat-i-KO-don)
BALLOON FLOWER

Platycodon grandiflorus

Hardiness: *Zones 4-9*

Flowering season: *summer*

Height: *10 to 36 inches*

Flower color: *blue, white, pink*

Soil: *well-drained, acid loam*

Light: *full sun to partial shade*

The balloon flower derives its common name from the fat, inflated flower buds it produces. These pop open into spectacular cup-shaped 2- to 3-inch-wide blossoms with pointed petals.

Selected species and varieties: *P. grandiflorus*—deep blue flowers on slender stems above neat clumps of blue-green leaves; 'Album' has white flowers; 'Shell Pink', pale pink flowers; 'Mariesii' is a compact variety 18 inches tall with bright blue flowers. 'Double Blue' has bright blue double flowers on 2-foot stems.

Growing conditions and maintenance: Space balloon flowers 18 inches apart. Pink varieties develop the best color when grown in partial shade. Propagate from seed to flower the second year or by division.

Polygonum
(po-LIG-o-num)
SMARTWEED, KNOTWEED

Polygonum bistorta 'Superbum'

Hardiness: *Zones 4-9*

Flowering season: *summer*

Height: *6 inches to 3 feet*

Flower color: *pink, white, red*

Soil: *moist loam*

Light: *full sun to light shade*

Although the genus *Polygonum* contains many weeds familiar to gardeners, it also boasts a few highly ornamental species with colorful flower spikes held above neat mats of foliage.

Selected species and varieties: *P. affine* (Himalayan fleeceflower)—spikes of rose pink flowers 6 to 9 inches tall above dark green leaves turning bronze in fall; 'Superbum' produces crimson flowers. *P. bistorta* (snakeweed)—pink flowers like bottle brushes on 2-foot stems above striking clumps of 4- to 6-inch-long wavy green leaves with a white midrib; 'Superbum' grows to 3 feet.

Growing conditions and maintenance: Space polygonums 1 foot apart. Himalayan fleeceflower thrives in full sun; snakeweed prefers some shade. Propagate by division in spring. Use *P. bistorta* wherever you need a spreading ground cover; plant *P. affine* alongside a path or at the front of a border.

Potentilla
(po-ten-TILL-a)
CINQUEFOIL

Potentilla nepalensis 'Miss Wilmott'

Hardiness: *Zones 5-8*

Flowering season: *spring to summer*

Height: *2 to 18 inches*

Flower color: *white, yellow, pink, red*

Soil: *well-drained, sandy loam*

Light: *full sun to light shade*

Cinquefoil's neat, compound leaves, with three to five leaflets arranged like fingers on a hand, grow in spreading clumps of foliage. The open-faced flowers, which have five petals arranged around a ring of fuzzy stamens, resemble wild roses. Cinquefoils are effective creeping between stones in the rock garden and as a ground cover on dry slopes.

Selected species and varieties: *P. atrosanguinea* (Himalayan or ruby cinquefoil)—dark red 1-inch-wide flowers and five-fingered 8-inch green leaves with silvery undersides on plants 12 to 18 inches tall; 'Fire Dance' flowers have a scarlet center and a yellow border on 15-inch stems; 'Gibson's Scarlet' has bright scarlet flowers on 15-inch stems; 'William Rollinson' grows to 18 inches with deep orange and yellow semidouble flowers; 'Yellow Queen' grows bright yellow flowers with a red center on 12-inch stems above silvery foliage. *P. nepalensis* (Nepal cinquefoil)—a bushy species with cup-shaped flowers in shades of salmon, rose, red, orange, and purple, often flowering throughout the summer; 'Miss Wilmott' is a dwarf variety 10 to 12 inches tall with cherry red flowers; 'Roxana' has coppery orange petals surrounding red centers on 15-inch stems. *P.* x *tonguei* (staghorn cinquefoil)—apricot-colored flowers with red centers on trailing stems 8 to 12 inches long above evergreen foliage. *P. tridentata* (wineleaf cinquefoil) [also classified as *Sibbaldiopsis tridentata*]—clusters of tiny white flowers blooming late spring to midsummer on 2- to 6-inch plants with shiny, leathery evergreen leaves that turn wine red in the fall; 'Minima' is a low-growing cultivar (3 inches high) that performs well as a ground cover. *P. verna* (spring cinquefoil)—a prostrate, fast-spreading plant that grows 2 to 3 inches high and produces golden yellow flowers ½ inch wide; 'Nana' has larger flowers than the species and grows slightly higher.

Growing conditions and maintenance: Plant smaller cinquefoils 1 foot apart and larger species 2 feet apart. Potentillas prefer a poor soil; they will produce excess leafy growth if raised in fertile soil. Wineleaf cinquefoil develops its best fall color in acid soils. Cinquefoils are generally short-lived perennials and grow best in areas with mild winters and summers. *P. verna* can be invasive; its stems may root, forming a broad mat. Propagate from seed or by division every 3 years in spring or fall.

Primula
(PRIM-yew-la)
PRIMROSE

Primula japonica 'Postford White'

Hardiness: *Zones 3-8*

Flowering season: *spring*

Height: *2 to 24 inches*

Flower color: *wide spectrum*

Soil: *moist loam*

Light: *partial shade*

Neat, colorful primroses produce clusters of five-petaled blossoms on leafless stems above rosettes of tongue-shaped leaves, which are evergreen in milder climates. More than 400 species of primroses in nearly every color of the rainbow offer the gardener a multitude of choices in height and hardiness.

Selected species and varieties: *P. auricula* (auricula primrose)—fragrant, bell-shaped flowers in yellow, white, or other hues on plants 2 to 8 inches tall; hardy to Zone 3. *P. denticulata* (Himalayan primrose)—globe-shaped clusters of purple flowers with a yellow eye on 8- to 12-inch stalks; varieties are available in strong red, pink, and white flower tones; to Zone 6. *P. helodoxa* (amber primrose)—soft yellow flowers on 24-inch stems; to Zone 6. *P. japonica* (Japanese primrose)—whorls of white, red, pink, or purple flowers on 2-foot stalks; 'Miller's Crimson' has deep red blossoms; 'Postford White', white flowers; to Zone 6. *P. x polyantha* (polyanthus primrose)—flowers singly or in clusters on 6- to 12-inch stems in a wide choice of colors; to Zone 4. *P. sieboldii* (Japanese

star primrose)—nodding heads of pink, purple, or white flowers on 12-inch stalks. *P. vulgaris* (English primrose)—fragrant single flowers in yellow and other colors on 6- to 9-inch stems.

Growing conditions and maintenance: Space primroses 1 foot apart in moisture-retentive soil. Water deeply during dry periods. Himalayan, amber, and Japanese primroses require a boglike soil. English and polyanthus primroses tolerate drier conditions, while other species mentioned fall somewhere in between. Polyanthus primroses are short-lived and often treated as annuals. Japanese star primroses go dormant after flowering. Propagate primroses from

Primula x polyantha

seed or by division every 3 to 4 years in spring. Auricula and Japanese star primroses can also be propagated from stem cuttings, Himalayan primroses from root cuttings. Plant primroses in masses with spring bulbs, or use as border plants.

Rudbeckia
(rood-BEK-ee-a)
CONEFLOWER

Rudbeckia fulgida 'Goldstrum'

Hardiness: *Zones 3-9*

Flowering season: *summer*

Height: *1 to 4 feet*

Flower color: *yellow*

Soil: *moist to dry*

Light: *full sun to partial shade*

Rudbeckias are annuals, biennials, and perennials from open woodlands and meadows throughout most of the United States. Their gay yellow daisylike flowers, with a fringe of narrow petals surrounding a prominent center, are favorites among wildflower gardeners. These plants bloom prolifically on wiry stems above vigorous clumps of deeply cut foliage.

Selected species and varieties: *R. fulgida* 'Goldstrum'—bright yellow flowers with brown centers, growing from midsummer to frost on compact 2-foot plants. *R. grandiflora* (large coneflower)—1½ to 3 feet tall. Flowers up to 6 inches or more across have drooping petals and a brown cone-shaped center. *R. nitida*—bright yellow petals surrounding extremely large 2-inch centers on 2- to 7-foot stems. *R. subtomentosa* (sweet coneflower)—1 to 4 feet tall with 3-inch flowers with dark centers.

Growing conditions and maintenance: Plant coneflowers 1½ to 2 feet apart. Propagate from seed or by division every 2 years in spring. Coneflowers are a good choice for southern gardens.

Salvia
(SAL-vee-a)
SAGE

Salvia farinacea 'Victoria'

Hardiness: *tender or Zones 4-10*

Flowering season: *spring to fall*

Height: *1 to 6 feet*

Flower color: *blue, purple, white, red*

Soil: *well-drained loam*

Light: *full sun*

Whorled spikes of tiny, hooded, summer-to-fall-blooming flowers line the tips of salvia's erect stems above soft, sometimes downy leaves. Salvias are particularly effective in masses that multiply the impact of their flowers. Tender perennial salvias that cannot withstand frost are grown as annuals in Zone 8 and colder.

Selected species and varieties: *S. argentea* (silver sage)—branching clusters of white flowers tinged yellow or pink on 3-foot stems above rosettes of woolly, gray-green, 8-inch leaves. *S. azurea* ssp. *pitcheri* var. *grandiflora* (blue sage)—large, deep blue flowers on stems to 5 feet lined with gray-green leaves. *S. farinacea* (mealy-cup sage)—violet-blue or white flowers from midsummer to frost on 2- to 3-foot stems; 'Blue Bedder' has deep blue flowers on 8-inch clusters on compact plants to 2 feet tall. *S. haematodes* (meadow sage)—airy sprays of lavender-blue flowers from early to midsummer on plants to 3 feet tall. *S. jurisicii* (Jurisici's sage)—dangling lilac or white flowers on stems 12 to 18 inches tall. *S. officinalis* (common sage)—whorls of tiny white, blue, or purple flowers above wrinkled, hairy, aromatic gray-green leaves, which can be used as a seasoning for food; 'Purpurascens' has purple-tinged leaves; 'Tricolor', leaf veins turning from cream to pink and red as foliage ages. *S. sclarea* 'Turkestanica' [also called *S. sclarea* var. *turkestana* or var. *turkestaniana*]—rosy pink flower spikes tipping 3-foot stems above wrinkled, hairy leaves. *S.* x *superba* (perennial salvia)—violet-purple flowers in dense whorls around 4- to 8-inch spikes from late spring to early summer on rounded plants to 3 feet tall; 'Blue Queen' grows 18 to 24 inches tall; 'East Friesland' has deep purple blossoms on 18- to 24-inch plants; 'May Night' grows to 24 inches with intense violet-blue flowers.

Salvia officinalis 'Purpurascens'

Growing conditions and maintenance: Sage grows best in dry soils; its roots should not stay wet over winter. Because they vary in hardiness, particular care must be given to selection of species. Garden sage is hardy to Zone 4; Pitcher's salvia and perennial salvia, to Zone 5; meadow sage and Jurisici's sage, to Zone 6; mealy-cup sage, to Zone 8 and evergreen in Zone 9. Plant smaller salvia varieties 18 inches apart, larger ones 2 to 3 feet apart. Removing spent flowers encourages reblooming. Propagate by division in spring or fall, from cuttings, or, except for perennial salvia, from seed.

Santolina
(san-to-LEE-na)
LAVENDER COTTON

Santolina chamaecyparissus

Hardiness: *Zones 6-8*

Flowering season: *summer*

Height: *18 to 24 inches*

Flower color: *yellow*

Soil: *well-drained to dry loam*

Light: *full sun*

Santolina forms a broad, spreading clump of aromatic leaves, with slender stems topped by tiny yellow flower buttons. The foliage makes an attractive edging for a bed or walkway, or can be used as a low-growing specimen in a rock garden. It can also be sheared into a tight, low hedge.

Selected species and varieties: *S. chamaecyparissus*—up to 24 inches tall with equal or greater spread, forms a broad, cushionlike, evergreen mound. Leaves are silvery gray-green and ½ to 1½ inches long; yellow flowers bloom in summer and are often removed to maintain clipped hedge. *S. virens*—green toothed-edged leaves in dense 18-inch clumps.

Growing conditions and maintenance: Lavender cotton is a tough plant, well suited to adverse conditions such as drought and salt spray. It prefers dry soils of low fertility and becomes unattractive and open in fertile soils. Avoid excess moisture, especially in winter. Space plants 18 to 24 inches apart. Prune after flowering to promote dense growth, or shear anytime for a formal, low hedge. Propagate from seed or from stem cuttings taken in early summer.

Saxifraga
(saks-IF-ra-ga)
SAXIFRAGE, ROCKFOIL

Saxifraga umbrosa

Hardiness: *Zones 7-9*

Flowering season: *late spring to early summer*

Height: *4 to 24 inches*

Flower color: *white, pink, rose, bicolored*

Soil: *moist, well-drained, neutral, fertile*

Light: *full to dappled shade*

An ideal plant for rock gardens, saxifrage's rosettes of leaves form a mat from which runners or stolons spread. The red threadlike runners of strawberry geranium, which is also grown as a houseplant, produce baby plants. Delicate flowers rise above foliage in spring.

Selected species and varieties: *S. stolonifera* (strawberry geranium, beefsteak geranium)—18- to 24-inch branched stems bearing 1-inch-wide white flowers above 4-inch-tall clumps of round, hairy leaves with white veins and red undersides, up to 4 inches wide. *S. umbrosa* (London-pride)—18-inch-high clumps of 2-inch-long oval leaves, pea green above and red beneath, with white, pink, rose, or bicolored flower sprays on 6-inch stems from late spring to early summer.

Growing conditions and maintenance: Saxifrages grow best in neutral, rocky soil but will tolerate other soils as long as they are very well drained but evenly moist. Generously enrich the soil with leaf mold or peat moss. Plant 8 to 10 inches apart in spring, and mulch lightly to overwinter. Apply an all-purpose fertilizer in spring. Propagate by dividing after flowering.

Sedum
(SEE-dum)
STONECROP

Sedum 'Autumn Joy'

Hardiness: *Zones 3-10*

Flowering season: *spring to fall*

Height: *3 inches to 2 feet*

Flower color: *white, yellow, orange, red, pink*

Soil: *well-drained loam*

Light: *full sun to light shade*

Stonecrops are valued for both their flowers and their foliage, which add color and rich texture to a garden over a long season. Their thick, succulent leaves vary in color from bright green to blue-green to reddish green. Individual flowers are small and star-shaped, with 5 petals. Generally borne in dense clusters that cover the plant, they attract butterflies to the garden. The blooming season varies among species from spring to fall, with some flowers even persisting into winter. Sedums are easy to grow and tolerate drought, making them well suited to rock gardens and dry borders. They can be used as individual specimens, in groupings of three or more, or massed as a succulent ground cover.

Selected species and varieties: *S. aizoon* (Aizoon stonecrop)—yellow flowers above bright green leaves on stems 12 to 18 inches tall, blooming from spring to summer; 'Auranticum' has deep yellow flowers and red-tinted stems. *S.* 'Autumn Joy'—rosy pink flower buds that form above gray-green leaves on 2-foot stems in midsummer, turn red before opening bronze-red in fall, and turn golden brown if left in place for the winter. *S. kamtschaticum* (orange stonecrop)—6 to 9 inches tall with a wide-spreading habit, excellent for rock gardens, grows small orange-yellow flowers in summer; 'Variegatum' produces deep orange flowers and green leaves with a broad white margin blushed with pink. *S. maximum* (great stonecrop)—greenish yellow, star-shaped flowers in late summer above oval, gray-green leaves on stems up to 2 feet tall; 'Atropurpureum' has red flowers and maroon leaves. *S. rosea* (roseroot)—tiny yellow or purple flowers atop clumps of 12-inch stems with small toothed leaves; *S. rosea integrifolium* has pink to red-purple flowers. *S.* 'Ruby Glow'—ruby red fall flowers above purple-gray foliage on compact plants 8 inches tall; a good choice for the front of a border. *S. sieboldii* (Siebold stonecrop)—dense heads of pink flowers effective throughout fall above nearly triangular blue-gray leaves on 6- to 9-inch somewhat trailing stems. *S. spectabile* (showy stonecrop)—a heat-tolerant

Sedum kamtschaticum

species with bright pink flowers that bloom from late summer till frost on 18-inch stems; 'Brilliant' has raspberry red flowers; 'Carmen', rose pink flowers; 'Variegatum', bright pink flowers atop leaves variegated yellow and green; 'Meteor', large wine red blooms; 'Stardust', white flowers that stand out against blue-green leaves; Zones 3-10. *S. spurium* (two-row stonecrop)—pink, red, or white summer flowers on vigorously spreading evergreen stems 3 to 6 inches tall that make a tough evergreen ground cover; 'Bronze Carpet' has pink flowers and red-brown foliage; 'Coccineum' has scarlet blooms; 'Dragon's Blood' produces purple-bronze leaves and deep crimson star-shaped flowers; 'Red Carpet' has bronze leaves and red flowers; 'Variegatum', green leaves with creamy pink margins. *S.* 'Vera Jameson'—a slightly larger hybrid of *S.* 'Ruby Glow' at 12 inches tall, with bronze foliage and magenta flowers.

Sedum spurium

Growing conditions and maintenance: Stonecrops are tough plants that spread without becoming invasive. Space *S. sieboldii* 1 foot apart, other species 1½ to 2 feet apart. They tolerate almost any well-drained soil, even if it is dry and sterile. Stonecrops can be left undivided for many years, but can be propagated by division in spring or from stem cuttings taken in summer.

Silene
(sy-LEE-ne)
CAMPION, CATCHFLY

Silene schafta

Hardiness: *Zones 4-8*

Flowering season: *summer to fall*

Height: *4 inches to 2 feet*

Flower color: *white, pink, red*

Soil: *well-drained, sandy loam*

Light: *full sun to light shade*

Campions produce star-shaped, five-petaled flowers on branching stems for several weeks during the growing season. The plant's tufts of low-growing, narrow foliage sometimes spread.

Selected species and varieties: *S. schafta* (moss campion)—rose pink or purple flowers on 12-inch stems above 6-inch rosettes of hairy, oblong, light green leaves. *S.* 'Robin's White Breast'—white flower bells above dense 8-inch mounds of silvery gray leaves. *S. virginica* (fire-pink catchfly)—clusters of pink to red flowers on sticky 2-foot stems above flat rosettes of evergreen leaves.

Growing conditions and maintenance: Space campions 12 inches apart. Propagate from seed or by division in spring.

Solidago
(sol-i-DAY-go)
GOLDENROD

Solidago canadensis

Hardiness: *Zones 3-10*

Flowering season: *summer, fall*

Height: *1 to 10 feet*

Flower color: *yellow*

Soil: *moist, well-drained to dry*

Light: *full sun to partial shade*

The upright stems of goldenrods are tipped with eye-catching clusters of yellow flowers in summer and fall. These tough, dependable perennials are native to meadows and prairies in Canada and throughout most of the United States. They make excellent cut flowers, and butterflies feed on their nectar.

Selected species and varieties: *S. caesia* (blue-stemmed goldenrod, wreath goldenrod)—slender blue- or purple-tinged stems 1 to 3 feet with small arching sprays of yellow flowers in late summer and fall; Zones 4-8. *S. canadensis* (Canada goldenrod)—2 to 4 feet tall with branching flower clusters in late summer; Zones 3-10. *S. juncea* (early goldenrod)—up to 6 feet or more in height with arching clusters of flowers from mid- to late summer; Zones 3-7. *S. missouriensis* (Missouri goldenrod)—an early-blooming goldenrod with nodding flower clusters on reddish stems 1 to 2 feet tall from mid- to late summer; Zones 4-8. *S. nemoralis* (gray goldenrod)—up to 2 feet high with plume-shaped flower clusters in late summer and fall; Zones 3-9. *S. odora* (sweet goldenrod)—2 to 5 feet tall with large flower clusters from midsummer through fall and neat, bright green foliage that smells like anise when crushed; Zones 3-9. *S. rugosa* (rough-leaved goldenrod)—2 to 5 feet tall with flower sprays composed of thin, arching stems for 3 to 4 weeks in fall; Zones 3-8. *S. sempervirens* (seaside goldenrod)—large branching clusters of flowers on stems to 8 feet tall in late

Solidago odora

summer and fall above a clump of narrow evergreen leaves up to 16 inches long; Zones 4-8.

Growing conditions and maintenance: Space goldenrods 18 to 24 inches apart. These plants thrive in full sun in soils of average fertility. *S. caesia* also tolerates partial shade. *S. sempervirens* tolerates salt spray and can be pinched in early summer to encourage compact growth. Most goldenrods are aggressive growers and may need dividing every 2 to 3 years. *S. caesia, S. odora,* and *S. sempervirens* are less vigorous growers than the others and easier to keep within bounds. Propagate goldenrods by seed or division. Propagate hybrids by division.

Stokesia
(sto-KEE-zi-a)
STOKES' ASTER

Stokesia laevis 'Blue Danube'

Hardiness: *Zones 5-9*

Flowering season: *summer*

Height: *12 to 18 inches*

Flower color: *lavender, blue, white*

Soil: *well-drained, sandy loam*

Light: *full sun*

The showy, fringed flowers of Stokes' aster bloom on branched flowerstalks rising from neat rosettes of shiny, narrow, straplike leathery leaves that are evergreen in warmer climates. Stokes' aster is excellent in bouquets.

Selected species and varieties: *S. laevis*—solitary flower heads 2 to 5 inches across, blooming over a 4-week season in summer; 'Blue Danube' has 5-inch clear blue flowers; 'Blue Moon', lilac flowers; 'Jelitto' has 4-inch-deep blue blossoms; 'Silver Moon' blooms white.

Growing conditions and maintenance: Space *Stokesia* 18 inches apart. Mulch over winter in colder climates. Propagate the species from seed, and the species and its hybrids by division in the spring.

Verbena
(ver-BEE-na)
VERBENA, VERVAIN

Verbena canadensis 'Rosea'

Hardiness: *Zones 6-8*

Flowering season: *summer to fall*

Height: *4 inches to 5 feet*

Flower color: *pink, red, purple*

Soil: *well-drained loam*

Light: *full sun*

Verbena's tiny flowers bloom in flat, dainty clusters on wiry stems.

Selected species and varieties: *V. bonariensis* (Brazilian verbena)—fragrant purple flowers on stems to 5 feet. *V. canadensis* (rose verbena)—rose pink blossoms in rounded clusters on dense mats of creeping stems 6 inches tall; 'Rosea' produces fragrant rose-purple flowers blooming almost continuously. *V. peruviana* (Peruvian verbena)—crimson flowers on trailing stems 4 inches high. *V. tenuisecta* (moss verbena)—lavender flower clusters on 1-foot stems.

Growing conditions and maintenance: Space Brazilian verbena plants 2 feet apart, smaller forms 1 foot apart. Rose verbena is hardy to Zone 6, other species to Zone 8. Propagate from seed or from cuttings taken in the late summer.

Veronica
(ve-RON-i-ka)
SPEEDWELL

Veronica 'Sunny Border Blue'

Hardiness: *Zones 4-8*

Flowering season: *spring to summer*

Height: *6 inches to 4 feet*

Flower color: *blue, pink, white*

Soil: *well-drained loam*

Light: *full sun to light shade*

Clumps of spreading stems lined with soft-textured, narrow leaves and tipped with long spikes of tiny, spring to summer flowers make speedwell a good choice for fillers or naturalizing.

Selected species and varieties: *V.* x hybrids—plants 12 to 24 inches tall; 'Sunny Border Blue' produces blue flowers. *V. incana* (silver speedwell, woolly speedwell)—pale lilac-blue flowers above low clumps of silver-gray foliage; 'Minuet' has pink flowers and gray-green leaves; 'Saraband', 12- to 18-inch plants with violet-blue flowers. *V. longifolia* (long-leaf speedwell)—plants to 4 feet; 'Icicle' has white flowers; var. *subsessilis,* lilac blooms. *V. spicata* (spike speedwell)—18-inch plants; 'Blue Fox' has lavender-blue flower spikes; 'Red Fox', rose-to-pink blooms. *V. teucrium* [also called *V. austriaca* ssp. *teucrium*] 'Crater Lake Blue'—compact 12- to 18-inch plants with wide spikes of deep blue flowers.

Growing conditions and maintenance: Plant speedwell 1 to 2 feet apart. Remove spent flowers to extend bloom. Propagate from seed or cuttings or by division in spring or fall.

Veronicastrum
(ve-ro-ni-KAS-trum)
CULVER'S ROOT

Veronicastrum virginicum

Hardiness: *Zones 4-8*

Flowering season: *summer*

Height: *3 to 6 feet*

Flower color: *white, pale lavender, pink*

Soil: *well-drained, acid loam*

Light: *full sun to partial shade*

Veronicastrum produces branched clusters of tiny flower spikes on tall, erect stems. Its leaves are arranged in tiered whorls that ascend the stem.

Selected species and varieties: *V. virginicum* (blackroot)—tiny tubular flowers packed densely along 6- to 9-inch flower spikes on stems 6 feet tall in clumps 18 to 24 inches wide; 'Roseum' grows pink flowers; 'Album', white flowers. Veroniscastrum is a good background plant for the garden.

Growing conditions and maintenance: Space veronicastrum 18 to 24 inches apart in moderately acid soil. Plants that are grown in shade may require staking for support. Propagate plants by division in the fall.

Viola
(Vy-O-la)
VIOLET

Viola canadensis var. rugulosa

Hardiness: *Zones 3-9*

Flowering season: *spring and fall*

Height: *3 to 12 inches*

Flower color: *yellow, white, rose, violet*

Soil: *moist, well-drained loam*

Light: *partial shade*

Violets produce dainty blossoms that have 2 upper petals and 3 lower petals joined into a short spur on thin stems. Leaves are heart shaped.

Selected species and varieties: *V. canadensis* (Canada violet)—white flowers with a yellow eye; *V. canadensis* var. *rugulosa* has narrower, wrinkled leaves with hairy undersides. *V. cornuta* (horned violet)—pansylike flowers on plants with evergreen leaves; 'Lord Nelson' has deep violet flowers. *V. cucullata* (marsh blue violet)—white flowers with purple veins; 'Royal Robe' has deep blue flowers. *V. odorata* (sweet violet)—fragrant flowers in shades of violet, rose, and white; 'Alba' has white blossoms; 'Czar', deep violet flowers. *V. tricolor* (Johnny-jump-up)—tricolored violet blue-and-yellow flowers.

Growing conditions and maintenance: Space violets 8 to 12 inches apart. Propagate from seed or by division.

Agapanthus
(ag-a-PAN-thus)
LILY-OF-THE-NILE

Agapanthus africanus

Hardiness: *tender or Zones 8-10*

Type of bulb: *rhizome*

Flowering season: *summer*

Height: *18 inches to 5 feet*

Soil: *moist, well-drained*

Light: *full sun*

Domed clusters of five-petaled, star-shaped flowers with prominent stamens rise on leafless, hollow stalks from graceful clumps of straplike evergreen leaves that persist after the flowers fade. Agapanthus makes dramatic border specimens or pot plants and can be used as long-lasting cut flowers. Its seedpods add interest to dried arrangements.

Selected species and varieties: *A. africanus* 'Albus' (African lily)—clusters of 30 or more 1½-inch white flower stars on stems to 3 feet tall. *A. praecox* ssp. *orientalis* (Oriental agapanthus)—up to 100 white or blue flowers clustered on stems to 5 feet tall above 3-foot-long leaves that are up to 3 inches wide and sometimes striped yellow; 'Peter Pan' is an 18-inch dwarf cultivar with blue blossoms.

Growing conditions and maintenance: Plant rhizomes 24 inches apart in spring for summer bloom, setting the tops of the bulbs just below the soil line. In colder areas, grow plants in pots, moving them indoors before frost. They bloom best when slightly potbound. Cut stems back after flowers fade. Propagate by dividing rhizomes every 4 or 5 years in spring.

Allium
(AL-lee-um)
FLOWERING ONION

Allium cernuum

Hardiness: *Zones 3-9*

Type of bulb: *true bulb*

Flowering season: *spring to summer*

Height: *6 inches to 5 feet*

Soil: *moist, well-drained*

Light: *full sun to partial shade*

Related to edible culinary species, flowering onions produce showy 2- to 12-inch flower clusters, usually in dense spheres or ovals composed of hundreds of tiny blooms packed tightly together, but sometimes in loose, dangling or upright airy domes of larger flowers. Each stout, leafless hollow stem holds a single flower well above a low rosette of grassy or straplike leaves that die back after the bulbs produce their blooms. Many species smell faintly like onion or garlic when cut or bruised, but a few are sweetly fragrant. Mass alliums for effect in spring or summer beds or borders; strategically site larger flowering onions as dramatic garden accents; and interplant smaller species with ground covers or in a rock garden. Alliums are striking as cut flowers or in dried bouquets. Some flowering onion species will naturalize, and a few are suitable for forcing. Rodent pests find flowering onion bulbs unappealing.

Selected species and varieties: *A. aflatunense* (ornamental onion, Persian onion)—4-inch purple flower globes in late spring on 2- to 4-foot-tall stems above 4-inch-wide foliage; Zones 4-8. *A. atro-* *purpureum*—2-inch wine red spheres on 2- to 3-foot stems in late spring above narrow 18-inch leaves; Zones 3-9. *A. caeruleum* (blue garlic, blue globe onion)—deep blue blossoms in dense 2-inch globes on 2-foot stems in late spring above narrow 10- to 18-inch-long leaves; Zones 3-9. *A. carinatum* ssp. *pulchellum* (keeled garlic)—carmine flower clusters on stems to 2 feet in summer; 'Album' has white flowers; Zones 3-9. *A. cernuum* (nodding wild onion)—loose clusters of 30 to 40 delicate pink flowers dangle atop 8- to 18-inch stems in late spring above rosettes of grassy 10-inch leaves; Zones 3-9. *A. christophii* (stars-of-Persia)—spidery late spring flowers with a metallic luster growing in lacy clusters up to 10 inches across on stout stems to 2 feet growing from rosettes of 1-inch-wide leaves up to 20 inches long; Zones 4-8.

Allium christophii

A. flavum (small yellow onion)—dangling 2-inch clusters of yellow bell-shaped flowers on 1-foot stems in summer; Zones 4-9. *A. giganteum* (giant ornamental onion, giant garlic)—lilac-colored summer flower globes 6 inches across on stems to 5 feet rising from clumps of leaves 2 inches wide and up to 30 inches long; Zones 5-8. *A. jesdianum*—dense clusters of deep violet flowers; Zones 4-9. *A. karataviense* (Turkestan onion)—pale rose 3-inch or larger flower clusters on 10-inch stems above broad straps of attractive, spreading blue-green foliage in late spring; Zones 4-9. *A. macleanii*—red-violet blossoms clustered at the tips of 3-foot stems in late spring above broad, shiny foliage; Zones 4-9. *A. moly* (lily leek, golden onion)—flat clusters of ¾- to 1-inch flowers; 'Jeannine' has long-lasting 2- to 3-inch vivid yellow flowers on 12-inch stems in summer above blue-green leaves with a metallic sheen; Zones 3-9. *A. neapolitanum* 'Grandiflorum' (daffodil garlic, Naples garlic)—loose, open 3-inch clusters of up to 30 fragrant 1-inch white flower stars on 12- to 18-inch stems in late spring; Zones 6-9. *A. nigrum*—white spring flowers touched with gray on 2-foot stems; Zones 4-9. *A. oreophilum*—open clusters of fragrant 2-inch rosy pink blossoms on 4-inch stems in late spring; Zones 4-9. *A. rosenbachianum* 'Album'—silvery white 4-inch

Allium sphaerocephalum

flower clusters on stems to 3 feet in late spring above 2-inch-wide leaves up to 20 inches long; Zones 5-9. *A. roseum* 'Grandiflorum' (bigflower rosy onion, rosy garlic)—3-inch pinkish white flower globes in late spring on stems to 15 inches, frequently with tiny bulbils appearing after the flowers fade; Zones 5-9. *A. schubertii*—spidery pink-violet flowers in clusters up to a foot or more across on 1- to 2-foot stems in summer above distinctively wavy, inch-wide foliage; Zones 4-9. *A. sphaerocephalum* (drumstick chive, roundheaded leek, roundheaded garlic)—densely packed 2-inch oval heads of deep purple, bell-shaped summer flowers on 3-foot stems rising from clumps of hollow cylindrical leaves up to 24 inches long; Zones 4-8. *A. stipitatum* 'Album'—6-inch spheres of white flowers on stems to 4 feet in late spring above 2-inch-wide leaves; Zones 4-9. *A. triquetrum* (three-cornered leek, triangle onion)—dangling white flowers striped with green on unusual triangular 18-inch stems rising from clumps of deep green leaves 10 to 15 inches long throughout spring; Zones

4-9. *A. unifolium*—rose flowers on 12- to 18-inch stems in late spring; Zones 4-9. *A. ursinum* (bear's garlic, ramsons, wood garlic)—2½-inch flat-topped clusters of white flowers with a strong garlicky odor on 12- to 15-inch stems in late spring; Zones 4-9. *A. zebdanense*—white blossoms clustered on 12-inch stems in late spring; Zones 4-9. *A. hybrids*—'Globemaster' has durable large purple blooms on 2- to 3-foot stems; 'Lucy Ball', deep lilac clusters on stems to 4 feet in summer; 'Purple Sensation', purple flowers on 30-inch stems in spring; Zones 4-9.

Growing conditions and maintenance: Plant flowering onions in fall in northern zones, in spring or fall in warmer areas. Set bulbs at a depth two to three times their diameter, spacing smaller bulbs 4 to 6 inches apart, larger ones 12 to 18 inches. Alliums suitable for naturalizing include *A. aflatunense*, *A. karataviense*, *A. moly*, *A. neapolitanum*, *A. oreophilum*, *A. sphaerocephalum*, and *A. triquetrum*, although *A. triquetrum* can be invasive. Alliums may be left undisturbed in the garden for years until diminished bloom signals that bulbs are overcrowded. Both pleasantly scented *A. neapolitanum* and low-growing *A. schubertii* are suitable for forcing; plant several bulbs per 6-inch pot or bulb pan. Cut stems back after flowers fade, but allow foliage to die back before removing it. Protect bulbs with winter mulch north of Zone 5. Propagate by separating and replanting tiny bulblets that develop at the base of parent bulbs, by potting tiny bulbils that appear amid flower clusters, or by sowing seed, which will grow blooming-size bulbs in 2 years.

Anemone
(a-NEM-o-nee)
WINDFLOWER

Anemone coronaria

Hardiness: *Zones 3-9*

Type of bulb: *tuber or rhizome*

Flowering season: *spring*

Height: *3 to 18 inches*

Soil: *moist, well-drained*

Light: *full sun to light shade*

Windflowers carpet a border with drifts of daisylike flowers held above whorls of attractively divided leaves resembling flat parsley. Single or double rows of petals surround a prominent cushion of anthers in a contrasting color, often with a halo of cream or white separating it from the main petal color. Mass windflowers for a tapestry of color beneath spring-flowering shrubs and trees or allow them to naturalize in woodland gardens. Anemones can be forced as houseplants, and the taller ones make good cut flowers.

Selected species and varieties: *A. apennina* 'Alba' (Apennine windflower)—inch-wide white flowers tinged blue on 6- to 12-inch stems; Zones 6-9. *A. blanda* (Grecian windflower)—2-inch single- or double-petaled flowers with prominent yellow centers on 3- to 8-inch stems; 'Blue Star' has light blue flowers; 'Blue Shades', light to dark blue blooms; 'Charmer', deep pink flowers; 'Pink Star', very large pink blossoms; 'Radar', reddish purple flowers with a white center; 'Rosea', rosy pink blooms; 'Violet Star', violet flowers with a white center; 'White Splendor', long-lasting, large white flowers; Zones 5-8. *A. coronaria* (poppy anemone)—'de Caen' hybrids grow 18 inches tall with single rows of petals; 'Mr. Fokker' has blue flowers; 'Sylphide', deep violet blooms; 'The Bride', pure white flowers. St. Brigid hybrids produce semidouble rows of petals; 'Lord Lieutenant' has bright blue flowers; 'Mt. Everest', white flowers; 'The Admiral', red-violet blooms; 'The Governor', deep scarlet flowers. 'Hollandia' has bright red flowers; Zones 6-9. *A. nemorosa* (wood anemone)—1-inch-wide white flowers tinged pink with yellow centers

Anemone blanda

on 6- to 10-inch stems; 'Alba Plena' has double petals; Zones 4-8. *A. ranunculoides* (buttercup anemone)—yellow blossoms on 6-inch stems; 'Flore Pleno' has semidouble yellow petals giving a ruffled appearance; 'Superba', large flowers above bronzy foliage; Zones 3-9.

Growing conditions and maintenance: Plant windflowers in the fall, massing them for best effect. Soak tubers overnight before setting them out 2 inches deep and 3 to 6 inches apart. *A. apennina* and Grecian windflower can be grown north of Zone 6 by setting tubers out in spring, then lifting them for storage in fall. *A. apennina*, Grecian windflower, and poppy anemone can be forced for houseplants. *A. apennina*, Grecian windflower, wood anemone, and buttercup anemone all naturalize well, although the latter two can be invasive. Anemones need constant moisture, though not soggy conditions, to bloom at their best. Propagate windflowers from seed or by division in late summer after foliage fades.

Arisaema
(a-ris-EE-ma)
DRAGONROOT

Arisaema triphyllum

Hardiness: *Zones 4-9*

Type of bulb: *tuber*

Flowering season: *spring*

Height: *1 to 3 feet*

Soil: *moist, acid*

Light: *partial to full shade*

Arisaemas produce a fleshy spike called a spadix nestled within an outer leaflike spathe, which folds over the spadix like a hood. Glossy, three-lobed leaves taller than the spathe and spadix persist throughout the summer. The spadix ripens to a cluster of attractive red fruit in fall. Use arisaemas in wildflower or woodland gardens or along stream banks, where they will slowly spread out and naturalize.

Selected species and varieties: *A. dracontium* (green-dragon)—green spathe enfolding a 4- to 10-inch green or yellowish green spadix on 1-foot stems. *A. sikokianum*—ivory spadix within a spathe that is deep maroon banded in green on the outside and ivory at its base on the inside, on 1-foot stems. *A. triphyllum* (jack-in-the-pulpit, Indian turnip)—green to purple spadix within a green to purple spathe striped purple, green, white, or maroon inside on 1- to 2-foot stems.

Growing conditions and maintenance: Plant arisaemas in fall, setting tubers 4 inches deep and 1 foot apart in soil that is constantly moist but not soggy. Propagate by division in early fall.

Arum
(A-rum)
ARUM

Arum italicum

Hardiness: *Zones 6-9*

Type of bulb: *tuber*

Flowering season: *spring*

Height: *12 to 18 inches*

Soil: *moist, acid*

Light: *partial shade*

Italian arum *(Arum italicum)* is noteworthy for its attractively marbled, arrow-shaped leaves, which appear in fall and persist through the winter. Inconspicuous flowers appear in spring, lining a fleshy, fingerlike spadix enfolded by a leaflike hood called a spathe, which rises to a sharp point. Most gardeners grow arum for the plump cluster of glossy, brightly colored berries that follows the flowers in summer. Arum will naturalize in moist woodland or wildflower gardens.

Selected species and varieties: *A. italicum* 'Marmoratum' [also called 'Pictum'] (Italian arum)—narrow, waxy leaves veined in cream or silver followed by a creamy yellow or yellow-green spadix and thick clusters of brilliant orange berries.

Growing conditions and maintenance: Plant Italian arum in late summer, setting tubers 3 inches deep and 1 foot apart in soil that is moist but not soggy. Propagate from seed or by division in late summer. Caution: Both the foliage and berries of Italian arum are poisonous and must be kept out of the reach of children.

Babiana
(bab-ee-AH-na)
BABOON FLOWER

Babiana stricta

Hardiness: *tender or Zones 9-11*

Type of bulb: *corm*

Flowering season: *spring*

Height: *8 to 12 inches*

Soil: *moist, well-drained*

Light: *full sun*

Baboon flowers produce 1½-inch fragrant flowers with pointed petals surrounding a contrasting eye; the blooms last as long as 5 weeks in the garden. Flowers grow in clusters on stems rising from stiff, sword-shaped leaves. Use baboon flowers in borders or grow them in containers as patio specimens.

Selected species and varieties: *B. stricta*—flowers in shades of cream, blue, lilac, and crimson; 'Purple Sensation' produces white-throated purple flowers; 'White King', white petals streaked blue on their undersides surrounding a deep blue eye; 'Zwanenburg Glory', lavender to violet petals splashed with white.

Growing conditions and maintenance: Plant baboon flowers in fall, setting corms 6 inches deep and 6 inches apart. North of Zone 9, plant corms in spring and lift after foliage fades in fall for replanting the following spring. Propagate from seed or by removing and planting the cormels that develop around parent bulbs every 3 to 4 years.

Caladium
(ka-LAY-dee-um)
ANGEL-WINGS

Caladium bicolor 'Aaron'

Hardiness: *tender or Zones 10-11*

Type of bulb: *tuber*

Flowering season: *summer*

Height: *1 to 2 feet*

Soil: *moist, well-drained*

Light: *partial shade to shade*

Exotic caladiums form clumps of intricately patterned translucent leaves that eclipse their insignificant flowers. The arrow-shaped leaves, rising continuously throughout summer, are vividly marbled, shaded, slashed, veined, and flecked in contrasting colors to brighten shady borders or decorate indoor gardens.

Selected species and varieties: *C. bicolor* [formerly *C.* x *hortulanum*]—foot-long arrow- or heart-shaped leaves; 'Aaron' has green edges feathering into creamy centers; 'Candidum' is white with green veining; 'Fannie Munson', pink-veined red edged in green; 'Festiva', rose-veined green; 'Irene Dank', light green edged in deeper green; 'June Bride', greenish white edged in deep green; 'Pink Beauty', a pink dwarf spattered with green; 'White Christmas', white with green veining.

Growing conditions and maintenance: Plant in spring when night temperatures remain above 60°F, setting the tubers 2 inches deep and 8 to 12 inches apart. North of Zone 10, lift and dry tubers in fall to replant the next spring. Provide high humidity and temperatures of 60°F or more. Propagate by division in spring.

Camassia
(ka-MA-see-a)
CAMASS, QUAMASH

Camassia quamash

Hardiness: *Zones 5-9*

Type of bulb: *true bulb*

Flowering season: *spring*

Height: *1 to 4 feet*

Soil: *moist, well-drained, sandy*

Light: *full sun to light shade*

Camass's spires of inch-wide flowers like tiny stars with a fringe of narrow, pointed, sometimes double petals open from bottom to top over several weeks. Naturalize camass in damp wildflower gardens, alongside streams or ponds, or among other spring-blooming bulbs.

Selected species and varieties: *C. cusickii* (Cusick quamash)—up to 300 flowers on stalks 3 to 4 feet tall; 'Zwanenburg' has horizontal stalks upturned at their ends. *C. leichtlinii* (Leichtlin quamash)—up to 40 flowers on stems to 4 feet; 'Alba' produces white blossoms; 'Blue Danube', very dark blue; 'Sempiplena', double-petaled creamy white to yellow. *C. quamash* (common camass)—foot-long spires on 2-foot stems; 'Orion' is very deep blue. *C. scilloides* (Atlantic camass, eastern camass, wild hyacinth)—blue or white ½-inch flowers on 2½-foot stems.

Growing conditions and maintenance: Plant camass bulbs in fall, setting them 4 inches deep and 6 to 9 inches apart. Provide shade where summers are dry. Bulbs can be lifted to remove offsets but are best left undisturbed unless flowering declines. Otherwise, propagate from seed.

Canna
(KAN-ah)
CANNA

Canna 'Brandywine'

Hardiness: *tender or Zones 8-11*

Type of bulb: *rhizome*

Flowering season: *summer to fall*

Height: *18 inches to 6 feet*

Soil: *moist, well-drained*

Light: *full sun*

Cannas produce a continuous show of bold 4- to 5-inch flowers with a tousled arrangement of petal-like stamens in strong colors from summer through frost. The flowers, which are sometimes bicolored, are carried on clumps of stiff, erect stems. The broad, bold leaves, up to 24 inches long, are usually a deep, glossy green but are sometimes bronzy red or striped or veined in white or pink. They line the stems to provide a dramatic backdrop to the flowers. Mass these coarse-textured plants at the back of borders in casual groupings or formal patterns, or grow dwarf cultivars as edgings or in patio containers.

Selected species and varieties: *C.* x *generalis* (canna lily)—standard varieties grow 4 to 6 feet tall; 'Black Knight' has deep velvet red flowers and bronze foliage; 'City of Portland', rosy salmon flowers above green leaves; 'Gaiety', yellow flowers edged in orange; 'Los Angeles', coral pink blooms above green foliage; 'The President', bright red flowers and deep green leaves; 'Red King Humbert', red flowers above bronzy foliage on very tall stems; 'Richard Wallace', canary yellow blossoms and green foliage; 'Rosamund Cole', red-and-gold bicolored blossoms; 'Stadt Fellbach', peach flowers with yellow throats fading to pink; 'Wyoming', rugged red-orange flowers and reddish bronze leaves. Dwarf varieties of this species grow to less than 3 feet tall; 'Ambrosia' has pinky orange blossoms on 18-inch stems; 'Brandywine', scarlet flowers on 3-foot stems; 'Pfitzer's Chinese Coral', rich coral pink blossoms; 'Pfitzer's Crimson Beauty', bright red flowers on 18-inch stems; 'Pfitzer's Primrose Yellow', soft yellow blooms; 'Pfitzer's Salmon', unusually large salmon pink flowers; 'Pretoria', yellow-orange flowers above deep green leaves striped with cream.

Growing conditions and maintenance: In Zones 9 and 10, set cannas out as bedding plants in spring, planting the rhizomes 4 to 6 inches deep; space standard cultivars 2 feet apart, dwarf cultivars 1 foot apart. Provide ample moisture and high humidity during the growing season. Cannas can remain in the ground year round in frost-free areas; in Zone 8, provide a protective winter mulch. North of Zone 8, start cannas for beds or containers indoors 4 weeks before night temperatures reach 60°F; in fall, cut foliage back to 6 inches and lift rhizomes for winter storage. Pinch each container-grown rhizome back to a single shoot for largest flowers. Propagate cannas from seed, soaking seeds for 48 hours before planting to loosen their tough outer coats; or by division in spring, sectioning to allow no more than two buds per piece.

Crinum
(KREE-num)
SPIDER LILY

Crinum x powellii

Hardiness: *tender or Zones 7-11*

Type of bulb: *true bulb*

Flowering season: *spring, summer, fall*

Height: *2 to 4 feet*

Soil: *moist, well-drained, fertile*

Light: *full sun to light shade*

Crinums produce whorls of lilylike flowers with a spicy fragrance over a long season of bloom. Each cluster blooms atop a stout stem rising from a clump of deep green, sword-shaped, evergreen or deciduous leaves. The blossoms are either funnel shaped with thick, ridged petals curving backward, or lacy and spidery with narrow, straplike petals. Crinum's unusual bulbs, about the size of a grapefruit, have elongated necks up to 1 foot long and bloom best when they are crowded. In warmer areas, plant them where they can remain undisturbed for several years. They do especially well at the edges of ponds and streams where there is constant moisture, slowly naturalizing into large clumps. In northern areas, sink bulbs in tubs, which can be moved indoors to a greenhouse or conservatory for the winter.

Selected species and varieties: *C. americanum* (Florida swamp lily)—up to 6 white flower funnels in late spring or summer on 2-foot stems before leaves appear. *C. asiaticum* (grand crinum, poison bulb)—up to 50 heavily scented white flowers with straplike petals and pink stamens in summer on stalks to 4 feet. *C. bulbispermum* (Orange River lily)—a dozen or more pink or white flower trumpets with rose-striped petals in fall on 3-foot stems above deciduous foliage. *C. moorei* (Cape Coast lily, long-neck swamp lily)—10 to 20 rose red flower funnels in summer on 4-foot stalks rising from bold evergreen leaves. *C. x powellii* (Powell's swamp lily)—six to eight red flower trumpets touched with green at their base on 2-foot stalks rising from evergreen leaves up to 4 feet long; 'Album' has white flowers. *C.* 'Cecil Houdyshel'—profuse pink flowers. *C.* 'Ellen Bosanquet'—wine red summer flowers above evergreen foliage.

Growing conditions and maintenance: Outdoors, plant crinums so that the necks of the bulbs remain above ground and the bulbs are 2 to 3 feet apart. Keep constantly moist for best bloom. In tubs, allow no more than 1 to 2 inches of soil space between the sides of the bulbs and their container. With southern exposure and heavy mulching to protect them from frost, *C. bulbispermum* and *C. x powellii* sometimes thrive in Zones 7-8. *C. moorei* and *C.* 'Ellen Bosanquet' make excellent tub specimens. Propagate species from seeds, which sometimes begin forming roots while still on plants. Remove seeds as soon as they ripen and sow immediately to reach flowering-size bulbs in 3 years; hybrids may revert to their parent forms. Both species and hybrids can be propagated by removing and replanting the small offsets growing alongside mature bulbs in spring.

Crocus
(KRO-kus)
CROCUS

Crocus chrysanthus 'Cream Beauty'

Hardiness:	*Zones 3-8*
Type of bulb:	*corm*
Flowering season:	*winter, spring, fall*
Height:	*2 to 8 inches*
Soil:	*well-drained*
Light:	*full sun*

Delicate bowls of color in an otherwise drab landscape, crocus flowers hug the ground on short stems from late winter through midspring. There are also fall-blooming species, not to be confused with the flowers commonly known as autumn crocus, which are actually *Colchicum*. Narrow, grassy crocus leaves are sometimes attractively banded down their centers in gray-green or white and may appear before, at the same time as, or after several flowers rise from each small corm. They last several weeks before dying back. Some are fragrant. Each flower has six wide petals that open into a deep, oval cup shape, then relax into a round, open bowl. Crocuses are available in a broad range of hues, and are often striped, streaked, or tinged with more than one color. Prominent yellow or orange stigmas decorate the center of each blossom. Those of *C. sativus* are the source of saffron for many culinary uses; it takes more than 4,000 flowers to produce an ounce of the precious herb. Mass crocuses for best effect in beds, borders, and rock gardens. They naturalize easily and are often planted as edg-

ings and allowed to ramble in lawns. Force them for indoor winter display.

Selected species and varieties: *C. ancyrensis* 'Golden Bunch'—winter-to-spring-blooming flowers that are yellow outside, orange fading to yellow inside, on 2-inch stems above 12-inch leaves; Zones 6-8. *C. angustifolius* 'Minor' (cloth-of-gold crocus)—deep yellow flower cups flushed with mahogany outside on stems 2 inches or less in winter to spring; Zones 5-8. *C. biflorus* (Scotch crocus)—white or lilac flowers veined or tinged purple with yellow throats on 4-inch stems in winter to spring; ssp. *alexandri* is white feathered with purple; ssp. *weldenii* 'Fairy', white with purple blotches; Zones 5-8. *C. chrysanthus* (snow crocus)—late winter flowers

Crocus ancyrensis

bloom on 4-inch stems before the 12-inch leaves appear; 'Advance' produces peachy yellow flowers touched with violet; 'Ard Schenk', long-lasting white blooms; 'Blue Bird', blooms that are blue-violet outside, creamy inside; 'Blue-Pearl', petals that are lavender outside touched with bronze at their base, white inside blending to a yellow throat; 'Cream Beauty', long-lasting creamy yellow blooms; 'Dorothy', long-lasting yellow flowers feathered with bronze; 'Gipsy Girl', profuse, long-lasting yellow flowers streaked reddish brown; 'Lady-killer', petals violet-purple outside, creamy white inside; 'Miss Vain', pure white blossoms with lemon yellow throats; 'Prins Claus' is a dwarf cultivar with long-lasting white flowers blotched in blue; 'Snow Bunting' has white flowers with lilac streaking and yellow throats; 'Zwanenburg Bronze', reddish brown petals striped with yellow; Zones 4-8. *C. etruscus* 'Zwanenburg'—lilac flowers veined with deep purple appearing the same time as the white-striped leaves in winter to spring; Zones 3-8. *C. flavus*—yellow to orange flowers appearing on 7-inch stems at the same time as the grassy foliage in winter to spring; 'Golden Yellow' [formerly *C. vernus*

Crocus chrysanthus 'Zwanenburg Bronze'

'Yellow Giant'] has rich yellow blossoms; Zones 4-8. *C. kotschyanus* [formerly *C. zonatus*]—rose lilac flowers splashed with orange in fall; Zones 5-8. *C. medius*—lilac to purple flowers with deep purple veining on stems to 10 inches in fall; Zones 6-7. *C. minimus*—pale violet to white flowers with prominent red-orange stigmas on 2- to 3-inch stems in spring; Zones 5-8. *C. ochroleucus*—white to pale cream petals tinged with orange on 3- to 6-inch stems in fall; Zones 5-8. *C. pulchellus*—bright lilac blossoms with yellow interiors appearing the same time as the leaves in fall; 'Zephyr' is pure white; Zones 6-8. *C. sativus* (saffron crocus)—lilac or white fall flowers on 2-inch stems with prominent stamens that are dried and used for flavoring and coloring in cooking; Zones 6-8. *C. serotinus* ssp. *clusii*—fragrant, purple-veined pale lilac flowers with creamy throats on 3- to 4-inch stems appearing at the same time as sparse foliage in fall; ssp. *salzmannii* is similar but with sparser leaves and no fragrance; Zones 6-8. *C. sieberi* (Sieber crocus)—fragrant late-winter-to-spring flowers; ssp. *atticus* has white flowers streaked with purple on 2- to 3-inch stems; ssp. *sublimis* 'Tricolor', lilac blue flowers with white banding at the edge of a yellow

throat; 'Firefly', white flowers touched with violet; 'Hubert Edelsten', deep purple to soft lilac flowers on 4-inch stems; 'Violet Queen', deep violet blooms on 3-inch stems; Zones 7-8. *C. speciosus*—light blue fall flowers with darker blue veining and prominent orange stigmas on 3- to 6-inch stems; 'Artabir' grows fragrant light blue flowers with conspicuous veining; 'Cassiope', lavender-blue blooms with creamy yellow throats; 'Conqueror', clear blue flowers; var. *aitchisonii*, pale lilac flowers veined with deeper lilac, the largest of all crocus blossoms; Zones 5-8. *C. tomasinianus*—lilac to purple flowers appearing at the same time as leaves in late winter to spring, reputed to be rodent resistant; 'Barr's Purple' yields large royal purple flowers; 'Ruby Giant', large violet blooms; 'Whitewell Purple' is reddish purple; Zones 5-9. *C. vernus* (Dutch crocus, common crocus)—large flowers on stems to 8 inches tall appearing at the

Crocus tomasinianus

same time as leaves in late winter to spring; 'Flower Record' is deep purple; 'Jeanne d'Arc', white; 'Paulus Potter', shiny reddish purple; 'Pickwick', white striped with lilac and splashed with purple at its base; 'Remembrance', bluish purple; 'Striped Beauty', lilac striped with white. *C. versicolor* 'Picturatus'—white flowers striped in purple with yellow throats on 5½-inch stems in late winter to spring; Zones 5-8.

Growing conditions and maintenance: Plant corms 3 to 4 inches deep and 4 to 5 inches apart in groups. They are not fussy about soil, but good drainage is essential. Space more closely in pots for forcing, allowing six to eight corms per 6-inch pot

or shallow bulb pan, and setting the corms 1 inch deep. Hold potted corms at 40°F until roots form, then bring indoors at 65°F for flowering. Crocuses can also be forced in colorful bulb vases designed especially for the purpose with a pinched

Crocus vernus 'Jeanne d'Arc'

waist to suspend the corm just above the water line; when roots fill the vase, bring the corm into sunlight in a warm room for blooming. After forcing, allow foliage to die back, then plant corms out in the garden for reflowering the following spring. Cultivars of Dutch crocus are especially recommended for forcing. *C. ancyrensis* 'Golden Bunch', *C. speciosus* cultivars, and *C. vernus* 'Pickwick' are among the easiest crocuses to naturalize. To plant crocuses in lawns, cut and lift small patches of grass, place the corms, then replace the sod. Plant spring-flowering varieties from September to November, fall-flowering ones no later than August. Where crocuses have established themselves in lawns, avoid mowing in spring until the foliage of spring-flowering crocuses dies back; in fall, postpone mowing once the buds of fall-blooming species have broken through the ground until their flowers fade and foliage withers. Crocuses are easily grown from seed and self-sow freely, a characteristic that somewhat offsets the attractiveness of the corms to mice, chipmunks, and squirrels. Otherwise, propagate by lifting and dividing crowded clumps after foliage dies back, removing and replanting the smaller cormels that develop alongside mature corms. Buy *C. kotschyanus* only from reputable dealers who propagate their own bulbs, as collection in the wild has endangered this species.

Cyclamen
(SIK-la-men)
PERSIAN VIOLET

Cyclamen persicum

Hardiness: *Zones 6-9*

Type of bulb: *tuber*

Flowering season: *fall, winter, spring*

Height: *3 to 12 inches*

Soil: *moist, well-drained, fertile*

Light: *light shade*

Cyclamen's unusual, sometimes fragrant, flowers have petals swept back from a prominent center or eye. The petals are sometimes twisted, double, ruffled, shredded, or ridged, giving the delicate, inch-long blossoms the appearance of exotic birds or butterflies. Each flower rises on a slender stem from a clump of long-lasting heart- or kidney-shaped leaves that are sometimes marbled green and gray above or reddish underneath. Multiple flower stalks appear over a long season of bloom. While the florist's cyclamen, popular as a houseplant, is a tender pot plant, other cyclamens are hardy species that will spread in wildflower gardens, rock gardens, and shady borders, naturalizing into low ground covers beneath both deciduous and evergreen plantings.

Selected species and varieties: *C. africanum*—rose to carmine fall flowers above large, fleshy 6-inch leaves with wavy edges; Zones 8-9. *C. cilicium* (Sicily cyclamen)—twisted pink or light rose blossoms with a dark rose eye on 3-inch stems in fall above leaves with silver centers; Zones 7-8. *C. coum*—white to carmine flowers with purple blotches blooming from winter to spring on 3- to 6-inch stems above green or marbled leaves with reddish undersides; 'Album' is white; 'Roseum', pale pink. *C. graecum*—fall-blooming rose flowers with a deep carmine eye, sometimes scented; Zones 7-9. *C. hederifolium* [also called *C. neopolitanum*] (baby cyclamen)—pink or white, sometimes fragrant, flowers with a crimson eye on 3- to 6-inch stems blooming from summer to fall above marbled leaves; 'Album' is white; Zones 6-9. *C. persicum* (florist's cyclamen, common cyclamen)—rose, pink, or white, sometimes fragrant flowers, with dark eyes on 6- to 12-inch stems

Cyclamen repandum

above marbled leaves with toothed edges in winter; Zone 9. *C. repandum*—deep pink flowers in late spring or early summer and spotted leaves.

Growing conditions and maintenance: Plant cyclamen's flat, cormlike tubers in summer or fall, setting them ½ inch deep and 4 to 6 inches apart in soil that has a neutral to alkaline pH. Provide an annual topdressing of leaf mold. Pot florist's cyclamen's large tuber-corms individually in pots and maintain plants at temperatures of 60° to 65°F throughout the blooming period. Cyclamens do not produce offsets, but plants self-sow seed freely. Propagate from seed to reach blooming size in 3 years or by transplanting the self-sown seedlings in summer or fall.

Dahlia
(DAH-lee-a)
DAHLIA

Dahlia 'Tamjoh'

Hardiness: *tender or Zones 9-11*

Type of bulb: *tuber*

Flowering season: *summer to fall*

Height: *12 inches to 8 feet*

Soil: *moist, well-drained, fertile*

Light: *full sun*

Dahlias reliably brighten the flower border over a long season of bloom with highly diverse blossoms varying from flat-faced, single-petaled types to round, dense mounds of petals. Dahlia sizes are as variable as petal forms, with some flowers only a few inches across and others the diameter of a dinner plate. Related to daisies, dahlias have a central disk of tightly packed disk flowers surrounded by one or more rows of petal-like ray flowers that are sometimes doubled, curved inward, twisted, cupped, or rolled into tiny tubes. Colors range widely, and some dahlias are bicolored or variegated, with petals tipped, streaked, or backed with contrasting color. The more than 20,000 cultivars available to modern gardeners descend from a few wild species cultivated by Aztec botanists. For the garden trade, dahlias are classified by the shape and arrangement of their ray flowers and coded according to flower size. Dwarf dahlias are cultivated in sunny beds or borders as low-growing bushy edgings, standard dahlias as medium to tall fillers or as exhibition-size specimens. The largest dahlias are diffilcult to use in the home garden simply because of their size—those with the largest blooms can have stems the thickness of broomsticks. Thus, the plants with smaller flowers are easier to work into a bed or border design. Regardless of their size, all dahlias make long-lasting cut flowers.

Selected species and varieties: *Single dahlias*—one or two rows of flat petals surrounding a flat, central disk; 'Bambino White' is a dwarf cultivar with 1-inch flowers on 14-inch bushes. *Anemone-flowered dahlias*—a central disk obscured by a fluffy ball of short, tubular petals and rimmed by one or more rows of longer, flat petals; 'Siemen Doorenbosch' has flat lavender petals surrounding a creamy central pincushion on 20-inch plants. *Collarette dahlias*—central disks surrounded by a collar of short, often ruffled or cupped petals, backed by a second collar of broader, flat petals; 'Jack O'Lantern' has an inner collar streaked

Dahlia 'Hullins Carnival'

yellow and orange and deep orange outer petals on 4-foot plants; 'Mickey' has a yellow inner collar backed by deep red outer ray flowers on 3-foot bushes. *Peony-flowered dahlias*—two or three overlapping layers of ray petals, often twisted or curled, surrounding a central disk; 'Japanese Bishop' grows dark orange flowers on 3-foot plants; 'Jescott Julie' has petals that are orange above, burgundy below, on 3-foot stems. *Formal decorative dahlias*—double rows of flat, evenly spaced petals covering the central disk; 'Duet' has crimson petals tipped with white on 3-foot plants; 'Orange Julius', orange petals edged in yellow on 4-foot stems. *Informal decorative dahlias*—double rows of randomly

spaced flat petals hiding the central disk; 'Gay Princess' is pink with creamy centers on 4-foot plants. *Ball dahlias*—cupped, doubled petals crowding spirally into round domes or slightly flattened globes; 'Nijinsky' has purple flowers on 4-foot stems; 'Rothsay Superb', red blooms on 3-foot plants. *Pompom dahlias*—small round balls of tightly rolled petals less than 2 inches in diameter; 'Amber Queen' is golden amber to bronze on 4-foot stems; 'Chick-a-dee', wine red touched with pink on 3-foot plants. *Cactus dahlias*—straight or twisted petals rolled like quills or straws over half their length to a pointed tip; 'Border Princess' is apricot bronze to yellow on 2-foot stems; 'Brookside Cheri', salmon pink on 4-foot plants; 'Juanita', ruby red on 4-foot stems. *Semicactus dahlias*—flat petals curling over less than half their length into tubes at their tips; 'Amanda Jarvis' produces rose flowers on 3-foot stems; 'Bella Bimba', apricot pink blooms on 4-foot plants. *Star dahlias*—two or three rows of short petals curving inward. *Chrysanthemum-type dahlias*—double rows of petals curving inward and hiding the central disk. *Water lily-flowered dahlias*—short petals tightly clasped over the central disk like a water lily bud, surrounded by several rows of broad, flat petals; 'Lauren Michelle' has petals that are rosy lavender above, purple below on 4½-foot stems; 'Gerry Hoek', shell pink flowers on 4-foot plants.

Within each of these classifications, dahlias are also coded by size: Giant or AA dahlias have flowers more than 10 inches wide; large or A, 8- to 10-inch flowers; medium or B, 6- to 8-inch flowers; small or BB, 4- to 6-inch blooms; miniature or M, flowers up to 4 inches across; pompom or P, blossoms under 2 inches.

Growing conditions and maintenance: Plant dahlia tubers in spring, placing those of taller cultivars in a hole 6 to 8 inches deep and covering them with 2 to 3 inches of soil. Space the holes 3 to 4 feet apart. As shoots develop and extend above ground level, remove all but one or two and add soil to fill the hole. Plant tubers of shorter cultivars 2 to 3 inches deep and 1 to 2 feet apart. In transplanting potted seedlings, position them

2 inches deeper than the depth of their pot. Stake all but dwarfs, pompoms, and miniatures. Dahlias bloom 2½ to 4 months after planting. To keep plants blooming continuously, give them at least an inch of water weekly while blooming, and mulch with 2 to 3 inches of manure, compost, or ground peat moss to retain moisture and provide nutrients. To produce bushy plants, pinch out terminal leaf buds when leaves first appear and again when the first lateral branches emerge. To develop large, exhibition-size blossoms, prune all lateral side shoots and remove all but the center bud when flower buds appear. Remove faded flowers before they go to seed to prolong blooming period. For long-lasting cut flowers, pick dahlias while it is cool and stand cut stems in hot water, 100° to 160°F, in a cool, shaded location for several hours before arranging. Propagate dahlias from seed started indoors in very early spring to flower that season, from stem cuttings, or by dividing tubers in spring.

Eranthis
(e-RAN-this)
WINTER ACONITE

Eranthis hyemalis

Hardiness: *Zones 4-7*

Type of bulb: *tuber*

Flowering season: *late winter to spring*

Height: *2 to 4 inches*

Soil: *moist, well-drained, fertile*

Light: *full sun to light shade*

Often blooming before the snow has melted, winter aconites produce cheery buttercup-like flowers composed of waxy, curved petals cradling a loose pompom of frilly stamens. Each almost stemless blossom opens above a tiny ruff of oval, pointed leaves. The blossoms close tightly to protect themselves during cold nights, then reopen the next day with the sun's warmth. Winter aconites readily naturalize into golden ground covers in woodland or rock gardens.

Selected species and varieties: *E. cilicica* (Cilician winter aconite)—1½-inch-deep yellow flowers on 2½-inch stems with bronzy foliage. *E. hyemalis*—inch-wide yellow flowers on 2- to 4-inch stems.

Growing conditions and maintenance: Plant winter aconite tubers in late summer or very early fall to allow roots time to establish themselves for late-winter blooming. Soak the brittle roots overnight, then set tubers 2 to 3 inches deep and 3 inches apart where they will receive sufficient moisture. Winter aconites self-sow readily. Propagate from seed or by dividing the tiny tubers in late summer.

Erythronium
(eh-rith-RONE-ee-um)
DOGTOOTH VIOLET

Erythronium 'Kondo'

Hardiness: *Zones 3-8*

Type of bulb: *corm*

Flowering season: *spring*

Height: *6 inches to 2 feet*

Soil: *moist, well-drained, fertile*

Light: *partial to full shade*

Native woodland wildflowers, dogtooth violets produce delicate, nodding lilylike blooms with petals curved back to reveal prominent stamens and anthers either singly or in small clusters. The flowers rise from pairs of oval, pointed leaves that are often marbled or mottled in gray, brown, or bronze. Mass dogtooth violets in woodland gardens or as a spring ground cover beneath deciduous shrubs, where they will naturalize into colonies.

Selected species and varieties: *E. citrinum*—clusters of 1½-inch white or cream flowers with pale lemon throats on 10- to 12-inch stems; Zones 6-8. *E. dens-canis* (dogtooth fawn lily, European dogtooth violet)—single white to pink or purple flowers 2 inches across with blue or purple anthers on 6- to 12-inch stems above leaves marbled brown and bluish green; 'Charmer' produces pure white flowers touched with brown at their base above leaves mottled with brown; 'Frans Hals', royal purple blooms with a green throat; 'Lilac Wonder' is soft lilac with a brownish base; 'Pink Perfection', bright pink; 'Purple King', reddish purple with a white throat above brown-

spotted leaves; 'Rose Queen', rosy pink; 'Snowflake', pure white; var. *japonicum* is a miniature only 4 to 6 inches tall with violet flowers tinged purple at the base; var. *niveus* is pale pink; Zones 3-8. *E. grandiflorum* (glacier lily, avalanche lily)—golden yellow flowers with red anthers in clusters on 1- to 2-foot stems. *E. revolutum* (mahogany fawn lily, coast fawn lily)—1½-inch white to pale lavender flowers aging to purple on 16-inch stems; 'White Beauty' is a dwarf producing 2- to 3-inch white flowers with yellow throats on 7-inch stems above leaves veined in white; Zones 3-8. *E. tuolumnense* (Tuolumne fawn lily)—1¼-inch

Erythronium grandiflorum

yellow flowers touched with green at the base on 12-inch stems above bright green 12-inch leaves; Zones 3-8. *E. hybrids*—'Citronella' yields lemon yellow flowers on 10-inch stems; 'Jeannine', sulfur yellow blooms; 'Kondo', greenish yellow blossoms touched with brown at the base; 'Pagoda', pale yellow flowers with a deeper yellow throat on 10-inch stems.

Growing conditions and maintenance: Plant dogtooth violets in summer or fall, placing the corms 2 to 3 inches deep and 4 to 6 inches apart. Dogtooth violets often take a year to become established before blooming. Provide adequate moisture in summer after flowers and foliage fade. Propagate from seed to bloom in 3 to 4 years or by removing and immediately replanting the small cormels that develop at the base of mature corms in late summer or fall.

Fritillaria
(fri-ti-LAH-ree-a)
FRITILLARY

Fritillaria imperialis

Hardiness: *Zones 3-8*

Type of bulb: *true bulb*

Flowering season: *spring*

Height: *6 inches to 2½ feet*

Soil: *moist, well-drained, sandy*

Light: *full sun to light shade*

From the imposing, musky-scented crown imperial bearing a garland of blossoms aloft on stout stalks to small, dainty woodland species with single blooms on wiry stems, fritillaries produce nodding flower bells in unusual colors and patterns in a variety of forms to accent spring gardens. The flowers have prominent, colorful stamens and are often striped, speckled, or checkered in a wide range of hues. Touching the petals sometimes produces a small "tear" from reservoirs of nectar at the base of each petal. The often glossy leaves are highly variable, sometimes appearing in whorls extending halfway up the flower stalk, sometimes alternating from one side of the stem to the other throughout its length, occasionally growing in a tuft at the stem's base. Mass fritillaries in wildflower gardens, rock gardens, or perennial borders where other plants will fill in when their foliage dies down in early summer.

Selected species and varieties: *F. ac-mopetala*—purple-striped olive green flower bells tinged lighter green inside on 18-inch stalks; Zones 3-8. *F. assyriaca*—lime-green and violet blossoms on 12- to 20-inch stems; Zones 3-8. *F. bi-flora* 'Martha Roderick' (mission bells, black fritillary)—four to six brownish orange flower bells with white spots in their centers on 15-inch stems; Zones 3-8. *F. camschatcensis* (Kamchatka lily, black sarana)—one to six 1-inch purple-brown-and-black flower bells on wiry

Fritillaria meleagris

2-foot stems; Zones 3-8. *F. davisii*—plum purple blossoms on dainty plants 6 to 10 inches tall; Zones 3-8. *F. imperialis* (crown imperial)—bold 30-inch stalks, the lower half lined with whorls of glossy, pointed leaves, the tip crowned by a tuft of shorter leaves with a ring of large, 2-inch flower bells with dangling yellow stamens below it; 'Maxima Lutea' is lemon yellow; 'Rubra Maxima', dark red; Zones 4-7. *F. meleagris* (snake's-head fritillary, checkered lily, guinea hen tulip, leper lily)—1½-inch flower bells checkered dark maroon and white on 8- to 10-inch stems; 'Alba' is pure white; Zones 3-8. *F. michailovskyi*—up to five deep purplish red-and-yellow flower bells with their tips flipped daintily outward on 4- to 8-inch stems; Zones 5-8. *F. pallidiflora*—up to a dozen pale yellow and green 1- to 1½-inch flower bells flecked with brown and red, borne in the upper leaf joints along arching 18-inch stems; Zones 3-8. *F. persica*—up to 30 velvety purple blossoms lining 30-inch stems; 'Adiyaman' yields inch-wide plum flowers; Zones 4-8. *F. pudica* (yellow fritillary, yellow bell)—¾-inch yellow-orange flowers tinged purple in clusters of three on 9-inch stems; Zones 4-8. *F. purdyi* 'Tinkerbell'—six or seven dainty white flower bells striped rusty brown on the outside and spotted red inside on 6-inch

stems above a low rosette of 6-inch leaves; Zones 5-8. *F. uva-vulpis*—solitary purplish gray flower bells edged in yellow on 12- to 18-inch stems; Zones 3-8. *F. verticillata*—1¼-inch cup-shaped pale yellow blossoms flecked with green outside and spotted purple inside lining 2-foot stems, the tips of the upper leaves elongating into tendrils; Zones 6-8.

Growing conditions and maintenance: Plant fritillaries in late summer or fall, setting large bulbs 4 inches deep and 12 inches apart, smaller bulbs 2 inches deep and 8 inches apart. Bulbs may take a year to become established in new locations before they flower. Most fritillaries like full sun and very well drained soil, but *F. camschatcensis, F. meleagris,* and *F. pallidiflora* prefer light shade and moist soil. For all fritillaries, avoid sites with cold, wet soils, and reduce watering once

Fritillaria pudica

foliage dies back. Both *F. imperialis* 'Rubra Maxima' and *F. persica* are endangered in the wild; buy bulbs from reputable growers selling stock propagated by themselves or other growers rather than purchased from collectors. The skunklike odor of crown imperial is said to repel mice, chipmunks, and other rodents. Propagate fritillaries by removing and replanting bulb offsets in late summer or early fall to reach flowering size in 3 to 4 years; or by removing and planting bulb scales to produce bulblets.

Galanthus
(ga-LANTH-us)
SNOWDROP

Galanthus nivalis

Hardiness: *Zones 3-8*

Type of bulb: *true bulb*

Flowering season: *winter to spring*

Height: *6 to 12 inches*

Soil: *moist, well-drained, sandy*

Light: *full sun to light shade*

Snowdrops produce small white flowers that often bloom before the last snow melts. Each winged blossom is composed of three longer petals almost concealing three shorter, inner petals tipped with green. A single flower dangles from a slender stem above two to three grassy leaves. Snowdrops rapidly naturalize under deciduous shrubs or on lawns, in rock gardens, and in woodland borders. They can also be potted as houseplants.

Selected species and varieties: *G. elwesii* (giant snowdrop)—1½-inch blossoms on flower stalks to 12 inches above blue-green leaves. *G. nivalis* (common snowdrop)—1-inch blooms on 4- to 6-inch stems; 'Flore Pleno' produces double flowers; 'Sam Arnott', large, fragrant blossoms; 'Viridi-apice' has both its outer and inner petals tipped with green.

Growing conditions and maintenance: Plant bulbs 3 inches deep and 3 inches apart in late summer or fall. For indoor bloom, pot bulbs in fall, placing four to six bulbs 1 inch deep in each 4-inch pot. Snowdrops self-sow readily and can be propagated from seed or by lifting and dividing the clumps of bulbs that form.

Gladiolus
(glad-ee-O-lus)
CORN FLAG

Gladiolus communis ssp. byzantinus

Hardiness: *tender or Zones 4-11*

Type of bulb: *corm*

Flowering season: *spring to fall*

Height: *1 to 7 feet*

Soil: *well-drained, fertile*

Light: *full sun*

Gladiolus produce showy spikes of 1½- to 5½-inch flowers above fans of stiff, sword-shaped leaves. The closely spaced flowers open from bottom to top on alternate sides of the stiff flower stems. Abundant, sometimes fragrant, flowers open one at a time to provide several weeks of bloom. Use tall gladiolus in groups at the back of a border, shorter species in rock gardens or mixed in borders with spring bulbs. Gladiolus make long-lasting cut flowers; shorter species can be forced for indoor bloom.

Selected species and varieties: *G. callianthus* [formerly classified as *Acidanthera bicolor*] 'Murielae'—fragrant 2- to 3-inch white flowers with purple throats on 2-foot stems in summer; Zones 7-11. *G. carneus* (painted lady)—white, cream, mauve, or pink blossoms flecked purple on 2-foot stems, blooming spring to summer; Zones 9-11. *G.* x *colvillei* (Coronado hybrid)—2-inch scarlet flowers blotched yellow on branching 2-foot stems in spring; Zones 7-11. *G. communis* ssp. *byzantinus* (Byzantine gladiolus)—white-streaked burgundy flowers on 2-foot stems in spring to summer;

Zones 5-11. *G.* hybrids—ruffled, waved, crimped, or frilled flowers in shades of white, yellow, red, purple, blue, or green, sometimes bicolored or multicolored, on stems to 7 feet in summer through fall; 'Nova Lux' is pure velvety yellow; 'Red Bird', flaming red; 'Priscilla', white-feathered pink with a yellow throat; 'Royal Blush' has deep rose red petals edged in white; 'White Knight' is pure white; tender. *G. nanus* [also classified as *Babiana nana*]—spring- to- summer-blooming dwarf plants 1 to 2 feet tall; 'Amanda Mahy' is salmon with violet splotches; 'Desire', cream; 'Guernsey Glory' has pink to purple petals with red edges and cream blotches; 'Impressive' is pinkish white splotched deep rose; 'Prins Claus', ivory with purple spotting; Zones 4-11.

Growing conditions and maintenance: Work well-rotted manure or other organic matter deeply into the soil a year before planting. North of Zone 8, plant hardy gladiolus in fall, tender ones in spring. Set large corms 4 to 6 inches deep and 6 to 9 inches apart, smaller ones 3 to 4 inches deep and 4 to 6 inches apart. Provide ample water while growing and blooming. North of Zone 8, tender gladiolus should be dug in fall for replanting in spring. Early-blooming hybrids flower 90 days after planting, midseason varieties in 110 days, and late midseason ones in 120 days. To avoid fungus problems, do not plant gladiolus in the same location from year to year. Pick for cut flowers as the first bloom begins to open, leaving four to five leaves to feed the corm. Propagate by removing the cormels that develop around mature corms.

Haemanthus
(heem-ANTH-us)
BLOOD LILY

Haemanthus katherinae

Hardiness: *tender or Zones 9-11*

Type of bulb: *true bulb*

Flowering season: *summer*

Height: *12 to 18 inches*

Soil: *moist, well-drained*

Light: *full sun to light shade*

Blood lilies produce frothy clusters of tubular flowers with colorful protruding stamens cradled within broad, petal-like bracts or in spherical clusters atop stout, leafless stems. While sometimes grown outdoors in warm zones, they bloom best as root-bound container specimens.

Selected species and varieties: *H. albiflos* (white paintbrush)—2-inch flower clusters with yellow-orange stamens within greenish white bracts on 12- to 18-inch stems. *H. coccineus* (Cape tulip)—3-inch clusters of 1-inch flowers with golden stamens within red bracts on 12-inch stems. *H. katherinae* [also known as *Scadoxus multiflorus* ssp. *katherinae*] (Catherine-wheel)—over 200 small 2½-inch pink-red flowers in 9-inch globes on 18-inch stems. *H. multiflorus* (salmon blood lily)—up to 200 inch-long coral red flowers with spiky stamens in 3- to 6-inch spheres on 18-inch stems.

Growing conditions and maintenance: Plant 6 to 8 inches apart outdoors or in pots, with the tip of the bulb at the soil surface. Start potted lilies in spring, then dry off and store over winter. Propagate from seed or from bulb offsets.

Hippeastrum
(hip-ee-AS-trum)
AMARYLLIS

Hippeastrum 'Bold Leader'

Hardiness: *tender or Zones 9-11*

Type of bulb: *true bulb*

Flowering season: *spring*

Height: *1 to 2 feet*

Soil: *moist, well-drained, sandy*

Light: *full sun*

Spectacular amaryllis, with its flowers that can be as large as 8 inches across, is sometimes grown in sunny borders in warmer zones but is most renowned as a pot plant for indoor forcing.

Selected species and varieties: *H.* hybrids—'Apple Blossom' is cherry pink flushed white; 'Bold Leader', signal red; 'Double Record' has double white flowers veined and tipped red; 'Lady Jane', deep salmon orange double flowers; 'Orange Sovereign', bright orange blooms; 'Picotee', white petals rimmed red; 'Red Lion', velvety red flowers; 'Scarlet Baby' is a red miniature with two to three flower stems; 'White Christmas' is white.

Growing conditions and maintenance: Outdoors in Zones 10-11, plant in fall or spring, setting bulbs 6 inches deep and 1 foot apart. Indoors, plant the bulb with its top third out of the soil in a pot 2 inches wider than the bulb. Pot from late fall through winter; blooms in 5 to 8 weeks. Keep bulb barely moist until growth starts. After flowering, remove stem and fertilize until foliage dies. Dry bulb off for repotting. Propagate by separating offsets after foliage dies or from seed.

Hyacinthus
(by-a-SIN-thus)
HYACINTH

Hyacinthus 'Blue Jacket'

Hardiness: *Zones 3-7*

Type of bulb: *true bulb*

Flowering season: *spring*

Height: *4 to 12 inches*

Soil: *well-drained, fertile*

Light: *full sun*

With their heady fragrance, hyacinths are a classic bulb in the spring border. When first planted, most produce a single stiff, cylindrical cluster of inch-wide flower stars crowded on all sides of formally erect stems. Petal tips curve backward gracefully, giving the dense clusters a frilly appearance, an effect that is heightened when flowers are shaded in two tones of the same color. In subsequent years, flower stems grow longer and clusters become looser and more informal. The blooms last up to 2 weeks in the garden above straplike leaves at the base of the flower stalks. There are doubled cultivars with whorls of petals in graduated sizes engulfing each tiny blossom, and multiflora cultivars that produce several flower stems with widely spaced blossoms from each bulb. Mingle hyacinths with other spring bulbs in beds and borders, or force them indoors in pots or special glass hyacinth vases. They last almost a week as cut flowers.

Selected species and varieties: *H. orientalis* (Dutch hyacinth, common hyacinth, garden hyacinth)—clusters of star-shaped blossoms in an array of colors above foot-long leaves; 'Anne Marie' is pastel pink aging to salmon; 'Blue Giant' has large pastel blue clusters; 'Blue Jacket' is deep purple with paler petal edges; 'Blue Magic', purple-blue with a white throat; 'Carnegie', elegant pure white; 'City of Harlem', pastel lemon yellow; 'Delft Blue', porcelain blue with paler edges; 'French Roman Blue' is a multiflora cultivar with blue blooms; 'Gipsy Queen', yellow-tinged clear orange; 'Hollyhock' has flowers with double red petals on 4-inch stalks; 'Jan Bos' is clear candy-apple red in slender spikes; 'Lady Derby', rosy pink; 'Lord Balfour' has clusters of rose purple blossoms; 'Oranje Boven' is salmon; 'Peter

Hyacinthus 'Anne Marie'

Stuyvesant', deep purple-blue; 'Pink Pearl', deep luminescent pink; 'Snow White' is a white multiflora variety; 'Violet Pearl' is lilac-rose aging to silver.

Growing conditions and maintenance: Outdoors, plant bulbs in fall, setting them 4 to 6 inches deep and 6 to 8 inches apart. Indoors, allow 4 or 5 bulbs per 6-inch pot. Plant indoor bulbs in fall as well; specially prechilled bulbs will bloom earlier than ordinary bulbs. Keep potted bulbs damp in a dark location below 50°F for about 12 weeks or until roots fill the pot and bulbs show 2 inches of leaf growth. Then move the pots into filtered sunlight at a temperature no higher than 65°F. If using special hyacinth vases, suspend bulb above (but not touching) the water and treat the same as potted bulbs. 'Anne Marie' and 'Blue Jacket' are particularly good cultivars for forcing. Hyacinths are hard to propagate but sometimes form offsets alongside mature bulbs that can take up to 6 years to reach blooming size.

Ipheion
(IF-ee-on)
IPHEION

Ipheion uniflorum

Hardiness: *Zones 5-10*

Type of bulb: *true bulb*

Flowering season: *spring*

Height: *4 to 6 inches*

Soil: *acid, well-drained loam*

Light: *full sun to light shade*

An ipheion bulb sends up several flowering stalks, each flower rising on a single stem from clumps of grassy leaves, for a long period of bloom. The flowers have tiny pointed petals surrounding a cluster of bright orange stamens. They are faintly mint scented, whereas the leaves give off an onion odor when bruised. The leaves appear in fall, and persist all winter and through the blooming period until the bulbs go dormant in summer. Plant ipheion in woodland or rock gardens, in meadows, or among paving stones, where it will rapidly naturalize. It can also be forced indoors for midwinter bloom.

Selected species and varieties: *I. uniflorum* [formerly *Brodiaea uniflora* and *Tritilea uniflora*] (spring starflower)— 1-inch white flowers tinged blue; 'Wisley Blue' is light blue with a white center; 'Rolf Fiedler', deep electric blue.

Growing conditions and maintenance: Plant ipheion in late summer or fall, setting bulbs 3 inches deep and 3 to 6 inches apart. Provide winter mulch in Zones 5-6. Pot bulbs 1 inch deep for forcing. Propagate spring starflowers by dividing clumps of bulb offsets.

Iris
(EYE-ris)
FLAG, FLEUR-DE-LIS

Iris reticulata 'Harmony'

Hardiness: *Zones 5-9*

Type of bulb: *rhizome; true bulb*

Flowering season: *spring or summer*

Height: *4 to 24 inches*

Soil: *well-drained, sandy*

Light: *full sun*

Most irises, including the dramatic, tall bearded types, grow from rhizomes—although a few species, including the delicate *I. reticulata,* are bulbous. Dwarf irises, which are sometimes scented, bloom on short stems before their grassy leaves have fully emerged. The leaves continue to grow to their full length after flowers fade. Bokara and Dutch iris emerge simultaneously with their leaves and produce their flowers on tall, erect stems. All irises have complex flowers composed of three drooping outer petals known as falls and three erect inner petals called standards. The falls are marked with contrasting color at their bases and are sometimes crested with a raised ridge or punctuated by a pair of small protrusions called horns. The shorter standards, appearing in a complementary or contrasting color, may be curved, frilled, or wavy. Flowers last 1 to 3 weeks in the garden. Dwarf irises are ideal in rock gardens and at the edge of borders. Dutch irises, some of which are fragrant, naturalize easily, rapidly forming large clumps in sunny beds. Both Bokara and Dutch irises make excellent cut flowers lasting up to 2 weeks. Irises can also be forced for indoor bloom.

Selected species and varieties: Rhizomatous bearded iris hybrids are classified according to plant height as dwarf, intermediate, and tall, and are then further subdivided by flower size and season.

Dwarf bearded iris hybrids derive many of their characteristics from the parent species, *I. pumila* and *I. chamaeiris*. Miniature dwarf bearded iris—less than 10 inches tall with 1½- to 2½-inch flowers in midspring; 'Already' has wine red flowers; 'Angel Eyes', white flowers with blue spots on falls; 'Sky Baby', ruffled blue blooms. Standard dwarf bearded iris—10 to 15 inches tall with 1½- to 2½-inch blossoms that appear a week later than those of miniatures; 'Baby Snowflake' has white flowers; 'Bingo', velvety purple flowers; 'Early Sunshine', yellow

Iris cristata

flowers; 'Red Dandy', wine red flowers.

Intermediate and border bearded iris—2- to 4-inch flowers on plants 15 to 28 inches tall, with intermediates blooming in midspring, borders in late spring to early summer; 'Little Angel' has white flowers; 'Lemonade', white falls on yellow blossoms.

Tall bearded iris—plants that grow upward of 28 inches tall with flowers to 8 inches across in late spring to summer; 'Cindy' has red-bearded white flowers; 'Charade', ruffled medium blue flowers; 'May Magic', light pink blossoms.

Reblooming bearded iris—varying heights and flower sizes, blossoming in spring and again anytime from midsummer to fall; 'Autumn Bugler' has violet flowers with dark purple falls.

I. cristata (crested iris)—blue or white

Iris pseudacorus

flowers with yellow or white crested ridges on 6- to 9-inch plants in early to midspring; 'Shenandoah Sky' grows pale blue flowers; 'Summer Storm', deep blue. *I. sibirica* (Siberian iris)—deep blue, violet, or white flowers 2 inches wide on stems to 4 feet tall in late spring.

Bulbous irises: *I. bucharica* (Bokara iris)—2- to 2½-inch-wide spring flowers with yellow falls touched with white on 18-inch stems; Zones 5-9. *I. danfordiae* (Danford iris)—a dwarf iris producing fragrant, spring-blooming, 4-inch single flowers with bristlelike canary yellow standards, falls splotched green and orange, and leaves growing to 12 inches; Zones 5-9. *I. hollandica* (Dutch iris)—fragrant 4-inch spring-to-summer flowers growing singly or in pairs on 15- to 24-inch stems; 'Angel's Wings' has pale blue standards and royal blue falls with white-rimmed yellow blotches; 'Blue Ideal', sky blue blooms on 20-inch stems; 'Blue Magic', deep blue-purple falls; 'Golden Harvest' is golden yellow shading to orange; 'Ideal' has dusty gray-blue falls blotched orange; 'Purple Sensation', deep violet falls with yellow blotches rimmed by royal blue; 'White Wedgewood' is pure white; Zones 6-9. *I. pseudacorus* (yellow flag)—2-inch light yellow flowers with a brown blotch on the falls, blooming in late spring to early summer on stalks to 5 feet tall. *I. reticulata*—very fragrant, spring-blooming 3- to 9-inch dwarf plants, violet purple with white-bordered orange crests on falls and leaves to 18 inches; 'Cantab' is pale turquoise blue with white-rimmed orange blotches on its falls; 'Edward', dark blue spotted in orange; 'Gordon', medium blue with yellow-ridged falls; 'Har-

mony', pale blue standards and royal blue falls with white-rimmed yellow splotches; 'Ida', light blue falls marked in yellow; 'Joyce', lavender blue standards and deep sky blue falls touched with yellow and green; 'J. S. Dijt', fragrant, rich purple standards and blue falls marked with yellow; 'Natashcha', snow white tinged blue with orange splashes on falls; 'Pauline', violet standards and dark purple falls marked with a blue-and-white variegated blotch; 'Purple Gem', deep violet standards and rich plum purple falls; 'Spring Time', pale blue standards and deep violet falls spotted purple and yellow and tipped with white; Zones 5-9.

Growing conditions and maintenance: Space dwarf bearded and crested irises

Iris sibirica 'Harpswell Haze'

1 foot apart. Allow 1½ feet between taller types. Most irises grow best in full sun, but crested iris prefers partial shade. Bearded irises thrive in a well-drained neutral loam. Siberian irises need constant moisture and a soil high in organic matter. Propagate by dividing the rhizomes or clumps after flowering. Plant bulbous dwarf irises in spring, Dutch irises in spring or fall, setting bulbs 4 inches deep and 3 to 6 inches apart and massing them for best effect. *I. reticulata* prefers slightly alkaline soil. North of Zone 8, place Dutch irises in sites protected from wind and cover with winter mulch. Allow foliage to mature through summer. Both dwarf and Dutch irises do best when allowed to form thick clumps over 3 to 5 years, after which flowering will probably diminish. Lift while dormant and propagate by removing and replanting the quantities of small offsets that form alongside mature bulbs in fall.

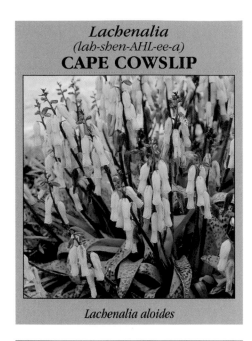

Lachenalia
(lah-shen-AHL-ee-a)
CAPE COWSLIP

Lachenalia aloides

Hardiness:	*tender or Zones 9-10*
Type of bulb:	*true bulb*
Flowering season:	*spring*
Height:	*6 to 12 inches*
Soil:	*moist, well-drained, sandy*
Light:	*full sun*

Cape cowslips bear long spikes of drooping, tubular flowers above broad, oval, pointed leaves. The waxy, inch-long flowers are often tinged and tipped in multiple colors, and the fleshy leaves and stems are marbled purple. Cape cowslips are rock-garden plants where winters are warm and are grown as container specimens elsewhere. They make long-lasting cut flowers.

Selected species and varieties: *L. aloides* (tricolored Cape cowslip)—yellow petals tinged green and touched with red; 'Pearsonii' is golden yellow with maroon tips; 'Aurea', bright yellow-orange. *L. bulbifera* (nodding Cape cowslip)—coral pink to red, tipped with green and purple.

Growing conditions and maintenance: Plant Cape cowslips outdoors in fall, setting bulbs 1 inch deep and 2 inches apart. Indoors, set five to six bulbs 1 inch deep in a 6-inch pot. Propagate by removing the bulblets that grow alongside mature bulbs or, for *L. bulbifera,* potting the small bulbils that develop in the plant's leaf joints.

Lilium
(LIL-ee-um)
LILY

Lilium columbianum

Hardiness:	*Zones 3-9*
Type of bulb:	*true bulb*
Flowering season:	*late spring to fall*
Height:	*2 to 8 feet*
Soil:	*moist, well-drained, fertile*
Light:	*full sun to light shade*

Funnel-shaped lily flowers are composed of six overlapping pointed petals called tepals. Sometimes smooth, sometimes wavy or frilled, the tepals are flecked with raised spots, often in a contrasting shade. The flowers curve backward to varying degrees from almost flat or bowl-shaped faces to flaring trumpets to tightly rolled tiny turbans. Curling stamens carry anthers dusted with pollen in vivid colors. Lilies offer a wide range of colors and color combinations, with tepals flushed or striped in contrasting hues in addition to their spots. They bloom on flower stalks, either singly or in clusters, at the tips of stiff, erect stems lined with short, grassy leaves. Flowers may face upward or outward or may nod from arching stalks. Up to 50 often highly fragrant flowers may appear on a single stem. The wide range of choices allows fanciers to plant lilies for continuous bloom throughout the summer. Lilies attract attention when planted in borders, where they quickly develop into spreading clumps. They can also be grown in patio containers, forced for indoor bloom, or used as long-lasting cut flowers.

Selected species and varieties: *L.* hybrids—thousands of hybrids grouped into divisions of plants with similar flower size, height, form, and bloom time. *Division 1. Asiatic hybrids:* Early-summer-flowering compact lilies, usually 2 to 4 feet tall, divided into up-facing, outward-facing, and pendent subgroups based on the form of their 4- to 6-inch flowers, which are borne singly or in clusters; 'Avignon' is mellow orange; 'Connecticut

Lilium 'Avignon'

King' has flat-faced, upright yellow blossoms with gold throats; 'Enchantment King', upright red-orange blooms with black spotting; 'Grand Cru' is yellow with tepal centers flushed maroon; 'Melon Time' has apricot-orange upright flowers; 'Mona' is clear yellow with yellow spots; 'Montreux', lightly spotted dusty rose; 'Roma', deep cream with few spots; 'Rosefire', clear reddish gold without spotting. *Division 2. Martagon hybrids:* Late-spring-flowering plants 3 to 6 feet tall with 3- to 4-inch nodding flowers like tiny turbans; 'Mrs. R. O. Backhouse' produces yellow-orange flowers flushed with rose; 'Paisley hybrids' are yellow-orange spotted maroon. *Division 3. Candidum hybrids:* 3- to 4-foot-tall or taller plants flowering from late spring to early summer with tiered clusters of 3- to 4-inch tiny turbans; 'Cascade Strain' produces fragrant pure white flowers. *Division 4. American hybrids:* Lilies to 7 or 8 feet, flowering from late spring to midsummer with tiers of up to 30 or more tiny Turk's caps; 'Bellingham Hybrids' are 3- to 4-inch midsummer-blooming flowers in shades of yellow, orange, and red. *Division 5. Longiflorum hybrids:* Fragrant, outward-facing flower trumpets blooming in midsummer, though the familiar Easter lily is often forced for earlier bloom; 'Casa Rosa' has 6-inch pink blossoms. *Division 6. Trumpet hybrids* [also called *Aurelian hybrids*]: Summer-flowering lilies 4 to 6 feet tall with large 6- to 10-inch flowers that are either trumpet shaped, sunburst shaped, bowl shaped, or nodding; 'Black Dragon' yields creamy 6-inch white flower trumpets flushed with purple on the outside; 'Golden Splendor', fragrant golden yellow trumpets flushed copper outside; 'Pink Perfection', large deep pink trumpets. *Division 7. Oriental hybrids:* Mid- to late-summer-blooming garden favorites from 2 to 8 feet tall bearing trumpet-shaped, flat-faced, or bowl-shaped flowers up to 12 inches across or trusses of smaller turban-shaped flowers; 'Casa Blanca' has pure white trumpets with orange anthers; 'Imperial Crimson', fragrant flat-faced white flowers blushed with pink; 'Imperial Gold', fragrant, flat-faced white flowers banded with yellow and spotted in crimson; 'Star Gazer', erect, deep carmine flowers up to 8 inches across with wavy tepals spotted dark red and rimmed in white on compact stems;

Lilium 'Rosefire'

'White Mountain', upward-facing white trumpets with golden throats. *Division 8. Miscellaneous hybrids:* Reserved for future hybrids not fitting any previous division. *Division 9. Species lilies: L. auratum* (gold-banded lily, gold-rayed lily, mountain lily)—up to 30 bowl-shaped, fragrant 10-inch-wide white flowers with tepals banded in gold down their centers and spotted with crimson on 4- to 6-foot stems blooming in mid- to late summer. *L. canadense* (Canada lily, meadow lily,

yellow lily)—3-inch dangling, bowl-shaped yellow to red-orange flowers spotted with crimson on stems to 6 feet in early to midsummer. *L. candidum* (Madonna lily, white lily)—fragrant trusses of shimmering white trumpets with

Lilium candidum

yellow throats on 2- to 4-foot stems in early summer. *L. columbianum* (Columbia lily, Columbia tiger lily, Oregon lily)—tiered clusters of nodding 2-inch yellow to red turbans spotted maroon on 5-foot stalks in summer. *L. hansonii* (Japanese Turk's-cap)—loose spikes of 2½-inch yellow-orange turbans spotted purple on 2- to 5-foot stems in early summer. *L. henryi*—20 or more dangling light orange turbans with green throats on stems to 8 feet in late summer. *L. lancifolium* [also called *L. tigrinum*] (devil lily, tiger lily)—up to 25 nodding 5-inch orange or red Turk's caps spotted with purple on 6-foot plants in midsummer. *L. martagon* (Martagon lily, Turk's-cap lily, turban lily)—tiered clusters of up to 50 nodding light purple-rose flower turbans spotted with dark purple and unpleasantly scented on stems to 6 feet in midsummer; 'Album' is a pure ivory. *L. monadelphum* (Caucasian lily)—bell-shaped 5-inch yellow flowers tinged and spotted purple on 4- to 5-foot stems in early summer. *L. pumilum* (coral lily)—up to two dozen inch-wide, lacquer red nodding Turk's caps on compact 1- to 2-foot plants in early summer. *L. regale* (regal lily)—fragrant, outward-facing white flower trumpets flushed purple outside with gold throats inside, clustered like a crown atop 3- to 5-foot stems in midsummer. *L. speciosum* (showy Japanese lily)—fragrant, nodding Turk's caps rimmed in

white on 4- to 5-foot stems in late summer to early fall; 'Album' is pure white; 'Rubrum', white blushed and spotted with crimson; 'Uchida', deep reddish pink with a white throat and crimson spots. *L. superbum* (American Turk's-cap lily, swamp lily, lily royal)—deep yellow-orange 3-inch flowers with maroon spots nodding in trusses on 5- to 8-foot stems in midsummer. *L.* x *testaceum* (Nankeen lily)— 3-inch apricot turbans spotted red on 4- to 6-foot plants in midsummer.

Growing conditions and maintenance: With the exception of *L. candidum* and its *Division 3* hybrids, plant lilies in spring or fall, setting bulbs 2 to 3 times deeper than their diameter. Space bulbs 1 foot apart. Plant *L. candidum* and its hybrids with bulb tips an inch below the surface in fall. Mulch lilies to keep roots cool and moist in summer, protected from frost in winter. *L. auratum* and *L. speciosum* will not tolerate lime in the soil. *L. auratum, L. canadense,* and *L. speciosum* are susceptible to the lily mosaic virus. *L. lancifolium* is a carrier of the virus, which does not harm it but is spread to other lilies by aphids; buy only disease-free stock and plant far from other lilies. Stake taller lilies for support. For pots and patio containers, choose compact lilies and set bulbs deep enough to allow space for stem roots. Propagate lilies by removing and replanting the small bulblets that grow along the underground stem or by removing and potting the tiny black bulbils that appear in the leaf joints of some species.

Mertensia
(mer-TENZ-ee-a)
BLUEBELLS, LUNGWORT

Mertensia virginica

Hardiness: *Zones 3-8*

Type of bulb: *rhizome*

Flowering season: *spring*

Height: *18 to 24 inches*

Soil: *moist, well-drained, fertile*

Light: *light shade to full sun*

Mertensia produces loose clusters of nodding flower bells over several weeks. The blossoms dangle near the top of stems lined with oval, pointed, soft green leaves. Foliage dies back by midsummer. Bluebells will slowly grow into large clumps in woodland borders, rock gardens, and wildflower gardens, and provide textural contrast when interplanted with spring bulbs such as narcissus and tulip.

Selected species and varieties: *M. virginica*—(Virginia bluebells, Virginia cowslip, Roanoke bells)—inch-long pale dusty blue flowers with tiny curling crests at the tip of each petal.

Growing conditions and maintenance: Plant Virginia bluebells in fall, setting the tips of crowns just at the soil surface with buds facing up. Space crown sections 1½ to 3 feet apart. When purchasing Virginia bluebells, look for nursery-propagated crowns; refuse plants collected in the wild. To propagate, divide crowns in fall, making sure each section has at least one bud.

Narcissus
(nar-SIS-us)
DAFFODIL

Narcissus 'Dutch Master'

Hardiness: *Zones 3-10*

Type of bulb: *true bulb*

Flowering season: *late winter to late spring*

Height: *4 to 18 inches*

Soil: *well-drained*

Light: *full sun to shade*

Daffodil flowers, growing either singly or in small clusters, bloom atop stout, hollow stems above clumps of narrow, glossy, grasslike leaves. Mature bulbs produce two or more stems. The 1- to 4-inch-wide flowers sometimes face upward or arch downward but most often face out. Each bloom consists of an outer ring of six petals called the perianth and a raised center called a corona, which may be an almost flat small cup, a large cup of medium length, or, when it is very long, a trumpet. The edges of the corona may be ruffled, fringed, flared, frilled, or split. The petals of the perianth may be pointed or round, overlapping or separate. Colors range the spectrum. Species narcissus are renowned for their sweet, intense fragrance. Hybrids of the species number in the thousands, and the genus is grouped into 12 divisions for identification. There are miniature cultivars within almost every division. Group them in borders, beds, and woodland or rock gardens, or scatter them to naturalize on lawns and in meadows. All narcissus make excellent cut flowers, and all, particularly some of the species,

are excellent for forcing. All parts of narcissus are poisonous.

Selected species and varieties: The 12 divisions are based on the shape of the corona, its size relationship to the perianth, and, sometimes, the species from which the plants originated. *Division 1. Trumpet daffodils:* One flower per 16- to 20-inch stem, with the corona a trumpet as long as or longer than the perianth petals; 'Arctic Gold' is deep yellow; 'Bravoure' has white petals and a yellow cup; 'Dutch Master' is all yellow, good for forcing; 'Las Vegas' has giant white petals and a yellow corona; 'Little Beauty' is a 6-inch miniature with white petals and a golden yellow trumpet; 'Little Gem' is an all-yellow miniature; 'Lunar Sea' has soft yellow petals and a white cup; 'Mount

Narcissus 'Gigantic Star'

Hood', white petals with a cream trumpet; 'Spellbinder', yellow-green flowers with a corona aging white; 'Unsurpassable' is golden yellow with extremely large trumpets. *Division 2. Large-cup daffodils:* One flower on each 12- to 20-inch stem, the corona ranging in size from one-third the length of the petals to almost their length; 'Accent' has white petals and a pink corona; 'Ambergate', red corona and orange petals blushed red; 'Camelot' is a long-lasting golden yellow bloom; 'Carlton' has two shades of yellow and is vanilla scented; 'Ceylon' has yellow petals and an orange cup and grows vigorously; 'Daydream' is translucent yellow with a cup maturing to white; 'Flower Record' has white petals and a yellow corona rimmed red; 'Gigantic Star' is an extremely large pale yellow-orange bloom with a vanilla scent; 'Ice Follies' has creamy white petals and a flat yellow cup aging white; 'Kissproof', copper yellow petals, a red-orange cup; 'Pink Charm', white petals, a corona banded salmon; 'Redhill', ivory petals, a deep red-orange corona; 'Salome', ivory petals, a pale yellow corona aging to salmon pink;

Narcissus 'Ice Follies'

'St. Keverne' is all yellow; 'St. Patrick's Day', bright yellow with a flat white corona; 'White Plume', pure white. *Division 3. Small-cup daffodils:* One flower per 10- to 20-inch stem, with the corona less than a third the length of the perianth petals; 'Barrett Browning' is early flowering with a white perianth and an orange to red corona; 'Birma' has deep yellow petals with a red cup. *Division 4. Double daffodils:* One or more flowers per 12- to 16-inch stem, with either the perianth petals or the corona or both doubled, the corona sometimes a tuft of tousled petals almost as wide as the perianth instead of a cup; 'Bridal Crown' has cream petals, deep red-orange centers; 'Cheerfulness' is a single white bloom flecked yellow; 'Erlicheer' yields eight or more fragrant, white-petaled flowers with yellow-tinged centers on each stem; 'Flower Drift' is ivory with a ruffled yellow-orange center; 'Pencrebar' is a bright orange miniature cultivar less than 6 inches tall; 'Sir Winston Churchill' has fragrant white petals with orange centers; 'Tahiti' is deep yellow with a red center; 'Unique', ivory white with an extremely frilled golden center. *Division 5. Triandus hybrid daffodils:* Two or more drooping flowers per 10- to 12-inch stem, with the perianth petals flared backwards; 'Hawera' is less than 6 inches tall with clusters of tiny yellow bells; 'Liberty Bells' is soft yellow; 'Petrel' produces up to 7 fragrant white

flowers per stem; 'Thalia' grows two or more fragrant white flowers, resembling orchids, per stem. *Division 6. Cyclamineus hybrid daffodils:* One flower on each short stem—under 8 inches—with a trumpet-shaped corona and perianth petals swept backwards; 'February Gold' is yellow; 'Jack Snipe' has rounded white petals and a fringed yellow cup; 'Jenny' is pure white; 'Jet Fire' has red-orange petals with yellow cups; 'Jumblie' is a miniature, under 6 inches, with yellow petals swept back from a pencil-thin yellow-orange corolla; 'Peeping Tom' is lemon yellow; 'Tête-à-Tête' is a miniature under 6 inches with buttery yellow petals and a corona flushed orange. *Division 7.*

Narcissus 'Jack Snipe'

Jonquilla hybrid daffodils: Three to 6 fragrant flowers on a round 10- to 14-inch stem with small cups; 'Baby Moon' is a miniature, under 6 inches, with fragrant yellow blooms; 'Bell Song' is fragrant, with white petals and a pink corona; 'Pipit', fragrant, with pale yellow petals and a white corona; 'Quail' is orangey yellow; 'Sun Disk', a yellow miniature, under 6 inches, with very rounded petals; 'Suzy' is fragrant, with yellow petals and a deep red-orange corona; 'Trevithian' has curled yellow petals and a frilled corona and is very fragrant. *Division 8. Tazetta hybrid daffodils:* Three to 20 fragrant flowers with almost flat coronas per 6- to 14-inch stem; 'Avalanche' has a perianth crowded with doubled white petals and a yellow corona; 'Geranium', fragrant white petals and a yellow-orange cup; 'Minnow', a miniature under 6 inches, has white petals and a bright yellow cup; 'Scarlet Gem', yellow-orange petals enfolding a deep red-orange corona with

frilled edges. *Division 9. Poeticus hybrid daffodils:* One fragrant flower per 12- to 16-inch stem with rounded pure white perianth petals and a tiny, brilliantly colored, disk-shaped, flat corona; 'Actaea' has brilliant white petals with deep green

Narcissus 'Minnow'

stamens tucked within a deep orange disk rimmed red. *Division 10. Species and wild forms:* N. bulbocodium var. conspicuus (hoop-petticoat daffodil)—petals reduced to tiny pointed projections around smooth, flaring yellow coronas like ladies' hoopskirts on 6- to 10-inch stems. N. jonquilla (jonquil)—2-inch golden yellow flowers with flat coronas in clusters on 12-inch stems. N. papyraceus (paper-white narcissus)—clusters of up to a dozen very fragrant flowers on 16-inch stems, excellent for forcing; 'Galilee' has pure white late blooms; 'Israel', creamy yellow petals and a deep yellow corona; 'Jerusalem' is pure white; 'Ziva', a very early white. N. poeticus var. recurvus (pheasant's-eye narcissus)—1½- to 3-inch blossoms with back-swept white petals and a flat, disk-shaped yellow to red corona on 8- to 16-inch stems. N. pseudonarcissus ssp. obvallaris (Tenby daffodil)—rich deep yellow 2- to 3-inch flowers with ruffled and flared trumpets on 10-inch stems. N. tazetta (bunch-flowered narcissus, polyanthus narcissus)—4 to 8 fragrant blooms with a white perianth and yellow corona; 'Canaliculatus' has very fragrant blossoms with backswept white petals ringing a yellow cup on 6-inch stems; 'Grand Soleil d'Or', a deep yellow perianth and bright orange cup on 12-inch stems. *Division 11. Split-corona daffodils:* One upward-facing flower with a flattened corona split one-third or more of its length on each 14- to 20-inch stem; 'Cassata' has white petals and a ruffled lemon yellow cup aging to white; 'Colbanc' is pure white with an "eye" of deep green stamens; 'Mondragon' is golden yellow and deep orange; 'Palmares' has white petals and pink ruffled centers; 'Tricollet', white petals around an orange corolla. Plants in the Division 11 subdivision *Papillion daffodils* resemble floral butterflies; 'Sorbet' is an ivory butterfly type with a sunny yellow center. *Division 12. Miscellaneous daffodils:* All daffodils not belonging to any of the previous divisions.

Growing conditions and maintenance: Plant narcissus in fall, setting the bulbs, which can range from ¼ to 2 inches in diameter, into the ground at a depth three

Narcissus bulbocodium

times the width of the bulb and spacing them 1 to 3 inches apart, depending on their size and the effect desired in the garden. Allow foliage to sprawl and to die back for at least 6 weeks in early summer before removing it. Fragrant *N. tazetta* and its hybrids are hardy only in Zones 9 and 10 but are among the choicest daffodils for forcing because they require no chilling. To force plants into bloom, buy prechilled bulbs or chill all daffodil bulbs except those of *N. tazetta* and its hybrids before potting them 1 inch deep in containers. Propagate narcissus by removing and immediately replanting the small bulblets that develop at the base of mature bulbs as soon as foliage withers, or dry the bulbs and hold them for replanting in fall. Bulblets take several years to grow to blooming size.

Puschkinia
(push-KIN-ee-a)
PUSCHKINIA

Puschkinia scilloides var. libanotica 'Alba'

Hardiness: *Zones 4-9*

Type of bulb: *true bulb*

Flowering season: *spring*

Height: *4 to 6 inches*

Soil: *moist, well-drained*

Light: *full sun to light shade*

Puschkinia's wands of tight, oval buds open first into loose clusters of tiny flower bells and finally into small stars on slender stems rising from tufts of narrow leaves like those of daffodils. The plants naturalize easily into drifts of blooms to carpet rockeries or beds and make an attractive border edging.

Selected species and varieties: *P. scilloides* var. *libanotica* (striped squill)— ½-inch bluish white flowers striped darker blue above 6-inch leaves; 'Alba' is pure white.

Growing conditions and maintenance: Plant bulbs in fall, setting them 2 inches deep and 6 inches apart. Group them in small colonies for best effect. They bloom best when left undisturbed. Propagate by removing the small bulblets that grow alongside mature bulbs.

Ranunculus
(ra-NUN-kew-lus)
BUTTERCUP, CROWFOOT

Ranunculus asiaticus

Hardiness: *tender or Zones 9-11*

Type of bulb: *tuber*

Flowering season: *spring and summer*

Height: *10 to 18 inches*

Soil: *moist, very well drained, sandy*

Light: *full sun*

Buttercups produce quantities of saucer-shaped flowers over a long season of bloom. There are many hybrids, so thickly doubled that flowers become colorful domes of whorled overlapping petals. Each tuber may produce five or six dozen flowers up to four at a time throughout the season on stems lined with ferny leaflets. Buttercups can be used in borders and rock gardens, and they excel as cut flowers.

Selected species and varieties: *R. asiaticus* 'Tecolote Giants' (Persian buttercup)—flowers up to 5 inches across in pastel shades of pink, rose, yellow, tangerine, and white, with bi- and tricolors.

Growing conditions and maintenance: Plant Persian buttercups in fall, soaking the tubers overnight then setting them in the soil with the claws down with the tops 1½ inches deep. Space them 8 inches apart. Crowns are subject to rot, so sites with fast drainage are essential for success. Tubers go dormant in summer. North of Zone 9, treat plants as annuals, setting them out in spring and lifting them in fall for winter storage. Propagate from seed or by dividing tubers.

Rhodohypoxis
(ro-do-hi-POKS-is)
RHODOHYPOXIS

Rhodohypoxis baurii

Hardiness: *Zones 6-10*

Type of bulb: *rhizome*

Flowering season: *summer*

Height: *3 to 4 inches*

Soil: *well-drained, sandy*

Light: *full sun*

Rhodohypoxis sends up tufts of 3-inch, stiff, grassy leaves covered with downy hairs in spring, followed by dainty, flat-faced blossoms that appear throughout the season. Each blossom sits atop a slender stem; the plants produce several flowering stems at a time. Dwarf rhodohypoxis are excellent planted among paving stones and will form colonies in rock gardens or borders. They can also be grown as container specimens.

Selected species and varieties: *R. baurii* (red star)—1- to 1½-inch white, pink, rose, or red flowers with petals crowded closely together at the center, obscuring the stamens.

Growing conditions and maintenance: Plant rhodohypoxis in fall, setting rhizomes 1 to 2 inches deep and 2 to 3 inches apart. Protect rhizomes with winter mulch in Zones 5 and 6. North of Zone 6, treat rhodohypoxis as an annual, planting in spring and lifting in fall, or grow it in shallow containers, allowing 4 or 5 rhizomes per 6-inch bulb pan. They are best left undisturbed, but clumps of rhizomes can be lifted and separated for propagation in spring as leaves begin to show.

Sanguinaria
(sang-gwi-NAR-ee-a)
BLOODROOT

Sanguinaria canadensis

Hardiness: *Zones 3-9*

Type of bulb: *rhizome*

Flowering season: *spring*

Height: *6 to 14 inches*

Soil: *moist, well-drained, rich*

Light: *partial shade*

Bloodroot is one of the loveliest spring-blooming woodland wildflowers native to eastern North America, and its large round blue-green leaves make an attractive ground cover. The plant is named for its red sap, root, and stems.

Selected species and varieties: *S. canadensis* (bloodroot, red puccoon)—solitary white flower to 1½ inches across with gold stamens on a 6- to 10-inch stalk. Each flower bud is surrounded by a furled leaf when it emerges. When fully expanded, the leaves are up to 1 foot across and have five or more lobes whose edges curl slightly upward.

Growing conditions and maintenance: Bloodroot thrives in rich, moist soil and benefits from added organic matter. It does best when planted beneath deciduous trees, where it receives bright sunshine before the trees leaf out and partial shade for the rest of the growing season. Mulch lightly with deciduous leaves in winter. Propagate by seed planted immediately after collection, or by dividing rhizomes in fall or early spring.

Tulipa
(TOO-lip-a)
TULIP

Tulipa 'Plaisir'

Hardiness: *Zones 2-8*

Type of bulb: *true bulb*

Flowering season: *spring*

Height: *6 to 28 inches*

Soil: *well-drained, sandy, fertile*

Light: *full sun*

Synonymous with spring to many gardeners, tulips' egg-shaped buds unfold into a profusion of forms ranging from inverted bells to flat saucers, stars, urns, deep cups, and lilylike shapes, sometimes with the petals reduced to mere ribbons. Petals may be smooth, curled, frilled, crisped, ruffled, flared, doubled, or waved. Tulips come in every color except true blue and are often striped, edged, flecked, flushed with contrasting color, or "flamed" in a zigzag variegated pattern. The hundreds of tulip species and thousands of hybrids are sorted by botanists into groups with similar origins, shapes, and bloom times. Species tulips, also called wild tulips or botanical tulips, generally have very early flowers on strong, sturdy stems, and are the parents of the taller hybrids, which bloom at various times throughout spring. The botanical *Kaufmanniana*, *Fosteriana*, and *Greigii* tulips merited their own divisions in the latest shuffling of botanical nomenclature. Low-growing species tulips can be grown in rock gardens or as edgings for beds or borders and may naturalize where conditions are right for their growth. Plant taller hybrids in informal groupings or formal patterns where they will produce blooms for several years before requiring renewal. Tulips can be forced for indoor bloom and make excellent cut flowers.

Selected species and varieties: Hybrids and species tulips are organized into 15 divisions used in the garden trade. *Division 1. Single early tulips:* Among the

Tulipa 'Apricot Beauty'

first to flower, in very early spring, on 6- to 14-inch stems with smooth petals in neat cups; 'Apricot Beauty' is salmon edged in apricot; 'Princess Irene', orange-splashed purple. *Division 2. Double early tulips:* Bowls of ruffled, doubled petals up to 4 inches across on 12-inch stems in early spring; 'Monte Carlo' is deep, clear yellow; 'Peach Blossom' has honey-scented soft rose petals edged with cream. *Division 3. Triumph tulips:* Satiny-smooth flowers in midspring on 18- to 24-inch stems; 'Attila' is pale purple-violet; 'New Design', cream flushed pink and apricot with leaves edged pinky cream. *Division 4. Darwin hybrid tulips:* Large, smooth-petaled ovals opening into flat cups up to 7 inches across in midspring on stems to 36 inches; 'Daydream' has yellow petals aging to apricot-flushed orange; 'Golden Parade', bright yellow petals edged in red; 'Pink Impression', purplish pink. *Division 5. Single late tulips* [includes Cottage and Darwin tulips]: Distinctly rectangular flower cups, some with pointed petals, in late spring on stems to 30 inches; 'Blushing Beauty' is yellow to apricot-blushed rose; 'Georgette' has clusters of butter yellow blooms with the edges aging to red; 'Halcro' is raspberry with a

yellow base; 'Maureen', cool white; 'Mrs. J. T. Scheepers', pure yellow; 'Queen of the Night', deep maroon, almost black. *Division 6. Lily-flowering tulips:* Urn-shaped buds open in late spring into lily-like flowers with curved, pointed petals on 24-inch stems; 'Red Shine' is deep ruby red with blue center; 'White Triumphator', pure white. *Division 7. Fringed tulips:* Late-spring flowers with very finely fringed petals on 14- to 24-inch stems; 'Burgundy Lace' is deep wine; 'Fringed Elegance', yellow flecked with pink. *Division 8. Viridiflora green tulips:* Late-spring flowers with petals in varying degrees of green on 18-inch stems; 'Spring Green' is ivory white with the center of the petals slashed green. *Division 9. Rembrandt tulips:* Petal color is "broken," or variegated, with elaborately patterned stripes and blotches on 18- to 30-inch stems in midspring; 'Cordell Hull' is white streaked with red. *Division 10. Parrot tulips:* Tousled petals, exotically fringed, waved, crisped, and flared, on flowers blooming in late spring on stems to 24 inches; 'Flaming Parrot' is deep yellow flamed with crimson. *Division 11. Double late tulips* [also

Tulipa dasystemon

called *peony-flowered tulips*]: Bowls of doubled petals in late spring on 16- to 24-inch stems; 'Angelique' is deep pink shading to pale pink; 'Miranda', two shades of red with a yellow base. *Division 12. Kaufmanniana tulips:* Urn-shaped buds opening into large flowers with curved petals on stems under 12 inches in very early spring; 'Ancila' is soft rosy pink outside, white inside; 'Show Winner', deep scarlet. *Division 13. Fosteriana tulips:* Enormous blossoms in

early spring on stems to 18 inches; 'Juan' is orange with a yellow base. *Division 14. Greigii tulips:* Flowers on strong, 8- to 16-inch stems above attractively purple-mottled foliage; 'Czar Peter' is red rimmed with white; 'Red Riding Hood', deep red-orange with a black base. *Division 15. Species tulips:* T. bakeri 'Lilac Wonder'—rosy purple cups with yellow bases on 6-inch stems; Zones 5-9. *T. batalinii* 'Bright Gem'—yellow cups of pointed petals flushed orange, 6 inches tall; Zones 3-8. *T. clusiana* var. *chrysantha* (golden lady tulip)—deep saucers, yellow inside, crimson edged with yellow outside, 12 inches tall; Zones 3-9. *T. dasystemon* (Kuen Lun tulip)—clusters of white flower stars tinged bronze and green, 4 inches tall; Zones 4-8. *T. linifolia* (slimleaf tulip)—curled, pointed electric red petals and red-rimmed leaves, 6 inches tall; Zones 4-8. *T. pulchella* 'Violacea' (red crocus tulip)—tiny purple-red ovals tinged green at bases, 3½ inches tall; Zones 5-8. *T. turkestanica*—clusters of white flower stars tinged violet, 5 inches tall; Zones 5-8.

Growing conditions and maintenance: Plant tulips in late fall, at a depth equal to three times their diameter. Space according to bulb size. Plant up to 40 hybrid bulbs per square yard or up to 60 smaller species bulbs per square yard. Note, however, that the famous variegation of Rembrandt tulips is caused by a virus that does not hurt them but can be harmful if spread to lilies and other tulips by aphids. Site Rembrandts far from susceptible plants. In Zones 9 and 10, tulips must be prechilled. Buy them in that condition or prechill them yourself by placing them in a vented paper bag in the refrigerator at 40°F for 9 to 12 weeks before setting them out; in modern frost-free refrigerators, however, you run the risk of drying them out. T. bakeri 'Lilac Wonder', T. clusiana var. chrysantha, and the hybrids 'Burgundy Lace', 'Flaming Parrot', 'Golden Parade', 'Halcro', 'Maureen', 'Menton', and 'Mrs. J. T. Scheepers' require no prechilling and may naturalize in warm zones. Allow foliage to ripen before mowing or removing it. Tulips tend to disappear over time; either treat them as annuals or dig and replant bulbs every 2 to 3 years as flowering diminishes.

Veltheimia
(vel-TY-mee-a)
RED-HOT POKER

Veltheimia bracteata

Hardiness: *tender or Zones 10-11*

Type of bulb: *true bulb*

Flowering season: *late winter to spring*

Height: *15 to 20 inches*

Soil: *well-drained, sandy*

Light: *full sun*

Red-hot poker's oval clusters of up to 50 flower buds open from bottom to top into long, drooping funnels with curled lips. Clusters are carried on sturdy stems above attractive rosettes of glossy green leaves with wavy edges. Both leaves and stems are attractively mottled. Use red-hot poker outdoors in warm climates; grow as a pot plant elsewhere.

Selected species and varieties: *V. bracteata*—2-inch pink-red or pink-purple blossoms with green-and-white flecked lips above foliage and stems marbled green and purple.

Growing conditions and maintenance: Outdoors in Zones 10 and 11, plant red-hot poker bulbs 1 inch deep and 6 to 10 inches apart in fall. In pots, group several of the large, 6-inch bulbs together in large bulb pans for best effect. Plant them 4 to 6 inches apart with the top third of the bulb exposed and allow bulbs to dry off during summer dormancy. Propagate by removing bulb offsets after foliage withers.

Zantedeschia
(zan-tee-DES-ki-a)
CALLA LILY

Zantedeschia aethiopica

Hardiness: *tender or Zones 9-10*

Type of bulb: *rhizome*

Flowering season: *summer or fall*

Height: *2 to 3 feet*

Soil: *moist to well-drained*

Light: *full sun to partial shade*

Calla lily's gracefully curved and sculpted flowers have a cool, formal elegance few other blooms can match. Petal-like spathes curl into elongated trumpets with a flared lip pulled to a point. The waxy spathe curls around a colorful, sometimes fragrant, fingerlike spadix bearing the true flowers, which are tiny and inconspicuous. Up to 12 or more blossoms bloom at the same time amid broad, stalked, arrow-shaped leaves with wavy edges that are often heavily flecked and spotted with white for added interest. In warm zones, calla lilies are eye-catching specimens for beds or borders and will naturalize where conditions suit them. Elsewhere they are grown as annuals or as pot plants for patio or indoor use. Callas are prized as cut flowers.

Selected species and varieties: *Z. aethiopica* (common calla, giant white calla, arum lily, trumpet lily)—fragrant, snowy white flowers 10 inches long on 2-foot plants; 'Perle Von Stuttgart' is somewhat smaller than the species, with abundant blossoms. *Z. albomaculata* (spotted calla, black-throated calla)—

5-inch white flowers with purple throats on 2-foot plants. *Z. elliottiana* (golden calla, yellow calla)—6-inch golden yellow flowers, tinged greenish yellow on the outside, on 2½-foot plants. *Z. rehmannii* (red calla, pink calla)—3-inch pink flowers on 18- to 24-inch plants. *Z.* hybrids—'Black-Eyed Beauty' produces creamy white blossoms veined green, with a black throat or eye rimming the spadix; 'Black Magic' is yellow with a black eye; 'Cameo', salmon; 'Harvest Moon' is yellow with a red eye; 'Pink Persuasion', purple-pink; 'Solfatare' is a creamy pale yellow with a black eye.

Zantedeschia rehmannii

Growing conditions and maintenance: Outdoors in Zones 8-10, plant calla lilies in spring or fall, setting rhizomes 1 to 4 inches deep and spacing them 1 to 2 feet apart. Calla lilies tolerate boggy conditions and can be grown with their roots in water at the edges of ponds. North of Zone 8, start them indoors in early spring and transplant them outside after all danger of frost has passed for blooming in summer. Lift rhizomes in fall after foliage withers and store for winter. For pot culture, set growing tips of rhizomes at soil level and allow one root per 6-inch pot. Callas bloom about 2 months after planting. Golden calla lily can be propagated from seed. Propagate all calla lilies by dividing their rhizomes in spring or fall.

'ALBA SEMI-PLENA'

Classification: *alba*

Bloom period: *summer*

Height: *6 to 8 feet*

Hardiness: *Zones 4-10*

ARS rating: *8.6*

Date introduced: *prior to 1600*

'Alba Semi-plena' is also known as the White Rose of York. Its semidouble white flowers are 2½ inches across with prominent golden stamens, and they produce a powerful fragrance. Borne in clusters, flowers appear in midseason and do not repeat. Elongated orange-red hips appear in late summer and fall. The foliage is gray-green.

With sturdy, arching canes that develop a vase-shaped form, 'Alba Semi-plena' can be grown as a freestanding shrub for a specimen or for use in borders, or it can be trained as a climber on a wall, a trellis, or a fence. Like other alba roses, it tolerates some shade and is quite hardy and disease resistant.

'AMERICAN PILLAR'

Classification: *rambler*

Bloom period: *summer*

Height: *15 to 20 feet*

Hardiness: *Zones 5-10*

ARS rating: *7.5*

Date introduced: *1902*

The five-petaled single blossoms of 'American Pillar' are carmine-pink with white centers and golden stamens. Erupting once in midsummer, they are produced in large clusters that almost cover the entire plant. Flowers have no scent. Leaves are leathery, large, and dark green; canes are green and prickly.

The plant is very vigorous, growing to 20 feet, and is best used for climbing on a fence or arbor. Like other ramblers, it may be subject to mildew.

'BARONNE PRÉVOST'

Classification: *hybrid perpetual*

Bloom period: *summer to fall*

Height: *4 to 6 feet*

Hardiness: *Zones 5-10*

ARS rating: *8.5*

Date introduced: *1842*

The elegant 3- to 4-inch blooms of 'Baronne Prévost' are very double, with 100 petals that quarter and fold back on a green button-eyed center. Ranging from pale pink to deep rose pink, the recurring blooms are extremely fragrant. Buds are globular, leaves are medium green, and canes are very prickly.

Best grown as a freestanding shrub, 'Baronne Prévost' grows between 4 and 6 feet high with an approximately equal spread. The plant is vigorous, and it has a less awkward form than do most hybrid perpetuals. Also, the foliage is more attractive and disease resistant than that of most of the class.

'BETTY PRIOR'

Classification: *floribunda*

Bloom period: *summer to fall*

Height: *4 to 5 feet*

Hardiness: *Zones 4-10*

ARS rating: *8.2*

Date introduced: *1935*

The carmine-pink buds of 'Betty Prior' open to 2- to 3-inch cupped single blossoms that flatten with age and bear a light, spicy fragrance. Blossoms occur in large clusters so profuse that they can cover the entire bush. In cool weather, flowers remain carmine-pink, but as temperatures rise they become medium pink. The five petals surround yellow stamens that darken to brown. Foliage is medium green and semiglossy.

Plants are vigorous and bushy with a rounded form. One of the most popular floribundas ever, this rose is effectively used for mass plantings and hedges, in small groups, and singly in a bed. It is also very winter hardy and exceptionally resistant to black spot, but less so to mildew.

'BLAZE'

Classification: *large-flowered climber*

Bloom period: *spring to fall*

Height: *12 to 15 feet*

Hardiness: *Zones 5-10*

ARS rating: *7.4*

Date introduced: *1932*

Clusters of cup-shaped scarlet blossoms occur on both old and new wood of 'Blaze' throughout the growing season. Flowers are semidouble, 2 to 3 inches across, lightly fragrant, and nonfading, even in hot weather. Early flowers are somewhat larger than those produced later in the season. Dark green leathery foliage contrasts nicely with the continuous show of blooms.

This easy-to-grow rose has a vigorous, upright habit, and its canes are quick to reach their height of 12 to 15 feet, making it a good choice for fences, arbors, pillars, and porches. It is quite hardy but is somewhat susceptible to powdery mildew.

'BONICA'

Classification: *shrub*

Bloom period: *summer*

Height: *3 to 5 feet*

Hardiness: *Zones 4-9*

ARS rating: *9.1*

Date introduced: *1981*

'Bonica' (also called 'Meidomonac') is free flowering and easy to grow. Large, loose clusters of up to 20 flowers appear throughout the summer. Each spiraled bud opens to reveal a 2½- to 3½-inch double blossom with soft pink ruffled petals. The foliage is dark green and glossy. Bright orange hips appear in fall and remain attractive all winter.

The plant has a spreading habit with arching stems spanning 5 to 6 feet. This rose is not fussy about pruning; it can be maintained as a compact hedge or lightly tip pruned for a more informal appearance. 'Bonica' is an excellent choice for beds or borders, for massing, or for use as a hedge along a walk or driveway. It is highly disease resistant, exceptionally hardy, and tolerant of harsh climates. This is the first shrub rose to win the AARS award.

'BRIDE'S DREAM'

Classification: *hybrid tea*

Bloom period: *summer to fall*

Height: *3 to 4 feet*

Hardiness: *Zones 5-10*

ARS rating: *8.0*

Date introduced: *1985*

The large double flowers of 'Bride's Dream' are pale pink, high centered, and lightly fragrant. They usually occur singly on the stem and appear in great abundance throughout the growing season. Foliage is dark green, and stems bear brown prickles.

The plant is a strong grower with a tall, upright habit. It can be situated in beds or borders, and its flowers are excellent for cutting and exhibition. 'Bride's Dream' is judged by some growers to be the best hybrid tea in its color class.

'BUFF BEAUTY'

Classification: *hybrid musk*

Bloom period: *summer to fall*

Height: *5 to 6 feet*

Hardiness: *Zones 5-10*

ARS rating: *8.3*

Date introduced: *1939*

The color of the 3- to 4-inch double flowers of 'Buff Beauty' ranges from buff yellow to deep apricot, depending on weather conditions. Richly fragrant, flattened blossoms are borne in clusters. The abundant foliage emerges bronze-red, turning a glossy dark green as it matures. Canes are smooth and brown.

This rose is a very attractive plant with a graceful, arching habit and is often broader than it is tall. It requires a lot of space but makes a lovely specimen. It can also be trained to a pillar or wall, or can be used as a ground cover on banks.

'CAREFREE BEAUTY'

Classification: *shrub*

Bloom period: *summer to fall*

Height: *4 to 5 feet*

Hardiness: *Zones 4-10*

ARS rating: *8.5*

Date introduced: *1977*

'CATHERINE MERMET'

Classification: *tea*

Bloom period: *summer*

Height: *3 to 4 feet*

Hardiness: *Zones 7-10*

ARS rating: *8.1*

Date introduced: *1869*

'CELSIANA'

Classification: *damask*

Bloom period: *summer*

Height: *4 to 5 feet*

Hardiness: *Zones 4-10*

ARS rating: *8.8*

Date introduced: *prior to 1750*

'CHERISH'

Classification: *floribunda*

Bloom period: *summer to fall*

Height: *3 feet*

Hardiness: *Zones 4-9*

ARS rating: *8.3*

Date introduced: *1980*

The long, pointed buds of 'Carefree Beauty' open to semidouble medium pink flowers. Each blossom has 15 to 20 petals and bears a rich, fruity fragrance. Flowers appear in clusters of three to 20 and are produced freely all season. Foliage is a bright apple green.

This rose has a vigorous, bushy, spreading habit. It is easy to grow, as its name implies, and makes an excellent flowering hedge or garden shrub. Space plants 18 inches apart to form a dense hedge.

Flowers of 'Catherine Mermet' open a blush pink with lilac edges and change to soft beige as they mature. Inner petals often display yellow at the base. The double blossoms are 3 inches across and are borne singly or in small clusters on graceful stems. Their fragrance is strong and spicy. Leaves are copper colored when young, maturing to a medium green.

This rose is somewhat delicate, requiring nothing less than a warm, sunny spot and rich, well-drained soil. It is quite tender and is frequently grown in greenhouses. With an upright, arching habit, it is well suited for beds, borders, and specimen plantings. Flowers are excellent for cutting. Pruning should be restricted to removal of dead, weak, or spindly canes. It is moderately disease resistant and heat tolerant.

The semidouble, gently nodding blooms of 'Celsiana' are 3½ to 4 inches across, cup shaped, and deliciously scented. Borne in clusters, the flowers open a clear pink and fade to a soft blush as they age. Petals are silky textured and surround bright yellow stamens. The flower colors are complemented perfectly by gray-green foliage.

The plant has an upright habit with gracefully arching canes and makes a fine choice for a bed or border, where it can put on a midseason display of color. 'Celsiana' is disease resistant and very hardy.

The 3- to 4-inch double blossoms of 'Cherish' put out a light cinnamon fragrance and appear over a lengthy season. Borne both singly and in clusters of up to 20, the high-centered flowers are coral-apricot with a creamy white base. The spiraled buds open slowly, and the flowers are exceptionally long-lasting. New leaves are bronze red, turning very dark green and glossy with age.

The compact, symmetrical habit of the bush is somewhat spreading, making 'Cherish' an appropriate choice for beds and borders. It can also be used as a low hedge. Flowers are exceptional for cutting. Added to the long list of the rose's virtues are good disease resistance and hardiness. It is an AARS winner.

'COMMUNIS'

Classification: *moss*

Bloom period: *summer*

Height: *4 feet*

Hardiness: *Zones 4-10*

ARS rating: *7.7*

Date introduced: *late 1600s*

Considered by many to be the best moss rose, 'Communis' (also called 'Common Moss') produces mossy growths on its sepals, buds, and stems. Buds are rose pink, opening to pale pink, intensely fragrant double flowers that are 2 to 3 inches wide. Reflexed petals surround a green button eye. The abundant foliage is medium green.

'Communis' plants are moderate growers with an arching habit; they are usually slightly taller than they are broad. The rose is well suited to beds and borders, and is both disease resistant and hardy.

'CONSTANCE SPRY'

Classification: *shrub*

Bloom period: *midsummer*

Height: *6 to 15 feet*

Hardiness: *Zones 4-10*

ARS rating: *7.8*

Date introduced: *1961*

The light pink double or very double flowers of 'Constance Spry' resemble peonies. This rose blooms only once each year, but the display is dramatic, producing a wealth of 3½- to 5-inch flowers bearing a rich, myrrhlike fragrance. The flowers appear in clusters, showing up well against abundant dark green foliage. Canes bear lots of bright red prickles.

A very vigorous plant, 'Constance Spry' can either be pruned to maintain a large, rounded shrub or be trained to climb a fence, wall, tripod, or pillar, where it can grow as high as 15 feet.

'COUNTRY DANCER'

Classification: *shrub*

Bloom period: *summer to fall*

Height: *2 to 4 feet*

Hardiness: *Zones 4-10*

ARS rating: *7.5*

Date introduced: *1973*

The high-centered buds of 'Country Dancer', a Dr. Buck rose, open to large, flat, double flowers that are somewhere between deep pink and rosy red in color—and quite fragrant. The petals are slightly yellow toward their base, and they surround golden stamens. Flowers occur in clusters throughout the growing season. Foliage is dark green.

This rose is usually grown as a low, spreading shrub. It can also be used as a hedge. Canes can be trained to a pillar or fence but should be trained horizontally to obtain the best flowering display; canes that grow vertically will produce all of their flowers at the tips. Although it's extremely hardy, 'Country Dancer' is somewhat susceptible to black spot.

'DOUBLE DELIGHT'

Classification: *hybrid tea*

Bloom period: *summer to fall*

Height: *4 feet*

Hardiness: *Zones 5-10*

ARS rating: *8.9*

Date introduced: *1977*

Each blossom of 'Double Delight' is a uniquely colored combination of red and creamy white. The exact coloration depends on light and temperature, but generally the red begins at the petal tips and diffuses to a creamy center. The double flowers are 5½ inches across, borne singly on stems, and have a strong, spicy fragrance. Leaves are a medium matte green.

Its bushy form and free-flowering habit make this rose a fine choice for beds and borders. It is a superb cut flower, prized for its form, color, fragrance, and long vase life. 'Double Delight' is fairly disease resistant but is somewhat tender. It is an AARS winner.

'ESCAPADE'

Classification: *floribunda*

Bloom period: *summer to fall*

Height: *2½ to 3 feet*

Hardiness: *Zones 4-10*

ARS rating: *8.8*

Date introduced: *1967*

The 3-inch semidouble flowers of 'Escapade' are light mauve-pink or lilac to rosy violet with creamy white centers. They are borne in both large and small clusters, and each bloom has about 12 petals that surround amber stamens. Blooms commence in midseason, repeating consistently until a hard frost. The blooms are lightly fragrant. Leaves are light green and glossy.

'Escapade' plants have an upright, bushy habit and are vigorous growers. They are useful in beds and borders and can also be planted as a low hedge. The flowers are excellent for cutting.

'EUROPEANA'

Classification: *floribunda*

Bloom period: *summer to fall*

Height: *2 to 3 feet*

Hardiness: *Zones 4-10*

ARS rating: *9.0*

Date introduced: *1968*

Borne in large clusters, the double blooms of 'Europeana' are 3 inches across and cup shaped. Petals are deep crimson and have a velvety texture. Beginning in midseason, flowering continues prolifically until the fall. Leaves emerge bronze red, maturing to deep, glossy green with reddish tints.

This bush is quite robust. Its enormous flower clusters can cause the stems to bend under their weight, so it should be grouped with plants that will provide support for the flower-laden stems. Because it has a bushy, spreading habit, 'Europeana' is suitable for beds, borders, and low hedges. Flowers are good for cutting, and the plants are disease resistant and very hardy. This rose is an AARS winner.

'FANTIN-LATOUR'

Classification: *centifolia*

Bloom period: *late spring*

Height: *4 to 6 feet*

Hardiness: *Zones 4-10*

ARS rating: *8.2*

Date introduced: *unknown*

Although 'Fantin-Latour' has a relatively short bloom period and does not repeat, the quality of the blossoms makes up for its short season. Each 2- to 3-inch very double flower is composed of 200 petals, giving it the full appearance typical of centifolia roses. When it first opens, the pale blush pink bloom is cupped; it then flattens as it matures. The blossoms emit a delicate fragrance. Leaves are dark green, and canes are nearly smooth.

'Fantin-Latour' plants produce arching canes that usually reach 5 feet in height and a little less in spread. They perform well in a bed or border where their late-spring flower display is breathtaking. This is a very hardy rose, but its disease resistance is only moderate.

'FÉLICITÉ PARMENTIER'

Classification: *alba*

Bloom period: *early summer*

Height: *4 to 5 feet*

Hardiness: *Zones 4-10*

ARS rating: *8.6*

Date introduced: *1834*

The pale blush pink, very double blooms of 'Félicité Parmentier' open flat, then reflex to form a ball. As the 2- to 2½-inch flowers age, the tightly quartered petals fade to creamy white at their outer edges. Flowers are borne in clusters in profusion in early summer, but they do not repeat. Their fragrance is heady. Leaves are gray-green, and the abundant prickles are dark.

This rose has a bushy, compact habit, reaching 4 to 5 feet in height and 4 feet in width, and is less upright than most albas. The tidy form requires little pruning. It tolerates poor soil, partial shade, and climatic extremes, and is resistant to disease.

'FIRST EDITION'	'FRAU KARL DRUSCHKI'	'FRENCH LACE'	'GRUSS AN AACHEN'

Classification: *floribunda*

Bloom period: *summer to fall*

Height: *3½ feet*

Hardiness: *Zones 4-10*

ARS rating: *8.6*

Date introduced: *1976*

Classification: *hybrid perpetual*

Bloom period: *early summer and fall*

Height: *4 to 7 feet*

Hardiness: *Zones 5-10*

ARS rating: *7.8*

Date introduced: *1901*

Classification: *floribunda*

Bloom period: *summer to fall*

Height: *3½ feet*

Hardiness: *Zones 4-9*

ARS rating: *8.2*

Date introduced: *1981*

Classification: *floribunda*

Bloom period: *spring to fall*

Height: *2 to 3 feet*

Hardiness: *Zones 4-10*

ARS rating: *8.3*

Date introduced: *1909*

The pointed coral-orange buds of 'First Edition' open to luminous coral-rose blossoms with orange tints. The petals surround yellow anthers. Flowers are double, 2 to 2½ inches across, and lightly fragrant, and they are borne in flat-topped clusters. Their color deepens in cool weather. Foliage is glossy and medium green.

The bushes are vigorous and upright. They are suited to many uses, including beds and borders, low hedges, and containers. Flowers are excellent for cutting and exhibition, and the plants have good disease resistance. 'First Edition' is an AARS winner.

This rose produces a great abundance of double blossoms from high-centered buds in early summer and repeats the show in fall. The elegant white flower is 4 to 4½ inches across with 30 to 35 rolled petals that display a touch of lemon yellow at their base. Canes are nearly smooth, supporting leathery, coarse, light green foliage.

The plant is vigorous and erect, with stout branches and long, strong stems. The color and form of its flower makes it useful in combination with other roses, both in beds and in indoor arrangements. Buds are reluctant to open in damp weather, and leaves are susceptible to mildew.

Flowers of 'French Lace' are borne singly or in clusters of up to 12 and bloom continuously from early summer to frost. Buds are pointed, opening to flat, 3- to 4-inch double blossoms that are ivory with apricot tones and emit a light tea fragrance. The thorny canes produce small, dark green hollylike leaves.

Plants are well branched, bushy, and upright. Their attractive form and abundant flowering potential recommend them for use as a low hedge or in a bed or border. Flowers are long-lasting and beautiful in indoor arrangements. To top off its list of virtues, 'French Lace' is highly resistant to disease. It is an AARS winner.

Buds of 'Gruss an Aachen' are tinted with red-orange and yellow but open to reveal pale apricot-pink blooms that fade to creamy white. The flowers, reminiscent of old-garden roses, are 3 inches across, double, and cup shaped, with a rich fragrance. They are borne in clusters throughout the season. Leaves are rich green and leathery.

This rose has a low growing, bushy habit and is very free blooming, even in partial shade. It is a good choice for a bed or low hedge. The plants are quite hardy and disease resistant.

'HANNAH GORDON'

Classification: *floribunda*

Bloom period: *spring to fall*

Height: *3 feet*

Hardiness: *Zones 4-10*

ARS rating: *8.2*

Date introduced: *1983*

The large double flowers of 'Hannah Gordon' are white with bold cerise-pink markings and petal edges. Each bloom has about 35 petals and a light fragrance. Flowers appear continuously throughout the season. The foliage is large, medium green, and semiglossy.

Plants are upright, compact, and bushy. They are useful in beds and borders, can be very effective when massed, and also do nicely when used as a low hedge.

'HERITAGE'

Classification: *shrub*

Bloom period: *summer*

Height: *4 to 5 feet*

Hardiness: *Zones 4-10*

ARS rating: *8.7*

Date introduced: *1984*

The blush pink double flowers of this David Austin rose are colored a bit deeper toward their centers. Their form is exquisite, with the outer petals forming a deep cup around precisely arranged and folded inner petals. Profusely borne in clusters throughout the summer, they create a cloud of rich scent that is a blend of myrrh and lemon. Foliage is dark green and semiglossy. The canes have few thorns.

The plant is a robust grower with a bushy, upright habit. It is a fine addition to beds or borders, makes a wonderful hedge, and provides a long season of cut flowers. Plants are fairly disease resistant but may be susceptible to rust.

'ICEBERG'

Classification: *floribunda*

Bloom period: *summer to fall*

Height: *3 to 4½ feet*

Hardiness: *Zones 4-9*

ARS rating: *8.7*

Date introduced: *1958*

Throughout summer, 'Iceberg' produces large clusters with up to a dozen pure white blossoms that stand out beautifully against small, light green, glossy foliage. Buds are long and pointed with high centers. Each double flower is 2 to 4 inches across, somewhat flat, and sweetly scented.

'Iceberg' is an all-purpose rose in that the vigorous plant can be grown as a hedge or a border or as a container specimen, trained as a tree rose, or used for cutting flowers for indoor arrangements. It is bushy and well branched and is easily trained. A climbing version is also available, rated 8.8 by the ARS. Both forms are disease resistant.

'ISPAHAN'

Classification: *damask*

Bloom period: *spring to summer*

Height: *4 to 6 feet*

Hardiness: *Zones 4-10*

ARS rating: *8.7*

Date introduced: *prior to 1832*

The very fragrant, double blooms of 'Ispahan' (also called 'Pompon des Princes') appear in profusion over a 2-month period in early and midseason, but they do not repeat. Borne in clusters, the bright clear pink flowers are 2½ to 3 inches across, cup shaped, and loosely reflexing. They are long-lasting, holding both their shape and their color well. Foliage is small with a blue-green cast.

This rose is bushy and upright. With a flowering season that is remarkably long for a damask, it is valued both as a garden shrub and for cut flowers. The plant is vigorous, disease resistant, and quite hardy.

'JEANNE LAJOIE'

Classification: *climbing miniature*

Bloom period: *spring to fall*

Height: *8 feet*

Hardiness: *Zones 5-10*

ARS rating: *9.2*

Date introduced: *1975*

'Jeanne Lajoie' produces long, pointed buds that open to miniature two-toned pink flowers. Usually borne in clusters, the flowers are most abundant during cool weather. The high-centered blooms have 20 to 25 pointed petals and are lightly fragrant. In fall, this rose produces small orange hips. Foliage is lush, glossy, and dark.

A very vigorous grower, 'Jeanne Lajoie' is upright and bushy. It can be trained as a climber, or used as a freestanding shrub or hedge rose. Deadheading after its first flush of blooms will significantly increase later flowering. Plants are disease resistant and hardy.

'JOSEPH'S COAT'

Classification: *large-flowered climber*

Bloom period: *summer to fall*

Height: *8 to 10 feet*

Hardiness: *Zones 6-9*

ARS rating: *7.6*

Date introduced: *1964*

The clusters of double blossoms of 'Joseph's Coat' create an amazing riot of color, with yellows, pinks, oranges, and reds all present at the same time. The red and orange tones become more prominent in autumn. Buds are urn shaped, and unlike those of many climbers they occur on new wood. Flowers are 3-inch cups that are lightly fragrant, leaves are dark green and glossy, and canes are prickly.

The plant is tall and upright. It can be trained as a climber on a pillar, fence, or trellis or, because it is not very robust, can be allowed to grow as a loose, freestanding shrub. It is somewhat tender and prone to powdery mildew.

'JUST JOEY'

Classification: *hybrid tea*

Bloom period: *summer*

Height: *3 feet*

Hardiness: *Zones 5-10*

ARS rating: *7.7*

Date introduced: *1972*

Blossoms of 'Just Joey' are 4 to 6 inches across, composed of 30 exceptionally large petals with interestingly frilly edges. Buds are large, elegantly pointed, and brandy colored, opening to double apricot blooms that lighten as they mature. Flowers bear a deep fruity scent. Both the flowers and their fragrance are long-lasting. Leaves are large and glossy, and stems are prickly.

Plants are rather squat and spreading, with a moderate growth rate. They are fairly disease resistant. The flowers are particularly outstanding for indoor arrangements because of their large size and long vase life.

'LA MARNE'

Classification: *polyantha*

Bloom period: *spring to fall*

Height: *2 to 4 feet*

Hardiness: *Zones 5-10*

ARS rating: *8.3*

Date introduced: *1915*

The delicately fragrant, cup-shaped blooms of 'La Marne' appear continuously throughout the season; it is one of the most profusely blooming roses grown. Semidouble flowers are borne in loose clusters and are blush white with a vivid pink edge; their color deepens in cool weather. Foliage is dense and glossy.

This bushy, vigorous rose is tall for a polyantha. It is happiest in sunny, open locations. The luxuriant foliage and non-stop blooming ability make it a superb choice for a hedge or garden shrub, and it is a fine container specimen as well.

'LEANDER'	**'MARCHESA BOCCELLA'**	**'MUTABILIS'**	**'NASTARANA'**

Classification: *shrub*

Bloom period: *spring to summer*

Height: *6 to 8 feet*

Hardiness: *Zones 4-10*

ARS rating: *8.3*

Date introduced: *1982*

Classification: *hybrid perpetual*

Bloom period: *spring to fall*

Height: *4 to 5 feet*

Hardiness: *Zones 5-10*

ARS rating: *8.9*

Date introduced: *1842*

Classification: *China*

Bloom period: *summer to fall*

Height: *3 to 8 feet*

Hardiness: *Zones 7-10*

ARS rating: *8.2*

Date introduced: *prior to 1894*

Classification: *noisette*

Bloom period: *summer to fall*

Height: *3 to 4 feet*

Hardiness: *Zones 6-10*

ARS rating: *8.3*

Date introduced: *1879*

'Leander', a David Austin rose, produces a dizzying profusion of deep-apricot-colored flowers in spring and early summer. Borne in clusters, the blooms are small, and have a fruity fragrance. Although the rose is not considered a repeat bloomer, flowers may reappear later in the season. Semiglossy leaves are medium in both size and color.

This rose has a full habit, growing nearly as wide as it is tall, and makes a fine large garden shrub. It is among the most disease resistant of the English roses.

'Marchesa Boccella' (also known as 'Jacques Cartier') produces large, full flowers in repeat flushes throughout the growing season. Each very double bloom is delicate pink with blush edges. Borne in tight clusters on short, stiff stems, the blooms are very fragrant. The petals are more numerous but smaller than those of most hybrid perpetuals. Foliage is dense and bright green.

One of the finest of the class, this rose is a robust grower with a medium to tall erect form and is somewhat spreading. Its recurring flowering habit and lush foliage are suited to large beds and borders.

The pointed orange buds of 'Mutabilis' open to single blooms that start out sulfur yellow, change to coppery pink, and then deepen to crimson. All three colors can be present on a bush at the same time. Irregularly shaped flowers resemble butterflies, earning the plant the nickname butterfly rose. The flowers are very fragrant. Leaves emerge in an attractive shade of bronze.

If grown beneath the protection of a wall, these vigorous, robust plants are capable of reaching 8 feet in height with a 6 foot spread. In a more open site, plants usually reach only 3 feet. They benefit from regular feeding and abundant watering. 'Mutabilis' tolerates slightly alkaline soil and summer heat and humidity but is fairly tender.

The semidouble blooms of 'Nastarana' are white tinged with pink and appear in large clusters on new wood. Each flower is about 2 inches across and bears a pleasant tea rose fragrance. Flowering repeats well throughout the season. Leaves are smooth, oval, and medium green.

Plants are very vigorous, with an upright habit. They prefer an open, sunny site but are tolerant of partial shade. They also tolerate poor soils, summer heat, and humidity, but may require winter protection. They may be susceptible to mildew and black spot.

'NEARLY WILD'

Classification: *floribunda*

Bloom period: *spring to summer*

Height: *2 to 4 feet*

Hardiness: *Zones 4-10*

ARS rating: *7.6*

Date introduced: *1941*

The small, tapered buds of 'Nearly Wild' open to rose pink blooms that have five petals and are very fragrant. The flowers occur prolifically along the length of each stem. The main flowering season is spring, but some blooms appear through summer.

Plants are compact and bushy, and are often wider than tall. This rose makes an excellent ground cover for sunny banks; space plants 2½ to 3 feet apart. It can also be planted to cascade down a wall or trained to climb a low fence. Placed in front of taller shrubs, it provides good foreground color, and it makes a fine container specimen. 'Nearly Wild' tolerates slightly alkaline soil and is very hardy.

'PARTY GIRL'

Classification: *miniature*

Bloom period: *summer to fall*

Height: *12 to 15 inches*

Hardiness: *Zones 5-10*

ARS rating: *9.0*

Date introduced: *1979*

The pointed buds of 'Party Girl' open into apricot-yellow high-centered blooms. Borne singly or in clusters, each flower is 1 to 1½ inches across and bears a pleasant, spicy fragrance. Leaves are dark green and glossy.

This miniature is bushy and compact—and very versatile. It makes a lovely potted plant, indoors or out, and it's well suited for mixing into perennial borders or for edging a rose or shrub garden. The flowers are outstanding for cutting and exhibition. Plants are hardy and disease resistant.

'PAUL NEYRON'

Classification: *hybrid perpetual*

Bloom period: *spring and fall*

Height: *3 to 6 feet*

Hardiness: *Zones 5-10*

ARS rating: *8.1*

Date introduced: *1869*

The huge, very double blossoms of 'Paul Neyron' are the size of small plates, measuring 4½ to 7 inches across. They are colored pink to rose pink with lilac shading, and the petals are intricately swirled. Flowers are very fragrant and appear in spring and repeat in fall. Foliage is large and matte green, and canes are nearly smooth.

This hybrid perpetual is a strong, vigorous grower with an upright habit. It's a nice choice for beds or borders, and its spectacular blooms are exceptional in indoor arrangements. 'Paul Neyron' is significantly more disease resistant than other roses in this class.

'PLAYBOY'

Classification: *floribunda*

Bloom period: *spring to fall*

Height: *3 feet*

Hardiness: *Zones 4-10*

ARS rating: *8.1*

Date introduced: *1976*

The burgundy-bronze buds of 'Playboy' open to display large flowers that are a vivid blend of orange, yellow, and scarlet. Each 3½-inch bloom has 7 to 10 petals and a yellow eye. Borne in clusters, the flowers are delightfully fragrant and appear all season. In fall, spent blooms produce attractive hips. Foliage is dark and glossy.

'Playboy' is aggressive and easy to grow. The bushes are useful in beds and borders, and the long-stemmed flower sprays are long-lasting both in the garden and when cut for indoor arrangements. This rose is disease resistant and tolerates partial shade.

'QUEEN ELIZABETH'

Classification: *grandiflora*

Bloom period: *summer to fall*

Height: *4 to 7 feet*

Hardiness: *Zones 4-9*

ARS rating: *9.0*

Date introduced: *1954*

The 3½- to 4-inch double flowers of 'Queen Elizabeth' appear in a variety of soft pink shades in great abundance from summer to fall. They are borne singly or in clusters on extremely long stems, opening from pointed buds to lightly scented, cupped flowers. This was the first grandiflora rose introduced, and many consider it to be still the finest. Leaves are leathery, dark green, and glossy; stems are purplish brown and nearly thornless.

The tall, upright, vigorous plant is easy to grow and should not be overpruned. It can be effective planted either alone or in groups in beds or borders, or it may be used as a tall flowering hedge. The long-stemmed flowers are ideal for cutting and exhibition. Plants are disease resistant. This rose is an AARS winner.

'RISE 'N' SHINE'

Classification: *miniature*

Bloom period: *summer to fall*

Height: *12 to 16 inches*

Hardiness: *Zones 5-10*

ARS rating: *9.1*

Date introduced: *1977*

The 1½- to 2-inch blossoms of 'Rise 'n' Shine' are a bright, clear yellow, providing a dramatic contrast with foliage that is dark and glossy. The buds are long and pointed and open to high-centered flowers with 35 petals. Blossoms are borne singly or in clusters continuously throughout the summer, with a good repeat. They bear little fragrance.

Plants are upright and well branched, forming a short, rounded bush. They are perfect for edgings and containers and can easily be incorporated into beds or borders. They are easy to grow and disease resistant.

ROSA BANKSIAE BANKSIAE

Classification: *species*

Bloom period: *spring to early summer*

Height: *12 to 25 feet*

Hardiness: *Zones 8-10*

ARS rating: *8.6*

Date introduced: *1807*

The double white flowers of *R. banksiae banksiae* appear in profusion in spring and continue for up to 6 weeks. The flowers cover the plant during this period. Each blossom is less than 1 inch across, pure white, and extremely fragrant with the scent of violets. Leaves are long, light green, and shiny, and the canes are nearly thornless.

Where it is hardy, this rose is a fast, vigorous grower and is quite long-lived. It grows well on a tree, wall, or trellis but may become rampant where the growth is not controlled. The related variety *R. banksiae lutea* bears pale to deep yellow double flowers and is slightly hardier and less fragrant; its ARS rating is 8.8. Both varieties are known as the Lady Banks' Rose.

ROSA EGLANTERIA

Classification: *species*

Bloom period: *late spring*

Height: *8 to 14 feet*

Hardiness: *Zones 5-10*

ARS rating: *8.6*

Date introduced: *prior to 1551*

R. eglanteria is commonly called the sweetbrier or eglantine rose. Its single blush pink flowers are 2 inches across, with petals surrounding golden stamens. They appear singly or in small clusters in late spring. Bright red hips follow the flowers. The leaves are tough and dark green and are distinctly apple scented, while flowers are sweetly fragrant. Canes bear abundant prickles.

This is a large, vigorous rose with a rambling habit. It has become naturalized in North America and can be found growing in pastures. In the garden, plants should be heavily pruned to contain them and to encourage new growth, which is especially fragrant.

'ROSA MUNDI'

Classification: *gallica*

Bloom period: *summer*

Height: *3 to 4 feet*

Hardiness: *Zones 4-10*

ARS rating: *8.6*

Date introduced: *prior to 1581*

'Rosa Mundi' (*R. gallica versicolor*) is a sport of 'Apothecary's Rose' (*R. gallica officinalis*). Its 2- to 3-inch semidouble flowers are spectacularly striped crimson, pink, and deep pink over blush white. Borne singly or in small sprays, the very fragrant flowers open to wide and flattened cups. An occasional branch will revert to the deep-pink-colored flowers of its parent. Red hips appear in late summer. Leaves are a dark matte green, and stems are nearly smooth.

This upright, bushy rose is very hardy and tolerates summer heat and humidity. It is useful in beds or borders, and its flowers can be used for indoor arrangements and potpourri. This rose is somewhat prone to mildew.

'RUGOSA MAGNIFICA'

Classification: *hybrid rugosa*

Bloom period: *spring to fall*

Height: *4 to 6 feet*

Hardiness: *Zones 3-9*

ARS rating: *8.3*

Date introduced: *1905*

The deep red-purple to lavender petals of repeat-blooming 'Rugosa Magnifica' surround golden yellow stamens. The fragrant blooms are double and are followed by abundant large orange-red hips. Foliage is dense.

This shrub is a very vigorous grower with a wide-spreading habit. It is good in mixed-shrub plantings, as a specimen, or as a hedge. Like other hybrid rugosas, it is extremely hardy and disease resistant, adapts to a wide range of soils, and tolerates seaside conditions.

'SEXY REXY'

Classification: *floribunda*

Bloom period: *spring to fall*

Height: *3 feet*

Hardiness: *Zones 4-10*

ARS rating: *9.0*

Date introduced: *1984*

The 2½- to 3½-inch double flowers of 'Sexy Rexy' are carried in large clusters throughout the season. Each mildly fragrant blossom is composed of 40 or more medium to light pink petals. Flowers flatten as they mature. The abundant small leaves are light green and glossy.

This free-flowering rose is vigorous and bushy. It is effective in beds with perennials or in front of taller roses, where it can cover leggy stems. It also makes an attractive low hedge. Plants are very disease resistant.

'SHOWBIZ'

Classification: *floribunda*

Bloom period: *summer to fall*

Height: *2½ to 3 feet*

Hardiness: *Zones 4-10*

ARS rating: *8.6*

Date introduced: *1981*

The short, pointed buds of 'Showbiz' open to 2½- to 3-inch scarlet flowers. Blooming in large sprays, they are double and loosely cupped, with ruffled petals and bright yellow stamens, and have a slight fragrance. The abundant leaves are dark green and glossy.

This rose is bushy, low, and compact. A fine contribution to beds and borders with its boldly colored blooms and rich foliage, it can also be planted in numbers as an attractive low hedge or mass planting. The flowers are good for cutting, and plants are disease resistant. 'Showbiz' is an AARS winner.

'SIMPLICITY'	'SOUVENIR DE LA MALMAISON'	'SUN FLARE'	'SUNSPRITE'

Classification: *floribunda*

Bloom period: *summer to fall*

Height: *3 to 6 feet*

Hardiness: *Zones 4-10*

ARS rating: *8.1*

Date introduced: *1979*

Classification: *bourbon*

Bloom period: *summer to fall*

Height: *3 feet*

Hardiness: *Zones 5-9*

ARS rating: *8.4*

Date introduced: *1843*

Classification: *floribunda*

Bloom period: *summer to fall*

Height: *2 to 3 feet*

Hardiness: *Zones 4-10*

ARS rating: *8.1*

Date introduced: *1983*

Classification: *floribunda*

Bloom period: *spring to fall*

Height: *2½ to 3 feet*

Hardiness: *Zones 5-10*

ARS rating: *8.7*

Date introduced: *1977*

The 3- to 4-inch semidouble flowers of 'Simplicity' are borne in clusters. Each blossom is cupped or flattened, with 18 medium pink petals surrounding yellow stamens that darken with age. Flowers bear little fragrance. Foliage is a fresh light to medium green and is semiglossy.

Bushy and dense with graceful, arching canes, 'Simplicity' is an excellent choice for a hedge; when first introduced it was even marketed as a "living fence." It also works well in beds and borders, and the flowers are good for cutting. Plants are disease resistant.

The delicate blush pink blossoms of 'Souvenir de la Malmaison' are slightly darker toward the center. They are cupped when they first open but gradually flatten into flowers that are 4 to 5 inches across. As the blooms age they fade slightly to almost white. Flowers are double and quartered, with a rich, spicy fragrance. Foliage is medium green and glossy.

This rose is a bit of a challenge to grow. It thrives in hot, dry weather but does poorly during wet periods, when buds may refuse to open. Dwarf, bushy, and rounded, it is lovely in beds and borders. A climbing form, rated 8.2 by the ARS, reaches 6 to 8 feet and is well suited to growing up a pillar.

The small, pointed buds of 'Sun Flare' open to 3-inch flat, double blossoms. Colored bright lemon yellow, the flowers have 25 to 30 petals and a licorice fragrance. They are borne freely, mostly in large clusters but sometimes singly. The leaves are very glossy and deep green, providing a dramatic foil for the blooms.

Plants are vigorous, with a round, somewhat spreading habit. Attractive landscape plants, they are well suited to many purposes, including beds, borders, and hedges. Flowers are good for cutting. 'Sun Flare' is highly disease resistant, a rare trait in a yellow rose. It's an AARS winner.

The high-centered oval buds of 'Sunsprite' open to deep yellow flowers. Appearing in clusters of five or more, the blossoms are double, each with about 28 petals, and are richly scented. Flowers are borne continuously throughout the season. Foliage is light green and glossy.

This rose has a compact, upright habit. It is suitable for use in beds and borders, where its low growth neatly covers the base of taller, leggier plants. Its flowers are excellent for cutting and exhibition. It is disease resistant.

'TOUCH OF CLASS'	**'TUSCANY'**	**'UNCLE JOE'**	**'VARIEGATA DI BOLOGNA'**

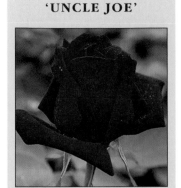

Classification: *hybrid tea*

Bloom period: *summer to fall*

Height: *4 feet*

Hardiness: *Zones 5-10*

ARS rating: *9.5*

Date introduced: *1984*

Classification: *gallica*

Bloom period: *spring*

Height: *3 to 4 feet*

Hardiness: *Zones 4-10*

ARS rating: *7.7*

Date introduced: *prior to 1820*

Classification: *hybrid tea*

Bloom period: *summer to fall*

Height: *5 feet*

Hardiness: *Zones 5-10*

ARS rating: *7.7*

Date introduced: *1971*

Classification: *bourbon*

Bloom period: *summer*

Height: *5 to 8 feet*

Hardiness: *Zones 5-9*

ARS rating: *7.6*

Date introduced: *1909*

'Touch of Class' produces spiraled orange buds whose color takes on coral and cream shading as they open and eventually evolves to pink. Flowers are 4½ to 5½ inches across and double. They have little or no fragrance. Usually borne singly on long stems, the blooms are attractively set off against dark green, semiglossy foliage.

This rose has a tall, upright, bushy habit. It is well suited to beds and borders, where it produces its flowers over a lengthy season. The long-stemmed blooms are long-lasting in indoor arrangements. Foliage is prone to mildew. 'Touch of Class' is an AARS winner.

The large semidouble flowers of 'Tuscany' are dark crimson to deep purple with a velvety texture. Petals are flat and are arranged around prominent yellow stamens, creating a dramatic contrast. Although very fragrant, the flowers are not as heavily scented as some gallicas. They appear in abundance in spring and do not repeat. Leaves are small and dark green.

The vigorous plants have a tidy, rounded form and are well suited to small gardens. The intense colors of the flowers make them spectacular in bloom. They are winter-hardy and tolerant of summer heat and humidity.

'Uncle Joe' (sometimes listed as 'Toro') bears its 6-inch double blooms singly on long stems. The buds open slowly to become high-centered medium to dark red flowers with a strong fragrance. The large, leathery leaves are a glossy dark green.

Plants are vigorous growers with a tall, upright habit. Their stems are quite strong and amply able to hold up the huge blossoms. This rose is suitable for beds and borders and is excellent for cutting. Cool, damp weather may stunt the production of flowers.

No two flowers of 'Variegata di Bologna' are exactly alike in coloration: Petals are white and individually striped with various shades of crimson and purple. The very double blooms are 3 to 4 inches across and globular, flattening and quartering with age. Borne in clusters of three to five, the blossoms bear a strong and long-lasting fragrance. They appear in abundance in midseason but repeat sparsely, if at all. Leaves are narrow and glossy; canes are nearly smooth.

The bushes are vigorous, upright, and slender, and are versatile in the landscape. Their long, flexible canes are easily trained to climb a fence, trellis, or pillar, or can be pegged. Heavy pruning will produce a more compact, 4- to 5-foot shrub suitable for borders. Flowers are good for cutting.

Abies
(AY-beez)
FIR

Abies concolor

Hardiness: *Zones 3-7*

Plant type: *tree*

Height: *30 to 50 feet or more*

Interest: *form, foliage*

Soil: *moist to dry, well-drained*

Light: *full sun*

White fir develops into a grand evergreen pyramid ideal as a specimen, screen, or vertical accent. The upper branches are upright in habit; the middle and lower, horizontal to descending. The trees bear flat, aromatic needles that have blunt tips and a glaucous coating. Greenish or purplish cones, up to 6 inches long, mature to a brown hue and fall apart when ripe.

Selected species and varieties: *A. concolor* (white fir, Colorado fir)—30 to 50 feet high (but reaching 100 feet under ideal conditions) by 15 to 30 feet wide, having a central trunk with whorled branches and producing bluish green, grayish green, or silvery blue needles up to 2½ inches long; 'Compacta' is a densely branched dwarf usually 3 feet high, with 1½-inch blue needles, acquiring an attractively irregular form as it matures.

Growing conditions and maintenance: Although white firs accept dry, rocky soils, they grow better in deep, sandy or gravelly loams. They withstand drought, heat, cold, and air pollution better than other firs. They tolerate light shade but fare best in full sun. Mulch well with shredded bark, woodchips, or leaves.

Acer
(AY-ser)
MAPLE

Acer griseum

Hardiness: *Zones 2-9*

Plant type: *shrub or tree*

Height: *6 to 75 feet*

Interest: *foliage, form, fruit*

Soil: *moist, well-drained*

Light: *full sun to partial shade*

The genus *Acer* includes a diverse group of deciduous plants ranging from towering trees with brilliant fall foliage to small, picturesque specimens ideal as centerpieces for ornamental beds. The mid-size maples included here are good specimen or patio trees. Flowers are usually inconspicuous, followed by winged seeds.

Selected species and varieties: *A. ginnala* (Amur maple, fire maple)—15 to 25 feet tall, usually branched close to the ground, with a canopy wider than its height, bearing serrated medium to dark green three-lobed leaves 1½ to 3 inches long that unfurl early in spring along with small, fragrant, yellowish white flower panicles, followed by winged fruits, often red, that persist to late fall; Zones 2-8. *A. griseum* (paperbark maple)—oval- to round-crowned tree 20 to 30 feet tall with up to an equal spread, clad in exfoliating reddish brown bark and producing dark green to blue-green leaves with three leaflets that may turn red in fall; Zones 4-8. *A. macrophyllum* (bigleaf maple, Oregon maple)—three- to five-lobed leaves 8 to 12 inches wide that turn yellow to orange in fall on a wide-crowned, 45- to 75-

foot-tall tree with fragrant greenish yellow flowers in nodding clusters that appear with the leaves in spring; hardy to Zone 5. *A. nigrum* [also classified as *A. saccharum* ssp. *nigrum*] (black maple)—a 60- to 75-foot-tall tree closely related to the sugar maple with drooping lobed leaves 3 to 6 inches wide that turn a brilliant yellow in fall; Zones 4-8. *A. palmatum* (Japanese maple)—slow-growing tree or multistemmed shrub 15 to 25 feet tall and at least as wide, with deeply cut leaves having five, seven, or nine lobes, and young stems that are reddish purple to green and become gray with age, Zones 5-8; 'Bloodgood' grows upright to 15 to 20 feet with maroon or reddish purple leaves that turn scarlet in fall, blackish red bark, and attractive red fruit; 'Dissectum' (threadleaf Japanese maple) is a small, pendulous, lacy shrub usually 6 to 8 feet tall, with drooping

Acer palmatum 'Dissectum'

green-barked branches that bear very finely divided pale green leaves with up to 11 lobes that turn yellow in fall; 'Dissectum Atropurpureum' has a moundlike appearance similar to 'Dissectum', with lacy purple-red new leaves that fade to green or purple-green and turn crimson or burnt orange in fall, as well as tortuous branching that is most apparent in winter. *A. rubrum* (red maple, scarlet maple, Canadian maple)—a medium- to fast-growing tree to 60 feet tall, and sometimes much taller, with ascending branches forming an irregular, oval to rounded crown 20 feet wide and with reddish twigs bearing red 1-inch flowers in early spring followed by red winged seeds, then small, shiny, three- to five-lobed green leaves yielding a dazzling fall color that is unreliable in the species but consistent among cultivars; 'Autumn Blaze' [*A.* x *freemanii*] is a fast-growing cultivar reaching 50 feet tall by 40 feet wide exhibiting superb orange-red fall color on its dense, oval to rounded crown, hardy to Zone 4; 'October Glory' has a round crown and vivid bright orange to red foliage in midfall, holding late into the season and coloring well in the South. *A. saccharum* (sugar maple, rock maple)—60 to 75 feet tall with a spread about two-thirds the height in a symmetrical crown bearing greenish yellow flowers in spring and three- or five-lobed medium to dark green leaves

Acer rubrum 'October Glory'

that turn yellow, burnt orange, or reddish in fall; Zones 3-8.

Growing conditions and maintenance: Most maples can withstand occasional drought; red maples grow naturally in wet soil. Bigleaf maples prefer a cool, moist climate like that of their native Pacific Northwest. Sugar and red maples prefer slight acidity but tolerate other soil types. *A. rubrum* 'Autumn Blaze' is said to be slightly more drought tolerant than true red maple cultivars. Amur and paperbark maples tolerate a wide range of acid and alkaline soils. Japanese maples need highly organic loam; amend the soil with peat moss or leaf mold before planting. The finely divided foliage of threadleaf maples often shows leaf burn in hot, dry climates; find a spot sheltered from strong winds, late spring frosts, and searing sun. Amur and sugar maples tolerate some shade. Large maples have extensive, fibrous root systems that crowd the soil's surface in search of water and nutrients, making it difficult to sustain significant plantings beneath them.

Aesculus
(ES-kew-lus)
BUCKEYE

Aesculus glabra

Hardiness: *Zones 3-7*

Plant type: *tree*

Height: *20 to 40 feet*

Interest: *foliage, form, buds*

Soil: *moist, well-drained, slightly acid*

Light: *full sun to partial shade*

One of the first trees to leaf out in spring, the buckeye (also called horse chestnut) is a low-branched, round-topped tree with deep green five-fingered compound leaves that turn a vibrant orange in fall. Its large greenish yellow spring flowers are usually lost amid the foliage. The fruit is a brown seed capsule with a prickly cover, considered by some to be a good-luck charm. Buckeyes cast deep shade, discouraging grass below. Plant them in a naturalized area or a mulched bed where leaf, flower, and fruit litter will not be a nuisance. The seeds are poisonous.

Selected species and varieties: *A. glabra* (Ohio buckeye, fetid buckeye)—20 to 40 feet tall with an equal spread, bearing medium to dark green leaflets 3 to 6 inches long that open bright green, followed by flower panicles up to 7 inches long, and later 1- to 2-inch oval fruit.

Growing conditions and maintenance: A native of rich bottomlands and riverbanks, the Ohio buckeye prefers deep loam. Mulch well to conserve moisture; dry soil causes leaf scorch. Prune in the early spring.

Aucuba
(aw-KEW-ba)
AUCUBA

Aucuba japonica 'Variegata'

Hardiness: *Zones 7-10*

Plant type: *evergreen shrub*

Height: *6 to 10 feet*

Interest: *foliage, fruit*

Soil: *moist, well-drained, fertile*

Light: *partial to deep shade*

A rounded, upright shrub with large, leathery leaves that are often marked with gold or yellow, aucuba brightens shady areas. An excellent transition plant between woodland and garden, it is also useful for hedges and borders. If a male plant is nearby, female aucubas produce scarlet berries that last all winter but are often hidden by the foliage. Leaf color remains unchanged throughout the seasons.

Selected species and varieties: *A. japonica* (Japanese aucuba, Japanese laurel, spotted laurel)—lustrous medium to dark green leaves 3 to 8 inches long and up to 3 inches wide that dominate tiny purple flowers borne in erect panicles in early spring and ½-inch-wide bright red berries; 'Variegata' (gold-dust plant) is female and has deep green leaves heavily sprinkled with yellow.

Growing conditions and maintenance: Aucuba prefers slightly acid loam but will tolerate other soils. Once established, it withstands moderate drought. Full shade is best to maintain leaf color; direct sun—particularly in warmer climates—tends to blacken the foliage. Prune to control height and maintain shape.

Betula
(BET-u-la)
BIRCH

Betula nigra

Hardiness: *Zones 2-9*

Plant type: *tree*

Height: *40 to 70 feet*

Interest: *bark, form, foliage*

Soil: *moist, acid*

Light: *full sun*

Birches grace the landscape with trunks of decorative bark and airy canopies of medium to dark green finely toothed leaves that flutter in the slightest breeze and turn yellow in fall before dropping. Male and female flowers, called catkins, are borne on the same tree. Birches create a light dappled shade and are lovely in groups or singly as specimens.

Selected species and varieties: *B. nigra* (river birch, red birch, black birch)—40 to 70 feet tall with a spread almost equal to its height, usually multitrunked, with cinnamon brown bark, peeling when young and becoming deeply furrowed into irregular plates with age, and nearly triangular leaves to 3½ inches long that often show brief fall color; Zones 4-9. *B. papyrifera* (paper birch, canoe birch, white birch, cluster birch)—a low-branched tree with reddish brown bark when young, aging to creamy white and peeling thinly to reveal reddish orange tissue beneath, growing 50 to 70 feet tall by 25 to 45 feet in spread, and bearing 2- to 4-inch roundish, wedge-shaped leaves turning a lovely yellow in fall; Zones 2-7. *B. pendula* (European white birch, silver

birch, warty birch, common birch)—graceful, drooping branches on a 40- to 50-foot-tall by 20- to 35-foot-wide tree with the bark on trunk and main limbs changing slowly from whitish to mostly black-on-white with age, golden brown twigs and slender branches bearing serrated, almost diamond-shaped leaves 1 to 3 inches long that hold later in the fall than do the other species but often show little fall color, Zones 2-7; 'Dalecarlica' (cutleaf weeping birch, Swedish birch) has pendulous branches that arc to touch the ground and dangling, deeply lobed and sharply toothed leaves.

Growing conditions and maintenance: Give birches optimum growing conditions and keep a sharp eye out for insects

Betula papyrifera

or disease. Although river birches can thrive in periodic flooding, most species need good drainage and grow best in loose, rich, acid loams. Paper birch and European white birch tolerate neutral soils, but river birch must have acid soil. Amend soil with peat moss, leaf mold, or finished compost. Add sand if the soil is heavy. Mulch to retain moisture and to protect from lawn-mower damage. All birches bleed heavily in late winter or early spring; prune in summer or fall. Bottom branches on paper birch can easily be removed to create a high-branched specimen tree. Although river birch and paper birch are resistant to the bronze birch borer, European white birch is quite susceptible and may succumb if a routine spraying program is not followed. Most birches live about 50 years.

Carpinus
(car-PY-nis)
HORNBEAM

Carpinus betulus 'Fastigiata'

Hardiness: *Zones 4-7*

Plant type: *tree*

Height: *30 to 60 feet*

Interest: *foliage, form, bark*

Soil: *well-drained*

Light: *full sun to partial shade*

A deciduous tree with crisp summer foliage, smooth gray bark, and a well-contoured winter silhouette, hornbeam (also called ironwood) makes a handsome specimen tree. Because it has dense foliage that takes well to pruning, however, it is often used as a hedge or screen. The dark green leaves may turn yellow or brown in fall. Hornbeam has extremely hard wood that was once used to make ox yokes.

Selected species and varieties: *C. betulus* (European hornbeam, common hornbeam)—pyramidal when young, maturing to a rounded crown, 40 to 60 feet tall under average conditions with a spread of 30 to 40 feet, bearing sharply toothed leaves 2½ to 5 inches long and 1 to 2 inches wide that remain unusually pest free; 'Columnaris' has a densely branched, steeple-shaped outline; 'Fastigiata' grows 30 to 40 feet tall with a spread of 20 to 30 feet, an oval to vaselike shape, and a forked trunk.

Growing conditions and maintenance: A highly adaptable and trouble-free plant, European hornbeam tolerates a wide range of soil conditions.

Ceanothus
(see-a-NO-thus)
WILD LILAC, REDROOT

Ceanothus arboreus

Hardiness: *Zones 7-11*

Plant type: *tree, shrub, or ground cover*

Height: *18 inches to 25 feet*

Interest: *flowers*

Soil: *well-drained to dry*

Light: *full sun*

Wild lilacs are widely used on slopes and in masses in West Coast gardens. They improve the soil by fixing nitrogen. Evergreen forms bloom in spring.

Selected species and varieties: *C. arboreus* (Catalina mountain lilac, feltleaf ceanothus)—blue plumes on a 25-foot-tall shrub or tree with 4-inch evergreen leaves; Zones 9-10. *C.* x *delilianus*—3-foot deciduous shrub with 4- to 6-inch blue flowers in summer and fall and dark green leaves 3 inches long; 'Gloire de Versailles' grows 6 feet tall with fragrant lavender-blue flowers; hardy to Zone 7. *C. griseus* var. *horizontalis* (Carmel creeper)—18 to 30 inches tall and 5 to 15 feet wide with light blue flower clusters 1 inch wide and glossy 2-inch-long evergreen leaves; hardy to Zone 8. *C. thyrsiflorus* 'Skylark' (blueblossom)—dark blue spikes bloom on a broad 3- to 6-foot-tall shrub with 2-inch-long evergreen leaves; hardy to Zone 8.

Growing conditions and maintenance: Wild lilacs thrive on rocky slopes that usually stay dry all summer. Plant them in light, sandy soil, and water only during their first season. Fast drainage is a must.

Cedrus
(SEE-drus)
CEDAR

Cedrus deodora

Hardiness: *Zones 6-9*

Plant type: *evergreen tree*

Height: *100 to 150 feet*

Interest: *form, foliage*

Soil: *well-drained*

Light: *full sun*

Cedars grow into magnificent specimen trees, their sweeping branches and great height best displayed on broad lawns.

Selected species and varieties: *C. atlantica* (Atlas cedar)—slowly reaches more than 100 feet tall and two-thirds as wide, appearing open and spindly when young but maturing into a flat-topped shape with bluish green or sometimes green to silvery blue inch-long needles and 3-inch-long cones that take 2 years to mature; 'Glauca' (blue Atlas cedar) has rich blue needles. *C. deodara* (deodar cedar)—pyramidal and more attractive when young than Atlas cedar, becoming flat topped and broad with age, growing 40 to 70 feet tall with a nearly equal spread but sometimes reaching 150 feet, with light blue to grayish green needles up to 1½ inches long, a gracefully drooping habit, and 3- to 4-inch cones; Zones 7-8.

Growing conditions and maintenance: Give both species ample room to develop in a site protected from strong winds. Atlas cedar grows best in moist, deep loam but will tolerate other soils as long as they are well drained. A moderately dry site is best for deodar cedar.

Chaenomeles
(kee-NOM-e-lees)
FLOWERING QUINCE

Chaenomeles speciosa 'Texas Scarlet'

Hardiness: *Zones 4-8*

Plant type: *deciduous shrub*

Height: *3 to 10 feet*

Interest: *flowers*

Soil: *moist to dry, acid*

Light: *full sun*

A thorny, rounded, spreading shrub, flowering quince's best attribute is its showy profusion of early-spring flowers before the foliage appears. The small, yellowish green quincelike fruits that ripen in fall can be used for jams and jellies but cannot be eaten raw. The shrub's dense, twiggy branching makes a coarse winter silhouette. Budded stems can be used for late-winter arrangements.

Selected species and varieties: *C. speciosa* (common flowering quince, Japanese quince)—6 to 10 feet tall with equal or greater width, usually with red or scarlet, but sometimes pink or white, flowers and lustrous dark green leaves that open bronzy red; 'Cameo' produces peachy pink double flowers; 'Nivalis', white flowers; 'Texas Scarlet', profuse tomato red flowers on a 3- to 5-foot plant.

Growing conditions and maintenance: Flowering quince adapts to most soils except the very alkaline. Full sun produces the best bloom. Restore vigor and improve flowering by cutting out older branches. Leaf spot and too much spring rain can cause a loss of foliage, but some leaf drop by midsummer is normal.

Chamaecyparis
(kam-ee-SIP-a-ris)
FALSE CYPRESS

Chamaecyparis obtusa

Cladrastis
(cla-DRAS-tis)
YELLOWWOOD

Cladrastis kentukea

Cornus
(KOR-nus)
DOGWOOD

Cornus florida

Hardiness: *Zones 4-8*

Plant type: *shrub or tree*

Height: *4 to 75 feet*

Interest: *form, foliage*

Soil: *well-drained, fertile, acid to neutral*

Light: *full sun to partial shade*

False cypresses are coniferous evergreen specimen trees with fan-shaped, flattened branch tips and scalelike foliage.

Selected species and varieties: *C. lawsoniana* (Lawson false cypress, Lawson cypress, Port Orford cedar)—40- to 60-foot columnar tree with massive central trunk, short ascending branches with drooping tips, and glaucous green to dark green foliage, Zones 5-7; 'Allumii' grows a narrow silvery blue spire to 30 feet. *C. obtusa* (hinoki false cypress, hinoki cypress)—dark green slender pyramid growing 50 to 75 feet tall; 'Crippsii' forms a broad pyramid with drooping golden yellow branch tips; 'Gracilis' takes a narrow conical form, 6 to 10 feet tall; 'Nana Gracilis' has very dark green foliage arranged in slightly curved sprays, making for an attractive accent plant 4 to 6 feet tall and 3 to 4 feet wide.

Growing conditions and maintenance: Although hinoki false cypress is moderately tolerant of light shade and drier climates, most other species prefer full sun in cool, moist climates. Provide partial shade in hot regions and protect from drying wind. Amend soil with peat moss or leaf mold to hold moisture.

Hardiness: *Zones 4-8*

Plant type: *tree*

Height: *30 to 50 feet*

Interest: *flowers, foliage, form, bark*

Soil: *well-drained*

Light: *full sun*

An excellent deciduous shade tree for small landscapes, yellowwood produces long, hanging panicles of fragrant flowers in mid- to late spring and a broad canopy of bright green foliage that turns yellow in fall. The bark is smooth and gray. Open, delicate, zigzag branching creates an airy form. The color of the interior wood gives the tree its name. Flowering is best every second or third year.

Selected species and varieties: *C. kentukea* [formerly called *C. lutea*] (American yellowwood, Kentucky yellowwood, virgilia)—low-branching habit with a rounded crown 40 to 55 feet wide, producing 3- to 4-inch-long compound leaves opening bright yellowish green before darkening slightly later, with flower clusters up to 14 inches long, and thin brown seedpods 4 to 5 inches long in fall.

Growing conditions and maintenance: Although it occurs naturally on rich, limestone soils, American yellowwood adapts to a wide range of soil types from acid to alkaline and is remarkably pest free. Once established, it is drought tolerant. Prune only in summer to prevent heavy sap bleeding.

Hardiness: *Zones 3-9*

Plant type: *large shrub or small tree*

Height: *15 to 30 feet*

Interest: *flowers, foliage, fruit, form, bark*

Soil: *well-drained*

Light: *bright shade to full sun*

Dogwoods can turn the spring landscape into a fairyland and in fall provide bright red fruit for birds. They may also offer red to reddish purple fall foliage, colorful bark, and low, layered branching for an attractive winter silhouette.

Selected species and varieties: *C. alternifolia* (pagoda dogwood, green osier)—strongly fragrant yellowish white flowers borne in flat clusters 1½ to 2½ inches wide on a horizontally branched tree growing 15 to 25 feet tall with a greater spread and tierlike habit, also bearing fruit that matures from green to red to blue-black; Zones 3-7. *C. florida* (flowering dogwood)—small tree with broad crown, usually 20 to 30 feet tall with an equal or greater spread, producing white flowerlike bracts lasting 10 to 14 days in spring before the leaves emerge, followed in fall by small glossy red fruits borne in clusters of at least three to four; Zones 5-9. *C. kousa* (kousa dogwood)—large shrub or small tree 20 to 30 feet tall and wide with exfoliating gray, tan, and brown bark and tiered branching, flowering in late spring after the leaves appear and lasting for up to 6 weeks, followed by pink to red fruit up to 1 inch wide in late summer to fall, when the leaves turn reddish purple or scarlet, Zones 5-8; var. *chinensis* (Chinese dogwood)—grows to 30 feet and has larger bracts than the species. *C. mas* (cornelian cherry, sorbet)—multistemmed shrub or small, oval to round tree 20 to 25 feet tall and 15 to 20 feet wide, branching nearly to the ground with attractive exfoliating gray to brown bark, bearing small clusters of yellow flowers for 3 weeks in early spring and bright red fruit in midsummer that is partly hidden by the lustrous dark green leaves, 2 to 4 inches long, that usually show little fall color; Zones 4-8.

Growing conditions and maintenance: Give flowering and pagoda dogwoods a moist, acid soil enriched with leaf mold, peat moss, or compost. Partial shade is

Cornus mas

best in hotter areas. Mulch to keep soil cool and prevent lawn-mower damage, which invites invasion by dogwood borers. Kousa dogwood prefers loose, sandy, acid soil, rich with organic matter, in sunny locations. It is more drought tolerant than flowering dogwood. Although adaptable to a wide range of soil types, cornelian cherry prefers moist, rich sites in sun or partial shade and is probably the best performer of the dogwoods for the Midwest. Susceptible to the usually fatal anthracnose, which has killed many dogwoods on the East Coast, flowering dogwood has a better chance of staying healthy if stress is reduced. The other dogwoods listed here appear not to be affected. For colder climates, the best bud hardiness in flowering dogwoods occurs in trees native to those regions.

Cotinus
(ko-TYE-nus)
SMOKE TREE

Cotinus coggygria 'Velvet Cloak'

Hardiness: *Zones 5-9*

Plant type: *shrub*

Height: *10 to 15 feet*

Interest: *fruiting panicles*

Soil: *well-drained*

Light: *full sun*

For most of the summer and early fall, smokebush almost explodes with puffy, smoky pink plumes, actually hairs arising from the 6- to 8-inch fruiting stalks as the tiny yellowish flowers fade. An eye-catching accent plant that often has colorful fall foliage, smokebush also works well in borders and groupings.

Selected species and varieties: *C. coggygria* (common smokebush, smoke plant, Venetian sumac, wig tree)—a loose and open multistemmed deciduous shrub, 10 to 15 feet wide, bearing 1½- to 3-inch-long leaves that unfurl pink-bronze in midspring, mature to medium blue-green, and sometimes show yellow-red-purple fall color and branched puffs changing to gray; 'Royal Purple' has purplish maroon leaves with scarlet margins, eventually turning scarlet all over; 'Velvet Cloak', purple plumes and velvety dark purple leaves throughout the summer before changing to reddish purple in fall.

Growing conditions and maintenance: Tolerant of a wide range of soils, smokebush demands only that a site be well drained. Too-rich or too-moist soil reduces bloom and subdues leaf color.

x *Cupressocyparis*
(kew-press-oh-SIP-ar-iss)
LEYLAND CYPRESS

x Cupressocyparis leylandii 'Silver Dust'

Hardiness: *Zones 6-10*

Plant type: *evergreen tree*

Height: *60 to 70 feet*

Interest: *foliage, form*

Soil: *adaptable*

Light: *full sun*

A dense, towering, columnar or pyramidal tree when left unchecked, x *Cupressocyparis*—a hybrid of *Cupressus* and *Chamaecyparis*—produces some of the fastest-growing and finest-textured screen or hedge plants available. The fanlike arrangement of bluish green scalelike needles appears soft and feathery.

Selected species and varieties: x *C. leylandii* (Leyland cypress)—a cross between *Cupressus macrocarpa* (Monterey cypress) and *Chamaecyparis nootkatensis* (Alaska cedar) that grows 3 feet a year or more to 70 feet tall and usually 10 to 18 feet wide, with reddish brown scaly bark; cultivars include silvery green, variegated, and golden yellow forms; 'Silver Dust' has creamy white markings on green foliage.

Growing conditions and maintenance: Leyland cypress grows best in moist, well-drained, moderately fertile loams but is very tolerant of almost any soil. Provide protection from drying winter winds. It is best transplanted from a container; field-grown plants are hard to ball and burlap. Unaffected by serious pests, it also resists sea winds and cold damage.

Fagus
(FAY-gus)
BEECH

Fagus sylvatica 'Atropunicea'

Hardiness: *Zones 3-9*

Plant type: *tree*

Height: *50 to 70 feet or more*

Interest: *form, foliage*

Soil: *moist, well-drained, acid*

Light: *full sun to dappled shade*

Long-lived beeches have massive trunks clad in smooth gray bark. In spring, as inconspicuous flowers form, silky leaves unfurl, turning bronze or ochre in the fall. Nuts are small but edible. Shallow rooted, often with branches sweeping the ground, beeches usually inhibit grass.

Selected species and varieties: *F. grandifolia* (American beech)—50 to 70 feet tall and almost as wide, with light gray bark and toothy leaves 2 to 5 inches long, dark green above and light green below. *F. sylvatica* (common beech, European beech, red beech)—usually 50 to 60 feet tall and 35 to 45 feet wide, with elephant-hide bark, branching close to the ground, Zones 4-7; 'Atropunicea' ['Atropurpurea'] (purple beech, copper beech) has black-red new leaves that turn purple-green; 'Aurea Pendula' is a weeping form with yellow new leaves aging to yellow-green; 'Dawyck Purple' grows in a narrow column with deep purple leaves.

Growing conditions and maintenance: Although both species listed here enjoy acid soil, European beech adapts to most soils. Best growth occurs in full sun.

Fargesia
(far-JEEZ-ee-a)
BAMBOO

Fargesia murielae

Hardiness: *Zones 5-9*

Plant type: *woody grass*

Height: *10 to 15 feet or more*

Interest: *form, foliage*

Soil: *adaptable*

Light: *partial shade*

Narrow, tapered dark green leaves flutter from purplish sheaths on slender purplish gray culms, or canes, that arch as they mature and spread to form mounded clumps. Use as a dramatic color and vertical accent in ornamental beds. Cut canes make good garden stakes.

Selected species and varieties: *F. murielae* [also classified as *Thamnocalamus spathaceus*] (umbrella bamboo)—slender bright green canes to 12 feet tall, aging to yellow, bend at the top under the weight of rich green leaves 3 to 5 inches long that turn yellow in fall before dropping; hardy to Zone 6. *F. nitida* [also classified as *Sinarundinaria nitida*] (clump bamboo, hardy blue bamboo, fountain bamboo)—hollow dark purple canes ½ inch in diameter and 10 to 15 feet tall (reaching 20 feet under optimum conditions) are coated with a bluish white powder when young and, after the first year, produce leaves to 7 inches long with bristly margins on one side.

Growing conditions and maintenance: As clumps begin to develop above soil level, divide and replant. Clump bamboo is less invasive than umbrella bamboo.

Fraxinus
(FRAK-si-nus)
ASH

Fraxinus pennsylvanica

Hardiness: *Zones 2-9*

Plant type: *tree*

Height: *45 to 80 feet*

Interest: *foliage*

Soil: *wet to dry*

Light: *full sun*

Ashes are moderate- to fast-growing trees that give light shade. In fall, the leaves may crumble after they drop, requiring little if any raking. Small greenish yellow flowers are borne on separate male and female trees in spring. Paddle-shaped winged seeds on female trees germinate easily and may become a nuisance. Select a male clone or a seedless variety.

Selected species and varieties: *F. americana* (white ash)—to 80 feet tall with an open, rounded crown, with compound leaves, dark green above and pale below, that turn a rich yellow, then maroon to purple in fall, hardy to Zone 3; 'Champaign County', to 45 feet, with a dense canopy of leaves. *F. pennsylvanica* (red ash, green ash)—50 to 60 feet tall with an irregular crown half as wide, bearing shiny green leaves that may turn yellow in fall, to Zone 3; 'Patmore', a seedless form, grows 45 feet tall, with a symmetrical, upright-branching crown; to Zone 2.

Growing conditions and maintenance: Though ashes prefer moist, well-drained soil, white ash tolerates dry and moderately alkaline soils, and green ash adapts to wet and dry soils and high salt.

Hamamelis
(*ba-ma-MEL-lis*)
WITCH HAZEL

Hamamelis x intermedia 'Arnold Promise'

Hardiness: *Zones 5-8*

Plant type: *shrub or small tree*

Height: *15 to 20 feet*

Interest: *flowers, foliage, fragrance*

Soil: *moist, well-drained*

Light: *partial shade to full sun*

Witch hazel brightens and perfumes the winter landscape with yellow to red ribbonlike flowers, then dazzles the fall garden with colorful foliage. Seed capsules explode on maturity in late fall, shooting seeds many feet away. Best located where their scent and bright flowers can be appreciated at close range, witch hazels are underused in American gardens.

Selected species and varieties: *H. x intermedia*—an upright-spreading shrub flowering yellow, red, or burnt orange on bare branches and bearing medium green leaves 3 to 4 inches long that turn yellow to red in fall; 'Arnold Promise', one of the best blooming cultivars, produces fragrant clear yellow flowers, each straplike petal up to 1 inch long, in late winter as well as reddish orange fall foliage; 'Jelena' [also called 'Copper Beauty'] produces copper-colored flowers and orange-red fall color.

Growing conditions and maintenance: Witch hazel grows best in slightly acid soil enriched with organic matter. If the plant becomes open, prune to encourage dense growth. Propagate by layering if a shrub—with cuttings if a tree.

Hydrangea
(*by-DRANE-jee-a*)
HYDRANGEA

Hydrangea arborescens 'Annabelle'

Hardiness: *Zones 3-9*

Plant type: *deciduous shrub or vine*

Height: *3 to 80 feet*

Interest: *flowers, foliage, bark*

Soil: *moist, well-drained*

Light: *bright full shade to full sun*

Hydrangeas produce flowers that change color through their bloom period, usually from white to purplish pink, then to brown. Most are shrubs, but the climbing hydrangea is a vine with twining stems and aerial roots that cling to rough surfaces. The flower clusters of hydrangeas consist of small, starlike, fertile flowers surrounded by larger, showier, sterile flowers, 1 to 1½ inches wide. The long-lasting blossoms are valued for fresh and dried arrangements and wreaths. All hydrangeas are coarse in texture, and some offer colorful fall foliage and attractive exfoliating bark.

Selected species and varieties: *H. anomala* ssp. *petiolaris* (climbing hydrangea)—climbs to a height of 60 to 80 feet, with flat-headed white flowers 6 to 10 inches wide, toothy leaves up to 4 inches wide, and attractive reddish brown peeling bark; Zones 4-7. *H. arborescens* (hills-of-snow, wild hydrangea, sevenbark, smooth hydrangea)—a rounded, fast-growing shrub, 3 to 5 feet high and wide, bearing serrated oval leaves up to 8 inches long, and 4- to 6-inch-wide, almost flat flower clusters with few sterile (e.g.,

showy) blooms, borne on new growth; 'Annabelle' produces symmetrical, extremely showy flower clusters up to 1 foot across. *H. paniculata* (panicle hydrangea)—a fast-growing, upright, often unkempt large shrub or small tree, 10 to 25 feet high and 10 to 20 feet wide, bearing minimally decorative flower panicles, 6 to 8 inches long that change from white to purplish pink in mid- to late summer, Zones 3-8; 'Grandiflora' (peegee hydrangea) is a far showier cultivar with mostly sterile flowers in panicles 12 to 18 inches long. *H. quercifolia* (oakleaf hydrangea)—a moderate-growing, 4- to 6-foot-high mound with shoots arising from the base but with few branches,

Hydrangea quercifolia

bearing erect flower panicles 4 to 12 inches long from mid- to late summer, rich brown, flaky bark on older stems, and large three- to seven-lobed deep green leaves that turn red, brownish orange, and purple in fall; hardy to Zone 5.

Growing conditions and maintenance: Hydrangeas are intolerant of drought at any time of year and wilt under hot afternoon sun in warmer climates. The heavy flower heads of *H. arborescens* 'Annabelle' can force stems to the ground. For better form, cut to the ground in late winter and feed lightly; flowers will form on new growth by early summer. It can be grown as a herbaceous perennial in colder climates. Peegee hydrangea produces its largest blooms and a cleaner form when all but 5 to 10 shoots are removed. Prune oakleaf hydrangeas after flowering, removing weak branches.

Ilex
(EYE-lex)
HOLLY

Ilex aquifolium 'Argenteo-marginata'

Hardiness: *Zones 4-10*

Plant type: *shrub or tree*

Height: *2 to 50 feet*

Interest: *foliage, fruit, form*

Soil: *moist, well-drained*

Light: *full sun to partial shade*

The genus produces a broad range of mostly evergreen plants in all sizes and shapes. Dense, lustrous foliage and a neat habit make shrub hollies ideal foundation plants, hedges, and background plants. The taller hollies make lovely specimen plants and effective screens. Tiny, sometimes fragrant spring flowers are inconspicuous. In most species, a female plant must be within 100 feet of a male to set fruit.

Selected species and varieties: *I.* x *altaclarensis* 'Wilsonii' (Altaclara holly)—a 30-foot-tall tree with spiny leaves up to 5 inches long and 3 inches wide and red fruit; Zones 7-9. *I. aquifolium* (common holly, English holly)—30 to 50 feet tall, with fragrant whitish flowers in spring, wavy leaves with spines, and red berries, Zones 6-9; 'Argenteo-marginata', a female, has dark green leaves edged with white; 'Boulder Creek', also a female, glossy black-green leaves. *I.* x *attenuata* 'Fosteri' (Foster Hybrids)—small pyramidal trees 10 to 25 feet high with small red berries; Zones 6-9. *I. cornuta* (Chinese holly, horned holly)—a dense, rounded shrub 8 to 10 feet tall,

with spiny rectangular leaves up to 4 inches long, small, fragrant spring flowers, and bright red berries lasting until late winter, Zones 7-9; 'Berries Jubilee' has large berry clusters and grows 6 to 10 feet tall; 'Carissa' is 3 to 4 feet tall and up to 6 feet wide, bearing oval leaves with only one spine; 'Needlepoint' has narrow, twisted leaves and a single spine. *I. crenata* (Japanese holly, box-leaved holly)—a dense, multibranched rounded shrub that grows slowly to 5 to 10 feet high and wide, with lustrous oval leaves ½ to 1 inch long and small black berries hidden under the foliage, Zones 5-8; 'Convexa' is a very dense cultivar that eventually grows to 9 feet tall and more than twice as wide, with ½-inch-long curved leaves and heavy fruit; 'Green Island' has an open habit, growing to 4 feet tall and 6 feet wide; 'Helleri' is 2 to 3 feet tall by 5 feet wide with ½-inch dull, very dark

Ilex cornuta

green leaves; 'Microphylla' has an upright habit and leaves smaller than the species. *I. decidua* (possum haw, winterberry)—a deciduous shrub or small tree to 15 feet, with glossy green leaves turning yellow in fall and orange to red berries that linger until the next spring; Zones 5-9. *I. glabra* (inkberry, Appalachian tea)—an upright, multibranched rounded shrub 6 to 8 feet tall by 8 to 10 feet wide, becoming open with age, with narrow-oval leaves 1 to 2 inches long and bearing small black berries, partly hidden by the leaves, from fall to the following spring, Zones 4-9; 'Compacta', a female, is a more tightly branched form 4 to 6 feet tall. *I.* x *meserveae* (Meserve Hybrids)—a group of dense, bushy shrubs 8 to 12 feet tall, with lustrous dark green or bluish

green leaves on deep purple stems, hardy to Zone 4; 'Blue Prince', a male, forms a broad pyramid; 'Blue Princess', known to grow as much as 15 feet high and 10 feet wide, has dark blue-green leaves and red berries. *I. opaca* (American holly)—a 40- to 50-foot tree, pyramidal when young, becoming open and irregular over time, with dull to dark yellow-green leaves and bright red berries persisting into winter; Zones 5-9. *I. pedunculosa* (long-stalked holly)—a moderately dense, large shrub or small tree, 15 to 20 feet tall, with dark

Ilex pedunculosa

green leaves, 1 to 3 inches long, and red berries borne on long stems in fall, usually not lasting into winter; Zones 5-8. *I.* x 'Sparkleberry'—forms a narrow column, with small red berries that persist well into winter and nearly black bark. *I. vomitoria* (yaupon, cassina—15 to 20 feet tall and less in width, with attractively irregular branches, gray to white bark, and a heavy fruit crop lasting till spring, Zones 7-10; 'Nana' grows 5 feet high and wide, with fruit often hidden by the foliage.

Growing conditions and maintenance: Although hollies tolerate partial shade, they prefer full sun. Most evergreen hollies do not endure hot, windy, or dry climates. For best results, provide a loose, well-drained loam. Chinese holly tolerates most soils and withstands drought. Japanese holly prefers moist, slightly acid soils. Inkberry, found naturally in swamps, thrives in wet, acid soils. American holly needs very well-drained, acid loam in wind-protected areas. Long-stalked holly tolerates heavy soils and drying wind. Yaupon withstands dry to wet sites and tolerates alkalinity. All species readily accept pruning.

Koelreuteria
(kol-roo-TEER-ee-a)
GOLDEN-RAIN TREE

Koelreuteria paniculata 'September'

Hardiness: *Zones 5-9*

Plant type: *tree*

Height: *30 to 40 feet*

Interest: *flowers, foliage, form*

Soil: *well-drained*

Light: *partial shade to full sun*

A delightful small tree to shade a garden bench or patio, the golden-rain tree produces airy sprays of yellow flowers in early summer on wide-spreading branches. Greenish balloon-shaped seed capsules turn yellow, then brown and papery in fall; the color change takes about 2 months. The dense canopy consists of large compound leaves that are medium bright green, changing to yellow before dropping in fall. Sparse branching gives the tree a coarse look in winter.

Selected species and varieties: *K. paniculata* (golden-rain tree, varnish tree)—rounded crown with spread equal to or greater than its height, bearing 6- to 18-inch-long leaves composed of seven to 15 toothed and lobed leaflets 1 to 3 inches long, purplish red when opening, and flower clusters 12 to 15 inches long and wide; 'September' flowers in late summer and is less hardy than the species.

Growing conditions and maintenance: Golden-rain tree tolerates a wide variety of conditions including drought. It grows best—about 1½ feet per year—in soil well amended with peat moss or leaf mold. Provide shelter from wind.

Ligustrum
(li-GUS-trum)
PRIVET, HEDGE PLANT

Ligustrum japonicum

Hardiness: *Zones 6-10*

Plant type: *shrub*

Height: *6 to 15 feet*

Interest: *foliage, flowers, fruit*

Soil: *adaptable*

Light: *full sun or shade*

Privet is grown primarily for its dense habit and lustrous foliage, which is highly amenable to heavy shearing. Usually used for hedges, screens, and foundation plants, privet can also be tailored into topiary specimens. White flowers, often considered malodorous, bloom in late spring or early summer, followed by black or blue-black berries.

Selected species and varieties: *L. japonicum* (Japanese privet, waxleaf privet, waxleaf ligustrum)—an upright, dense evergreen shrub 6 to 12 feet tall and up to 8 feet wide with 2- to 6-inch-high pyramidal flower clusters offsetting very dark green leaves 1½ to 4 inches long; Zones 7-10. *L. ovalifolium* 'Aureum' (California privet)—yellow leaves with a green spot in the center when planted in sun, heavily scented flower clusters 2 to 4 inches wide in summer, and shiny black berries on 10- to 15-foot densely arranged upright stems, semievergreen to evergreen in warmer climates.

Growing conditions and maintenance: Easily grown and undisturbed by insects or disease, privet adapts to almost any soil except those that are constantly wet.

Liquidambar
(li-kwid-AM-bar)
SWEET GUM

Liquidambar styraciflua

Hardiness: *Zones 5-9*

Plant type: *tree*

Height: *60 to 120 feet*

Interest: *foliage*

Soil: *moist, slightly acid*

Light: *full sun*

The sweet gum is a neatly conical tree whose star-shaped leaves linger till late fall and turn lovely shades of yellow, purple, and scarlet. Its name is derived from the fragrant, gummy sap, used in making perfume. The bark is deeply furrowed and resembles cork. Spiny globe-shaped fruits drop from late fall to early spring, a liability for patios, walkways, and barefoot walks in the grass.

Selected species and varieties: *L. styraciflua* (American sweet gum, red gum, bilsted)—narrow-pyramidal in youth, maturing into a semirounded crown with a spread two-thirds the height, the branches edged with corky wings and bearing glossy rich medium green leaves 4 to 7½ inches long and wide, with five to seven finely serrated, pointed lobes.

Growing conditions and maintenance: Although native to rich, moist bottomlands, sweet gum is tolerant of poor soils if they are neutral to slightly acid and reasonably moist. The roots need plenty of room to develop. Plant in spring in soil amended with peat moss or leaf mold. Sweet gum usually takes 2 to 5 years to become established. Prune in winter.

Liriodendron
(lir-ee-o-DEN-dron)
TULIP TREE

Liriodendron tulipifera

Hardiness: *Zones 4-9*

Plant type: *tree*

Height: *70 to 100 feet or more*

Interest: *foliage, form*

Soil: *moist, well-drained, slightly acid*

Light: *full sun*

A giant suitable only for large areas, the tulip tree is a columnar to oval deciduous tree with distinctive bright green foliage that turns golden yellow in fall. In mid- to late spring, tuliplike greenish white flowers with a deep orange blotch at the base of the petals appear high on the tree after the foliage unfurls. Conelike clusters of winged fruit persist into winter.

Selected species and varieties: *L. tulipifera* (yellow poplar, tulip magnolia, tulip poplar, whitewood)—fast growing with a spread of 35 to 50 feet and the potential of topping 100 feet tall, pyramidal when young, bearing lobed leaves up to 8 inches wide and long opening early in spring, and cup-shaped flowers 2½ inches wide with six petals, borne singly at or near branch tips.

Growing conditions and maintenance: Give tulip trees a moist, deep loam with plenty of room to grow. They prefer slightly acid soils but will tolerate neutral to slightly alkaline soils. Leaves occasionally turn black with a mold that grows on the sweet, sticky substance secreted by scale and aphids. In ideal soil, tulip trees may grow 2½ to 3 feet per year.

Magnolia
(mag-NO-lee-a)
MAGNOLIA

Magnolia stellata 'Royal Star'

Hardiness: *Zones 4-9*

Plant type: *shrub or tree*

Height: *10 to 80 feet*

Interest: *flowers, fragrance, fruit, foliage, form*

Soil: *moist to wet, acid, fertile*

Light: *partial shade to full sun*

Large or small, magnolias of any size make outstanding accent or specimen plants, their showy flowers sweet with fragrance in spring or summer, and their fat, conelike fruit capsules splitting open to expose red seeds in fall. The smaller forms make excellent patio or shade trees; the stately bull bay needs a broad lawn for best development and display of its huge leathery leaves and 8- to 12-inch cup-shaped flowers.

Selected species and varieties: *M. grandiflora* (bull bay, southern magnolia, evergreen magnolia)—dense evergreen pyramid 60 to 80 feet high and 30 to 50 feet wide, branching close to the ground, bearing fragrant creamy white six-petaled waxy flowers in late spring to summer against lustrous dark green leaves 5 to 10 inches long, and fruit capsules 3 to 5 inches long, Zones 7-9; 'Bracken's Brown Beauty', a densely branched, compact form to 30 feet tall, produces leathery leaves 6 inches long that are lustrous dark green above and rusty brown below, with 5- to 6-inch-wide flowers and 2- to 3-inch fruits; 'Little Gem' has a shrubby habit with small-

er leaves and 3- to 4-inch flowers that bloom from summer to fall on a 20-foot specimen. *M. stellata* (star magnolia)—dense, roundish to oval form, 15 to 20 feet high and 10 to 15 feet wide, with fuzzy gray winter buds opening to fragrant white 3- to 4-inch flowers, each with 12 to 18 strap-shaped petals, in late winter or early spring before the satiny dark green 2- to 4-inch leaves appear, Zones 4-8; 'Royal Star' has 25 to 30 pure white petals in each flower. *M. virginiana* (sweet bay, laurel magnolia, swamp

Magnolia virginiana

laurel, swamp bay, swamp magnolia)—creamy white, lemon-scented nine- to 12-petaled flowers 2 to 3 inches wide in late spring or early summer, followed by showy dark red seed clusters to 2 inches long, borne on a multistemmed deciduous or semievergreen shrub of open, spreading habit, 10 to 20 feet high and wide in the North, to 60 feet in the South, where it is evergreen; Zones 5-9.

Growing conditions and maintenance: *M. virginiana* grows well in wet soils; the other magnolias need moist, well-drained loam. Amend the soil with peat moss or leaf mold before planting. Mulch to conserve moisture and keep the roots cool. Feed with an acid fertilizer no later than midsummer to allow new growth time to harden off. Star magnolia's buds are easily killed by late winter freezes; provide a sheltered spot, and avoid southern exposure that would encourage buds to swell early. Bull bay can be a messy tree, dropping large leaves in spring and fall that are slow to decay; *M. grandiflora* 'Bracken's Brown Beauty' drops fewer leaves. Magnolias are surface rooters; do not underplant.

Mahonia
(ma-HO-nee-a)
OREGON GRAPE

Mahonia bealei

Hardiness: *Zones 5-10*

Plant type: *evergreen shrub or ground cover*

Height: *10 inches to 12 feet*

Interest: *flowers, fragrance, fruit*

Soil: *moist, well-drained, acid, fertile*

Light: *full to dappled shade*

Mahonia's lemon yellow flowers in earliest spring can perfume a shady garden. The grapelike berries, maturing in summer, are covered with a blue bloom and are relished by birds. Stiff and formal in habit, mahonia has leathery, hollylike, compound leaves that are blue-green in summer and purplish in winter.

Selected species and varieties: *M. aquifolium* (mountain grape, holly barberry) —slightly fragrant flowers borne in terminal clusters 2 to 3 inches long and wide on upright stems on a 3- to 9-foot-tall shrub; Zones 5-8. *M. bealei* (leatherleaf mahonia)—very fragrant flowers 6 to 12 inches wide and 3 to 6 inches long from late winter to early spring, and berries that turn from robin's-egg blue to blue-black on a 10- to 12-foot-tall shrub; hardy to Zone 7. *M. repens* (creeping mahonia)—spreading mat of stiff stems to 10 inches high, with deep yellow flowers in 1- to 3-inch-long racemes.

Growing conditions and maintenance: Mahonia needs a deep, loamy soil in a site protected from wind. Dry soils or too much sun will yellow leaves. Keep well watered, and mulch to retain moisture.

Malus
(MAY-lus)
APPLE

Malus 'Red Jade'

Hardiness: *Zones 5-8*

Plant type: *tree*

Height: *15 to 25 feet*

Interest: *flowers, fruit, fragrance, form*

Soil: *moist, well-drained, acid to nearly neutral*

Light: *full sun*

In spring, scented blossoms 1 to 2 inches wide cloak the entire length of the tree's branches, followed by small fruit that may linger into fall if birds allow. Although many crab apples flower and fruit heavily in alternate years, the types listed here are all annual bearers.

Selected species and varieties: *M. floribunda* (Japanese flowering crab apple, showy crab apple, purple chokeberry)— arching, rounded habit 15 to 25 feet tall and wide, with clusters of pink to red buds opening white, followed by red or yellow fruit; hardy to Zone 5. *M.* 'Prairiefire'—red buds opening to rosy red flowers, reddish new foliage, and maroon fruits, to 20 feet tall and rounded, very disease resistant. *M.* 'Red Jade'—weeping form 15 feet tall, with pendulous branches bearing deep pink buds that open to profuse white blooms, and red fruit.

Growing conditions and maintenance: Although easy to grow in average soil, crab apples do best in heavy loam. Any pruning should be done before summer, when buds are formed for the next year. Crab apples are susceptible to a number of diseases, including fire blight.

Nandina
(nan-DEE-na)
HEAVENLY BAMBOO

Nandina domestica

Hardiness: *Zones 6-9*

Plant type: *evergreen shrub*

Height: *2 to 8 feet*

Interest: *foliage, fruit, flowers, form*

Soil: *moist, fertile*

Light: *full shade to full sun*

Nandina's fine-textured bluish green foliage, emerging pink or coppery and often turning red to reddish purple in fall and winter, splays out from bamboo-like canes. In late spring or early summer, panicles of creamy flowers appear, followed by spectacular clusters of red berries that persist through winter. Nandina is suited for foundations or borders, in masses, or as a specimen.

Selected species and varieties: *N. domestica* (sacred bamboo)—erect habit, 6 to 8 feet tall, with compound leaves having sharply tapered leaflets, each 1½ to 4 inches long and half as wide, 8- to 15-inch-long clusters of tiny white flowers with yellow anthers, and heavy panicles of ⅓-inch berries; 'Harbour Dwarf' grows to 2 to 3 feet, forming a graceful mound.

Growing conditions and maintenance: Although nandina grows best in acid loam, it tolerates a wide range of other soils and withstands drought. Winter sun helps redden foliage. Plant in groups to improve berrying. If left unpruned, it becomes leggy; remove old canes or cut canes to various lengths to create a dense plant. Canes cannot be forced to branch.

Phellodendron
(fell-o-DEN-dron)
CORK TREE

Phellodendron amurense

Hardiness: *Zones 3-8*

Plant type: *tree*

Height: *30 to 45 feet*

Interest: *bark*

Soil: *adaptable*

Light: *full sun*

Cork tree is valued for the heavily ridged and furrowed gray-brown bark, resembling cork, that cloaks the few wide-spreading horizontal main branches on old trees. Inconspicuous yellowish green flowers bloom in late spring, followed by small clusters of black berries in late fall on female trees. Both flowers and fruit have a turpentine-like odor when they are bruised. Lustrous green compound leaves, like those of black walnut, cast a light shade and sometimes turn yellow in fall, lingering on the tree only briefly.

Selected species and varieties: *P. amurense* (Amur cork tree)—30 to 45 feet tall with equal or greater spread, with orange-yellow stems bearing glossy dark green leaflets to 4 inches long, and corky bark developing in old age. *P. chinense* (Chinese cork tree)—grows 30 feet tall, with dark yellow-green leaflets to 5 inches long on red-brown stems; hardy to Zone 5.

Growing conditions and maintenance: Cork tree tolerates drought, pollution, and a wide variety of soil types. It is easily transplanted and is usually pest free. Prune in winter.

Picea
(PYE-see-a)
SPRUCE

Picea abies 'Nidiformis'

Hardiness: *Zones 2-7*

Plant type: *tree or shrub*

Height: *3 to 60 feet or more*

Interest: *foliage, form*

Soil: *moist, well-drained, acid*

Light: *full sun to partial shade*

These needled evergreens form towering pyramids useful as windbreaks, screens, or single specimens. Smaller forms are good as accents or in groups.

Selected species and varieties: *P. abies* (Norway spruce)—a fast-growing pyramid with drooping branches, 40 to 60 feet tall (can reach 150 feet) and 25 to 30 feet wide, its medium green foliage maturing to dark green, bearing 4- to 6-inch cylindrical cones and often losing its form in old age; 'Nidiformis' (bird's-nest spruce) is a 3- to 6-foot-tall spreading mound. *P. glauca* (white spruce)—a tree aging to a narrow, dense spire 40 to 60 feet tall by 10 to 20 feet wide, with ascending branches, Zones 2-6; 'Conica' (dwarf Alberta spruce) is a neat, very slow growing (to 10 feet in 25 years) cone-shaped plant with light green foliage.

Growing conditions and maintenance: Spruces prefer moist, acid, deep loam but tolerate other soils with adequate moisture, especially in the first few years. They prefer sunny sites in cold climates. White spruce withstands heat and drought better than many other species.

Pieris
(PYE-er-is)
PIERIS

Pieris japonica 'Variegata'

Hardiness: *Zones 5-8*

Plant type: *evergreen shrub*

Height: *6 to 12 feet*

Interest: *foliage, flowers, buds*

Soil: *moist, well-drained, slightly acid*

Light: *full sun to light shade*

Clustered chains of greenish to red buds decorate this mounding shrub from late summer to the following spring, when they open into white or pink urn-shaped flowers. New foliage, tinged with reddish bronze, unfurls and retains that hue for weeks before turning a lustrous dark green. Japanese pieris makes a beautiful four-season specimen, and also works well in foundations and borders. Caution: Pieris buds and flowers are poisonous.

Selected species and varieties: *P. japonica* (Japanese pieris, lily-of-the-valley bush)—upright shrub 6 to 8 feet wide, with spreading branches bearing rosettes of shiny leaves and slightly fragrant 3- to 6-inch-long flower clusters; 'Compacta' grows densely to a height of 6 feet, with small leaves and prolific bloom; 'Crispa' has wavy leaves; 'Variegata' has leaves with creamy to silver margins.

Growing conditions and maintenance: Japanese pieris grows best in well-drained soil well supplemented with leaf mold or peat moss. Protect from strong winds. If protection is provided, it can be grown in Zone 4. Provide light shade where summers are hot.

Pinus
(PYE-nus)
PINE

Pinus strobus

Hardiness: *Zones 2-10*

Plant type: *evergreen tree*

Height: *6 to 90 feet*

Interest: *foliage, form, fruit*

Soil: *wet to dry*

Light: *full sun*

This diverse genus of needle-leaved evergreen conifers includes picturesque specimen and accent plants, towering screens, and lovely single shade trees.

Selected species and varieties: *P. arisata* (bristlecone pine)—a very slow grower, some examples of which are, at over 4,000 years old, the oldest living things on earth, reaching 8 to 20 feet tall with bluish white to dark green needles; Zones 4-7. *P. contorta* var. *contorta* (shore pine)—a 25- to 30-foot-tall tree with twisted trunk and branches; hardy to Zone 7. *P. densiflora* 'Umbraculifera' (Japanese umbrella pine)—upright-spreading, with umbrella-like crown to 9 feet tall or more, with exfoliating orange bark and bright to dark green needles; Zones 3-7. *P. edulis* [also classified as *P. cembroides* var. *edulis*] (pinyon, nut pine)—slow growing, 10 to 20 feet tall, with horizontal branches and an often flat crown, and dark green needles; hardy to Zone 5. *P. eldarica* (Afghanistan pine)—fast growing, 30 to 80 feet tall, with dark green needles to 6 inches long; hardy to Zone 7. *P. mugo* (mountain pine, mugo pine)—a broad pyramid to 20 feet tall or

a low, broad, bushy shrub, with usually medium green foliage; Zones 2-7. *P. nigra* (Austrian pine)—pyramidal shape broadening over time to a flat top with heavy, spreading branches, 50 to 60 feet tall by 20 to 40 foot wide, with dark green needles; Zones 4-7. *P. palustris* (longleaf pine, southern yellow pine, pitch pine)—a sparsely branched tree 55 to 90 feet tall, bearing needles to 9 inches long on mature trees and 10-inch cones; Zones 7-10. *P. strobus* (white pine)—a low-branched tree growing 50 to 80 feet tall and half as wide, pyramidal when young but becoming broad crowned with age, producing a dense growth of bluish green needles; Zones 3-8. *P. thunbergiana* (Japanese black pine)—an irregular pyramid usually 20 to 40 feet tall, with sometimes

Pinus thunbergiana

drooping, wide-spreading branches bearing dark green, crowded, twisted needles 2½ to 7 inches long and 1½- to 2½-inch cones; Zones 5-7.

Growing conditions and maintenance: Bristlecone pine does well in poor, dry soils but suffers in drying winds or pollution. Shore pine grows naturally in boggy areas. Japanese umbrella pine prefers well-drained, slightly acid soil. Afghanistan pine and pinyon thrive in desert conditions; the former also tolerates salt spray. Mountain pine needs moist, deep loam. Austrian pine tolerates alkaline soils, moderate drought, salt, and urban pollution but grows best where moisture is assured. White pine grows best in moist loams but is also found on dry, shallow soils and wet bogs; it is intolerant of air pollutants, salt, and highly alkaline soil. Japanese black pine thrives in moist loams but is tolerant of sand and salt.

Populus
(POP-yew-lus)
POPLAR, ASPEN

Populus tremuloides

Hardiness: *Zones 1-7*

Plant type: *tree*

Height: *40 to 90 feet*

Interest: *form, foliage, bark*

Soil: *adaptable*

Light: *full sun*

Quaking aspen is a fast-growing slender deciduous tree whose lustrous dark green leaves, turning yellow in the fall, quiver with the slightest breeze. The bark is smooth, creamy to greenish white, becoming dark and furrowed on old trees. Quaking aspens are best planted in groups rather than as single specimens. Invasive root systems also make them good for erosion control.

Selected species and varieties: *P. tremuloides* (quaking aspen, trembling aspen, quiverleaf)—slender and pyramidal in youth, developing a slightly more rounded crown with age, usually high branched and spreading 20 to 30 feet, with pointed, roundish, finely serrated leaves 1½ to 3 inches long and wide that turn medium yellow in fall.

Growing conditions and maintenance: The most widely distributed tree in North America, quaking aspen grows in almost any site except soggy soils. Best growth occurs, however, in moist, deep, well-drained soil. The wood is weak and easily broken by storms. Quaking aspens usually live less than 50 years. They tolerate drought, salt spray, and urban pollution.

Prunus
(PROO-nus)
CHERRY, APRICOT

Prunus subhirtella var. pendula

Hardiness: *Zones 4-10*

Plant type: *shrub or tree*

Height: *3 to 50 feet*

Interest: *flowers, foliage, fruit*

Soil: *moist, well-drained*

Light: *full sun to partial shade*

This huge genus ranges from shrubs and small to mid-size deciduous trees valued for their spring flowers to robust broad-leaved evergreens used for screens, foundation plants, and hedges. None of the species listed here have edible fruits.

Selected species and varieties: *P. caroliniana* (Carolina cherry laurel, mock orange)—an evergreen oval-pyramidal shrub or tree, 20 to 30 feet high and 15 to 25 feet wide, with lustrous dark green, sharply tapered, sometimes spiny leaves 2 to 3 inches long and 1 inch wide hiding black fruits, and heavily scented white flower clusters to 3 inches long in early spring, Zones 7-10; 'Bright 'n' Tight' has smooth-edged leaves smaller than the species on a tightly branched pyramid growing to 20 feet tall. *P. laurocerasus* (common cherry laurel, English laurel)—lustrous medium to dark green leaves 2 to 6 inches long and one-third as wide, slightly toothed and borne on green stems tightly branched on a broad 10- to 18-foot-tall evergreen shrub that produces heavily fragrant flowers in racemes 2 to 5 inches long, and purple to black fruit masked by the leaves, hardy

to Zone 6; 'Otto Luyken' is a compact form 3 to 4 feet tall and 6 to 8 feet wide that blooms profusely and has dark green leaves 4 inches long and 1 inch wide; 'Schipkaensis' has shorter, slightly narrower, smooth-edged leaves, to 5 feet high; hardy to Zone 5. *P. lusitanica* (Portugal laurel, Portuguese cherry laurel)—fragrant white clusters 6 to 10 inches long in late spring and dark purple cone-shaped fruits on a bushy shrub or tree 10 to 20 feet high with evergreen leaves 2½ to 5 inches long; Zones 7-9. *P. mume* (Japanese flowering apricot)—pale rose flowers in winter, after which shiny green leaves and yellowish fruit appear on a tree to 20 feet; Zones 6-9 (to

Prunus x yedoensis

Zone 10 in California). *P. subhirtella* var. *pendula* (weeping Higan cherry)—pink single flowers appear before the leaves on graceful, weeping branches on a 20- to 40-foot tree, followed by black fruit; Zones 4-9. *P.* x *yedoensis* (Japanese flowering cherry)—40- to 50-foot tree that bears pink or white flowers in spring before or as the leaves appear, black fruit, Zones 5-8; 'Akebono' has pink double flowers on a tree 25 feet high and wide.

Growing conditions and maintenance: As a rule, plant flowering fruit trees in full sun in well-worked loam; add sand to loosen heavy clay. Prune cherries only when necessary, removing crossed or ungainly branches. Laurels can thrive in full sun to partial shade in soil enriched with organic matter, usually enduring drought once established. In warmer climates, provide afternoon shade for Carolina cherry laurel, even in winter. Common cherry laurel is tolerant of wind and salt spray. Laurels take pruning well.

Pyrus
(PYE-rus)
PEAR

Pyrus calleryana 'Chanticleer'

Hardiness: *Zones 5-8*

Plant type: *tree*

Height: *to 40 feet*

Interest: *flowers, foliage*

Soil: *well-drained*

Light: *full sun*

Callery pears are showy trees that burst with white flowers in early spring. Their lustrous dark green leaves form a dense, symmetrical canopy until midfall, when they turn reddish purple and finally drop. Because the foliage appears early and remains late, Callery pear makes a good aerial privacy screen in urban gardens. Small fruit is inedible to humans but is enjoyed by birds in winter.

Selected species and varieties: *P. calleryana* 'Chanticleer' (Callery pear)—grows 35 feet high to 16 feet wide in 15 years, with a pyramidal crown narrower than some other cultivars in this species, bearing ⅓-inch-wide flowers in profuse 3-inch clusters and oval-rounded leaves to 3½ inches long.

Growing conditions and maintenance: Callery pears adjust to almost any well-drained soil and tolerate drought and pollution. Prune in late winter while still dormant. They tend to lose their tight form after 20 years or so, due to many branches arising close together on the trunk; 'Chanticleer' has stronger crotches than other cultivars and shows good resistance to fire blight.

Quercus
(KWER-kus)
OAK

Quercus ilex

Hardiness: *Zones 2-9*

Plant type: *tree*

Height: *40 to 100 feet or more*

Interest: *form, foliage*

Soil: *light to heavy, well-drained*

Light: *full sun*

Deciduous or evergreen trees that can provide the dominant structure and framework for the landscape, oaks have a central main trunk and usually stout horizontal branches supporting a broad canopy of dark green foliage. The leaves of deciduous forms often remain into winter. Small flowers form in spring, followed by acorns in late summer to fall.

Selected species and varieties: *Q. ilex* (holly oak, holm oak, evergreen oak)—reaching 40 to 70 feet high and wide, with leathery evergreen leaves, sometimes toothed and usually 1½ to 3 inches long, deep green above and yellowish to gray below; hardy to Zone 5. *Q. macrocarpa* (bur oak, mossy-cup oak)—spreading crown of heavy branches, usually 70 to 80 feet tall and at least as wide but has been known to top 100 feet, with 4- to 10-inch-long leaves, lobed near the stem, dark green above and whitish below, showing greenish yellow to yellow-brown fall color, and acorns, usually fringed, up to 1½ inches long; Zones 2-8. *Q. phellos* (willow oak)—narrow, slightly wavy, willowlike leaves up to 5½ inches long, turning yellow, yellow-brown, and reddish in fall, on

an oval crown 40 to 60 feet high and two-thirds as wide; Zones 5-9. *Q. robur* (English oak, truffle oak, common oak, pedunculate oak)—a short trunk leads to a broad, fairly open crown, 40 to 60 feet tall with equal spread under average landscape conditions (but can reach 100 feet tall), with 2- to 5-inch-long rounded-lobed leaves that are dark green above and pale blue-green below, showing no

Quercus robur

fall color, and oblong acorns; Zones 4-8. *Q. shumardii* (Shumard's oak, Shumard red oak)—grows 40 to 60 feet tall and wide, pyramidal when young but maturing to a spreading crown, with russet-red to red fall color on deeply lobed and sharply pointed leaves 4 to 6 inches long and 3 to 4 inches wide; Zones 5-9. *Q. suber* (cork oak)—trunk and main limbs clad in thick, corky bark on an evergreen tree 60 feet high and equally wide, bearing coarsely toothed 3-inch lobeless leaves that are dark green above, fuzzy gray below; Zones 7-9.

Growing conditions and maintenance: Oaks grow best in moist, deep soil, but most species fare well in a wide range of soil types as long as there is no hardpan present. Although oaks tolerate partial shade, they grow best, and stay healthier, in full sun. Holly oak can withstand inland drought and salt spray, but may become shrubby in exposed, seaside locations. Shumard oak tolerates either wet or dry sites. A good oak for desert conditions, cork oak needs well-drained soil and is drought resistant once established; its leaves yellow in alkaline soil. Do not compact or change the elevation of soil within the oak's root zone, which usually extends far beyond the canopy's reach.

Rhododendron
(roh-doh-DEN-dron)
RHODODENDRON

Rhododendron schlippenbachii

Hardiness: *Zones 4-8*

Plant type: *shrub*

Height: *2 to 12 feet*

Interest: *flowers, foliage*

Soil: *moist, well-drained, acid, fertile*

Light: *partial to bright full shade*

Over 900 species of rhododendrons and azaleas are included in the genus *Rhododendron*. Most rhododendrons are evergreen, have bell-shaped flowers, and often have scaly leaves. Most azaleas are deciduous, have funnel-shaped flowers, and have leaves that are never scaly. Both are effective in borders, groupings, and naturalistic shady gardens.

Selected species and varieties: *R. catawbiense* (Catawba rhododendron, mountain rosebay, purple laurel)—lilac-purple, sometimes purplish rose, flowers in midspring, 6 to 10 feet tall and not as wide; Zones 4-8. *R.* 'Gibraltar'—an upright deciduous shrub 8 to 12 feet tall and almost as wide with medium green leaves that turn orangish in fall and extra large, orange ruffled flowers. *R.* hybrids—'Blue Diamond' grows to 3 feet, with lavender-blue flowers, hardy to Zone 7; 'Bow Bells' has bright pink flowers, rounded leaves, and bronzy new growth to 4 feet, hardy to Zone 6; 'Cilpinense' grows to 2½ feet with light pink flowers fading to white, its buds reliably hardy only in Zone 8; 'Moonstone' grows to 2 feet, with pale pink flowers turning creamy yellow, reliably hardy to Zone 7; 'Ramapo' has blue-green new foliage and violet-blue flowers, 2 to 4 feet tall, to Zone 5; 'Scarlet Wonder', 2 feet tall, with bright red flowers and shiny, quilted foliage, to Zone 6. *R. mucronulatum* (Korean rhododendron)—a deciduous shrub of rounded, open habit, 4 to 8 feet tall and wide, with rosy purple flowers in late winter, followed by 1- to 4-inch-long medium green leaves that are aromatic when crushed and turn yellow to bronzy red in fall. *R.*

Rhododendron 'P.J.M.'

'P.J.M.'—3 to 6 feet tall and wide, with lavender-pink flowers borne profusely in early to midspring and dark green evergreen leaves 1 to 2½ inches long turning plum in fall and winter. *R. schlippenbachii* (royal azalea)—a rounded deciduous shrub 6 to 8 feet tall and wide bearing fragrant, pale to rosy pink flowers 2 to 3 inches wide as new leaves unfurl bronze, later turning dark green before changing to yellow, orange, or red in fall.

Growing conditions and maintenance: Make sure that soil is well drained, and add peat moss or leaf mold liberally. Set plant so that the top of the rootball is an inch or two above the surface of the soil. Mulch to conserve moisture and to keep roots cool. Water deeply in dry periods, particularly before the onset of winter. Evergreen types should be protected from hot afternoon sun and winter winds. Morning sun enhances bloom without stressing the plant. Foundation plantings run the risk of failing because lime leaching from structural cement sweetens the soil; in these cases, increase soil acidity with aluminum sulfate. Unlike other members of this genus, royal azalea does well in near neutral soils.

Stewartia
(stew-AR-tee-a)
STEWARTIA

Stewartia pseudocamellia

Hardiness: *Zones 5-9*

Plant type: *shrub or tree*

Height: *10 to 40 feet*

Interest: *flowers, foliage, bark*

Soil: *moist, well-drained, acid, organic*

Light: *partial shade to full sun*

Stewartia has camellia-like summer flowers and colorful fall foliage. A fine specimen tree, Japanese stewartia has exfoliating bark in cream, rusty red, and gray.

Selected species and varieties: *S. ovata* (mountain stewartia, mountain camellia)—creamy white flowers 2½ to 3 inches wide and oval leaves 2 to 5 inches long that turn orange to red in fall on spreading branches of a bushy shrub or small tree 10 to 15 feet tall and wide, with bark not as showy as that of Japanese stewartia. *S. pseudocamellia* (Japanese stewartia)—20 to 40 feet tall with open, spreading branches, producing white 2- to 2½-inch flowers with white filaments and orange anthers amid 1½- to 3½-inch leaves that turn vibrant yellow, red, and reddish purple in fall; Zones 5-7.

Growing conditions and maintenance: Stewartia is difficult to transplant and should be put into the ground as a 4- to 5-foot-tall balled-and-burlapped plant and not moved again. Dig a large hole and amend the soil liberally with peat moss, leaf mold, or compost. In warmer climates, provide some afternoon shade. Stewartias rarely need pruning.

Syringa
(si-RING-ga)
LILAC

Syringa reticulata

Hardiness: *Zones 3-8*

Plant type: *tree or shrub*

Height: *3 to 30 feet*

Interest: *flowers, fragrance*

Soil: *moist, well-drained*

Light: *full sun*

Deciduous staples of gardens past, lilacs produce fat, highly scented flower clusters after their dark green pointed-oval leaves have appeared.

Selected species and varieties: *S. patula* [formerly classified as *S. velutina*] 'Miss Kim' (Manchurian lilac)—fragrant 4- to 6-inch-long icy blue bloom clusters open from purple buds in late spring to early summer on a 3- to 6-foot-tall shrub. *S. reticulata* [formerly classified as *S. amurensis* var. *japonica*] (Japanese tree lilac)—20 to 30 feet tall, with branches spread stiffly 15 to 25 feet before becoming more arching and graceful with age, with an oval to round crown and creamy white, privet-scented terminal flower clusters 6 to 12 inches long and wide for 2 weeks in early summer, and reddish brown cherrylike bark; Zones 3-7.

Growing conditions and maintenance: Lilacs grow best in loose, slightly acid loam, but they adjust to both acid or slightly alkaline soil. Prune after flowering and remove crowded branches; lilacs need good air circulation. Japanese tree lilac is unusually pest free and resistant to mildew.

Taxodium
(taks-ODE-ee-um)
CYPRESS

Taxodium distichum

Hardiness: *Zones 4-9*

Plant type: *tree*

Height: *50 to 70 feet or more*

Interest: *form, foliage, bark*

Soil: *moist, sandy, acid*

Light: *full sun*

These stately deciduous conifers have sage green needlelike foliage that turns bright orange-brown in fall. In swampy areas or along the edge of a lake, the shaggy reddish brown main trunk is flanked by narrow root projections that reach out of the water in kneelike bends to collect oxygen for the tree. Inconspicuous flowers bloom in spring, and fragrant green to purple cones 1 inch across mature to brown. Use common bald cypress as a dramatic fine-textured vertical accent in the garden, or plant in groups along the edge of a pond.

Selected species and varieties: *T. distichum* (common bald cypress, swamp cypress, tidewater red cypress)—new foliage opens bright yellow-green in graceful sprays amid short, ascending branches on a slender pyramid 50 to 70 feet high or more by 20 to 30 feet wide.

Growing conditions and maintenance: Although common bald cypress makes its best growth in moist to wet deep, sandy loams, it is surprisingly tolerant of dry soil and low fertility. It is also very resistant to strong winds, and is seldom seriously bothered by disease or insects.

Viburnum
(vy-BUR-num)
ARROWWOOD

Viburnum carlesii

Hardiness: *Zones 4-9*

Plant type: *shrub*

Height: *3 to 12 feet*

Interest: *flowers, fruit, foliage*

Soil: *moist, well-drained*

Light: *full sun to partial shade*

The mostly deciduous, highly ornamental viburnums listed here offer snowy clouds of flowers in spring and often colorful berries that may persist well into winter. Others are valued for their fragrance, reddish fall foliage, or branching patterns. Viburnums are useful in shrub borders, as screens, or as specimens.

Selected species and varieties: *V. carlesii* (Korean spice viburnum)—pink buds open to white, domelike, enchantingly fragrant flower clusters 2 to 3 inches wide on a rounded, dense shrub 4 to 8 feet tall and wide, followed by ineffective black fruit in late summer; Zones 4-8. *V. davidii* (David viburnum)—turquoise blue fruits on an evergreen mound 3 to 5 feet high that also produces dull white flower clusters 2 to 3 inches wide; Zones 8-9. *V. dilatatum* (linden viburnum)—8 to 10 feet tall and 6 to 8 feet wide, bearing flat, creamy white clusters to 5 inches wide in late spring, bright red or scarlet berries that ripen in fall and persist into winter, and semilustrous dark green leaves 2 to 5 inches long, sometimes turning russet-red in fall, Zones 5-7; 'Catskill' is a dwarf form 5 to 6 feet

tall and 8 feet wide with dark green leaves that turn yellow, orange, and red in fall, and dark red fruit clusters that ripen in late summer and linger until midwinter. *V. plicatum* var. *tomentosum* (doublefile viburnum)—layered, tierlike, horizontal branches on a plant 8 to 10 feet tall and wide. Flat, pure white flower clusters 2 to 4 inches wide on 2-inch stems consisting of fertile nonshowy flowers rimmed by a ring of showy sterile flowers, followed by red berries that turn black in summer. Coarsely toothed, prominently veined leaves 2 to 4 inches long that turn reddish purple in fall, Zones 5-8; 'Mariesii' has larger sterile flowers and slightly longer flower stems; 'Shasta' grows 6 feet tall and 10 to 12 feet

Viburnum setigerum

wide, with 4- to 6-inch wide-spreading flower clusters that obscure the leaves. *V. setigerum* (tea viburnum)—a multistemmed shrub 8 to 12 feet tall and 6 to 8 feet wide, with 3- to 6-inch-long blue-green leaves, once used to make tea, and unremarkable 1- to 2-inch white flower clusters but with a profuse crop of bright red berries in fall; Zones 5-7.

Growing conditions and maintenance: Viburnums grow best in slightly acid loam but tolerate slightly alkaline soils. Amend the soil with peat moss or leaf mold to increase moisture retention, and add sand if soil is poorly drained. Allow enough lateral room for the plant to fully develop; prune if necessary after flowering.

Picture Credits

Gordon Morrison/designed by Elizabeth Heekin Bartels—drawing by Luanne Urfer, Landscape Architect. 116: Lefever/Grushow/Grant Heilman Photography, Inc. 117: Drawing by Luanne Urfer, Landscape Architect. 118: Art by Gordon Morrison/designed by Luanne Urfer, Landscape Architect—drawing by Luanne Urfer, Landscape Architect. 119: Art by Gordon Morrison/ designed by Luanne Urfer, Landscape Architect—drawing by Luanne Urfer, Landscape Architect. 120: Lefever/Grushow/ Grant Heilman Photography, Inc. 121: Drawing by Luanne Urfer, Landscape Architect. 122: Art by Gordon Morrison/designed by Elizabeth Heekin Bartels—drawing by Luanne Urfer, Landscape Architect. 123: Art by Gordon Morrison/designed by Elizabeth Heekin Bartels—drawing by Luanne Urfer, Landscape Architect. 124, 125: Leonard G. Phillips. 126: Jerry Pavia. 127: © Robert Holmes. 128: Art by George Bell. 129: Art by Stephen R. Wagner—Bernard Fallon/designed by Chris Rosmini. 130: Bernard Fallon/designed by Barry Campion. 131: Jerry Pavia; art by Andrew Lewis/ARCOBALENO. 132: Jerry Pavia. 133: Dency Kane/designed by Robert Levenson and Kathe Tanous, East Hampton, N.Y. 134, 135: Jerry Pavia. 136, 137: Dency Kane/designed by Robert Levenson and Kathe Tanous, East Hampton, N.Y.—art by Andrew Lewis/ARCOBALENO. 138: Art by George Bell. 139: Leonard G. Phillips—art by George Bell. 140: © Walter Chandoha. 141: Bernard Fallon/designed by Laura Cooper. 142, 143: Jerry Pavia; art by Stephen R. Wagner. 144: Jerry Pavia/designed by Sydney Baumgartner. 145: © Anita Sabarese. 146: Jerry Pavia. 149: Art by Sharron O'Neil. 150, 151: Roger Foley/designed by Karen Burroughs and Gary Hayre, Ashton, Md. 152: Roger Foley. 153: Leonard G. Phillips/designed by Donna L. Hearn and Howard A. Wynne. 155: Jerry Pavia. 156: Robert Walch/designed by Andrew Hartnagle and Wayne Stork, Doylestown, Pa. 158, 159: Roger Foley/designed by Oehme, van Sweden and Associates, Inc. 160, 161: © Michael S. Thompson. 162: Leonard G. Phillips/designed by Sally Wheeler and Tom Gilbert, Cismont Manor Farm. 163: © Michael S. Thompson—art by Fred Holz. 164, 165: Rosalind Creasy—Gay Bumgarner; Stephen Swinburne/courtesy The Cook's Garden, Londonderry, Vt. 166: Jerry Pavia. 167: Roger Foley. 168, 169: © Walter Chandoha; Gay Bumgarner; © Karen Bussolini. 170: Jane Grushow/Grant Heilman Photography, Inc. 171: Jerry Pavia/designed by Louise G. Smith. 172, 173: Jerry Pavia—Jerry Pavia/William T. Smith, Landscape Architect, ASLA, Atlanta. 174: Jerry Pavia. 175: Charles Mann. 176: Jerry Pavia. 177: Art by Allianora Rosse. 178: Chart by John Drummond, Time-Life Books, Inc.; Clive Nichols, Reading, Berkshire, U.K. 179: © Alan and Linda Detrick; Jerry Pavia. 180, 181: Jerry Pavia—Jerry Pavia/designed by Lutsko Associates, San Francisco. 182: Jerry Pavia. 183: Richard Shiell. 185: © David McDonald/Photogarden/designed by Northwest Perennial Alliance. 187: Carole Ottesen—Joanne Pavia. 188, 189: © Cynthia Woodyard—Jerry Pavia. 190, 191: © Michael S. Thompson; Brent Heath. 192: Ken Druse/The Natural Garden. 193: Bernard Fallon/designed by Sandy Kennedy. 194: © Cynthia Woodyard. 195: Lauren Springer—© Cynthia Woodyard. 196: © Karen Bussolini—© Alan and Linda Detrick. 197: Jerry Pavia/courtesy Diane and Jon Spieler, garden designed by Johnathan Plant, Los Angeles. 198: © Karen Bussolini. 199: Charles Mann. 200: Art by Andrew Lewis/ARCOBALENO. 201: Leonard G. Phillips/designed by John B. Welch. 202, 203: Rob Proctor; Catriona Tudor Erler. 204: © Lynne Harrison—© Walter Chandoha. 205: © Dency Kane. 206: Charles Mann. 207: Carole Ottesen. 208: Jerry Pavia. 209: Carole Ottesen. 210, 211: Charles Mann; Jerry Pavia. 212: © Alan and Linda Detrick. 213: Jerry Pavia. 214, 215: © Walter Chandoha; © Alan and Linda Detrick. 216, 217: © R. Todd Davis (2); © Alan and Linda Detrick—C. Colston Burrell. 218, 219: © judywhite (2)—© R. Todd Davis. 224: Art by Davis Meltzer and Rebecca Merrilees. 225: Art by Lorraine Mosley Epstein. 226: Art by Nicholas Fasciano (2)—Fred Holz. 227: Art by Nicholas Fasciano—Robert E. Hynes—Fred Holz—Sharron O'Neil. 236, 237: Maps by John Drummond, Time-Life Books, Inc. 239-243: Jerry Pavia. 244: Joanne Pavia; Jerry Pavia (2). 245: Joanne Pavia; Jerry Pavia (2). 246: Joanne Pavia; Jerry Pavia (2). 247-250: Jerry Pavia. 251: Joanne Pavia; Jerry Pavia (2). 252, 253: Jerry Pavia. 254: Jerry Pavia; Joanne Pavia; Jerry Pavia. 255-263: Jerry Pavia. 264: Jerry Pavia; © Walter Chandoha; Jerry Pavia. 265, 266: Jerry Pavia. 267: Joanne Pavia; Jerry Pavia (2). 268: Jerry Pavia; Joanne Pavia; Jerry Pavia. 269: Jerry Pavia. 270: Joanne Pavia; Jerry Pavia. 271: Jerry Pavia (2); Joanne Pavia. 272: Joanne Pavia; Jerry Pavia (2). 273, 274: Jerry Pavia. 275: Jerry Pavia; Joanne Pavia; Jerry Pavia. 276: Jerry Pavia. 277: Jerry Pavia (2); Steven Still. 278: Joanne Pavia; Jerry Pavia; Joanne Pavia. 279, 280: Jerry Pavia. 281: Jerry Pavia (2); Joanne Pavia. 282, 283: Jerry Pavia. 284: Joanne Pavia; Jerry Pavia (2). 285: Jerry Pavia; Joanne Pavia; Jerry Pavia. 286: Jerry Pavia (2); Steven Still. 287: Jerry Pavia. 288: Joanne Pavia; Jerry Pavia (2). 289: Joanne Pavia; Jerry Pavia (2). 290: Joanne Pavia; Jerry Pavia; Joanne Pavia. 291: Jerry Pavia (2); Joanne Pavia. 292: Jerry Pavia (2); Joanne Pavia. 293, 294: Jerry Pavia. 295: Jerry Pavia (2); © R. Todd Davis. 296: Jerry Pavia; Joanne Pavia; Jerry Pavia. 297: Jerry Pavia. 298: Joanne Pavia (2); Jerry Pavia. 299: Jerry Pavia; Joanne Pavia; Jerry Pavia. 300: Jerry Pavia; Steven Still; Jerry Pavia. 301: Jerry Pavia; Joanne Pavia; Jerry Pavia. 302: Jerry Pavia. 303: Jerry Pavia; Joanne Pavia; Robert S. Hebb. 304, 305: Jerry Pavia. 306: © Michael S. Thompson. 307: © Richard Shiell; © Michael S. Thompson; Brent Heath. 308: Joanne Pavia (2); Jerry Pavia. 309: Jerry Pavia. 310: Joanne Pavia (2); Jerry Pavia. 311: Joanne Pavia. 312: Joanne Pavia; Jerry Pavia. 313: Jerry Pavia. 314: Jerry Pavia; Joanne Pavia (2). 315: Jerry Pavia. 316: Joanne Pavia; Jerry Pavia (2). 317: Jerry Pavia; Joanne Pavia. 318: Joanne Pavia (2); Jerry Pavia. 319: Jerry Pavia; Joanne Pavia; Jerry Pavia. 320: Jerry Pavia. 321: Jerry Pavia; Joanne Pavia; Jerry Pavia. 322: Jerry Pavia; Joanne Pavia. 323: Jerry Pavia. 324: Peter Haring; Jerry Pavia (3). 325: Jerry Pavia. 326: Peter Haring (2); Jerry Pavia (2). 327: Peter Haring; Jerry Pavia (3). 328: Jerry Pavia; Joanne Pavia; Peter Haring (2). 329: Jerry Pavia (2); Joanne Pavia; Jerry Pavia. 330, 331: Jerry Pavia. 332: Jerry Pavia (2); Peter Haring; Jerry Pavia. 333: Jerry Pavia; Peter Haring; Jerry Pavia (2). 334: Jerry Pavia (2); Peter Haring (2). 335: Jerry Pavia; Peter Haring; Jerry Pavia (2). 336: Jerry Pavia (2); Peter Haring (2). 337: Jerry Pavia; Peter Haring; Jerry Pavia (2). 338: Jerry Pavia. 339: Richard Shiell (2); Jerry Pavia. 340: © Alan and Linda Detrick; © Hal H. Harrison/Grant Heilman Photography, Inc.; Thomas E. Eltzroth. 341: © Saxon Holt; Jerry Pavia; Richard Shiell. 342: Dency Kane; Jane Grushow/Grant Heilman Photography, Inc.; Jerry Pavia. 343: Jerry Pavia. 344: Jerry Pavia; Michael Dirr (2). 345: Dency Kane; Jerry Pavia; Joanne Pavia. 346: Jerry Pavia (2); Dency Kane. 347: Jerry Pavia (2); Richard Shiell. 348: © R. Todd Davis (2); C. Colston Burrell. 349: Jerry Pavia. 350: © R. Todd Davis; Jerry Pavia; Richard Shiell. 351: Jerry Pavia (2); Grant Heilman/Grant Heilman Photography, Inc. 352: Jerry Pavia. 353: Jerry Pavia (2); Dency Kane. 354: Jerry Pavia; Joanne Pavia; Jerry Pavia. 355: Jerry Pavia (2); Dency Kane.

Time-Life Books is a division of **TIME LIFE INC.**

TIME LIFE INC.
PRESIDENT and CEO: George Artandi

TIME-LIFE BOOKS
PRESIDENT: Stephen R. Frary

TIME-LIFE CUSTOM PUBLISHING

Vice President and Publisher: Terry Newell
Vice President of Sales and Marketing: Neil Levin
Director of Editorial Development:
Jennifer Louise Pearce
Director of Special Sales: Liz Ziehl
Managing Editor: Donia Ann Steele
Production Manager: Carolyn M. Clark
Quality Assurance Manager: James King

Editorial Staff for
The Big Book of Garden Design

Project Manager: Linda Bellamy
Design: Mallow Design
Picture Coordinators: Ruth Goldberg,
Kimberly Grandcolas
Special Contributors: Celia Beattie (proofreader),
Lina B. Burton (index), Ruth Goldberg (cover
copy), Joyce B. Marshall (copy editor)

Editor: Janet Cave
Administrative Editor: Roxie France-Nuriddin
Art Directors: Cindy Morgan-Jaffe, Alan Pitts,
Sue Pratt
Picture Editors: Jane Jordan, Jane A. Martin
Text Editors: Sarah Brash, Darcie Conner John-
ston, Paul Mathless
Associate Editors/Research and Writing: Megan
Barnett, Sharon Kurtz, Katya Sharpe, Robert
Speziale, Karen Sweet, Mary-Sherman Willis
Senior Copyeditor: Anne Farr
Contributors: Jennifer Clark, Catherine Harper
Parrott (picture research); Vilasini Balakrishnan,
Cyndi Bemel, Susan S. Blair, Dena Crosson, Meg
Dennison, Catriona Tudor Erler, Catherine Hack-
ett, Adrian Higgins, Marie Hofer, Ann Kelsall, Bon-
nie Kreitler, Jocelyn G. Lindsay, Peter Loewer,
Carole Ottesen, Rita Pelczar, Ann Perry, Roseanne
Scott, Marianna Tait-Durbin, Margaret Stevens,
Susan Gregory Thomas, Olwen Woodier (research
and writing); Margery duMond, Marfé Ferguson-
Delano, Bonnie Kreitler, Gerry Shremp, Lynn
Yorke (editing); John Drummond (art)
Correspondents: Christine Hinze (London),
Christina Lieberman (New York). Valuable assis-
tance was also provided by Liz Brown (New York).

Library of Congress Cataloging-in-Publication Data
The Big book of garden design : simple steps
to creating beautiful gardens / by the editors of
Time-Life Books.
p. cm.
ISBN 0-7835-5280-7
1. Gardens—Design. 2. Landscape gardening.
3. Plants, Ornamental. 4. Gardens—United States—
Design. 5. Landscape gardening—United States.
6. Plants, Ornamental—United States.
I. Time-Life Books.
SB473.B485 1998   712'.6—dc21   97-31251   CIP

**Books produced by Time-Life Custom Publishing are available at a special bulk discount
for promotional and premium use. Custom adaptations can also be created to meet your
specific marketing goals. Call 1-800-323-5255.**